ISBN 978-0-259-39531-7
PIBN 10815319

1 MONTH OF
FREE
READING

at

www.ForgottenBooks.com

By purchasing this book you are eligible for one month membership to ForgottenBooks.com, giving you unlimited access to our entire collection of over 1,000,000 titles via our web site and mobile apps.

To claim your free month visit:
www.forgottenbooks.com/free815319

English
Français
Deutsche
Italiano
Español
Português

www.forgottenbooks.com

Mythology Photography **Fiction**
Fishing Christianity **Art** Cooking
Essays Buddhism Freemasonry
Medicine **Biology** Music **Ancient**
Egypt Evolution Carpentry Physics
Dance Geology **Mathematics** Fitness
Shakespeare **Folklore** Yoga Marketing
Confidence Immortality Biographies
Poetry **Psychology** Witchcraft
Electronics Chemistry History **Law**
Accounting **Philosophy** Anthropology
Alchemy Drama Quantum Mechanics
Atheism Sexual Health **Ancient History**
Entrepreneurship Languages Sport
Paleontology Needlework Islam
Metaphysics Investment Archaeology
Parenting Statistics Criminology
Motivational

A

TREATISE

ON

ANCIENT PAINTING,

CONTAINING

OBSERVATIONS

ON THE

RISE, PROGRESS, and DECLINE of that Art
amongft the *Greeks* and *Romans*;

THE

High Opinion which the Great Men of Antiquity had of it ; its
Connexion with POETRY and PHILOSOPHY ; and the Ufe that
may be made of it in Education :

To which are added

Some REMARKS on the peculiar Genius, Character, and Talents of
Raphael, Michael Angelo, Nicholas Pouffin, and other Celebrated Modern
Mafters ; and the commendable Ufe they made of the exquifite Remains of
Antiquity in PAINTING as well as SCULPTURE.

The Whole illuftrated and adorned with

FIFTY PIECES of ANCIENT PAINTING ;

Difcovered at different times in the Ruins of Old *Rome*, accurately engraved from
Drawings of *Camillo Paderni* a *Roman*, lately done from the Originals with
great Exactnefs and Elegance.

By GEORGE TURNBULL *LL. D.*

———*Eft etiam illa Platonis vera, & tibi Catule, certe non inaudita vox, omnem doctrinam harum ingenuarum, & humanarum Artium, uno quodam Societatis vinculo contineri, ubi enim perfpecta vis eft
rationis ejus, qua caufæ rerum, atque exitus cognofcuntur, merus quidam quafi omnium confenfus doctrinarum,
concentufque reperitur.* Cicero de Oratore, *Lib.* 3.

ΟΣ τις μὴ ἀσπάζεται τὴν ζωγραφίαν, ἀδικεῖ τὴν ἀλήθειαν, ἀδικεῖ δὲ κ̀ σοφίαν ὁπόση ἐς ποιητὰς ἥκει, φορὰ γὰρ ἴση
ἀμφοῖν ἐς τὰ τῶν ἡρώων εἴδη, κ̀ ἔργα. ξυμμετρίαν τὲ ὐκ ἐπαινεῖ, δι᾽ ἣν κ̀ λόγος ἡ τέχνη ἅπτεται.
Philoftrati Imagines.

LONDON:

Printed for the AUTHOR ; and fold by A. MILLAR, at *Buchanan's* Head, over-againft
St. *Clement's* Church, in the *Strand.*
M.DCC.XL.

T O

The RIGHT HONOURABLE

H E N R Y

Lord Vifcount *Lonfdale*, &c.

This T R E A T I S E is humbly dedicated

By his LORDSHIP'S

Moft Devoted,

and Obedient Servant,

GEORGE TURNBULL.

SUBSCRIBERS NAMES.

A.
*H*IS *Grace the Duke of* Argyle.
 His Grace the Duke of Athol.
The Right Honourable the Earl of Aberdeen.
The Right Reverend Ifaac *Lord Bifhop of*
 St. Afaph.
The Honourable Sir John Anftruther *Bart.*
James Abercrombie *Efq;*
John Armftrong *M. D.*
The Advocates *Library at Edinburgh.*
Mr. William Adams, *Architect.*

B.
The Right Honourable Earl of Bute.
The Right Honourable Lord Belhaven.
The Right Honourable Lord Brook.
The Honourable George Baillie.
The Honourable William Berkely.
Sir John Baird *Bart.*
Bell Boyle *Efq;*
William Briftow *Efq; two Books.*
John Briftow *Efq;*
Jofiah Burchet *Efq; Secretary to the Ad-*
 miralty.
James Baillie *M. D.*
Robert Burd *M. D.*
Robert Barket *M. D.*
Beaupre Bell *M. A.*
Robert Blackwood *Efq;*
John Blackwood *Efq;*
Alexander Blackwood *Efq;*
Mr. Stephen Le Bas.

C.
The Right Honourable Lord Cathcart.
The Right Honourable Lord Cornbury.
The Honourable William Cecil.
The Honourable Brigadier James Campbell.
Colin Campbell *Efq;*
John Cotton *Efq;*
John Cotton, *jun. Efq;*
Evelyn Chadwick *Efq;*
Thomas Calderwood *Efq;*
Alexander Cunningham *M. D.*
Trinity-College, *Cambridge.*
St. John's-College, *Cambridge.*
John Campbell, *of Stackpool-Court, Efq;*

D.
His Grace the Duke of Devonfhire.
The Right Honourable the Lord Deskford.
The Right Reverend Thomas *Lord Bifhop*
 of Derry, *four Books.*
The Honourab. Lieutenant-General Dormer.
Sir James Dafhwood *Bart.*
Sir Francis Dafhwood *Bart.*
Sir James Dalrymple *Bart.*
Andrew Ducarrel *Efq;*
Robert Dundafs *Efq;*
James Douglafs *M. D.*
Mr. Robert Dodfley, *fix Books.*

E.
The Right Honourable the Earl of Effex.
The Right Honourable the Earl of Eglinton.
The Right Honourable the Earl of Egmont.
The Right Honourable Lord Erskine.
Sir Richard Ellys *Bart.*
Major Edwards.

F.
Henry Furnefe *Efq;*
Martin Folkes *Efq;*
John Forbes *Efq;*
The Reverend Dr. Freind.
Mr. David Faulconer.
John Freind *Efq;*
Thomas Fotheringham *Efq;*

G.
His Grace the Duke of Gordon.
The Right Honourable Lord Guernfey.
Colonel Guife.
Roger Gale *Efq;*

H.
The Right Honourable the Lord Hardwick,
 Lord High-Chancellor of Great-Britain.
The Right Honourable the Earl of Had-
 dington.
The Right Honourable Lord Hertford.
The Right Honourable Lord Harcourt.
The Right Honourable Lord George Hay.
The Right Honourable Lord Hope.
The Honourable Charles Hope.
Sir James Hall.
William Harvey *Efq;*
Nathaniel Hickman *Efq;*
Mr. John Hall.
The Reverend Mr. John Horfley.
The Reverend Mr. Robert Hamilton.
Mr. Gavin Hamilton, *12 Books.*
Mr. Henry Hume.
John How *Efq;*
Mr. William Hollier.

I.
The Right Honourable Lord Irwin.
Theodore Jacobfon *Efq;*

L.
The Rt. Honourable the Earl of Loudon.
The Right Honourable the Lord Lonfdale,
 two Books.
The Honourable Lord Linton.
The Honourable Anthony Lowther.
Matthew Lamb *Efq;*
Erneft Leflie *Efq;*
John Lockhart *Efq;*
James Loch *Efq;*
Thomas Lidderdale *M. D.*
Sir Darcy Lever *Knt. L L. D. of Alkrington.*

[A]   M,

M.

His Grace the Duke of Marlborough.
The Right Honourable the Earl of March-
   mont.
The Rt Honourable the Earl of Middlefex.
The Rt Honourable Lord Sherrard Mannors.
The Right Honourable Lord Manfel.
The Right Honourable Lord Monfon.
The Honourable William Murray.
Sir Patrick Murray Bart.
Sir Charles Moore Bart.
The Honourable Thomas Maynard Efq;
William Morehead Efq; five Books.
Henry Moore Efq;
Andrew Mitchel Efq;
Mr. Andrew Mitchel, Apothecary.
Mrs. Efther Medina.
Richard Mead M. D. Reg. eight Books.
——— Monroe M. D.
The Reverend Dr. Conyers Middleton.
Daniel Mackercher Efq;

N.

James Newfham Efq;
Robert Nugent Efq;

O.

The Right Honourable the Earl of Oxford.
The Right Honourable Arthur Onflow Efq;
   Speaker of the Houfe of Commons.
Exeter College, Oxford.
Captain John Osborn.

P.

His Grace the Duke of Perth.
The Right Honourable Lord Primrofe.
Sir Erafmus Philips Bart.
John Philips Efq;
The Honourable William Pulteney Efq;

Q.

His Grace the Duke of Queensberry.
Her Grace the Dutchefs of Queensberry.

R.

The Right Honourable the Earl of Rock-
   ingham.
The Right Honourable the Countefs of
   Rockingham.
Henry Rolle Efq;
John Robarts Efq;
Andrew Reid Efq; two Books.
Mr. James Robertfon, Merchant, in Lynn.
John Richardfon Efq;
Mr. ——— Richmond, at Paris, four Books.

S.

His Grace the Duke of Somerfet.
The Rt Honourable the Earl Stanhope.
The Right Honourable the Earl of Stair.
The Honourable John Spencer Efq;
The Right Honourable the Countefs of
   Shaftesbury.
The Right Honourable Lady Anne Strode.
William Strode Efq; two Books.
Samuel Strode Efq;
William Stuart Efq;
The Honourable Edward Southwell Efq;
Richard Sommers Efq; Commiffioner of his
   Majefty's Cuftoms.
Alexander Strahan Efq;
George Sinclair Efq;
Sir Hans Sloan Bart. M. D.
Sir Brownlow Sherrard Bart.
Sir Hugh Smithfon Bart.
Alexander Stuart M. D.
The Reverend Mr. Jofeph Spence.
Mr. Stephen Slaughter.
Alexander Stuart Efq;
Mr. ——— Serjeant.

T.

The Moft Honourable the Marquis of
   Tweeddale.
The Right Honourable Lord Talbot.
Sir Edmund Thomas Bart.
The Reverend John Taylor LL. D.
The Reverend Mr. Thomas Turnbull.
Jofeph Townfhend Efq;
James Thomfon Efq

U.

Alexander Udney Efqs

W.

The Hon. Thomas Watfon Efq; fix Books.
The Right Reverend Benjamin Lord Bifhop
   of Winchefter.
Andrew Wauchope Efq; 13 Books.
James Wauchope Efq;
William Wauchope Efq;
Colonel Edward Wauchope.
Sir James Weemyfs.
Mr. Robert Weems, two Books.
The Reverend Mr. Robert Wallace.
William Wyndham Efq;

Y.

Hitch Younge Efq;

Z.

Mr. John Zachary.

EPISTLE

Right Honourable the Lord Vifcount *Lonfdale*,

Upon Education, and the Defign of this Eſſay on Painting, &c.

MY LORD,

I Should not have adventur'd to dedicate this Eſſay to your Lordſhip did it aim at nothing higher (as ſome may imagine from the Title) than merely to recommend to our Youth a Taſte in Painting as an ingenious and innocent Amuſement. That Art is indeed diſcourſed of at great length in this Treatiſe ; but in ſuch a manner as affords me full room to give my Sentiments, or rather the Sentiments of ſome of the greateſt Men of Antiquity concerning Education. A Subject, my Lord, of the higheſt Importance, and to the mature Conſideration of which your real Love of Mankind, and ſincere Concern for their Happineſs, muſt have often led your penetrating Mind.

IN ſhewing wherein the real Excellence of Painting conſiſts, and the happy uſe that was or might be made of it in forming Youth to Virtue and a good Taſte of all the Arts ; I am naturally led to animadvert upon ſeveral Miſtakes in Education ; and to ſhew the neceſſity of combining in it all the Liberal Arts and Sciences, in order to accompliſh moſt ſucceſsfully its acknowledged End ; which is to form and improve betimes in young Minds the Love of true Knowledge, and the Love of Society, Mankind, and Virtue ; and to inſtil into them at the ſame time a right Notion of the better ways of explaining, recommending, embelliſhing or enforcing upon the Mind any Truth, or any Virtue ; one or other of which muſt be the End of *Language* of whatever ſort ; that is, of every Art that pretends to inſtruct or move us.

SO thoroughly, my Lord, am I convinced of the Uſefulneſs of the Deſign that runs throughout the whole of this Eſſay, which is humbly offered to your Lordſhip by a Heart that often indulges itſelf with the higheſt delight in admiration of Parts and Virtues united together, which I am not here allowed to be ſo particular upon as I could wiſh : So fully, my Lord, do I feel the Importance of the Scope that is chiefly kept in view throughout the following Treatiſe, that I would gladly take advantage of the noble Image now before me ; and entering upon that Subject here, make an Experiment on myſelf of a Rule preſcribed by many ancient Writers as verify'd in their own Experience. Would you, ſay they, attain to a kind of Inſpiration in handling any Subject ; imagine you are ſpeaking or writing to one who thoroughly underſtands it ; has it fully at heart ; and like whom you would chuſe to be able to think and expreſs your Sentiments : And then let your Thoughts flow freely, as you are warm'd and directed by that pleaſing, elevating Fancy. I am ſufficiently authoriſed, my Lord, by ancient Examples to ſet forth the Moment of my Deſign, and the Truth of the Principles upon which it is built, in this kind of Dedication : And I dare not preſume to addreſs your Lordſhip in the modern way of Panegyrick, though I am ſure every one will ſay, that in order to draw the moſt amiable Character, all that is neceſſary on this occaſion is to hit the Likeneſs, and to paint a true one.

'TIS impoſſible, my Lord, to reflect one moment upon Human Nature without perceiving, that its right or wrong State depends as neceſſarily upon Education, as that of a Plant upon proper Culture. Though Man be eſſentially different from every merely mechanical Being that never acts, but is in all caſes paſſive, or moved by Springs and Cauſes abſolutely independent of it; becauſe Man hath an active Principle in his Frame, and a certain Sphere of Power or Dominion aſſigned to him by Nature, in virtue of which, many Operations and Effects, both within and without his Mind, are dependent as to their Exiſtence or Non-exiſtence upon his own Will : Tho' this be as certain as Conſciouſneſs can render any Fact; yet our acting well or ill, the right or wrong Exerciſe of our ſeveral Powers muſt depend upon the Principles and Habits we have early imbib'd and contracted, for theſe make us what we are ; theſe conſtitute our Temper and Diſpoſition ; by them we are moved and influenced in all our Choices and Purſuits. Wherefore not to think of modelling theſe aright in Education, is to neglect the only End it pretends to have in view, which is to mould us into a good Form or Temper. To give a wrong Caſt to them by Education is to employ the forming Art to miſhape, and deform or deprave us. The Buſineſs of Education is by cultivating and perfecting all our Powers and Affections, all our Faculties, and all the Movements by which we are ſet to work, to make Man ſuch as he ought to be ; that is, ſuch as his greateſt Dignity and Happineſs require he ſhould be : Or, in other words, to inſtil into him ſuch Principles, and to form within him ſuch Deſires, Affections and Habits as will lead him right in all his Purſuits and Employments ; and to inure him to ſuch Exerciſes of his Powers and Faculties as will render them moſt vigorous ; moſt ſerviceable to himſelf and to Society on every occaſion.

RIGHT Education, if it be not the one thing needful, it is at leaſt abſolutely neceſſary to private or publick Happineſs. The beſt Laws without proper care about it are Mockery : They may enſnare Men, but they can go but little way in reſtraining them ; and none at all in forming or mending them : Whereas proper Education would in a great meaſure prevent the neceſſity of Laws and their Sanctions, by framing betimes a right Diſpoſition in us that would naturally, and as it were neceſſarily produce what good Laws can only command. If the moving Powers, or Springs of Motion, and all the Wheels be found and right, all muſt go well in moral Nature as well as in Mechaniſm.

EVERY one who hath the Perfection and Happineſs of Mankind ſo ſincerely at heart as your Lordſhip, muſt have often reflected upon the great End of Education, and the proper Methods of gaining that End ; and conſequently muſt have wondered to find a very powerful and exceeding uſeful Principle in our Make intirely overlooked in it, as if it had nothing

thing to do with our Conftitution; and that is, the Influence of Habits early formed. This is the more furprizing, becaufe the Reality and Strength of this Principle in our Natures is fo univerfally acknowledged, that in every Nation it is and always has been a vulgar Proverb, That Cuftom is a fecond Nature. The Power of Habit is readily owned by all: But what is done, my Lord, in the forming Art that is founded upon this Principle; or what proper means are ufed conformably to this acknowledged Truth, early to eftablifh good Habits in young Minds, either in refpect of Inftruction or Difcipline?

THE Whole of Education muft confift in the Formation of right Habits: For what we call Temper is nothing elfe but natural Propenfions formed by repeated Exercifes into ftrong and lafting Habits. Every Affection, every Power, and every Propenfion muft be originally of Nature: Art cannot create: All it can do is to cultivate and perfect what Nature hath planted: But 'tis Art and repeated Exercife that work natural Powers into Strength, or natural Affections into Temper. Some proper Difcipline or Regimen is therefore neceffary to accomplifh the principal Scope of Education, if to produce virtuous Habits be fuch. And what can be juftly called cultivating and improving Underftanding or Reafon, but forming one by proper Exercife into the confiderative Temper, or the Habit of deliberating and computing before one chufes or acts? 'Tis certainly Pleafure and Pain that move us: Nothing can be the Object of Affection or Defire but Pleafure; or, on the other hand, the Object of Averfion and Diflike but Pain. Pleafures of Senfe, of Contemplation, of Sentiment, of Self-approbation, and their Oppofites, are all but fo many different forts of Pleafures and Pains. And let Metaphyficians debate and wrangle as long as they will, this muft neceffarily be true, and be no more than an identical Propofition, that what is pleafing is pleafing, and that Pleafure alone can be pleafant. But it is Reafon's Bufinefs to examine, compute and ballance Pleafures and Pains of all kinds: And then is Reafon well formed; or formed into a really ufeful Principle, when the Mind hath acquired the Habit of computing before it acts; and of computing readily as well as truly: Which Habit or Temper can only be attained by inuring the Mind betimes to think and reafon before it acts, that is, to compare and ballance Pleafures and Pains before it chufes.

NOW in forming this Habit, which not only conftitutes the wife but the free Man, there are two things to be taken care of. One is to inure Youth to reafon, or compute from Experience only; that is, from Facts afcertained by Obfervation, and not from abftract, imaginary Theories and Hypothefes. The other is to inure them to imploy their Reafon chiefly about thofe Objects and Connexions in Nature, which have the neareft relation to human Life and Happinefs. In order to both which 'tis manifeft, that they ought to be taught to take a juft View of human Nature, and to confider Man as he really is, neither as a merely fenfitive Being, nor as a merely moral one; but as a compound of moral and fenfitive Powers and Affections. For in the human Make thofe Powers and Affections are fo blended together, that it is impoffible to avoid Errors concerning Man's Duties or Interefts, if any of them are confidered feparately, that is, independently of the reft.

IT were eafy, my Lord, to point out feveral falfe Doctrines that take their Rife from dividing thofe conftituent Parts of our Frame from one another, which are really infeparable in the Nature of things. To mention no other Inſtance at preſent: Hence, I think, it is that ſome have railed in ſuch a vague, undetermined manner againſt Luxury, as if all Pleaſures ought to be deſpiſed by wiſe and good Men, and therefore baniſhed human Society, but thoſe that are abſolutely neceſſary to our Subſiſtence; or thoſe that produce Enjoyment and Satisfaction of the very nobleſt kind.   In the general, confuſed way of declaiming againſt Luxury, all the Pleaſures of Imagination, and all the ornamental Arts are damn'd as abſolutely ſuperfluous, and as unworthy of our Attention in any degree: Nay Cleanlineſs, not to ſay, Elegance, is condemned and interdicted, as if Nature had given Man Eyes, Ears, and other Senſes, with a natural Taſte and Reliſh of Proportion, Beauty, and Harmony, to no purpoſe.

THE happy Conſequence of inuring Youth to reaſon from Experience alone; and to reaſon firſt and chiefly about thoſe things that have the neareſt relation to Life, and with which it is therefore our Intereſt to be very early acquainted, would be, that the natural Deſire of Knowledge, which is implanted in us on purpoſe to impel us to ſeek after that Science, which is as neceſſary to guide our Conduct, as Light is to ſhew us our Road, would not be miſled into a way of gratifying itſelf by Enquiries quite remote from the practice of the World.   And I am apt to imagine, my Lord, that more are ignorant of Life, and quite Strangers to the World and human Affairs, in conſequence of employing their Minds about Objects that have little or no concern with Men and Things, than through mere Stupidity or Want of Capacity.   It is falſe Learning that is the moſt dangerous Enemy to the true, or that moſt effectually ſupplants it.   Nothing therefore is of greater Importance in Education, than to render Youth betimes capable of diſtinguiſhing uſeful Enquiries, from thoſe that ought only to have the place of Amuſements, like a Game at Cheſs or Piquet: And for that reaſon it would be of more conſequence to exerciſe young People in often reviewing, with attention, a well-calculated Table of Arts and Sciences, in reſpect of their different degrees of Utility, than any other Categories or Arrangements of Ideas whatſoever, that are called Logick in the Schools, though ſuch likewiſe may have their uſe.

BUT at the ſame time that the Habit of reaſoning well and readily is formed by inuring Youth to Reaſon; the Faculty of expreſſing known Truths clearly and ſtrongly may be likewiſe acquired.   It is neceſſary that a Teacher ſhould take the moſt gradual, regular, clear, and full Method of explaining and proving Truths; or that he ſhould proceed ſtep by ſtep with his Scholars: And therefore that didactick Art will of courſe be learned by them at the ſame time that Knowledge itſelf is acquired in that way.   But there is an *Eloquence* of another kind that ought not to be neglected in the Formation of Youth; and that would ſoon be attained by them, were but this one Rule obſerved in Education, to inure Students after they have been led to the Knowledge of any Truth in the didactick way, to find out the propereſt Methods of expreſſing it conciſely and ſtrongly; or of giving a convincing, emphatical View of it in few Words.   This laſt would be teaching them the Language in which Men ought to ſpeak to Men about the ſame Truths that can only be conveyed into raw, unformed Minds in a more ſlow and tedious manner.   After young People underſtand any Truth, it is neither unpleaſant nor unprofitable; but on the contrary it is very fit to employ them in conſidering how ſeveral celebrated Authors have choſen to repreſent it in different Lights, each according to his own Genius; or in order to adapt it to ſome particular Caſt of Underſtanding; and then in vying with them in finding out other ways of

expreſſing

expreffing the fame Truth with due Force and Perfpicuity. But we commonly begin in Education with Words, as if there were any other way of
trying or judging Words and Phrafes, or Signs of any kind, but by examining whether they are propet Expreffions of the Truths they are intended
to fignify; whether they are equal, fuperiour, or inferiour to other Expreffions of the fame Truths in refpect of the fole End of Language, which
is to convey Sentiments with Clearnefs and Efficacy. The chief thing
indeed is to have juft or true Sentiments; that is, to have right Apprehen-
fions of Nature : But that Knowledge may take faft hold of our Minds,
dwell with us and afford us variety of delight; and that we may be capable of imparting it to others, fo as to render it the Source of manifold
Entertainment, as well as of Information to them; the various proper
ways of proving, embellifhing, and enforcing Truths muft be taught and
ftudied. And therefore in proportion as one acquires Knowledge, he
ought likewife to learn Languages; or to be made acquainted with all the
better ways of evincing and impreffing any Truths on the Mind.

I may be thought by fome perhaps to take Language in a very uncommon Senfe. But that I have ufed it in its jufteft, as well as its moft comprehenfive Meaning, will be obvious to every one who but reflects, that
there can be but two Objects of human Inquiry, Truths themfelves, that
is, real Connexions in Nature or Facts; and the various manners of making Truths underftood and felt. Whence it plainly follows, that the didactick Style, Oratory, Poetry, and likewife all the Arts of Defign, Painting,
Statuary and Sculpture, fall properly under the Idea of Language. And
therefore if right Education ought to teach and inftruct in Truths, and in
the various good Methods or Arts of conveying Truths into the Mind; no
fooner is one led into the Difcovery of any Truth, than he ought to be
imployed in comparing and examining feveral different ways by which it
may be unfolded, proved, embellifhed, and enforced by Oratory, Poetry,
or Painting. For to apply this general Obfervation to Painting, which is
commonly reckoned fo remote from Philofophy; nothing is more evident
than, that Pictures which neither convey into the Mind Ideas of fenfible
Laws, and their Effects and Appearances, nor moral Truths, that is, moral Sentiments and correfponding Affections, have no Meaning at all :
They convey nothing, becaufe there is nothing elfe to be conveyed. But,
on the other hand, fuch Pictures as anfwer any of thefe Ends, muft for
that reafon fpeak a Language, the Correctnefs, Strength, Purity and Beauty
of which it muft be well worth while to underftand as a Language : More
efpecially fince there is indeed no other way of trying the Propriety, Force
and Beauty of a poetical Image, but by confidering the Picture it forms in
the Imagination, as a Picture.

ALL the inftructing or moving Arts confidered in this light, that is,
as fo many Methods of conveying Truths agreeably or ftrongly into the
Mind; or of exciting our Affections by means of Ideas fitted to move them,
muft belong to Education, and ought to be employed by Philofophy every
ftep it makes. For feveral fuch Arts being compared together, muft naturally confpire to give a jufter Notion of the fupreme Beauty and Excellence
of any Language, in confequence of the fole End common to all Languages, than can be acquired by any of them, if feparately ftudied : And
being combined, they muft neceffarily have a multiplied Force in impreffing any piece of Knowledge on the Mind.

b   ONE

ONE great Error then in modern Education conſiſts in imagining, that Philoſophy, Rhetorick, Poetry, and the other Arts ought to be taught ſeparately; whereas in reality it is Philoſophy or the Knowledge of Nature that ought to be taught; and the proper way of giving a juſt Notion of Oratory, Poetry, and the other Arts of illuſtrating, embelliſhing and impreſſing Truths, is by ſhewing every ſtep Philoſophy advances, what theſe Languages have done, or may do to exhibit and enforce any Truth with all its Effects and Conſequences. And this, my Lord, is what I have endeavoured to illuſtrate in the following Eſſay.

BUT, my Lord, if to ſeparate the inſtructing or moving Arts from Philoſophy be a very detrimental miſtake in Education, ſince it divides Languages from Things; muſt it not be yet a more pernicious one to ſever moral from natural Philoſophy; or not to carry on our Enquiries about Man and his Relations and Connexions in Nature (which is moral Philoſophy) in the ſame manner, and conjunctly with our Enquiries into the Laws and Connexions of the ſenſible World, (the Knowledge of which is called natural Philoſophy) as one continued Reſearch into Fact and Truth, or into real Connexions in the ſame united Syſtem: And that with a practical View, or in order to obſerve what uſeful Maxims and Rules for human Life and Society may be inferred from any Diſcovery made in that Science? On the one hand, every Diſcovery in Nature that may be rendered ſubſervient to the Uſe or Ornament of Society really adds to Man's Property and Dominion in Nature: And whatever Knowledge is conducive to the good of Mankind, is in effect moral Science. On the other hand, every Enquiry about the Conſtitution of the human Mind, is as much a queſtion of Fact or natural Hiſtory, as Enquiries about Objects of Senſe are: It muſt therefore be managed and carried on in the ſame way of Experiment; and in the one caſe as well as in the other, nothing ought to be admitted as fact, till it is clearly found to be ſuch from unexceptionable Experience and Obſervation. He who hath the real good of Society ever before his Eyes in his Studies, certainly imploys his Underſtanding to a very uſeful Purpoſe, and from a very laudable Motive: Such a one will let no Truth, he may find out, eſcape him, without enquiring moſt ſtrictly what advantage may be derived from it to Mankind; and he will value his Diſcoveries proportionably. And Man being a compound Creature, *nexus utriuſque mundi*, (as he is called by ſome Philoſophers) the Knowledge of the natural World is not leſs requiſite to his Happineſs than that of the moral. All the Neceſſities and Conveniencies of Life and Society require the Science of natural Connexions as well as of moral ones. Nay, to ſtudy human Nature can be nothing elſe but to enquire into that nice blending and intermingling of natural and moral Parts by which it is conſtituted: And Concluſions deduced from moral Powers and Affections, conſidered apart from ſenſitive ones, cannot make *Human Morality*, if Man really is a moral Being, intimately related to and connected with the Laws of the ſenſible World. An exact Theory of Morals can only be formed from a full and accurate Review of the various natural Principles or natural Diſpoſitions of Mankind, as theſe ſtand related to one another, and to ſurrounding Objects. And indeed one cannot reflect upon the great Improvements that have been made in Philoſophy, in all its Parts, ſince it hath been cultivated in the obvious and only way of purſuing it, without promiſing to one's ſelf a very happy Enlargement of moral Philoſophy, ſo ſoon as it ſhall be purſued in the ſame manner; that is, as Philoſophers ſhall endeavour in the later, as they have done in the former, to find out from Experience, Analogies, Agreements and Harmonies of Phænomena; or, in other words, to reduce Appearances to general Laws. That the Know-ledge of Nature, of human Nature in particular, is yet so very imperfect, is certainly owing to dividing or severing natural and moral Philosophy from one another; or to our not giving due Application to collect from Experience the general Laws to which Phænomena of the moral sort are reducible, in like manner as several Phænomena of the sensible World have been reduced to a few simple general Laws, which have at the same time been found to be wisely and fitly established in respect of the Good and Order they produce; for all Phænomena of whatever sort can only be ex-plained or accounted for in that way: All that Explication of Phænomena can mean, is the reducing them to some general Law or Principle: And therefore all other Attempts towards the Advancement of real Know-ledge are to no purpose.

IN consequence of the View that hath been briefly delineated of Phi-losophy and Languages, it is manifest, that the right way of teaching true Philosophy, must be teaching at the same time Science and Languages: And therefore it must be forming at the same time Reason, Imagination, and Temper. 'Tis plainly forming Reason to discover or prove Truths; and Imagination to embellish and enforce, that is, to paint them. And that it is forming the Temper, is no less obvious, since Temper means no-thing else but certain Affections worked into Habits, or become as such the Bent and Disposition of our Mind. But Affections can only be wrought into Habit or Temper by being often exercised and worked; and the Ex-ercisers or Workers are Sentiments duly conveyed and enforced by Reason and Imagination.

THIS is yet more evident when we consider, that what is principal with respect to Reason in Education, is, as hath been said, to form betimes that deliberating, computing Temper by which the Mind becomes Master of itself, and able to resist all the most inviting Promises and Solicitations of Objects, till their Pretensions have been fairly canvassed. This Temper is what is properly called Virtue or Strength of Mind: without it one must be feeble and unsteady, unable to act a reasonable or becoming part in Life; nay, the Sport of contradictory Passions and Appetites. It is by it alone that one can attain to that Harmony and Consistency of Affections and Manners which create Peace and Joy within, and command Respect and Love from all around; even from the most Dissolute and Vitious; for Nature can never be rendered quite insensible to the Beauty and Charms of wise and good Conduct.

A due Consideration of those Maxims will naturally lead every think-ing Person to discover Absurdities of many kinds in Education, that no doubt have frequently come a-cross your Lordship's Mind. Hence we may see the Error of the famous *Lycurgus*, since his manner of Education nei-ther served to produce a right Temper, nor a sufficient variety of Genius, or consequently of Happiness in Society; but, on the contrary, tended to make Men savage and ferocious, and at the same time cunning and deceit-ful; and to exclude from human Life many excellent Virtues and agreeable Affections, as well as Philosophy, and all the fine Arts.

HENCE we may see, on the other hand, the Error in *Athenian* Edu-cation; the Youth there being more employed about Languages than Things: Whence it was that *Athens* was so over-run with that Deluge of Sophistry, which *Socrates* was continually opposing; and that too many applied

applied themſelves to the embelliſhing Arts, or the Arts of Imagination, in proportion to the number of thoſe who applied to the Study of Nature; or to drawing Conſequences from the real Knowledge of Nature for uſe and practice in Life, and to be the Objects of the imitative and ornamental Arts. Whence proceeded in a great meaſure the fatal Abuſe, Degeneracy and Corruption of the fine Arts among them, before the *Romans*, who had theſe Arts from *Greece*, gave any attention to them.

HENCE likewiſe appears the neceſſity of treating Morals in another way than *Puffendorf*, *Grotius*, and moſt other celebrated modern Doctors of moral Philoſophy have done; ſince their Concluſions (tho' they be generally true) are neither deduced from a right, that is, a full View of the human Conſtitution, and our Relations and Connexions in Nature; nor are moral Doctrines explained and enforced in their Writings by the propereſt Terms of Expreſſion: On the contrary, all inſinuating, beautifying, and captivating Lights in which moral Truths may be repreſented, that at once enlighten and warm the Mind, are rather avoided by them. I can't help, my Lord, obſerving one thing farther on this Subject, that if one may reaſon at all from Authorities in Morals, as thoſe Writers chiefly do, the propereſt way of reaſoning from Authorities about Morals would be by ſhewing; that almoſt all the Truths which relate more immediately to human Life and good moral Conduct are ſo evident, that in all Ages and in all Countries they have been converted into Proverbs or familiar Sayings; and, which is very ſurprizing, they have been expreſſed very nearly by the ſame Images in all Countries, notwithſtanding all the Diverſities of Genius, Temperament, and Language that have prevailed in the World. Whence it would appear how common, how univerſal good Senſe is, and always hath been.

ANOTHER Error in Education is no leſs manifeſt from what hath been ſaid, which is, that it is not contrived in order to explore, and give free Scope and ſuitable Culture to all different Genius's. Education is generally carried on in the ſame uniform way, without any regard to the natural variety of Genius amongſt Mankind; as if it were done on purpoſe to diſappoint the kind Intention of Nature in diverſifying Men's Diſpoſitions and Talents: At leaſt, proper Meaſures are not taken in Education to invite different Genius's to diſcloſe themſelves; or after they are known to give ſuitable Culture to each that appears, in order to improve it to its natural Perfection and uſeful End. Diverſity of Genius amongſt Men is however no leſs neceſſary to the Enlargement of human Happineſs and Perfection in the Sum of things, than variety of Herbs and Plants is to the Beauty and Utility of the ſenſible World. And ſure it is not more abſurd to propoſe one way of training and forming all young People, than to think of one ſort of Culture for all kinds of Vegetables.

THERE is another Diverſity among Mankind that is as little attended to in forming Youth as that juſt mentioned; the remarkable variety amongſt us in reſpect of different Propenſities to certain Affections. And yet this later Diverſity, if it be not quite inſeparable from the former, is no leſs requiſite than it to the End of Nature in making Man, which is the general Good of the Kind. Some are naturally hot and fiery, others are cold and phlegmatick; ſome are prone to Anger, ſome to Love, ſome to Ambition, and others to Quiet and Eaſe; ſome, in one word, to one Paſſion, and ſome to another: And all theſe Varieties are ſo many different Seeds that require each its peculiar Culture; and which might, each by

proper

proper Methods of Education, be improved into that ufeful Temper of which it is the natural Seed or firft Principle. Nature doth nothing in vain, whether in the material or moral World : Whatever Foundations it hath laid for Art to work upon, are well intended: And as Art and Culture can only perfect what Nature hath begun; fo the Improvement of natural Faculties and Difpofitions being wifely left to ourfelves, to neglect the due Culture of any Power, Quality, or Affection Nature hath formed in human Breafts, is to defpife, or at leaft to over-look its kind and generous Provifion for our extenfive Happinefs in the beft way of providing for us; which is by furnifhing us with a proper variety of Materials and Talents for our own Cultivation and Improvement into Goods.

FROM what hath been faid, it is fufficiently evident in general, what ought to be the chief Aim of Inftruction; and how it ought to be managed in order to perfect our Faculties of Reafon and Imagination, and to produce betimes in our Minds good and ufeful Habits. And at the fame time it is obvious, that teaching cannot be fufficient, but that fome early Difcipline or Regimen is abfolutely neceffary to gain the principal End of Education; fince it is by proper practice alone that any Virtue can be rendered habitual to the Mind; or be early confirmed into Temper.

HAVING thus, my Lord, laid open fome Errors in Education, I wifh I were able to propofe a proper Scheme of it: But that requires a mafterly Projector, a very expert moral Architect. All I am capable of doing is to throw afide fome Rubbifh; and fhew the Foundations upon which the noble Building muft be raifed: That Building which would effectually make human Society happy; or at leaft without which it is impoffible, Men can arrive at that Perfection and Happinefs Nature plainly intended them for; but left to themfelves to build, that they might have the Satisfaction of confidering it as their own Acquifition. We are certainly defigned by our Maker for whatever Dignity and Happinefs we are qualified to attain to by the proper Exercife of our natural Powers and Affections. And as that alone, which is fo acquired, is moral Perfection, Virtue or Merit, and alone can afford the Pleafure of Self-approbation; fo Mankind's being made able to arrive at their higheft Perfection and Happinefs only by their united Force, is the neceffary Bafis of focial Union, and of all the noble Enjoyments refulting from focial Intercourfe and well-form'd Government.

IF any one thinks meanly of our Frame and Rank, let him ferioufly confider the Riches and Fullnefs that appears in Nature as far as we can extend our Enquiries; and how every Being in the Scale of Life within our Obfervation rifes in due degree: Let him then confider how neceffary the Exiftence of fuch a Species as Man is to the afcending Plenitude of Nature; to its *Fullnefs and Coherence*; and let him impartially examine our Conftitution, and the Provifion made for our Happinefs; the Excellence to which our natural Powers and Difpofitions may be improved and raifed by good Education and proper Diligence; or the Dignity and Felicity to which we may attain by the Study of Wifdom and Virtue, efpecially in well-regulated Society; for he will plainly fee, that though there be good reafon to think that there are various Orders of rational Beings in the Scale of Exiftence, the loweft of which is fuperiour to Man, yet he is crowned with Glory and Honour, is well placed, and hath a very confiderable Dominion allotted to him: Let him attentively confider feveral glorious Characters in Hiſtory : Or rather let him turn his Eyes with me towards a living Example of Worth and Greatneſs, to have a place in whoſe Eſteem is indeed Merit, that cannot be reflected upon, without feeling a noble Ambition more and more to deſerve it ; nor declared to the Publick without bringing one's ſelf under the ſtrongeſt Obligations to take particular care of one's Conduct. I am,

MY LORD,

Your Lordſhip's

Moſt Obedient,

Humble Servant,

London, Ap. 25.
1739.

GEORGE TURNBULL.

A

A
PREFACE,

Education, Travelling, and the Fine Arts.

A *Preface is now generally expected, and I fall in more readily with that established Custom, because it gives me an opportunity of premising something to the following Treatise that is by no means improper or unnecessary.*

THOUGH one of the principal Ends I proposed to myself in this Essay on Painting, *&c. be to prepare young Travellers for seeing Statues, Sculptures, and Pictures to better advantage than they can possibly do if they have not previously turned their Thoughts a little that way ; Yet I am far from thinking it the chief Design of Travel to examine the Productions of the Fine Arts even with the greatest Accuracy, or in the most intelligent, philosophical manner ; and much less in order to become an Antiquary or Virtuoso, in the common Acceptation of that Character ; or to see the Remains of ancient Arts very superficially, and to set up for a Critick of them upon so slight a Foundation.*

THERE are Subjects of a more important Nature than Paintings and Sculptures, in whatever light they are considered, that ought principally to employ the Thoughts of a Traveller, who has it in his View to qualify himself for the Service of his own Country, by visiting foreign ones. But one Point aimed at in this Treatise is to shew how mean, insipid, and trifling the fine Arts are when they are quite alienated from their better and nobler, genuine Purposes, which, as well as those of their Sister Poetry, are truly philosophical and moral : that is, to convey in an agreeable manner into the Mind the Knowledge of Men and Things ; or to instruct us in Morality, Virtue, and human Nature. And it necessarily follows, that the chief Design of travelling must be somewhat of greater moment than barely to learn how to distinguish an original Medal from a counterfeit one, a Greek *from a* Roman *Statue, or one Painter's Hand from another's ; since it is here proved, that even with regard to the Arts of Design that kind of Knowledge is but idle and trivial ; and that by it alone one has no better title to the Character of a Person of good Taste in them, than a mere verbal Critick hath to that of a polite Scholar in the* Classicks.

LET us consider a little the pretended Reasons for sending young Gentlemen to travel : They may be reduced to these two. " *That they may see the* " *Remains of ancient Arts, and the best Productions of modern Sculptors and* " *Painters ;*" *and* " *That they may see the World and study Mankind.*"

NOW as for the first, how it should be offered as a Reason for sending young Gentlemen abroad, is indeed very unaccountable, when one considers upon what footing Education is amongst us at present ; unless it could be thought that one may be jolted by an Italian *Chaise into the Knowledge and Taste that are evidently prerequisite to travelling with advantage, even in that view ; or that*

such

fuch Intelligence is the neceffary, mechanical Effect of a certain Climate upon the Underftanding; and will be inftantaneoufly infufed into one at his Arrival on Claffick Ground. For in our prefent Method of educating young Gentlemen either in publick Schools or by private Tutors, what is done that can in any degree prepare them for making proper and ufeful Reflexions upon the fine Arts, and their Performances? *Are not the Arts of Defign quite fever'd in modern Education not only from Philofophy, their Connexion with which is not fo obvious, or at leaft fo generally acknowledged; but likewife from claffical Studies, where not only their Ufefulnefs muft be readily owned by all who have the flighteft Notion of them, but where the want of proper Helps from ancient Statues, Bas-reliefs and Paintings for underftanding ancient Authors, the Poets in particular, is daily felt by Teachers and Students?* It is not more ridiculous to dream of one's acquiring a ftrange Language merely by fucking in foreign Air, than to imagine that thofe who never have been directed at home into the right manner of confidering the fine Arts ; thofe who have no Idea of their true Beauty, Scope, and Excellence (not to mention fuch as have not the leaft notion of Drawing) that fuch fhould all at once fo foon as they tread Italian Soil become immediately capable of underftanding thefe Arts, and of making juft Reflexions upon their excellent Productions. And yet this is plainly the cafe with regard to the greater part of our young Travellers. And for that reafon I have endeavoured in the following Effay to lead young Gentlemen and thofe concerned in their Education, into a jufter Notion of the Fine Arts than is commonly entertained even by the Plurality of their profeffed Admirers ; by diftinguifhing the fine Tafte of them from the falfe Learning that too frequently paffes for it ; and by fhewing in what refpects alone the Study of them belongs to Gentlemen, whofe high Birth and Fortune call them to the moft Important of all Studies ; that, of Men, Manners and Things, or Virtue and publick Good. And this I have attempted to do by fetting to view the Opinions which fome of the greateft Men of all Ages have had of their trueft Excellence and beft Scope ; and not by Arguments of my own Devife ; or for which I have no better Authority than my own Judgment.

AS for the other principal End of Travel, commonly comprehended under the general Phrafe of feeing the World, and acquiring the Knowledge of Mankind, it is a Subject that requires a much more comprehenfive Knowledge of the World than I can pretend to, to treat it as it ought to be. Having however in the following Difcourfe on Painting fhewn, what Notions fome very great Men, of ancient Times in particular, entertained of that Art ; and having made the beft ufe I could of their Sentiments and Reafonings about the fine Arts, to fet them in a due light ; I fhall juft remark here, with regard to travelling, that ancient Philofophers, Legiflators, Patriots and Politicians thought Travel neceffary, and accordingly travelled. But why did they travel ; or at what time of Life did they fet about it? They travelled after they were Men of Reading and Experience ; and they travelled to fee different States and to acquire more Experience in human Affairs ; or a more extenfive Knowledge of Mankind. And indeed he who hath been in the World, and rightly underftands what knowing the World means, he, and he alone is qualified for travelling. Seeing the World is a very familiar Phrafe; it is almoft in every one's mouth. But how few diftinctly comprehend its full Import and Signification? The Ancients travelled to fee different Countries, and to have thereby Opportunities of making folid Reflexions upon various Governments, Laws, Cuftoms and Policies, and their Effects and Confequences with regard to the Happinefs or Mifery of States, in order to import with them into their own Country, Knowledge founded on Fact and

Obfervation,

Obfervation, from which, as from a Treafure of Things new and old, fure and folid Rules and Maxims might be brought forth for their Country's Benefit on every Emergency. For this is certain, that the real Knowledge of Mankind can no more be acquired by abftract Speculation without ftudying human Nature itfelf in its many various Forms and Appearances, than the real Knowledge of the material World by framing imaginary Hypothefes and Theories, without looking into Nature itfelf : And no lefs variety of Obfervations is neceffary to infer or eftablifh general Rules and Maxims in the one than in the other Philofophy. But how can one be fuppofed fit for fuch ferious and profound Employment, before he hath very clear and diftinct Ideas of Government and Laws, and of the Interefts of Society ; or who by previous Education hath not been put into the way of making Reflexions on thofe ufeful Subjects ?

I have often heard a very young Nobleman (the Advantage of whofe uncommon Parts, and equal Virtues, may his Family, his Friends, and his Country long continue to enjoy) remark abroad, " That though all our young " Gentlemen of Fortune are fent to travel at a certain Age, promifcuoufly " or without diftinction ; yet it is very eafy to find out whether one be fit for " travelling or not ; fince he alone is fo, who takes pleafure in reading Hi- " ftory, not merely for his Amufement, but in order to lay up in his Mind " truly ufeful Knowledge ; and who, after having been inured for a con- " fiderable time to fuch a ferious and profitable Train of deep-thinking about " Men and Things ; and having thus conceived a clear Notion of the things " to be obferved and enquired into in his Travels in any foreign Country, is " able to form to himfelf a proper Plan of Travels, in order to accomplifh " fome manly, rational Defign." Such only are qualified to travel : Before fuch a Turn of Mind be well eftablifhed by Reading, Converfation, and fome Practice in the World, it is as abfurd to fend one abroad to ftudy Mankind, as to think of coming at Perfection in any Science without the Knowledge of its Elements or firft Principles. It is really like employing one to meafure without a Standard, or count without Arithmetick.

IN order to travel with Advantage through any foreign Country, one ought to have not only a very full Knowledge of the Laws, Conftitution, Hiftory and Interefts of his own Country, (which is feldom the cafe) ; but he ought likewife to have as full and thorough a Knowledge of that foreign Country he intends to vifit, as can be learned at home from Books and Converfation: And he ought certainly to have very juft and well-digefted Notions of Government, and civil Policy, and its Ends : Otherwife he goes indeed abroad not knowing whither he goes, or what he goes to fee ; without any Scheme ; and abfolutely unqualified to compare, or make right Judgments of Men and Things.

IF Parents fend their Sons fo young abroad, for no other reafon but merely that they may be for fome time out of their fight, (I wifh it could be likewife faid, that they fent them out of Harm's way) in fuch a cafe is it to be wondered at, that young Gentlemen go abroad without any other view but to make ufe of their Diftance from all Checks, to fling themfelves headlong into Pleafure, and give full fwing to their Appetites ; and that thus they bring back with them broken Conftitutions, and a worfe Habit of Mind ?

IF young Gentlemen are early fent abroad for any of the inferiour Parts of Liberal Education, there muft be great Defects in our own at home, which ought

d to

to be remedied, in order to put an end to a Neceſſity ſo riſquous, in what-ever View we take of it. If the Exerciſes are ſo neceſſary to compleat Education, that young Gentlemen are ſent very young into France *on that account, (and certain genteel, manly Exerciſes are undoubtedly requiſite to form a fine Gentleman) why have we them not in our own Schools and Uni-verſities in their proper Place and Seaſon ?*

IT *cannot be ſaid, that it is to learn Good-manners and a polite Mien and Carriage, that our young Gentlemen muſt be ſent ſo early into* France, *without doing injuſtice to our own Fair Sex, by Converſation with whom they would quickly be poliſhed into a Behaviour far preferable to that con-tracted abroad. 'Tis no doubt owing to our ſending our Youth to be poliſhed in* France *into genteel, pretty Behaviour (as it is called) a Complement that has been paid to that Nation by the* Britiſh *in particular, too, too long, that the* French *are the only People in the World who have the very extraordi-nary Politeneſs to tell all Strangers, that they alone underſtand* Le ſçavoir vivre ; *and the* Commerce de la vie. *That ſurely cannot be the reaſon for ſending young Gentlemen betimes into Country-Towns in* France, *ſince it is well known how awkard the People of the beſt Faſhion at* Caen, Angers, *or* Beſançon, *for inſtance, appear to the Court-bred at* Verſailles *or* Paris, *the Center of* French *Politeneſs. 'Tis the Fair Sex in every Country that is the Source of good Breeding, and that regulates genteel Manners : And thanks to our untravelled Ladies for their better Notion of a fine Gentleman ; ſince it is chiefly by their means that any of our young Travellers who return from* France *Fops and Coxcombs, are ever recovered from their* French *Flutter-ing, Volatility, and Impertinence, and reſtored to that native Plainneſs and Seriouſneſs of the* Britiſh ; *of which, if ever we become generally aſhamed, all that is Grave and Great amongſt us, andth at exalts us above every ſlaviſh Country, muſt be on the Brink of Ruin.*

IF *it is ſaid, that they are ſent early into* France *to learn the* French *Language, that they may have a Tongue to travel with afterwards ; I ſhall only ſay, that very many have acquired in conſequence of a right Edu-cation at home, not only* French *but* Italian, *to a very great degree of Per-fection, without having neglected Languages of greater Uſefulneſs, by the Help of which they may early imbibe Sentiments much better becoming a free People, than they can from* French *or* Italian *Authors : Sentiments that will beſt ſerve to maintain Love of Liberty and publick Spirit in that due Vigour neceſſary to uphold a free Conſtitution. And there are, on the other hand, but few Examples of very great Progreſs made abroad in* France *in the* French *Language, by ſuch as had not made conſiderable Advances in it before they left their own Country.*

THO' *it appears from what hath been ſaid, who alone are qualified to travel ; and that very few young People can be ſo, at leaſt till ſound Poli-ticks, and the Knowledge of the World have a greater ſhare in our Educa-tion ; yet it is with the higheſt Satisfaction I ſay it, that I have met with ſome very young Gentlemen abroad who travelled to very great advantage. I have already mentioned a very juſt Remark of one in his Travels ; and I would name him and a great many more, did I not fear to offend their Modeſty. One very extraordinary Inſtance I cannot chuſe but relate, to ſhew young Travellers what Diſpoſition of Mind is neceſſary to travelling pro-fitably. A Nobleman who ſet out to travel very young, not ſatiſfied with having very well digeſted the Plan of his Travels before he left* England, *upon his Arrival in ―― ſat down ſeriouſly to review his paſt Education ;*

and

and to confider what remained for him to do, to fit himfelf for being fervicé-
able to his Country in the high Station to which his Birth entitled him.
Having then for fome time maturely weigh'd the chief Ends of travelling,
and confidered the Preparation it requires, he wrote, by way of Directory
to himfelf, an excellent Performance, in Imitation of the ancient Fable of
Prodicus concerning the Choice of Hercules. Wifdom and Pleafure accoft
him as they did Hercules. The latter courts him to fling himfelf into her
foft Arms, and to give full Scope to every Fancy and Appetite that promifes
him pleafure, without being at the trouble of examining its Pretenfions. But
Wifdom advifes him to think of Virtue and true Honour; of his Country and
its Good; and to travel in order to qualify himfelf for worthy Purfuits and
Employments at home. He by asking Wifdom what Defign one ought chiefly
to propofe to himfelf in travelling, puts her upon pointing out to him the chief
Purpofes and Advantages of Travel, and the Qualifications neceffary for gaining thefe Ends : Upon which he refolves to beftow fome time at the Univerfity,
where he then was, upon Hiftory, the Laws of Nature and Nations, and other
fuch previous Studies; and then to travel on condition that Wifdom would go
along with him, keep his Country ever in his Heart and Eye, and preferve
him from the contagious Vices of the World. He was able to form to himfelf
in this manner an excellent Scheme of travelling, and having purfued it as
one could not but expect from fuch rare Virtue and Prudence, his Country
now reaps the happy Fruits of his Knowledge and Integrity. If one would be
great and amiable, let him imitate * * *, and be happy by fo doing.

THE World is fufficiently ftuffed with Books of Travels, but in almoft
all of them I have been able to get into my Hands, the main End of travelling is over-looked; and as if the Knowledge of Mankind had nothing
to do with it, every thing elfe is treated of in them but that alone. The
greater part of them are filled up with general Notices of Buildings, Statues,
Bas-reliefs and Pictures, that are to be feen in Italy in particular, which
do not even fuperfede the neceffity of having recourfe to the very defective
Originals from which they are taken, that are to be found in every Town,
under the Title of a Guide to Foreigners, for that place. Mr. B—— has
wrote a Book, from the Title of which one would naturally expect a Treatife
upon the principal Purpofes and Ends of travelling, and the right Method
of accomplifhing thefe Ends. But tho' he calls it An Effay on the Utility
of Travel, after telling us, that it is fit to carry good Maps with us of
the Countries we intend to vifit, and giving us fome other fuch-like profound
Advices, he immediately falls into learned, or rather advent'rous Difcuffions
about Medals, Gems, and Talifmans, as if collecting fuch Rarities were to
be a Gentleman's chief Employment abroad ; and the Knowledge of Men
and Things were quite foreign to his purpofe. Hardly will any one of our
Travellers fay, that M—— is a fufficient Guide, or that he with all his
commendable Zeal againft Popery ; all his ridiculous Anecdotes of Priefts,
Friars, and Nuns, and all his fage Counfels about carrying with us Bed-
Linen, Knives, Forks, Spoons, a Blunderbufs, &c. has quite exhaufted the
Subject.

BUT tho' we ftill want fomething more full upon the chief Purpofe of
travelling, than hath been yet written, for the Direction and Affiftance
of our young Travellers ; Lord Bacon hath a Chapter upon it in his moral
Effays, that well deferves to be often read, and maturely pondered before
one fets out, and to be frequently returned to, and read over and over
again abroad. In Mr. Addifon's Travels there are fome excellent Obfervations upon Men and Things ; but his Remarks will chiefly ferve to fhew, how
well

well verſed in the Claſſicks one ought to be, in order to have agreeable En-
tertainment in ſeeing the Scenes of celebrated Actions, and the Remains of
ancient Arts.

   LORD MOLESWORTH *in his Preface to his Account of* Denmark, *ſhews*
what advantage one who thoroughly underſtands the Value of a free Conſti-
tution, and hath withal a humane, generous Soul, will reap in enſlaved
Countries, by ſeeing, or rather feeling the miſerable Effects of lawleſs Power.
Travelling into ſuch Kingdoms he thinks neceſſary to thoſe who are born in
free Countries; becauſe as one is in danger of forgetting the Value of Health,
whilſt he enjoys an uninterrupted Courſe of it; ſo amidſt the happy Fruits
of Liberty, a Senſe of its ineſtimable Worth may be loſt, or at leaſt conſider-
ably impaired.   But, on the other hand, if one hath not very juſt Notions
of Government; and a very benign, as well as penetrating Mind, may be
not be dazzled by the glaring Pageantry and falſe Magnificence of the Courts.
of Tyrants; and become enamoured of the Worſhip paid by a ſlaviſh Com-
monalty to the Nobles, and think the Homage and Submiſſion they are obliged
to render in their turn to their deſpotick Lord, ſufficiently compenſated by the
Power left them to tyrannize over their Inferiours.

   LORD MOLESWORTH'*s Account of* Denmark *points out to Travellers the*
Things that ought to be inquired into abroad : And thoſe who having read
that excellent Treatiſe, Sir William Temple'*s Account of the United Pro-*
vinces, Busbequius'*s Epiſtles, and ſome other ſuch Books, have learned what they*
ought principally to endeavour to know in foreign Countries; and have al-
ready taken the propereſt Methods of getting ſatisfaction about all theſe Mat-
ters with regard to their own Country; thoſe alone are fit to travel; and
ſuch can't fail to return from abroad freighted with very uſeful Knowledge.
But ſuch, as far from being prepared for thoſe important Enquiries, have
not ſo much as the leaſt Taſte of the fine Arts before they travel; what elſe
can be expected from them, but that they ſhould entirely give themſelves up
abroad to ſhameful, ruinous Pleaſures, to Dreſs, Gallantry and Play; and that
amongſt People not of the higher Rank : not merely becauſe it is eaſier to
have acceſs to the lower; but rather becauſe they meet amongſt them with
more of that vile, pernicious Flattery and Cringing, by which they were cor-
rupted at home, not by Servants and Paraſites alone.

   I have only mentioned theſe few things about Travel, leſt any one ſhould
imagine, that having wrote upon Painting chiefly for the Uſe and Aſſiſtance
of young Travellers, I looked upon it to be the principal Deſign of travelling
to get acquainted with Antiquities, or with the Hands and Pencils of Pain-
ters.   And having ſufficiently declared my Sentiments on that head, I ſhall
now take advantage of another received Cuſtom in Prefaces, and give ſome
ſhort Account of the following Eſſay.   A Reader now-a-days as naturally
expects that in a Preface, as one does an Advertiſment, where there is any
Rarity to be ſeen, with ſome general Information of the Entertainment of-
fered for his Money.   And this is ſo much the more neceſſary, with regard to
this Treatiſe, becauſe it is impoſſible to expreſs fully in the Title of it a
Deſign ſo new and comprehenſive : And ſome may have imagined that it is
only a Treatiſe for Painters.

   THE Deſign of the Eſſay on the Riſe, Progreſs, *and* Decline of Paint-
ing among the Greeks, &c. *is to ſet the Arts of Deſign in a juſt Light;*
and to point out in particular the excellent Uſe that may be made of them in
Education.

IN ihe firſt Chapter it is obſerved, that the Arts of Deſign are very ancient ; more ancient than the Fables concerning Apollo, Minerva, Vulcan, *the* Muſes *and* Graces, *and conſequently than the Story of* Dædalus. *But whatever may be determin'd with reſpect to their Antiquity in practice,* Homer *certainly had very perfect Notions of them in all their Parts and Qualities; and a very high Idea of their Power, Extent and Uſefulneſs, not only to charm and pleaſe, but to inſtruct in the moſt important Points of Knowledge.* Virgil *likewiſe has not ſcrupled to ſuppoſe not only Sculpture but Painting as anciently in uſe as the Siege of* Troy ; *and he had the ſame Opinion of their Dignity, Utility, and Excellence. The beſt ancient Philoſophers entertained the ſame Sentiments concerning thoſe Arts; their Fitneſs in particular, to teach human Nature; to diſplay the Beauties of Virtue and the Turpitude of Vice; and to convey the moſt profitable Inſtructions into the Mind in the moſt agreeable manner. Accordingly they employ'd them to that noble purpoſe, frequently taking the Subjects of their moral Leſſons from Paintings and Sculptures with which publick Porticoes at* Athens, *where the Philoſophers taught, were adorn'd. Some Moderns of our own Country, who are own'd to have come neareſt to the beſt Ancients in agreeable as well as uſeful Writing, have earneſtly inculcated the like Notion of the polite Arts, and recommended them together with the manly Exerciſes as neceſſary to complete a truly Liberal Education. Thus the Concluſion, that is principally aim'd at in this Eſſay, comes out with a conſiderable degree of Evidence in the firſt Chapter.*

IN order to give a juſt View of the Excellence and Uſefulneſs of the fine Arts, it is requiſite to give a fair Repreſentation of the Perfection to which they have been improved at any time. Some may ſuſpect, that Men of fine Imaginations have carry'd theſe Arts further in Speculation than they have ever been actually brought to, or than they can really be advanced. Thoſe who have conceiv'd, whether from Deſcriptions of Poets, or from ſeeing a few good Pictures, ſome Idea of what they may be really able to perform, if duly cultivated and improved, will naturally be deſirous of knowing what Progreſs they had made in ancient Times; and by what Means and Cauſes that chiefly happen'd. And in truth it is hardly poſſible to ſet their Power, Extent, and Merit in a better light, than by ſhewing what they have actually produced. Now this is attempted in the ſecond Chapter.

BUT before I entered upon the Hiſtory of the Art, it was proper to obſerve in an Eſſay, chiefly intended to ſhew the Uſefulneſs of Painting and its Siſter Arts in Education, That tho' the more ancient Treatiſes on Paintings are loſt ; inſomuch that we have nothing preſerv'd to us that was expreſſly written on that Subject, except what is to be found in Pliny *the Elder, and the two* Philoſtratus's *Works ; yet ſuch was the ancient Manner of Education, and of explaining any particular Art or Science, that in their Diſcourſes upon Poetry, Eloquence, Morals and other Subjects, many excellent Remarks are made for the Illuſtration of theſe Subjects upon the different Talents and beſt Performances of ancient Painters ; the eſſential Qualities of good Painting, and the Riſe, Progreſs and Decline of that Art : which Obſervations when laid together in proper Order, will be found to furniſh not only a very full Hiſtory of the Art, but a juſt Idea of its Uſefulneſs in Education ; or for the Improvement of the Heart as well as of the Imagination and Judgment. Accordingly the firſt Chapter ends with an Obſervation to that purpoſe upon the Authorities from which the following Account of ancient Painting is brought, and upon the ancient Manner of uniting all the Arts and Sciences in Liberal Education.*

e

IN the *fecond Chapter an Account is given by way of Parallel, of the chief Talents and Qualifications of the more remarkable Painters in the two moft diftinguifh'd Ages of the Art, that of* Apelles *and that of* Raphael; *in which it is fhewn by what fimilar Means and Caufes it advanced to fo like a degree of Perfection at both thefe Periods. The Analogy between thofe two Ages of Painting in many Circumftances is indeed furprifing; but it is well vouch'd, and not imagined; and therefore abftractly from all other Confiderations, it is, by itfelf, a Phænomenon well worth a Philofopher or Politician's Attention. This Hiftory is given by way of Parallel; becaufe it was thought it would not be difagreeable to fee two Ages of the Art, as it were, at one View; but chiefly becaufe it is very difficult to convey clear Ideas of the Talents of Painters merely by Words; and thofe who are at a lofs to underftand any ways of fpeaking that are ufed in defcribing the Abilities of any ancient Painter, will be beft fatisfied by having recourfe to the Pictures (or good Prints of them) of thofe Mafters among the Moderns, to whom the like Qualifications are afcribed. In this double Hiftory frequent Opportunities occur of fetting to view the Connexion of the polite Arts with true Philofophy, and their Serviceablenefs in fhewing the Beauties and Deformities of Life and Manners, and in leading to juft Notions of Nature, and of all the Arts, and likewife of good moral Conduct; more particularly in drawing the Characters of* Apelles, Pamphilus, Euphranor, Nicias *and* Metrodorus; *and in commenting upon fome Paffages of* Cicero *and* Quintilian, *concerning the like Progrefs of Painting and Oratory among the* Greeks, *and fome of the Caufes and Means of their Improvements.*

THIS Effay is divided into Chapters, becaufe it is neceffary to return again and again to the fame Subject, in order to fet it in various Lights and Views.

AND in the third the fame Subject is refum'd, but purfu'd in another manner. It is likewife about the Progrefs of Painting among the Greeks. *In it fome of the beft Pictures of the moft celebrated ancient Artifts are confider'd, fuch as feem'd moft proper to fhew the Perfection at which Painting in all its parts had arriv'd in* Greece; *to evince the Excellence of the fine Arts; and to confirm the Conclufion that is principally aim'd at, the Connexion of Painting with Poetry, and of both with Philofophy: which in the end of that Chapter is illuftrated by a Paraphrafe on what the two* Philoftratus's *have faid on that Subject in their Books of Pictures. To which Reflexions a few others are added upon the equal Extent of Painting with Poetry, and the fimilar Diverfity both thofe Arts admit of, that do likewife no lefs plainly follow from the Examples of ancient Painting defcrib'd in this Chapter.*

IN the fourth, after fome Obfervations upon the Colouring and Drawing of the Ancients, and their Knowledge of Perfpective; fome of the moft effential Qualities of good Painting; fuch as Truth, Beauty, Greatnefs, Eafe and Grace are more particularly confider'd. And for this end, two Dialogues of Socrates, *one with a Painter, and another with a Statuary, are examin'd and commented upon at great length. After which feveral Paffages of* Ariftotle, Cicero, Quintilian, *and other Authors, relative to thefe Qualities of good Painting, are explain'd. And in difcourfing on them, Painting having been all along compar'd with Poetry, in order to give a right Idea of both, the Chapter ends with a fhort View of the principal Queftions, by which, in the Senfe of ancient Criticks, Pictures as well*

as

às Poems ought to be try'd and examin'd ; which shews the Consideration of both to be a very improving and truly philosophical Employment.

IN *the fifth Chapter, an Enquiry is made concerning the Progress of Painting among the* Romans; *in which it being quickly found out, that Painting never came to so great Perfection among them as in* Greece ; *some Reflections are made upon the moral Causes, to which the Progress and Decline of all the Arts, of Painting in particular, are afcrib'd by ancient Authors. Some had been already mentioned in the second Chapter, relating to the Talents and Characters of Painters, and the Encouragement of that Art; but several others of more universal Concern are here touch'd, such as the mutual Union and Dependance of all the Arts, and their Connexion with Liberty, Virtue, publick Spirit and true Philosophy.*

The sixth Chapter sheweth the excellent Uses to which the Greeks *chiefly employ'd the Arts of Design ; and the high Opinion which some of the greatest Men of Antiquity entertain'd of their real Dignity and Excellence, on account of their Tendency to promote and encourage Virtue, and to give Lustre, Beauty and Taste to human Life. After which there is some Reasoning to shew how necessary the fine Arts are to the truest Happiness of Man and the real Grandeur of Society. And last of all the Objections made against the polite Arts are remov'd : Such as, that* Plato *banish'd them from his ideal Republick ; and what is said by others of their Tendency to soften and effeminate Men, and of their having been one principal Cause of the Ruin of the* Roman *State.*

BUT *all these Enquiries being chiefly intended to prepare the way for a philosophical Consideration of the fine Arts ; in the seventh Chapter it is shewn, that good Taste of Nature, of Art, and of Life, is the same ; takes its Rise from the same Dispositions and Principles in our moral Frame and Make ; and consequently that the most successful way of forming and improving good Taste, must be by uniting all the Arts in Education agreeably to their natural Union and Connexion. To illustrate this more fully, our Capacity of understanding Nature, delighting in it, and copying after it, either in Life and Conduct ; or by the imitative Arts; is shewn to arise from our natural Love of Knowledge ; our Sense of Beauty natural and moral ; our publick and generous Affections, and our Love of Greatness ; to improve and perfect which Dispositions is certainly the principal Scope of Education. Then the properest way of teaching Oratory, Poetry, Logick, natural or moral Philosophy is enquired into ; and Painting is prov'd to be requisite to the most agreeable as well as profitable Method of explaining and teaching all these Arts and Sciences. Whether Education is consider'd with respect to the Improvement of Imagination, of Reason, or of the Heart,. Painting is shewn to be of excellent use. In considering the Nature and End of Philosophy, Pictures are prov'd to be proper Samples or Experiments either in natural or moral Philosophy ; and they are shewn to be as such, of admirable Efficacy to fix our Attention in the Examination of Nature, the sole Object of all Knowledge,. the Source of all Beauty, and the Standard of all the imitative Arts. To confirm this some moral Pictures are describ'd. And after having remarked, that in reading and explaining the Classick Authors to Pupils, Sculptures and Pictures ought for many reasons to have their place, and to be often referr'd to ; this Chapter concludes with observing, that this Scheme of Education only requires, that Drawing be early taught, which, as* Aristotle *long ago asserted, is not only necessary to Liberal Education, but to that of Mechanicks.*

THE

THE last Chapter points out some other very useful and entertaining Enquiries about Pictures, besides those that regard Truth and Beauty of Composition. For though that be the main thing in Painting as well as in Poetry; yet so like are these Arts in every respect, that some other Researches are equally pleasing and profitable with respect to both: Such as how the distinguishing Genius of a Painter, as well as that of a Poet, appears in all his Works; and what use modern Painters have made of the Antique, in like manner as the best modern Poets have done of the ancient ones.

THESE Enquiries are recommended as being not merely about Hands and Styles, but about Men and Things, and for that reason they are not barely suggested; but in order to put young Travellers into the way of them, some Observations are offer'd with respect to the distinguishing Talents, Genius and Characters of several of the most famous modern Masters, and the happy and laudable Use they made of the exquisite Remains of Antiquity in Sculpture and Painting.

THIS Work concludes with some few Remarks upon the fifty Pieces of ancient Painting now engraved with great Exactness and Elegance from excellent Drawings. Several Observations are made on them in the preceding Chapters; but here some Reasons are given for publishing them. It is a part of Antiquity that deserves to be made known, and that must therefore be very acceptable to all Lovers of Antiquity. Which is more, they serve to prove that the Accounts given in this Essay of ancient Painting, from ancient Authors, may be depended upon, or are not exaggerated. But they are publish'd chiefly in order to excite those, who are concern'd in Education, to make a proper use of the ancient Remains of Antiquity in Painting and Sculpture, in explaining ancient Authors to their Scholars; and to induce Travellers instead of republishing Statues and Bas-reliefs that have been often well engraved, to enquire after such as have not yet been made publick, by which either the Taste of Art may be improv'd, or any light may be given to ancient Authors. Some Account is added of the Originals, their Sizes, where they were found, and where they are, &c. It never was my Intention to enter in this Essay upon any mythological or classical Discussions about any Remains of ancient Arts; yet some few Passages of the Classicks that occur'd to me upon considering some of these ancient Paintings, are inserted, for the sake of those, who perhaps may never have thought of the mutual Light which ancient Authors and ancient Pieces of Art cast one on the other, though that hath been taken notice of by many Writers. And I am exceedingly glad that I can tell the Publick, that one much fitter for that learned, as well as polite Task, has far advanced in such a Work, which cannot fail to be of great use to Teachers and Students of Poetry, History, Sculpture, and Painting; and in particular to Travellers, as far at least as Improvement in good Taste of the fine Arts is concern'd in Travel, so equal is the Undertaker to that useful Design.

*ALL I have further to add is, that I am exceedingly indebted to a late excellent Commentary in French on Pliny's Book of Painting; as likewise to the same Author's Notes in French, added to a very correct Edition of the Latin Text *; and that I have not scrupled to make use of such English Translations and Paraphrases upon several Passages of ancient Authors relative to my Subject, as seemed to me to do justice to the Originals: But all that I have borrowed of that, or of any kind, is acknowledged in the marginal Notes; where the more important Passages of ancient*

Authors

---

* By Mr. D. D. London 1725.

Authors commented upon in the Text, are also inserted for the most part at full length, and in the original Languages. Mr. Pope's *Observations on the Shield of* Achilles *make a great part of the first Chapter. And indeed as an Essay on the Antiquity of Painting would have been very imperfect without taking notice of the fine Ideas* Homer *had of that Art; so it would have been vain and arrogant to have attempted any thing on that Subject after so masterly a Performance upon it. 'Tis very difficult not to indulge one's self in praising when the Heart is full of Esteem. But it very justly would have been accounted presumptuous and assuming in me, to do more than mention Mr.* Pope *when I quote any part of his Writings. It belongs to those of established Fame to dispense it, and to me to endeavour to merit it.*

I have received very little assistance from any of the few Writers upon ancient Painting, (for they do little more than copy from Pliny*) except* Junius **, and to him I frankly own I owe so much, that had he not obliged the World with his very learned Performance, I should never have attempted what I have done. But at the same time those who have read that Author will immediately perceive from the Account already given of this Essay, that I have pursued quite a different Scheme; and that I can have but very little in common with him except certain Authorities from ancient Authors. And with regard to those he quotes, I have left out not a few, as having very little relation to my Subject; many I have made a very different use of from what he does; and very many Passages of ancient Authors are to be found in this Treatise, which had either escaped him, or did not fall within his Plan. To give a just Idea of truly Liberal Education is my principal view throughout the whole; or by explaining the Relation of Painting to Philosophy, which is generally reckoned so remote from it, and its Usefulness in Education, to unfold at full length the Truth and Importance of that Saying of* Plato: " *That all the Liberal Arts and Sciences have a strict* " *and intimate Affinity; and are closely united together by a certain common* " Bond; *and that they cannot be sever'd from one another in Education, with-* " *out rendering any of the Arts that is taught very defective and imper-* " *fect; and Education very narrow and stinted, and incapable of produ-* " *cing that universal good Taste which ought to be its Aim." And that is quite a different Subject from what* Junius *had in view, tho' he likewise occa-sionally takes notice of this natural and inseparable Connexion and Union of all the Liberal Arts and Sciences. As I have no right to give any Advice to Artists; so I have no where attempted to do it, or assumed any higher Character to myself than that of a Collector from the Ancients. Yet if any Artists should think or say that Artists alone can judge of their Performances, I would just ask such, for whom they paint, if it is for Artists only. They surely have no reason to complain, when one not of the Profession endeavours to the utmost of his power to do justice to their Art, and to shew what ex-cellent useful Entertainment it is capable of affording to all who will but consider it as a Species of Poetry, as it ought to be. All however I pre-tend to, is to have acted the part of a Compiler, and to have digested into the best Order I could the Sentiments of ancient Authors about Painting, that are scattered thro' many of their Treatises on other Subjects: But in doing so, I did not think myself obliged merely to translate, I have oftener commented or paraphrased.*

LET me just subjoin, that I flatter myself the virtuous Intention with which this Work is wrote, will atone with my Readers for many Imperfec-

f   *tions*

---

* Francifcus Junius de Pictura veterum.

tions in it, besides those in Language, with regard to which I can't forbear saying, that I have ever had the same Idea of too great nicety about Style, as of over-finishing in Pictures.   *I need not make any Apology for inserting so many Passages from ancient Poets in the Text, since the practice is common ; those who like the original Authors from which they are quoted, will be pleased to find them applied to proper purposes ; and very few Translations of ancient Poets are so equal to the Originals as that of* Homer, *that I could adventure to make the same use of them I have done of it.*   *I return my most hearty Thanks to all those who have generously encouraged this Work ; and I hope they will not blame me for its not being published precisely at the time mentioned in the Proposals, since (not to say that very few Authors have so exactly kept to their time as I have done) I can assure them, the Hindrances that retarded this Work were absolutely inevitable.*   *Not having leave to mention those Gentlemens Names who were pleased to take the trouble of revising my Papers, and to favour me with their Animadversions upon them, all I can do is to assure them, I reckon myself exceedingly obliged to their very friendly Corrections and Amendments.*

N. B. If this Essay had been printed upon a Paper of the Size that was at first intended, it would have far exceeded the number of Sheets proposed. But it was afterwards thought proper, for the sake of the Copper-Plates, to print it upon a Paper of a much larger Size, tho' the Author's Expence be thereby not a little augmented.

THE

THE

PRINCIPAL CONTENTS of this Essay

DIGESTED INTO

A Regular Connected Summary.

CHAP. I. *Contains Observations upon the Antiquity of the Arts of Design, of Painting in particular ; and the just Notions which we are led to form of their Dignity, and Usefulness, by many Descriptions of Sculptures and Pictures in* Homer *and* Virgil, *in the following Order.*

The Learned have proved Painting to be very ancient by several Arguments : Arguments taken from ancient Fables, from the Nature of Things ; and from History. *p.* 1, *and* 2.

Though *Pliny* says it was not known at the Siege of *Troy* ; yet he owns that Sculpture was : Whence it follows, that Design must have been understood at that time ; and he justly wonders at its very quick Progress, on supposition that it began later. *p.* 3.

Homer, who is rigidly exact in his Accounts of Customs and Arts, represents Painting, or something equivalent to it to have been then in use : And whether the Practice of that Art be so ancient or not, 'tis plain, he had very perfect Ideas of it in all its parts: Accordingly he was not only regarded by ancient Criticks as the Father of Oratory and Poetry ; but by ancient Painters as their Legislator and Inspirer. —— *p.* 3.

And indeed a very good Reasoning of *Cicero* to prove, that Oratory as well as Poetry must have been at a very considerable degree of Perfection at that Period, equally extends to Painting, of which *Homer* shews such a thorough Skill and Taste. —— *p.* 4.

Mr. *Pope's* excellent Dissertation on the Shield of *Achilles* is inserted here, in which it is considered as a Piece of Painting which was never done before by any Critick ; for by it *Homer's* compleat Knowledge and high Opinion of that Art are put beyond all doubt; and the Art itself is set in a most just and delightful Light.

Some Authorities are added to prove, that it was considered by the Ancients in the same View. —— *p.* 5, *to* 12.

That *Virgil* had the same high Opinion of the Arts of Design, and equally delighted in bringing Ornaments to his Poem from them, appears by several Descriptions of Pictures and Sculptures, and other Works of Taste in his *Æneid* ; from the historical Paintings in particular, with which he adorns *Juno's* Temple, and the Effect he describes them to have had upon *Æneas.* —— —— *p.* 12.

Every one who is capable of understanding and relishing those beautiful Descriptions, must upon reading them anticipate the Conclusion chiefly aimed at in this Essay ; and immediately perceive and acknowledge the Lustre and Taste the fine Arts duly improved and applied would give to human Life and Society ; and the use that might be made of them in Education. —— —— *p.* 13.

And we find in ancient History that several Philosophers actually made a very happy use of them in teaching Morals in particular ; frequently taking the Arguments of their Lectures from the Pictures with which their Schools were adorned. —— *p.* 14, *and* 15.

But because I propose to give a History of the Art, and also to shew at fuller length what Opinion some of the greatest Men of Antiquity had of Painting, and wherein they placed its chief Excellence and Usefulness, it is proper to premise an Observation upon the Notion which the Ancients entertained of the natural Union and Connexion of all the Liberal Arts and Sciences ; upon ancient Logick ; and the ancient manner of explaining any Art or Science : for very little being left to us which was expressly written by any Ancient on Painting, 'tis only in consequence of their way of illustrating any one Art, by comparing it with all the others, that we can know their Sentiments concerning that Art. —— —— *p.* 16,17.

The Design of this Essay is to dispose into proper Order the Reflexions of *Socrates, Plato, Aristotle, Cicero, Plutarch, Quintilian,* and other ancient Authors that are scattered occasionally through their Treatises on other Subjects ; and thus to give a full Idea of the Art and the Use that might be made of it in Liberal Education. —— *p.* 18.

Chap. II. *Contains Observations upon the Perfection to which Painting was brought in* Greece ; *and upon some of the Means and Causes of its Improvement, in the following Order.*

Because

Euphranor

Euphranor is a Painter of a furprizing Character among the Ancients; he had many wonderful Talents : And juft fuch a one was *Michael Angelo* among the Moderns. They had both the fame Excellencies; and they both erred in the fame manner; that is, on the fide of Greatnefs. —— —— —— *p.* 30.

Antidotus, Scholar to *Euphranor,* was a Painter of the fame Genius and Character with *Andrea del Sarto,* Scholar to *Michael Angelo :* They were both heavy but diligent ; they had not enough of the poetical Fire equally requifite to Painting and to Poetry. *p.* 30.

Nicias had excellent Qualifications, and a very high Idea of the Sublimity and Ufefulnefs to which the Art might be brought : he confidered Painting as a Species of Poetry: And indeed all the great Mafters had the fame high Notion of the Art, and ftrove accordingly to carry it to its utmoft Beauty and Strength, by proper Methods of Study ; and thus it was that the Art was brought amongft them to fo great Perfection. This we learn from *Socrates,* from *Maximus Tyrius,* from *Cicero* and *Quintilian.* It was fo likewife with regard to the beft modern Mafters, and thus was the Art perfected by them. —— —— —— —— *p.* 31, 32.

A. Carrache by his juft Notions of Painting faved or rather reftored the Art from falfe Tafte and Ruin : He formed feveral excellent Painters, who by his Inftructions became able to oppofe with fuccefs a falfe Tafte that had already gained a great Afcendant at *Rome, Guido* in particular. —— —— *p.* 33.

Paufias, Scholar to *Pamphilus,* painted chiefly in the encauftiek way ; and he had much the fame Tafte with *Giov. da Udina,* Scholar to *Raphael,* who excelled in grotefque Decorations. —— —— —— *p.* 33.

Athenion is greatly praifed by the Ancients for the fame Excellence, as *Giulio Romano* amongft the Moderns; that is, for Erudition : and thefe two were deficient in Colouring in the fame refpect. —— —— *p.* 34.

Pyreicus painted low Subjects, like the *Baffans* among the Moderns, and had as well as they his Admirers. —— —— *p.* 34.

Callicles and *Calades* painted chiefly in Miniature; but had great Talents either for Comedy or Tragedy in Painting. But *Timomachus* excelled in doing tragical Pictures ; or in moving Horror and Pity, which is the End of Tragedy. He had that Excellence afcribed to the *Florentine* Mafters, called the *Furia* by Artifts. —— *p.* 34, 35.

Nicearchus, like *Guido* and *Parmeggiano,* excelled in expreffing the foft, tender Affections. —— —— *p.* 35.

The feveral Qualifications of a good Painter were in ancient, as well as modern Times, divided among many Mafters. Some were only underftood and admired by Artifts. Some by all. Some excelled in one part of Painting, and fome in another. *p.* 35.

Erigonus was an inftance of an extraordinary Genius, and what it is able to attain to with very little Affiftance. He was a common Servant to *Nealces;* but quickly became a great Painter, meetly by the Strength of his natural Difpofition and Parts. And we have two fuch Examples among the modern Painters *Polydore* and *Michael Angelo,* both of *Carravaggio.* —— —— —— *p.* 35.

Amongft the Antients fome Women were excellent Paintreffes: fo likewife amongft the Moderns, *Varro* gives a fine Character of *Lala,* and her Works. —— *p.* 36.

The laft of the *Greek* Painters I mention is *Metrodorus,* who was a good Philofopher as well as Painter, and had a confiderable hand in forming *Scipio,* one of the greateft Men that ever liv'd. We may learn from *Scipio's* Character what Education ought to aim at ; and from his Education how this End can only be accomplifh'd; even by uniting all the fine Arts and the manly Exercifes with Philofophy. —— —— *p.* 37.

But it may be ask'd, were there no Painters before *Apollodorus? Quintilian* names fome. But cenfures thofe pretended *Virtuofi* who valued their Pieces more upon account of their Antiquity than their real Excellence. —— —— *p.* 37.

This Cenfure however does not fall on thofe who are curious about the Hiftory of Arts; but on thofe who fondly doat on Ruft and Ruins. —— —— *p.* 38.

The Art began in *Greece* according to the oldeft Accounts we have of it, in the fame way it did in *Italy* at the Revival of Painting; and proceeded in the fame Manner from the firft rude Defigners in *Greece* like to *Cimabue, Giotto* and others among the Moderns, to *Panænus, Polygnotus* and a few others the firft of a Succeffion of Painters among the *Greeks,* equal to *Maffaccio* and *Mantegna* among the Moderns. —— *p.* 39.

It is difficult to fix the Age of the firft rude Defigners mention'd among the *Greeks.* But it plainly appears by all Accounts that the Art, at whatever Period it began, or was reviv'd, advanc'd to Perfection very gradually This is evident from what *Cicero* and *Quintilian* tell us of the fimilar Progrefs of Oratory, Sculpture, and Painting. *p.* 39, 40, 41.

Cicero and *Columella,* and other Antients give us a fine Picture of the Times in which polite Arts were improv'd; of the Spirit, Emulation, and Attachment to the Truth of Art that prevail'd amongft Artifts; and of the Care and Zeal of great Men to encourage that Spirit. —— —— —— —— —— *p.* 42.

Chap. III. *Contains Observations on some Pictures described by ancient. Authors ; on the just Notions the Ancients had of the Art, and of its Connection with Poetry and Philosophy, in this Order.*

That

That whole Story, as it is told by *Homer*, affords several fine Subjects for the Pencil: The last part of it, *Ulysses* surprising *Nausicaa* and her Damsels, was painted by *Polygnotus* in the various Gallery at *Athens*. And *Homer's* Comparison taken from *Diana* was painted by *Apelles*. *Virgil* very probably had an eye not only to *Homer's* Description; but to *Apelles's* Picture done to vie with it, in his Descriptions of *Diana* and *Venus*. —————————————————————— *p.* 56.

His superiour Excellence above all the other Painters of his time in giving Grace and Greatness to his Pictures, appears from the Accounts given us of his *Venus Anadyomene ;* of his Picture representing War, to which *Virgil* alludes ; of his *Alexander* with Thunder in his Hand ; of his *Hero* and *Leander* ; and of the Graces. And the Serviceableness of Painting in representing the Beauties of Virtue, and the Deformities of Vice, is obvious from his Picture of Calumny described by *Lucian*. —————— *p.* 57, 58.

The Subjects of *Nicomachus's* Pictures were truly poetical. Such were his Rape of *Proserpine*, and *Ulysses* acknowledged by his Dog *Argus*, a Subject taken from *Homer ;* his *Apollo*, *Diana*, a Bacchanalian Piece ; his *Scylla*, and other Pieces. —*p.* 59.

Euphranor excelled in painting Gods and Heroes. He had painted all the Divinities, *Theseus*, and several Heroes, and some Battle-pieces : 'Tis observable, that though he had a masterly grand Taste, yet he neglected no part of the Art, and was famous for painting Hair to great perfection, and in a very picturesque Gusto. —— *p.* 60.

Cydias painted the *Argonautick* Expedition in a truly heroick, grand Taste. And the truth of the Character given of *Nicias* appears from the Perfections ascribed to several Pictures done by this great Master, to his *Danaë*, his *Calypso*, his *Io*, his *Juno*, his *Perseus*, his *Alexander*, and several Pieces. —————— *p.* 60, 61.

That *Timomachus* was justly said to have excelled in Tragedy ; and that there is the tragick Stile in Painting, as well as in Poetry, is plain from what is said of his *Ajax*, his *Medea*, his *Orestes*, his *Iphigenia*, and his *Medusa :* to excell in which tragick Subjects, so as to avoid the painful and disagreeable, or the too horrible, is, as ancient Authors have observed, extremely difficult. —————— *p.* 61, 62.

There are Examples among the Ancients of all the Parts and Qualities of Painting. *Aristophon*, *Socrates*, and others, did historical and allegorical Pieces. The first of these was a very ancient Painter, he was Brother to *Polygnotus*. —— *p.* 62.

The *Danaë*, and the *Stratonice*, and the *Hercules* ascending to Heaven, by *Artemon*, are highly commended. *Ctesilochus* was a Libertine Painter. *Nealces* had a great regard to the *Costume*. *Simus* painted the Goddess *Nemesis*, with all her proper Symbols. *p.* 63.

Theodorus had painted in several Pieces all the remarkable Fates in the *Trojan* War : These Pictures were at *Rome* in *Virgil's* time, as he had seen them, so probably he had them in view in his Description of the Pictures representing the *Trojan* War, in *Juno's* Temple at *Carthage*. The same Artist had painted *Clytemnestra*, and other tragical Subjects. He had also painted *Cassandra*, to which Picture, which was at *Rome* in *Virgil's* time, the Poet no doubt had an Eye. It is not derogatory from *Virgil* to suppose that he borrowed Images from the Arts of Design ; and his doing it must have considerably augmented the pleasure of his Readers, who were acquainted with the Pictures he thought worthy of being described or alluded to. From those Instances that have been mentioned, the strict Alliance between Painting and Poetry is obvious : And other Proofs of it might be brought. —————— —————— *p.* 63, 64.

Theon painted *Orestes*, and used a very fine Stratagem in producing it to view at the publick Contests. —————— *p.* 65.

The burning of *Troy*, the Nativity of *Minerva*, and *Diana*, were finely painted by *Aregon*. —————— —————— —— *p.* 65.

There were some who only painted Portraits, as *Dionysius*. But the *Dionysius*, of whom *Aristotle* speaks, was a History-Painter, as we shall see afterwards. —— *p.* 65.

The Battle of the *Argians* was nobly painted by *Onatas ;* and the Ancients seem to have delighted much in martial Pieces, which are indeed truly moral Pictures. *p.* 65.

A great many other ancient Pictures are particularly describ'd or alluded to by ancient Writers ; but those that have been mention'd sufficiently confirm the Truth of what the two *Philostratus's* have said of the Excellence of Painting ; its relation to Poetry, and the Connexion of both these Sister-Arts with Philosophy ; which is the Conclusion chiefly aim'd at in this Essay. —————— —————— *p.* 66, 67.

To what these Authors have said, the Examples of Painting that have been brought, authorize us to add, that Painting and Poetry admit of the same Variety : and accordingly the Antients divided Painting as well as Poetry into the Epic, Tragic, Comic, Pastoral, &c. The End of both these Arts is the same, to instruct, move, and delight. And the Ancients well understood when the Epic Majesty and Sublimity, the Comic Mask, or the Tragic Buskin might be ascrib'd to Pictures as well as to Poems. *p.* 67, 68.

Chap.

Chap. IV. *Contains farther Remarks on some of the more essential Qualities of good Painting, as they are explain'd to us by ancient Authors; the poetical ones chiefly, Truth, Beauty, Unity, Greatness, and Grace in Composition, in the following Order.*

I confine myself to what the Ancients have said. *Socrates* represents moral Imitation as the chief End of Painting, and shews how serviceable the Art may be in exhibiting Characters, and in recommending the Beauty of Virtue. ———— *p.*81,82. So *Aristotle* likewise.

Other Philosophers being sensible of the Power and Charms of Painting, have endeavoured to force it into the Service of Vice. But *Socrates* made a better use of it, and one more suited to the natural Genius and Tendency of the Art, as well as more proper to display its Efficacy and Sublimity : All the good Qualities of the fine Arts are united and connected together like the moral Graces and Virtues. · So that it is hardly possible to discourse of any one of them singly and apart from the rest. *p.*82,83.

Painting admits of the Sublime as well as Writing, and it is the same in both. There is a Sublimity peculiar to some Subjects ; such in particular are virtuous Characters and Tempers severely tried : but there is a Greatness in Manner that may be attained to in Painting, whatever the Subject be. ———— ———— *p.*83, 84.

It consists in producing Surprizes by a well-chosen variety, and in contrasting artfully : in both which ancient Painters eminently excelled ; as they did likewise in concealing Bounds, which is the third thing essential to Greatness of Manner. *p.*85, 86.

There is Ease in Painting as well as in Writing : some Subjects are peculiarly called easy ones ; but Ease, whether in Writing or Painting, as it is opposed to the stiff, affected and laboured, is the same, and attainable by the same Rules as far as it is attainable by Study and Rules ; for it must be in a great measure of Nature's Growth, and it is chiefly learned in the School of the World. *p.*86, 87.

The Perfection of all the Arts consists, according to *Cicero*, in the Decorum, and is well defined by him. It is the same that he in other places, and *Quintilian* after him, call Simplicity and Frugality. Art must imitate Nature in its just Reserve, without niggardliness ; in retrenching the Superfluous, and adding Force to what is principal in every thing. ———— *p.* 88.

Grace can hardly be defined ; it is different from Beauty and Greatness : it is not peculiar to one Character : it extends even to the Folds of the Draperies. Several ingenious Writers have made good and useful Observations upon the Airs of Heads, Proportions, Contrasts and Attitudes to be found in the Antiques, that have Grace and Greatness, which deserve our Attention. All the Pieces now published have these excellent Qualities ; the Airs of Heads, Attitudes, and Draperies, are exceeding beauteous and graceful. I cannot better describe this Quality than by translating a Passage of *Lucian* as well as I can, where he calls upon Painting to do a Master-piece, and paint a more beautiful, graceful Woman than ever had been seen in real Life, in which he likewise most pleasantly represents all the different Qualifications of the best ancient Masters. *p.* 89, 90, 91.

In order to infuse Grace and Greatness into one's Works, the Painter must possess it himself in Habit, and then will it insinuate itself into his Performances naturally, and have the same good Effect upon their Beholders, that *Tibullus* ascribes to it in outward Behaviour. ———— ———— *p.*91.

The Perfection the Arts of Design had arrived at in Grace, cannot be wholly ascribed to the extraordinary Genius of the Artists : that would be doing injustice to a People who produced the best Models, either with respect to external or moral and inward Beauty and Proportion for Artists to imitate or copy after, that ever appeared in the World. *Reubens* ascribes the outward Beauty and Grace of ancient Works to the excellent Patterns they had of it before their Eyes. And the same reason extends to the other superiour Beauty and Grace belonging to the Mind, not less remarkable in their Pieces. ———— ———— . *p.* 92, 93.

Modern Masters only imitated and endeavoured to equal the Copies of the Ancients, which they did from Nature, far superiour to what we now see, at the same time striving to excel it. And it cannot surely be thought to have been of small Consequence to the imitative Arts and Artists to have had the most perfect Originals to copy after, or rather to endeavour to surpass. ———— ———— *p.*93.

From what hath been said, we see by what Questions or Principles, in the Sense of ancient Criticks, Pictures as well as Poems ought to be tried ; and that the Examination of both is truly philosophical Employment. It is the Study of Nature, with the Assistance of good Copies. ———— ———— ———— *p.*93, 94.

Chap. V. *Contains Observations on the Rise and Decline of Painting among the* Romans ; *the State of the other Arts, while it flourished among the* Greeks *and* Romans ; *and the Causes natural and moral to which its Declension is ascribed, in the following Order.*

It is acknowledged by all the *Roman* Writers that Philosophy, and all the Liberal Arts, came from *Greece* to *Rome*, and that it was very late before they were encouraged by the *Romans*, Painting in particular. ———— ———— *p.*94.

muft

muft be allowed to have a great fhare in the Phænomenon. His Account of Facts is juft; but with regard to his Conclufions I beg leave to obferve, that the Ancients, *Cicero* in particular, have juftly remarked, that when a State is inwardly unfettled, or in outward Danger, the Defire of Knowledge, and Love of Arts is not likely to rife and fpread. This Temper is the Produce of Peace; but of what Peace? Of Peace refulting from Profperity, and Liberty fix'd upon a folid Foundation, and guarded by the Love of Liberty's watchful jealous Eye. But they have alfo obferved, that nothing is more dangerous to Virtue, true Philofophy, and all the Arts, than Opulence and profound Quiet and Eafe, and the Vices which, as it were, naturally fpread from that Source. Hence the ancient Proverb, *Plus nocuere togæ, quam loricæ.* *p.* 107, 108.

This Obfervation, founded on Experience, well deferves the Politician's Attention. But not to leave our prefent Subject; with regard to what this Author fays of phyfical Caufes, I would only obferve, that in confequence of our Frame, phyfical Caufes muft needs have a very great Influence on our Minds; but ftill moral Caufes muft be principal with refpect to moral Appearances or Effects. And this Influence of natural Caufes does evidently not extend fo far as to render Progrefs in Virtue and Knowledge quite beyond our own power. The chief Dependence of Virtue, and the Arts upon Caufes not in our power, is in the nature of Things a focial Dependence, *viz.* our Dependence upon the right Frame of the Government we live under, and upon our Education. ——— *p.* 108, 109.

This Author at the fame time that he commends the *Englifh* Genius, afcribes our not having had any great Painters wholly of our own Growth to our Air, Diet, and other fuch Caufes. But other Reafons fufficient to explain the Fact are too obvious. *p.* 110.

From what hath been faid, we fee how neceffary a free and publick-fpirited Government is to produce and uphold all the liberal Arts, as well as all the Virtues. *p.* 110.

Chap. VI. *Contains Obfervations on the Ufes to which Painting and Sculpture were employed among the Ancients: the noble Purpofes to which they ought to be employed, in order to adorn human Society, promote and reward Virtue and publick Spirit; and upon the Objections that are brought againft the Encouragement of them, in this Order.*

Pictures and Sculptures were applied to preferve the Memory of great Men and great Deeds, and to beget a noble Emulation to imitate fuch Examples. All their Heroes, all their Poets, all their Philofophers, all their ingenious Artifts were honoured by having their Pictures put up in publick Places. And proper Symbols were given to Pictures or Statues reprefenting the diftinguifhing good Qualities of each Perfon. Several Examples of this are given, as how *Homer* was painted, *Achilles*, feveral Heroes, &c. ——— *p.* 110, 111.

But this was not all, ancient Artifts excelled in expreffing the peculiar Characters of Perfons in their Portraits or Statues. And ——— *p.* 112, 113.

Great Deeds were painted in the hiftorical way; ancient Shields were adorned with fuch Reprefentations. ——— *p.* 114.

Philopæmon recovered the *Achaian* Youth from Effeminacy by a noble Stratagem, which fhews how our natural Tafte of Beauty may and ought to be improved by Education. *p.* 115.

To confirm all this, feveral ancient Monuments of great Men and their illuftrious Deeds are mentioned; the good Effect of the ancient funeral Panegyricks among the *Greeks* and *Romans* is taken notice of. Pictures reprefenting great Men and their excellent Deeds were placed in the Temples. So likewife were moral Pictures. The allegorical Picture of *Cebes* was an Ornament of a Temple of *Saturn*. There were Places throughout all *Greece* for publick Meeting and Converfation, called *Lefche*, that were adorned with Pictures and Sculptures. ——— *p.* 116, 117, 118.

The publick Libraries at *Rome*, after the Model of thefe in *Greece*, were adorned with Pictures and Sculptures. Which Libraries were dedicated or confecrated in a very folemn manner. ——— *p.* 119.

Atticus was at great pains to preferve the Images of illuftrious Men. So was *Marcus Varro.* ——— *p.* 119.

Private Libraries were adorned in like manner. ——— *p.* 120.

The Conclufions that follow from all this are manifeft. Hence appears the true and beft Ufe of the fine Arts; and that Pictures ought to be fet up to publick View, and not to be excluded from fight. ——— *p.* 120.

M. Agrippa was very zealous againft fhutting up Pictures in private Houfes, an Evil that begun to prevail in his time. The *Topham* Collection was given to *Eton* College on terms worthy of an *Afinius Pollio*, a *Varro*, or a *Marcus Agrippa*. ——— *p.* 120.

Pictures

Chap. VII. *Contains Obfervations on the Samenefs of good Tafte in all the Arts, and in Life and Manners ; on the Sources and Foundations of rational Pleafures in our Natures ; and the Ufefulnefs of the fine Arts in a Liberal Education, in this Order.*

3. With a Sense and Love of Greatness, which Taste leads the Mind to be particularly pleased with Objects that are in themselves great, or have a Greatness in their Manner. Such Objects wonderfully elevate the Mind, and delightfully prove its force. *p*. 133.

This is a true Account of natural Philosophy, of our natural Qualifications for the pursuit of it, and of the Pleasures arising from it according to *Plato*, Lord *Verulam*, and Sir *Isaac Newton*. And hence we may learn how moral Philosophy also can only be improved. —————— · ——— ——————— ——— *p*. 133, 134.

Now the same Faculties and Dispositions that qualify us for the Study of Nature, do likewise fit us for the Imitation of Nature. 1. For the Imitation of Nature in Life and Conduct; in Beauty, Order, Truth, Consistency and Harmony of Life and Manners; for imitating the Wisdom, the Simplicity, the Greatness and Goodness of the allgoverning Mind, that made and ruleth over all in the Regulation of our Affections and Behaviour. ——— ——— ——— *p*. 134.

Cicero reduces all the Virtues to the suitable Improvements of those four Dispositions in our Nature, by which we are eminently distinguished above other Animals; the Love of Truth, the Love of Union and Society, the Love of Power and Greatness, and the Love of Beauty, Harmony, and Order. ——— ——— *p*. 135.

The Capacity of Virtue necessarily pre-supposes a Sense of moral Beauty and Greatness, and a social Principle: and so does our Capacity of enjoying and delighting in the Order, Harmony, Goodness and Greatness of Nature. We may therefore justly argue, that if there be such a thing in Nature as Order, Beauty, Goodness, and Greatness, we ought to imitate it in the Government of our Affections, and in our Conduct; and if we are capable of forming any Notion to ourselves of moral Beauty, Fitness and Greatness in Conduct; there must be moral Order, Beauty, Fitness and Greatness in Nature itself throughout all its Oeconomy and Administration. ——— *p*. 136.

But, 2. We are qualified by Nature for the Imitation of Nature by ingenious Arts, by the same Faculties and Dispositions which fit us for the Study of Nature, and the Imitation of it in our Conduct. ——— ——— ——— *p*. 136.

All Arts are Imitations of Nature. But Poetry, Sculpture and Painting are peculiarly called imitative Arts. We are made by Nature prone to Imitation. Hence the Origin of all the Arts that imitate Nature, and vie with it. Now we are qualified for imitating the Beauty, Truth, Simplicity, Goodness and Greatness of Nature in these Arts, by the same Dispositions just mentioned. This will appear by recalling to mind what hath been said of the more essential good Qualities of Painting; of Truth, Beauty, Grace and Greatness in that Art. And we may justly reason in this manner, that if the reality of these Qualities is acknowledged in one instance, either in Nature itself, in our moral Conduct, or in the imitative Arts; their reality must of necessity be owned throughout them all. Virtuosi must therefore either give up their beloved Arts, or own the reality of Virtue. ——— ——— *p*. 136, 137.

To illustrate this, it is proper to observe, 1. The strict Analogy that there is between our Sense of Beauty in material Objects, and our Sense of Beauty in moral ones; and the strict Analogy that there is universally between the corporeal and moral, or intellectual World, as far as our Observation can go. ——— *p*. 138.

2. The inseparable Connexion throughout all Nature, of Truth and Beauty with Utility. Both these are much insisted upon by the Ancients. ——— *p*. 139.

3. Who tell us also in their way of explaining the Beauty and Perfection of the imitative Arts; that these Arts ought not too strictly to adhere to any particular Object of Nature, but to take their Idea of Beauty from Nature in general, and to endeavour to do as Nature does, to make a good Whole; because these Arts cannot take in all Nature, but a part only; therefore whatever they represent ought to be a perfect Whole, as Nature itself, where all is managed for the best, with perfect Frugality and just Reserve; its wise Author being profuse to none, but bountiful to all: never employing in one thing more than enough; but with exact Distribution and Oeconomy retrenching the Superfluous, and adding force to what is principal in every thing. This seems to be *Cicero*'s Meaning when he is speaking of *Zeuxis*, and giving the Reason why he collected Beauties from many different Originals, to make one perfect Piece. ——— *p*. 140.

In order to such Imitation of Nature, 'tis obvious that Art must set off what is principal by proper Contrasts; for thus in Nature itself is every thing heightned or strengthen'd. *p*. 141.

4. It is likewise worth Observation in the 4th place, that the chief Pleasures excited in us by ingenious Imitations of human Life and Manners pre-suppose a moral and publick Sense: They could not otherwise have an agreeable Effect upon us; or give us such exquisite Touches of Joy. And reciprocally, if the reality of a moral Sense and social Affection in our Natures be owned, it must necessarily follow, that the chief Pleasures we can receive from Imitations or Fictions, must be of a moral and social kind. *p*. 142.

5. To these Observations it may be justly added, that Man is so made as to be greatly delighted with whatever presents him with a high Idea of the Perfection to which human Nature may be improved by due Culture. And for this reason all the Improvements of the fine Arts must be exceeding delightful to human Contemplation. *p*. 142.

i   The

The Conclufions that naturally follow from thofe Principles that have been laid down concerning our moral Make and Conftitution; and that were inferred from them by the better Ancients, are, —————— —————— *p.* 142.

That Man is fitted and qualified by Nature for a very noble degree of Perfection and Happinefs: not merely for fenfitive, but chiefly for rational Happinefs. And Happinefs is not unequally diftributed by Nature upon fuppofition, that our chief Happinefs is from the Exercifes of Reafon and Virtue. For all Men may have the Pleafures of Reafon, Virtue, and Religion to a very high pitch: that is in every one's own power. And in a good and well-conftituted Government, even the lower Ranks of Men will have the Pleafures arifing from the Sciences, and from well-improved Arts, in a very confiderable degree. —————— —————— —————— *p.* 143.

We may juftly infer from the preceding Account of human Nature, that our Author muft have a moft perfect moral Difpofition, or be infinitely good and benevolent, fince he hath made us capable of difcerning and delighting in moral Order, Beauty, Truth and Goodnefs. —————— —————— *p.* 143.

But the Conclufion which chiefly belongs to our prefent purpofe regards Education; namely, that it muft be its chief End to improve to due perfection our Underftanding, our Imagination, and our Senfe of Beauty natural and moral: And that the propereft Method of accomplifhing that End muft be by combining together in Education all the Liberal Arts and Sciences agreeably to their natural Union, Connexion, and Dependency. —————— —————— —— —— *p.* 143, 144.

To illuftrate this 'tis only neceffary to reflect upon the ancient Method of teaching Oratory and Poetry, and of explaining the effential Qualities of good Painting. All thefe Arts are truly philofophical; and as the Confideration of them neceffarily leads to a moft profound Examination of Nature, of human Nature in particular, fo Philofophy cannot advance one ftep without bringing Examples from them: And the true Defign of genuine Logick is to point out the common Union and Connexion of all the Liberal Sciences and Arts, in order to furnifh us with a proper Directory for our right Procedure in queft of Truth and Knowledge. —— —————— *p.* 144, 145.

But the Ufefulnefs of the Arts of Defign will appear more clearly if we confider what Philofophy is, and how it ought to be taught; for Pictures are plainly Samples either in natural or in moral Philofophy: And the beft way of teaching the one or the other Philofophy is by Samples or Experiments. Landfcapes or Views of Nature's vifible Beauties are Samples or Experiments in natural Philofophy; whether they are Copies after particular Parts of real Nature, or imaginary Compofitions. They are Samples of the Beauties or Harmonies which refult from Nature's Laws of Light and Colours; for by thefe all the vifible Beauties of the fenfible World are produced: And thus they are proper means for forming and improving our Eye, or our Senfe of vifible Beauty in the fame way that mufical Compofitions are the proper means of improving an Ear for Mufick. So *Plutarch* and other Ancients have juftly remarked. —————— *p.* 145.

Now as for moral or hiftorical Pictures, they are plainly Samples or Experiments in the Philofophy which teaches human Nature, its Operations and Paffions, and their Effects and Confequences. It is acknowledged that Poetry by its Imitations affords very proper Samples to the moral Philofopher's Contemplation. And it is no lefs evident that moral Pictures muft likewife furnifh equally proper Samples in the fame way. The imitative Arts are for that reafon recommended by *Ariftotle* as better teaching human Nature than merely didactick Philofophy; nay, than Hiftory itfelf: They are, faith he, more *Catholick* or *Univerfal.* That all moral Pictures are Samples of human Life and Manners, is too evident to be infifted upon. And the Advantage of teaching moral Philofophy by means of fuch Samples confifts in this. The Mind is highly delighted with the double Employment of comparing Copies with Originals; and is thereby rendered more attentive to Nature itfelf than it can be without fuch Helps. And which is more, as certain delicate Veffels in the human Body cannot be perceived by the naked Eye, but muft be magnified in order to be difcerned; fo without the help of Magnifiers not only would feveral nice Parts of our moral Frame efcape our Obfervation; but no Features or Characters of the moral fort would be fufficiently attended to. Now the imitative Arts become Magnifiers in the moral way by means of reprefenting Affections, and their Workings, and Confequences in fuch Circumftances as are moft proper to fet them in the ftrongeft, the moft affecting and moving Lights. *p.* 146, 147.

Poetry hath its Advantages above Painting; and Painting hath its Advantages above Poetry. But without entering into a very idle Queftion about the Precedency of thofe two excellent Arts, which naturally go hand in hand with Philofophy, and mutually affift and fet off one another to great advantage; it is evident that both have this manifeft pre-eminence in teaching human Nature above Philofophy itfelf, as it proceeds in the dry way of mere Definition and Divifion, that they find eafier accefs into the Mind, and take firmer hold of it. And which is yet more, whereas Philofophers moft commonly have fome favourite Hypothefis in view, the Imitators of human Life, Poets and Painters, exhibit Affections and Characters as they conceive, or rather as they feel them, without fuffering themfelves to be biaffed by any Scheme. They follow the

Impulfe

Impulſe of Nature itſelf, and paint as ſhe dictates to them, or rather as ſhe moves them. How proper Samples moral Pictures are in teaching moral Philoſophy, that is, in exhibiting human Nature to view, and in recommending Virtue, and diſcountenancing Vice, will be evident, if we call to mind the noble Effects of ſeveral excellent Pictures; or the Influence which thoſe have naturally and neceſſarily on every Mind : *Raphael's* Cartoons in particular, and his *Parnaſſus*, School of *Athens*, and Battle of *Conſtantine*, &c. ⸻ ⸻ ⸻ *p.* 148, 149.

Hence we may ſee, that the Liberal Arts ought not to be ſever'd from Philoſophy in teaching it. In whatever View Education is conſidered, the Aſſiſtance of the Arts of Deſign is uſeful, nay neceſſary: whether we conſider it as intended to improve our Reaſon, our Imagination, or our Temper ; all the liberal Arts combine naturally together to effectuate any of theſe excellent Purpoſes in the beſt, that is, the moſt agreeable and ſucceſsful manner. And the reaſon is, becauſe, as hath often been obſerved by the Ancients, Beauty, Truth and Greatneſs are the ſame in Nature, in Life, and in Arts. Virtue is every where the ſupreme Charm or Beauty : And the moral *Venus* dreſt by the fine Arts (which are properly the Hand-maids to Philoſophy, or its beſt Miniſters) *glows with double Charms.* Whilſt ancient Philoſophers taught and recommended Virtue, taking the Arguments of their moral Diſcourſes from moral Pictures, the *living Leſſon ſtole into the Heart with more prevailing Force than dwells in Words ;* and round ſuch ſage Inſtructors the Breaſts of their noble Diſciples glow'd with an ardent Flame, Philoſophy not animated by living Examples cannot kindle. *p.* 150.

This Scheme of Education, as comprehenſive as it appears, and really is, may be eaſily put in practice. It only ſuppoſes the Principles of Deſign to be early taught ; which, as *Ariſtotle* wiſely obſerved, is not more neceſſary to liberal Education than to the Improvement of mechanick Arts. ⸻ ⸻ *p.* 151.

The Education of the ancient *Greeks* is well worth our Conſideration and Imitation in every reſpect : Their Muſick was quite a different thing from what now paſſes under that name. And with the Liberal Arts and Sciences they conjoined in Education certain manly genteel Exerciſes abſolutely neceſſary to the Formation of truly fine Gentlemen ; or to fortify againſt Effeminacy ; to give Grace and Vigour at once to the Body and to the Mind; and thus to qualify Youth early for the Service of their Country in the Arts of War or Peace. ⸻ ⸻ *p.* 152.

But I have accompliſhed my principal Deſign if what I have ſaid of the Uſefulneſs of the Arts of Deſign in Philoſophy and Education, be found in any degree conducive either to give a juſter Notion of the fine Arts than is commonly entertained even by their profeſſed Admirers ; or to give a more comprehenſive View of the Ends Education ought to aſpire at, than is generally apprehended, or at leaſt purſued. *p.* 152.

Chap. VIII. *Contains ſome Obſervations on the particular Genius, Characters, Talents, and Abilities of the more conſiderable modern Painters ; and the commendable Uſe they made of the ancient Remains in Painting as well as Sculpture ; and upon the Pieces of ancient Painting now publiſhed, in the following Order.*

It is plain from what hath been ſaid of the Analogy between Painting and Poetry, and the Foundations of a good Taſte of either in our Natures, that a juſt Notion of Truth of Compoſition is the principal thing in both theſe Arts. And that it is as eaſy to become a good Judge of the one as of the other. ⸻ *p.* 152, 153.

And there is indeed no uſeful Enquiry with regard to Poetry, to which there is not ſome analogous or correſpondent Reſearch with reſpect to Painting. There is the like Character with relation to the later, as that of the mere *verbal Critick* in the former : And it muſt be no leſs agreeable to obſerve what good Uſes modern Painters have made of ancient Works ; than to enquire into the happy and laudable Imitations of ancient Poets by modern ones. ⸻ ⸻ *p.* 153.

It muſt likewiſe be very entertaining to obſerve the peculiar Genius of a Painter diſcovering itſelf in his Works, in the ſame manner as it is to trace that of an Author, of a Poet in particular, in his Productions. ⸻ ⸻ *p.* 154.

Servile imitators in both Arts are equally deſpicable. And Painters ought to borrow Aſſiſtances from ancient Works, in the ſame way that a good Poet imitates an ancient one ; that is, as *Virgil* imitated *Homer.* Painters as well as Poets ought to ſtudy their own Turn and Genius, and give free and fair play to it. But as there is a remarkable difference between the Poets who are not acquainted with the Ancients, and thoſe who are ; ſo there is a no leſs ſenſible difference between the Painters who ſtudied the Antique, and thoſe who did not. *Raphael*, the beſt of modern Painters, formed himſelf into his beſt manner by ſtudying the Antique ; and aſcribed all his Perfection to the Aſſiſtances he received from theſe excellent Models. He not only ſtudied and held in great Admiration the ancient Statues and Bas-reliefs, but likewiſe the ancient Paintings : He was at great pains to make or get good Drawings after all the Pieces of that

kind

The Conclufion aimed at throughout this Effay is briefly this, *That Virtue is the fupreme Charm in Nature, in Affections, in Manners, and in Arts.*

ERRATA.

PAG. 25, in the Notes (25) read *dixiffe*.
51. l. 5. Inftead of *new* read *young*.
59. In the laft Quotation from *Virgil* read *fpelunca*,
87. In the Notes (71) inftead of *Hefiodum* read *Hefiodium*.
126. In the Notes (76) read *dubitas* inftead of *dabitis*.
104. In the Notes (50) read *aufus* inftead of *aufus*.
108. l. ult. read *have in confequence of our Frame and Conftitution a very great Influence upon our Minds, and all our Intellectual or moral Powers*.

And in the Notes (60) read *contagia* inftead of *contagia*. And l. 5. read *primum illa rata funt? arrogantia quæ*, &c.
112. after *fo Manilius*, read — *cujufque ex ore profufo*.
143. l. pen. read *argues* inftead of *writes*.
171. l. 1. read *Volupia*.

Read in feveral places *thofe* inftead of *thefe*, and *vice verfa*.
And be pleafed to excufe feveral other fuch-like Errors.

A N

E S S A Y

On the Rife, Progrefs, and Decline of

PAINTING

Among the *Greeks* and *Romans*.

CHAP. I.

Obfervations upon the Antiquity of the Arts of DESIGN, *of* PAINTING *in particular; and the juft Notions which we are led to form of their Dignity and Ufefulnefs, by many Defcriptions of* SCULPTURES *and* PICTURES *in* Homer *and* Virgil.

THAT the Art of PAINTING was in high repute, and brought to a confiderable degree of Perfection in very ancient Times, is the unanimous Opinion of *Voffius, Dati, Junius, Bulengerus, Fraguier,* and almoft all the Learned who have written on that Subject: many Arguments are brought to prove it (1).

That Painting is very ancient, is the unanimous Opinion of the Learned; and feveral Arguments are brought to prove it.

From ancient Fables.

PLATO and other ancient Authors tell us, it was the *Sun*, the firft and ableft of Painters, that taught Men to defign and paint. And what elfe can thefe Writers mean? what elfe can that known Story of a Shepherdefs circumfcribing her Lover's Shadow in order to preferve his Image, and other fuch like Fables concerning its Origin, fignify; but that this imitative Art, which is equally ufeful and pleafant, and to which Nature points and invites us fo ftrongly, by retracing or copying her own Works in various manners, muft have been very early attempted. Man is made prone to Imitation for many wife and kind Reafons. By this Principle he is at once qualify'd and excited to ftudy Nature, and copy after her, and thereby to learn feveral Arts. And the Stories of *Apollo, Minerva, Vulcan,* the Mufes and Graces, fuppofe the Arts already invented; and therefore the Arts of Defign are older than thefe very ancient Fables, and confequently than the Story of *Dædalus.*

" THE ingenious Abbé *Fraguier* (2), in his Difcourfe on the Antiquity of Painting, fays,
" he was led by the Confideration of the near Refemblance and ftrict Alliance between
" Poetry and Painting, to enquire which of the two is moft ancient. 'Tis agreed they are
" Sifters, their Intention and Scope is the fame; and the Means they employ for attaining
" their

(1) See *Ger. Joh. Voffius in quatuor artibus popularibus*; graphices fect. 4. Idem *Voffius lib.* 3. *cap.* 45. *de origine & progreffu Idololatriæ,* docet picturam (quæ cælaturam etiam, fculpturamque complectitur) antiquorem effe temporibus Iliacis, contra quam a Plinio proditum eft.
See alfo *Francifci Junii Catalogum pictorum, aliorumque artificum, in articulo Aaron.*
Vafari's Lives of the Painters, tom. 1. p. 64. *proemio delle vite,* & tom. 2. *littera di M. Gio. Battifta,* &c. The Teftimonies cited by thefe Writers from ancient Authors, facred and profane. Sciographia quidem inventa eft a Sauria, equum in fole circumfcribente: Graphicen invenit Crato, in tabula dealbata umbras viri ac mulieris inungens; a Virgine vero inventa eft Coroplaftice; fiquidem amore alicujus capta, circumfcripfit dormientis quafi umbram in pariete; pater deinde multum oblectatus fimilitudine, ufque adeo indifcreta (figulinam enim exercebat) lineamenta exculpta opplevit argilla: Is typus etiam nunc affervatur Corinthi. His fuccedentes Dædalus & Theodorus Milefius, Statuariam & Plafticen

adinvenerunt. *Athenagoras Legat. pro Chriftianis,* & *Fran. Jun. de pictura veterum in Catalogo. Crato pictor.*

(2) *Differtation de l'ancienneté de la Peinture,* par M. l'Abbé *Fraguier, dans l'Hiftoire de l'Academie Royale des Infcriptions & Belles Lettres,* tom. 1. p. 75.—L'homme qui eft ne imitateur, & dans qui l'inclination a imiter n'eft, peut-etre, pas une vertu, fe porta naturellement a l'imitation. Tout aidoit en luy ce penchant. L'ignorance le fortifioit, comme elle le fortifie encore aujourd'huy dans les enfans.—Les Objets qu'il avoit fous les yeux fembloient l'inviter au plaifir de l'imitation, & la nature elle-mefme, qui par le moyen des jours & des ombres, peint toutes chofes, ou dans les eaux, ou fur les corps dont la furface eft polie, luy apprenoit à fatisfaire fon gouft pour l'imitation. Il fatisfaifoit doublement tout à la fois, puifqu'en imitant les corps & les retraçant, il imitoit auffi la nature, qui les retrace & les imite en tant de façons differentes. Ainfi le Soleil, que Platon nomme ingenieufement le plus habile de tous les peintres, apprit aux hommes les commencements de la peinture.—On dit,

B   par

From the Nature of things.

" their common End are extremely like. But which is eldest ? 'Tis natural (faith he) to
" imagine that a certain rude way of delineating Objects, preceded the Invention of thofe
" arbitrary Marks by which Writing is form'd; and Writing is not improbably, fuppofed to
" be more antient than Poetry. It was not to draw Letters that the Pencil was firft taken
" up: Men had certainly effay'd to reprefent Objects by tracing their Forms; that is, to
" paint them, before they thought of combining Letters into Words in order to fignify
" Ideas. Nature leads firft to that which is eafieft and moft obvious; it advances by flow
" Steps to what is more remote from Invention. We may therefore pronounce in favour
" of Painting, that the precedence to it ; but fuch a Precedence (as often happens in
" great Families) is only due to it in point of Antiquity. For Poetry, according to the
" nature of things, muft have been the Fruit of gradual Refinement, of Politenefs cultivated
" by means of Writing; whereas Painting might have taken its Rife in very unimproved
" times, and while Mankind had no notion of Letters."

TO this effect the Abbé *Fraguier* reafons. And what appears fo probable in Theory, and
is, as he obferves, not obfcurely intimated to us by feveral ancient Apologues, many con-
curring Teftimonies of Hiftorians put beyond all doubt (3).

From Hiftory.

AS far as Hiftory reaches back, it prefents us with manifeft Proofs of the Antiquity of all
the Arts of Defign. The firft Writers of Hiftory were not a little indebted to thefe Arts for
their beft Materials and fureft Vouchers in compiling their Records : Painting, Sculpture,
and other Monuments, having been employed in the moft ancient Times to preferve the
Memory of Facts, and likewife to reprefent religious and philofophical Opinions.

BUT not to dwell long on Arguments from which nothing can be learned but barely the
Antiquity of a ruder fort of Painting ; I fhall only add, that one of our own beft Authors
feems to be of the fame Opinion with refpect to the Antiquity of that Art. " Defcription,
" faith he, runs further from the things it reprefents than Painting, for a Picture bears a
" near refemblance to its Original, which Letters and Syllables are wholly void of. Colours
" fpeak all Languages; but Words are underftood only by fuch a People or Nation. For
" this reafon, though Mens Neceffities quickly put them on finding out Speech, Writing
" is probably of a later Invention than Painting; particularly we are told that, in *America*,
" when the *Spaniards* firft arrived there, Expreffes were fent to the Emperor of *Mexico* in
" paint, and the News of this Country delineated by the Strokes of a Pencil ; which
" was a more natural way than that of Writing, though at the fame time much more im-
" perfect ; becaufe it is impoffible to draw the little Connections of Speech, or to give the
" Picture of a Conjunction or an Adverb (4)."

IT will be more inftructive as well as entertaining, to give my Readers a View of fome
other Reafonings on this Subject; which, at the fame time that they prove the very ancient
Practice and Efteem of Painting, afford no inconfiderable Infight into its chief Rules and
Beauties. And fuch are the Arguments brought from the Writings of *Homer*, the beft
and moft antient of Authors; and who is likewife very juftly called by *Cicero* (5), *Lucian* (6),
and others, the beft of Painters.   *PLINY*

---

par exemple, qu'une bergere, &c. il y a mille petits contes
femblables, qui, Vrais ou faux, ne fervent qu'à confirmer
ce qu'on Vient de dire, & ne font que des applications
particulieres d'un principe générale, & comme des apologues inVentez pour l'explication d'une Vérité.

Picturam, Cælaturam, Statuariam ab infima Antiquitate
repeti polle oftendi, cum Seruch Abrahami aVus Statuarius
& *Ardexarremide* fuerit. Memnon fuit antiquiffimus in
Ægypto Pictor & Statuarius. *Vid. Diodor. Siculum*, lib. 2.
*de Simandii Regis Ægyptii Sepulchro, cujus ambitus milliare
unum amplectus eft.*—Sculptus deinde eminens ceteris Rex
variis coloribus, erant deinceps Ægypti deorum omnium
Imagines. Sequebatur Bibliotheca in qua infcriptum,
Animi Medicamentum ; poft quam Domus erat in qua
20 Lectifternia Jovis & Junonis. Ibi picta Animalia fa-
cris apta. *Bulengerus de Pictura*, &c. lib. 1. cap. 9.

(3) Afferunt Ægyptii, literas, aftrorum curfus, Geo-
metriam, artefque plurimas ab fe fuiffe inVentas ; nonnulli has in Ægypto inveniffe quendam nomine Memnona
affirmant: fed apud eos Animalium Effigies loco literarum erant. *Died. Sic.* lib. 1.
See two Differtations in the *Memoires de Litterature tirez
des regiftres de l'Academie Royale des Infcriptions*, &c. par
M. l'Abbé *Anfelme.* The firft is in the 4th tome, p. 380.
The other, tome 6, page firft. Sur les monumens qui ont
ferVi de memoires aux premiers Hiftoriens ; where he fays
—Les evenemens fameuX eftoient reprefentez fur les bafes
des ftatues, des trépieds, des autels, dans les portiques, dans
les temples : & l'on peut dire que les anciens ont peint fuc-
ceffivement toute l'hiftoire, d'abord groffierement, & dans
la fuite avec plus de delicateffe. Many Teftimonies are
brought from *Herodotus, Diodorus Siculus*, and other ancient Authors, to proVe the Antiquity of the defigning
Arts :—and likewife from the facred Writings, the Command of God forbidding the Worfhip of Images.—The

able Artifts employed to work about the Tabernacle in
Gold, and Silver, and Brafs, *Exod.* xxxi. 2. And the
account that is given of the Origin of Images and Ido-
latry, in the Book of *Wifdom*, chap. xiv. ver. 15, 16, 17,
18, &c. For a Father afflicted with untimely mourning,
when he hath made an Image of his Child (now taken
away, now honoured him as a God, which was then a
dead Man, and delivered to thofe that were under him
Ceremonies and Sacrifices. Thus in procefs of time gra-
ven Images were worfhipped by the commandments of
Kings : Whom Men could not honour in prefence, becaufe they dwelt far off, they took the counterfeit of his
Vifage from far, and made an exprefs Image of a King
whom they honoured.—Alfo the fingular diligence of the
Artificer did help to fet forward the Ignorant to more
Superftition : for he—forced all his Skill to make the
Refemblance of the beft fafhion.

Euhemerus, in his ἱερὰ ἀναγραφὴ, feems to have given
the fame account of the Origin of Superftition, in
order to proVe its abfurdity ; according to the accounts
given of his Work by Heathen Writers, compared with
what is faid by the Fathers of the Church. See a Differtation on his Life and Works in *les Memoires de Litterature*, tome 8. p. 97.

(4) See Spectator, Vol. 6. N°. 416. and *Antonio de
Solis's Conqueft of Mexico.*

(5) Traditum eft etiam, Homerum cæcum fuiffe, at
ejus picturam, non poefim videmus. Quæ regio, quæ
ora, qui locus Græciæ, quæ fpecies formæ, quæ pugna,
quæ acies, quod remigium, qui motus hominum, qui
ferarum, non ita expictus eft, ut, quæ ipfe non viderit,
nos ut viderimus effecerit ? *Tufc. Quæft.*

(6) Μάλλον ἢ τὸν δεῖξιν τῶν γραφῶν Ὁμήρου, παεῤντε
Εὐφράνορος ἢ Ἀπίλλου, Ἀιδύμιζαν Imagines.

PLINY expressly says, that the Art of Painting was unknown in the times described by the Iliad : But, acording to that Author, the Art of Carving was in use at the Siege of *Troy*; and consequently Design, which is the most essential part of Painting, was then understood : And when he observes, that Painting does not appear to have been known at that time, he wonders how an Art (7), beginning so late, came so soon to its Perfection.

HOMER is reckoned so rigidly exact in describing the Customs, Manners, and Practices of Times, and Countries, that ancient Historians pay a very great regard to his Authority, and scruple not to build upon it (8). And therefore we can hardly doubt but that Painting was practised even at that early Period, since he represents it, or something equivalent to it, to have been then in use. But whether this Art was arrived to any degree of Excellence at the time of the *Trojan* War or not, *Homer* himself must be allowed by every one who understands the many lively and elegant Descriptions of Carvings, Statues, Sculptures, Tapestries, Pictures and Ornaments of all kinds, that occur in that divine Poet, to have had very perfect Ideas of all the Arts of Design, not only of Statuary and Sculpture, but of Painting. Tho' the Name of the Art is not to be found in his Writings, yet the Art itself is plainly described as it consists in Design and Colouring. So highly was he charmed with these Arts, that he has enriched his Poems with an infinite variety of Beauties derived from that delightful Source. It is indeed impossible to give a more perfect Notion of their End, Use, Power, and Excellence, than he hath done by his Descriptions of several Works of an exquisite, masterly Taste. Hence as he is universally owned, by all Criticks, ancient and modern, to be the Father of Poetry and Oratory, insomuch that all the Precepts and Examples of these Arts are taken from him; so he was likewise regarded by the best ancient Painters as their Inspirer, Teacher and Director. Were certain ancient Treatises on Painting still in being, of which we hardly know any thing but their Titles, it is highly probable we should find their Authors paying no less Homage to his Authority than the best Criticks on Eloquence and Poetry have always done. For this we are sure of, that the best ancient Statuaries and Painters studied from his Writings (9) : from his Writings they took almost all their Ideas and Subjects : whatever Affections, Passions, Virtues, Vices, Manners, Habits or Attitudes they drew ; whatever Characters of Gods, Demi-Gods, or Men and Women they represented, they had *Homer* always in their view as their best-Pattern to copy after. *Zeuxis* was considered by the Painters as their Legislator with respect to Divinities and Heroes, because he had followed *Homer* as his; so a very good Author tells us (10). It was *Homer*'s Paintings, say several other Writers (11), that awakened and kindled the Conceptions of the most eminent Sculptors and Painters, while they strove to keep up to the Truth, Beauty, and Grandeur of the Ideas he had impressed on their Imagination. His Descriptions became the Characters which were pursued by the great Masters, and in all Works of a good Taste. Now, what the *Roman* Orator says of *Homer* (12) with respect to Poetry and Rhetorick, holds equally good with regard to Painting : All these Arts must have been greatly improved, and in high esteem, before, or in his time, otherwise he could not have had such a consummate Idea of them in all their Parts and Qualities. No Art or Science starts all at once into Perfection : all things, natural or moral, advance to Vigour and Maturity by gradual steps. Can therefore these Arts, of which *Homer* shews so perfect a Taste and Knowledge, be supposed to have been but in embryo and hardly known in his time; or to have as yet produced nothing truly beautiful and elegant? Can any one consider his Descriptions of *Minerva*'s Ægis, *Achilles*'s Shield, the Buckler of *Agamemnon* (13), and several other such Works of the

Marginal notes:

Pliny says it was not known at the time of the Trojan War : But owns that Sculpture was, and therefore Design was.

He wonders at its quick Progress on that supposition.

Homer makes it so old, and is rigidly exact in his Accounts of Manners and Arts.

Whatever be as to that, he himself certainly had very perfect Ideas of the Art.

He was regarded by ancient Criticks as the Father of Poetry and Oratory.

And by ancient Painters as their Inspirer and Legislator.

Cicero's Argument with regard to the other Arts, will hold equally good with respect to Painting.

Several Descriptions in Homer referred to.

---

(7) Nullam artium celerius consummatam cum Iliacis temporibus non fuisse eam appareat. *Plin.* 35.

(8) *Strabo* in the first Book of his Geography, near the beginning, has these Words, δε (Ὁμηρος) ὁ μόνον ἐν τῷ φράσει τῶν ποιητῶν ἀριστ' κ. τ. λ.) Qui non solum universos priores ac posteriores Virtute poetica superavit ; sed etiam ipsa ferme rerum civilium, quæ ad vitam spectant, experientia. And in the same Book, afterwards, he adds, τὴν γὰρ ἐκείνου ποίησιν φιλοσοφίας πᾶσας νομίζω. κ. τ. λ.) Illius enim poesin sapientiæ studium esse, ac Philosophiam universi æstimant, non ut inquit Eratosthenes, qui, ad intelligentiam & mentem poemata judicari non debere, jubet, nec ullam ex Poetis Historiam esse petendam. So *Pausanias* in several places.

(9) *Strabo*, lib. 8. Ἀπομνημονεύουσι ᾗ τὸ Φειδίου κ. τ. λ.) Unum de Phidiæ memoriæ proditum est, ab eo Pandæno responsum, qui cum Phidiam interrogaret, quodnam ad exemplar Jovis statuam facturus esset, ad Homeri respondit Imaginem, quam hisce versibus explicavit :
Ἦ, καὶ κυανέησιν ἐπ' ὀφρύσι νεῦσε Κρονίων.
Ἀμβρόσιαι δ' ἄρα χαῖται ἐπερρώσαντο ἄνακτος,
Κρατὸς ἀπ' ἀθανάτοιο· μέγαν δ' ἐλέλιξεν Ὄλυμπον.

(10) *Quintilian*, lib. 12. Nam Zeuxis plus membris corporis dedit, id amplius atque augustius ratus, atque, ut existimant, Homerum secutus, cui validissima quæque forma etiam in fœminis placet. Ille Vero ita circumscripsit omnia, ut eum Legumlatorem vocent, quia deorum atque heroum effigies, quales ab eo sunt traditæ, cæteri tanquam ita necesse sit, sequuntur.

(11) *Strabo ut supra.* Vide *Junius de Pictura veterum. Phidias.* Phidias Homeri versibus egregio dicto allusit, (inquit Val. Maximus lib. 3. cap. 7. exemplo ext. 4.) simulacro enim Jovis Olympii perfecto, quo nullum præstantius aut admirabilius humanæ fabricæ manus fecit ; interrogatus ab amico, quonam mentem suam dirigens, vultum Jovis, propemodum ex ipso cœlo petitum, eboris Lineamentis esset amplexus : illis se versibus, quasi magistris, usum respondit : so Macrobius. Saturnal. l. 5. c. 14.

(12) *Cicero de Clar. Orat.* cap. 10. Neque enim jam Troicis temporibus tantum laudis in dicendo Ulyssi tribuisset Homerus, & Nestori,—nisi jam tum ellet honos Eloquentiæ, &c. ibid. cap. 18. At in Actione, Nicomacho, Protogene, Apelle, jam perfecta sunt omnia, & nescio an reliquis in rebus omnibus idem eveniat. Nihil est enim simul & inventum & perfectum.

(13) *The beaming Cuirass next adorn'd his Breast,*
The same which once King Cinyras *possest :*
Three glittering Dragons to the Gorget rise,
Whose imitated Scales against the Skies
Reflected various Light, and arching bow'd,
Like colour'd Rainbows o'er a show'ry Cloud.
(Jove's wondrous Bow, of three celestial dyes,
Plac'd as a sign to Man amid the Skies.) Iliad B.ii. l. 25.

His Buckler's mighty Orb was next display'd,
That round the Warrior cast a dreadful shade ;
Tremendous Gorgon frown'd upon its Field,
And circling Terrors fill'd th' expressive Shield :

Within.

the moſt perfect Deſign, and doubt of *Homer's* having ſeen ſome Performances of that kind, that had helped to raiſe his Imagination to ſuch noble Conceptions of what the fine Arts in their higheſt Perfection can produce? But if all ſhould be aſcribed to the unaſſiſted Strength of an extraordinary Genius; yet ſcarce any one can read theſe Deſcriptions without feeling the charming Power of the ingenious Arts, without falling in love with them, and expatiating moſt agreeably in his own Fancy upon the manifold wonders they are capable of performing.

THE Paſſages of *Homer* that are referred to by the Abbé *Fraguier*, are inſerted in the Notes.

INDEED Mr. *Pope* ſeems to have put this quite out of diſpute in his Obſervations on the Shield of *Achilles.* Monſieur *Boivin* (14) had entirely removed the main Objection made by ſome Criticks againſt this Buckler, that it is crouded with ſuch a multiplicity of Figures, as could not poſſibly be repreſented in the compaſs of it. But Mr. *Pope* has conſidered it

as a piece of Painting, which was never done before by any modern Critick; and by ſo doing has fully proved *Homer's* perfect Knowledge of Painting, and ſet the Art itſelf in the fineſt light. As it would be vain to attempt any thing after him; ſo it would be an unpardonable Injury to the Art, in ſuch a Collection as I have propoſed, of the beſt Obſervations on its Antiquity and Uſefulneſs, not to give that excellent Diſcourſe at its full length.

" THERE is reaſon to believe that *Homer* did in this, as he has done in other Arts, (even " in Mechanicks) that is, comprehend whatever was known of it in his time; if not (as " is highly probable) from thence extend his Ideas yet farther, and give a more enlarged " notion of it. Accordingly, it is very obſervable, that there is ſcarce a Species or Branch " of this Art which is not here to be found; whether Hiſtory, Battle-Painting, Landskips, " Architecture, Fruits, Flowers, Animals, &c.

" I think it poſſible that Painting was arrived to a greater degree of Perfection, even " at that early Period, than is generally ſuppoſed by thoſe who have written upon it. " *Pliny* expreſſly ſays, that it was not known in the time of the *Trojan* War. The ſame " Author, and others, repreſent it in a very imperfect State in *Greece,* in or near the " Days of *Homer.* They tell us of one Painter, that he was the firſt who begun to ſhadow; " and of another, that he fill'd his Out-lines only with a ſingle Colour, and that laid on " every where alike: But we may have a higher notion of the Art, from thoſe Deſcrip- " tions of Statues, Carvings, Tapeſtries, Sculptures upon Armour, and Ornaments of all " kinds, which every where occur in our Author; as well as from what he ſays of their " Beauty, the Relievo, and their Emulation of Life itſelf. If we conſider how much it is " his conſtant practice to confine himſelf to the Cuſtom of the Times whereof he writ, it " will be hard to doubt but that Painting and Sculpture muſt have been then in great practice " and repute.

" THE Shield is not only deſcribed as a piece of Sculpture, but of Painting: the Out- " lines may be ſuppoſed engraved, and the reſt enamel'd, or inlaid with various-colour'd " Metals.

Within its Concave hung a ſilver Thong,
On which a mimick Serpent creeps along,
His azure Length in eaſy Waves extends,
Till in three Heads th' embroider'd Monſter ends. Ib. l. 43, &c.

See alſo his Deſcription of *Paris's* Armour, II. iii. l. 410.

O'er her broad Shoulders hangs his bottid Shield,
Dire, black, tremendous! round the Margin roll'd,
A Fringe of Serpents hiſſing guards the Gold:
Here all the Terrors of grim War appear,
Here rages Force, here tremble Flight and Fear,
Here ſtorm'd Contention; and here Fury frown'd,
And the dire Orb portentous Gorgon crown'd. Il. v. l. 911.

Two rows of ſtately Dogs, on either hand,
In ſculptur'd Gold and labour'd Silver ſtand.
Theſe Vulcan form'd with Art divine, to wait
Immortal Guardians at Alcinous' Gate;
Alive each animated Frame appears,
And ſtill to live beyond the pow'r of Years. Od. B. vii. l. 118, &c.

Meantime, to beauteous Helen, from the Skies
The various Goddeſs of the Rainbow flies:
Her in the Palace, at her Loom ſhe found;
The golden Web her own ſad Story crown'd,
The Trojan Wars ſhe weav'd (herſelf the Prize)
And the dire Triumphs of her fatal Eyes. Iliad B. iii. l. 169.

Around her next a heav'nly Mantle flow'd,
That rich with Pallas' labour'd Colours glow'd;
Large Claſps of Gold the Foldings gather'd round,
A golden Zone her ſwelling Boſom bound.
For beaming Pendants tremble in her Ear,
Each Gem illumin'd with a triple Star.
Then o'er her Head ſhe caſt a Veil mote white
Than new-fall'n Snow, and dazzling as the Light.
Laſt her fair Feet celeſtial Sandals grace. Il. B. xiv. l. 207.

While ſhe with Work and Song the time divides,
And thro' the Loom the golden Shuttle guides. Odyſ. B. v. l. 78.

——————With earneſt gait
Seek thou the Queen along the Rooms of State;
Her royal Hand a wond'rous Work deſigns,
Around, a Circle of bright Damſels ſhines,
Part twiſt the Threads, and part the Wool diſpoſe,
While with the purple Orb the Spindle glows. Odyſ. B. vi. l. 365.

(14) This Author ſuppoſes the Buckler to have been perfectly round: He divides the convex Surface into four concentrick Circles. The Circle next the Center contains the Globe of the Earth and the Sea in miniature: he gives this Circle the Dimenſion of three Inches. The ſecond Circle is allotted for the Heavens and the Stars: he allows the Space of ten Inches between this and the former Circle. The third ſhall be eight Inches diſtant from the ſecond. The Space between theſe two Circles ſhall be divided into twelve Compartments, each of which makes a Picture of ten or eleven Inches deep. The fourth Circle makes the Margin of the Buckler: and the Interval between this and the former, being of three Inches, is ſufficient to repreſent the Waves and Currents of the Ocean. All theſe together make but four Foot in the whole in diameter. The Print annex'd to it will ſerve to prove, that the Figures will neither be crouded nor confuſed, if diſpoſed in the proper Place and Order. See Mr. *Pope's* Obſervations on the Shield. The Argument for the Antiquity of Painting from *Homer's* Deſcription of this Shield, is thus ſtated by *Bulengerus,* lib. 1. cap. 3. *de Pictura,* &c.

Nulla ars celerius conſummata eſt, cum Iliacis temporibus non fuiſſe apparet, inquit Plinius. Imò Iliacis temporibus fuiſſe apparet, ex clypeo Achillis apud Homerum. Excipies Homerum æqualem non fuiſſe Iliaco excidio.

" Metals. The variety of Colours is plainly diftinguifh'd by *Homer*, where he fpeaks of
" the Blacknefs of the new-open'd Earth, of the feveral Colours of the Grapes and Vines;
" and in other places. The different Metals that *Vulcan* is feign'd to caft into the Furnace,
" were fufficient to afford all the neceflary Colours : But if to thofe which are natural to the
" Metals, we add alfo thofe which they are capable of receiving from the Operation of
" Fire, we fhall find that *Vulcan* had as great a variety of Colours to make ufe of as any
" modern Painter. That enamelling or fixing Colours by fire, was practifed very an-
" ciently, may be conjectur'd from what *Diodorus* reports of one of the Walls of *Babylon*,
" built by *Semiramis, that the Bricks of it were painted before they were burn'd, fo as
" to reprefent all forts of Animals*, lib. 2. chap. 4. Now it is but natural to infer, that
" Men had made ufe of ordinary Colours for the Reprefentation of Objects, before they
" learnt to reprefent them by fuch as are given by the Operation of Fire ; one being much
" more eafy and obvious than the other, and that fort of Painting by means of fire being
" but an Imitation of the Painting with a Pencil and Colours. The fame Inference will be
" farther enforc'd from the Works of Tapeftry, which the Women of thofe times inter-
" weaved with many Colours; as appears from the Defcription of that Veil which *Hecuba*
" offers to *Minerva* in the fixth Iliad, and from a Paffage in the twenty-fecond, where
" *Andromache* is reprefented working Flowers in a Piece of this kind. They muft cer-
" tainly have known the ufe of Colours themfelves for Painting, before they could think
" of dying Threads with thofe Colours, and weaving thofe Threads clofe to one another,
" in order only to a more laborious Imitation of a thing fo much more eafily performed
" by a Pencil. This Obfervation I owe to the Abbé *Fraguier*.

" IT may indeed be thought, that a Genius fo vaft and comprehenfive as that of *Homer*,
" might carry his Views beyond the reft of Mankind ; and that in this Buckler of *Achilles*
" he rather defign'd to give a Scheme of what might be performed, than a Defcription of
" what really was fo : And fince he made a God the Artift, he might excufe himfelf from
" a ftrict Confinement to what was known and practifed in the time of the *Trojan* War.
" Let this.be as it will, it is certain that he had, whether by Learning, or by Strength of Genius,
" (though the latter be more glorious for *Homer*) a full and exact Idea of Painting in all its
" parts ; that is to fay, in the Invention, the Compofition, the Expreffion, *&c.*

" THE Invention is fhewn in finding and introducing in every Subject, the greateft, the
" moft fignificant, and moft fuitable Objects. Accordingly in every fingle Picture of the
" Shield; *Homer* conftantly finds out either thofe Objects which are naturally the principal,
" thofe which moft conduce to fhew the Object, or thofe which fet it in the livelieft and
" moft agreeable Light : Thefe he never fails to difpofe in the moft advantageous Manners,
" Situations, and Oppofitions.

" NEXT, we find all his Figures differently characterized, in their Expreffions and At-
" titudes, according to their feveral Natures : The Gods (for inftance) are diftinguifh'd in
" Air, Habit and Proportion, from Men, in the fourth Picture ; Mafters from Servants, in
" the eighth ; and fo of the reft.

" NOTHING is more wonderful than his exact Obfervation of the Contraft, not only
" between Figure and Figure, but between Subject and Subject. The City in peace is a
" Contraft to the City in war : Between the Siege in the fourth Picture, and the Battle in
" the fixth, a piece of Paifage is introduced, and rural Scenes follow after. The Country
" too is reprefented in war in the fifth, as well as in peace in the feventh, eighth, and ninth.
" The very Animals are fhewn in thefe two different States, in the tenth and the eleventh.
" Where the Subjects appear the fame, he contraftes them fome other way : Thus the firft
" Picture of the Town in peace having a predominant Air of Gaiety, in the Dances and
" Pomps of the Marriage ; the fecond has a Character of Earneftnefs and Sollicitude, in the
" Difpute and Pleadings: In the Pieces of rural Life, that of the·Plowing is of a different
" Character from the Harveft, and that of the Harveft from the Vintage. In each of thefe
" there is a Contraft of the Labour and Mirth of the Country People : In the firft, fome
" are Plowing, others taking a Cup of good Liquor ; in the next, we fee the Reapers
" working in one part, and the Banquet prepar'd in another ; in the laft, the Labour of
" the Vineyard is reliev'd with Mufick and a Dance. The Perfons are no lefs varied, old
" and young, Men and Women : There being Women in two Pictures together, namely
" the eighth and ninth, it is remarkable that thofe in the latter are of a different Character
" from the former ; they who drefs the Supper being ordinary Women, the others who
" carry Baskets in the Vineyard, young and beautiful Virgins : And thefe again are of an
" inferiour Character to thofe in the twelfth Piece, who are diftinguifh'd as People of Con-
" dition by a more elegant Drefs. There are three Dances in the Buckler ; and thefe too
" are varied.: that at the Wedding is in a circular Figure, that of the Vineyard in a row, that

" in

excidio. In ipfo clypeo Vulcanus fecit fcienter artificiofa
multa, Terram, Cœlum, Marc, Solem indefeffum, Lunam orbiculatam. *Idem* apud Hefiodum ex clypeo Her-
culis apparet, fi ehini erat Cælatura, erat & Pictura,   quæ utræque pedetentim, & per gradus, non uno tempore abfolutionem confecutæ funt. Excipies Picturam
fuiffe ætate Hefiodi non Herculis. Sed ante Herculem
pictura fuit fub Mofe, & ante Mofem fub Abrahamo.

C

" in the laſt Picture, a mingled one. Laſtly, there is a manifeſt Contraſt in the Colours;
" nay, even in the Back-grounds of the ſeveral Pieces : For example, that of the Plowing
" is of a dark tint, that of the Harveſt yellow, that of the Paſture green, and the reſt in
" like manner.

" THAT he was not a Stranger to aerial Perſpective, appears in his expreſſly marking
" the diſtance of Object from Object : He tells us, for inſtance, that the two Spies lay a
" little remote from the other Figures; and that the Oak under which was ſpread the
" Banquet of the Reapers, ſtood apart. What he ſays of the Valley ſprinkled all over with
" Cottages and Flocks, appears to be a Deſcription of a large Country in perſpective. And
" indeed a general Argument for this may be drawn from the number of Figures in the
" Shield; which could not be all expreſs'd in their full Magnitude : And this is therefore
" a ſort of proof that the Art of leſſening them according to Perſpective was known at
" that time.

" WHAT the Criticks call the *Three Unities*, ought in reaſon as much to be obſerved
" in a Picture as in a Play; each ſhould have only one principal Action, one Inſtant of
" Time, and one Point of View. In this Method of Examination alſo the Shield of *Homer*
" will bear the teſt : He has been more exact than the greateſt Painters, who have often
" deviated from one or other of theſe Rules; whereas (when we examine the Detail of
" each Compartiment) it will appear,

" FIRST, that there is but one principal Action in each Picture, and that no ſuper-
" numerary Figures or Actions are introduced. This will anſwer all that has been ſaid of
" the Confuſion and Croud of Figures on the Shield, by thoſe who never comprehended
" the Plan of it.

" SECONDLY, that no Action is repreſented in one Piece, which could not happen
" in the ſame inſtant of time. This will overthrow the Objection againſt ſo many different
" Actions appearing in one Shield; which, in this caſe, is much as abſurd as to object
" againſt ſo many of *Raphael's* Cartons appearing in one Gallery.

" THIRDLY, it will be manifeſt that there are no Objects in any one Picture, which
" could not be ſeen in one point of View. Hereby the Abbé *Terraſſon's* whole Criticiſm
" will fall to the ground, which amounts but to this, that the general Objects of the Hea-
" vens, Stars and Sea, with the particular Proſpects of Towns, Fields, &c. could never be
" ſeen all at once. *Homer* was incapable of ſo abſurd a Thought, nor could theſe heavenly
" Bodies (had he intended them for a Picture) have ever been ſeen together from one Point;
" for the Conſtellations and the Full Moon, for example, could never be ſeen at once with
" the Sun. But the celeſtial Bodies were placed on the Boſs, as the Ocean at the Margin
" of the Shield : Theſe were no parts of the Painting, but the former was only an Orna-
" ment to the Projection in the middle, and the latter a Frame round about it : In the ſame
" manner as the Diviſions, Projections or Angles of a Roof are left to be ornamented at
" the Diſcretion of the Painter, with Foliage, Architecture, Groteſque, or what he pleaſes:
" However his Judgment will be ſtill more commendable, if he contrives to make even
" theſe extrinſical Parts, to bear ſome alluſion to the main Deſign. It is this which *Homer*
" has done, in placing a ſort of Sphere in the middle, and the Ocean at the border, of a
" Work, which was expreſſly intended to repreſent the Univerſe.

Theſe Pictures on   " I proceed now to the Detail of the Shield; in which the Words of *Homer* being firſt
the Shield are the   " tranſlated, an attempt will be made to ſhew with what exact Order all that he deſcribes
moſt ancient Pieces " may enter into the Compoſition, according to the Rules of Painting."
of Painting.

And therefore in-
ſerted here.   THE SHIELD OF ACHILLES DIVIDED INTO ITS SEVERAL PARTS.

                              The Boſs of the Shield. 1.

Verſe 483. Ἐν μὲν γαῖαν, &c.] " HERE *Vulcan* repreſented the Earth, the Heaven,
" the Sea, the indefatigable Courſe of the Sun, the Moon in her full, all the celeſtial Signs
" that crown *Olympus*, the *Pleiades*, the *Hyades*, the great *Orion*, and the *Bear*, commonly
" called the Wain; the only Conſtellation, which, never bathing itſelf in the Ocean, turns
" about the Pole, and obſerves the Courſe of *Orion*."

                                                                                    THE

1. Then firſt he form'd th'immenſe and ſolid Shield ;	Th' unweary'd Sun, the Moon compleatly round ;
Rich, various Artifice emblaz'd the Field ;	The ſtarry Lights that Heav'n's high Convex crown'd ;
Its utmoſt Verge a threefold Circle bound ;	The Pleiads, Hyads, with the northern Team ;
A ſilver Chain ſuſpends the maſſy round,	And great Orion's more refulgent Beam ;
Five ample Plates the broad Expanſe compoſe,	To which around the Axle of the Sky,
And godlike Labours on the Surface roſe.	The Bear revolving, points his golden Eye,
There ſhone the Image of the Maſter Mind :	Still ſhines exalted on th'etherial Plain,
There Earth, there Heav'n, there Ocean he deſign'd ;	Nor bathes his blazing Forehead in the Main.

THE Sculpture of thefe refembled fomewhat of our terreftrial and celeftial Globes, and took up the Center of the Shield : 'Tis plain by the huddle in which *Homer* expreffes this, that he did not defcribe it as a Picture for a point of Sight.

THE Circumference is divided into twelve Compartiments, each being a feparate Picture ; as follow :

FIRST COMPARTIMENT. *A Town in Peace.* 1.

῍Ε, δὲ δύω ποίησε πόλεις, *&c.*] " HE engraved two Cities ; in one of them were re-
" prefented Nuptials and Feftivals.   The Spoufes from their Bridal-chambers, were conducted
" thro' the Town by the light of Torches.   Every Mouth fung the hymeneal Song : The
" Youth turn'd rapidly in a circular Dance : The Flute and the Lyre refounded : The Wo-
" men, every one in the Street, ftanding in the Porches, beheld and admired."

IN this Picture, the Brides preceded by Torch-bearers are on the Fore-ground : The Dance in circles, and Muficians behind them : The Street in perfpective on either fide, the Women and Spectators in the Porches, *&c.* difpers'd thro' all the Architecture.

SECOND COMPARTIMENT. *An Affembly of the People.* 2.

Λαοι δ' ἐν ἀγορῷ, *&c.*] " THERE was feen a number of People in the Market-place,
" and two Men difputing warmly : The occafion was the payment of a Fine for a Murder,
" which one affirm'd before the People he had paid, the other deny'd to have receiv'd ; both
" demanded, that the Affair fhould be determin'd by the Judgment of an Arbiter : The Ac-
" clamations of the Multitude favour'd fometimes the one Party, fometimes the other."

HERE is a fine Plan for a Mafter-piece of Expreffion ; any Judge of Painting will fee our Author has chofen that Caufe, which, of all others, would give occafion to the greateft variety of Expreffion : The Father, the Murderer, the Witneffes, and the different Paffions of the Affembly, would afford an ample Field for this Talent even to *Raphael* himfelf.

THIRD COMPARTIMENT. *The Senate.* 3.

Κήρυκες δ' ἄρα λαὸν ἐρήτυον, *&c.*] " THE Heralds rang'd the People in order : The
" reverend Elders were feated on Seats of polifh'd Stone, in the facred Circle ; they rofe
" up and declared their Judgment, each in his turn, with the Sceptre in his hand : Two Ta-
" lents of Gold were laid in the middle of the Circle, to be given to him who fhould pro-
" nounce the moft equitable Judgment."

THE Judges are feated in the Center of the Picture ; one (who is the principal Figure) ftanding up as fpeaking, another in an Action of rifing, as in order to fpeak : The Ground about them a Profpect of the Forum, fill'd with Auditors and Spectators.

FOURTH COMPARTIMENT. *A Town in War.* 4.

Τὴν δ' ἑτέρην πόλιν, *&c.*] " THE other City was befieged by two glittering Armies :
" They were not agreed, whether to fack the Town, or divide all the Booty of it into two
" equal parts, to be fhared between them : Mean time the Befieged fecretly arm'd themfelves
" for an Ambufcade.   Their Wives, Children, and old Men were pofted to defend their
" Walls : The Warriors march'd from the Town with *Pallas* and *Mars* at their head : The
" Deities were of Gold, and had golden Armours, by the Glory of which they were diftin-
" guifh'd above the Men, as well as by their fuperior Stature, and more elegant Proportions."

THIS Subject may be thus difpofed : The Town pretty near the Eye, a-crofs the whole Picture, with the old Men on the Walls : The Chiefs of each Army on the Fore-ground :
Their

1. *Two Cities radiant on the Shield appear,*
The Image one of Peace and one of War,
Here facred Pomp and genial Feaft delight,
And folemn Dance, and hymeneal Rite ;
Along the Street the new-made Brides are led,
With Torches flaming, to the nuptial Bed :
The youthful Dancers in a Circle bound
To the foft Flute, and Cittern's filver Sound :
Thro' the fair Streets, the Matrons in a row,
Stand in their Portions, and enjoy the fhow.

2. *There, in the Forum fwarm a num'rous Train :*
The fubject of Debate, a Townfman flain :
One pleads the Fine difcharg'd, which one deny'd,
And bade the Publick and the Laws decide :
The Witnefs is produc'd on either hand ;
For this, or that, the partial People ftand.

3. *Th' appointed Heralds ftill the noify Bands,*
And form a Ring with Scepters in their hands ;

On Seats of Stone, within the facred place,
The rev'rend Elders nodded o'er the cafe ;
Alternate, each th' attefting Scepter tack,
And rifing folemn, each his Sentence fpake.
Two golden Talents lay amidft, in fight,
The Prize of him who beft adjudg'd the right.

4. *Another part (a Profpect differing far)*
Glow'd with refulgent Arms, and horrid War.
Two mighty Hofts a leaguer'd Town embrace,
And one would pillage, one wou'd burn the place.
Meantime the Townfman, arm'd with filent care,
A fecret Ambufh on the Foe prepare :
Their Wives, their Children, and the watchful Band
Of trembling Parents on the Turrets ftand.
They march ; by Pallas and by Mars made bold ;
Gold were the Gods, their radiant Garments Gold,
And Gold their Armour : Thefe the Squadron led,
Auguft, divine, fuperiour by the head.

Their different Opinions for putting the Town to the Sword, or sparing it on account of the Booty, may be exprefs'd by some having their Hands on their Swords, and looking up to the City, others stopping them, or in an action of persuading against it. Behind, in prospect, the Townsmen may be seen going out from the Back-gates, with the two Deities at their head.

HOMER here gives a clear instance of what the Ancients always practifed ; the distinguishing the Gods and Goddesses by Characters of Majesty and Beauty somewhat superiour to Nature ; we constantly find this in their Statues, and to this the modern Masters owe their grand Taste in the Perfection of their Figures.

Fifth Compartiment. *An Ambuscade.* 5.

Οἶ δ' ὅτε δὴ ῥ' ἵκανον, *&c.*]   " BEING arrived at the River where they designed their " Ambush (the place where the Cattle were water'd) they difpofed themfelves along the Bank, " cover'd with their Arms : Two Spies lay at a distance from them, observing when the Oxen " and Sheep should come to drink. They came immediately, followed by two Shepherds, " who were playing on their Pipes, without any apprehension of their danger."

THIS quiet Picture is a kind of Repose between the last, and the following active Pieces. Here is a Scene of a River and Trees, under which lie the Soldiers, next the Eye of the Spectator ; on the farther Bank are placed the two Spies on one hand, and the Flocks and Shepherds appear coming at a greater distance on the other.

Sixth Compartiment. *The Battle.* 6.

Οἷ μὲν τὰ περιδόντες, *&c.*]   " THE People of the Town rush'd upon them, carried off " the Oxen and Sheep, and kill'd the Shepherds. The Besiegers sitting before the Town, " heard the Outcry, and mounting their Horses, arrived at the Bank of the River ; where " they stopp'd and encounter'd each other with their Spears. Discord, Tumult, and Fate " raged in the midst of them. There might you see cruel Destiny dragging a dead Soldier " thro' the Battle ; two others she seiz'd alive ; one of which was mortally wounded ; the " other not yet hurt : The Garment on her Shoulders was stain'd with human Blood : The " Figures appeared as if they lived, moved, and fought, you would think they really dragged " off their dead."

THE Sheep and two Shepherds lying dead upon the Fore-ground. A Battle-piece fills the Picture. The allegorical Figure of the *Parca* or Destiny is the principal. This had been a noble Occasion for such a Painter as *Rubens*, who has, with most Happiness and Learning, imitated the Ancients in these fictious and symbolical Persons.

Seventh Compartiment. *Tillage.* 7.

Ἐν δ' ἐτίθει νειὸν μαλαχὴν, *&c.*]   " THE next Piece represented a large Field, a deep " and fruitful Soil, which seem'd to have been three times plow'd ; the Labourers appear'd " turning their Plows on every side. As soon as they came to a Land's end, a Man pre- " fented them a Bowl of Wine ; cheared with this, they turn'd, and worked down a new " Furrow, desirous to hasten to the next Land's end. The Field was of Gold, but look'd " black behind the Plows, as if it had really been turn'd up ; the surprizing effect of the Art " of *Vulcan.*"

THE Plowmen must be represented on the Fore-ground, in the action of turning at the end of the Furrow. The Invention of *Homer* is not content with barely putting down the Figures, but enlivens them prodigiously with some remarkable Circumstance : The giving a Cup of Wine to the Plowmen must occasion a fine Expression in the Faces.

EIGHTH

5. *A place for Ambush fit, they found, and stood*
Cover'd with Shields, beside a silver Flood.
Two Spies at distance lurk, and watchful seem
If Sheep or Oxen seek the winding Stream.
Soon the white Flocks proceeded o'er the Plains,
And Steers slow-moving, and two Shepherd-Swains ;
Behind them, piping on their Reeds, they go,
Nor fear an Ambush, nor suspect a Foe.

6. *In Arms the glitt'ring Squadron rising round,*
Rush sudden ; Hills of slaughter heap the Ground,
Whole Flocks and Herds lie bleeding, on the Plains,
And, all amidst them, dead, the Shepherd-Swains.
The bellowing Oxen the Besiegers hear ;
They rise, take horse, approach, and meet the War ;
They fight, they fall, beside the silver Flood ;
The waving Silver seem'd to blush with Blood.
There Tumult, there Contention stood poffefs'd ;
One rear'd a Dagger at a Captive's Breast ;

One held a living Foe, that freshly bled
With new-made Wounds ; another dragg'd a dead ;
Now here, now there, the Carcasses they tore :
Fate stalk'd amidst them, grim with human Gore.
And the whole War came out, and met the Eye ;
And each bold Figure seem'd to live, or die.

7. *A Field deep furrow'd, next the God design'd,*
The third time labour'd by the sweating Hind ;
The shining Shares full many Plowmen guide,
And turn their crooked Yokes on ev'ry side.
Still as at either end they wheel around,
The Master meets 'em with his Goblet crown'd ;
The hearty Draught rewards, renews their Toil ;
Then back the turning Plow-shares cleave the Soil :
Behind, the rising Earth in ridges roll'd,
And sable look'd, tho' form'd of molten Gold.

EIGHTH COMPARTIMENT. *The Harveft.* 8.

Ἐν δ' ἐτίθει τέμενⒼ, &c.] " NEXT he reprefented a Field of Corn, in which the
" Reapers work'd with fharp Sickles in their Hands; the Corn fell thick along the Furrows
" in equal rows : Three Binders were employed in making up the Sheaves : The Boys at-
" tending them, gather'd up the loofe Swarths, and carried them in their Arms to be bound :
" The Lord of the Field ftanding in the midft of the Heaps, with a Scepter in his Hand, re-
" joices in filence : His Officers, at a diftance, prepare a Feaft under the Shade of an Oak,
" and hold an Ox ready to be facrificed ; while the Women mix the Flower of Wheat for the
" Reapers Supper."

THE Reapers on the Fore-ground, with their Faces towards the Spectators ; the Gatherers
behind, and the Children on the farther Ground. The Mafter of the Field, who is the
chief Figure, may be fet in the middle of the Picture with a ftrong light about him, in the
Action of directing and pointing with his Scepter : The Oak, with the Servants under it, the
Sacrifice, &c. on a diftant Ground, would all together make a beautiful Groupe of great variety.

NINTH COMPARTIMENT. *The Vintage.* 9.

Ἐν δ' ἐτίθει ϛαφυλῆσι, &c.] " HE then engraved a Vineyard loaden with its Grapes :
" The Vineyard was Gold, but the Grapes black, and the Props of them Silver. A Trench
" of a dark Metal, and a Palifade of Tin encompafs'd the whole Vineyard. There was one
" Path in it, by which the Labourers in the Vineyard pafs'd : Young Men and Maids carried
" the Fruit in woven Baskets : In the middle of them a Youth play'd on the Lyre, and charmed
" them with his tender Voice, as he fung to the Strings (or as he fung the Song of *Linus* :)
" The reft ftriking the Ground with their Feet in exact time, follow'd him in a Dance, and
" accompanied his Voice with their own."

THE Vintage fcarely needs to be painted in any Colours but *Homer's*. The Youths
and Maids toward the Eye, as coming out of the Vineyard : The Enclofure, Pails, Gates, &c.
on the Fore-ground. There is fomething inexpreffibly riant in this Piece, above all the reft.

TENTH COMPARTIMENT. *Animals.* 10.

Ἐν δ' ἀγέλην ποίησε Βοῶν, &c.] " HE graved a Herd of Oxen, marching with their
" Heads erected ; thefe Oxen (inlaid with Gold and Tin) feem'd to bellow as they quitted
" their Stall, and run in hafte to the Meadows, thro' which a rapid River roll'd with refound-
" ing Streams amongft the Rufhes : Four Herdfmen of Gold attended them, follow'd by
" nine large Dogs. Two terrible Lions feized a Bull by the Throat, who roar'd as they
" dragg'd him along ; the Dogs and the Herdfmen ran to his refcue, but the Lions having torn
" the Bull, devour'd his Entrails, and drank his Blood. The Herdfmen came up with their
" Dogs, and hearten'd them in vain ; they durft not attack the Lions, but ftanding at fome
" diftance, bark'd at them, and fhun'd them."

WE have next a fine Piece of Animals, tame and favage : But what is remarkable, is, that
thefe Animals are not coldly brought in to be gazed upon : The Herds, Dogs, and Lions are
put into action, enough to exercife the Warmth and Spirit of *Rubens*, or the great Tafte of
Julio Romano.

THE Lions may be next the Eye, one holding the Bull by the Throat, the other tearing
out his Entrails : A Herdfman or two heartening the Dogs : All thefe on the Fore-ground.
On the fecond Ground another Groupe of Oxen, that feem to have been gone before, toffing
their Heads and running ; other Herdfmen and Dogs after them : And beyond them, a Profpect of the River.

ELEVENTH

8. *Another Field rofe high with waving Grain ;*
With bended Sickles ftand the Reaper-train :
Here ftretch'd in Ranks the levell'd Swarths are found,
Sheaves heap'd on Sheaves, here thicken up the Ground.
With fweeping Stroke the Mowers ftrow the Lands ;
The Gath'rers follow and collect in Bands ;
And laft the Children, in whofe Arms are born
('Too fhort to gripe them) the brown Sheaves of Corn.
The ruftick Monarch of the Field defcries
With filent Glee, the Heaps around him rife.
A ready Banquet on the Turf is laid,
Beneath an ample Oak's expanded Shade.
The Victim-Ox the fturdy Youth prepare;
The Reapers due Repaft, the Womens Care.

9. *Next, ripe in yellow Gold, a Vineyard fhines,*
Bent with the pond'rous Harveft of its Vines ;
A deeper dye the dangling Clufters fhow,
And curl'd on filver Props, in order glow :
A darker Metal mix'd, intrench'd the place ;
And Pales of glitt'ring Tin th' Enclofure grace.

To this, one Path-way gently winding leads,
Where march a Train with Baskets on their Heads,
(Fair Maids, and blooming Youths) that fmiling bear
The purple Product of th'autumnal Year.
To thefe a Youth awakes the warbling Strings,
Whofe tender Lay the Fate of Linus *fings ;*
In meafur'd Dance behind him move the Train,
Time foft the Voice, and anfwer to the Strain.

10. *Here Herds of Oxen march, erect and bold,*
Rear high their Horns, and feem to lowe in Gold,
And fpeed to Meadows on whofe founding Shores
A rapid Torrent thro' the Rufhes roars :
Four golden Herdfmen as their Guardians ftand,
And nine four Dogs compleat the ruftick Band.
Two Lions rufhing from the Wood appear'd,
And feiz'd a Bull the Mafter of the Herd :
He roar'd, in vain the Dogs, the Men withftood,
They tore his Flefh, and drank the fable Blood.
The Dogs (oft' chear'd in vain) defert the Prey,
Dread the grim Terrors, and at diftance bay.

ELEVENTH COMPARTIMENT. *Sheep.* 11.

ʹΕν δὲ νομὸν, &c.] " THE divine Artift then engraved a large Flock of white Sheep,
" feeding along a beautiful Valley. Innumerable Folds, Cottages, and enclos'd Shelters,
" were fcatter'd thro' the Profpect."

THIS is an entire Landskape without human Figures, an Image of Nature folitary and
undifturb'd : The deepeft Repofe and Tranquillity is that which diftinguifhes it from the others.

TWELFTH COMPARTIMENT. *The Dance.* 12.

ʹΕν δὲ χορὸν, &c.] " THE skilful *Vulcan* then defign'd the Figure and various Mo-
" tions of a Dance, like that which *Dædalus* of old contrived in *Gnoffus* for the fair
" *Ariadne.* There the young Men and Maidens danced hand in hand ; the Maids were
" drefs'd in linen Garments, the Men in rich and fhining Stuffs : The Maids had flowery
" Crowns on their heads ; the Men had Swords of Gold running from their fides in Belts
" of Silver. Here they feem to run in a ring with active Feet, as fwiftly as a Wheel runs
" round when tried by the Hand of the Potter. There, they appeared to move in many
" Figures, and fometimes to meet, fometimes to wind from each other. A multitude of
" Spectators flood round, delighted with the Dance : In the middle two nimble Tumblers
" exercifed themfelves in Feats of Activity, while the Song was carried on by the whole
" Circle."

THIS Picture includes the greateft number of Perfons : *Homer* himfelf has group'd
them, and mark'd the manner of the Compofition. This Piece would excel in the different Airs of Beauty which might be given to the young Men and Women, and the graceful Attitudes in the various manners of dancing : On which account the Subject might be
fit for *Guido*, or perhaps could be no where better executed than in our own Country.

THE BORDER OF THE SHIELD. 13.

ʹΕν δ' ἐτίθει ποταμοῖο, &c.] " THEN laftly, he reprefented the rapid Courfe of the
" great Ocean, which he made to roll its Waves round the Extremity of the whole Cir-
" cumference."

THIS (as has been faid before) was only the Frame to the whole Shield, and is therefore but lightly touch'd upon, without any mention of particular Objects."

This Shield was con-   'TIS not improper to add to this beautiful Differtation, that the Shield of *Achilles* was
fidered by the fame   confidered by the Ancients in the fame light, as a Mafter-piece of picturefque Sculpture.
View by the An-   This appears from a Paffage of the eldeft *Philoftratus* in his Life of *Apollonius Tyaneus* (14) :
cients : And this   And the fame Author tells us, that this kind of Painting was very anciently practifed. In
kind of Sculpture   a Picture defcribed by the youngeft *Philoftratus*, called *Pyrrhus* or *Myfi* (15), *Pyrrhus's*
was very ancient.   Shield is painted according to *Homer's* Defcription, becaufe *Vulcan's* Armour was yielded
to him by *Ulyffes* : On which occafion *Philoftratus* fhews us its feveral Beauties confidered
as a Picture. How fine an Idea the Ancients had of *Homer's* grand and comprehenfive
Defign, which was no lefs than to draw the Picture of the whole World in the compafs
of this Shield, may be judged, as Mr. *Pope* obferves, from that Verfe of *Ovid* ; where he
calls it

—— *Clypeus vafto cælatus imagine mundi.* Met. l. 13.

AND

11. *Next this, the Eye, the Art of* Vulcan *leads*
Deep thro' fair Forefts, and a Length of Meads ;
And Stalls, and Folds, and fcatter'd Cots between ;
And fleecy Flocks that whiten all the Scene.

12. *A figur'd Dance fucceeds : Such one was feen*
In lofty Gnoffus, *for the* Cretan *Queen,*
Form'd by Dædalean *Art. A comely Band*
Of Youths and Maidens, bounding hand in hand ;
The Maids in foft Cymars of Linen dreft ;
The Youths all graceful in the gloffy Veft ;
Of thofe the Locks with flow'ry Wreaths inroll'd,
Of thefe the Sides adorn'd with Swords of Gold,
That glitt'ring gay, from filver Belts depend.
Now all at once they rife, at once defcend,
With well-taught Feet : Now fhape, in oblique ways,
Confus'dly regular, the moving Maze :
Now forth at once, too fwift for Sight they fpring,
And undiftinguifh'd blend the flying Ring :
So whirls a Wheel, in giddy Circle toft,
And rapid as it runs, the fingle Spokes are loft.
The gazing Multitudes admire around ;
Two active Tumblers in the Centre bound ;
Now high, now low, their pliant Limbs they bend,
And gen'ral Songs the fprightly Revel end.

13. *Thus the broad Shield complete the Artift crown'd*
With his laft Hand, and pour'd the Ocean round :

In living Silver feem'd the Waves to roll,
And beat the Buckler's Verge, and bound the whole.

(14) *Lib.* 2. *cap.* 22. Ταύτῃ ὃ ὦ Δάμι. κ. τ. χ.) Ifta
autem, O Dami, Pori juffu artificiofe elaborata opera,
non ærariæ artis folum effe dicemus, nam pictorum inftar
habent ; neque picta duntaxat, quoniam arte æraria funt
concinnata. Verum induftriæ ea ftatuamus unum virum,
artis pictoriæ juxta & ærariæ peritum, quale apud Homerum Vulcani opus in Achillis clypeo repræfentatur.
Plena enim & ifta interficientium atque interfectorum,
terramque madere fanguine diceres, quamvis ære fit elaborata. Ibid. *cap.* 20. Τὸ ὃ Τάξιλα μέγεθος μὲν ἔιναι κτ
τὴν Νίνον. κ. τ. λ.) Taxila urbem magnitudine ab antiqua Nino non multum differre, &c.—Tabulæ æneæ in
quovis pariete erant defixæ, picturas exhibentes. Pori
nempe & Alexandri gefta delineata erant orichalco, argentoque & auro, atque ære nigro, elephanti, equi, milites, galeæ & clypei, haftæ & tela, gladifque ex ferro
omnia. Er quæ egregia picturæ eft indoles : Verbi gratia,
fi a Zeuxide vel Polygnoto, aut Euphranore aliquid fit
profectum, qui in umbris rite exprimendis, & animandis
quafi picturis, reductis item & eminentibus repræfen-
tandis operam pofuere ; eam hic quoque apparere inqui-
unt. Materiæ autem varia genera colliquefcendo coaluere
perinde atque colores. Suaviffimi vero etiam mores,
Pictura expreffi funt.

(15) *Philoft.* Icones 10.

AND it is indeed aftonifhing, (faith he) how, after this, the Arrogance of fome Moderns could unfortunately chufe the nobleft Part of the nobleft Poet for the Object of their blind Cenfures. Their Criticifms, whatever effect they may have on fome other parts, yet when aimed againft this Buckler, are quite weak and impotent: ·

> *Poftquam arma dei ad Vulcania ventum eft*
> *Mortalis mucro, glacies ceu futilis, icta*
> *Diffiluit.*

*Virgil likewife a-
bounds in Defcrip-
tions of Sculptures
and Pictures: And
afcribes th fame
Antiquity to Paint-
ing as Homer.*

VIRGIL has imitated *Homer* in every thing, and abounds no lefs in beautiful De-fcriptions of Statues, Sculptures, Carpets, Veftments, and other Pieces of curious Defign and exquifite Workmanfhip (16). He was charmed with thofe of *Homer*, and therefore would give the fame Ornaments to his Poem. And 'tis no fmall Confirmation of the Ar-gument for the Antiquity of Painting taken from *Homer's* Writings, that *Virgil*, who is juftly faid by Criticks to be the moft exact and judicious of all Poets, fpeaking of the fame Times, has not fcrupled to fuppofe Painting as well as Sculpture to have been then at its higheft Perfection.

*Some of Virgil's
Defcriptions refer-
red to Sculptures,
&c.*

THE Armour of *Æneas*; his Shield particularly, with all its prophetick Sculptures, re-prefenting the future Annals of *Italy*, are defcribed with the greateft Elegance; and the De-fcription is with good reafon introduced by the Hero's Admiration and Joy at the fight of them (17).

> *Proud of the Gift, he rowl'd his greedy Sight*
> *Around the Work, and gaz'd with vaft delight,*
> *He lifts, he turns, he poizes, and admires*
> *The crefted Helm, that vomits radiant Fires:*
> *He fhakes the pointed Spear; and longs to try*
> *The plated Cuifhes, on his manly Thigh,*
> *But moft admires the Shield's myfterious Mould,*
> *And* Roman *Triumphs rifing on the Gold;*
> *For thofe, embofs'd, the heavenly Smith had wrought*
> *(Not in the Rolls of future Fate untaught)*
> *The Wars in order, and the Race divine,*
> *Of Warriors iffuing from the* Julian *Line.*   Dryden, Æn. 8.

" 'TIS (18) happy that *Virgil* has made a Buckler for *Æneas* as well as *Homer* for
" *Achilles.* The *Latin* Poet, who imitated the *Greek* one, always took care to accom-
" modate thofe things which time had chang'd, fo as to render them agreeable to the Pa-
" late of his Readers; yet he hath not only charg'd his Shield with a great deal more work,
" fince he paints all the Actions of the *Romans* from *Afcanius* to *Auguftus*; but has not
" avoided any of thofe Manners of Expreffion which offend the Criticks. We fee there
" the Wolf of *Romulus* and *Remus*, who gives them her Dugs one after another.

> *They fuck'd fecure, while bending back her Head,*
> *She lick'd their tender Limbs, and form'd them as they fed.*

" The Rape of the *Sabines*, and the War which followed it: *Metius* torn by four Horfes, and
" *Tullus* who draws his Entrails thro' the Foreft: *Porfenna* commanding the *Romans* to
" receive *Tarquin*, and befieging *Rome*: The Geefe flying to the Porches of the Capitol,
" and giving notice by their Cries of the Attack of the *Gauls*. We fee the *Salian* Dance,
" and the Pains of the Damn'd; and farther off, the Place of the Blefs'd, where *Cato* pre-
" fides: We fee the famous Battle of *Actium*, where we may diftinguifh the Captains:
" *Agrippa* with the Gods, and the Winds favourable; and *Anthony* leading on all the
" Forces of the Eaft, *Egypt*, and the *Bactrians*. The Fight begins, the Sea is red with
" Blood, *Cleopatra* gives the Signal for a Retreat, and calls her Troops with a Siftrum.
" The Gods, or rather the Monfters of *Egypt*, fight againft *Neptune, Venus, Minerva,*
" *Mars* and *Apollo*: We fee *Anthony's* Fleet beaten, and the *Nile* forrowfully opening
"   his

---

(16) *Arte laboratæ vefles, oftroque fuperbo:*
Ingens argentum menfis; cælatapue in auro
Fortia facta patrum, feries longiffima rerum
Per tot ducta viros antiquæ ab origine gentis,&c. Æn. 1. 641.

Victori chlamydem auratam, quam plurima circum
Purpura Mæandro duplici Melibœa cucurrit
Intextufque puer, frondofâ regius Idâ,
Veloces jaculo cervos curfuque fatigat,
Acer, anhelanti fimilis; quem præpes ab Ida
Sublimem pedibus rapuit Jovis armiger uncis.
Longævi palmas nequicquam ad fidera tendunt
Cuftodes, fævitque canum latratus in auras, &c. Æn. 5. 250.

Quinetiam veterum effigies ex ordine avorum
Antiqua è cedro, Italufque paterque Sabinus
Vitifator, curvam fervans fub imagine falcem;
Saturnufque fenex, Janique bifrontis imago
Keftibulo aftabunt· aliique ab origine reges,
Martia qui ob patriam pugnando vulnera paffi,&c.Æn 7.177.

Vid. ibid. lib. 7. ver. 657, & 785.

(17) *Ille deæ donis & tanto lætus honore,*
Expleri nequit, atque oculos per fingula volvit:
Miraturque, interque manus & brachia verfat
Terribilem criftis galeam flammafque vomentem,
Fatiferumque enfem, Loricam ex ære rigentem,
Sanguineam, ingentem: qualis cum cærula nubes
Solis inardefcit radiis, longeque refulget.
Tum leves ocreas electro auroque recocto,
Haftamque & clypei non enarrabile textum.
Illic res Italas, Romanorumque triumphos,
Haud vatum ignarus ventarique infcius ævi,
Fecerat ignipotens: illic genus omne futuræ
Stirpis ab Afcanio, pugnataque in ordine bella,
Fecerat, &c.   Æn. 8. 617.

(18) This Defcription of the Shield is given in Mr. Pope's Words. See his Obfervations on the Shield of *Achilles.* Iliad 18.

" his Bofom to receive the Conquer'd. *Cleopatra* looks pale and almoft dead at the thought
" of that Death fhe had already determined; nay we fee the very Wind *Iapys* which haftens
" her Flight: We fee the three Triumphs of *Auguftus*; that Prince confecrates three hun-
" dred Temples, the Altars are filled with Ladies offering up Sacrifices, *Auguftus* fitting at
" the Entrance of *Apollo's* Temple, receives Prefents, and hangs them on the Pillars of the
" Temple; while all the conquer'd Nations pafs by, who fpeak different Languages, and
" are differently equipp'd and arm'd."

Pictures in the Temple of Juno *at* Carthage.

VIRGIL not only defcribes Sculptures but Pictures. The whole *Trojan* War is painted
in the Temple of *Juno* at *Carthage.* And thefe Defcriptions are fo much the more worthy
of our particular attention, that in all probability, (as there will be occafion to fhew afterwards) they were taken from real Pictures at *Rome* in *Virgil's* time.

Their Effect on Æneas.

ÆNEAS faw the whole Hiftory of the *Trojan* War painted in order on the Wall.
And what Opinion the *Latin* Poet had of the Power and Excellency of the Art, is delightfully fet forth to us by the Effect which they had upon his Hero. He feeds his Mind with
pictured Story, conceives Hopes, and is moft tenderly moved. *Servius* very well obferves
on the Paffage, that 'tis only a humane, generous People, that can delight in fuch Reprefentations; and that fuch Pictures as *Virgil* defcribes, muft needs have a very humanizing Influence upon all who have the Seeds of Virtue and Generofity in their Hearts. The Pictures
are thus defcribed:

> Sidonian Dido *here with folemn State*
> *Did* Juno's *Temple build, and confecrate :*
> *Enrich'd with Gifts, and with a golden Shrine;*
> *But more the Goddefs made the Place divine.*
> *On brazen Steps the Marble Threfhold rofe,*
> *And brazen Plates the Cedar Beams inclofe :*
> *The Rafters are with brazen Cov'rings crown'd,*
> *The lofty Doors on brazen Hinges found.*
> *What firft* Æneas *in this place beheld,*
> *Reviv'd his Courage, and his Fear expel'd.*
> *For while, expecting there the Queen, he rais'd*
> *His wond'ring Eyes, and round the Temple gaz'd;*
> *Admir'd the Fortune of the rifing Town,*
> *The ftriving Artifts, and their Arts renown :*
> *He faw in order painted on the Wall,*
> *Whatever did unhappy* Troy *befall :*
> *The Wars that Fate around the World had blown,*
> *All to the Life, and ev'ry Leader known.*
> *There* Agamemnon, Priam *here he fpies,*
> *And fierce* Achilles *who both Kings defies.*
> *He ftop'd, and weeping faid, O Friend ! ev'n here*
> *The Monuments of* Trojan *Woes appear !*
> *Our known Difafters fill ev'n foreign Lands :*
> *See there, where old unhappy* Priam *ftands !*
> *Ev'n the mute Walls relate the Warrior's Fame,*
> *And* Trojan *Griefs the* Tyrians *Pity claim.*
> *He faid, his Tears a ready Paffage find,*
> *Devouring what he faw fo well defign'd ;*
> *And with an empty Picture fed his Mind.*
> *For there he faw the fainting* Grecians *yield,*
> *And here the trembling* Trojans *quit the Field,*
> *Purfu'd by fierce* Achilles *through the Plain,*
> *On his high Chariot driving o'er the Slain.*
> *The Tents of* Rhefus *next, his Grief renew,*
> *By their white Sails betray'd to nightly View.*
> *And wakeful* Diomede, *whofe cruel Sword*
> *The Centries flew; nor fpar'd their flumb'ring Lord.*
> *Then took the fiery Steeds, e'er yet the Food*
> *Of* Troy *they tafte, or drink the* Xanthian *Flood.*
> *Elfewhere he faw where* Troïlus *defy'd*
> Achilles, *and unequal Combat try'd.*
> *Then, where the Boy difarm'd with loofen'd Reins,*
> *Was by his Horfes hurry'd o'er the Plains :*
> *Hung by the Neck and Hair, and drag'd around,*
> *The hoftile Spear yet fticking in his Wound ;*
> *With tracks of Blood infcrib'd the dufty Ground.*
> *Mean time the* Trojan *Dames opprefs'd with Woe,*
> *To* Pallas' *Fane in long Proceffion go,*
> *In hopes to reconcile their heav'nly Foe :*

They

They weep, they beat their Breasts, and rend their Hair,
And rich embroider'd Vests for Presents bear :
But the stern Goddess stands unmov'd with Pray'r.
Thrice round the Trojan *Walls* Achilles *drew*
The Corps of Hector, *whom in Flight he slew.*
Here Priam *sues, and there, for Sums of Gold,*
The lifeless Body of his Son is sold.
So sad an Object, and so well express'd,
Drew Sighs and Groans from the griev'd Hero's Breast :
To see the Figure of a lifeless Friend,
And his old Sire his helpless Hand extend.
Himself he saw amidst the Grecian *Train,*
Mix'd in the bloody Battel on the Plain,
And swarthy Memnon *in his Arms he knew*
His pompous Ensigns, and his Indian *Crew,*
Penthisilea *there, with mighty Grace,*
Leads to the Wars an Amazonian *Race :*
In their right Hands a pointed Dart they wield;
The left, for Ward, sustains the Lunar Shield.
Athwart her Breast a golden Belt she throws,
Amidst the Press alone provokes a thousand Foes ;
And dares her Maiden Arms to Manly Force oppose.
Thus, while the Trojan *Prince employs his Eyes,*
Fix'd on the Walls with Wonder and Surprize;
The beauteous Dido, *with a num'rous Train,*
And Pomp of Guards, ascends the sacred Fane.

IF those charming Descriptions do not fully prove, that the designing Arts were arrived at a very great pitch of Beauty, and Perfection, in the most ancient Times; they shew at least *Homer's* and *Virgil's* exact Knowledge, and thorough good Taste of them; what high Conceptions they had form'd of their Power and Dignity, as well as Agreeableness. And indeed these masterly Passages have been quoted here, not merely to prove the Antiquity of the ingenious Arts, but chiefly to give a just View, in the beginning of this Discourse, of their End, and Extent; or of what they are able to perform and ought principally to aim at. Every one who is capable of understanding and relishing those delightful Descriptions, must be naturally led by them, to many pleasant, and useful Reflections, upon the Beauty and Usefulness of Painting and Sculpture. He will immediately reflect upon the Elegance, Grace, and Taste, those Arts, when duly improved, must give to human Society. Not stopping there, he will enlarge with pleasure in his own fancy, upon the many happy Effects they would produce, if skilfully employed in Education, at once to form and enrich the Imagination, and to humanize and improve the Heart. And thus he will anticipate the Conclusion, which it is the main Design of this Essay to confirm and illustrate by several Considerations.

ARTS, that are able to produce such Works as have been described, must certainly be acknowledged capable of furnishing the most worthy Amusements to reasonable Beings, and the most becoming graceful Ornaments to human Life. 'Tis indeed these Arts alone, that, taking a right turn, and being duly promoted, can effectually discountenance, and banish all that brutish Sensuality, which is the Disgrace and Bane of Mankind. A rich Soil, if not sown with good and wholesome Seeds, and duly cultivated, will soon be over-spread with the most noxious Weeds; and in opulent States, if the elegant Arts are not carefully cherished and encouraged, gross Voluptuousness will spring up in their room, and they will quickly be over-run with Vices not more pernicious than abominable.

BUT this is not all : Those Descriptions of Paintings and Sculptures shew us, that the Arts of Design ought not to be considered merely as ornamental : There is hardly any useful Truth, or important Lesson in Philosophy, which may not be most agreeably insinuated into young and tender Minds by good Pictures. For what is it that this Art cannot represent, in the most expressive, touching manner ? Cities delightful in peace, or formidable in war ; the Labours of the Country, or the Fruits of those Labours in the Harvests and Vintages ; the pastoral Life in its Pleasures and Dangers ; and in a word, all the Occupations, all the Ambitions and Diversions of Mankind, were painted on *Achilles's* Shield : For, all this, the Poet well knew, the Art was able to perform. And what a variety of Characters, Passions, and Actions in like manner doth *Virgil* represent, as painted in *Dido's* Temple, or engraved on the Buckler and Armour of *Æneas* ! There is no Beauty in the natural World, no Passion in the human Breast, no Vicissitude in Life, no Blessing, no Calamity, no Virtue, no Vice, which those ingenious Arts, Painting in particular, cannot exhibit to our Sight, the most powerful of our Senses, in the most lively affecting manner.

These Descriptions from Homer *and* Virgil *give a just Idea of the Use, Power, and End of Painting.*

Thus we are led to anticipate the main Conclusion aimed at in this Essay.

The Taste and Lustre these Arts give to Society.

E   IF

IF therefore our Schools for Education were fuitably furnifhed with good Paintings and Sculptures, what equally profitable and delightful Leffions might be given from them, on the moft philofophical, momentous Subjects, and, at the fame time, upon the real Ufefulnefs and Excellence of the fine Arts! We are told, that the Schools at *Athens,* in which the Youth were inftructed and formed, being adorned with Sculptures and Paintings, the Philofophers often took the Arguments of their Lectures from them; and fo at the fame time explained fome moral Truth, and pointed out the Beauty and Elegance of the ingenious Picture or Sculpture reprefenting it. Thus *Zeno* (19) and feveral other Philofophers are faid to have taught moral Philofophy; or to have ftrongly inculcated upon the Youth, who flock'd to hear them with Delight, Benevolence, Fortitude, Temperance, the Love of Society, Liberty, Mankind, and every truly ennobling Virtue, with all their happy Confequences, and Effects in the Breafts which they adorn, and in human Society. To this manner of teaching *Perfius* alludes:

The ancient Philofophers made ufe of them in teaching Morals.
Zeno, Socrates, Cebes.

> *Haud tibi inexpertum curvos deprendere mores,*
> *Quæque docet Sapiens braccatis illita Medis*
> *Porticus, infomnis quibus & detonfa juventus*
> *Invigilat, filiquis, & grandi pafta pollentâ.*
> *Et tibi quæ Samios diduxit litera ramos,*
> *Surgentem dextro monftravit limite callem.* 'Sat.}.

SO *Cicero,* when he tells us that the philofophical *Portico,* (*fapiens Porticus*) taught, that Virtue and Virtue only is true Happinefs. We find *Socrates* (20), the beft of Philofophers, who had been a Sculptor in his Youth, frequently giving Leffons to the Painters and Statuaries, upon the Knowledge of human Nature, that is requifite, in order to imitate Manners, and exprefs Paffions in their Works; and often making ufe of thofe Arts, for inftructing the Youth in Virtue, correcting their Manners, and giving them juft Notions of moral Beauty. He was wont to fay, that, from hewing and polifhing a Block of Marble into the Figure of a Man, he had learned what muft be done in order to reform and polifh Mankind into their becoming, lovely Shape. In fine, one of the moft agreeably inftructive Pieces of Morality left us by the Ancients, is an Explication of a Picture, the allegorical Picture of *Cebes.* 'Tis exceeding pleafant to obferve, in reading the Hiftory of thofe times, with what eagernefs and fatisfaction the noble *Grecian* Youth followed and heard a *Socrates*; and perhaps one of the chief reafons why Philofophy now-a-days hath fuch a forbidding and rugged Afpect, and doth not produce the fame happy Effects it is faid to have done in thofe ancient Times, is, its being now fever'd in Education, by a fatal Error, from the ingenious fprightly Arts, as if they were too light and airy to bear it company. Hence thofe heavy Complaints of the Dronifhnefs and Infipidity of Philofophy, which formerly was wont to delight and charm as well as to inftruct. Whence elfe is it, that philofophical Education is found to ftand fo much in need of Redrefs, and Amendment from that excellent School we call the World, and from the polite Arts? Nor have the Arts fuffer'd lefs by this unnatural Separation, for if they do not receive their Subjects and Rules, their Materials and Inftructions, from true Philofophy, they muft become infipid, and trifling, if not corrupt, mere Tinfel; they may flatter the Senfe, but they cannot give any Employment, nor confequently any Entertainment, to the Reafon and Underftanding.

ONE who has not been a little converfant in Pictures, Statues, and Bas-reliefs, will not be able to enter fully into the Beauties of thofe defcrib'd by *Homer* and *Virgil,* and far lefs to underftand this Conclufion. But let any one, who doubts of the Power of thofe Arts to inftruct and move, or to awaken pleafing and ufeful Reflections in the Mind, make the Experiment on himfelf at *Hampton-Court*; let him but give that attention to *Raphael's* Cartons, which it is hardly poffible to with-hold, if one chances to caft his Eye on them: for however unacquainted he may be with Pictures, if he is not an utter Stranger to Nature, to Humanity, he fhall foon feel fuch noble and virtuous Sentiments arife in his Mind, as may fully convince him of the Aptitude of this powerful Art to tell an inftructive or moving Story, in the moft agreeable and lively manner, and to infpire Men with the beft Ideas and Difpofitions. The excellent Reflections (21), which are naturally, and, as it were, neceffarily called up, by thofe beft Performances of the beft of Painters, in the Breaft of every heedful Beholder, are elegantly defcribed by an excellent Author, in one of the Spectators, to prove the fitnefs of the Art to teach Morals, move the Affections in a wholefome way, and to inftill the beft Principles into the Mind, with the moft lafting Impreffion.

Raphael's Cartoni a proof of this.

AND, left any one, whether Virtuofo, or Philofopher, may have rafhly conceived a prejudice againft my Intention, of fhewing the Ufefulnefs of the Arts of Defign in Education, as a whimfical fingular Conceit, imagining that they are quite remote from Philofophy,

---

(19) See *Diogenes Laertius* in *Zenone.*

(20) This Paffage from *Xenophon* is given at full length in the beginning of the fourth Chapter. See *Joannis Meurfii Athenæ Atticæ,* lib. 1. cap. 5. where

there is a long Account of the *Pœcile* at *Athens,* and its Ornaments, where the Philofophers often taught.

(21) Thefe Reflections are quoted in the feventh Chapter.

fophy, and merely for Amufement : It may not be improper to mention here two other modern Authors, who feem to have had the very fame Ideas of the Ufefulnefs of all the Liberal Arts in Education, which, as it hath already appeared, and will be more fully proved afterwards, the beft ancient Poets and Philofophers had conceived of them.

THE firft I fhail mention is *Milton*, who, in his moft inftructive Dialogue on Education (22), clearly proves the abfolute neceffity of uniting the fine Arts and the manly Exercifes with Philofophy, in order to render the Education of young Gentlemen truly liberal and complete.

Milton and Shaftefbury quoted to prove that this Notion is not whimfical or fingular.

THE other is my Lord *Shaftesbury* (23). He is univerfally acknowledged to have had a very mafterly Tafte of all the polite Arts, and to have treated the moft important Subjects in moral Philofophy, in the moft agreeable manner ; and how often do we find him, in his Writings, regretting the unhappy Confequences that arife from feparating the ingenious Arts, and the liberal Exercifes, from Philofophy in the Formation of our Youth. Both thofe great Men had formed themfelves by the Study of the beft Ancients, whofe conftant Doctrine it was, that all the liberal Arts and Sciences are clofely bound and connected together by a ftrict, natural relation ; that they have all one Object, one End, one Rule and Meafure ; and that good Tafte in them all muft be the fame, becaufe the Principles upon which Beauty and Truth in Nature, in moral Conduct, and in every Art depend, are the fame. They have but one common Enemy, Luxury, or a falfe Tafte of Pleafure; and to guard, defend, and fortify againft the Diforder and Ruin which that introduces into the Mind, and brings upon Society, ought to be the main Defign of Education : Which can only be done, by eftablifhing early, in the tender, docile Mind, a juft Notion of Pleafure, Beauty, and Truth, the generous Love of publick Good, and a right Tafte of Life, and of all the Arts which add to the Happinefs or Ornament of human Society. Thus alone can the Youth be qualify'd for publick Service, and for delighting in it ; and thus only can they learn at the fame time how to recreate themfelves at hours of leifure, in a manly virtuous way, or without making one ftep towards Vice.

BUT having taken notice of the high Opinion which feveral of the greateft Men of Antiquity, and fome who are owned to have come the neareft to them among the Moderns, had of Painting, and of the excellent Ufes to which it might be rendered conducive ; it is fit to inquire a little into the Progrefs this Art is faid to have made at any time ; what it hath ever been really able to accomplifh ; or to what Perfection it hath actually been brought, that we may fee whether Painting ever came up to thefe great Ideas of its Power and Extent ; or whether this Art hath not been carried in Speculation, by Men of fine Imaginations, far beyond the Life, Power and Beauty, to which it ever really attained. But before I enter upon that Subject, it feems requifite to premife an Obfervation on that ancient manner of teaching and explaining the Liberal Arts and Sciences, in confequence of which it is that Painting is fo fully handled by feveral ancient Authors in their Writings on other Subjects. This is neceffary, becaufe the moft ancient Writers on Painting being loft, it is commonly imagined that very little more can be known of ancient Painting but what is preferved to us in *Pliny*. And the Ufefulnefs of Painting in liberal Education, which is the Point chiefly aimed at in this Effay, will evidently appear, before we advance any further, from the very Confideration of the Nature of thofe ancient Treatifes, from which the following Account of Painting is chiefly brought.

A preliminary Remark upon the ancient manner of explaining the Sciences.

THE great Error In Education, or in teaching the liberal Arts and Sciences, amongft the Moderns, [as Lord *Verulam* hath obferved (24)] is the not keeping the clofe Union and ftrict Connection of all the Arts and Sciences in view. " After the Diftribution of " particular Arts and Sciences Men have abandoned Univerfality : They forgot the natural " and neceffary Coherence of all the Portions of Knowledge ; the intimate Relation and " Dependance of all Truths. But let this be a general Rule, and let it be always remem" ber'd, that all Partitions of Knowledge be accepted rather as Lines and Veins, than for " Sections and Separations ; and that the Continuance and Entirenefs of Knowledge be " preferved. For the contrary hereof hath made particular Sciences become barren, fhallow " and erroneous, while they have not been nourifh'd and maintained from the common " Foun-

Lord Verulam's *Obfervation on ancient Logick.*

(22) Thefe Authors do not indeed exprefsly mention Pictures. But their Scheme of Education confifts in uniting all the fine Arts with Philofophy and the manly Exercifes. See the whole Treatife of *Milton* on Education, and what he fays there of Logick and Poetry particularly.

(23) In feveral parts of his Characterifticks, particularly in his Advice to an Author, p. 333. " It feems " indeed fomewhat improbable, that according to mo" dern Erudition, and as Science is now diftributed, our " ingenious and noble Youths fhould obtain the full ad" vantage of a juft and liberal Education, by uniting the " Scholar-part with that of the real Gentleman and

" Man of Reading. Academies for Exercifes, fo ufeful " to the Publick, and effential in the Formation of a " genteel and liberal Character, are unfortunately neg" lected. Letters are indeed banifh'd, I know not where, " in diftant Cloifters and unpractifed Cells, as our Poet " has it, confined to the Commerce and mean Fellow" fhip of bearded Boys. The fprightly Arts and Sciences " are fever'd from Philofophy, which confequently muft " grow dronifh, infipid, pedantick, ufelefs, and directly " oppofite to the real Knowledge and Practice of the " World and Mankind, &c."

(24) *Francifci Baconi Opera*, Vol. 2. Of the Advancement of Learning.

" Fountàin. So we fee *Cicero* the Orator complained of *Socrates* and his School (25),
" that he was the firft that feparated Philofophy and Rhetórick ; whereupon Rhetorick be-
" came an empty, verbal Art."

'TIS indeed (according to all the Ancients) by giving a large Profpect into the vaft and
extenfive Continent of Knowledge; and by prefenting, in due time, to the Mind, a clear
View of the great Aim and Scope of all Study and Science; of the plain and obvious way,
by which alone the Knowledge of any part of Nature can be acquired ; of the Commu-
nity, (fo to fpeak) of all the Liberal Arts and Sciences ; and of the Samenefs of good Tafte
in them all; it is by thefe Methods alone that Education can open and enlarge the Mind
as it ought, or fit and ftrengthen it for fuccefsfully purfuing, and improving any particular
Branch of Science, to which one may be afterwards determined chiefly to betake himfelf.
" And therefore, the fame Author juftly holds it to be a great Error, that Scholars, in
" Univerfities, come too foon and too unripe to Logick and Rhetorick, Arts fitter for
" Graduates than for Children and Novices : For thefe two taken rightly, are the graveft
" of Sciences, being the Arts of Arts, the one for Judgment, the other for Ornament : And
" they are the Rules and Directions how to fet forth and difpofe Matter : And therefore,
" for Minds empty and unfraught with Matter, and which hath not gathered that which
" *Cicero* calleth (*fylva & fupellex*) ftuff and variety ; to begin with thofe Arts (as if one
" fhould learn to weigh, meafure, or paint the Wind) doth work but this Effect, that the
" Wifdom of thofe Arts which is great and univerfal is almoft made contemptible, and
" is degenerate into childifh Sophiftry and ridiculous Affectation. And farther, the un-
" timely learning of them hath drawn on by confequence the fuperficial and unprofitable
" teaching and writing of them, as fitteth indeed to the Capacity of Children."

The Logick of Plato's School.

LOGICK or Dialectick is called rational Philofophy, becaufe it hath Science, Knowledge and good Tafte for its Object. Now, according to *Plato*, after Students have been
for fome time practifed in Geometry, natural Philofophy, and moral Reafonings ; after their
Minds are richly furnifhed with a great variety of Ideas, clear Conceptions, and folid Judgments from various Reading and Inftruction, this Science is of ufe to give them an united
View of the Confent, Harmony, and Dependance of all the Arts and Sciences ; of the Analogy and ftrict Relation of all Truths. To fet young unfurnifhed Minds, fays *Plato*, to
furvey the Materials of Knowledge, and to range them into order, according to their different Relations, Dependencies, and Analogies : To fet them to form and collect Rules for their
future Progrefs in Science, and their Security againft Error ; or to examine and criticize
the teaching and adorning Arts with that view, is no lefs abfurd, than it would be to employ one to review, clafs, and difpofe houfhold Furniture and Utenfils, who is utterly unacquainted with their Ends and Ufes, or with the domeftick Arts. It is the fame as to bid
one count without Arithmetick, or meafure without a Standard. The Habit of Reafoning
can only be acquired by various practice in it. Till one is acquainted with different ways of
Reafoning, and every fort of Evidence, how can he make Reafon, Knowledge, Evidence,
and Enquiry into Truth, or the feveral Manners of teaching, perfuading, and refuting, the
Objects of his Speculation and Criticifin ?

Its Ufefulnefs.

TILL the Mind hath been exercifed by manifold ufe about different Truths, and hath
laid up by due Information a large Stock of Knowledge, the Houfe is very empty : There
are no Materials to be furvey'd, inventoried, and ranged. But after Students have been
taught to inquire into feveral parts of Nature, after they have been inured to reafon about
different Connections and Relations of things, and have imbibed Inftruction from every
particular Art ; from Hiftory, natural and moral, from Poetry, Philofophy, and even from
the Arts of Defign : Then it is highly proper to give them a large and comprehenfive View of
the vaft Extent of Philofopy ; and of the Unity of all the Arts and Sciences that inquire into
Nature, and pretend to explain its Laws and Appearances, or to imitate and emulate them :
Then it is time to prefent them with a Map of the Sciences, fhewing their Divifions and
Partitions, and the Reafons for which they are fo diftributed and divided ; and, at the fame
time, the Unity, the Continuance, the Entirenefs of the whole Body of Science. This
is the Bufinefs of Logick ; and this was the ancient Method of Education in the beft
Schools (26).

HENCE

(25) We find the Paffage he fpeaks of in *Cicero de Ora-*
tore, lib. 3. 16. where he is giving an account of the different *Familiæ Philofophorum*, as he calls them. Inventi
funt, qui cum ipfi doctrina, & ingeniis abundarent, a
re autem civili, & a negotiis, animi quodam judicio
abhorrerent, hanc dicendi exercitationem exagitarent atque contemnerent :——Hinc diffidium illud exiftit quafi
Linguæ atque cordis, abfurdum fane & inutile, & repre-
hendendum, ut alii nos fapere, alii dicere docerent, &c.

(26) Nonne igitur tibi videtur Dialectica effe veluti
Culmen & Apex in fummo faftigio collocata ? Neque
ulla Difciplina hac effe fuperior, fed illa omnium Difci-
plinarum finem in fe omnino habere.——Arbitror quoque & de univerfo illo ordine quem ad eas res omnino

omnes a nobis commemoratas adhibuimus, hoc pacto
conftituendum : fi mutua illarum communitas atque cognatio recte componatur, & quæ confentaneè ex ipfarum
natura conficiantur, perite colligeretur, futurum inde
ut proprie quædam rationes ex his eliciantur, quæ ad in-
ftituti argumenti cognitionem fint collaturæ : Neque in-
anem in illis operam, fed & utilem & opportunam adhi-
bitum iri : Sin minus, infructuofam plane futuram illarum rerum confiderationem.——Hæc vero Dialectices ratio fola ita progreditur, ut fublatis hypothefibus ad ipfum
fimplex impermixtumque principium pergat, ut & firmum
fibi fundamentum fubfternat, oculumque animi cœno
quodam Barbarico revera demerfum atque defoffum fenfim
trahat, deducatque furfum, earum artium quas fupra ex-
pofuimus, veluti fociarum & famulatum præfidiis atque
adjumentis

HENCE it is, (as all who are acquainted with the better Ancients must have observed) *The ancient Manner of explaining the Arts.* that, in explaining any particular Art whatsoever, they have carefully laid the Foundations of universal good Taste, in all the Arts.   They are at pains to shew on every occasion, by proper Comparison, that the most essential Rules of Oratory, Poetry, or any other Art whatsoever, extend to all the Arts, and produce similar good Effects in them all.   They seem always to have it in their Eye, to point out the Unity, or Sameness of good Taste, to whatever Subject it is applied; the Sameness of the Principles on which it every where depends; and in general the strict Union and Connection of all the Liberal Arts and Sciences.

CICERO highly commends the School of *Plato* (27), for insisting so much, in all *Cicero commends Plato's Maxim concerning the Unity of the Sciences; and in treating of Oratory explains the other Arts.* their philosophical Discourses, on the intimate Relation, and strict Alliance of all the liberal Arts and Sciences; and recommending it so strongly, to all the Lovers of Science, to keep that Union and Harmony always before their Minds: And in the Books of *Cicero* on Oratory, we have a remarkable Instance of this ancient way of handling any particular Art; for, whether he is giving the History of Eloquence, and its Improvements; or explaining its Scope, Foundations and Precepts, he constantly brings his Illustrations from the other Arts, from Painting and Sculpture particularly.   So that however remote from one another these Arts may seem to be at first sight, they are soon found, in his way of treating them, to reflect very great light upon one another, and to have a very close and friendly Correspondence.   And thus every Reader is most agreeably, as well as advantageously, instructed by him, at the same time, in the principal Rules and Beauties; and Faults and Imperfections of almost all the Arts.   From *Cicero* we learn, how Eloquence was improved, and perfected, in a manner very analogous to the gradual Progress and Advancement of Painting and Sculpture; how they set out, as it were, in the same way; and went on, acquiring, step by step, new Force and Beauty by like means; till, at last, they were brought very nearly, each to its true Dignity and Perfection.

HE and other ancient Authors shew us whence this must proceed, by very proper Remarks on the Analogy of these Arts in several respects; on the common Causes and Means of Improvement and Perfection, or of Degeneracy and Corruption in all the Arts.   They shew us, that, as distinct as their several Provinces are, the Rules belonging to them all are the same; all their Beauties and Perfections are resolvable into the same Sources; they are supported, nourished and perfected by the same means; and they sink, are corrupted, or take a wrong turn, thro' the same bad Influence, and in the same manner : When one is tainted, the Infection soon spreads over all the rest; no matter where it begins, they all quickly shew the Symptoms and Marks of the same Contagion.

QUINTILIAN imitates *Cicero* in this agreeable way of discoursing on Rhetorick; *Quintilian follows his Example.* and hardly moves one step, without bringing, in like manner, apt Comparisons and Similitudes to illustrate its Rules and Principles, from the other Arts, from Painting and Sculpture in particular.

ARISTOTLE had led the way, having taken the same Method in explaining Rhetorick and Poetry. . And, in general, we find the ancient Philosophers mixing their Criticisms *Aristotle had led the way; and all the ancient Authors intermix Criticism with their moral and other Pieces.* on the Arts with their profoundest Pieces of Philosophy, to the mutual advantage of Philosophy, and of the Arts; as well as with their other politer Treatises occasionally wrote for publick use.   So *Plato* in many of his Dialogues, as for instance in his *Phædrus,* where an entire Piece of the Orator *Lysias* is criticized in form.   Such an Author was *Varro;* and

---

adjumentis utens.——Nonne hæc prudens cautio est ut juniores, videlicet homines illas minime tractent? Neque enim re latet, Arbitror ubi primum, Adolescentes differendi illam artem atque rationem capessunt, ea cognitione continuò ad contradictiones abuti, imitantes eos qui harc artem adhibent refutando mendacia, & Veritati illustrandæ.   Ipsos vero videre est illa facultate exultantiores conari ut alii alios redarguant, veluti catuli, iis cum quibus res est, disputatione distrahendis & discerpendis.——At vir ætate provectior atque maturior ab hac infania declinabit ultro : Ac hominem investigandæ veritatis gratia differentem imitabitur potius quam eum qui jocandi causa versutiis decipulisque dat operam : Quin & ipse moderatior erit & hanc artem ex infami illustrem reddet. *Plato de Rep. l.* 7. *p.* 533, 534, 539. Edit. *Steph.*
It belongs not to my present purpose to insist long on this Subject; but the Logick delineated by *Plato* in his Books *de Republica,* and his other Treatises, well deserves the mature Consideration of those who are concerned in Education, and teaching the Sciences; so very different is it from that Science which commonly takes the name of Logick.   See what *Milton* says on this Subject in his Treatise of Education, vol. 1. of his Works, p. 139.
   " And now lastly will be the time to read with them
   " those organick Arts, which enable Men to discourse

" and write perspicuously, elegantly, and according to
" the fitted Stile of lofty, mean, or homely.   Logick
" therefore, so much as is useful, is to be referred to this
" due place, with all her well-coucht Heads and To-
" picks, until it be time to open her contracted Palm into
" a graceful and ornate Rhetorick taught out of the
" Rule of *Plato, Aristotle, Phalereus, Cicero, Hermo-
" genes, Longinus.*   To which Poetry would be made
" subsequent, or indeed rather precedent, as being less
" subtle and fine, but more simple, sensous and passion-
" ate, &c."

(27) Ac, nequis a nobis hoc ita dici forte miretur, quod alia quædam in hoc facultas sit ingenii, neque hæc dicendi ratio, aut Disciplina : ne nos quidem huic cuncti studio penitus unquam dediti fuimus.   Etenim omnes Artes, quæ ad Humanitatem pertinent, habent quoddam commune vinculum, & quasi cognatione quadam inter se continentur.   *Cicero pro Archia Poeta ab initio.*   Est etiam illa Platonis Vera, Et tibi, Catule, certe non inaudita vox, omnem Doctrinam harum ingenuarum, & humanarum artium, uno quodam Societatis Vinculo contineri, ubi enim perspecta vis est rationis ejus, qua causæ rerum, atque exitus cognoscuntur, mirus quidam omnium quasi consensus Doctrinarum, concentusque reperitur.   *Cic. de Orat. lib.* 3. 6.

F

and in this manner do *Plutarch, Dionysius Halicarnasseus, Lucian,* and several others, also write on various Subjects.

NOW hence it comes about, that, tho' none of the more ancient Treatises on Painting are extant, yet we may gather a great deal concerning the Perfection to which that Art was brought amongst the Ancients; and the Opinion which the greatest Men of Antiquity had of its true Dignity and Excellence, from Authors who have, not expressly, written of it. It is therefore by disposing under proper Heads, the Observations with relation to Painting, which are scatter'd thro' many Authors, and adding them to *Pliny's* short History of this Art, that it is now proposed to give a just Idea of it, of its Connection with Poetry, Oratory, and Philosophy, and of its Usefulness in Education; a fair Representation of the Perfection it had arrived at amongst the *Greeks,* and of the Esteem in which it was held by the best Judges in ancient Times.

The Design of this Essay, is, to collect and dispose into proper Order the Observations that lie scatter'd thro' many ancient Treatises on Painting, and to add these to Pliny's *Account of the Art.*

CHAP. II.

Observations upon the Perfection to which Painting *was brought in* Greece, *and some of the Means and Causes of its Improvement.*

A Parallel proposed between two Ages of Painting, as the most agreeable way of shewing to what Perfection the Art was brought in both.

LET us then inquire a little into the State of Painting in *Greece,* while the Arts flourish'd there, and into the principal Causes and Means by which it was so highly improved in the most ancient Age of it described to us.

NOW perhaps it may not be a disagreeable way of pursuing that Design, to attempt it by way of parallel; that is, by comparing the Characters, Talents and Accomplishments of the chief Masters in *Greece,* about the time of *Apelles,* with those of the more distinguish'd Painters about that of *Raphael:* Or in general by comparing the Accounts that are given of the Progress and Perfection of the Art in that latter Period of it, with those that are transmitted to us, of its Improvements and Advances in the other. Nothing is more entertaining and profitable, than to compare Men with Men, and Times with Times; or the State of an Art at one Period, with its Condition and Circumstances at another. Similarity in moral Effects, is not less agreeable and satisfactory to the Mind than in natural ones: Nor is it more the natural Philosopher's Business, to trace Analogies of Appearances in the one, than it is the moral Philosopher's, to observe them in the other. There is indeed a Likeness between these two Ages of the Art in many Circumstances, which is very surprising; and it is by itself for that reason a Phænomenon well worth the Philosopher's Attention. It cannot be unpleasing to see two Ages of the Art at one view. And there is yet another Advantage that arises from giving this History by way of Parallel, for it being very difficult to convey clear Ideas of the Talents of Painters merely by Words, such as are at a loss to understand any of the ways of speaking about the Abilities of ancient Masters, may be satisfied by having recourse to the Pictures (or good Prints of them) of modern Masters, to whom the like Qualifications are ascrib'd.

Apelles and Raphael compared.

FIRST of all, there is a very remarkable Likeness in Genius, Abilities and Character, between the two noted Chiefs of the Art, *Apelles* and *Raphael,* by whose Works it hath acquired its highest Glory. For this reason, the last is commonly called the second *Apelles,* or *Apelles* revived. They are describ'd to have been of the same Temper, Turn, and Disposition of Mind (1). And therefore 'tis not to be wonder'd, that the Pictures of the former, are said to have been of the same Character with those of the latter, or to have had the same distinguishing Excellencies. "Effects are always proportional and similar to " their Causes." Like Causes will produce like Effects in the moral as well as in the natural World; and therefore as Works are to one another, so are their Authors. Or, in other Words, if Authors are of a like Temper and Genius, their Performances will likewise bear a very strong resemblance; for the Character of the Author will always discover itself in his Productions.

A Likeness of Genius.

RAPHAEL and *Apelles* had both graceful Persons; and yet more graceful Minds. They were both humane, open, free, easy, well-bred Men. They both throughly understood Good-Manners, or Beauty and Decency in Life and Behaviour, and had great Souls; and those good Qualities eminently distinguish'd their Works. Beauty, Sweetness, Spirit, Freedom, Ease, Truth, Grace and Greatness gave inimitable Charms to every thing that
came

(1) Il ne lui échapoit jamais rien de ce qui pouvoit servir à l'embellissement & a la perfection de ses peintures. Il savoit si bien mettre les figures en leur place, que dans la composition de ses tableaux, on y voit une beauté d'ordonnance qui ne se rencontre point ailleurs. Il peut bien être qu'il n'ait point dessiné un nud plus doctement que Michel Ange; mais son goût de dessiner est bien meilleur & plus pur.
Je trouve que celui qui a dit que les hommes se peignent eux-mêmes dans leurs ouvrages, a parfaitement bien ren-

contré a l'egard de Raphaël. Car on rapporte de lui qu'il sembloit qu'a sa naissance les Graces fussent descenduës du Ciel pour le suivre par tout, & lui servir de fidélles compagnes pendant sa vie; ayant toûjours paru gracieux dans ses actions & dans ses mœurs aussi-bien que dans ses tableaux: de sorte que la douceur, la politesse & la civilité ne rendoient pas sa personne moins chere à tout le monde, que ses peintures rendoient son nom célébre par toute la terre. *Les Vies de Peintres.* Felibien.

came from their Pencils. They are called the two greateſt Painters that ever were, becauſe no other ever poſſeſs'd ſo many of the excellent Qualities belonging to a perfect Painter, in ſuch a high degree as thoſe two did, almoſt equally; that is, in the ſame Senſe that *Homer* and *Virgil* are ſaid to have been the beſt of Poets. 'Tis for the ſame, moſt eſſential, exₑcellent Talents of a Painter, that they are both ſo greatly celebrated. Modern Writers ſpeak of the Accompliſhments of the one, in the ſame terms, as ancient Authors, of the other. They both excelled in a fine Taſte and Choice of Nature (2); an Idea of Beauty and Grace beyond the power of Words to expreſs; a copious, rich Invention, a refin'd Imagination, a correct Judgment, and an elegant, ſweet and gracious, yet bold, ſublime, and maſterly Manner of Painting. They both knew what to chuſe, and how far to go; what to emulate in Nature, and when to ſtop or give over. They both knew how to imitate Nature, without following it too cloſely, or copying after it too ſtrictly; well knowing that the Art allows not the Imitator to bring all Nature into his Piece, but a part only. They underſtood how to take their Notion of Beauty, not from one particular Object, but from the various Parts of Nature; and thus they were capable to compoſe coherent, great, and beautiful Pictures. This is the Sum of what is ſaid in praiſe of either; and theſe are the higheſt Endowments of a Painter. 'Tis this Intelligence and Taſte, which alone can form Pictures that never cloy a skilful Eye, but grow in Beauty and Excellence, in proportion as the Underſtanding of their Admirers refines and improves. So the Works of *Apelles* are ſaid to have done; and ſo thoſe of *Raphael* are known to do.

They excelled in Beauty, Grace and Uſefulneſs.

BUT as their Excellencies were the ſame, ſo likewiſe, (very nearly at leaſt) were their Imperfections. *Apelles* yielded to *Aſclepiodorus* in the exact Obſervance of Symmetry and Proportion; and to *Echion*, in what is called, by Painters, the Ordonnance, that is, in the Ordering and Diſpoſition of the Figures. Now *Raphael*, as he was thought ſomewhat inferiour to *Michael Angelo* in the Part of Deſign, ſo he was to *Titian* in the Union and Harmony of Colouring.

In what they were both deficient.

APELLES not only performed divinely with his Pencil, but his Pen was equally ingenious and elegant: For the three Volumes he wrote on the principal Beauties and Secrets of the Art, were highly eſteem'd: *Pliny* probably had received great aſſiſtance from them, in this part of his univerſal Hiſtory of Nature and Arts. But we may form a juſt Notion of his Temper and Genius, from the Ingenuity and Greatneſs of Mind, which appear'd equally in doing juſtice to himſelf, and to his Rivals; in acknowledging his own Defects, and in cenſuring others. He treated all his Competitors with great Candour, Modeſty, and Good-humour; he was exceedingly communicative; never found fault without a reaſon, and ever in the mildeſt way; he ſeem'd to be more quick and ready in deſcrying Beauties than Defects, and more willing to commend than to condemn. He was not aſhamed to acknowledge frankly in what he came ſhort of any one; nor was he ſo narrow-minded and invidious as to grudge others their due praiſe: But at the ſame time as he could not but know his own Excellence, ſo he ſcrupled not to claim his right, with an unarrogant Aſſurance that well becomes true Merit, and that can never offend thoſe who are conſcious of any of thoſe good Qualities in which the Mind naturally exults (3). The truly virtuous Satisfaction

Apelles's Character.

His Humanity.

(2) Sìo doveſſi paragonare ad Apelle alcuno de' moderni, non cambierei Raffaello; perdomi di riconoſcere in lui non tanto l'eccellenza dell' ingegno, quanto la finezza dell' arte: ma di più quelle medeſime maniere, e quegli ſteſſi coſtumi, che reſero l'uno, e l'altro grati oltremodo a' Principi dell' età loro. Amendue corteſi, arguti, grazioſi, di grande inVentiVa, e fantaſia, amici della gloria, e inclinati agli amori. Tutti due premiati, onorati, amati, ammirati. *Dati, vit. d'Apelle.* Felibien, tom. 1. p.182. At in Ætione, Nicomacho, Protogene, Apelle, jam perfecta ſunt omnia. *Cic. de Clar. Orat.*

*Apellæ cuperent te ſcribereceræ.*Stat.Sylv.l.1.in quoDomit *Clarus fronde Jovis, Romani fama Cothurni,*
  Spirat Apellea redditus arte memor. Mart. l.2. Ep.19.
——*O Apella, O Zeuxis pictor,*
Cur numero eſtis mortui? hinc eXemplum
    ut pingeretis:
Nam alios Pictores nihil moror huiuſmodi
    tractare exemplar. Plaut. in Pœnulo.

Fuit Apelles non minoris ſimplicitatis quàm artis. Præcipua Apellis in arte venuſtas fuit, cum eadem ætate maximi Pictores eſſent; quorum opera cum admiraretur, collaudatis omnibus, deeſſe iis unam illam Venerem dicebat, quam Græci χάριτα Vocant: Cætera omnia contigiſſe, ſed hac ſolâ ſibi neminem parem. Idem & aliam gloriam uſurpavit, quum Protogenis opus immenſi laboris, ac curæ ſupra modum anxiæ, miraretur: Dixit enim, omnia ſibi cum illo paria, aut illi meliora, ſed uno ſe præſtare, quod manum ille de tabula non ſciret tollere: Memorabili præcepto, nocere ſæpe nimiam Diligentiam.
——Fuit enim Comitas illi, propter quam & gratior Alexandro Magno, frequenter in officinam ventitanti: Nam, ut diximus, ab alio pingi ſe vetuerat Edicto:—

Comiter ſuadebat—tantum erat Auctoritatis Viro in regem alioqui iracundum.——Apelles & in Æmulis benignus. *Plin. lib.* 35.

Ingenio & Gratia, quam in ſeipſo maxime jactat, Apelles eſt præſtantiſſimus. *Quintil. Inſt.* lib. 12. c.10.

Elegans formarum ſpectator. *Athenæus, lib.* 13. c. 6.

See *Ælian.* Hiſt.var.12. 41. *Plut. in Demetrio Poliorcete.*

Cum primis illud Alexandri præclarum, Quod Imaginem ſuum, quo certior poſteris proderetur, noluit a multis Artificibus Vulgo contaminari: ſed edixit univerſo Orbi ſuo, nequis Effigiem regis temere aſſimilaret, ære, colore, cælamine; Quin ſolus eum Polycletus ære duceret, ſolus Apelles coloribus delinearet.——Eo igitur omnium metu factum, ſolus Alexander ut ubique Imaginum ſummus eſſet: Utque omnibus ſtatuis, & Tabulis, & Toreumatis idem Vigor acerrimi Bellatoris, idem Ingenium maximi Honoris, eadem Forma Viridis Juventæ, eædem Gratia reliſcinæ frontis cerneretur. *Apuleius in Florid. Plin. Hiſt. Natur. lib.* 7. c. 37.

Apelli fuit perpetua conſuetudo nunquam tam occupatam Diem agendi, ut non Lineam ducendo exerceret Artem: Quod ab eo in ProVerbium Venit.——Amphioni de poſitione cedebat; plura ſolus prope quam ceteri omnes contulit; voluminibus etiam editis, quæ Doctrinam eam continent.

(3) Of this Self-Confidence there is a Saying of *Melanthius* the Painter, recorded by *Diogenes Laertius, lib.*4. *in Polemone.* Μελάνθιος ὁ ζωγράφος ἐν ταῖς περὶ ζωγραφικῆς φησὶ δεῖν αὐθάδειάν τινα καὶ σκληρότητα τοῖς ἔργοις ἐπιτρέχειν, ὁμοίως δὲ τοῖς ἤθεσιν: *Val. Max.* lib.3. c.7. gives an Inſtance of this in *Zeuxis.* This and other Inſtances are brought by *Ariſtides, tom.* 3. *Orat.* 5. *de Paropthegmate:* In which he aſſerts, Magnum ſui fiduciam non

Satisfaction with one's self on the account of real Merit, is diftinguifh'd from ill-founded Vanity, Pride, and Self-Conceit, by this agreeable Characteriftick which always attends it, that while it looks with a friendly encouraging Afpect on any valuable Accomplifhment in others, it never allows one to fit down contented, as if there were no higher Attainments to be purfued than thofe he is already mafter of; but is on the contrary the keeneft In-

His Diligence to improve himfelf.

centive to Progrefs and Improvement. And accordingly, *Apelles,* far from imagining himfelf at the Top of Perfection, continued, after all the Advances he had made, and the Glory he had juftly acquired, indefatigably to afpire after greater Excellence in his Art. He was thus an Example to Painters of the earneft and perfevering, emulous Zeal that alone can perfect the Artift and the Arts, of Diligence and Care to improve one's Ideas and Tafte of Beauty and Greatnefs; Diligence and Ambition to excel one's felf as well as all

His excellent Advice to Painters.

others: And, at the fame time, he, by his modeft Cenfure of *Protogenes,* has left one of the beft and moft inftructive Leffons to Painters, with regard to that Over-carefulnefs and too rigorous, anxious Exactnefs in correcting and finifhing, by which Pictures are deadned, difpirited, and lofe all Grace (4). He well knew the Difference between Nicety or Concinnity, and true Elegance; how neceffary to Grace and Beauty, and the Perfection of Works of Genius and Fancy, Eafe, Freedom, and the Hiding of Art and Labour are: And therefore he owned that he only had the Advantage of *Protogenes* in this refpect, that he had found out the Secret of difcerning when to ftop and lay afide his Pencil; whereas *Protogenes* not knowing when to give over, his Works appeared too laboured, and had not the Spirit, Eafe, and Grace, that are the great Charms in Painting: An important Leffon in all the Arts, and often applied by *Cicero* and *Quintilian* to Oratory (5).

Raphael's Charac-ter.

NOW *Raphael* is praifed for the fame Courteoufnefs to his Rivals, Affability and Communicativenefs to all; the fame readinefs to commend whatever is excellent, and to learn from every one; the fame Ambition to be ever improving, without which any degree of Self-confidence is infufferable Arrogance. And what that Grace means in which *Apelles* fo greatly excelled all his Competitors, can only be underftood and learned from *Raphael* or *Corregio's* Works. For that *Je-ne-fçay-quoi* of Sweetnefs duely mixed with Freedom and Greatnefs, that at the fame time touches the Heart and fooths the Imagination, cannot be defined by Words or taught by Rules; it is in a peculiar Senfe the Gift of Nature, and can only be diftinguifh'd by the Eye, and felt within one.

ONE Circumftance more is well worth our Obfervation with regard to thofe two greateft Painters, that as *Apelles* is highly praifed for hitting the beft Likenefs of Perfons, and exhibiting their Minds as well as their Bodies (6); fo *Raphael's* Portraits have always been exceedingly admired on the fame account, and judged expreffive of the Souls of the Perfonages they reprefented, and not merely of their outward Forms.

PAINTING then had arrived to fuch a pitch of Perfection and Excellence amongft the *Greeks* in *Apelles,* that none hath ever been able to come near him but *Raphael,* who had the fame Temper, Genius and Turn of Mind.

How Apelles was formed by Pamphi-lus.

BUT how came it to fuch a height of Perfection? *Pamphilus* the Mafter of *Apelles* had joined to the Art of Painting, the Study of all the Liberal Arts and Sciences, which enlarge, elevate, and enrich the Mind; of Mathematicks efpecially, without the Help of which, he ufed to fay, that it was impoffible to bring Painting to Perfection. And thus he contributed exceedingly to the Improvement and Reputation of the growing Art. He had the Intereft to procure certain valuable Privileges (7) and Advantages to its Students

and

---

non dedecere magnas Animas, neque Artificibus eximiis crimen fuperbiæ protinus impingendum, cum fibimet ipfis non plus quam æquum eft tribuunt. This is the Scope of the whole Oration.

(4.) 'Tis thus *Pliny* himfelf defcribes the bad Effect of Over-diligence in the Character of *Callimachus, Nat. Hift.* 34. 8. Callimachus femper Calumniator fui, nec finem habens Diligentiæ, ob id Cacizo-technos appellatus, memorabili exemplo adhibendi curæ modum. Hujus funt faltantis Lacænæ, emendatum opus, fed in quo gratiam omnem diligentia abftulerit. Hunc quidem & Pictorem fuiffe tradunt.

(5) In omnibus rebus videndum eft quatenus: etfi enim fuus cuique modus eft, tamen magis offendit nimium quam parum. In quo Apelles Pictores quoque eos peccare dicebat, qui non fentirent quod effet fatis. *Cic. Orator. n.* 22. Et ipfa emendatio finem habet. *Quint. Inft. lib.* 10. *c.*4. Utiliffima eft diffimulata fubtilitas, quæ effectu apparet, habitu latet. *Senec. in Pro. lib.* 1. *Contro.*

(6) Apelles pinxit imagines fimilitudinis adeo indifcretæ, ut (incredibile dictu) Apion grammaticus fcriptum reliquerit, quendam a facie homines addivinantem, quos

Metopofcopos vocant, ex his dixiffe, aut futuræ mortis annos, aut præteritæ. Pinxit & Antigoni Regis imaginem altero lumine orbam,- primus excogitata ratione vitia condendi. Obliquam namque fecit ut quod deerat Corpori, Picturæ deeffe videretur, tantumque eam partem e facie oftendit, quam totam poterat oftendere. *Plin. lib.* 35.

N. B. Once for all 'tis proper to obferve with regard to the Chronology of the ancient Painters, That *Zeuxis, Parrhafius, Melanthius,* and *Pamphilus* were contemporary. They are placed in the 95th Olympiad, A.M.3604. *Apollodorus* was likewife contemporary with *Zeuxis.* Before them were *Phidias, Panænus* and *Polygnotus.* This laft in the 90th Olympiad, A.M. 3582. The two former were Brothers, and flourifh'd in the 84th Olympiad, A.M. 3560. *Ariftides* and *Protogenes* were contemporary with *Apelles. Euphranor* was Scholar to *Ariftides, Paufias* to *Pamphilus,* &c.

(7.) Eupompus docuit Pamphilum Apellis præceptorem. ——Ipfe (Pamphilus) Macedo natione, fed primus, in Pictura, omnibus literis eruditus, præcipue Arithmetice & Geometrice, fine quibus negavit artem perfici poffe. Docuit neminem minoris talento, annis decem; quam mercedem ei Apelles & Melanthius dedere. Et hujus auctoritate effectum eft, Sicyone primum, deinde & in

tota

and Profeffors, which greatly ennobled the Art in the Opinion of the World; and fo were no inconfiderable Incentives to thofe to apply themfelves to it who are moft likely to fucceed in Painting, or indeed to improve any ingenious Art : But, which is of principal moment, he firft introduced the Cuftom at *Sicyon*, that was foon followed throughout all *Greece*, of teaching the Elements of Defign very early in the Schools amongft the Liberal Arts; by which means, no doubt, Painting became in a little time generally underftood by all who had a liberal Education, and confequently was very highly relifh'd and efteem'd. We may eafily conceive, that the Art muft have gained very great Improvements from a Painter fo univerfally well acquainted with all the Parts of polite Literature, with Philofophy, and every other ufeful Science; and who imployed every Branch of his Scholarfhip towards perfecting his favourite Profeffion. For this, like every other Art, can only be advanced, and improved, in proportion as its Scope, Extent, Power and Excellence are fully comprehended; and in confequence thereof all neceffary Aids from the other Sciences are called upon to affift, and perfect it. This uncommon Genius not only practifed the Art with great Succefs, but taught it and wrote of it with equal Applaufe (8). And to his Inftruction was owing an *Apelles* in a great meafure; fo true it is, that the beft natural Genius, as well as the beft Soil, requires proper Culture; and that Art and Nature muft confpire together to produce truly beautiful, generous Plants (9). So *Horace* fpeaking of Painting as well as Poetry,

His Character and Accomplifhments.

> —— *Ego nec Studium fine divite vena*
> *Nec rude quid profit video ingenium. Alterius fic*
> *Altera pofcit opem res, & conjurat amice.* Hor. Art. Poet.

NOW fuch a Genius was *Leonardo da Vinci* in the latter Age of Painting; and to his like Abilities and Accomplifhments is the Improvement of the Art at that Period afcribed. He was one of the compleateft Scholars and fineft-Gentlemen of that Age; a Perfon of very extraordinary natural Endowments, and of vaft acquired Parts; he was particularly well-skilled in the Mathematicks; in thofe Parts of that Science at leaft which relate more immediately to the Arts of Defign. He not only fhewed the Ufefulnefs of that Science to a Painter by his Performances and Writings; but gave in the general, by his Works and Leffons, a larger Notion and a higher Idea, than had been hitherto conceived, of the Grandeur, Truth, and Sublimity the Art is capable of attaining, and ought to afpire after. And thus he had fo great a fhare in kindling the Ambition and Emulation of Painters; in directing them to the right Method of improving the Art, and in procuring juft Efteem to its Students and Profeffors; that he is juftly faid to be one of thofe who in any Age have contributed the greateft fhare towards the Advancement of Painting to its true Dignity and Glory. By his Intereft an Academy of Painting was founded at *Milan*, which was under his Direction for a long time; and conduced not a little to promote the Knowledge, Tafte, and Love of the then growing Art. He practifed it, taught it, and wrote of it with great Approbation. And to him we are chiefly indebted for the Perfection of a *Raphael*, who foon learned from his Inftructions to quit *Perugino* his firft Mafter's dry, ftiff, infipid Manner, to form greater and nobler Ideas, and to paint with more Spirit and Strength : To which good Qualities his own natural Genius quickly added that Grace, in which no other ever came fo near to *Apelles*.

Leonardo da Vinci, by whom Raphael was formed, had the fame Talents with Pamphilus. They were both Mathematicians, &c.

THE chief Excellence of *Pamphilus*, and *Leonardo da Vinci*, feems to have confifted in giving every thing its proper Character; in the Truth of their Defign, and the Grandeur of their Conceptions. And it is obfervable, that, as *Pamphilus* ftudied under *Eupompus*, who valued himfelf upon ftudying Nature, the great Miftrefs of Painters, imitating her with Tafte and Judgment, and not fervilely following any Artift (10); fo *Leonardo da Vinci*,

And they both had Mafters of the fame Turn and Genius.

tota Græcia, ut pueri ingenui, omnia ante, Graphicen, hoc eft, Picturam, in Buxo docerentur, recipereturque ea ars in primum gradum liberalium. Semper quidem bonos ei fuit, ut ingenui exercerent; mox ut honefti; perpetuo interdicto ne fervitia docerentur, &c. *Plin. Nat. Hift.* 35.
Floruit circa Philippum, & ufque ad fucceffores Alexandri Pictura præcipue, fed diverfis virtutibus. Nam cura Protogenes, ratione Pamphilus ac Melanthius, &c. *Quin. Inft* 12. 10.

(8) *Suidas* mentions him as a Writer on Painting.

(9) Ut ager quamvis fertilis, fine cultura fructuofus effe non poteft, fic fine Doctrina animus; ita eft utraque res fine altera debilis. *Cic. Tufc. Quæf. lib.* 2.

(10) Tradunt Lyfippum primo ærarium fabrum, audendi rationem cepiffe Pictoris Eupompi refponfo: eum enim interrogatum, quem fequeretur antecedentium? dixiffe, demonftrata hominum multitudine, naturam ipfam imitandam effe, non artificem. *Plin. l.* 34. *c.* 8.
Of *Andrea Verrocchio*, Mafter to *Pietro Perugino*, and *Leonardo da Vinci*, *Vafari* thus fpeaks—Fù ne tempi fuoi

Orefice, profpettivo, fcultore, intagliatore, pittore, e mufico. Ma in vero nell' arte della fcultura, e pittura, hebbe la maniera alquanto dura, e crudetta : come quello che con infinito ftudio fe la guadagnò più che col beneficio, ò facilità della natura — in giovanezza atteſe alle fcienze, e particolarmente alla geometria——fono alcuni difegni di fua mano nel noftro libro, fatti con molta pacienza, e grandiffimo giudicio, in fra i quali fono alcune tefte di femina con bell' arte, & acconciature di capelli, quali per la fua bellezza Leonardo da Vinci fempre imitò : fonui ancora dua cavalli con il modo delle mifure, e centini da fargli di piccoli grandi, che venghino proportionati e fenza errori.——Andrea dunque usò di formare, con forme cofi fatte, le cofe naturali, per poterle con più commodità tenere inanzi, & imitarle, cioè mani, piedi, ginocchia, gambe, braccia, e torfi. Dopo fi cominciò al tempo fuo a formate le tefte di coloro, che morivano con poca fpefa; onde fi vede : ogni cafa di Firenze fopra i camini, ufci, fineftre, e cornicioni infiniti di detti ritratti, tanto ben fatti, e naturali, che paiono vivi. *Vit. de Pittore di Gio. Vafari. See Il Ripofo di Borghini.*
See likewife *Leonardo da Vinci* on Painting, the *Englifh* Tranflation, what he fays of Nature, p. 32. A Painter ought to have his Mind continually at work, and to

G   make

Vinci, who hath very strongly recommended by his Writings the Study of Nature's Laws and Beauties to all who would arrive at any Perfection in Painting, had a Master (*Andrea Verrocchio*) who was very well skill'd in Opticks and several other Sciences, and a very assiduous Student and imitator of Nature. Thus it was by similar Talents of its Professors, that the Art was brought to so equal Perfection in those two Ages of it.

Zeuxis the best Colourist amongst the Ancients.

From whom he learned the Art.

ZEUXIS is esteemed the best Colourist amongst the ancient Painters; but *Apollodorus* had opened the Door by which he enter'd into the profoundest Secrets of the colouring Art. *Pliny* tells us (11), the famous Statuaries who flourished before his time must certainly have been great Masters of Drawing, if the Painters were not : But he was the first, it seems, who remarkably excelled in mingling, or laying on Colours, or in both; and in the Distribution of Lights and Shadows. He is celebrated for his good Choice of Nature, and for giving Beauty, Strength, and Relief to his Figures, far beyond what any Painters before him had been able to do. He understood how to give every thing the Touches which are most proper and suitable to them, such as distinguish them from each other, and give the greatest Spirit and Truth to a Picture. This is that great and difficult Art which *Pliny* calls *species rerum exprimere, i. e.* to exhibit the things themselves. The Colouring of *Apollodorus* is spoken of in such a manner by the Ancients, that he seems to have made some Discovery in the Use of Colours, that produced as new and surprizing Effects at that time as the Secret of Oil-colours did, when, being found out by *Jean Van Eyk* in *Flanders*, it was brought into *Italy* by *Antonello* of *Messina*, tho' not of the same kind'; for it does not appear that the Art of preparing Colours with Oil was known to the Ancients, as highly as their Colouring is commended for all the charming Effects Colouring ever hath, or can possibly produce.

APOLLODORUS is greatly praised for his Intelligence of Colours, and of the Clair-obscure and the illusive Power to which he had thereby raised the Art : And yet *Zeuxis* (12), according to the same Authors, so far out-stripped him in this part of Painting, that they seem not to know how to express the superiour Beauty, Union, Harmony, and Melodiousness of his Compositions. Must not Colouring then have been exceedingly perfect ? Whatever *Zeuxis* painted was the thing itself, with such Propriety, Union, Tenderness, Harmony of Colours, and such a charming Relief was it expressed : All he did was Nature; but beautiful Nature; the most perfect Nature : So that by him Painting was rendred a compleatly deceiving and enchanting Art. This is the Substance of what is said in his praise.

So Titian *amongst the Moderns.*

NOW the same Excellencies are justly ascribed to *Titian* : His Colouring is wonderfully glowing, sweet and delicate ; it is real Life ; but Life seldom seen : for in such great Masters Art really excels Nature ; or at least Nature in her most common Effects.

From whom he learned the Art.

HERE again we see Art advancing to Perfection by gradual steps, as all things in Nature do, from Infancy to Vigour and Ripeness (13). Many Improvements had been already made in Colouring ; and it was *Titian*'s Fellow-Scholar and Rival, who first found out the admirable Effects of strong Lights and Shadows, and began to make choice of the warm glowing agreeable Colours, the Perfection and entire Harmony of which were afterwards to be found in *Titian*'s Pictures. His first, were in a dry mean manner ; and it may be justly said, that he improved more by the Emulation that was between him and his Fellow-Disciple, than by all the Instructions he had received from *Bellini* their Master ; in like manner as the great Improvements *Zeuxis* made in the same part of Painting, are attributed chiefly to the Rivalship betwixt him and *Apollodorus*, and his Contests with *Parrhasius* (14).

ZEUXIS

make Remarks on every Subject, &c.—p. 34. among other things I shall not scruple to deliver a new Method, &c.—p. 50. take notes of the Muscles, &c.—p. 67. when you understand Anatomy and Perspective, take all occasions of observing different Attitudes and Gestures of Men in different Actions, &c.

(11) Ab hoc (Apollodoro) fores apertas Zeuxis Heracliotes intravit.——Audentemque jam aliquid, penecillum, ad magnam gloriam perduxit. *Plin.* 35. He speaks often in the same Stile of other Artists, Evecta supra humanam fidem ars est successu, mox & audacia, *lib.* 34. *c.7.* Apollodorus Atheniensis primus species exprimere instituit, primusque gloriam penecillo jure contulit.—— In luminibus artis primus refulsit, neque ante eum tabula ullius ostenditur quæ teneat oculos. *Plin.* 35. Apollodorus pictor qui mortalium primus invenit rationem commiscendi Colores, & exactam umbrarum expressionem, Atheniensis erat. *Plutarch. Bellone an pace*, &c.

(12) Zeuxis atque Parrhasius, non multum ætate distantes, circa Peloponnesiaca ambo tempora (nam cum Parrhasio sermo Socratis apud Xenophontem invenitur)

plurimum arti addiderunt. Quorum prior luminum umbrarumque rationem invenisse, secundus examinasse subtilius lineas traditur. *Quintil. Inst. lib.* 12. *c.*10. Zeuxidis aut Polygnoti aut Euphranoris tabulæ, sectantur opacum quid, ac spirans, & recedens aliquid & eminens. *Philost. de vit. Apol. lib.* 2. *c.* 9. Equidem respondet Aristodemus Homerum in pangendis carminibus epicis admiratus sum maxime : In Tragœdia Sophoclem : In Statuaria Polycletum : In Pictura Zeuxin. *Xenop. Apomnem. c.* 4. An pateretur hoc Zeuxis, aut Phidias, aut Polycletus, nihil se scire, cum in his effet tanta solertia ? *Cic. Acad. l.* 2. *& de Orat. lib:* 3. Nam & Zeuxidis manus vidi, nondum vetustatis injuria victas, & Protogenis rudimenta, cum ipsius Naturæ veritate certantia. *Petron. Satyr.*

(13) Nihil est in Natura rerum omnium, quod se universim profundat & quod totum repente evolet ; sic omnia quæ fiunt, quæque aguntur acerrime, lenioribus principiis Natura ipsa prætexuit. *Cic. de Orat. lib.* 2.

(14) In eum Apollodorus versus fecit, artem ipsi ablatam Zeuxin ferre secum. Descendisse Parrhasius in certamen

ZEUXIS is cenfured by fome for making his Heads, and all the Extremities too big. *Quintilian* fays, he was thought to have made his Bodies always larger than Life; and to have imitated *Homer* in that refpect, who has been obferved to give even his Women a Largenefs approaching to mafculine. And doubtlefs (faith this Author) he imagined by fo doing, that he gave more Dignity and a nobler Air to his Figures (15). But the greateft Fault with which this Painter is charged, is his not having painted Manners. Tho' *Pliny* mentions a *Penelope* by *Zeuxis*, in which he (16) feemed to have expreffed her modeft, foft Character and Manners; and fome other Pieces that do not deferve that Cenfure: yet *Ariftotle* and others have remarked that Defect in this renowned Colourift (17.)

They are cenfured for the fame Defects and Faults.

NOW the fame Fault is found with *Titian*, and with all the Painters in general of the *Venetian* School, who fo eminently excelled in Colouring. And thus it hath been obferved in ancient Times as well as modern, that as the beft Colourifts have failed in that other moft effential part of Painting; fo, on the other hand, thofe who excelled in correct Defign and juft Expreffion, were defective in Colouring : So limited is human Perfection, or fo extremely difficult it is to excel in many things, as an excellent ancient Author obferves on this Subject (18.)

IT is however entirely a modern Difpute which of thefe Parts is the moft excellent. From what is faid of *Zeuxis*, on account of his not having ftudied Expreffion enough, by that excellent Critick of all the polite Arts, the *Stagyrite*, (at the fame time that his fweet, harmonious, enchanting Colouring is fo exceedingly praifed) and from a Converfation of *Socrates* (19) with the beft Artifts of his time, (in which he fhews that the Reprefentation of Manners is the principal Beauty of the imitative Arts) we may learn that the beft Judges in ancient Times were not at a ftand what to think when the Soul was not expreffed by a Picture, however fine the Flefh and Blood might be. They could not but admire the Art which was able to go fo far as to give the moft plaufible Appearance of real Life, a very fine Carnation (as the Painters call it) to a Figure ; but at the fame time they regretted, that the fame admirable Skill and Dexterity had not the other Talent, of exhibiting Manners and the Qualities of the Mind, joined with it ; in order to make the Art not merely wonderful and pleafing to the Sight, but inftructive too in Morals, by which means it might have become as ufeful as it was agreeable. And what indeed are fine Proportion and regular Features in real Life, if a Soul is wanting; or if there is neither Senfe nor Meaning in the Countenance and Gait, no Spirit, no Vivacity, nothing that befpeaks Intelligence, nor any one Quality of the Mind; or, in a word, if no Manners are expreffed ? Does not an Idiot-Look deftroy the Effect of all the outward Charms of Shape, Colour, and Stature ; and rob the Fair-one of all her Power to touch our Hearts, though formed in all the Exactnefs of Features, and with all the Beauty of the fineft Complexion ? We may judge what it is that ftrikes and enchants, by the Praifes that are extorted fo foon as we are touched. For if it is not fome particular outward Expreffion in the Turn of Features, or in the Air and Mien, of fomething that dwells within; if it be not this which charms, why is it that we naturally and immediately cry out, what a fprightly Look ! what a graceful Mien ! what a majeftick Air ! what a foft gentle Look ! how much Goodnefs and Sweetnefs ! what Affability, what Humanity, what Freedom of Mind, or what Sagacity and Judgment ! And muft it not then be the fame in an Art which imitates Life ? Can there be Beauty in the fineft unmeaning Portrait, fince there is none in fuch a real Face ? Or is it poffible that the famous *Helen* of *Zeuxis* (20) could have been efteemed the moft perfect Model of female Beauty, if it expreffed none of the feminine Affections and Graces, but had an infipid; fenfelefs Countenance and Air ? How very unvaluable muft a Picture of *Penelope* have been, if it did not reprefent her as *Homer* hath done, in comparifon of one that did ?

Of the Difpute about Colouring, Defign, and Expreffion, to which the preference is due.

The Sentiments of ancient Criticks about it.

Swift

---

tàmen cum Zeuxide traditur ; Et cum ille detuliffet Uvas pictas tanto fucceffu ut in fcenam Aves devolarent. There is a *Greek* Epigram, alluding to thefe Grapes, in the Anthol : thus tranflated by *Grotius*.

  Vix eft ab avis his ut abftineam manum,
  Ita me Colorum forma deceptum trahit.

(15) Zeuxis plus membris corporis dedit, id amplius atque auguftius ratus ; atque (ut exiftimant) Homerum fecutus : cui validiffima forma, etiam in fœminis placet. *Quint. Inft. l. 12. c. 10.* So *Pliny*, Deprehenditur tamen Zeuxis ceu grandior in capitibus articulifque ; alioqui tantus diligentia, &c. *Plin. 35.*

(16) Mores pinxiffe videtur. *Ibidem.*

(17) Plurimorum juniorum Tragœdiæ funt fine moribus, & multi prorfus poetæ funt tales : Ita quoque inter Pictores Zeuxis fe habet ad Polygnotum. Polygnotus enim eft bonus morum pictor, at Zeuxidis pictura nullos habet mores. *Arift. Poet. c. 6.*

(18) *Diodorus Siculus, lib. 26.* makes this Obfervation, Fieri nequit ut Natura mortalis, etiamfi fcopum fibi propofitum affequatur, comprehenfionem omnium fine ulla

reprehenfione obtineat. Neque enim Phidias, in magna habitus admiratione ob fimulacrorum eburneorum fabricationem ; neque Praxiteles qui lapideis operibus eximiè admifcuit affectiones animi ; neque Apelles aut Parrhafius, artem pictoriam experienter temperatis coloribus ad fummum faftigium provehentes, tantam in fuis operibus experti funt felicitatem, ut peritiæ fuæ effectum prorfus irreprehenfibilem exhiberent. Cum enim homines effent, ac primas obtinerent in iis quæ fibi agenda fufceperant, nihilominus tamen propter imbecillitatem humanam in multis a propofito fibi fcopo aberrarunt.

(19) *Xen. Apomnem. c. 10.* Ergo Statuariam, fubjecit Socrates, animi actiones, per formam, repræfentare oportet.

(20) Zeuxis Pictor in magna erat admiratione apud Crotoniatas. Huic Helenam pingenti, miferunt pulcherrimas quas penes fe habebant Virgines, ut eas infpiceret nudas : Ex multis itaque partibus, pulcherrimum quodque in animo comprehendens ars, conftruxit opus perfectæ pulchritudinis Ideam repræfentans. *Dion. Halic.* So *Cicero de Inventione. Valerius Maximus* tells us, Cum pinxiffet Helenam, quid de eo opere homines cenfuri effent, expectandum non putavit, fed protinus hos verfus adjecit ex Iliad 3. ver. 156.

3

Swift from above defcends the royal Fair ;
Her beauteous Cheeks the Blufh of Venus *wear*
Chaften'd with coy Diana's *penfive Air.*   Odyf. B. 17.

SOME Criticks, being aware of this, have endeavour'd to reconcile what *Ariftotle* fays
of *Zeuxis,* with the Praifes given to him by others : *Pliny* in particular, by means of that
Divifion of Affections very generally received amongft Philofophers, into foft and rough,
fmooth and boifterous (21). And it hath indeed been remark'd at all times, that fome
Painters have excelled in reprefenting the one kind, and fome in expreffing the other. But
this Diftinction between Paffions, tho' *Pliny* himfelf ufes it afterwards in his Character of
Ariftides, is not fufficient to reconcile what he fays of *Zeuxis,* with the Account of his
Pictures given by *Ariftotle,* who had much better Opportunities of being acquainted with
their Perfections or Imperfections : For, according to *Pliny,* he had not only painted the
Manners of *Penelope,* that is to fay, the foft, tender, modeft Virtues that make her Character in the Odyffey ; but likewife other Subjects in which he had expreffed the violent
Paffions ; as for example, *Hercules* yet an Infant ftrangling the Serpents before his trembling Mother (22) : But *Ariftotle* exprefly fays, on the other hand, that there are no Manners in his Pictures.

WHEN therefore all the Accounts that are given us of *Zeuxis* are compared together,
what is faid by *Ariftotle,* with refpect to the want of Manners in his Pictures, muft be
underftood in the fame way as the like Charge againft *Titian* or the *Venetian* School in
general, that is, in a comparative Senfe, or in refpect of other Mafters who chiefly ftudied
Expreffion, and eminently excelled in it ; as the beft Mafters of the *Roman* and *Florentine*
School among the Moderns : And, amongft the Ancients, *Apelles, Ariftides, Timanthes,*
and others. It feems manifeft that *Zeuxis,* like *Titian,* far excelled all in Colouring, but
was like him alfo inferiour to many in Expreffion.

BUT whatever may be determined with regard to this Cenfure of *Zeuxis,* it was, in
the Opinion of the Ancients, but the loweft Attainment of a Painter, to be able to give
the trueft Appearance of Fiefh and Blood, or a fine natural Colouring to Bodies, however
rare and difficult a Talent that may be : Correctnefs of Defign, and Truth of Expreffion,
are, according to them, the chief Excellencies ; for the fake of which, Defects in Colouring will be eafily forgiven and over-looked by the moft underftanding ; that is, by thofe
who feek from Pictures not merely Gratification or Pleafure to the Senfe, but Employment and Entertainment to their Underftanding, and agreeable wholefome Exercife to their
Affections : In order to gain which great Ends of Painting, Pictures muft be animated by
Minds ; they muft have Souls ; Characters and Manners muft be painted.

ON the other hand, however, it is owned, by the fame Ancients, to be by the skilful
Management of Colours, that the fpecious Appearances of Objects are reprefented, and
that the Pencil afpires after compleat Deceit, and a full Command over our very Senfe :
And confequently, it is not mere Drawing, however correct, and expreffive, but Painting,
by the united Force of different Colours, that can be called the throughly imitative and
illufive Art (23).

THO' *Apelles* could not have given Beauty and Grace to his Pictures, nor have deferved
the high Praifes that are beftowed upon him by the confenting Voice of all ancient Writers,
had he not underftood Defign, Proportion and Expreffion extremely well ; yet he was excelled in Symmetry and Proportion by *Afclepiodorus,* as he himfelf generoufly acknowledged : And *Ariftides* feems to have furpaffed him in reprefenting the Paffions. As for
Symmetry and Proportion, it was *Parrhafius* the Contemporary of *Zeuxis* who firft fully
underftood and obferv'd it.

HE is highly commended for the Softnefs, Delicacy, and Elegance of his Out-line. *Pliny*
expatiates with delight upon his excelling eminently in rounding off his Figures, fo as to
detach them from the board, and to make them ftand out with great Strength and Relief.
                                                                                      This

---

(21) See this Divifion explained at large, *Quint. Inft.
l.* 10. *c.* 2.

(22) Fecit & Penelopen, in qua pinxiffe mores Videtur ; & Athletam ;——Et Hercules infans, Dracones
ftrangulans, Alcmena matre coram pavente & Amphitry-
one. *Plin. lib.* 35.
   As for the reading *amores* inftead of *mores* in P*liny,* it
not only implies that *Zeuxis* did not paint the *Penelope* of
Homer, (but another *Penelope* of a lafcivious proftituted
Character: which cannot be admitted :) But it fuppofes
Amoroufnefs and Lafcivioufnefs painted, and yet no
Manners expreffed, which is manifeftly abfurd. *Mores*
in Poetry is always underftood in a general Senfe, comprehending not only the good Affections and Manners,
but all the Affections and Manners of whatever kind,

whether good or blameable. A Character either in
Painting or Poetry is faid to be *bene morata,* or to have
Manners, if it is a probable, confiftent, well-drawn
Character, whether it be moral or immoral, as we
call it.
   See *Cicero de Off. lib.* 1. *c.* 28. Sed tum fervare illud
Poetas dicimus, quod deceat, cum id quod quaque per-
fona dignum eft & fit, & dicitur. So *Horace,*
         *Interdum fpeciofa locis, morataque recte,
         Fabula.——*   Art. Poet. 319.

(23) εν γραφαις κινηπικωτερον εςι χρωμα γραμμης, δια
το αισθηικωλον και αποτηλον. *Plut. de Poet. Aud Apollodorus* is called the firft great Light among the Painters, becaufe thofe before him only underftood Drawing ;
he is the firft who began to colour agreeably.

This is indeed a very masterly part; and as *Pliny* says of the ancient Painters, so it may be likewise said of the Moderns, " Tho' many have succeeded very well in Painting the " middle Parts, very few have been able to come up to the throughly illusive way of termi- " nating the Extremities, so as to give them a just degree of Roundness, and make them fly " off, inviting the Eye to look behind them, and promising as it were to discover what " they hide (24)." But this wonderful Art ought rather to be called the Subtility than the Sublimity of Painting (25), which last belongs more properly to the poetical Part of it, consisting in Greatness of Invention and Composition ; Nobleness of Ideas ; Energy of Expression, and a grand Taste joined with Beauty and Grace. *Praised.*

THE same *Parrhasius* is also much commended for the sprightly, significant Airs of his Heads, and the Comeliness and Sweetness he gave to his Countenances. Now *Corregio* amongst the Moderns excelled in many of these Qualities : He was not correct in Design ; but his Pencil was wonderfully soft, tender, beautiful, and charming : He painted with great Strength and Heightening, and there was something truly grand in his Manner : He understood how to distribute his Lights in a way wholly peculiar to himself, which gave an extraordinary Force and Roundness to his Figures. This Manner is said by some Artists (26) to have consisted in extending a large Light, and then making it lose itself insensibly in the dark Shadowings which he placed out of the Masses. It is this Art, say they, that gives his Pictures so great Roundness, without our being able to perceive from whence such Force proceeds, and so vast a Pleasure to the sight : And in this part the rest of the *Lombardy* School copy'd him. His Manner of designing Heads, Hands, and Feet, (say they) is very great, and well deserves Praise and Imitation : He had also found out certain natural and unaffected Graces for his Madonna's, his Saints, and little Children, which were proper to them, and are wonderfully pleasing. *He may be compared with Corregio in some respects, tho' the latter was not equal to the former in Correctness of Design.*

Corregio's Excellence.

IN several other Circumstances there is a great Affinity and Likeness between this eminent modern Painter and *Protogenes*, Contemporary of *Apelles*, and one of the greatest ancient Masters, as we shall afterwards observe. But with regard to *Parrhasius*, it is worth our attention, that *Socrates* the Philosopher was often with him (27); and, no doubt, this Painter had received very great Instruction and Assistance from one, who together with his Knowledge of Nature, that of human Nature in particular, must have had a very good Idea of Design, having been bred to Sculpture in his younger Days (28). To his Conferences with this Philosopher, it is not unreasonable, in some measure, to ascribe his Skill of Symmetry and exact Observance of it ; but more especially his admirable Dexterity in Painting such a variety of shrewd, sly, quaint, entertaining Looks : For in this he is said to have made great proficiency (29), and to have shewn a vast Fertility of Genius and Imagination. This appears sufficiently from the Description that is given of his Picture of the People of *Athens,* representing by several well-distributed and judiciously-managed Groupes in one Piece, a very considerable Diversity of Humours, Tempers and Characters. *How much Parrhasius may have profited by his Conversations with Socrates.*

NOW *Socrates* is famous for his deep Insight into Human Nature, and his vast Comprehension of Men and Manners ; for his ironical humorous Turn, and the wonderful Facility with which he could assume any Mien, or put on any Character, in order to accomplish more successfully, his truly philosophical Design of stripping all false Appearances of Wit, Learning or Virtue, of their artificial Varnish, and exposing them in their native Colours.

(24) Primus (Parrhasius) symmetriam Picturæ dedit : Primus argutias vultus, elegantiam capilli, venustatem oris ; confessione artificum, in lineis extremis palmam adeptus. Et hæc est in Pictura summa sublimitas. Corpora enim pingere & media rerum, est quidem magni operis ; sed in quo multi gloriam tulerint : Extrema corporum facere & definentis picturæ modum includere, rarum in successu artis invenitur : ambire enim debet se extremitas ipsa & sic definere, ut promittat alia post se ; ostendatque etiam quæ occultat. *Plin.* 35.
Ludovicus Demontiosius says, Sic malim legere (extrema corporum facere, & definentis Picturæ modo illudere rarum in successu artis invenitur.) Nam definentis Picturæ modum includere quid fit nescio, sed definentis Picturæ modo spectantibus illudere, hoc artis est, *Lud. Demont. Comment. de Sculp. & Pict. Antiq.*

(25) This is called by others *Subtilitas*. Parrhasius examinasse lineas subtilius, traditur. *Quint. Inst. lib.* 12. *c.* 10. Tanta enim subtilitate extremitates imaginum erant ad similitudinem præcisæ, ut crederes etiam animorum esse picturam. *Petron. Arb. Satyr.* And Pliny himself afterwards, Ferunt artificem protinus, contemplatum subtilitatem, discisse, &c. The Sublime in Painting is that which he describes afterwards in the Character of *Timanthes,* and what *Varro* ascribes to *Euphranor.*

(26) See *Felibien* and Mr. *Graham's* Lives of the Painters.

(27) *Xen. Apom. cap.* 10. Præterea siquando cum aliquibus colloqueretur, qui artificia noffent, etiam his proderat. There follows a Conversation of *Socrates* with *Parrhasius,* and another with a Stauary.

(28) Socrates filius erat Sophronisci lapidarii, & Phænaretes obstetricis, (quemadmodum & Plato in Theæteto ait) genere Athenienfis, Pago Alopecensis. Duris Vero & servisse eum ac lapides sculpsisse tradit: Esse vero illius etiam gratias illas quæ sunt in arce, vestibus indutæ. Timon in Syllis dicitur eum vocasse λιθόξοον. *Diog. Laer. lib.* 2. *in Vita Socratis.* In ipso arcis Atheniensis introitu, Mercurium, quem Propylæum vocant, & gratias fecisse dicunt Sophronisci filium Socratem, cui inter homines Apollinis Delphici oraculum sapientiæ primas detulit. *Pausan. lib.* 1. Suidas in *Socrat.* *Maximus Tyrius, Differt.* 22.

(29) *Quas aut Parrhasius protulit, aut scopas ;*
Hic saxo, liquidis ille coloribus
*Soleri nunc hominem ponere, nunc Deum:*Hor.l.4.Od.8.
Et cum Parrhasii tabulis, signisque Myronis,
Phidiacum vivebat ebur.—   Juvenal. Sat. 8.

Date mihi Zeuxidis artem, & Parrhasii Sophismata, *Hymmerius apud Photium.* Pliny commends *Myron* for the same Quality, Myron numerosior in arte quam Polycletus & in symmetria diligentior. *Plin. lib.* 34. *cap.* 8.

H

lours (30). *Parrhafius*'s Houfe being much frequented by the People of the firft Diftinction, was often, we are told, the Scene of *Socrates*'s Difputes, Conferences, and Lectures. There he frequently took occafion, in his noted, peculiar manner, to give found and wholefome Advices, or fevere Rebukes; and to hold Converfations on the profoundeft Subjects in Philofophy and Morals, under the fpecious Appearance of only intending to criticize a Picture, and unfold the Beauties and Excellencies of the Arts of Defign. It is not therefore to be doubted, but the Painter muft have been confiderably beholden to this moft witty, ingenious Philofopher, for the Advances he had made in one of the moft difficult, moft ufeful, and moft philofophical Parts of the Art; in reprefenting, truly, and naturally, a great variety of Manners and Characters. *Socrates*'s chief Talent and peculiar Excellence confifted in the very fame Dexterity which diftinguifh'd that Painter, with whom he was fo converfant, that is, in being able to paint Mankind, the Men of *Athens* in particular, with Truth and Spirit; in giving due Propriety, Force, and Relief to the Characters and Perfonages he had a mind to exhibit; or in making, either the Faults and Imperfections, or the Beauties and Excellencies he drew, fo evident, fo palpable, that they could not but ftrike, and make a very deep Impreffion.

margin: Socrates and Parrhafius had the fame Talents.

IF we look into the Lives of *Raphael, Leonardo da Vinci,* of the *Carraches, Dominichin,* and all the Painters who excelled in reprefenting the Paffions and Manners, we fhall find them all to have been no lefs obliged to the Inftructions and Converfation of Philofophers, than *Parrhafius* was to *Socrates*: Being perfuaded that the grand Ufefulnefs of Painting confifted in that Art, they took all neceffary pains to underftand human Nature, and to be able, by a skilful Imitation of its various Workings and Motions, to touch the Heart, and make inftructive Impreffions upon it.

PARRHASIUS, tho' he greatly excelled in painting human Paffions and Manners, was however out-done by *Timanthes* in a trial of Skill betwixt them; the Subject of which was *Ajax* and *Ulyffes* contending for the Arms of *Achilles*. *Timanthes*'s Picture was preferred by a great Plurality of Suffrages; fo great a Mafter of Expreffion muft he likewife have been (31).

margin: Parrhafius furpaffed by Timanthes.

THE latter is chiefly renowned for the wonderful Invention and perfect Judgment that appeared in his Works. It was not the mechanical, but rather the poetical Part in which he was fo eminent. For tho' he had a very light, and, at the fame time, a bold Pencil; yet there was more Genius, Invention, Spirit and Compafs of Thought in his Pictures, than Ability of Hand. It was his Ideas and the Talents of his Mind, that were chiefly admired, in confequence of that mafterly way he had, of awakening great Thoughts and Sentiments, by his ingenious Works, in the Breafts of Spectators; his wonderful Talent of fpreading their Imaginations, and leading them to conceive in their own Minds more than was expreffed by his Pictures. In all his Works, fays *Pliny*, there was fomething more underftood than was feen; and tho' there was all the Art imaginable, yet there was ftill more Ingenuity than Art (32). This is the true Sublime in Painting, as well as in Poetry and Oratory. *Longinus* in giving an account of the reafon why the true Sublime hath fuch a powerful and pleafing Effect, defcribes it juft as *Pliny* does this Excellency, he and all ancient Authors afcribe to *Timanthes* above all the other Painters.

margin: His Character.

margin: He excelled in what may be called the Sublime in Painting. It is defcribed by Pliny as Longinus defines it in Writing.

" WE are fo framed by Nature, fays *Longinus,* that our Mind is wonderfully exalted
" by the true Sublime. It raifes itfelf, glories and triumphs with high delight in fuch Sen-
" timents, as if itfelf had invented what it hears. If therefore any thing is pronounced by
" one never fo well verfed in the Arts of Eloquence, that feems grand and towering, but
" at the fame time not fink deep into the Mind, awaken and elevate it, leaving behind
" it *more to be contemplated than is expreffed*; but on the contrary, being pondered, falls
                                                                                    " from

(30) In hoc genere Fanius in Annalibus fuis Africanum hunc Æmilianum dicit fuiffe, & eum Verbo Græco appellat '*Eíρωνα*: Sed, uti ferunt, qui melius hæc norunt, Socratem, opinor, in hac ironia diffimulantiaque longe lepore, & humanitate omnibus præftitiffe. Genus eft perelegans, & cum graVitate falfum, cumque Oratoriis dictionibus, tum urbanis fermonibus accommodatum. *Cic. de Orat. l.* 2. Primum, inquam, deprecor, ne me, tanquam Philofophum, putetis fcholam Vobis aliquam explicaturum: quod ne in ipfis quidem Philofophis magnopere unquam probavi. Quando enim Socrates, qui parens philofophiæ jure dici poteft, quidquam tale fecit? eorum erat ifte mos, qui tum Sophiftæ nominabantur: quorum e numero primus eft aufus Leontinas Georgias in conventu poffcere quæftionem, id eft, jubere dicere, qua de re quis vellet audire. Audax negotium; dicerem impudens, nifi hoc inftitutum poftea tranflatum ad philofophos noftros effet, Sed & illum, quem nominaVi, & ceteros Sophiftas, ut e Platone intelligi poteft, lufos videmus a Socrate. Is enim percunctando, atque interrogando elicere folebat eorum opiniones, quibufcum differebat, ut ad ea quæ il refpondiffent, fiquid videretur, diceret. *Cic. de fin. lib.* 2. *ab initio.*

Tum etiam vita univerfa ironiam habere Videtur, qualis eft vita Socratis. Nam ideo dictus '*Eíρων*, id eft agens imperitum, & admirator aliorum tanquam fapientium, ut quemadmodum *AΛΛηγορίαν* facit continua *Μεταφορά*, fic hoc Schema facit troporum ille contextus. *Quint. Inft. lib.*9. 2. Nam illa, qua plurimum eft Socrates ufus, hanc habuit Viam, cum plura interrogaffet, quæ fateri adverfario neceffe effet, noviffimè id de quo quærebatur, inferebat, cui fimile conceffiffet, id eft, inductio. *Quint.lib.* 5. *c.*11.

(31) Ergo magnis fuffragiis fuperatus a Timanthe, Sami, in Ajace armorumque judicio; —Timanthi vel plurimum adfuit ingenii. Ejus enim eft Iphigenia, oratorum laudibus celebrata: Qua ftante ad aras peritura, quum mœftos oppinxiffet omnis, præcipue patruum, & triftitiæ omnem imaginem confumpfiffet, patris ipfius voltum velavit, quem digne non poterat oftendere. *Plin.* 35. *Cic. de Orat. Quint. Inft. lib.* 11. *cap.* 13. *Val. Max. lib.* 8. *cap.* 2. *Exemplo externo* 6to.

(32) In unius hujus operibus intelligitur plus femper quam pingitur, & cum fit ars fumma, ingenium tamen ultra artem eft. *Plin. ibidem.*

" from its firſt Appearance of Loftineſs ; ſuch Sayings have no right to be called Sublime,
" ſince the Effect periſhes with the Sound that conveyed them.   For that alone is truly
" great and ſublime which tranſports the Hearer into a laſting Admiration : It is over-
" powering and cannot be withſtood, but entering into the Mind with irreſiſtible Force,
" takes firm hold of it, and makes an indelible Impreſſion upon it (33)."

THIS is the beſt Explication that can be given of the Talent of *Timanthes*, of expreſ- *The ſame in Paint-*
ſing more than he painted : It is hardly to be underſtood by a ſhorter Commentary, or *ing.*
without comparing it with what is defined to be the Sublime in the other Arts.   But how
far Painting can go, or what it can do in this ſublime way, will be beſt conceived by *It may be beſt un-*
means of *Raphael*'s Pictures, and thoſe of *Nicolas Pouſſin*, who of all the modern Painters *derſtood from Ra-*
poſſeſſed that extraordinary Sublimity of Genius in the higheſt degree.   In ſeveral of their *phael and Pouſſin's*
Pieces there is a Force and Energy which wonderfully erects and ennobles the Mind, in- *Pictures.*
flames the Imagination, and lights up the Underſtanding, calling up great and elevated Conceptions, which make ſo much the more forcible Impreſſion on the Mind, becauſe the
Spectator really imagines them entirely his own Product, and, as it were, only hinted to
him occaſionally by the Pictures he admires.   Let any one reflect on what it is that ſo
highly pleaſes, and tranſports him, when he conſiders any of *Raphael*'s Cartons, or of
Pouſſin's Sacraments, and he will immediately reſolve it principally into this ſurprizing
Art of affording an inexhauſtible Source of true and great Thoughts to the Spectator, in
which the Mind exults as its own, more being ſuggeſted by theſe ſublime divine Pieces
than is fully expreſſed.

. *POUSSIN* was ſo great a Maſter of Expreſſion, that he is juſtly reckoned among *Pouſſin praiſed for*
the chief, if not the greateſt, for Painting the inward Sentiments, Affections, and Move- *his Skill in expreſſing*
ments of the human Heart (34).   Tho' he failed like *Ariſtides* in his Colouring, and fell as *the Paſſions.*
far ſhort of *Raphael* as the other is ſaid to have done of *Apelles* ; yet he deſerves the ſame *And this the Talent*
Character that is given of that great ancient Maſter ; who, as *Pliny* and others tell us, was *of Ariſtides.*
the firſt who by Genius and Study attained to the compleat Science of exhibiting Manners and
Paſſions of all ſorts.   They both excelled in painting all kinds of Affections, not only the
ſoft and tender, but the ſtrong and impetuous.   As defective as *Ariſtides* was in his Colouring, for it was dry and harſh, yet his Pictures were eagerly ſought after, highly eſteemed
and purchaſed at very high Prices (35) ; ſo greatly was his Skill in diſplaying human Nature,
and in touching the Heart valued ; and ſo will *Pouſſin*'s likewiſe for ever be by all Men of true
Taſte : The reaſon is obvious ; nothing affects the Heart like that which is purely from itſelf, and of its own growth. " The moſt delightful, the moſt engaging, and pathetick of
" all Subjects which Poets ſing or Artiſts form, is that which is drawn from moral Life or
" from the Affections and Paſſions."   Other Imitations may pleaſe, but theſe intereſt us.
This is the Excellence that is likewiſe aſcribed to *Dominichin* amongſt the Moderns.   While
Guido's Pictures, by the Beauty and Sweetneſs of his Pencil, charm the Eye ; the natural,
and ſtrong Expreſſion of Paſſions in the other's violently move and agitate the Heart,
which (as *Felibien* juſtly obſerves) is one of the nobleſt Effects of Painting (36).

PROTOGENES was Contemporary with *Apelles* and *Ariſtides*, and he is claſſed *Protogenes Con-*
amongſt the beſt ancient Painters.   *Ariſtotle*, that excellent Judge of all the fine Arts, and *temporary with*
whoſe Talent indeed was more towards polite Learning and the Arts, than the more pro- *Apelles.*
found, abſtruſe Parts of Philoſophy, highly eſteemed the Genius and Abilities of this Painter.   He out of his regard to the Dignity and Excellence of the Art, as well as to the Re- *His Character and*
putation of this Painter, would gladly have perſuaded him to have employed his Talents *Turn, and how*
more worthily than in painting mere Portraits, Hunters, Satyrs, and ſuch inferiour Sub- *Ariſtotle endea-*
jects (37) ; to have try'd nobler Arguments, ſuch as the Battles of *Alexander*, which the Phi- *voured to perſuade*
loſopher *him to paint high*
and noble Subjects.

(33) Φύσιι γὰρ πως—συρῦται χαρᾶς ἢ μεγαλαυχίας, ὡς   Diſtinction is explained by *Quintilian*, and in what he
αὐτὰ γινύεσαμ ὅσιρ ἠκνσιν ἰ—μηδ' ἰξισπαλεῖσι τῆ διανοία   places the Excellency of Oratory, the Ancients made
πλέον τῶ λεγομῦρα τὸ ἀναθεωρεῖρθρον. Sect. 7.   that of Painting likewiſe chiefly to conſiſt ; as it is well
                                                     expreſſed by *Martial* :

(34) This is the Character *Felibien*, *Bellori*, &c. give   *Ars utinam mores animumque effingere poſſet :*
of *Nicolas Pouſſin*.   Je l'ai dejà dit, que ce ſçavant homme   *Pulchrior in terris nulla tabella foret.*
a même ſurpaſſé en quelque ſorte les plus fameux Peintres   Huc igitur incumbat orator, hoc opus ejus, hic labor eſt,
& Sculpteurs de l'antiquité qu'ils'eſt propoſé d'imiter, en   fine quo cetera nuda, jejuna, infirma, ingrata ſunt.
ce que dans ſes ouVrages on y Voit toutes les belles expreſ-   Adeo Velut ſpiritus operis hujus atque animus eſt in af-
fions qui ne ſe rencontroient que dans differens maitres.   fectibus. *Quint. lib.* 6. *c.* 3.
Car *Timomachus* qui repreſenta Ajax en colere, ne fut
recommendable que pour avoir bien peint les paſſions les   (36) Si la Beauté de pinçeau & la Grace qui paroit
plus Vehementes. Le talent particulier de Zeuxis, etoit   dans les tableaux du guide charmoit les Yeux : les fortes
de peindre des affections plus douces & plus tranquilles,   & naturelles expreſſions du Dominiquin touchoient beau-
comme il fit dans cette belle figure de Penelope, ſur le   coup l'eſprit, & emouvoient daVantage les paſſions de
viſage de laquelle on reconnoiſſoit de la pudeur & de la   ceux qui les conſideroient : ce qui eſt un des plus beaux
ſageſſe. Le ſculpteur Cteſilas fut principalement conſi-   effets de la Peinture. *Felibien* tells us, that *Nicolas Pouſſin*
deré pour les expreſſions de douleur. Mais—le Pouſſin   ſpoke in this manner of *Guido* and *Dominichin*, tom. 4.
les poſſedoit toutes. *Felibien.*   p. 16.

(35) Is omnium primus animum pinxit & ſenſus hu-   (37) ——Et matrem Ariſtotelis philoſophi ; qui ei
manos expreſſit, quæ vocant Græci ἤθη ; idem pertur-   ſuadebat ut Alexandri Magni opera pingeret, propter
bationes : durior paulo in coloribus. *Plin.* 35.   *Pliny*'s   æternitatem rerum. Impetus animi, & quædam artis
                                                                                                         libido

Protogenes *brought*
into Reputation very
generoufly by Apel-
les.

lòfopher thought more fuitable to the Art, giving it occafion to exprefs a great variety of lofty Ideas, inftructive Characters, and interefting, moving Paffions and Actions. But it feems his natural Genius and Inclination led him to other Subjects. What he moft delighted in appears to have been of the paftoral kind, things of a quiet and gentle Character. He lived at firft in great Poverty and Obfcurity, and for a long time only painted Galleys and Ships, and mere Still-Life (38) : But afterwards he applied himfelf to higher Subjects, with fuch good Succefs, that tho' he had ftill but little Reputation in his own Country, yet his Merit had come to the knowledge of *Apelles*, who being thereby induced to vifit him, was the firft who raifed him a Character at home (39). *Apelles* being charmed with his Works, payed him greater Prices for them than he asked ; and then gave out that he defigned to pafs them for his own. This, as it was faid, on purpofe to procure a Name to one who fo well deferved efteem, fo it had the defign'd Effect. The *Rhodians* then began to value him and his Works, and to be jealous of their Honour ; and therefore were glad to keep his Pictures in their own Country upon any terms. Thus was *Protogenes* very generoufly brought into Reputation by *Apelles*, who faid of him that he was equal to himfelf in every refpect, excepting only that not knowing when to give over, by too nice Correctnefs, and too laborious Finifhing, he flattened his Pieces; and rendered them ftiff, lifelefs, and ungraceful.

As Corregio *was*
by certain Painters
of eftablifh'd Fame.
Protogenes *and*
Corregio *had no*
Mafters, and lived
in a poor obfcure
way.

WHAT is very remarkable with regard to *Protogenes* is, that he feems to have had no Mafter ; or at leaft it is not known whofe Difciple he was (40). He appears to have arrived at the high Attainments *Apelles* fo much admired, by mere Strength of natural Genius, and that under a Load of Poverty and Obfcurity that naturally links and difpirits one (41) ; juft as *Corregio* did in the latter Age of Painting, under the fame difadvantageous Circumftances ; who is however univerfally acknowledged to have come the neareft of any to the modern *Apelles*, in his peculiar Talents and Excellencies : He was in like manner brought into Reputation at home by the Praifes his Works received from Painters of eftablifhed Fame, fo foon as they faw them. All the Writers on Painting, and of the Lives of the Painters, juftly admire the Force of thofe natural Parts in *Corregio*, which with little or no help from any Mafters, and without any opportunity of ftudying the antique Remains of Painting and Sculpture ; without the Affiftance of a liberal Education, and in a Situation the moft unfavourable to the Improvements of Imagination and Genius, could arrive to fuch a pitch of Perfection, and produce Works but a very little inferiour to thofe of *Raphael;* who with the beft natural Genius for Painting, had all the Advantages and Encouragements that are moft conducive to cultivate it,' and make it perfect : This is likewife the very Language of Antiquity with refpect to *Protogenes*.

The Tranquillity
with which Proto-
genes *painted in the*
Camp of the Enemy.

And a like Inftance
in Parmegiano,
who had likewife a
fweet tranquil Pen-
cil.

TO mention but one Circumftance more in *Protogenes*'s Character and Life ; the Tranquillity with which he poffefs'd himfelf at *Rhodes*, continuing to work while it was befieged ; and the ingenious Reply he gave to thofe who were fent by *Demetrius* to ask how he had the Courage to paint even in the very Camp of the Enemy, are much celebrated (42) : He anfwer'd with an eafy Smile, that he knew very well the Prince was not come to make war againft the fine Arts. Now we have almoft a parallel Inftance of the fame Command of Temper in a modern Painter (*Parmegiano*) who likewife had one of the gentleft, fweeteft, and moft gracious Pencils in the World. When *Charles* the Fifth had taken *Rome* by ftorm, fome of the common Soldiers, in facking the Town, having broke into his Apartments, and found him, like *Protogenes* of old, intent upon his work, were

fo

libido in hæc potius eum tulerunt. *Plin.* 35. Upon which Paffage Mr. *Durand* well obferves, Le confeil etoit bon, îl falloit honneur a Alexandre, a Ariftote, a Protogene, a la Peinture, & c'etoit le moyen d'Immortalizer un auffi beau pinçeau que le fien. Cependant, (continue notre auteur) impetus animi & quædam artis libido in hæc potius eum tulere, c. a. d. fi je ne me trompe, que Protogene, au lieu de fuivre l'avis du Phiiofophe, fe fentit plus de penchant, ou plus de gout pour les fujets mentionnez ci-deffus, comme le Parale, l'Hemionide, l'Ialyfe, le Satyre, *&c.* See his Notes on this Book of *Pliny.*

(38) Summa ejus paupertas initio, atque fumma intentio ; & ideo minor fertilitas—quidam & navis pinxiffe ufque ad annum quinquagefimum. *Plin.* 35.

(39) Septem annis dicitur Protogenes hanc picturam (Ialyfum) perfeciffe ferturque Apelles, opere confpecto, tam vehementer obftupuiffe, ut vox eum deficeret : Tandem Vero dixiffe, grandem laborem atque opus admirandum effe, non tamen habere gratias, propter quas a fe picta cœlum contingerent. Hæc tabula unà cum pluribus aliis Romam deportata, ibi quoque cum reliquis abfumpta eft incendio. *Plutarch.* in *Apoph. Regum,* &c. *&* in *Demetrio.* *Ælian. variæ* Hift. *lib.* 12. *c.* 41. *Aulus Gellius* Noct. Att. *lib.* 15. *c.* 3. Floruit circa Philippum, *&c.* —— nam curâ Protogenes, *Quint.* Inft. *lib.* 12. *c.* 10. Protogenis rudimenta cum ipfius naturæ Veritate certantia non fine quodam horrore tractavi. *Petron. Arbit.* Satyric. Cum culpandus non fit medicus, qui e longin-

qua mala confuetudine ægrum in meliorem traducit ; quare reprehendendus fit, qui orationem minus valentem, propter malam confuetudinem traducit in meliorem ? Pictores Apelles & Protogenes, fic alii artifices egregii non reprehendendi, quod confuetudinem Myconis, Dioris, Arymnæ, & aliorum fuperiorum non funt fecuti. *Varro, lib.* 8. *de L. L.*

(40) Quis eum docuerit non putant conftare. *Plin.* 35.

(41) Summa ejus paupertas. *Plin. ibid.*
Hunc, qualem nequeo monftrare, & fentio tantum,
Anxietate carens animus facit, omnis acerbi
Impatiens, Cupidus Sylvarum, aptufque libendis
Fontibus Aonidum : neque enim cantare fub antro
Pierio, Thyrfumve poteft contingere mæfta
Paupertas, atque æris inops, quo nocte dieque
Corpus æget.——   Juv. Sat. 7.

(42) Accitus a Rege, interrogatufque, qua fiducia extra muros ageret ? Refpondit, fcire fe cum Rhodiis illi bellum effe, non cum artibus. Difpofuit ergo Rex in tutelam ejus ftationes ; gaudens quod poffet manus fervare, quibus jam pepercerat: & ne fæpius avocaret, ultro ad eum venit hoftes, relictifque victoriæ fuæ Votis, inter arma & mediorum ictus fpectavit artificem : fequiturque tabulam illius temporis hæc fama, quod eam Protogenes fub gladio pinxerit. *Plin. ibid.* See *Felibien's* Account of *Parmegiano.*

3

fo aftonifh'd at the charming Beauty of his Pieces, that inftead of Plunder and Deftruction; which was then their Bufinefs, they refolved to protect him, as they afterwards did, from all manner of Violence.

PROTOGENES was not only famous for Painting, but likewife for many Figures which he made in Brafs (43) : And it is worth obferving, that in thefe two Ages of Painting I am now comparing, feveral of the moft eminent Painters in both, were alfo excellent Statuaries and Sculptors : They found their account not only in confulting the good Statues and Bas-reliefs of renowned Artifts; but likewife in making Models to themfelves of Clay, or other fuch Materials, and in frequently viewing them in different Situations ; as *Tintoret* in particular among the Moderns (44).

NICOMACHUS is juftly praifed for the great Lightnefs and Freedom of his Pencil, and the vaft Facility and Quicknefs with which he executed fome very good Pictures : And yet *Philoxenus* his Scholar is faid to have been ftill more expeditious (45). They both painted excellent Pieces; and, though they painted very faft, they do not feem to have deferved the juft and very inftructive Reproofs, *Apelles* and *Zeuxis* are faid to have given to certain Painters, who boafted of their having finifhed feveral Pictures in a very fhort time (46). It is however very remarkable, that *Petronius* fpeaks of a certain quick and compendious way of Painting, which, coming into vogue, was one great caufe of the Ruin of the noble Art (47). And good Pictures, like all other Works of durable Merit which conceal Art the moft, require the greateft fhare of Study, Time, and Labour to their Production. . Nothing is more difficult and artful than to hide Art. How accurately proportioned and skilfully laboured muft the Building be, which, tho' ftrong and folid, appears light and eafy ! The happy Thought fwims not on the Surface, but lies deep in the Mind ; and is found out by profound and fevere Search. It is with refpect to eafy Pictures, as it is with regard to eafy Writings, when fuch Works (to ufe the Words of an excellent (48) Author) fall under the perufal of an ordinary Genius, they appear to him fo natural and unlaboured, that he immediately refolves to compofe, and fancies that all he hath to do is to take no pains. Thus he thinks indeed fimply, but the Thoughts not being chofen with Judgment, are not beautiful ; he it is true exprefles himfelf plainly, but flatly withal. So true is it that Simplicity of all things is the hardeft to be copied, and Fafe to be acquired with the greateft Labour.

NICOPHANES a Painter of the fame Age is celebrated for the Elegance of his Defign, for his grand Manner, and the Majefty of his Stile : In all which, it is faid, few Mafters were to be compared to him. And he, like one of a truly noble Tafte, fenfible of the Force of his Genius, and of the Dignity of his Art, defpifed low Subjects. He thought Painting was capable of being really ufeful to Mankind, and of fomething more than merely innocent Amufement : And therefore he employed his Talents in painting hiftorical Subjects, tragical ones chiefly ; fo that he deferved to be called the Tragedian in Painting. His Manner, with all its Weight, Gravity, and Majefty, was however very gracious, pleafant, and eafy (49).

THE modern Mafters that are moft renowned for the Facility with which they executed their Works, are chiefly *Giov.* Penni, commonly called *Il Fattore, Tintoret, Tempefta,* and *Pietro da Cortona.* And none amongft the Moderns ever took more delight, or fucceeded better in painting great and noble Subjects taken from Hiftory, Poetry, ancient Fables and Allegories than *Annibal Cartache* ; who, having ftudied the Sweetnefs and Purity of *Corregio* at *Parma* ; the Strength and Diftribution of Colours of *Titian* ; and at *Rome* the Correctnefs of Defign and the Beautifulnefs of the Antique, made it appear by his wonderful Paintings in the *Farnefe* Palace, that he had acquired all thefe feveral Perfections to a very great degree. He was indeed as grand, and yet as graceful in his Stile, as *Nicophanes* is defcribed to have been ; inferiour to *Raphael* alone in either, as the latter was

to

Side notes:

Nicomachus *or* Philoxenus *had not eafy Pencils, and painted faft ; but did not deferve the Rebukes* Apelles *and* Zeuxis *gave to certain Painters who boafted of finifhing Pictures in a fhort time.*

A Remark on Eafe in Writing and Painting.

Nicophanes *commended for the high Notion he had of the Art, and the care he took to make it really ufeful.*

Several Moderns painted faft.

Cartache *made a fine Choice of Subjects.*

---

(43) Fecit & figna ex ære ut diximus. *Plin. ibid.* He gives an account of his Works of that kind, *lib.* 34. *c.* 8.

(44) See *Felibien, tom.* 3. *p.* 158.

(45) Nicomachus celeritate atque arte mira. Philoxenus celeritatem præceptoris confecutus, breviores etiamnum quaſdam picturæ Vias & compendiarias invenit. *Plin.* 35.

(46) Apelli pictor ineptus tabulam a fe pictam oftendens, hanc, inquit, fubito pinxi. Et ille : Etiam te tacente video feftinanter pictam. Miror autem quod non plures alias ifthoc temporis elaboraveris. *Plut. de lib. Educ.* Memorant Zeuxin, cum pictorem Agatharcum audivifiet, gloriantem quod cito & facile tabulas pingeret, dixiſſe, ego vero longo tempore. Facilitas enim efficiendi

& acceleratio non addit operi durabile pondus, ἐ̓λ̕ ἀπίσιαν : Tempus Vero robur addit. *Plut. in Pericle.*

(47) Pictura quoque non alium exitum fecit, poftquam Ægyptiorum audacia tam magnæ artis compendiariam invenit. *Petron. Satyric.* Nicomachi Vero tabulis, & carminibus Homeri, præter reliquam vim, Veneremque, etiam hoc adeft, quod expedite & cum fumma facilitate facta videantur. *Plutar. in Timoleonte. Vitruvius* ranks him with thofe Painters, Quos neque induftria, neque artis ftudium, neque folertia defecit. *Lib.* 3. *in Proœm.*

(48) Guardian, N°. 15.

(49) Adnumeratur his & Nicophanes, elegans & concinnus, ita ut venuftate ei pauci comparentur. Cothurnus ei & gravitas artis. *Plin.* 35.

T

to *Apelles* only : And in order to do juftice to his Art, he was ever taking affiftance from his learned Friends *Auguftino, Aguaccio,* and others (50).

Perfeus, nor none of Apelles's Scholars came near their Mafter.

WE had occafion to remark, fpeaking of *Apelles,* that the beft Genius, like the fineft Soil, requires proper Culture ; and the Neceffity of Genius appears evidently in the Character of *Perfeus.* He had all the Advantages of ftudying under an *Apelles,* who compofed three Volumes on Painting chiefly for this Difciple's Ufe; but he came not near to his Mafter in Delicacy, Charms, Noblenefs and Grace of Drawing ; nor did he, in Colouring, approach to the Truth and Sweetnefs of *Zeuxis* (51). He is placed however amongft the Painters of the firft Clafs, becaufe he was of *Apelles's* School : Though his Pictures had not any great Beauties, yet they had, it feems, no confiderable Faults : If they did not fhew Genius, they fhewed, at leaft, that he was bred in a School where nothing that was bad could be learned, and where Genius muft have made wonderful Progrefs. This feems to be the Meaning of the Character *Pliny* gives him : And it is in like manner obfervable, that few of *Raphael's* Scholars equalled their Mafter ; and yet their Works bear manifeft Marks of the excellent School in which they were formed.

Nor did thofe of Raphael approach to his Perfection.

Euphranor had wonderful Talents.

His Character.

BUT *Euphranor's* is a very furprizing Character amongft the ancient Painters : He was fo univerfal a Genius ; fo great a Mafter of feveral Arts and Sciences ; fuch an equally good Sculptor and Painter. His Conceptions were great and noble ; his Stile grand and mafculine. But he is faid to have fallen into the fame Fault with *Zeuxis,* of making his Heads too large. He was the firft who diftinguifh'd himfelf by reprefenting Gods and Heroes in their true Characters, and with becoming proper Majefty (52). Few were able, faith an excellent Judge, to afcend to his Sublimity and grand Tafte (53). He flourifh'd about the time of *Apelles* (54). Now juft fuch a vaft Genius was *Michael Angelo* : He excelled in Sculpture, Painting, and Architecture ; and was well verfed in feveral other Sciences and Arts ; in Anatomy particularly, of which, it is agreed, no Painter hath been a greater Mafter. In all his Works he was like *Euphranor,* ever equal to himfelf ; the fame great Tafte, the fame bold, afpiring, mafterly Genius appeared in them all. His Ideas were noble and elevated ; and he always chofe Subjects fuitable to the Grandeur of his Imagination, which was fertile, and daring almoft to extravagance : For if he erred, it was, like *Euphranor,* in being rather too great in his Manner.

Such a one was Michael Angelo a- mongft the Moderns.

ONE of the moft famous of thofe who were bred up under *Euphranor* was *Antidotus.* He was extremely diligent and induftrious, but very flow at his Pencil. He was very correct in Proportion and Symmetry, upon which his Mafter had writ an excellent Treatife ; but he was not of a lively, fertile Imagination ; and his Colouring was harfh and dry (55). Many of the *Florentine* School, and its great Mafter *Michael Angelo* himfelf, are reckoned very deficient in the colouring part, tho' they are highly praifed for their Correctnefs of Defign. And the fame Fault afcribed to *Antidotus* is found particularly in *Andrea del Sarto's* Pictures, which generally want Strength and Life through the natural Timoroufnefs and Anxiety of their Author, his Over-carefulnefs and Diligence about them (56).

Antidotus Scholar to Euphranor.

Compared with Andrea del Sarto. *Both too diligent and heavy.*

BUT *Antidotus* was more famed for having formed a *Nicias* than for his Pictures ; the *Nicias* fo celebrated for painting fine Women, and for his wonderful Dexterity in reprefenting all forts of Animals beyond any Mafter of his time ; which yet was but the leaft of his Accomplifhments. For no Painter is more highly extolled for the great Variety and noble Choice of his Subjects ; for his Skilfulnefs and Dexterity in the Diftribution of Lights and Shadows ; for the Roundnefs, Relief, and Morbidezza (as the *Italian* Painters call it) of his Figures ; and his Intelligence of the Keeping (57). But what is chiefly worth our notice with relation to this excellent Mafter, is the high and juft Notion he had of the Art,

Nicias Scholar to Antidotus.

His fublime Ideas of the Art, and excellent Qualifications.

(50) See *Felibien* and *Vafari.*

(51) Multum a Zeuxide & Apelle abeft, Apellis difcipulus Perfeus ad quem de hac arte fcripfit. *Plin.* 35. *Felibien* is much miftaken when he fays of *Perfeus,* Qu'il ecrioit un traité de fon art qu'il dedîa a fon maitre.

(52) Euphranor Ifthmius——docilis, & laboriofus ante omnes, & in quocunque genere excellens, ac fibi æqualis. Hic primus Videtur & expreffiffe dignitates heroum, & ufurpaffe fymmetriam : fed fuit univerfitate corporum exilior ; capitibus articulifque grandior. Volumina quoque compofuit de fymmetria & coloribus. *Plin.* 35. Euphranorem admirandum facit quod & cæteris omnibus ftudiis inter præcipuos, & pingendi fingendique mirus artifex fuit. *Quint.* 12. 10.

(53) Neque ille Callicles quaternûm digitûm tabulis nobilis cum effet, tamen in pingendo afcendere potuit ad Euphranoris altitudinem. *Varro de vit. pop. Rom. apud Sofipatrum, lib.* 1.

(54) He was Scholar to *Ariftides Thebanus* (*Apellis Æqualis*) already mentioned. And *Pliny* places him in the time of *Alexander.* Item & Alexandrum & Philip-

pum in quadrigis, *lib.* 34. 8. See the *French* Notes upon this Book often cited.

(55) Euphranoris autem difcipulus fuit Antidotus.—— Ipfe diligentior quam numerofior, & in coloribus feverior. *Plin.* 35.

(56) See *Felibien* and *Vafari.* This is the Fault *Quintilian* fpeaks of in other Works of Genius. At plerofque videas hærentes circa fingula, & dum inveniunt, ac dum inventa ponderant ac dimetiantur ; quod etiamfi idcirco fieret, ut femper optimis uterentur, admiranda tamen hæc infælicitas erat, quæ curfum animi refrœnat, & calorem cogitationis extinguit morâ ac diffidentiâ. *Quint. lib.* 8. *in Prœmio.*

(57) Euphranor maxime inclaruit difcipulo Nicia ·A· thenienfi : qui diligentiffime mulieres pinxit ; lumen & umbras cuftodivit, atque, ut eminerent e tabulis picturæ maxime curavit. *Plin.* 35. Nicias pictor filius Nicomedis in pingendis animalibus, ætatis fuæ longe præftantiffimus, habuit fepulchrale monumentum, inter eorum tumulos, quibus publicæ fepulturæ honorem impertiendum judicabant Athenienfes. *Paufanias, lib.* 1.

Art, and the noble Subjects he chofe to reprefent in order to do juftice to it, and employ it fuitably to its Excellence and Dignity. *Zeuxis, Parrhafius, Pamphilus, Apelles, Euphranor,* as we are often told by ancient Authors, by *Maximus Tyrius* in particular, and all the greateft ancient Mafters were great Admirers and Copiers of *Homer*; and fo was he likewife. He often faid, that Painting ought not to be proftituted to adorn trifling, low, unworthy Objects; but that it ought to be employed to reprefent great Actions, Battles, Victories, Triumphs, Gods, Heroes, Virtues, and fuch like fublime Subjects, in which its Beauty, Power, and Majefty might be difplayed. A Picture (faid he) ought to be confidered as a Species of Poetry, for fo it really is, being capable of the fame Invention, and Sublimity. The fame Spirit is required to animate, and the fame Judgment to conduct both: What is. below the Dignity of Poefy, is no lefs unworthy of Painting: There is no Subject of the former too great for the latter, or that may not be as much ennobled by the one as by the other (58). *He confidered Painting as a poetical Art.*

INDEED not *Nicias* only, but all the great Painters in any Age of Painting have had the fame true Ideas of their Art: And fuch Conceptions of it alone can produce a great Artift: Without fuch a juft Notion of the Scope, Aim, and Extent of that Art, all Attempts will be but low and groveling, far beneath the Sublimity it is capable of rifing to, and by which its Merit and Excellence ought to be meafured. *So all the great Mafters among the Ancients. And thus chiefly was the Art perfected by them.*

IN order to become an Orator, fays *Cicero* (59), one muft have conceived a juft Idea of the high Perfection Eloquence may attain, and ought to afpire at; he fhould keep that Picture or Model always before his Eye to animate and infpire him as well as to direct him in his Studies; in like manner as one who defires to become a Mafter of the Art of Painting, muft endeavour firft to have a juft Notion of the principal End and Excellence of that Art, and keep that ever in his view. Thus it was in fact that the beft Mafters, ancient and modern, arrived at Perfection. They had firft formed a juft Conception of the Excellence and Merit, to which a good Genius by due Application, and a right Courfe of Study might advance the Art: And that Idea being always prefent in their Minds, inflamed their Imagination, exalted their Conceptions, and pufh'd them on vigoroufly to the Studies and Efforts in which they had fuch happy fuccefs: And in proportion as they fucceeded they became more bold and daring, and aimed at higher Marks. Having the Truth, the Probability, the Sublimity, Majefty, Beauty and Grace, at which Painting ought to afpire, deeply impreffed on their Minds; they were at due pains to replenifh their Underftanding, expand and enrich their Imagination, correct and chaftife their Judgment and Tafte, by reading the beft Hiftorians and Poets; but chiefly by the Obfervation and Study of Nature, whofe Rival they confidered their Art to be. This is the Advice *Leonardo da Vinci* gave to all his Scholars, "Above all to be affiduous in contemplating Nature, in "order to emulate and rival her; to let none of her various Appearances efcape their "Obfervation, and to give all diligence to form a juft Tafte of her Simplicity, Beauty, "and Majefty." And *Pamphilus* who had been at fo much pains to improve his Mind by every Art and Science, and had formed an *Apelles*, who fhewed fo perfect a Tafte of beautiful Nature, no doubt had received, early, the fame excellent Advice from *Eupompus* his Mafter, who was (as has been obferved) a bufy Student of Nature, and look'd upon it as the Painter's beft Guide, to which all others ought to fubmit. This was the conftant Language of all the great Painters, ancient and modern (60), concerning Painting and the good Tafte of Nature requifite to excel in that Art. Thus it was that the Art improved, and that the Painters became able to be Poets or Creators; able to chufe from Nature with Intelligence and Tafte, and to form by the power of their own Fancy great and beautiful Works. This excellent Art can only be advanced and improved by calling in all the other Arts and Sciences to nourifh, and invigorate it; and by fuch a juft Conception of its true Excellence and real Beauty, as directs and prompts to proper Study, in order to attain

What Socrates, Cicero, and others fay on this Subject.

Cicero.

to

(58) Nicias pictor etiam hoc ftatim ab initio non parvam effe pictoriæ artis partem contendebat, ut artifex fumptâ materiâ fatis copiosâ pingeret, neque artem in minutias concideret, veluti aviculas aut flores; Verum eam potius navalibus equeftribufque præliis impenderet: Ubi variæ equorum formæ exhiberi folent; currentium nempe, adverfariis recto corporis ftatu obfiftentium, in genua denique procidentium: Equitum Vero alii jaculantes, alii ex equis decidentes, repræfentantur. Arbitrabatur enim ipfum quoque argumentum non minus aliquam artis pictoriæ partem effe, quam fabulæ poetarum præcipuam in ipfa poefi vim obtinere judicantur. *Demetr. Phaler. de Elocut. Sec.* 76.

(59) Attamen quoniam de oratore nobis difputandum eft, de fummo oratore dicam neceffe eft. Vis enim, & natura rei, nifi perfecta ante oculos ponitur, qualis, & quanta fit, intelligi non poteft. *De Orat. lib.* 3. 22.

Non enim quæro, quis fuerit, fed quid fit illud, quo nihil poffet effe præftantius: quod in perpetuitate dicendi non fæpe, atque haud fcio an unquam, in aliqua autem parte eluceat aliquando, idem apud alios denfius, apud

alios fortaffe rarius. Sed ego fic ftatuo, nihil effe in ullo genere tam pulchrum, quo non pulchrius id fit, unde illud, ut ex ore aliquo, quafi imago, exprimatur; quod neque oculis, neque auribus, neque ullo fenfu percipi poteft: Cogitatione tantum & mente complectimur. Itaque & Phidiæ fimulacris, quibus nihil in illo genere perfectius videmus, & his picturis quas nominavi, cogitare non poffumus pulchriora. Nec Vero ille artifex, cum faceret Jovis formam aut Minervæ, contemplabatur aliquem e quo fimilitudinem duceret: fed ipfius in mente infidebat fpecies pulchritudinis eximia quædam, quam intuens, in eaque defixus, ad illius fimilitudinem, artem, & manum dirigebat. Ut igitur in formis, & figuris, eft aliquid perfectum, & excellens, cujus ad cogitatam fpeciem imitando referuntur ea, quæ fub oculos ipfa cadunt: fic perfectæ eloquentiæ fpeciem animo videmus, effigiem auribus quærimus. *Cic. ad M. Brutum, ab initio. Vid. Rhetor. lib.* 2. *ab initio.*

(60) See what *Lamazzo* fays of a high Idea of Painting, Idea del tempio, &c. p. 12.

Quintilian.

to perfection in it. To this great Art we may justly apply what is said of Oratory, " That " it resembles Fire which is fed by the Fewel, inflamed by Motion, and gathers strength " by burning. For the Power of the Genius is augmented by the abundance of the Matter " to supply it : And it is impossible to make a great or magnificent Work, if either the " Materials be wanting, or Judgment to dispose them rightly (61)."

Socrates.

Maximus Tyrius.

Cicero.

WE are told by the best Philosophers what ought to be the Scope and Study of those who would arrive at Perfection in the designing Arts; and what really was the Aim and Pursuit of the Ancients whose Works were so perfect. For thus *Socrates* accosts *Parrhafius* in the Conference between them recorded by *Xenophon*: When you Painters would represent some perfect Form, do you not collect from many Objects those Beauties, which, when skilfully combined together, make a most beautiful Whole (62)? *Maximus Tyrius* speaking of the ancient Sculptors and Statuaries, says (63), " They chose with admirable " Discernment and Taste, the most beautiful Parts out of many Bodies, and of these scat- " tered Excellencies made one perfect Piece : But this Mixture and Combination is done " with so much Judgment and Propriety, that they seem to have taken but one Model of " consummate Beauty for their Imitation. For Art ought thus to aim at somewhat more " perfect than Nature, which yet shall appear natural ; and therefore let us not imagine " that we can ever find one natural Beauty that can dispute with the Statues of the great " Masters." In fine, how the ancient Painters attained to that exquisite Idea of Beauty, Simplicity and Greatness, in which the Excellence of their Works consisted; is finely represented to us by *Cicero*, in order to shew how a Notion of perfect Eloquence must be in like manner formed, by setting to view a *Zeuxis* chusing from many beautiful Women, the several Graces and Charms, that being put together with Judgment and Taste, composed his famous *Helen*, that most compleat Form and Standard of female Beauty. What *Cicero* makes this famous Painter say is very remarkable : " Set before me some of your " most beautiful Virgins, whilst I paint the Picture I have promised you, that truth may be " transferred from the living Original into my mute Copy (64)."

It was so with regard to the modern Masters.

THE modern Masters who brought Painting to so great Perfection, had the same Notion of the Art, and of the Method of Study that is requisite to produce Works of good Taste, and uncommon Beauty. This evidently appears from the Accounts that are given us of *Raphael, Michael Angelo, Titian, Guido, Rubens, Poussin*, and many others; and from the Writings of *Leonardo da Vinci*, and other Authors upon this Art.

A Saying of Carrache.

How he saved Painting from false Taste an' Ruin.

I shall only observe farther upon this Subject, that *Annibal Carrache* was wont to say, as *Nicias*, That Painting ought not be called merely mute Poesy, because as Poets paint by Words, and he is the best Poet who draws the best and most lively Pictures ; so Painters ought to speak with their Pencil and Colours, and he is the best Painter whose Pictures speak most powerfully to the Heart (65). Now this Painter saved the Art from being quite corrupted and lost, by his just Notion of its real Beauty and Perfection. For tho' *Raphael* had raised the Art to the highest Pitch of Taste and Sublimity, it soon began to decline. About the time of the *Carraches* it was already sadly degenerated in all the Schools, because they no longer studied and pursued that which is necessary to the Perfection of Painting.

THERE were then two Parties at *Rome* that divided all the Students of the Art, and which of them wandered farthest from Truth and Beauty is hard to determine ; the one following Nature too closely, and servilely imitating her just as they found her, without any Choice or Taste ; and the other without studying Nature at all, abandoning themselves entirely to the Conduct of their own capricious Imaginations. It was then that the *Carraches* appeared,

(61) Ars magna, sicut flamma, materiâ alitur & motibus excitatur & urendo clarescit. Crescit enim cum amplitudine rerum vis ingenii : nec quisquam clarum & illustre opus efficere potest, nisi qui materiam parem invenit. *Quint. Dialog. an sui sæcu. Orat.* &c.
Impetus ex dignitate rei cujusque concipitur ; perinde remissus acriorve prout illa digna est peti. *Senec. Epist.* 89.

(62) The Passage hath been often referred to, and is given at full length at the beginning of the fourth Chapter.

(63) *Maximus Tyrius*, Dissert. 7.
So *Plato*, Pictorum facultas nullum in pingendo terminum habere videtur, sed semper inumbrando, & deumbrando, vel quomodocunque aliter a pictoribus id vocetur, nec cessat unquam ; non enim potest fieri ut ad pulchriora expressioraque incrementum non habeatur. *Plato de Leg. lib.* 6.

(64) *Cic. Rhet. lib.* 2. *ab initio.* " Præbete igitur mihi, " quæso, ex istis virginibus formosissimis, dum pingo id, " quod pollicitus sum vobis, ut mutum in simulacrum ex

" animali exemplo Veritas transferatur." He adds the reason why a Painter ought not to take his Idea of Beauty from one particular part, but from many Objects of Nature. " Ille autem quinque delegit ; quarum nomina " multi poetæ memoriæ tradiderunt, quod ejus essent " judicio probatæ, qui verissimum pulchritudinis habere " judicium debuisset. Neque enim putavit, omnia, quæ " quæreret ad venustatem, uno in corpore se reperire " posse, ideo quod nihil, simplici in genere, omni ex " parte perfectum, natura expolivit. Itaque tanquam " ceteris non sit habitura quod largiatur, si uni cuncta " concesserit, aliud alii commodi aliquo adjuncto incom- " modo muneratur." And then he goes on to shew that the fame must be done in Oratory : Quod quoniam nobis quoque voluntas accidit ut artem dicendi perscriberemus, non unum aliquod proposuimus exemplum,—— ac si par in nobis hujus artis, atque in illo pictuæ, scientia fuisset, fortasse magis hoc suo in genere opus nostrum, quam ille in sua pictura eniteret, &c.

(65) So *Bellori* in his Life of *Annibal Carrache*.
See *Felibien* and *Du Pile* their Lives of the Painters, and il Microcosmo della Pittura di *Francisco Scannelli da Forli*, l. 1. p. 57.

appeared, and fo happily found out, and revived the true Genius of Painting, by their juſt Ideas of the Art, and of the beſt way of ſtudying and imitating Nature; joining with the Study of Painting the other Sciences that are neceſſary to form a good Taſte, and to furniſh Ideas and Rules to the Pencil. The *Carraches* poſſeſſed amongſt them all the various parts of uſeful polite Learning, as well as all the Beauties and Excellencies of the Deſigning Arts; and it was by uniting their different Forces and Talents that they reſtored the Art, and brought it again to ſuch an eminent degree of true Beauty, in oppoſition to the falſe Taſte that was already far ſpread, and had almoſt entirely corrupted and deſtroyed it (66).

TO them we owe *Guido, Albano, Dominichino,* and ſeveral other excellent Maſters. What is told to this purpoſe at great length by all the Writers of the Lives of the famous Painters, is well worth being repeated. *Lewis Carrache* (67) when he had well examined the Works of *Carravagio,* was not a little ſurprized to find them in ſuch vogue; there being nothing in them but a bold Contraſt of Lights and Shadows, and ſervile Exactneſs in imitating the moſt common Nature; no Decorum, no Grace, no Elegance of Choice or Judgment. As for *Annibal,* he could not refrain from complaining of thoſe, who by encouraging this new Manner, greatly contributed to the Ruin of good Taſte in Painting. I ſee nothing, ſaid he, in thoſe Pictures which are ſo highly praiſed but a new manner, that, far from deſerving Applauſe, is truly blameable. I don't know but any other Novelty would gain equal Approbation: And I think one might take a very effectual way to mortify the Author of this new Taſte, which is ſo highly cried up at preſent. For that effect I would paint in a quite oppoſite manner to *Carravagio*; I would oppoſe to his ſtrong and fierce Colouring, one quite tender and languid; and inſtead of confined Lights falling upon Objects from on high, I would paint all the Figures in open Air, and fully enlightened: Far from hiding in Darkneſs, as he does, the Parts that are moſt difficult to paint, by very black Shades; I would expoſe my Figures in full light, and ſhew every part performed with perfect Skill and Taſte. He only aims at copying Nature as it appears in more common Objects, without ſelecting from Nature what is moſt exquiſite and beautiful; and, on the contrary, I would make choice of what is moſt perfect in Nature; only paint agreeable, fine Parts, and compoſe of theſe a pleaſing, beauteous Whole, giving my Figures a charming Union and a Greatneſs which is but rarely ſeen in Nature itſelf. Whilſt *Annibal Carrache* diſcourſed in this manner of *Carravagio's* Works, *Guido* liſtened to him with great attention; and having well digeſted theſe Advices, he immediately ſet about to put them in execution, which he did with ſuch ſucceſs, that his Manner from this time, which was quite the reverſe of *Carravagio's,* was ſoon preferred to it, being found far more ſweet and agreeable. *Carravagio* oppoſed him with all his Power and Intereſt; but *Guido* continued to paint in his more enlightened, gracious manner, in ſpite of all his oppoſition; being perſuaded, that it would quickly meet with general Approbation, and be univerſally eſteemed more pleaſing than the oppoſite, obſcure, and almoſt deformed Manner of *Carravagio.* And ſo it happened, for in a very ſhort ſpace of time after *Guido* betook himſelf to that manner of Painting, he came into high Reputation, and was employed in the greateſt Works.

PAUSIAS of *Sicyon* was Scholar to *Pamphilus,* but he chiefly painted in the Encauſtick Way: For *Pamphilus* his Maſter had likewiſe practiſed and taught that other Art (68). He was chiefly famous for adorning Vaults, Ceilings, and Walls in that manner, and excelled in doing Fruits and Flowers; the laſt particularly, for he was in Love with *Glycera,* who it ſeems firſt introduced into *Greece* the Cuſtom of young People's wearing Garlands or Chaplets of Flowers, and compoſed them with great Dexterity and exquiſite Taſte. She was continually contriving new Models for them; and he being frequently with her, uſed to imitate her Deſigns, and vie with her by his Art. He was excellent at Fore-ſhortening his Figures, a difficult Task that ſeldom has a pleaſing effect. His moſt renowned Picture was the Portrait of his Miſtreſs in a ſitting Poſture, making a Garland of Flowers; for a Copy of which *L. Lucullus* gave a very high Price.

Pauſias Scholar to Pamphilus, painted chiefly in the Encauſtick Way, (this explained in the marginal Notes.)

THIS Painter ſeems to have had much the ſame Taſte as *Giovanni d'Udina,* one of *Raphael's* Diſciples, who by the agreeable Variety and Richneſs of his Fancy, and his peculiar

He had much the ſame Taſte with Gio. d'Udina for groteſque Decorations.

(66) See *Felibien* and *Bellori.*

(67) See *Felibien,* tom. 3. p. 495, &c.

(68) Pamphilus quoque, Apellis præceptor, non pinxiſſe tantum Encauſta, ſed etiam docuiſſe traditur Pauſian Sicyonium primum in hoc genere nobilem,——Ceris pingere ac picturam inurere, quis primus excogitaverit, non conſtat. *Quidam Ariſtidis inventum putant; poſtea conſummatum a Praxitele. Sed aliquanto vetuſtiores Encauſtæ picturæ extitere, ut Polygnoti & Nicanoris & Arceſilai, Pariorum. Lyſippus Æginæ picturæ ſuæ inſcripſit 'Ενικαυσην: Quod profecto non feciſſet, niſi Encauſtica inventa. Plin. lib. 5. cap. 20, 21. Ratio inurendæ ceræ hodie nos fugit. Eam tamen diſerte exponit. Plin. lib. 35. cap. 11. Encauſto pingendi duo fuiſſe antiquitus genera conſtat: Cera, & in Ebore, ceſtro, id eſt, veruculo, donec claſſes pingi cœpere. Hoc tertium acceſſit, reſolutis igne ceris, penecillo utendi; quæ pictura in navibus nec ſole, nec ſale, ventiſque corrumpitur. Ceſtrum eſt veruculum, ſeu ſcalprum ignitum, a Xαλω uro. Ceræ tabulatis navium, aut liminibus januarum affigebantur, extendebantur, deinde igne reſolvebantur, & veruculo ignito inurebantur, incidebantur, pingebantur, ut ſpecies quælibet pictura exprimi poſſent. Ceræ illæ variis coloribus erant incoctæ, tandem penecillus adhibebatur, ut ceræ liquefactæ diffunderentur, & coloribus imbuerentur. Bulengerus de Pictura, &c. lib. 1. cap. 6, and 7. See likewiſe P. Hardouin's Pliny upon this place, the French Notes upon this Book of Pliny, and the Commentary on Boileau dans l'Art Poetique, le Commencement du Chant. 3.

K

peculiar Happiness in expreſſing all ſorts of Animals, Fruits, Flowers, and the Still-Life, both in Baſſo-relievo and Colours, acquired the Reputation of being the beſt Maſter in the World for Decorations and Ornaments in Stucco and Groteſque (69).

Athenion greatly praiſed by the Ancients for his Erudition. ATHENION, Diſciple to *Glaucion* a Painter of *Corinth*, is likewiſe highly praiſed by the Ancients, and by ſome equalled to *Nicias.* 'Tis ſaid that in all probability he would have been left behind by none, if he had lived to improve thoſe Talents, which the Works he did when very young diſcovered. His Colouring inclined rather to the harſh and diſagreeable ; but he is greatly celebrated for his Learning and deep Science, for the Erudition that appeared in his Pictures. So is likewiſe *Giulio Romano* amongſt the Moderns, who *As Giulio Romano among Moderns.* not underſtanding exactly the Lights and Shadows, or the Harmony of Colours, is frequently harſh and ungraceful, and had a harder and drier manner than any of *Raphael's* School. They were both very converſant in the Poets, aſſiduous Students and Imitators of *Homer* in particular ; and great Maſters of the Qualifications required in a grand Deſigner (70).

Pyreicus painted low Subjects like the Baſſans. AMONGST the Ancients *Pyreicus* got the nick-name of *Rhyparographus*, from the ſordid and mean Subjects to which he applied himſelf, ſuch as Barbers or Shoe-makers Shops, Kitchins, Animals, Herbage, and the Still-Life (71) : Like the *Baſſans* amongſt the Moderns, whoſe Performance is alſo admirable, tho' the Subjects are low. Such Pieces in all Ages have had their Admirers. The ſmalleſt Pictures of *Pyreicus* were more eſteemed by ſome, and bought at higher Rates, than the nobler Works of many other Maſters. *Pyreicus* chiefly painted little Pieces.

Callicles.
And Calades. CALLICLES alſo excelled ſo exceedingly in Mignature Works, that he was reckoned but little inferiour to the great Maſters. And tho' the Invention of *Calades* was more noble, he too preferred Comedy to Tragedy ; that is, he choſe rather to paint mean, common Subjects than great Events. But *Antiphilus*, who likewiſe painted ſmall Pieces only, knew how to repreſent both high and low Life. He had a delicate Pencil, and a very great *Their Talents for Comedy and Tragedy in Painting.* command of it (72): When he attempted Tragedy, or ſublime and elevated Subjects ; or to move Pity, Horror, or the greater Paſſions, he had excellent ſucceſs. And the comical Humour he ſhewed on other occaſions in painting fantaſtical, ludicrous Ideas, hath made him very famous, for having amuſed himſelf in painting one very ridiculouſly dreſſed ; he was highly delighted with that Figure, and called it his *Gryllus* ; whence ever afterwards groteſque Figures, and Chimæras were called amongſt the Painters by that Name. It is the ſame *Antiphilus* who was juſtly puniſhed by *Ptolemy* for calumniating the innocent and generous *Apelles* (73).: He was originally of *Egypt*, but bred up under *Cteſidemus* an excellent *Greek* Painter.

BUT not to take notice of any others at preſent amongſt thoſe who only painted in Mignature, I ſhall juſt mention a few more, who did great Works, and excelled in the
                                                                                                best

(69) Pinxit & ipſe penecillo Parietes Theſpiis, cum reficerentur ; quondam a Polygnoto picti : multumque comparatione ſuperatus exiſtimabatur, quoniam non ſuo genere certaſſet. Idem & Lacunaria primus pingere inſtituit & cameras ; nec ante eum taliter adornare mos fuit. ——Amavit in juventa Glyceren, municipem ſuam, inventricem coronarum ; certandoque imitatione ejus, ad numeroſiſſimam florum varietatem perduxit artem illam. Poſtremo pinxit ipſam ſedentem cum corona, quæ e nobiliſſimis tabula, adpellata eſt Στεφανήπλοκος, ab aliis Στεφανόπωλις quoniam Glycere coronas vendirando ſuſtentaverat paupertatem. Hujus tabulæ exemplar, quod Apographon vocant, L. Lucullus duobus talentis emit Dionyſiis, Athenis Pauſias autem fecit & grandis tabulas, &c. *Plin. lib.* 35. 21. In the ancient groteſque Paintings at *Rome* upon the Vaults and Walls, Girls with Garlands of Flowers, or carrying Baſkets of Flowers in their Hands were common ; and other Figures like thoſe *Athenian* Virgins called the *Canephoræ*, often mentioned by *Pauſanias*, and called by Pliny, lib. 36. *Ciſtiferæ* ; Braſs Statues of which Pliny, by *Polycletus*, are thus deſcribed by *Cicero.* Ænea præterea duo ſigna, non maxima, verum eximia venuſtate, Virginali habitu atque veſtitu, quæ manibus ſublatis ſacra quædam more Athenienſium virginum repoſita in capitibus ſuſtinebant. Canephoræ ipſæ vocabantur. *Cic. in Verrem, lib.* 4. 3. There are ſeveral ſuch Figures in the Collection of Drawings after the antique Paintings at *Rome*, by the elder *Bartoli*, that formerly belonged to the *Maſſini* Family, and is now in Dr. *Richard Mead's* Library.

(70) Niciæ comparatur & aliquando præfertur Athenion.——Auſterior colore, &in auſteritate jucundior, ut in ipſa pictura eruditio eluceat. Qui niſi in juventa obiiſſet nemo ei compararetur. *Plin.*35. 21. See the Notes in *French* ; and with regard to *Giulio* it is ſaid :

Julius a puero muſarum eductus in antris,
Aonias reſeravit opes, graphicâque poeſi

Quas non viſa prius, ſed tantum audita poetis,
Ante oculos ſpectanda dedit ſacraria Phœbi:
Quoſque coronatis complevit bella triumphis
Heroum fortuna potens, caſuſque decores,
Nobilius reipſâ antiqua pinxiſſe videtur.
Freſnoy de Arte Graphica.

See *Du Pile's* Notes on that Paſſage, where he ſays, " It appears, that *Julio Romano* form'd his Ideas, and " made his Guſto from reading *Homer*, and in that imi- " tated *Zeuxis* and *Polygnotus*, who (as *Maximus Tyrius* " relates) treated their Subjects in their Pictures, as " *Homer* did in his Poetry." He painted ſeveral parts of *Homer* in the *St. Sebaſtian* Palace.

(71) —— Minori pictura celebres in penecillo, e quibus fuit Pyreicus, arte paucis poſtferendus. Is propoſito neſcio an deſtruxerit ſeſe quoniam humilia quidem ſecutus, humilitatis tamen ſummam adeptus eſt gloriam. Tonſtrinas, ſutrinaſque & pinxit ſimilia : Ob hoc cognominatus ῥυπαρογραφΘ : In his conſummatæ voluptatis quippe eæ pluris veniere quam maximæ multorum. *Plin.* 35. 18.

(72) Parva & Callicles fecit. Item Calades, comicis tabellis : utraque Antiphilus : namque & Heſionam nobilem pinxit ; idemque, jocoſo nomine, Gryllum, deridiculi habitus pinxit ; -unde hoc genus picturæ Grylli vocantur. *Plin. ibid.* Facilitate eſt præſtantiſſimus Antiphilus. *Quint. Inſt. lib.* 12. c. 10. *Varro* joins with him *Lyſippus.* Tua hæc villa tam & oblita tabulis eſt, nec minus ſignis ornata at meam veſtigium ubi nullum Lyſippi aut Antiphili videbis. *De re Ruſ. l.* 2. c. 2. Picturæ ſtudioſis nihil profuerit cognoviſſe Apellis, Protogenis & Antiphili opera, niſi & ipſi manum admoverint operi. *Theon. Sophiſt. Progymnaſm. cap.* 1.

(73) Antiphilus, falſa accuſatione, Apellem in diſcrimen Vitæ adduxit apud Ptolomeum regem. *Lucian de Calumn.* and Pliny in his Account of *Apelles*, lib. 35.

best Talents belonging to the Art of Painting. The Works of *Timomachus* are highly celebrated by the ancient *Greek* and *Latin* Poets. He seems to have excelled in expressing the furious Passions, in painting terrible Subjects, and in violently agitating the Mind (74). There was great Motion or rather Fury in most of his Pieces. This is likewise the Character of many Masters in the *Florentine* School.

Timomachus excelled in Tragedy, or in moving Horror and Pity.

NICEARCHUS was most eminent for treating the calm, soft and tender Affections, like *Guido* and *Parmegiano* among the Moderns, tho' he likewise knew how to represent the other sort. *Cratinus* had a particular Turn and Genius for the comick. And *Eudorus* shone in all sorts of scenical Decorations, of which he had a very fertile, elegant Taste (75).

Nicearchus in expressing, like Guido and Parmegiano, the soft, tender Affections, and several Masters had different Talents and Genius's.

CLESIDES is not more remarkable for knowing how to employ his Pencil to gratify his Vengeance, than *Stratonice* for shewing a generous Example by doing justice to good Painting, even when employed to blacken and defame herself. There was another *Antiphilus*, beside him already mentioned, who painted Hunters and all sorts of Animals with wonderful Subtlety and Dexterity. Some Masters excelled in the Exactness and Severity of the Execution, and their Works were chiefly esteemed by Artists; it being only very skilful ones that could discern their principal Beauties. Such a one was *Mecophanes* Disciple of *Pausias* (76). There was nothing, it is said, in his Performances, not one Stroke of the Pencil, not one single Tinct that was not directed with vast Intelligence, and that had not a very skilful Meaning to an Artist's Eye.

Some were only, or most esteemed by Artists.

OTHERS, like *Nealces* and *Socrates* (77), had so clear and perspicuous a manner of Composition, that their Performances were not admired by learned Eyes only, but gave full Satisfaction to the most accurate Judges, at the same time that they gave Pleasure to every ordinary Beholder. They deserved the Character *Cicero* gives of *Phidias's* Statues in a fine Compliment he makes to *Hortensius* the Orator (78). " The Genius of *Q. Hor-* " *tensius* when very young, like one of *Phidias's* Statues, was no sooner discovered than " approved." He seems to have studied not only natural Truth and Evidence; but likewise to have had a just regard to what the Painters call the *Costume*, and to have given every thing he painted all its properest and most distinguishing Characteristicks. Some delighted in painting the Chimæras and Monsters (79) described by Poets; others in presenting the Wars and Victories they have celebrated. The greater Genius's naturally chose proportionally great and elevated Subjects (80).

Nealces and Socrates by all.

THE extraordinary Disposition of *Erigonus* towards the Art is worth our notice; for tho' he only attended *Nealces* as a common Servant to pound his Colours; yet merely by seeing his Master work, without any Instruction from him he penetrated so far into the greatest Secrets of the Art, that he became an excellent Painter, and by his Lessons formed several very eminent Artists (81).

Erigonus had an extraordinary Genius. He was a common Servant to Nealces. And without much help became a good Painter.

AMONGST the Moderns, in *Polydore* of *Caravaggio* we have a like instance of Genius; for tho' brought up to no better Employment than carrying Stone and Mortar in the new Buildings of Pope *Leo* X at *Rome*, yet at last being strongly sollicited by his Genius to try his Talent in Designing, with a little Assistance from one of *Giovanni d'Udina's* Scholars, and his own Application to the Study of the Antiques, he became in a short time so able an Artist, that he had the honour of contributing much to the finishing those renowned Works in the *Vatican*. *Michael Angelo* of *Caravaggio*, the first of the *Roman* School that

So Polydore *of* Caravaggio. *And* Michael Angelo *of* Caravaggio,

(74) Timomachus Byzantius, Cæsaris dictatoris Ajacem & Medeam pinxit. Timomachi laudantur & Oresses; Iphigenia in Tauris;—præcipue tamen ars ei savisse in Gorgone visa est. *Plin. ibid.* The common Reading is (*Cæsaris dictatoris ætate*) justly corrected in the *French* Notes, because he could not be contemporary with *Cæsar*. He is always mentioned amongst the ancient ones; so Pliny, lib. 7. c. 38. *Apelles, Aristides, Timomachus*, &c. And in the 35th Book, speaking of the imperfect Works of the Masters, Illud vero perquam rarum ac memoria dignum, etiam suprema opera artificum, imperfectasque tabulas, sicut Irin Aristidis, Medeam Timomachi, &c. *cap* 23. His *Medea* is reckoned among the most ancient Pieces of Art, by *Cicero*, in his 4th against *Verres*, where there is a long Catalogue of the greatest Curiosities of Painting and Sculpture in *Greece* carried off by *Verres*.

(75) Nicearchus Venerem inter Gratias & Cupidines; Herculemque tristem insaniæ pœnitentia.——Cratinus comœdos——Eudorus scena-spectator.——Clesides, reginæ Stratonices injuria. Nullo enim honore exceptus ab ea, pinxit volutantem cum Piscatore, quem reginam amare sermo erat——Regina tolli vetuit, utriusque similitudine mire expressa. *Plin. ibid.*

(76) Sunt quibus Mecophanes, ejusdem Pausiæ discipulus, placeat diligentia, quam intelligant soli artifices;

aliàs durus in coloribus. *Plin. ibid.* It is of such Painters *Cicero* speaks, when he says, Quam multa vident Pictores in umbris, & eminentia quæ nos non videmus. *Acad.* lib. 4.

(77) Nam Socrates jure omnibus placet;——Nealces, Venerem, ingeniosus & solers in arte, &c.

(78) Q. Hortensii ingenium admodum adolescentis, ut Phidiæ signum, simul aspectum & probatum est. *Cic. de clar. Orat.*

(79) This is the Character *Quintilian* gives of *Theon Samius*. Concipiendis visionibus, quas φαντασίας vocant, Theon Samius est præstantissimus. *Quint. Inst.* 12. 10. *Plutarch. de Poetis audiendis* severely censures those who paint πράξεις αʹτόπους.

(80) Is porro quo generosior, celsiorque est, hoc majoribus velut organis commovetur, ideoque & laude crescit in umbris, & impetu augetur, & aliquid magnum agere gaudet. *Quint. Inst. lib.* 1. c. 2.

(81) Non omittetur inter hos insigne exemplum: nam Erigonus tritor-colorum Nealcæ pictoris, in tantum ipse profecit ut celebrem etiam discipulum reliquerit, &c. *Plin.* 35. For the Characters of the two Painters that follow, see *Felibien*.

that diftinguifh'd himfelf by his Intelligence of the Clair-obfcure, was alfo like his Coun-tryman *Polydore* no better than a Day-Labourer; till having feen fome Painters at work upon a Brick-wall which he had prepared for them, he was fo charmed with their Art, that he immediately applied himfelf to the Study of it; and in a few Years made fo con-fiderable a Progrefs, that at *Venice, Rome,* and in feveral other Parts of *Italy,* he was cry'd up and admir'd by all the young Students, as the Author of a new Stile of Paint-ing; which however was like to have proved very fatal to the Art.

Some Women famous for Painting amongst the Moderns.

Some ancient Pain-treffes.

Lala in particular. Her Character from Varro.

A S amongft the Moderns, the Daughter of *Tintoret, Marietta Tintoretta;* the Daughter of *Profpero Fontani;* the Daughter of *Vincentino;* *Sophonisba Anguifciola;* Madam *Schurman;* *Rofalba,* and feveral other Ladies, have made very great Advances in Painting, and procured very confiderable Honour and Fame to themfelves and the Art by their Works; fo there were not wanting amongft the ancient Ladies feveral very eminent Ge-nius's for Painting. *Pliny* fays, that *Timarete* was the firft of her Sex who acquired con-fiderable Reputation by Painting; a *Diana* done by her, having been plac'd in the Temple of *Ephefus,* amongft the Works of the moft famous Mafters (82). *Irene* not only had a very good hand at Portraits; but likewife painted hiftorical Pieces with great judgment. *Calypfo, Alcifthene, Ariftarete,* and others, are highly commended (83). But of all the Painters of that Sex *Lala* is the moft celebrated. *Varro* makes honourable mention of her in his Treatife of the Liberal Arts. He fays fhe would not marry, becaufe Family-Cares are apt to diftract the Mind, and are hardly compatible with that Freedom, that Force of Genius, and that Lightnefs and Eafinefs of the Pencil, which are the great Charms of Painting. While fhe was very young fhe painted Portraits either on Wood or Ivory, or in Wax, to great perfection, of her own Sex efpecially. She drew herfelf with excellent Tafte in the Attitude of a Girl at her Toilet, admiring her own Charms in the Mirror; and an old Woman, fo natural, that nothing could go beyond it. In fine, he remarks, that fhe poffeffed many excellent Talents, that feldom meet together, in a very eminent degree: She had an exceeding light and eafy Pencil, and painted with great Freedom, Ex-pedition and Facility; and, at the fame time, as for the Likenefs, the Colouring, and the Keeping, fhe fo greatly excelled in them all, that her Pictures commonly bore a higher Price than thofe of *Denis* and *Sopolis,* the beft Face-Painters of her time (84); whofe Works (faith he) do now adorn the Cabinets of the Curious (85). Thefe two were *Greeks* by Birth, but painted at *Rome* a great many Portraits of both Sexes. The firft of them was furnamed the *Anthropographos,* or the Man-Painter, becaufe he only did Portraits.

The laft Greek Painter mentioned is Metrodorus.

A good Philofopher as well as Painter.

He flourifhed in the time of Æmilius.

Had a confiderable fhare in forming one of the greateft Men that ever lived, Cornelius Scipio.

Scipio's Character.

T H E laft of the *Greek* Painters I fhall mention is indeed one, who, on many accounts, deferves our particular attention. 'Tis the famous *Metrodorus;* of whom, it is difficult (fay ancient Authors) to decide whether he was a greater Painter or Philofopher: He too was fo excellently skilled in Architecture and Poetry, that he wrote a Treatife upon each of them; both which were highly efteemed. So far are Painting and Phi-lofophy from being at fuch variance, or fo remote from one another as is commonly apprehended, that thefe two Arts were his chief delight. He had fo high a Reputation for the one and the other equally, at *Athens;* that when *Æmilius,* after defeating *Per-feus,* and fubduing all *Macedonia,* demanded of the *Athenians* one of their beft Philofo-phers to educate his Children, and an able Painter to direct the Ornaments of his Triumph: The Magiftrates of *Athens* unanimoufly determined that *Metrodorus* was equally qualify'd for both, and fent him to the *Roman* General; giving him to underftand, that they had provided him with one Perfon who has fully accomplifh'd to fatisfy him in all that he defired of them, when he ask'd a Philofopher and a Painter (86). A very extraordinary Encomium! hardly fince that time to be parallelled in Hiftory, but verified by that General's Experience and Approbation. It was under this Painter's Care that *Scipio's* Education was finifhed. He who was at once fo brave a Warrior, fo great a Con-queror, fo good a Citizen, and fo polite a Scholar; fo generous a Patron and Encou-rager of the fine Arts in peace, and the great Bulwark of his Country in war. He to whom we owe, in a great meafure, a *Terence,* and his fine Comedies; and who de-lighted fo much in the Converfation of the Hiftorian *Polybius* and the Philofopher *Pane-tius,*

---

(82) Timarete Miconis filia Dianam in tabula, quæ Epheft eft, in antiquiffimis picturis. *Plin.* 35. Fuit & alius Micon, qui minoris cognomine diftinguitur; cujus filia Timarete & ipfa pinxit. *Plin.* 35.

(83) Irene Cratini pictoris filia & difcipula, puellam quæ eft Eleufinæ: Calypfo, fenem & præftigiatorem Theodo-rum: Alcifthene, Saltatorem, Ariftarete, Nearchi filia & difcipula, Æfculapium. *Plin.* 35.

(84) Lala Cyzicena, perpetua Virgo Marci Varronis ju-Venta, Romæ, & penecillo pinxit & Ceftro, in Ebore, imagines mulierum maxime; ac, Neapoli, Anum in grandi tabula; fuam quoque imaginem ad fpeculum, Nec ullus in pictura velocior manus fuit: artis Vero tantum, ut multum manipretio antecederet celeberrumos eadem ætate pictore, Sopolin & Dionyfium quorum ta-

bulæ Pinacothecas implent. *Plin. ibid.* See the Notes in French.

(85) Dionyfius nihil aliud quam homines pinxit, ob Id Anthropographos cognominatus. *Plin. ibid.* There is another, *Dionyfius Colophonius,* mentioned by *Ælian,* *Ariftotle,* and others, of whom afterwards.

(86) ——Ubi eodem tempore erat Metrodorus, pictor, idemque Philofophus, in utraque fcientia magnæ aucto-ritatis. Itaque cum L. Paulus, devicto Perfeo, petiffet ab Athenienfibus ut quam probatiffimum Philofophum mit-terent fibi, ad erudiendos liberos; Itemque pictorem, ad triumphum excolendum: Athenienfes Metrodorum ele-gerunt, profeffi eundem in utroque defiderio præftantiffi-mum. Quod Ita Paulus quoque judicavit. *Plin.* 35. *Plutarch. in Æmil.*

tius, that they were always with him : He who kept in his Houſe *Pacuvius;* who was, ſay Hiſtorians, both Poet and Painter : He, in one word, who never counſelled, ſpoke, or did what was not worthy of a true *Roman,* and who divided his time between great Actions and elegant Studies. Such was the Pupil of *Metrodorus ;* and from this Example we may learn what happy Effects the polite Arts, joined with true Philoſophy in Education, muſt produce, when they meet with a Genius capable of Improvement ; the great Advantages of a truly Liberal Education, and the many excellent Qualities that are requiſite to compleat the Character of one duly qualified to inſtruct and form the Youth of Birth and Fortune (87). It is one of ſuch a great and amiable Character, that the Education of Perſons of high Rank and Diſtinction ought to be intended and calculated to form; one fit to ſerve his Country in peace and war ; one of an heroick Mind ; a ſincere Lover of his Country, and of a benevolent generous Diſpoſition ; utterly abhorring Villany, Effeminacy, and all vicious Pleaſures; one who loves the Liberal Arts, underſtands them, and delights in them, and in uſeful Converſation ; one whoſe Amuſements and Recreations, as well as Occupations, are manly and ingenious ; and who, next to the Glory of great and virtuous Deeds, hath higheſt ſatisfaction in thoſe Arts which are ſo fitted to recommend them and perpetuate their Memory. To ſuch Inſtruction and Education Philoſophy, and all the fine Arts, muſt concur with the manly genteel Exerciſes, as they did in that of *Scipio :* Any one of theſe being wanting, Education is deficient ; nor will the reſt be able to produce that compleat Effect a liberal one ought to aim at.

What Education ought to aim at.

Was accompliſhed in his by uniting together the fine Arts and the genteel manly Exerciſes.

THO' this be no Digreſſion from my main Subject, yet to return to what is now more immediately under Conſideration, we may ſee by this ſhort Sketch of Characters, that the Art was arrived to as great Dignity and Perfection amongſt the ancient *Greeks,* in and about the time of *Apelles,* as amongſt the *Romans* in and about the time of *Raphael ;* or at leaſt that *Ariſtotle, Socrates, Varro, Cicero, Pliny, Quintilian,* and others who have mentioned the ancient Painters and their Works, underſtood, as well as the beſt Judges amongſt the Moderns, in what the Beauty and Excellence of this Art lies ; and what are the requiſite Talents and Perfections of a great Painter. There is no Accompliſhment aſcribed to any of the great modern Maſters, which is not to be found in the Character of ſome ancient Painter in a very eminent degree, whether relating to Invention, Deſign, Diſpoſition, Proportion, Colouring, Clair-obſcure, Rounding, Relief, Beauty, Sweetneſs, Strength, Boldneſs, Majeſty, Grace, or any other Excellence in the Pictures which the greateſt modern Hands have produced. And we find it was the ſame Idea of the Art, and the ſame Method of Study, that formed the great Painters in every Age.

BUT were there no conſiderable Painters amongſt the *Greeks* before *Apollodorus,* and thoſe others named as the moſt perfect Maſters ? *Quintilian* names ſome that were more ancient, and at the ſame time makes a ſevere Reflection upon certain pretended Virtuoſi in his time, who, it ſeems, were fondeſt of the Pictures which had nothing to recommend them but merely their Antiquity, having been done when Painting was in a very low State, in compariſon of the greater Beauty and Perfection to which it was afterwards advanced. They preferred, ſays he, the Works of certain old Maſters, to much nobler Pictures; either out of a ſuperſtitious Veneration for what is very ancient ; or through a ridiculous Affectation of appearing profounder Judges than others, and capable of diſcerning Beauties where leſs learned Eyes could find none (88). But this Cenſure cannot fall on thoſe who are curious in collecting Drawings and Pictures now-a-days, as far back as they can go, in order to have Examples of the Progreſs of the Art ; nor on thoſe who are inquiſitive about the Riſe, Origin, and Progreſs of any Art whatſoever. For the Invention and Improvements of ingenious Arts will always be juſtly eſteemed one of the moſt important Branches of Hiſtory, by all who have juſt Notions of the true Dignity of Mankind, and of their beſt Employments. And it is only by a Collection of Drawings and Pictures ranged hiſtorically, [as in a Cabinet in *London* I have often viſited with pleaſure (89)]; ſo that one may there ſee all the different Schools, and go from one to another, tracing the Progreſs of each, and of every Maſter in each : It is only by ſuch a judiciouſly diſpoſed Collection,

But were there no Painters before Apollodorus ?

Quintilian names ſome. But cenſures thoſe pretended Virtuoſi who valued Pieces more upon account of their Antiquity than their Excellence.

On whom this Cenſure does, and does not fall.

(87) P. Scipio Æmilianus, vir avitis Publii Africani, paterniſque Lucii Pauli virtutibus ſimillimus, omnibus belli ac togæ dotibus, ingeniique ac ſtudiorum eminentiſſimus ſæculi ſui, qui nihil in Vita niſi laudandum aut fecit, aut dixit ac ſenſit.——Neque enim quiſquam hoc Scipione elegantius interValla negotiorum otio disjunxit : Semperque aut Belli aut Pacis ſerviit artibus, ſemper inter arma ac ſtudia verſatus, aut corpus periculis, aut animum diſciplinis exercuit. *Vel. Paterc. lib.* 1. *c.*12, & 13. Vid. *Excerpta Polybii.* Itaque ſemper Africanus Socraticum Xenophontem in manibus habebat, cujus imprimis laudabat illud, quod diceret, eoſdem labores non eſſe æque graveis imperatori ac militi, quod ipſe honos laborem leviorem facit imperatorium. *Cic. Tuſc. Quæſ. lib.* 2. *ſub fin.* Tu Videlicet ſolus Vaſis Corinthiis delectaris? Tu illius æris temperationem, tu operum lineamenta ſolertiſſime perſpicis? Hæc Scipio ille non intelligebat, homo doctiſſimus, atque humaniſſimus? Tu ſine ulla bona arte;

fine humanitate, ſine ingenio, ſine literis, intelligis, & judicas ? Vide, ne illa non ſolum temperantia, ſed etiam intelligentia, te, atque iſtos, qui ſe elegantes dici volunt, vicerit. Nam quia, quam pulchra eſſent, intelligebat idcirco exiſtimabat, ea, non ad hominum luxuriem, ſed ad ornatum ſanorum, atque oppidorum eſſe facta, ut poſteris noſtris monumenta religioſa eſſe videantur. *Cic. in Ver. lib.* 4. 44.

(88) Primi quorum quidem opera non vetuſtatis modo gratia viſenda ſunt, clari pictores fuiſſe dicuntur Polygnotus atque Aglaophon, quorum ſimplex color tam ſui ſtudioſos adhuc habet, ut illa prope, rudia ac velut futuræ mox artis primordia, maximis, qui poſt eos extiterunt, auctoribus præferant proprio quodam intelligendi, ut mea opinio fert, ambitu. *Quint. lib.* 12. *c.* 10.

(89) Mr. *Richardſon's.*

L

lection, that the Hiſtory of the Art of Deſigning and Painting can be fully repreſented or learned. Deſcription is not ſufficient ; the beſt Writer cannot poſſibly expreſs all that is to be obſerved and read in ſuch a Series of Examples and Monuments.

It falls on thoſe who doat on Ruſt and Ruins.

QUINTILIAN's Sarcaſm is only levelled againſt thoſe who are ſo blindly devoted to Antiquity, that they can ſee no Charms but in that which is very old ; and fondly doating on Ruſt, Ruins, or bad Workmanſhip, becauſe it hath a certain degree of Antiquity, neglect Works that have real Merit, and from which ſomething that is uſeful may be learned ; on ſuch, in a word, as meaſure things by any other Standard than their Perfection and Uſefulneſs. Monuments of a rude, beginning, or declining Art, deſerve their place, nay are neceſſary in the Hiſtory of an Art ; but merely to collect its firſt groſs, imperfect, abortive Attempts, or its Dregs and Refuſe, without ſeeking after Examples of its higher Improvements, is a Taſte that juſtly provokes to cry out with *Cicero* on the like occaſion, *Quæ eſt autem in hominibus tanta perverſitas, ut, inventis frugibus, glande veſcantur ?*

A few Obſervations on the firſt rude Painters in both Ages. The Moderns from Cimabue *to* Maſſaccio.

I ſhall therefore but juſt make a few Obſervations upon the firſt and earlieſt Notices that we have of Painting amongſt the *Greeks*, and compare them with the Accounts that are given of its Progreſs when the Art was revived in *Italy* ; that is, from *Cimabue* to *Maſſaccio, Mantegna, Antonello* of *Meſſina,* and ſome others, who are reckoned the firſt whoſe Works deſerve attention, on any other account than as Specimens of the low and mean Beginnings of Painting, during all that Period which we may call the Infancy of modern Painting. Hitherto not only Painters work'd in Diſtemper, the Secret of preparing Colours with Oil not being found out ; but their Colouring was ſo imperfect, that they are only ſaid to have marked their Lines with Colours, and are rather reckoned Deſigners than Painters, and but very indifferent Deſigners too. *Maſſaccio* was the firſt who began to obſerve Perſpective, draw with ſome degree of Correctneſs, give any Relief, Life or Motion to his Figures, or colour them agreeably. But after him, eſpecially when the part of painting with Oil-colours was generally known, the Art in all its parts improved very faſt, and went on daily gathering new Strength, till at laſt Colouring was perfected by *Titian,* and Deſign by *Michael Angelo* ; and *Raphael,* as it were, infuſed its Soul into this fine Body, by ſuperadding Beauty and Grace to what they had formed and ſhaped in perfection. As for *Cimabue,* he was of the ſame kind with the groſs and ignorant Painters, ſent for by the Government of *Florence,* under whom he ſtudied. *Giotto* began indeed to ſhake off ſomewhat of the Rudeneſs and Stiffneſs of theſe *Greeks :* He endeavoured to give better Airs to his Heads, and more of Nature to his Colouring, with ſomething like Action in his Figures : He attempted likewiſe to repreſent the Paſſions ; but he fell far ſhort, not only of true Expreſſion, but of that Livelineſs of the Eyes, that Tenderneſs of the Fleſh, and that Strength of the Muſcles in real Life, which was afterwards attained to by the great Maſters in their Pictures. This was the low State of Painting in his time ; and all the Maſters after him (till *Maſſaccio*) made but ſmall Improvements ; ſo that the Art continued almoſt at a ſtand for a Century, or at leaſt it advanced but ſlowly. Now as it is natural to think that the Art muſt have begun, and advanced in like manner (90), very ſlowly at every Period of it ; when it was firſt found out ; or when at any time, after having been loſt and buried, it roſe again as it were from the dead : ſo we have almoſt the ſame Accounts of a certain Succeſſion of Painters in *Greece* from *Ardices* to *Cimon Cleonæus,* who is deſcribed to have been the beſt of them. And it is only in the Characters given of theſe Artiſts, that we find the Beginnings of Painting deſcribed by ancient Writers. They alſo ſeem to have been rather Deſigners than Painters, and but very indifferent Deſigners too. Nay the Art appears to have been in a more imperfect State in their time, than in that of *Giotto* and his immediate Succeſſors : For before *Ardices* of *Corinth* (91), *Telephanes* of *Sicyon,* and *Crato* of the ſame City, Painting was no better than what ſerved juſt to repreſent the bare Shadow of a Man, or any Animal ; which was done by circumſcribing the Figure they intended to expreſs, whatever it was, with a ſingle Line only ; a ſimple manner of Drawing called *Sciographia.* They began to add new Lines (by way of Shadowing to their Figures) which gave them ſome appearance of Roundneſs, and a little more Strength. And this manner was called *Graphice :* But ſo imperfect ſtill was this way of delineating Objects, that they found it not unneceſſary to write under every Piece, the Name of what it was deſigned to repreſent. It was *Cleophantus* a *Corinthian* who firſt attempted to fill up his Out-lines : But that he did with one ſingle Colour laid on every where alike ; whence his Pieces and thoſe of *Hygiemon, Dinias* and *Charmas* got the Name of *Mono-chromata,* or

The Art began the ſame way in Greece.

The firſt rude Painters or rather Deſigners in Greece.

Pictures

---

(90) It muſt be ſo with reſpect to all Arts. So *Lucretius* obſerves :

  Navigia, atque agriculturas, mœnia, leges,
  Arma, vias, veſteis, & cætera de genere horum,
  Præmia, delicias quoque vitæ funditus omneis,
  Carmina, picturas, & dædala figna polire
  Uſus, & impigris ſimul experientia mentis
  Paulatim docuit pedetentim progredientis.
  Sic unum quidquid paulatim protrahit ætas
  In medium, ratioque in luminis eruit oras.

  Namque aliud ex alio clareſcere corde videbunt
  Artibus, ad ſummum donec venére cacumen.
                                        Lucret. L. 5. ſub finem.

(91) Primi exercuere Ardices Corinthius, & Telephanes Sicyonius, ſine ullo etiamnum hi colore ; jam tamen ſpargentes lineas intus ; ideo & quos pingerent ad_ ſcribere inſtitutum. Primus invenit eos colores, teſtâ ut ferunt, trita, Cleophantus Corinthius.

Pictures of one Colour (92) : Some little Improvements were made by *Eumarus* ; but he was excelled by *Cimon Cleonæus*, who is said to have found out the Art of Painting historically, and to have designed his Figures in variety of Postures : He was the first who distinguished the Joints and Muscles in Bodies, and attempted to imitate the Folds in Draperies ; yet the highest Encomium given even to him by *Ælian* and others, is, that he found Painting in its mere Infancy ; in a very weak imperfect State, and brought it to some small degree of Strength and Perfection.   And thus we see how the Art hath always begun and advanced.

THE question is, how to fix the Age of these Painters or Designers.   For *Panænus* and *Polygnotus* (93) are the first amongst the *Greeks* of any uninterrupted Succession of good Painters that can be distinctly traced, who seem to have been equal to *Massaccio*, *Mantegna*, &c. amongst the Moderns.   But the Art could not have arrived all at once to such a degree of Perfection as is ascribed to them ; it is contrary to the natural Course of things to suppose it ; and therefore they must have had some immediate Predecessors, as *Massaccio* had, by whom the Art was a little improved and advanced ; yet those Mo-nochromatists were long before them, and no others are named in History as the first Essayers of the Art, or who had not arrived at very considerable Perfection.   It is upon this Principle, that no Art is invented and perfected at once, and that according to the nature of things Painting, like other Arts, must have advanced gradually, and from very small Beginnings to any very considerable Pitch of Excellence : 'Tis upon this Principle, which can bear no dispute, that *Pliny* blames the *Greeks* for not being more exact in their Accounts of their Painters ; since it is impossible that *Panænus* could have been so good a Painter, or that the Art could have been in so great a degree of Perfection in his time, as it appears to have been, if it had not been very much cultivated before him.   What is more, we are told by *Pliny* and others, that there were very excellent Painters long before *Panænus*.   There is mention made of a celebrated Battle-piece by *Bularchus* a Painter, for which *Candaules* King of *Lydia*, the last of the *Heraclides*, gave a very high Price (94).   And *Pliny* speaks of excellent Pictures in *Italy*, which tho' fresh in his time, were older than the Foundation of *Rome*, and painted by *Grecians* (95).   From all which he very justly concludes, that these very rude imperfect Painters, or rather Monochromatists, must have been long before those good Painters.

WHAT then can we with any probability infer from all this, but that, setting aside the Arguments which have been brought from *Homer's* exact Knowledge of Painting, to prove its very great Antiquity, that Art must have been very anciently in great Reputation and Per-fection ; and that it may have undergone many Revolutions in *Greece*, or have been lost and revived again there, perhaps more than once : But this I leave to others to determine. It is sufficient to our purpose to observe, that at whatever time it begun to be cultivated, it must in all probability have begun and proceeded, as it did when it was revived in *Italy* in the latter Age of it, by very ordinary low *Greek* Painters, from *Cimabue* their Disciple to *Massaccio* ; or as it did in the time of the *Greek* Monochromatists that have been men-tioned.   And we find it advancing from a *Massaccio* to a *Raphael*, in the same manner that it did from *Panænus* to an *Apelles*, with wonderful Celerity.

'Tis difficult to fix the Age of these Greek Painters.

But Panænus seems the first of a Succession of Painters a-mong the Ancients, equal to Massaccio among the Moderns.

Pliny mentions very old good Pictures.

What it is reasonable to conclude from all this.

The Art at what-ever Period it began, or revived, advanced to Perfection very gradually.

TO

(92) Quod si recipi necesse est, simul adparet multo vetustiora principia esse ; eosque, qui Monochromata pinxerint, quorum ætas non traditur, aliquanto ante fuisse Hygiemonem, Dineam, Charmadem, & qui pri-mus in pictura Marem Feminamque discreverit, Euma-rum Atheniensem, figuras omnis imitari ausum ; quique inventa ejus excoluerit, Cimonem Cleonæum. Hic Ca-tagrapha invenit, hoc est, obliquas imagines & varie for-mare vultus, respicientes, suspicientesque, vel despicien-tes ; Articulis membra distinxit ; Venas protulit ; præ-terque in Veste Rugas & Sinus invenit. *Plin.* 35. Ci-mon Cleonæus artem adhuc rudem plurimum provexit, eoque discipulos suos majorem popofcit mercedem quam priores artifices. *Æl. var. Hist. l.* 8. *c.* 8.   In the An-thology there are two *Greek* Epigrams on him ; one of which is thus translated by *Grotius* : .

Ista Cimon pinxit minime rudis ; omne sed est qui
   Culpet opus : Nec tu, Dædale, liber erat.

'Tis in allusion to these Monochromata that *Cicero* plea-santly calls *Epicurus's* Gods Dii Monogrammi, non enim venis, & nervis, & ossibus continentur,——Nec iis cor-poribus sunt, ut aut casus aut ictus extimescant, aut mor-bos metuant ex defatigatione membrorum. Quæ verens Epicurus Monogrammos Deos & nihil agentes commen-tus est. *Cic. de Nat. Deor. lib.* 2.

(93) Panænus quidem frater Phidiæ, etiam prælium Atheniensium adversum Persas, apud Marathona factum, pinxit : adeoque jam colorum usus increbuerat, adeoque ars perfecta erat ut in eo prælio Iconicos duces pinxisse tradatur,——Primusque omnium certavit cum Timagora Chalcidense——alii quoque, post hos, clari fuere, sicut Polygnotus Thasius, qui primus mulieres lucida Veste

pinxit : Capita earum mitris versicoloribus operuit ; plu-rimumque pictura primus contulit. *Plin.* 35.

(94) In confesso perinde est Bularchi pictoris tabulam in qua erat Magnetum prælium, a Candaule rege Lydiæ Heraclidarum novissimo, qui & Myrcilus vocitatus est, repensam auro. Tanta jam dignatio picturæ erat, id circa ætatem Romuli acciderit necesse est : duo enim de vicesima Olympiade interiit Candaules ; aut, ut quidam tradunt, eodem anno quo Romulus, nisi fallor ; mani-festa jam tum claritate artis, atque absolutione. Quod si recipi necesse est, simul adparet multo vetustiora princi-pia esse, &c. *Plin.* 35.

(95) Hunc, (Cleophantum Corinthium) aut eodem nomine alium fuisse, quem tradit Cornelius Nepos secu-tum in Italiam Demaratum Tarquinii Prisci regis Romani patrem, fugientem a Corintho tyranni injurias Cypseli mox docebimus. Jam enim absoluta erat pictura etiam in Italia. Extant certe hodieque antiquiores urbe pic-turæ, Ardeæ in ædibus sacris : quibus equidem nullas æque miror tam longo ævo durantis in orbitate tecti, veluti recentis, &c. *Plin.* 35.   When he comes to men-tion the *Roman* Painters in the same Book, he says, De-cet non fileri & Ardeatis templi pictorem, præsertim ci-vitate donatum ibi, & carmine, quod est in ipsa pictura his versibus :

Dignis. Digna. Loca. Picturis. Condecoravit.
Reginæ. Junoni. Supremi. Conjugi. Templum.
Marcus. Ludius. Elotas. Ætolia. Oriundus.
Quem. Nunc. Et. Post. Semper. Ob. Artem. Hanc. Ardea
                              Laudat.
Ea sunt scripta antiquis literis Latinis. See *Julii Bulen-geri de Pictura & Statuaria lib.* 1. *c.* 9.

All that hath been said confirmed from Cicero and Quintilian in their Accounts of the like Progress of Oratory to that of Statuary and Painting.

'TO confirm the Truth of all that hath been said of the gradual Improvements that were made in Painting, and of the various Talents of its chief Improvers amongst the *Greeks*, I shall bring some Passages from *Cicero* and *Quintilian*, which contain the Substance of what hath been said on that Head, and that will serve to prove, at the same time, the Truth of the Observation, upon the manner in which these Authors have treated Oratory, premised to this Discourse.

Quintilian.

" IT remains [says *Quintilian* (96)] to speak of all the several kinds of Oratory, that
" being the third Branch of my first Division; for I promised to treat of the Art, the
" Artist, and the Work. Oration is the Orator's Work: And there are many Forms of
" it, as I shall prove; which, tho' the Art and Artist appear in them all, are very distinct,
" not only in Species, as one Statue or Picture is from another; but even in kind, as the
" *Tuscan* and *Grecian* Statues; or the *Asiatick* and *Athenian* Orators. These however
" which I call Works of a different kind, as they have their Authors, so likewise they have
" their Lovers; and there is no such thing yet as a perfect Orator, nor perhaps any per-
" fect Art of whatever sort; not only because each kind hath some peculiar Excellency,
" but because one Manner is not equally agreeably to all; and that partly on account of
" the various Genius's of Times, and partly because each particular Person hath his own
" proper Taste and Aim. The first Painters whose Works are visited not barely for Anti-
" quity's sake are *Polygnotus* and *Aglaophon*, whose imperfect Colouring some, thro' an
" Affectation of appearing more than ordinary Judges, prefer to the Works of the great
" Masters who came afterwards, tho'. their Pictures were but the Presages, the first Dawn-
" ing of a rising Art. After them flourished *Zeuxis* and *Parrhasius*, both about the *Pe-
" loponnesian* War; for *Xenophon* gives us a Conference between the latter and *Socrates*.
" These Artists greatly improved Painting; the first having found out the Art of distribu-
" ting Light and Shade with Truth and Agreeablenss; the other excelling in the Precision
" of his Out-line, and the Elegance of his Colours; *Zeuxis* copied *Homer*, and so be-
" came to the succeeding Painters a Model, whom it was necessary to imitate in drawing
" the Forms of the Gods and Heroes. The Art of Painting was in its highest Perfection
" about the time of *Philip*, and to the Successors of *Alexander*; but the various Qualities
" requisite to its Perfection were divided amongst many Professors. To *Protogenes* is
" ascribed Exactness in finishing, or rather Over-diligence. To *Pamphilus* and *Melanthius*
" a thorough Intelligence and Observance of Symmetry and due Proportions in their Fi-
" gures; to *Antiphilus* Facility or Ease; and to *Theon* the *Samian* a vast Fertility of Ima-
" gination even to Capriciousness. To *Apelles* is unanimously allowed what he claimed,
" Ingenuity and Grace far superiour to all that went before him: And *Euphranor* was
" highly admired for what is indeed very rare; for he was not only an excellent Painter,
" but a great Master of many other Arts; a Sculptor of the first Rank, as well as a sub-
" lime Painter.

" THE same Progress, with the same Diversity of Talents happened in Statuary. For the
" first Professors of that Art, *Calon* and *Egesius* did not far surpass the *Tuscans*, but were
" almost as stiff and hard: The Statues of *Calamis* were not so cold and dead; but those
" of *Mycon* were still much softer and nearer to Life: *Polycletus* added at once Correct-
" ness and Grace to his: To him is the Pre-eminence given; but that he too might not pass
" uncensured, Force and Energy is said to have been wanting to make his Works perfect.
" He represented Men with more Grace than is to be found in Nature: But he could not
" come up to the Majesty of the Gods; not daring to attempt any thing but soft and beard-
" less Cheeks, he avoided imitating venerable Age. But what was wanting in *Polycletus* is
" ascribed to *Phidias* and *Alcamenes*. *Phidias* excelled whether in exhibiting Gods or
" Men: None rivalled him in working in Ivory, as his *Minerva* of *Athens* and his *Olym-
" pian Jupiter* sufficiently prove; the last of which is said to have increased the religious
" Awe of the People, so fully was the Authority of the God expressed. *Lysippus* and
" *Praxiteles* were the best Copiers of Nature, for *Demetrius* studied Truth more than
" Beauty; he followed Nature too strictly.

" NOW

(96) Superest ut dicam de genere orationis. Hic erat propositus a nobis in divisione prima locus tertius: nam ita promiseram me de arte, de artifice, de opere dicturum. Cum sit autem rhetoris atque oratoris opus oratio, pluresque ejus forma, sicut ostendam, in omnibus his & ars est, & artifex, plurimum tamen invicem differunt, nec solum specie, ut signum signo, & tabula tabulæ, & actione actio, sed genere ipso, ut a Græcis Tuscanicæ statuæ, & Asianus eloquens Attico. Suos autem hæc operum genera quæ dico, ut autores, sic amatores habent, atque ideo nondum est perfectus orator, ac nescio an ars ulla, non solum quia aliud in alio magis eminet, sed quod non una omnibus forma placuit, partim conditione vel temporum, vel locorum, partim judicio cujusque ac proposito.—— Similis in statuis differentia: nam & duriora, & Tuscanicis proxima Calon atque Egesias; jam minus frigida calamis; molliora adhuc supra dictis Myron fecit. Diligentia ac Decor in Polycleto supra cæteros, cui quan-

quam a plerisque tribuetur palma, tamen ne nihil detrahatur, deesse pondus putant. Nam ut humanæ formæ decorem addiderit supra Verum, ita non explevisse Deorum autoritatem Videtur, quin ætatem quoque graviorem dicitur refugisse, nihil ausus ultra leves genas. At quæ Polycleto defuerunt, Phidiæ atque Alcameni dantur. Phidias tam diis quam hominibus efficiendis melior artifex traditur. In ebore Vero longe citra æmulum, vel si nihil nisi Minervam Athenis, aut Olympium in Elide Jovem fecisset, cujus pulchritudo adjecisse aliquid etiam receptæ religioni Videtur, adeo majestas operis Deum æquavit. Ad veritatem Lysippum & Praxitelem accepisse optimè affirmant. Nam Demetrius tanquam nimius in ea reprehenditur, & fuit similitudinis quam pulchritudinis amantior. In oratione Vero si species intueri Velis, totidem pene reperies ingeniorum, quot corporum formas, sed fuerunt quædam genera dicendi conditione temporum horridiora, alioquin magnam jam vim ingenii

Quintilian.

" NOW Oratory advanced in like manner: If we examine the different Kinds or
" Forms of it, we shall find almost as many Genius's and Turns of Mind as of Features and
" Complexions : Some sorts of Oratory, as well as of Painting and Statuary, were more
" unformed in consequence of the Rudeness and Unpoliteness of the times; but even these
" shewed great Strength and Vigour of Genius. Such were amongst us (*Romans*) the
" *Lælii*, the *Africani*, the *Cato's*, the *Gracchi*. Those may be called the *Polygnotius's*,
" and the *Calones* : Let *L. Crassus* and *Q. Hortensius* be placed in the middle Rank. After
" them arose a vast Growth of excellent Orators; but who had each his distinct Talents and
" Perfections, tho' they flourish'd much about the same time.———In *Cæsar* we admire the
" Nervous, in *Brutus* the Severe, in *Callidius* the Subtile, in *Cassius* the Bitter, in *Pollio* Cor-
" rectness, in *Sulpitius* Smartness, in *Messala* Dignity, in *Calvus* the Pure and Venerable.——
" Even in those I have seen; we commend the Fertility of *Seneca*, the Strength of *Africanus*,
" the mature Judgment of *Afrus*, the Sweetness of *Crispus*, the Elegance of *Secundus*,
" and the harmonious Cadences of *Trachalus*. As for *M. Tullius* he was not merely a
" *Euphranor* eminent in many Qualities; but in him were united, in their highest degree,
" all the Perfections which distinguish'd or gain'd a Name to any other.———Yet some even
" of his Contemporaries blamed him, calling him the *Asiatick*, as too pompous, swoln and
" redundant."

Cicero.

CICERO gives us a shorter account of the gradual Progress of the Arts of Design, almost to the same effect, and with the like view, in order to illustrate the parallel Advancement of Eloquence. " Who (saith he) that is conversant in Antiquity, doth not know
" that the Statues of *Canachus* were lame and too stiff? Those of *Calamis* were not so
" hard and rigid, but nearer to Life and softer : *Myron's* are justly pronounced beautiful,
" yet they were not quite Nature. Those of *Polycletus* are much more natural and lively,
" and indeed, in my Opinion, perfect. Painting improved in the same way; and the
" Painters who brought the Art to its Perfection, rose above one another by like steps.
" For, in that Art, do we not admire the drawing and specious Appearances in the Pic-
" tures of *Zeuxis*, *Polygnotus* and *Timanthes*, who employed but four Colours? And
" is not all perfect in *Ætion, Nicomachus, Protogenes*, and *Apelles* ? And may I not
" say, that the same happens throughout all the Arts, and indeed throughout all Nature?
" 'Tis not to be doubted but there were Poets before *Homer*, whom none afterwards
" could rival.——Our own first Productions in Poetry were as rude and stiff as the Statues
" of *Dædalus*.——And so it was likewise with regard to our Oratory."

Cicero.

. IN another place *Cicero* remarks, that there is the same Diversity in the Arts of Speaking and Painting (97) : And that in either of these, amidst a great variety of Forms and Manners, each of which is very commendable in its kind, or hath its particular Excellence, it
is not easy to determine which is the best. Painting, saith he, tho' the Art be but one,
yet like every Art and every Thing in Nature, admits of a great variety of Beauties and
Perfections (98) : And therefore Painters, as well as Orators, may be very different from one
another; and yet all of them may deserve high praise, and be justly pronounced admirable, each in his own peculiar Sphere and Excellence. There is indeed a best, a highest
Perfection in every Art, a supreme Beauty to which it is extremely hard to reach; and
which was never compassed by any Orator, Poet, or Painter, in any Production however
perfect,

ingenii præ se ferentia. Hinc sunt Lælii, Africani,
Catones, Gracchique, quos tu licet Polygnotos vel Calones appelles. Mediam illam formam teneant L. Craf-
sus, Q. Hortensius. Tum deinde efflorescat non multum
inter se distantium tempore, oratorum ingens proventus,
hinc vim Cæsaris, indolem Cœlii, subtilitatem Callidii,
gravitatem Bruti, acumen Sulpitii, acerbitatem Cassii,
diligentiam Pollionis, dignitatem Messalæ, sanctitatem
Calvi reperimus. In his etiam quos ipsi vidimus, copiam
Senecæ, vires Africani, maturitatem Afri, jucunditatem
Crispi, sonum Trachali, elegantiam Secundi. At M.
Tullium non illum habemus Euphranorem circa plurium
artium species præstantem : sed in omnibus quæ in quoque laudantur, eminentissimum, quem tamen & suorum
temporum homines incessere audebant ut tumidiorem ; &
Asianum, & redundantem, & in repetitionibus nimium,
&c. *Quint. l. 12.* Quis enim eorum, qui hæc minora
animadvertunt, non intelligit, Canachi signa, rigidiora
esse, quam ut imitentur veritatem? Calamidis dura illa
quidem, sed tamen molliora, quam Canachi. Nondum
Myronis satis ad veritatem adducta, jam tamen quæ non
dubites pulchra dicere. Pulchriora etiam Polycleti, &
jam plane perfecta, ut mihi quidem videri solent. Similis in pictura ratio est, in qua Zeuxim, & Polygnotum,
& Timantem, & eorum qui non sunt usi plus quam quatuor coloribus formas & lineamenta laudamus. At in
Ætione, Nicomacho, Protogene, Apelle, jam perfecta
sunt omnia, & nescio an reliquis in rebus omnibus idem
eveniat. Nihil est enim simul & inventum, & perfectum. Nec dubitari debet quin fuerint ante Homerum
poetæ, &c. *Cic. de clar. Orat.* 18.

enim sunt judicia, ut in Græcis : nec facilis explicatio,
quæ forma maxime excellat. In picturis alios horrida,
inculta, abdita, & opaca : contra alios nitida, læta, col-
lustrata delectat. Quid est, quo præscriptum aliquod,
aut formulam exprimas, cum in suo quodque genere
præstet, & genera plura sint ? Hac ego religione non
sum ab hoc conatu repulsus : Existimavique, in omnibus rebus esse aliquid optimum, etiam si lateret : idque
ab eo posse, qui ejus rei gnarus esset, judicari. Sed quoniam plura sunt orationum genera, eaque diversa, neque
in unam formam cadunt omnia, &c.

(98) Natura nulla est (ut mihi videtur) quæ non habeat in suo genere res complureis dissimileis inter se, quæ
tamen consimili laude dignentur. Nam & auribus multa
percipimus, quæ etsi nos vocibus delectant, tamen ita
sunt Varia sæpe, ut id quod proximum audias, jucundis-
simum esse Videatur : & oculis colliguntur pene innume-
rabiles voluptates, quæ nos ita capiunt, ut unum sensum
dissimili genere delectent, & reliquos sensus voluptates ob-
lectent dispares, ut sit difficile judicium excellentis maxime suavitatis. At hoc idem quod est in naturis rerum,
transferri potest etiam ad arteis. Una fingendi est ars,
in qua præstantes fuerunt Myro, Polycletus, Lysippus :
qui omnes inter se dissimiles fuerunt : sed ita tamen, ut
neminem sui Velis esse dissimilem. Una est ars, ratioque
picturæ, dissimillimique tamen inter se Zeuxis, Aglaophon, Apelles : neque eorum quisquam est, cui quidquam
in arte sua deesse Videatur. Et, si hoc in his quasi mutis
artibus est mirandum, & tamen Verum : quanto admirabilius in oratione, atque in lingua ? &c. *Cicero de Orat.
lib. 3. 7.*

(97) *Cicero ad Brutum.* 11.——Fac alium Attio, varia

M

Cicero.

perfect, to such a degree as came up fully to the Idea of it in the Mind of the Author or Artist. But the ingenious Arts flourish, prosper, and bring forth a goodly rich Harvest of various Fruits, all exceeding beautiful, and pleasant, though of different Hues and Qualities, when due Honour is render'd to every Person of Merit, and to every Advancement toward Perfection of whatever sort; not to those of the first Class alone, but to the second and third, to each kind, Order or Rank of Ability and Excellence (99). Thus every Genius, every Virtue, every Power in the Soul is quickened to exert itself, and every one strives to his utmost, giving all diligence to excel, in something truly praise-worthy. The genuine Spirit, that alone can animate and fructify the Arts, is by such means stirred up, and maintained in due Warmth and Vigour. Every one becomes emulous of surpassing the rest in some Perfection : No one satisfies himself with his Attainments, and the honour these may have already acquired him; but takes a higher Mark, and imagining somewhat of a more perfect kind than he hath hitherto produced, sets himself with all his collected Talents to surpass his own most admired Works. Success duly honoured redoubles the Force and Ardour of the Mind.

Cicero and Columella.

THIS is the Picture *Columella, Cicero,* and other ancient Authors have drawn, of the Temper and Spirit by which alone the Virtues and Arts can be promoted and animated (100). And thus it was, they tell us, with respect to Painting, Poetry, Oratory, and all the ingenious Arts, when they flourished in *Greece.* Hence it came about, that tho' *Demosthenes* far excelled all the Orators, as *Apelles* all the Painters; yet there were a great many other justly renowned Orators and Painters, besides these two, who had very great and peculiar Abilities and Excellencies. The same happened in the latter Age of Painting; the like Spirit pushed it on to its Perfection at that Period; so that tho' *Raphael* was superiour to all, yet there were many other Painters who deserved high Praises, and had each very great and distinguishing Qualifications.

Cicero.

CICERO tells us what that supreme Beauty and Excellence in all the Arts is, which it is so difficult to explain, and yet more to acquire (101) : It is called by the *Greeks* το πρέπον; and we may call it with the *Romans* the Decorum. It is the chief Excellence (saith he) in Life and Manners, as well as in the Arts. But of this afterwards. What is now under Consideration is the equal and analogous Advancement of Painting, in two different Ages of it, and the principal Means and Causes by which it was promoted to so great Perfection in both. And doubtless the Emulation among Painters arising from the Love of the Art, and the Encouragement given to every Kind and Degree of Merit in it, by the Rewards and Honours that were chearfully conferred on all who excelled in any part of the Profession, was one chief reason of its Improvement in both these Periods.

PAINT-

(99) Quod fiquem aut natura sua, aut illa præstantis ingenii vis forte deficiet, aut minus instructus erit magnarum artium disciplinis : teneat tamen eum cursum quem poterit. Prima enim sequentem, honestum est in secundis, tertiisque consistere. Nam in poetis, non Homero soli locus est (ut de Græcis loquar) aut Archilocho, aut Sophocli, aut Pindaro : sed horum vel secundis, vel etiam infra secundos. Nec vero Aristotelem in philosophia deterruit a scribendo amplitudo Platonis : nec ipse Aristoteles admirabili quadam scientia, & copia, cæterorum studia restinxit. Nec solum ab optimis studiis excellentes Viri deterriti non sunt, sed ne opifices quidem se artibus suis removerunt, aut Ialysi quem Rhodi Vidimus, non potuerunt, aut Coæ Veneris pulchritudinem imitari. Nec sim ulacro Jovis Olympii, aut Doryphori statua deterriti, reliqui minus experti sunt, quid efficere, aut quo progredi possent : quorum tanta multitudo fuit, tanta in suo cujusque genere laus, ut, cum summa miraremur, inferiora tamen probaremus. In oratoribus vero, Græcis quidem, admirabile est quantum inter omneis unus excellat. Attamen, cum esset Demosthenes, multi oratores, magni, & clari fuerunt, & antea fuerant, nec postea defecerunt. Quare non est eur eorum, qui se studio eloquentiæ dediderunt, spes infringatur, aut languescat industria. Nam neque illud ipsum, quod est optimum, desperandum est : & in præstantibus rebus, magna sunt ea, quæ sunt optimis proxima. *Ad Brut. 2.*

(100) Rectissime dixit M. Tullius in oratore, par est eos, qui generi humano res utilissimas conquirere, & perpensas exploratasque memoriæ tradere concupiverint cuncta tentare.——Summum enim culmen affectantes, satis honeste vel in secundo fastigio conspiciemur. An Latiæ musæ non solos Adytis suis Accium & Virgilium recepere, sed eorum & proximis, & procul a secundis sacras concessere sedes ? Nec Brutum, aut Cœlium, Pollionemque cum Messala & Catulo deterruere ab eloquentiæ studio fulmina illa Ciceronis. Nam neque ille ipse Cicero territus cesserat tonantibus Demostheni Platonique. Nec parens eloquentiæ, Deus ille Mæonius, vastissimis fluminibus facundiæ suæ posteritatis studia restinxerat, ac ne minoris quidem famæ opifices per tot jam sæcula videmus

laborem suum destituisse, qui Protogenem & Apellem cum Parrhasio mirati sunt : Nec pulchritudine Jovis Olympii Minervæque Phidiacæ, sequentis ætatis attonitos piguit experiri, Bryaxin, Lysippum, Praxitelem, Polycletum, quid efficere aut quousque progredi possent. Sed in omni genere scientiæ, & summis admiratio Veneratioque, & Inferioribus merita laus contingit. *Colum. in Præf. lib. 1^{mi}. & Re Rust.* Nequeo temperare mihi, quin rem sæpe agitatam animo, neque ad liquidum ratione perductam, signem stylo. Quis enim abunde mirari potest, quod eminentissima cujusque professionis ingenia, in eandem formam & idem ætati temporis congruant spatium, & quemadmodum clausa capsa, alioque septo, diversi generis animalia, nihilominus separata alienis, in unum quæque corpus congregantur ; ita cujusque clari operis capacia ingenia, in similitudinem & temporum & professuum, semetipsa ab aliis seperaverint ? Hoc evenisse tragicis, comicis, philosophis, historicis, grammaticis, plastis, pictoribus, sculptoribus, ut quisque temporum inititerit notis, reperiet eminentia cujusque operis artissimis temporum claustris circumdata. Hujus ergo præcedentisque sæculi ingeniorum similitudines congregantis & in studium par & in emolumentum, causas cum semper requiro, nunquam reperio quas Veras esse confidam, sed fortasse versimilis, inter quas has maxime. Alit æmulatio ingenia ; & nunc invidia, nunc admiratio incitationem accendit ; maturesque, quod summo studio petitum est, ascendit in summum, difficilisque in perfecto mora est ; naturaliterque quod procedere non potest, recedit. *Vel. Pat. Hist. lib. 1. cap. 16, 17.*

(101) Sed est eloquentiæ, sicut reliquarum rerum fundamentum, sapientia. Ut enim in vita, sic in oratione, nihil est difficilius, quam, quid deceat, Videre. πρέπον appellant hoc Græci : Nos dicamus sane decorum. De quo præclare, & multa præcipiuntur, & res est cognitione dignissima. Hujus Ignoratione non modo in vita, sed sæpissime & in poematis, & in oratione peccatur. After some Explication of this Decorum, he remarks how much *Apelles* and *Timanthes* observed it. *Cic. ad M. Brut. Orat. 21.*

PAINTING flourifhed (faith *Pliny*) and produced truly noble and excellent Works, Pliny. while the Art was duly countenanced and recompenfed; being in high requeft amongft Princes, Rulers, and all great Men (102). And was it not fo likewife in the latter Age of Painting, was not the Art in high Reputation amongft Popes, Princes, Cardinals, and all the Great and Powerful of that Age? What Honours and Rewards were not moft willingly paid to all the great Maiters; to the Art in general, and to all its Students and Profeffors? Honour (faith *Cicero*) enlivens and cherifhes the Arts: They droop and languifh when they are not duly efteemed and encouraged (103). Ambition and Emulation are the very Soul of the Arts, without which they are timid, fluggifh, inactive, and dare not look up towards Perfection.

OF Emulation and its happy Effects, in confequence of the Honours beftowed upon in- *Of different Schools* genious Artifts, we have many Inftances in both the Ages now under our Examination (104). *among the Ancients,* There was not only an ardent Rivalfhip and Competition amongft all the greateft Mafters, *as well as among* each exerting his utmoft to be the firft, or at leaft not to be the laft; but, which is a Cir- *the Moderns.* cumftance well worth obferving in this Parallel, in both thefe Ages of Painting, there were different Schools of that Art, each of which had its particular Tafte, and favourite Excel- lence, upon which it valued itfelf, and for which it claimed fuperiour Fame to all the reft. And this Emulation amongft different Schools had a ftronger and more extenfive Influence, *The Emulation that* to promote the Art in all its Qualities and Parts, than Rivalfhip betwixt particular Perfons *proceeded from* could poffibly have had. The Honour and Name of the School to which each Mafter *thence.* owed his Education, and was particularly attached, became an additional Incentive to him, and confpiring with his defire of private Glory, made his Efforts to improve fo much more warm and zealous, as they were indeed by this means more generous: For to gain Fame to a Body or Society is certainly a more noble and enlarged View, than that defire of Efteem which looks not beyond one's felf; and confequently is a Motive of double force, and excites to proportionally greater Enterprizes.

AS in the latter Age of Painting the *Florentine*, the *Lombard*, and the *Roman* Schools were in vigorous Emulation, while, at the fame time, every Mafter in each School vied with all the reft of his Affociates, and ftrove to be the firft in Fame of his own School; fo it likewife happened in the firft Age of Painting, in which there were likewife different Schools, almoft from the very firft Origin of the Art. Thefe different Schools had com- munication with one another, the Tafte, Works, and Excellencies of each were known to all the reft, and they reciprocally profited by one another.

THE chief Schools in ancient Times were at *Sicyon*, *Rhodes*, *Corinth* and *Athens*; and all thefe produced great Mafters, and contended warmly for the Victory and Pre-emi- nence (105). It was *Eupompus* of *Sicyon*, an excellent Artift, (faith *Pliny*) whofe Autho- rity was fo confiderable, that, whereas before him there were only two Schools of Painting, the *Afiatick* and the *Greek*, three were from that time diftinguifhed, the *Attick*, *Sicyonian* and *Ionick* (106). Now in like manner, in the time of the *Bellini*, two Schools were eftablifhed in *Italy*, which were remarkably different from one another. The one was the School of *Venice*, and of all *Lombardy*, the other of *Florence*, and of *Rome*. For though, even then, there was a very confiderable difference between the Painters of *Florence* and thofe of *Rome*; yet it was not till *Raphael's* time, that the School of *Rome* acquired its beft Manner, and proved like the *Athenian* of old under *Apelles*, the moft perfect and excellent of them all.

IT is not eafy, from the Accounts we have of the different ancient Schools and Mafters, to form a decifive Notion of the particular Tafte of each, or to clafs the ancient Mafters
according

(102) Primumque dicemus de pictura: Arte quondam nobili, cum expeteretur a regibus, populifque, & illos nobilitante, quos effet dignata pofteris tradere. *Plin.* 35. *ab init.*

(103) An cenfemus, fi Fabio, nobiliffimo homini, laudi datum effet, quod pingeret, non multos etiam apud nos futuros Polycletos & Parrhafios fuiffe? Honos alit arteis, omnefque incenduntur ad ftudia gloriâ: jacentque ea femper, quæ apud quofque improbantur. *Cic. Tufc. Quæf. lib.* 1. *ab init.*

(104) We have already taken notice of the Competition between *Zeuxis* and *Apollodorus*, *Apelles* and *Protogenes*, *Timanthes* and *Parrhofus*; fee the Effects of it in *Plutarch's* Life of *Pericles*, by whom *Phidias* was appointed Super- intendant of the Works at *Athens.*

(105) Rhodiorum pietati dedit hoc Minerva, ut omnis generis fimulacra fcientiffime fabricarent; propterea quod mortalium primi aram ftruxerunt apud fe natæ. See the Scholiaft upon *Pindar. Olymp. Od.* 7. *Pliny* fpeaking of *Sicyon* fays, Diu fuit illa patria pictura, *lib.* 35. *c.* 5. Maxime Sicyone & Corinthi adauctum eft pingendi fin- gendique & omne hujufmodi artificium. *Strab. Geog. lib.* 8. De Corintho teftatur Orofius, *lib.* 5. *c.* 3. Quod

per multa retro fæcula velut officina omnium artificum, atque artificiorum fuit, & emporium commune Afiæ & Europæ. Florebat adhuc gloria Sicyoniæ doctrinæ atque elegantioris picturæ, tanquam quæ fola priftinum fplen- dorem refervaffet illibatum. Quapropter etiam Apelles ille, apud omnes jam habitus in fumma admiratione, non dubitavit eo proficifci ac Sicyoniorum artificum familia- ritem talento emercari; magis e re fua fore judicans ex- iftimationis eorum, quam artis participem fieri. *Plut. in Arato.* Urbs Athenienfium multarum benigna mater & nutrix fuit artium; quarum alias prima reperit & in lucem protulit; aliis honorem, vim, & incrementa con- tulit: Non minimum vero ab hac urbe provecta ornata- que eft ars pingendi. *Plut. Bellone an Pace, &c.* Solon cum videret hominibus quotidie in Atticam undique propter fecuritatem & libertatem confluentibus urbem compleri, —traduxit ad artificia cives, tulitque legem, ne filius pa- rentem, qui ipfum non docuiffet artem, cogeretur alere. *Plutarch. in Solone.*

(106) Eupompi auctoritas tanta fuit, ut diviferit pic- turam in tria genera, quæ ante eum duo fuere, Helladi- cum, & quod Afiaticum adpellabant: propter hunc, qui erat Sicyonius, divifo Helladico tria facta funt; Ionicum, Sicyonium, Atticum. *Plin.* 35.

The Character of the chief ancient and modern Schools.

according to their different Schools, as thofe of the latter Age are commonly ranged. Yet it feems very probable from what hath been faid of them, that they were diftinguifhed very nearly in the fame manner as the Schools of *Rome, Florence,* and *Lombardy* are : The firft of which ftudied Majefty and Grandeur, with Simplicity and Purity : The fecond Fury and Motion : The third Sweetnefs and Agreeablenefs.

How the State of one Art in the fame Country, may be conjectured from that of any other Art in the fame Country and Time.

WE may form this Judgment of the ancient Schools of Painting, from what Writers tell us of the State of the other Arts in thefe Seats of Learning and Politenefs ; of their Oratory in particular. *Cicero* and *Quintilian* give us a particular Account of the diftinguifhing Qualities of the *Afiaticks, Rhodians* and *Athenians* in that refpeft ; correfponding, as they have obferved, to the different Natures and Tempers of each People. And no doubt the fame Differences prevailed with regard to all the other Arts amongft them : The fame Caufes would naturally produce the fame Effefts, or operate in a like manner on them all. Accordingly it hath been often obferved, that wherever the Arts have flourifhed at any time, one may judge of them all from the Charafter and Genius of any one of them. They will all partake of the fame prevailing Temperature or Tafte. The general or national Charafter of a People may be conjeftured from the State of the Arts amongft them : and reciprocally, the State of the Arts amongft any People may be pretty certainly divined from the general, prevalent Temper and Humour of that People, as it difcovers itfelf by other Symptoms in their Government, Laws, Language, Manners, *&c.* (107.)

Of the Emulation promoted by the ancient Contefts.

BUT not to infift longer on this Remark, 'tis univerfally acknowledged, that the publick Contefts and Prizes, in which anciently Painting, Statuary, and all the liberal Arts, as well as the manly Exercifes, had a fhare, contributed exceedingly to fire the Ambition of ingenious Artifts, and to refine and improve the publick Tafte (108). As in Poetry and Eloquence an Audience and Authors mutually improve one another ; fo muft it be likewife with reference to all the other Arts. A good Eye is formed in the fame manner as a good Ear. And therefore when one confiders the Nature of the publick Entertainments and Feftivals throughout *Greece,* at *Athens* more efpecially, in which all the ingenious Arts bore a part, it is no longer matter of wonder that the *Athenians* had ·fuch an univerfal good Tafte in them all ; or that even the Vulgar had a very refined Notion of Painting, and Statuary, as well as Poetry, Eloquence, and every other polite Art.

Lord Shaftefbury *quoted.*

" WHATEVER flourifhed, [fays an incomparable (109) Author] or was raifed to any " degree of Correftnefs or real Perfeftion in any Science or Art, was by means of *Greece* " alone ; and in the hand of that fole, polite, moft civilized and accomplifh'd Nation. " Nor can this appear ftrange when we confider the fortunate Conftitution of that People. " For tho' compofed of different Nations, diftinft in Laws and Governments, divided by " Seas and Continents, difperfed in diftant Iflands ; yet being originally of the fame Ex- " traft, united by the fame Language, and animated by that focial publick free Bent, which, " notwithftanding the Animofity of their feveral warring States, induced them to ereft fuch " heroick Congreffes and Powers as thofe which conftituted the *Amphiftonian* Councils, " the *Olympick, Ifthmian,* and other Games ; they could not but naturally polifh and re- " fine each other. It was thus they brought their beautiful and comprehenfive Language " to a juft Standard, leaving only fuch variety in the Dialefts, as render'd their Poetry in " particular fo much the more agreeable. The Standard was in the fame proportion car- " ried into the other Arts, the feveral Species found, and fet apart ; the Performers and " Mafters in every kind honour'd and admir'd : And laft of all even Criticks themfelves " acknowledged and received as Mafters over all the reft. From Mufick, Poetry, Rheto- " rick, down to the fimple Profe of Hiftory ; through all the plaftick Arts of Sculpture, " Statuary, Painting, Architefture, and the reft ; every thing Mufe-like, graceful and ex- " quifite, was rewarded with the higheft Honour, and carried on with the utmoft Ardour " and Emulation."

Mr. Rollin *quoted.*

THESE publick Conteftations, and the Advantages of them to the Arts and Sciences, have been often confidered. There is a very juft Account of them in Mr. *Rollin*'s univerfal Hiftory from the beft Authorities. And in another excellent Performance of his on Education,

(107) At Vero extra Græciam magna dicendi ftudia fuerunt, maximique huic laudi habiti honores, illuftre oratorum nomen reddiderunt. Nam ut femel e piræo eloquentia evefta eft, omnes peragravit infulas, atque ita peregrinata tota Afia eft, ut fe externis oblineret moribus, omnemque lilam falubritatem Atticæ difonis quafi fanitatem perderet, ac loqui pene dedifceret. Hinc Afiatici oratores non contemnendi quidem nec celeritate, nec copia, fed parum preffi & nimis redundantes. Rhodii fanitores, & Atticorum fimiliores, &c. *Cic. de Clar. Orat.* 13. Semper oratorum eloquentiæ moderatrix·fuit auditorum prudentia. Omnes enim, qui probari volunt, voluntatem eorum, qui audiunt, intuentur, ad eamque, & ad eorum arbitrium, & nutum, totos fe fingunt & accommodant. Itaque Caria, & Phrygia, & Myfia, quod minime politæ, minimeque elegantes funt, adfciverunt, aptum fuis auribus opimum quoddam, & tanquam adipatæ

diftionis genus, quod eorum Vicini (non ita lato interjefto mari) Rhodii nunquam probaverunt, Græci multo minus, Athenienfes vero funditus repudiaverunt, &c. *Cic. ad Brutum.* 8. Mihi autem orationis differentiam feciffe, & dicentium & audientium naturæ videntur, quod Attici limati quidem & emunfti, nihil inane aut redundans ferebant. Afiana gens tumidior & jaftantior. Tertium mox qui hæc dividebant, adjecerunt genus Rhodium, quod velut medium effe atque ex utroque mixtum volunt, &c. *Quint. Inft.* 12. 10.

(108) Quinimo certamen pifturæ, etiam florente·eo (Panæno)inftitutum eft Corinthi ac Delphis primufque omnium certavit cum Timagora Chalcidenfe fuperatus ab eo Pythius. *Plin.*35. So early were thefe Contefts inftituted.

(109) *Shaftesbury's Character.* Vol. III. p. 138.

cation, and the *Belles Lettres* (110), fpeaking of the good Effects of that noble Emulation, which the publick Honours and Rewards that were given in *Greece* to all ingenious Men excited; he mentions a very rare Inftance of Goodnefs and Generofity, in modern Times, that is indeed above all praife, and that had very noble Effects.   " Mr. *Colbert* (fays he) fet " apart forty thoufand Crowns a year to be diftributed, amongft thofe, chiefly, who had dif- " tinguifh'd themfelves in any Art or Science; and told thofe Gentlemen whom he had entrufted " with the care of making ingenious Men known to him, that if any Perfon of Merit was " in Diftrefs, or in pinching Circumftances, throughout *France*, whom he could relieve, the " horrid Guilt muft lie upon themfelves."

IN the latter Age of Painting, tho' no fuch publick Contefts took place, yet vaft Encouragement was given by the Great to all good Artifts: And Emulation being thus kindled and maintained, they ftrove to out-do one another, that they might have the honour to be employed in great Works. As in *Greece* many different Artifts were often fet together to work in the fame Temple, Portico, or other publick Building; fo likewife in *Italy* were Painters employed in adorning the fame Church or Palace, that they might thus be induced to vie the more earneftly with one another.

IT is particularly taken notice of by *Pliny* and others, that the ancient Painters and Statuaries difdained not to liften to the Remarks even of the illiterate and uninftructed, and to obferve the Effects which their Works had upon them.   It was cuftomary amongft them to expofe Pictures and Statues to publick view, to the common Criticifm of all, not only in the publick and folemn Congreffes, but at all times (111).   And thus the Artift had excellent Opportunities of taking many very ufeful Hints, and making feveral important Obfervations for the Improvement of his Art.   The frequent Confluence of Spectators to fee their Works, gave the Artifts occafions of remarking how People of different Orders, Characters, Ages, Tempers, Education and Manners were varioufly affected by their Imitations of Nature: It formed an excellent School for them to ftudy Nature in.   And indeed it is an Error to fuppofe that the Learned only can judge of good Performances, or of the Arts that imitate Nature, and have it for their Aim to touch and move the Heart.   This Practice of the ancient Painters, which was likewife followed by Orators and Poets, of trying their Works upon untaught Nature, proceeded on a true Obfervation often repeated by *Cicero* and others; that the Unlearned are feldom wrong in their Judgment about what is good or bad in any of the Arts; and that the chief difference between the Learned and the Vulgar confifts in this, that the latter are not able to apply Rules and Maxims, but judge merely from what they feel; whereas the former can reafon about their feeling from Principles of Science and Art.   *Cicero* infifts at great length on this Obfervation (112).   But *Quintilian* difpatches the whole matter in one very juft and expreffive Sentence.   " *Docti rationem Artis in-* " *telligunt, Indocti Voluptatem.*"

WHAT regard the beft modern Painters likewife paid to the Sentiments and Feelings of the Vulgar, in whom Nature expreffes herfelf juft as fhe is moved, without any Affectation or Difguife, we learn from feveral Stories in their Lives, of their clofe and careful Attention to the Effects which their Pictures had even on ordinary Women and Children;

(110) *De la Maniere d'Enfeigner, &c.* par Mr. *Rollin*, p. 420.   With regard to the Effect of Encouragement and Emulation in modern Times, I need only put my Readers in mind, how, after the Death of Pope *Leo* X, the Arts were in danger, when *Adrian* fucceeded, who had no Tafte, infomuch that he had fpoke feveral times of deftroying the fine Paintings of *Michael Angelo* in the Chapel of the *Vatican*; but not living long, the Arts revived again under *Clement* VII.

(111) Ut enim pictores, & ii, qui figna fabricantur, & Vero etiam poetæ, fuum quifque opus a Vulgo confiderari vult: ut, fiquid reprehenfum fit a pluribus, id corrigatur: hique & fecum, & cum aliis, quid in eo peccatum fit, exquirunt: fic aliorum judicio permulta nobis & facienda & non facienda, & mutanda, & corrigenda funt. *Cic. de Of. lib.* 2. 41.   Apelles perfecta opera proponebat in pergula tranfeuntibus, atque ipfe poft tabulam latens, Vitia quæ notarentur aufcultabat, vulgum diligentiorem judicem quam fe præferens: feruntque a futore deprehenfum quod in crepidis una pauciores intus feciffet anfas: eodem, poftero die, fuperbo ex emendatione priftinæ admonitionis, cavillante circa crus, indignatum profpexiffe, denuntiantem ne fupra crepidam judicaret. *Plin.* 35.——Quandoquidem hoc Phidiam quoque feciffe perhibent quo tempore apud Elios Jovem jam abfolverat. Stetiffe enim illum poft januam, ubi primum opus in lucem productum hominibus vifendum oftendiffet, fubaufcultaffeque quid quifque fpectantium laudaret aut reprehenderet.   Ceterum hic quidam nafum reprehendebat— alius vero faciem——Deinde digreffis fpectatoribus, rurfus

Phidiam femet concludentem correxiffe, atque ad multorum opinionem, & judicium imaginem emendaffe. Neque enim mediocre aut contemnendum effe exiftimabat populi tam numerofi Confilium, fed hoc fibi perfuaferat neceffario fore, ut multi femper plus quam unus perviderent: Tametfi ipfe femet Phidiam effe non ignorabat. *Lucian. de Imag.*   Rhodiis in admiratione fuere Ialyfus & Satyrus, columnæ adftans, cui columnæ perdix adfiftebat atque adeo tabula lilhac primum pofita, perdix tantopere traxit hominum oculos, atque in fe defixos tenuit, ut Satyrum nemo admiraretur quanquam elaboratiffimum. ——Videns igitur Protogenes ipfum opus factum effe quoddam quafi additamentum ad opus, perdicem delevit. *Strabo, lib.* 14. p. 652.

(112) Illud autem nequis admiretur, quonam modo hæc vulgus imperitorum in audiendo notet; cum in omni genere, tum in hoc ipfo magna quædam eft vis, incredibilifque naturæ.   Omnes enim tacito quodam fenfu, fine ulla arte aut ratione, quæ fint in artibus ac rationibus recta ac prava, dijudicant: Idque cum faciunt in picturis & in fignis, & in aliis operibus, ad quorum intelligentiam a natura minus habent inftrumenti; tum multo oftendunt magis in verborum, numerorum, vocumque judicio; quod ea funt in communibus infixa fenfibus, neque earum rerum quenquam funditus natura voluit effe expertem.——Mirabile eft, cum plurimum in faciendo interfit inter doctum & rudem, quam non multum differat in judicando.   Ars enim cum a natura profecta fit, nifi natura moveat ac delectet, nihil fane egiffe videatur, &c. *Cic. de Orat. lib.* 3. 50.

The regard paid by
modern Painters to
common Judgment.

Children: I shall only mention one *Bellori* and *Coypel* tell us (113) of *Annibal Carrā-che*; he had observed an old Woman mightily moved by a famous Picture of *Dominichin*, representing the Flagellation of St. *Andrew*, and describing all the Passions in it to her Child with great Emotion; but having remark'd, that a Picture of *Guido's*, in the same Church, of another Martyrdom, did not equally touch her; when a Dispute happened afterwards about these two Pictures, he only told this Story, leaving it to every one to judge to which the Preference was to be given; on supposition, that touching and moving the Affections was the chief End and Excellence of the Pencil.

BUT however that be, this is certain, that all the Arts in *Greece* were polished, and brought to Perfection chiefly by means of Criticism. This is acknowledged with regard to Poetry and Oratory: And it was no less so with respect to the other Sister-Arts. The good Performers in each Art found their account in encouraging fair Enquiries into the Truth and Beauty of every Art: They cordially fell in with such a proper Method of procuring just Esteem to themselves. They who were true and faithful to their Arts were

The Arts polished by
Criticism.

naturally most desirous of improving and refining the publick Taste, that in return they might be rightly and lastingly applauded; and therefore they not only encouraged the criticizing Art, but joined themselves in this most effectual way of preventing the Publick's being imposed on by the false Ornaments and affected Graces of mere Pretenders. Criticks are, as it were, the Interpreters to Artists, who unfold and explain the Excellencies of their Works to the People, and thus lead them to a thorough Intelligence of Truth and Perfection in Arts: And therefore it is the Impostor only that is afraid of them, or endeavours to discredit their Pretensions to correct and instruct. Accordingly, in ancient Times, whilst the gravest Philosophers, (who were Censors of Manners, and Criticks of a higher degree) disdained not to exert their Criticism on the inferiour Arts, and claimed it as the indisputable right of true Philosophy to give Laws to them all; Criticism was held in due repute; it gained a Hearing; did justice to every degree of Merit; taught to distinguish the true from the false; and quickly made good Taste universal: And no wonder that it did so, for as it is in Life, so it is in Arts; it costs much greater Labour and more violent Struggling to vitiate and corrupt our Taste, than to improve it.

IT is indeed a remarkable Circumstance in those two Ages of Painting we are comparing, that, in both, several Artists were capable of doing justice to their own Arts by their excellent Pens. In the first Age of it, whilst the Art was duly cultivated in

Ancient Painters,
Philosophers, and
others wrote well on
the fine Arts.

Greece, had Reputation, and produced Works of exquisite Taste and Genius, not only did some Artists write Treatises on Painting which were highly esteemed; but several other great Men thought it not below them to display the Beauties of this Art, and to recommend it to the publick Esteem, by celebrating the Praises of the great Masters, their excellent Works, and of the Art itself. *Apelles* (114), *Asclepiodorus*, *Pamphilus*, *Melanthius*, *Euphranor*, *Pasiteles*, *Protogenes*, *Theomnestus*, *Hypsicrates*, all of them renowned Painters, are said to have wrote on the Art, or to have explained its Rules and Principles, and criticized its Productions with great Judgment and Elegance: And thus they added no less to the Honour of the Art by their Writings, than by their Pictures. But not only these and other Painters, but several Philosophers, and others of distinguished Reputation for Science and good Taste, are likewise reported to have wrote the Lives of the famous Painters and Statuaries, and Treatises upon the designing Arts: Such as *Democritus* the Philosopher, of whom *Diogenes* gives so great a Character, comparing him to the *Olympian* Victors in the *Pancrasin*, for his universal and extraordinary Abilities in all the Liberal Arts and Sciences. He was Contemporary with *Socrates*, whom we find in *Xenophon's* Memoirs of him, not unfrequently conversing with Painters and Statuaries about Matters equally relating to Philosophy and the fine Arts. *Plato* not only loved the Art, but painted himself, and was often with the famous Artists. *Diogenes Laertius* in his Account of *Democritus* the Philosopher, mentions another of that Name an *Ephesian*, who also wrote upon the Temple of *Diana* of the *Ephesians*, and its Ornaments; amongst which were several Pictures by *Apelles* and other great Masters, and the famous *Diana* by *Timareta*, the first of the few Ladies who gained Fame by Painting. *Duris* is also highly praised for two Works, one on Sculpture, and the other on the Art of Painting. *Diogenes Laertius* mentions him in his Life of *Thales*. *Menechmos* of *Sicyon* wrote of the famous Artists, as we are told by *Athenæus*: And he and *Diogenes Laertius* both mention *Menodotus*, who had composed a Treatise of the famous Painters, and a Description of all the admirable Pieces of Art in the Temple of *Juno* at *Samos* his native Country. *Adeus, Alcetus, Antigonus, Menander, Alexis*, and several more, are likewise mentioned with great Applause, as good Writers on the plastick Arts, amongst whom was one *Polemon* a very highly esteemed Author; not improbably the same, of whom *Strabo* speaks, who had wrote several Books of Geography. He wrote a Treatise of Pictures; a Description of those at *Sicyon*;

a

---

(113) See *Coypel* on Painting, and *Leonardo da Vinci*, *p*. 35; While a Painter is employed in designing or painting, he ought to listen with attention to the different Sentiments which different People entertain of his Performance: There being no body, how ignorant in Painting soever, but who, &c.

(114) See *Junius de Pictura veterum*, and the *French* Translation of *Pliny's* Book on Painting, with the *Latin* Text. *Lond.* 1725.

a third Volume on the Lives of feveral great Painters dedicated to *Antigonus*; and a fourth on the capital Pictures in the Veftible of the Citadel at *Athens.*   Now fuch Works as thofe that have been mentioned, muft no doubt have contributed very confiderably towards the Promotion of the Arts, and of a good Tafte of them in ancient times.   And in like manner, in the latter Age of Painting, the Works of *Leonardo da Vinci, Alberti, Albert Durer, Bramante, Armenini, Allori, Baglioni, Vafari, Lomazzo, Borghini, Zuccaro, Ridolfi, Scanelli da Forli, Pino, Ludovico Dolci,* and others, very greatly conduced to the Inftruction of Painters, and to the Knowledge and Efteem of the Art; whilft it was thus fhewn to be really a Science that requires great Parts, various Learning and Knowledge, much Study as well as a fine Genius; and that it is capable of producing the nobleft Works, and of being employed to the beft and worthieft Purpofes.   The Arts being juftly explained and criticized, become fully underftood; and when they are underftood, they will be efteemed, loved, and promoted.

So feveral among the Moderns wrote, and did honour to the Art by their Writings.

ONE Circumftance more, in this Parallel between thefe two noted Ages of Painting, deferves to be confidered, that in the firft Age, or amongft the *Greeks,* Statuary and Sculpture being brought to great Perfection before Painting (115); the Painters profited not a little by the Advances thefe Arts had made.

Painting received affiftance from Sculpture and Statuary.

PHIDIAS the renowned Statuary was Brother to *Panænus*; and they feem to have been the firft that carried Painting to any confiderable height of Beauty and Elegance, or Truth and Correctnefs.   And juft fo in the latter Age of Painting, not only the good Painters and Statuaries were contemporary, and many Painters were excellent Sculptors; but, which is more, the Perfection to which Painting was improved in *Italy,* was in a great meafure owing to the digging up of the ancient *Greek* Statues, which, fo foon as they were difcovered, the Painters ftudied as Models.   It was from thefe exquifite Mafter-pieces of Art and Workmanfhip they learned to form a juft Idea and Tafte of Nature.   *Mantegna* one of the firft of the good Painters of that Age was a great Studier of the Antique; and arrived to all the Perfection he was Mafter of, by his continual Application to the Statues and Baffo-relievos: And that it was not inconfiderable, may be feen by his Triumphs of *Julius Cæfar,* at *Hampton-Court*; which are juftly faid to be the Triumphs of his Pencil.   The Hardnefs and Drynefs of his Manner, feems to be chiefly owing to his not underftanding fufficiently how to imitate the ancient Remains of Sculpture, without following them too fervilely in an Art of a different Genius; or to his not foftning and animating his Imitations of the Antiques from the living Beauties of Nature.   It was not till *Raphael* had found out this important Secret, that he made the true ufe of the Antique, and acquired his beft Manner.   In fine, the great Perfection to which he, and all the modern Mafters attained in Painting, were in a very great meafure owing to their juft regard to the antique Statues and Sculptures, and their unwearied ftudy of them; as I fhall afterwards have occafion more fully to obferve.

Among the Ancients.

Among the Moderns.

Mantegna ftudied the Antiques.

Raphael found out. the Art of imitating them well.

TO conclude, as there was a Greatnefs in the Manner of the firft-Painters in both thofe Ages of the Art; fo in both they degenerated in the fame way, by falling into the Effeminate and Languid.   " When it firft begun to revive in *Italy,* after the terrible " Devaftation of Superftition and Barbarity, (faith an excellent Painter and (116) Judge) " it was with a ftiff and lame Manner, which mended by little and little, till the " time of *Maffaccio,* who rofe into a better Tafte, and begun what was referved for *Ra-* " *phael* to compleat.   However, this bad Stile had fomething manly and vigorous; whereas " in the Decay, whether after the happy Age of *Raphael,* or that of *Annibal,* one fees " an effeminate languid Air: Or if it has not that, it has the Vigour of a Bully rather than " that of a brave Man.   The old bad Painting has more Faults than the modern, but this " falls into the infipid."   Now when we come to inquire into the Caufes, to which the Declenfion of Painting amongft the Ancients is afcribed, they will be found difcourfing of it juft in the fame manner.

How the Art began, and how it declined in both Ages.

MEANTIME we have feen, in this Chapter, a remarkable Likenefs in the Progrefs of Painting to its Perfection, at two different Periods.   It was cultivated and improved in the fame manner, and brought to a very like degree of Beauty and Excellence in both, by fimilar Steps, and by very analogous Means and Caufes.   We owe the Improvements of this Art in the laft Age of it to fuch a Succeffion of Mafters, as that, to which its Perfection in the firft is attributed by ancient Authors.   So like are thefe two Ages of Painting in every refpect, that there is hardly any Character of a Painter in the one Age, that hath not its Parallel in the other; nor indeed any remarkable Circumftance or Event with regard to the Art, or any of its Profeffors in the one, that was not, as it were, reiterated in the other.   Both, it is well known, were Ages in which all the other Parts of ufeful and polite Learning were greatly promoted and encouraged; and accordingly made very eminent

---

(115) Marmore fcalpendo primi omnium inclaruerunt Dipænus & Scyllis, geniti in Creta infula etiamnum Medis imperantibus,———Cum ii effent, jam fuerant in Chio infula Malas fculptor, dein filius ejus Mixiades———Non omittendum, hanc artem tanto vetuftiorem fuiffe quam picturam aut ftatuariam,———Et ipfum Phidiam tradunt fcalpfiffe Marmora——Alcamenem docuit in primis nobilem.   *Plin.* 36. 4.

(116) Vide two Difcourfes by Mr. *Richardfon, p.* 78.

eminent Advances, as well as Painting and Sculpture. And indeed, I need not stay to prove, that it is by no means likely, that Painting, which stands so much in need of help from all the other Arts, could have made such a wonderful Progress in the last Age of it, if the Taste of all politer Literature had not been revived at that time by the Study of ancient Authors, and the Remains of ancient Arts, and had not been very earnestly cultivated. In both Ages of the Art the Learned willingly gave all the assistance they were able to the Artists, of whom many were themselves very learned, and every one was exceeding willing to take Instructions from those who were (117).

CHAP. III.

Observations on some Pictures described by ancient Authors ; on the just Notions the Ancients had of the Art, and of its Connection with Poetry and Philosophy.

The Design of all Art is to instruct, delight and move.

THAT we may have a more compleat Notion of the Perfection at which the Art of Painting arrived amongst the *Greeks*; and of what the Art is capable to perform in teaching, delighting or moving; it is not improper to consider some few Pictures of ancient Masters.

The oldest Paintings described are very masterly, and in a great Taste.
Those in the Pœcile at Athens.
By Panænus, Polygnotus and Micon.

NOW the oldest Paintings which are celebrated by ancient Authors, for the Beauty and Taste of the Composition, as well as for the Noblenefs of the Subjects, are those with which the various Portico at *Athens* was adorned. It was so called on account of the great variety of excellent Pictures painted by several good Masters, which so extremely beautified and enriched it. Here *Panænus*, Brother to *Phidias* the celebrated Statuary, *Micon* and *Polygnotus*, all famous Painters, had exerted their utmost Skill and Art (1). The last is particularly renowned for having contributed a large share towards the adorning that Portico gratuitously; whereas the others received pay. For this instance of his Generosity and publick Spirit, confiderable Privileges and Honours were unanimously decreed to him by the *Amphictyonian* Council (2); and he was greatly praised by the Poet *Melanthius* (3).

THE most remarkable Pictures of *Panænus* and *Polygnotus* are fully described by *Pausanias* in his Account of this Portico; I shall only mention a few of their principal Beauties. The Subjects were truly grand, poetical, executed with much Judgment and Spirit, and in a very sublime Taste of Design. *Polygnotus's* Subjects were chiefly taken from *Homer*, whom he is said to have highly admired, and constantly studied. In his Picture of *Ulysses's* Descent into Hell, he represented the infernal River with so much Art, that not Fishes, but rather Shades of

(117) The Analogy between the two remarkable Ages of Painting, which I said in the beginning of this Chapter, is so surprising and worthy of our Attention, may be thus briefly stated, for the sake of those who may be desirous to have a compendious View of it.

The Art in both Ages advanced at first very slowly ; came to a certain Pitch, and then made a stand for some time : But beginning afterwards in both to soar above the first small Advances, it improved exceeding fast, till it came in both to a degree of Perfection, the Description of which in the one, from the Works of *Apelles*, is precisely correspondent to that which is most justly given of it in the other, from the Works of *Raphael*. *Panænus* and *Polygnotus*, and a few others, with the assistance of the Sculptors and Statuaries, brought the Art to such Perfection in the first Age, as it was carried by *Massaccio*, *Mantegna*, and a few others in the last, with like help from Statues and Sculptures. As *Apollodorus* and *Zeuxis* perfected Colouring in the one, so did *Georgion* and *Titian* in the other, being Artists of very like Genius and Talents. As were *Eupompus*, *Pamphilus*, and *Apelles* to one another, and to the Art ; so were *Andrea Verrochio*, *Leonardo da Vinci*, and *Raphael*. As was *Euphranor* to those, so was *Michael Angelo* to these. *Corregio* was to the Art in his time, and his Contemporaries in many respects, as *Protogenes* was to the Art, and his Contemporaries. As *Erigonus* in the first Age, so was *Polydore* and *Michael Angelo da Carravagio* in the last : and as was *Nicias* and his Scholars in the one, so were the *Carraches* and their Scholars in the other. The Qualities of good Painting were divided amongst many Masters in the first Age, in like manner as in the last : And the different Schools were to one another in the one Age, just as in the other. The Learned in both chearfully lent their help toward the Improvement of the Art : And the Great in both highly rewarded, honoured and encouraged it. And in fine, the best Masters in both Ages had the same Ideas of the Art, took like Pains,

and followed like Methods for improving it, by studying Nature and Authors, who having formed a right Taste of Nature, had beautifully described and imitated several Parts of it ; by giving due Attention to the Criticisms of the Learned ; and even by observing the Effects of their Imitations upon pure untaught Nature in the Vulgar and Illiterate. This is the Phenomenon, which I said seemed to me to deserve a Philosopher's Attention, and from a just Representation of which one might have at once a clear View of the two most remarkable Progresses of Painting.

(1) See *Pausanias*, lib. 10. & *Meursii Ath. Att. lib.* 1. c. 5. *Hesychius*, *Suidas*. Similis in pictura ratio est ; in qua *Zeuxin* & *Polygnotum* & eorum qui non sunt usi plus quam quatuor coloribus, formas & lineamenta laudamus. *Cic. de clar. Orat. Quint. Inst. lib.* 12. c. 10. Oportet juniores non tam Paufonis opera contemplari, quam Polygnoti, aut siquis alius commode mores exprimit. *Arist. Polit. lib.* 8. c. 5. *De Poet.* c. 2. & c. 6. Polygnotus Thasius & Dionysius Colophonius duo pictores erant. Ac Polygnotus quidem pingebat magna ; & in perfectis certamina subibat : Dionysii Vero picturæ, excepta magnitudine, Polygnoti artem accuratissime imitabantur, atque in ea, passiones animi, mores, formæ habitudinem, vestium subtilitatem, & reliqua ad vivum exprimebant. *Ælion. Hist. lib.* 4. c. 3. *Plutarch. in vita Cimonis & in Timoleonte.*

(2) Unde major huic auctoritas ; siquidem Amphictyones quod est publicum Græciæ concilium, hospitia ei gratuita decrevere. *Plin. lib.* 5. c. 17.

(3) The Verses are recorded by *Plutarch* in his Life of *Cimon*.

Αὐτῷ ἴδ δαπάνεισι Θεῶν ναὸς ἀρρεύ τι
Κικρονίαν κόσμησε ξ ἡμιθέων ἀρρεάσιν.

of Pifhes were feen fwimming in it (4). His Colouring in fome Figures muft have been very good; for *Lucian* in his Images, fpeaking of a *Caffandra*, by this Painter, fitting in a Chair, fays it was exceedingly admired for the Gracefulnefs of the Eye-brows, and the beautiful Frefhnefs and Vermilion of the Complexion (5). *Panænus* painted the famous Battle of *Marathon*, in which ten thoufand *Greeks* routed an Army of thirty thoufand *Perfians* (6). *Cornelius Nepos* tells us all the Honour that was rendred to *Miltiades* for having delivered *Athens* and all *Greece* from the Slavery which threatned them; was, that in the Picture of this Battle he is the principal Figure, at the Head of all the other Captains juft going to engage the Enemy, and exhorting his Soldiers to Bravery. Several noted Heroes of both fides were diftinguifhed in this Picture, in fuch a manner that every one had his proper and peculiar Character: And there was a great variety of true and moving Expreffion throughout the whole. Certain Animals were introduced into fome of thefe ancient Pictures, with great Propriety and Tafte, that were extremely natural and well painted (7). In fine, nothing can be nobler in Compofition, ftronger in Expreffion, or more juft with regard to the Grouping, Contrafting or Difpofition of Figures, than thefe Pictures of *Panænus* and *Polygnotus* in this celebrated Portico, and other places, are defcribed to have been. So that it appears to be only in refpect of greater Knowledge of the Colouring-part, that *Pliny* calls *Apollodorus* the firft of the great Lights amongft the ancient Painters; and fays, that before him no Picture could detain the Eye agreeably. Thofe two Painters chofe great Subjects, and feem to have vied by their Art with Poetry and its fublimeft Mafters. Their Pictures had Manners, which, according to *Ariftotle*, is the Quality that renders Painting at once moft affecting and inftructive : They chiefly employed their Pencils to paint great Actions, or pleafing Fables and Allegories ; and defigned in a manly, vigorous Stile. Such was the Art in its firft beginnings ; before Colouring was fully underftood, Defign and Compofition were in great Perfection.

WE have already mentioned the *Penelope* and *Helen* of *Zeuxis*. *Pliny* fays he painted likewife a *Jupiter*, which was truly majeftick : He was feated on a Throne in this Picture with great magnificence, and the other Gods ftood by him (8). We may judge by the ancient Statues of *Jupiter*, and of the other Gods, how ancient Artifts diftinguifhed them ; and what fuperiour Majefty they gave to *Jupiter* (9). In this, no doubt, the Painters and Statuaries followed one another, and both the Poets. In one of the ancient Paintings now publifhed, *Jupiter* is reprefented on his Eagle ; and though he is careffing *Juno*, hath great Majefty in his Countenance.

The Pictures of Zeuxis.

Jupiter.

THERE was another Piece by *Zeuxis*, of a very different kind, which we may call a Centaur-piece : it is very particularly defcribed by *Lucian* in the following manner (10).
" This excellent Painter (faith he) was not fatisfied with painting common and trite Sub-
" jects, but was ever attempting fomething new, untried, and difficult : And having ima-
" gined any Idea, however rare, and extraordinary, he was able to execute it by his Pen-
" cil, juft as he had conceived it in his Fancy. Amongft the many Marvels of his Hand,
" was a female Hippo-centaur fuckling two young ones. The Original was loft with the
" reft of the noble Collection that was fent by *Sylla* into *Italy*, the Ship being caft away :
" But I have feen a very good Copy of it, which I fhall attempt to defcribe ; not that I
" pretend to great Skill in Painting, but becaufe it is yet very frefh in my Memory, having
" made a very deep Impreffion on my Imagination, when at *Athens* I was moft agreeably
" entertained in admiring the wonderful Performances of that charming Art.

A famous Centaurefs defcribed by Lucian.

" THIS Centaurefs is painted lying in a green Field, all the Parts in which fhe re-
" fembles a Mare are couched on the Ground, the hinder Legs are ftretched out backward ;
" but the uppermoft Parts in which fhe is Woman, ralfe themfelves up to a confiderable
" height. She is in the fame Attitude as a Horfe, when he is endeavouring to raife himfelf
" from

(4) Ὕδωρ ἔναι ποταμὸς ἔοικε δῖλα ὥς ὁ Ἀχίλεως, ᾳ τοι ἀμοίτε ἐν αὐτῳ πευκήτες, καὶ ἀμωδρα ὄντα ὅτι π τα ἰδῶ τῶν ἰχθύων σκιὰς μᾶλλον ἤ ἰχθῦς εἰκασιε. *Paufan. Phocic.* where thefe Pictures are fully defcribed. See fuch a Picture defcribed by *Philoftratus* in *Pifcatoribus.*

(5) In hac tabula Caffandræ potiffimum laudabant fuperciliorum decus, & ruborem genarum. *Lucian. in Imagin.*

(6) Panænus quidem frater Phidiæ, etiam prælium Athenienfium adverfum Perfas, &c. *Plin.*35. 17. *Paufanias, lib.* 5. *Strabo, lib.* 8. *Cor. Nepos in Miltiade.* Several other fine Pictures by *Panænus* are defcribed by *Paufanias* in his *Eliaca, p.* 158. *Edit. Wechel.* All the Labours of *Hercules* ; *Prometheus* chained to the Rock, and *Hercules* coming to deliver him ; *Ajax* and *Caffandra*, and *Achilles* fupporting *Penthefilea* juft expiring, &c.

(7) So *Paufanias*, and *Ælian. de Animal. lib.* 7. *c.* 38. Canem in pugna Marathonia, dominum fuum profequen-

tem, atque in confertos hoftes una cum domina irruentem;

(8) Magnificus eft & Jupiter ejus in throno. *Plin. lib.* 35. 'Tis probably to this Picture *Quintilian* has his eye in the place often cited, where he fays, that *Zeuxis* having followed *Homer*, the other Painters confidered him on that account as their Legiflator in reprefenting Gods and Heroes ; he having painted them agreeably to *Homer's* Defcriptions.

(9) The famous *Jupiter* of *Phidias* is defcribed by *Paufanias*, likewife fitting on a Throne. Sedet Deus in folio ex auro atque ebore fabricato. Capiti ejus impofita eft corona referens oleæ furculos. Dextera fert victoriam, ——læVa tenet pulcherrimum fceptrum varietate metallorum omnium efflorefcens. Avis autem fceptro infidens eft aquila.——Ad fingulos etiam folii pedes factæ funt quatuor victoriæ faltantium fpeciem referentes : Duæ aliæ ad plantam pedis pofitæ, &c. *Paufan. Eliac.* 156.

(10) Luciani Zeuxis vel Antiochus.—— λαιδανει τὴν ὀψιν, ἐκ δωτέρου εἰς τὸ ἔτερον ὑπαγουσίνη, &c.

O

" from the Ground, and get up.   One of the young fucks one of her lower Dugs as a
" Colt does a Mare; to the other she gives the Breast as a Woman to her Child, em-
" bracing and careffing it.   Above, in the upper part of the Picture, the Husband-Centaur
" looks at her, from a rifing Ground, with a smiling Countenance, only shewing the human
" Part of his Form, and holding a young Lion over his head, to fright the Infants.   All
" the Parts of this Work shew a very bold, clean Pencil, and a full Command of the
" Art: The Lights and Shadows are finely diftributed, and a great many Drolleries very
" proper to the Subject and finely imagined, make the Picture exceeding gay.   But what I
" principally admired, was the Richnefs of Imagination, and the Variety of Art that ap-
" peared in the Execution of this whimfical Subject: For the Male is exceeding ruftick, and
" quite horrible; he is covered with Hair, and has vaft large Shoulders; fmiles, but in a
" favage, ghaftly manner.   One half of the Female is like one of the moft beautiful, young,
" unbroken *Theffalian* Mares: And indeed the other half is of exquifite Beauty; a com-
" pleatly fine Woman, the Ears only excepted, which he hath made to refemble thofe of
" a Horfe.   And fo dextroufly are thefe different Parts joined, that it is almoft impoffible
" to exprefs, how the Commixtion eludes the Sight.   The youngeft of the Infants is favage
" and fierce as the Father; and tho' but new-born, already shews its furious Nature: I
" was delighted and furprized to fee, with what childifh Looks, natural to fuch Creatures,
" they flare at the young Lion, while they hang at the Breaft."   *Philoftratus,* in his Account of an ancient Picture of the Education of *Achilles,* admires the fame wonderful
Art of mixing the human Part with that of the Horfe, by fo infenfible a Tranfition, that
one could hardly difcern the Separation of one from the other, or where the one begun
and the other ended; fo nicely were they blended (11).

THE fame Dexterity is admired in the *Farnefe* Gallery at *Rome,* where *Perfeus* is painted
by the *Carraches,* changing Men into Stones: And in a Centaur carrying off *Deïanira,*
by *Guido,* a famous Piece: The fame Art appears in the Syren in this Collection of ancient
Paintings.   *Lucian* does not fatisfy himfelf with commending this Picture in the general,
but he points out the Beauties of it with very great Intelligence: And while Authors by fo
particular Defcriptions shew good Tafte, and a full Underftanding of the Art, their Opinion may be very juftly depended upon, even when they only praife or blame, without
entering into a long Detail of particular Beauties.   The fame Author defcribes a very beau-

*Echion's Charac-
ter and Abilities.*

tiful Compofition by *Echion,* (fo good a Painter that he is joined by *Cicero* (12), with
Protogenes, Apelles, and *Nicomachus,* as the four by whom the Art was brought to the
higheft pitch of Perfection.)   He mentions this Picture in his Book of Images, and gives a

*His Marriage of
Alexander.*

full Account of it in his *Herodotus* (13).   The Subject was the Marriage of *Alexander*
with *Roxana.*   The Painter *Echion* brought the Picture to be feen and tried in the *Olympian* Conteftations; and *Proxenides,* who at that time was appointed Judge, was fo
charmed with its Beauties and Excellencies, that he made him his Son-in-Law.   " If any one,
" fays *Lucian,* fhould afk what there might be fo extraordinary in that Compofition, that
" *Proxenides* was induced by it to give the Painter his Daughter in marriage; having feen
" an admired Copy of it, I am able to give fome account of the matter.   The Apartment is
" inexpreffibly rich and elegant; and the Nuptial-bed in it is finely adorned; near to which
" is the Virgin *Roxana,* a perfect Beauty, with modeft down-caft Eyes, expreffing a great re-
" verence for *Alexander,* who is at a little diftance reaching out a Crown to her.   Several
" *Cupids* are differently employed in this Piece; but all of them look exceeding fweet and
" chearful.   One ftanding behind her, wantonly draws afide her Veil, to fhew her Charms
" to the Bridegroom: Another is employed about her Feet, and takes off her Sandals that
" fhe may go to bed: A third wrapping himfelf in *Alexander's* Mantle, feems to pull him
" with all his force to the Lady.   Their Friend *Epheftion* is there as Paranymph, with a
" burning Torch in his Hand, and leans upon a beautiful Youth reprefenting *Hymeneus.*   On
" the other fide are other *Cupids* playing with *Alexander's* Arms: Two carry his Lance, and
" appear over-loaded with their Burden: Other two pull along one who lies upon his Shield,
" as if he was their Prince; having harneffed themfelves with its Thongs and Tackling.   An-
" other hiding himfelf at a diftance feems to wait in ambufcade, and prepare to furprize
" and fright his Companions when they come up to him.   Nor are thefe, fays *Lucian,* mere
" Puerilities or trifling Devifes of the Painter (14); but are brought into the Picture with great
" Propriety and Judgment, to fhew that *Alexander* loved *Roxana* without forgetting his
" Arms, and that he was at the fame time a Lover and a Warrior."   There is a fine Picture
of *Cupids* defcribed by *Philoftratus,* in which there is a delightful variety of Attitudes and
Contrafts; fome are pulling Fruit; fome are eating with great relifh; fome run after a Hare;
and others are fporting and playing (15).   This *Echion* appears to have excelled in the pleafant agreeable way of difpofing Figures, and in a good Tafte of Ordonnance and Compofition.   And he being fo highly commended by the Ancients, and Contemporary with
Apelles ; it is very juftly thought, that it muft have been to him that *Apelles* acknowledged
                                                                                            himfelf

---

(11) So likewife in the Centaurides defcribed by *Philoftratus* in his *Icones.*

(12) *Cic. de clar. Orat.* 18.   The place quoted above.

(13) Luciani Herodotus vel Action.

(14) Ου ΄παιδιά ΄η ΄ἄλλως ταῦτά ἐστιν ΄ουδε ΄μειзιγάσαι
ἐν ΄αυτοῖς ὁ Αετίων ΄ἀλλά ΄δηλοῖ ΄του ΄Αλιξάνδρου, και τον
εἰς ΄τα ΄πολιμικα ΄ἔρωτα, και ὅτι ΄ἅμα και Ρωξάνης ΄ηρα, και
΄των ΄ὅπλων ΄ουκ ΄ἐπιλάνθετο. Ibid.

(15) See *Philoftrat. jun. Icones in Amoribus.*

himself inferiour in Difposition and not *Amphion* ; no Painter of that Name being mentioned by any other of the Ancients (16) befide *Pliny*. He but juft mentions fome Pictures of *Echion*, with applaufe ; one reprefenting Tragedy, and another Comedy ; *Semiramis* when raifed to a Crown from a low Eftate ; an old Woman with a flaming Torch in her Hand ; another reprefenting a new Bride, with a charming beautiful Bafhfulnefs, with the modeft Blufh that fpreads a delightful Red over the Face, called the Vermilion of Virtue (17). *Virgil*, who was fo mafterly a Painter, hath defcribed it charmingly in his Picture of the beautiful *Lavinia:*

> *Accepit vocem lacrymis Lavinia matris*
> *Flagrantes perfufa genas, cui plurimus ignem*
> *Subjecit rubor, & calefacta per ora cucurrit.*
> *Indum fanguineo veluti violaverit oftro*
> *Siquis ebur, vel mixta rubent ubi lilia multâ*
> *Alba rosâ : tales virgo dabat ore colores. Æn. 12.*

So *Ovid* ⸺ *Ingenuas picta rubore genas.* Amor. lib. 1. El. 14.
This Modefty is charmingly reprefented in the Countenance of the Bride in the *Nozze Aldobrandine*, in this Collection.

TIMANTHES's *Iphigenia* is greatly celebrated by *Cicero, Quintilian, Valerius Maximus, Pliny*, and feveral others, for the Judgment he fhewed in it. Having expreffed a great variety of Grief and Affliction in the Countenances and Geftures of the Prieft, her Brother, Friends, Relations, and Admirers, he veiled the Father's Face, thus leaving the Spectators to meafure his inexpreffible Anguifh and Mifery, by the effect this Confeffion of the difficulty of expreffing it muft naturally have had upon their Minds (18). *Cicero* mentions this as a great proof of the Artift's Judgment, and of his Skill in the moft difficult part of Painting (19). And all the Ancients praife it as a fublime Thought, than which nothing could more powerfully move, and affect the Minds of Beholders (20.) *Nicholas Pouffin* hath deferved great applaufe, by his ingenious Imitation of this artful, fublime Device of *Timanthes* ; by reprefenting *Agrippina*, in his Picture of the Death of *Germanicus*, hiding her Face, and in fuch an Attitude of the profoundeft Grief and Sorrow, that fhe is felt to be afflicted beyond Expreffion, and far above all the other Perfons in the Piece. *Euripides* had employed the fame ingenious Stroke of Art in his Tragedy of *Iphigenia* ; making the Father *Agamemnon* turn away his Head, and hide his Face, quite over-power'd with Grief (21).

THE noble Thought (as *Euftathius* obferves) was originally *Homer's* (22) : But it was firft introduced into Painting by the judicious Hand of *Timanthes* ; who well underftood how to make the beft ufe of every Circumftance of a well-told Story in a good Poet, and to rival it in Painting. *Pliny* commends the ingenious Fancy, and good Effect in another Picture of *Timanthes*, reprefenting one of the *Cyclops* faft afleep, and young Satyrs meafuring his Thumb with their *Thyrfus*, and expreffing in their Looks their Wonder at the Vaftnefs of it (23). *Giulio Romano*, in imitation of that ancient Piece, did a *Polyphemus*, which appears of a prodigious Size by means of Satyrs and little Infants.

Timanthes's Iphigenia is highly praifed.

He imitated Homer, and was imitated by Nic. Pouffin.

His Cyclops another proof of his Ingenuity and Invention.

(16) See the *French Notes* on *Pliny*, fo often commended, p. 260. Nam Amphioni de pofitione cedebat, &c. 'Tis for thefe reafons I have Ventured to fay *Echion* inftead of *Amphion*, in my account of *Apelles*.

(17) Echionis funt nobiles picturæ : Liber pater: Item tragœdia & comœdia ; Semiramis ex ancilla regnum apifcens ; ('tis fo in the Manufcript of *Gronovius,* and is confirmed by him from feveral Paffages of *Tacitus*, fee his Remarks) anus lampadas ferens ; & nova nupta, verecundia notabilis. *Plin.* 35. 17.

(18) *Valerius Maximus*, lib. 8. c. 11. Exemp. ext. 6. Itaque pictura ejus, arufpicis, amicorum. & fratris lacrymis madet ; patris fletum fpectantis affectui æftimandum reliquit.—Nobilis pictor luctuofum immolatæ Iphigeniæ fupplicium referens, cum Calchanta triftem, mœftum Ulyffem, clamantem Ajacem, lamentantem Menelaum circa aram ftatuiffet ; caput Agamemnonis involvendo, nonne fummi mœroris acerbitatem arte exprimi non poffe confeffus eft ? &c.

(19) *Cicero* fpeaking of the Decorum in all Works of Genius, which he thus defines : (Quafi aptum effe, confentaneumque tempori, & perfonæ: quod cum in factis fæpiffime, tum in dictis valet, in vultu denique, & geftu, & inceffu : contraque item dedecere.) He gives this Example of it in Painting. Si denique pictor ille vidit, cum immolanda Iphigenia triftis Chalcas effet, mœftior Ulyffes, mœreret Menelaus, obvolvendum caput Agamemnonis effe, quoniam fummum illum luctum penecillo non poffet imitari. *Cic. Orat.* 22.

(20) *Quint. Inft.* lib. 2. c. 17. Confumptis affectibus non reperiens quo digne modo, patris vultum poffit exprimere, velavit ejus caput, & fuo cuique animo dedit æftimandum. So *Pliny*, lib. 35. c. 15. Ejus eft Iphigenia, oratorum laudibus celebrata : qua flante ad aras peritura, quum mœftos oppinxiffet omnis, præcipue patruum, & triftitiæ omnem Imaginem confumpfiffet, patris ipfius vultum velavit, quem digne non poterat oftendere.

(21) ⸺ *Ut vero Agamemnon vidit*
Puellam euntem ad cædem in Nemus,
Ingemuit : & retro vertens caput,
Emifit lacrymas, oculis veftem opponens.
                          Eurip. in Aulide. 1550.

(22) Poeta non inveniens aliquam doloris exfuperantiam, quam digne tanto mœrori fcenis adderet, operit eum ; neque tantum filentem facit, fed totum e confpectu velut amovet. Hinc Sicyonius pictor Timanthes pingens illam Iphigeniæ mactationem obvelavit Agamemnonem. *Euftath. in Il.* 24. ver. 163. Edit. Rom. p. 1343. This notable Circumftance in this Picture ; and feveral other Paintings, are thus defcribed in the *Ætna* of *Cornelius Severus*, by fome afcribed to *Virgil.*

Quinetiam Graiæ fixos tenuere tabellæ
Signave ; nunc Pophiæ rorantes arte capilli ;
Sub truce nunc parvi ludentes Cholchide nati,
Nunc triftes circa fubjecta altaria cervæ,
Velatufque pater, ⸺ &c.

(23) Sunt & alia ingenii ejus exemplaria : veluti Cyclops dormiens, in parvula tabella ; cujus & fic magnitudinem exprimere cupiens, pinxit juxta Satyros pollicem ejus metientes. *Plin. ibid.*

fants playing about him. *Pliny* says, this Painter perfectly underſtood how to repreſent the Vigour, Grandeur, and Majeſty of a Hero, God or Demigod (24) ; and the excellent Diſpoſition and the Perſpicuity with which he painted *Aratus's* Victory over the *Ætolians,* are highly praiſed by *Plutarch* (25) ; whom we ſhall often find commending the Art and its great Maſters, and all the States which encouraged and honoured it ; and ſhewing a very fine Taſte in his Deſcriptions of Pictures.

IN mentioning the various Accompliſhments of *Parrhaſius,* I forgot to ſpeak of his excellent Skill in painting Hair (26) ; the elegant, eaſy Diſtribution of which is very difficult, and adds a very great Beauty to a Head : And indeed as it is in Nature a very great Ornament, one of the greateſt Beauties in Men or Women ; ſo the Poets never neglect to deſcribe fine Hair : *Homer* gives that Charm to all his Goddeſſes and Heroines ; and ſo does *Virgil : Apollo* is always painted by the Poets with beautiful Hair : And therefore the ancient Statuaries and Painters were very emulous of excelling in that part.

Some Works of Parrhaſius.
Heroes by him, and Boys.

BUT *Parrhaſius* was chiefly admired for his Dexterity in characterizing different Tempers and Humours, and in expreſſing all ſorts of Affections and Manners. He painted two Boys repreſenting the Simplicity, Innocence and Security of Children (27). He likewiſe repreſented, agreeably to their Characters, *Agamemnon, Achilles, Ulyſſes, Æneas,* and ſeveral other ancient Heroes. *Carlo Dati* takes notice of an ingenious Conjecture about one of his Pieces mentioned by *Pliny* (28). *Pliny* (according to the ordinary Reading) ſays, he painted a Nurſe with a Child in her Arms. (" *Nutricem Creſſam, infantemque* " *in manibus ejus.*") But that Critick mentioned by *Dati* inclined to read *Infanteſque in mammis ejus.* " A Nurſe with a Child at each Breaſt ;" agreeable to a Paſſage in *Virgil,* which may poſſibly allude to this Picture ; his Deſcription of the Slave preſented to *Sergeſtus.*

Olli ſerva datur, operum haud ignara Minervæ,
Creſſa genus, Pholoe, geminique ſub ubere nati. Virg. l. 5. 284.

His Picture of the People of Athens.

THIS is certainly a more pictoreſque Subject, than a Woman with a Child in her Arms, and ſhe is deſcribed by *Pliny* to have been painted as a Nurſe. His moſt famous Picture, (and he was very probably aſſiſted in it by *Socrates,*) repreſented the People of *Athens.* This Piece *Carlo Dati* thinks difficult to comprehend, or to form a diſtinct Idea of, imagining that it was one ſingle Figure ; whereas it probably conſiſted of ſeveral judicious, well-underſtood Groupes : In it he had painted to the Life all the Viciſſitudes of Temper to which this jealous, ſpiritous People were liable. They were repreſented as of a fluctuating inconſtant Humour ; apt to be provoked and angry, yet very exorable ; cruel, yet compaſſionate and clement ; unjuſt and outragious, yet mild and tender, ſmooth and equitable ; haughty, vain-glorious, and fierce, yet at other times timid and ſubmiſſive (29). All theſe Varieties of Temper and Genius were nobly and perſpicuouſly expreſſed ; ſo that the *Athenians* might ſee their own Image in it as in a Mirror : With ſuch a Looking-glaſs, the Philoſopher already named, and ſome of their Poets, uſed frequently to preſent them. *Pauſanias* mentions a Picture very nearly of the ſame Genius, and Extent of Art and Invention, upon the Walls of the Square at *Athens,* called *Ceramicos,* repreſenting *Theſeus* in the midſt of the People, founding the Democracy, and eſtabliſhing its Laws and Conſtitutions (30.) For in ſuch a Picture, doubtleſs a very great variety of Humours, Diſpoſitions and Characters muſt have been painted.

His obſcene Pieces cenſured.

PLINY gives no account of his little obſcene Pieces, ſome of which are mentioned by *Suetonius* ; but on this, and every other occaſion, condemns the vile Proſtitution and Abuſe

(24) Pinxit & heroa abſolutiſſimi operis, artem ipſam compleXus Vires pingendi. (*Vires* is the true Reading, not *viros* ; ſee the *French* Notes, where it is VerY well tranſlated, la Vigueur, la preſtance d'un heros & d'un demi-dieu.)

(25) ——Factum hoc imprimis fecit illuſtre : Timanthes Vero pictor univerſam pugnam evidentiſſima diſpoſitione repræſentavit. *Plut. in Arato.*

(26) So *Pliny* in his Character of him (Elegantiam capilli). So *Lucian in Imaginibus. Pliny* commends a Statuary for the ſame Talent, Leontinus primus nerVos & Venas expreſſit, capillumque diligentius. *Lib.* 34.

(27) ——Et pueros duos in quibus ſpectatur ſecuritas & ſimplicitas ætatis :—Laudantur & Æneas, Caſtorque ac Pollux in eadem tabula : Item Telephus, Achilles, Agamemnon, Ulyſſes. Fæcundus artifex, &c. *Plin.* 35.

(28) *Carlo Dati* in his Life of *Parrhaſius.*

(29) Pinxit & Demon Athenienſium, argumento quoque ingenioſo : Volebat namque varium, iracun-

dum, injuſtum, ——Et omnia pariter oſtendere. *Plin. ibid.*

(30) In extremo pariete Theſeus pictus eſt, & Democratia unâ cum populo. Hæc pictura probat Theſeum æquabili reipublicæ adminiſtrationem Athenienſibus conſtituiſſe. *Pauſ. lib.* 1. *p.* 6. The People of *Athens* were frequently repreſented by Statuaries. Leocharis Jupiter & populus (ſpectabatur in pinæo retro porticum ad mare. *Pauſ. lib.* 1. *p.* 2. In quingentorum curia a Lyſone effictus videbatur populus. *Ibid. p.* 6. Such a Miracle of Art was that of *Euphranor.* Euphranoris Alexander Paris eſt : In quo laudatur, quod omnia ſimul intelligantur, Judex Dearum, amator Helenæ, & tamen Achillis interfector. *Plin.* 34. 8. The Talent *Parrhaſius* was ſo much maſter of, may be alſo learned from another Performance of his, deſcribed in the *Greek* Epigrams.

　Vidit & hunc, credo, miſerum Pæante creatum
　　Parrhaſius, forma eſt tam bene picta viri.
　Quippe ſubeſt oculis arentibus abdita quædam
　　Lachryma, ſeque dolor tam ferus intus agit.
　Eximium nemo te, pictor, in arte negabit :
　　Deſinere illius ſed mala, tempus erit.
Anthol. Græc. Ep. l. 4. c. 8. verſ. Hug. Grot.

Abuse of an Art, so capable of giving sound Instruction and wholesome Exercise to the Mind (31).

SENECA the Rhetorician, and other Declaimers, have harangued upon a Story of this *Parrhasius*, as if he had tormented an old Man most cruelly, that he might be able to paint the Tortures of *Prometheus* with greater force. But *Carlo Dati* very justly holds that Story for such a Calumny, as that very false one of the same kind, with which some have defamed *Michael Angelo* (32). *A false Story about him refuted.*

ACHILLES TATIUS has described two Pictures by *Evanthes* (33); the first is *Andromeda* chained to a Rock, and *Perseus* coming down from Heaven to deliver her from the Monster ready to devour her. The Rock to which she is chained is said to have been so natural, that it appeared really hollow, just sufficient to hold *Andromeda*: Her Fear was finely expressed, and nothing could be more frightful than the Monster, with all the complicated Windings of his Tail and expanding Jaws; his Head only was out of the Water, which seemed in motion by the Monster's raising himself up : But the Parts under the Water were also discernible. *Perseus* descends, with great Vigour and Bravery, to her relief, with his Faulchion, and his Shield terrible with the *Medusa*'s Head, that shaking her Hair entwined with Serpents, threatned irresistible Destruction. *Some Pictures by Evanthes described by Achilles Tatius. Perseus and Andromeda.*

ANOTHER in the same Temple represented *Prometheus* likewise tied to a Rock with iron Chains, and *Hercules* just coming to his Deliverance. *Prometheus* seems in the greatest Agony, the Eagle having already fixed her Pounces on him, and made a terrible Wound ; but at the same time Hope begins to dawn, for he sees *Hercules* coming. His Eye, as *Tatius* expresses it very picturesquely, has, at the same time, a Cast outward to *Hercules*, and inward to his own Pain ; and he adds, that 'twas impossible to look at this Picture without being most deeply moved and affected (34). *Prometheus, and Hercules coming to deliver him.*

HE likewise describes an ancient Picture of *Tereus* (35), *Philomela*, and *Progne*, which was full of Expression and Motion. It represented a Maid-servant holding a Veil in her Hand fully expanded, and *Philomela* pointing out with her Finger to *Progne*, the obscene and barbarous Treatment she had suffered from *Tereus*, which was wrought upon it: *Progne* is violently enraged and seems ready to tear the Picture; *Philomela* being painted on the Veil in the most moving Circumstances; just as *Ovid* tells the Story : *Philomela and Progne.*

                                        ————*Passos*

---

(31) See what *Pliny* says on this Subject, *lib.* 33. Heu prodigiosa ingenia! quot modis auximus pretia rerum. Accessit ars Picturæ ad aurum & argentum, quæ cælando cariora fecimus. Didicit homo naturam provocare. Auxere & artem vitiorum irritamenta. In poculis libidines cælari jubet ac per obscænitates bibere. So *lib.*14.c.22. Vasa adulteriis cælata, tanquam pet se parum doceat libidinis temulentia. *Cicero* distinguishes very well between *duo jocandi genera*, Unum illiberale, Petulans, flagitiosum, obscænum: Alterum, elegans, urbanum, ingeniosum, facetum. Quo genere etiam philosophorum Socraticorum libri referti sunt. *Cic. de off. lib.* 1. 29. And that *Parrhasius*'s lascivious Pictures, (eo genere Petulantis joci.) *Propertius* moralizes charmingly on this Subject.

Templa Pudicitiæ quid opus posuisse puellis,
  Si cuivis nuptæ quidlibet esse licet ?
Quæ manus obscænas depinxit prima tabellas,
  Et posuit costâ turpia visa domo :
Illa puellarum ingenuos corrupit ocellos,
  Nequitiæque suæ noluit esse rudes.
Ah ! gemat in terris ista qui protulit arte
  Jurgia subtacita condita Lætitia.
Non istis olim variabant tecta figuris,
  Cum paries nullo crimine pictus erat,
Sed non immerito velavit Aranea fanum, &c.
                        Prop. lib. 2. Eleg. 6.

(32) See *Carlo Dati* in his Life of *Parrhasius.*

(33) Achillis Tatii Alexandrini 'Ερωτικῶ five de Clytophontis & Leucippes amoribus, *Edit. Salmas. lib.* 3. *p.*1606. ——Sane pro puellæ magnitudine saxum excavatum erat ita, ut non arte aliqua fabrefactum, sed sponte natum cavum Pictura testari videretur, illud enim asperum, quomodo terra producere solet, Pictor effinxit. In illo sedebat puella eo aspectu, ut si pulchritudinem tantum considerare voluisses ; admiratione dignam imaginem : sin vero vincula etiam, & Cete ;——In vultu pulchritudini pallor admistus erat, hic genas occupans, illa ex oculis effulgens : Non tamen eo usque genæ pallebant, ut suus iis rubor deesset : nec oculorum fulgor adeo coruscabat, quin languore quodam, qualem in violis paulo ante succisis con-

spicimus, dehonestaretur. Ita pulchro timore puellam Pictor decoraverat.——Adversum puellam cetus ab imo mari emergens undas capite, quo una exstabat, findebat. Nam corporis major pars aquæ contegebatur : non tamen adeo quin humerorum umbra, squamarum ordines caudæ flexiones prospicerentur. Sanna ingenti & profundo hiatu ——inter cetum ac puellam Perseus e cœlo devolans in Belluam ferebatur——læva manu Gorgonis caput sustinebat, & pro scuto projiciebat horribile sane aspectu. Nam & torve intueri, & comam concutere, & serpentes vibrare, ac minitari obitum e pictura videbatur. Dextra ferro ejusmodi armata erat, ut & falx & gladius simul erat, &c. *Lucian*, in his Book *de Domo*, describes two Pictures of *Perseus* and *Andromeda*, in which two different points of time are exactly observed. In one, *Perseus* assisted by *Minerva* cuts off the *Medusa*'s Head : In the other with his Shield, upon which the *Medusa*'s Head was now engraved he attacks the Monster, and delivers *Andromeda*. Two circumstances, says Lucian, were remarkably touched by the Painter in this last Piece, Multa imitatione expressit artifex ille, Verecundiam puta Virginis & metum. Spectat enim & pugnam desuper ex rupe, & adolescentis audaciam amatoriam, & Belluæ visum intolerabilem.—— Perseus autem sinistrâ quidem ostendit Gorgonem, dextra Vero ense ferit. Et rursum, quantum quidem Belluæ illius Medusam aspexit jam saxum est. See *Ovid. Met.*1. 85.

(34) Ipse sane picturam quasi doloris sensum habentem miseratus fuisses.——Prometheus ipse spe metuque plenus erat, ac partim quidem Vulnus, partim Vero Herculem intuebatur : quem sane totis oculis contemplari volebat. Sed obtutus partem alteram dolor ad se rapiebat. *Achilles Tatius, ibid.*

(35) *Achilles Tatius, ibid. lib.* 5. *p.* 280. Capillis evulsis, cingulo soluto, Veste discissa, seminudum pectus, ostendebat ; dextraque oculis admota Tereuin vehementer incusabat ; sinistra Vero laceræ vestis parte mammas obtegere nitebatur : Mulierem Tereus totis ad se viribus trahebat, arcteque complexabatur. The same Author, *lib.*1. describes a charming Picture of the Rape of *Europa* ; of which afterwards.

P

> —————*Paſſos laniata capillos,*
> (*Lugenti ſimilis, cæſis plangore Lacertis*)
> *Intendens palmas, prò diris, Barbare, faĉtis,*
> '*Prò crudelis, ait!* &c.   Ovid. Met. l. 6. ver. 531.

Ariſtides's Piĉtures.
A dying Mother.

A R I S T I D E S (36), who was ſo famous for expreſſing the Paſſions, painted a Subjeĉt of the moſt moving kind, a dying Mother, whoſe wounded Breaſt the hungry undiſcerning Infant greedily ſnatches, even in her laſt Moments intereſting herſelf with the greateſt Tenderneſs, left her dear Child ſhould ſuffer by ſucking her Blood.

A Battle-piece.

HE likewiſe painted a Battle-piece, in which there muſt certainly have been a vaſt variety of Ideas, Paſſions and Attitudes; for it conſiſted of a hundred Figures, and was highly eſteemed. There was, it ſeems, no Confuſion in this complex Piece, the Figures were ſo judiciouſly aggrouped and contraſted: And what Force of Expreſſion, and Truth muſt have been in it, we may judge from the Charaĉter of the Painter, all whoſe ſingle Figures appeared to live, move and ſpeak. One was done by him in the Attitude of a Supplicant, which had, as it were, a moving Voice. Another repreſented *Byblis* dying of Love to her Brother: The Charaĉter of which Piĉture, together with the Subjeĉt, is very elegantly expreſſed by *Pliny,* in one Word, as *Gronovius* remarks, (ἀναπαυομενην.)

> —————————*palles, auditâ, Bybli, repulsâ,*
> *Et pavet obſeſſum glaciali frigore peĉtus.*   Ovid. Met. l. 9. ver. 580.

Perſons expiring.

HE could, it ſeems, expreſs with the greateſt truth the Languiſhing of Body or Mind (37); for *Attalus* gave a great Sum of Money for a Piĉture by him, of a Perſon quite exhauſted, and juſt expiring. *Apelles* delighted in this Subjeĉt (38); and ſo did likewiſe ſeveral of the beſt ancient Sculptors and Statuaries. *Pliny* mentions a wounded Man by *Cteſilaus,* in whom one might ſee how much Life remained (39). He alſo painted an old Man with a Lyre in his Hand, teaching a Boy to play; and an Aĉtor of Tragedy inſtruĉting a Pupil in that Art (40). *Strabo* ſpeaks of a *Hercules* done by him in the fatal Veſt, that *Déjanira* had preſented to him, diſtraĉted and out of himſelf with Exceſs of Rage (41).

The moſt celebrated Piĉtures of Proto-genes.
His Jalyſus.

THE two moſt celebrated Piĉtures of *Protogenes* are his *Jalyſus,* and his Satyr, both exceedingly praiſed by a great number of ancient Authors. It was his *Jalyſus* that charmed *Apelles.* It is ſaid to have been the Labour of ſeven Years, and *Protogenes* took care to give it a very good Body of Colours, that it might be a laſting Memorial of his admirable Pencil. The Painter while he was about this excellent Piece was exceeding abſtemious, and lived chiefly on Roots, to preſerve his Fancy clear, lively, and unclouded (42). We have many Inſtances of the Severity of the ancient Painters in their way of living. A parallel Story is told of *Nicias*; and *Horace's* excellent Rule extends not only to Poets, but to Painters, and all Authors:

> *Qui ſtudet optatàm curſu contingere metam,*
> *Multa tulit fecitque puer, ſudavit & alſit,*
> *Abſtinuit Venere & Vino,* &c.   Hor. de Art. Poet.

There was a Dog in this Piĉture warm and foaming, like one juſt returned from Hunting; in expreſſing which, fortune is ſaid to have favoured the Painter exceedingly: For being quite angry that he could not, by all his Art and Pains, come up to Nature, in painting the Foam about the Dog's mouth, he threw his Pencil againſt the Piĉture, and by this accidental ſtroke, was done to his ſatisfaĉtion, what, by all his Labour, he had not been able to perform. Let that Story be as it will, *Apelles* thought this Piĉture very beautiful; but rather too much laboured: whereas *Protogenes,* on the other hand, could hardly ever be contented with any of his own Works, or think them ſo near to Nature as he wiſhed to make all he did. As much as this Piĉture is commended by the Antients, not one of them

has

---

(36) Hujus piĉtura eſt; oppida capta; ad matris morientis e vulnere mammam adrepens infans, intelligiturque ſentire mater & timere, ne e mortuo laĉte, ſanguinem lambat——Idem pinxit prælium cum Perſis, centum homines ea tabula complexus——pinxit & ſupplicantem pene cum Voce: & Anapauomenen propter fratris amorem. *Plin.* 35. 17. The firſt is thus deſcribed in one of the *Greek* Epigrams:

> *Suge miſer! nunquam quæ poſthac pocula ſuges:*
> *Ultima ab exanimo corpore poc'la trahe.*
> *Expiravit enim jam ſaucia: Sed vel ab orco*
> *Infantem novit paſcere matris amor.*
>
> Anthol. l. 3. tit. 12.

(37) Pinxit & ægrum ſine fine laudatum; qua in arte tantum valuit, ut Attalus Rex unam tabulam ejus centum talentis emiſſe tradatur. *Plin. ibid. & lib.* 7. *c.* 38.

(38) Sunt inter opera ejus & expirantium imagines. *Plin. lib.* 35.

(39) This is the very Charaĉter, and chief Excellency of the dying Gladiator at *Rome.* Cteſilaus vulneratum, deficientem, in quo poſſit intelligi quantum reſtet Animæ, *lib.* 34.

(40) Speĉtata eſt & in æde fidei in capitolio, imago ſenis cum lyra puerum docentis. Tragœdum cum puero in Apollinis, &c. *Plin.* 35.

(41) *Strabo Geogr. lib.* 8. *p.* 381.

(42) Palmam habet tabularum, ejus Jalyſus, qui eſt Romæ dicatus in templo Pacis: Quem cum pingeret, traditur madidis lupinis vixiſſe quoniam ſimul famem ſuſtinerent & ſitim; ne ſenſus nimia cibi dulcedine obſtrueret. Huic piĉturæ quater colorem induxit ſubſidio injuriæ & Vetuſtatis ut decidente ſuperiore inferior ſuccederet. *Carlo Dati* explains this, Volendo dare un buoniſſimo corpo di colori a queſt' opera, nell' abozzarla, e nel finirla la ripaſſaſſe, e ſopra vi tornaſſe ſino a quattro Vole ſempre migliorandola, e piu morbida riducendola, come ſe proprio di nuovo la diſſigneſſe. Eſt in ea canis mire faĉtus ut quam pariter caſus pinxerit, &c. *Plin.* 35.

has given a particular Account of it. But if it was a View of a part of the *Rhodian* Country, as some imagine, there must have been the Image of some beautiful Youth in it, for which it was chiefly esteemed, and whose Name it took. For *Aulus Gellius* calls it a most wonderful Image or Picture of *Jalysus* (43), and *Cicero* joins it with the *Venus* of *Apelles* (44), and speaks of it as a Picture reprefenting some beautiful Youth: It therefore very probably reprefented *Jalysus* the Founder of *Rhodes* as a very comely Youth, in the Attitude of a Hunter returned from the Chafe, with his Dog fweating and foaming by him. And not improbably, the Scene was some beautiful part of the *Rhodian* Country, with a Profpect of the City of *Rhodes* perhaps at a little diftance. All the different Conjectures about it, and all the various ways of fpeaking of it amongft the Ancients, being laid together, this feems to be the moft probable Opinion that can be formed of that celebrated Piece ; by which, chiefly, *Rhodes* was faved, and by which the Painter gained the Favour of *Demetrius Poliorcetes* (the Befieger) to a degree that hath added not a little to the Reputation of both (45).

THE Satyr is more particularly defcribed ; which *Protogenes* feems to have been painting when the Siege was laid. It was a Satyr called *Anapauomenos* (46) ; becaufe he was in a reclining Pofture. He held a Flute in his Hand, like a Shepherd refting himfelf at the Foot of an old Oak, and finging the Charms of his Miftrefs, or the Pleafures of a Country Life. He feems to have chofen this Subject which required great Tranquillity and Quietnefs of Mind to fucceed in, on purpofe to be a Monument of the Undifturbednefs with which he poffeffed himfelf, and applied to his Work, in the midft of Enemies and Arms. *Strabo* fays, it was a Satyr refting upon a Pillar, on which was painted a Partridge ; that, being more admired than the Satyr, was afterwards effaced by the Painter, that the principal Subject might be attended to as it deferved (47).

His Satyr.

THERE is likewife some Difpute amongft Criticks about two other Works of his, one called *Paralus*, and the other *Hemionida* or *Nausicaa*. The greater part of the Learned (48), *Carlo Dati*, *Hardouin*, and others, underftand by thefe Names given to the Pictures, the Names of Ships he had painted. But, befides that even the fineft Ship is but one of the loweft Subjects of Painting ; it is plain that the principal Subject reprefented in thefe Pieces was not a Ship, fince *Pliny* fays, " That the Painter had added in thefe Pic-
" tures, by way of Parerga, or accidental Ornaments, feveral little Galliots to preferve the
" Memory of the fmall Beginnings from which his Pencil had rifen to fuch Glory and
" Honour. For he had for a long time painted only Ships and Galleys." *Cicero* exprefsly fpeaks of *Paralus* as a human Figure (49). And when it is called to mind, that, according to *Pliny*, and other ancient Writers, *Paralus* paffed for the firft Inventor of Ships (50) ; or the firft who had the Courage fo celebrated by Poets (51), to venture to Sea, we can no longer be at a lofs to find out what this famous Picture of *Protogenes* muft have been, and why it is called the noble *Paralus*. It certainly reprefented this firft and noble Sailor ; and in fuch a Picture where the Sea and Ships muft have been reprefented, other little Boats were very properly painted : As they were likewife in the other Picture called *Hemionida* or *Nausicaa* ; becaufe the Subject was *Nausicaa* with her attendant Maids driven by Mules, (according to *Homer's* Defcription) to the River, to wafh the Robes of State in preparation for her Nuptials (52).

His Nausicaa *from* Homer.

> *Now mounting the gay Seat, the filken Reins*
> *Shine in her Hand: Along the founding Plains*
> *Swift fly the Mules ; nor rode the Nymph alone,*
> *Around, a Beavy of bright Damfels fhone.*

They

---

(43) *Noctes Atticæ, lib.* 15. *c.* 3. In his ædibus erat memoratiffima illa imago Jalyfi, Protogenis manu facta, illuftris pictoris: cujus operis pulchritudinem, &c. So *Plutarch* and *Ælian* in Paffages already cited.

(44) *Orator. ab initio.* —— Qui aut Jalyfi quem Rhodi vidimus, non potuerunt, aut Coæ Veneris pulchritudinem imitari, *lib.* 4. *in Verrem*, N° 60. Quid Thefpienfeis ut Cupidinis fignum, propter quod unum vifuntur Thefpii ? Quid Cnidios ut Venerem marmoream ? Quid ut plctam Coos? Quid Ephefios ut Alexandrum ? Quid Cyzicenos ut Ajacem, aut Medeam ? Quid Rhodios ut Jalyfum ?— *Epif. ad Att. lib.* 2. *Ep.* 21.—Et ut Apelles, fi Venerem, aut fi Protogenes Jalyfum illum fuum cæno oblitum videret, magnam, credo acciperet dolorem.

(45) *Carlo Dati* gives us the various Opinions about this Picture in the Poftille to his Life of *Protogenes, chap.* 5, 6, and 7. where he obferves, that, according to *Suidas,* it was a Figure of *Bacchus.* We have given the Sum of all their Conjectures.

(46) Satyrus eft, quem Anapauomenon vocant ; & nequid defit temporis ejus fecuritati tibias tenens. *Plin.* 35. See the *French* Notes on this Paffage, and *Carlo Dati*'s Poftille, &c.

(47) *Strabo, lib.* 14. *p.* 652.

(48) See *Carlo Dati* as above, and the *French* Notes. *Pliny*'s Words are, Ubi fecit nobilem Paralum & Hemionida, quam quidam Naufcaam vocant ; adjecerit parvulas naves longas in iis, quæ pictores parerga appellant : ut adpareret a quibus initiis ad arcem oftentationis opera fua perveniffent.

(49) *Cic. in Verrem, lib.* 4. 60.

(50) *Plin. lib.* 7. *c.* 56. Longa nave Jafonem primum navigaffe Philoftephanus auctor eft ; Egefias Paralum.

(51) *Illi robur & æs triplex*
Circa pectus erat, qui fragilem truci
Commifit pelago ratem
Primus, &c.   Horat. Carm. lib. 3; Od. 3.
Juv. Sat. 12. ver. 57. de Raptu. lib. 1. ab initio.

(52) This Picture was called *Nausicaa*; becaufe the young Princefs of that Name was the principal Figure in it ; and *Hemionida* is ufed (as *Hermolaus Barbarus* obferves upon this Paffage of *Pliny*) as a Term of Art to exprefs a Virgin riding upon, or more properly drawn by Mules, ἐν ἡμιόνων

This

They seek the Cisterns where Pheacian *Dames*
Wash their fair Garments in the limpid Streams ;
Where gathering into Depth from falling Rills
The lucid Wave a spacious Bason fills.　Odyssey, B. 6. Pope's Transl. ver. 106:

PAUSANIAS, in his fifth Book of his *Eliacks,* speaks of a Bas-relief representing two Virgins drawn by Mules, of whom one guides the Reins, and the other had her Head covered with a Veil ; which was said to represent this very Subject, *Nausicaa* going with one of her Virgins to the River. Here is indeed a very pleasing Subject for a Picture, and very suitable to the Genius of this Painter : And the same Story of *Nausicaa* in *Homer* affords several Subjects equally calculated for such a Genius to paint. As when after washing the Robes, she is sporting with her Nymphs:

The Mules unharnefs'd range beside the Main,
Or crop the verdant Herbage of the Plain.
And while the Robes imbibe the solar Ray,
O'er the green Mead the sporting Virgins play :
(Their shining Veils unbound) along the Skies
Tofs'd and retofs'd, the Ball incessant flies.
They sport, they feast ; Nausicaa *lifts her Voice*
And warbling sweet, makes Earth and Heav'n rejoice.

The Sequel of that Story was painted by Polygnotus.　A S for the Sequel of the Story, *Ulysses* surprizing *Nausicaa* and her Damsels, it was painted in the various Gallery at *Athens* by *Polygnotus,* who it seems had done almost all the more beautiful picturefque Parts of *Homer.* So *Paufanias* tells us in his Atticks. And what an charming Subject is it for a Mafter of Expreffion and Grace ?

Wide o'er the Shore with many a piercing Cry
To Rocks, to Caves, the frighted Virgins fly ;
All but the Nymph : The Nymph stood fix'd alone,
By Pallas *arm'd with Boldnefs not her own.*
Meantime, in dubious Thought, the King awaits,
And, self-considering, as he stands, debates,
Distant his mournful Story to declare,
Or proftrate at her Knee addrefs the Pray'r.
But fearful to offend, by Wifdom sway'd
At awful Diftance he accofts the Maid.

Homer's *Compari-son taken from* Diana *painted by* Apelles.　*HOMER's* Comparifon taken from *Diana,* attended by her Nymphs, is exceedingly beautiful : And yet *Apelles* is thought to have out-done the Poet in painting that Subject (53).

A sylvan Train the Huntrefs Queen furrounds,
Her rattling Quiver from her Shoulder founds :
Fierce in the Sport, along the Mountain-brow
They bay the Boar, or chafe the bounding Roe :
High o'er the Lawn, with more majeftick Pace,
Above the Nymphs she treads with ftately Grace ;
Diftinguish'd Excellence the Goddefs proves ;
Exults Latona *as the Virgin moves,* &c.

AND it is not improbable that *Virgil* had this Picture of *Apelles,* as well as the Original whence it was taken, in his Eye, in his Defcription of the same Goddefs.

Qualis in Eurotæ ripis, aut per juga Cynthi
Exercet Diana choros ; quam mille fecutæ
Hinc atque hinc glomerantur Oreades ; illa Pharetram
Fert humero, gradienfque Deas fupereminet omnes
Latonæ tacitum pertentant Gaudia pectus.　Æn. lib. 1. ver. 504.

As well as in that other equally beautiful Defcription of *Venus.*

Virginis os habitumque gerens, & virginis arma
Spartanæ ; vel qualis equos Threiffa fatigat
Harpalyce, volucremque fuga prævertitur Hebrum.
Namque humeris de more habilem fufpenderat arcum
Venatrix, dederatque comam diffundere ventis
Nuda genu, nodoque finus collecta fluentes.　An. l. 21. ver. 328.

THE

This is the Explication of *Hermolaus* adopted by Mad. *Dacier.* See her Remarks on the *Odyffey.* Pope's Notes, *ibid.* And the *French* Notes on *Plin.* 35. See likewife *Carlo Dati.*

(53) Et Dianam facrificantium virginum choro mixtam, quibus Viciffe Homeri verfus videtur id-ipfum defcribentis. *Plin.* 35. 17.

THE moſt celebrated Pieces of that great Maſter *Apelles*, was his *Venus Anadyomenè*, or *Venus* coming out of the Sea (54). *Lucian* in his beautiful Dialogue entitled, *The Images*, where, in order to draw the Portrait of a Woman more charming than any he found exiſting, he borrows from all the beſt Sculptors and Painters their moſt maſterly Strokes, ſays, *Euphranor* ſhall paint her Hair; *Polygnotus* her Eye-brows, and the Vermilion of her Cheeks; but *Apelles* ſhall do all the reſt of her Body after the Model of his *Pancaſte*; that is to ſay, of his *Venus* which was done chiefly after the Life, from *Pancaſte* the *Theſſalian* Beauty, *Alexander*'s firſt Miſtreſs; whom he afterwards gave to *Apelles* upon his falling deeply in love with her (55). This *Venus* was a conſummate Beauty; ſo perfect a Piece, that, in *Auguſtus*'s time, this Picture being then at *Rome*, and a little ſpoil'd in ſome of the inferiour Parts, no Painter would adventure to repair it. It was in like manner, with the greateſt difficulty, that *Carlo Marratti*, as ſweet and gracious as his Pencil was, and as fine an Idea of Beauty as he had, was perſuaded to retouch ſome parts of *Raphael*'s Paintings in the little *Farneſe* at *Rome*. *Apelles* had alſo begun another *Venus*, which not living to finiſh, no Painter would ever undertake to compleat; ſo elegant were the Out-lines and Contours of this unfiniſh'd Piece (56). For that he had perfected the Head, and upper part of the Breaſt with admirable Art, *Cicero* tells us (57).

THESE charming Beauties are often celebrated by the Poets:

> *Formoſæ periere comæ: quas vellet Apollo,*
> *Quas vellet capiti, Bacchus ineſſe ſuo.*
> *Illis contulerim, quas quondam nuda Dione*
> *Pingitur humenti ſuſtinuiſſe manu.* Ov. Am. l. 2. El. 14.

Again, *Sic madidos ſiccat digitis Venus uda capillos.*
     Et modo maternis tecta videtur aquis. Triſt. l. 2. 526.

OVID there deſcribes ſeveral Pictures in the Palace of *Auguſtus*.

Again, *Ut Venus artificis labor eſt & gloria Coi*
     Æquoreo madidas quæ premit imbre comas. Ov. Ep. de Ponto, l. 4. Ep. 1.

AND there is an Epigram of *Auſonius* on the ſame Subject,

> *Emerſam Pelagi nuper genitalibus undis*
> *Cyprin Apellei cerne laboris opus;*
> *Ut complexa manu madidos ſalis æquore crines*
> *Humidulis ſpumas ſtringit utrâque comis.*
> *Jam tibi nos Cypri, Juno inquit & innuba Pallas,*
> *Cedimus, & formæ præmia deferimus.* Auſ. Ep. n. 104. in Ven. Anady.

AND another in the *Greek* Epigrams by *Antipater Sidonius*; thus tranſlated into *Latin* by *Grotius*:

> *Maternis primum de fluctibus emergentem*
> *Cyprin Apellei cerne laboris opus:*
> *Ut manibus mulcens reſperſos æquore crines,*
> *De madidis ſpumam cogit abire comis,*
> *Non tibi de forma poſthac certabimus, ipſæ*
> *Dicent, ſi videant, nata ſororque Jovis.* Anthol. l. 4. tit. 12.

HE painted the Image of War, with its Hands tied behind, led in triumph; and *Alexander* riding in a triumphal Car (58). To the firſt of which *Virgil* ſeems to have had an eye in theſe charming Lines (59).

———*Diræ*

(54) Venerem exeuntem e mari D. Auguſtus dedicavit in delubro patris Cæſaris, quæ AnadYomene vocatur; verſibus Græcis, tali opere dum laudatur, victo, ſed illuſtrato: Cujus inferiorem partem corruptam qui reficeret, non potuit reperiri. Verum ipſa injuria ceſſit in gloriam artificis. *Plin. ibid.*

(55) *Athenæus*, lib. 13. c. 6. ſays it was done after *Phryne.* Erat utique Phryne magis pulchra in iis partibus quæ non videntur quamombrem haud facile fuit eam conſpicere nudam: Induebatur enim tunica arcte carnes adſtringentem neque publicis utebatur Balneis. Frequentiſſimo tamen Eleuſiniorum conventu ſeriatiſque Neptuno diebus, in Græcorum omnium conſpectu, deponens Veſtes & ſolvens comas, ingreſſa eſt mare: adeo ut Venerem e mari emergentem ad hoc etiam exemplum pinxerit Apelles.

(56) Venerem Cois, ſuperaturus etiam ſuam illam priorem: Invidit mors, peracta parte; nec qui ſuccederet operi ad præſcripta lineamenta inventus eſt. *Plin.*

35. 17. *Ad præſcripta lineamenta*, this properly ſignifies the Contours in Sculpture and Painting. Tu Videlicet ſolus Vaſis Corinthiis delectaris?—Tu operum lineamenta ſolertiſſime perſpicis. *Cic. in Ver. l. 4.*
So a Poet contemporary with Pliny ſpeaks:
     Artificum veteres agnoſcere ductus.
And a little afterwards:
     Linea quæ veterem longe fateatur Achillem.
Stat. in Hercul. lib. 4.

(57) *Epiſt. ad Famil. lib.* 1. Ep. 9. Nunc ut Apelles Veneris caput, & ſumma pectoris politiſſima arte perfecit, reliquam partem corporis inchoatam reliquit.

(58) Item belli imaginem reſtrictis ad terga manibus, Alexandro in curru triumphante: Quas utraſque tabulas D. Auguſtus in fori ſui celeberrimis partibus dicaverat, &c.

(59) Alludit, juxta Turnebum, ad imaginem belli hoc habitu pictam ab Apelle, &c.

—— *Diræ ferro & compagibus arctis*
Claudentur belli portæ : Furor impius intus,
Sæva sedens super arma, & centum victus ahenis
Post tergum nodis, fremet horridus ore cruento. Virg. Æn. l. 1. 298.

*His Alexander
with Thunder in
his Hand.*

HIS *Alexander* is also famous, with Thunder in his Hand, which he seemed ready to dart; so strongly did the Hand and Thunder stand out from the Board (60). *Plutarch* tells us in his Life of *Alexander*, that, on account of this wonderful Picture, it was commonly said there were two *Alexanders*, the unconquerable Son of *Philip*, and the inimitable *Alexander* of *Apelles* (61). The same Author says (62), that in this Picture he had given *Alexander* a ruddier, or rather browner and more swarthy Complexion than his natural one. This the Painter probably thought might be done without diminishing the Likeness; and it was more agreeable to the Character of the Picture than a softer fairer Colour. He is said by *Pliny* to have painted Thunder and Lightning, and those other marvellous Appearances of Nature which it was thought impossible to imitate, and that none before him had dared to attempt (63). *Julio Romano* was able amongst the Moderns to rise to this marvellous Force of the Art; to thunder and set the Heavens on fire with his Pencil. This he did in his famous Paintings at *Mantua*, which are elegantly described by *Felibien* (64).

*Hero and Leander.
And the Graces.*

*A famous Picture
of Calumny descri-
bed by Lucian.*

BY *Apelles* likewise was painted the beautiful *Hero*, receiving her *Leander* at the Seaside, and drying him with her fair Hands (65). He had painted the Graces, *Pausanias* tells us (66), in their true Character; and that seems to have been the proper Subject for this Painter to exert his peculiar and distinguishing Talents upon. But I shall only mention one more celebrated Work of this Painter, his famous Picture of *Calumny*, one of the most noble moral Pictures that ever was attempted. This he did upon his being accused, to *Ptolemy*, by a Painter who envied his Merit and just Fame. On the right hand, in this Picture, sits a Person of Distinction and Authority; but with the Ears of *Midas*, reaching out his Hand to *Calumny*, who hastens to address herself to him, attended by Ignorance and suspicious *Jealousy*. *Calumny* appears grand and magnificent in her Dress, but her Face and Gait bewray the Fury and Malice that boil in her Heart. She holds a Flambeau in one Hand to kindle Discord and Strife; and with the other drags a young Man by the Hair, who, with Hands uplifted to Heaven, implores the Gods to defend his Innocence. Before her marches Envy with a pale ghastly Visage, a meager consumptive Body, and piercing Eyes. A Croud of young Women follow in her Train as her Servants and Ministers; in whose Countenances appear Guile, Cunning, Artifice, and false, deceitful, traitorous Smiles. *Repentance* comes up behind with a very lugubrous Air and Dress; who with great Confusion, and all in Tears, prepares to receive Truth, whom she discerns coming up to her, but at a considerable distance. *Lucian* (67), who describes this Work of *Apelles*, afterwards gives us an excellent Discourse upon not rashly believing Calumny, which is nothing else but a fine philosophical Lecture upon this truly moral Picture : And here we have a plain proof of the Instruction that may be given by the Pencil, and the excellent Use that might be made of the Art in Education, or in reading moral Lessons; rendring them more insinuating and impressive, as it would make them more pleasing and entertaining. All the Virtues (68) and Vices, with their Effects and Consequences, were painted and carved by the Ancients with proper Symbols : Hence the Origin and true Meaning of the Epithets given to them by the Poets, as Mr. *Addison* has shewn in his Dialogues on Medals, after *Augustini*, *Osellius*, and other Writers on these Subjects.

*The Subjects of
Nicomachus's Pic-
tures were poetical.*

NICOMACHUS, who had a very sweet, light, and delicate Pencil, was, it seems, a great Lover of the Poets and their Fables, and took almost all the Subjects of his Pictures from them. *Plutarch* gives him a very great Character, and at the same time gives us a very instructive Lesson in the Art, and a just Idea of the intimate Alliance between Painting and Poetry. The Verses of *Antimachus*, saith he, and the Pictures of *Dionysius*, though they are strong and masculine, and have Nerves and Vigour; yet they are constrained and forced; too much Labour and Affectation appears in them : But the Paintings of *Nicomachus*, like *Homer's* Poesy, with all their Grandeur, Force, and Beauty, have this additional
Charm,

---

(60) Alexandrum magnum fulmen tenentem——digiti eminere videntur & fulmen extra tabulam esse. *Plin. ibid.*

(61) Apelles pinxit fulminigerum Alexandrum, atque adeo accurate atque adtemperate, ut diceretur duos esse Alexandros : Unum Philippi filium insuperabilem; alterum Apellis inimitabilem. *Plutarch. de Fortu. vel. Virt. Alex.*

(62) In Alexandri vita.

(63) Pinxit & quæ pingi non possunt, tonitrua, fulgura, fulgitraque. *Plin. ibid.*

(64) Tom. 2. p. 118.

(65) Pinxit & hero nudam, eaque pictura naturam ipsam provocabat. *Plin. ibid.*

(66) *Pausanias, lib.* 9. p. 596.

(67) *Lucian. de Calum. non temere credens.*

(68) See *Lomazzo Trattato della Pittura*, p. 662, &c where he shews how Discord was painted by *Aristides*, as described by *Virgil*; Envy, as it is described by *Ovid*; and, in one word, how the Virtues, the Vices, the Blessings, the Calamities of human Life, the Graces, the Furies, &c. were painted agreeably to the Descriptions of them in the best Poets. He treats at great length of all sorts of Subjects and Compositions, and gives very useful Lessons to Painters.

Charm, that they seem to have been done with extreme Ease and Facility (69). His Rape of *His Rape of Pro-* *Proserpine* was highly esteemed, so poetically was it represented (70). He likewise painted *serpine, and a* a Victory drawn in a triumphal Chariot by four sprightly Horses that seemed to cut the *Victory.* Air. So is *Ceres*, or perhaps *Fortune*, represented in one of the Pieces annexed to this Discourse. But one of his most famous Pieces is *Ulysses* at the Gate of his own Palace in disguise, in the very point of time that his faithful Dog came and expired at his Feet thro' excess of Joy (71). *Ulysses* was painted as a simple Peasant in the Disguise *Minerva* had *Ulysses acknow-* given him, which no Painter had attempted to do before; so accustomed were they to see *ledged by his Dog* *Ulysses* always in the Habit of a Hero, with his Casque, or his Head quite uncovered. *Argus.* *Nicomachus* had emulated *Homer* in this admired Piece, and painted the Story as charmingly as he hath told it:

> *A Figure despicable old and poor*
> *In squalid Vests, with many a gaping Rent,*
> *Propt on a Staff, and trembling as he went ;*
> *Then resting on the Threshold of the Gate,*
> *Against a Cypress Pillar lean'd his Weight.*

> *Thus near the Gates conferring as they drew,*
> *Argus, the Dog, his ancient Master knew ;*
> *He not unconscious of the Voice, and Tread,*
> *Lifts to the Sound his Ear, and rears his Head,*
> *Bred by* Ulysses, *nourish'd at his Board,*
> *But, ah ! not fated long to please his Lord !*

> *He knew his Lord; he knew, and strove to meet,*
> *In vain he strove to crawl, and kiss his Feet ;*
> *Yet (all he could) his Tail, his Ears, his Eyes*
> *Salute his Master, and confess his Joys.*
> *Soft Pity touch'd the mighty Master's Soul ;*
> *Adown his Cheek a Tear unbidden stole,*
> *Stole unperceiv'd ; he turn'd his Head, and dry'd*
> *The Drop humane :*————

> *The Dog whom Fate had granted to behold*
> *His Lord, when twenty tedious Years had roll'd,*
> *Takes a last Look, and having seen him, dies ;*
> *So clos'd for ever faithful* Argus' *Eyes !*   Odyss. 17.

THERE are Medals with this Story upon the reverse, as is well known by the Curious.

HE had likewise painted an *Apollo* and *Diana*, that were extremely beautiful, just as they are described by the Poets ; and the Mother of the Gods upon a Lion's Back surrounded *Apollo, Diana,* with her Priests : A very gay *Bacchanalian* Piece with Satyrs rushing upon the *Bacchantes* *and other Pieces.* while they were employed about their Sacrifice, with lustful Rage (72). The true Charac- ter of a Satyr is admirably expressed in one of the ancient Paintings now published. He painted the Monster *Scylla* described by *Homer*, and afterwards by *Virgil*. Perhaps it is *The Scylla.* owing to *Virgil's* having seen this Performance, that he is thought to have excelled *Homer* in the Description of this Monster.

> *At Scyllam cæcis cohibet speluncæ latebris*
> *Ora exertantem, & naves in saxa trahentem.*
> *Prima hominis facies, & pulchro pectore virgo*
> *Pube tenus, postrema immani corpore Pristis,*
> *Delphinum caudas utero commissa luporum.*   Æn. 3. ver. 425.

IT

(69) *Plutarch. in Timoleonte.* Versus Antimachi & Pic- turæ Dionysii Colophoniorum ut ut vim habeant & insig- nem eximii splendoris vigorem (ἰσχὺν καὶ τόνον. It is the same word [τόνος] that *Pliny* himself makes use of in describing the Improvements in Colouring made by the Ancients, and which he translates Splendor.) Plurimum tamen laboriosæ, coactæque affectationis præ se ferunt : Nicomachi vero tabulis & carminibus Homeri, præter reliquam vim Veneremque, etiam hoc adest, quod expe- dite & cum eximia facilitate facta videantur. There is a famous Saying of his, with a judicious Reflection upon it in *Stobæus, Serm. 61. Ex Plutarcho de amore.* Non est idem judicium videndi, quemadmodum neque gustandi : Etenim visus visu, & auditus auditu, natura magis con- formatur & arte coexercitatur ad pulchri explorationem. Ad harmonias nimirum & modulos, musicorum ; ad for- mas vero ac species, pictorum ingenia plurimum valent.

Quamobrem quoque tradunt Nicomachum aliquando re- spondisse cuidam Idiotæ, qui Helenam Zeuxidis minime sibi pulchram videri dixerat, sume oculos meos & dea tibi videbitur. Ælian ascribes such another Saying to *Ni- costratus. Var. Hist. lib. 14. c. 47.*

(70) Pinxit & raptum Proserpinæ ;——Victoria quadri- gam in sublime rapiens. *Plin. ibid.*

(71) Hic primus Ulyxi addidit pileum. See *P. Har- douin, Montfaucon's Antiq.* and the French Notes on Pliny.

(72) Pinxit & Apollinem & Dianam ; Deûmque ma- trem in Leone sedentem : Item nobilis Bacchas, adrep- tantibus Satyris ; Scyllamque quæ nunc est Romæ in templo pacis. *Plin. ibid.*

IT is to be feen on Medals; and *Antonio Auguftini* mentions an ancient Statue at *Rome* of the *Scylla* reprefented in the fame manner (73).

Several Pictures by Euphranor. The twelve Gods.

SEVERAL Pictures of *Euphranor*, that vaft Genius for Painting as well as Sculpture, are highly extolled. The twelve greater Gods, as they are called, with all their proper Attributes, and in the Characters peculiar to each. An ancient Author fays, that he had made *Neptune*'s Image fo juft, true, and grand, with fuch Characters of divine Majefty, and yet

His Jupiter.

added fo much fuperiour Greatnefs to that of *Jupiter*, that his After-Labours did not come up to his Defign; but having, as it were, exhaufted his Imagination in thefe two, he fell fhort in the reft. They are all however greatly praifed: And *Euftathius* fays, that having meditated a long time in order to conceive a juft Idea of *Jupiter*; upon reading *Homer*'s Defcription of him in the firft Book of the *Iliad*, he cried out, that he had now a proper one to be emulated (74).

> *He fpoke, and awful bends his fable Brows;*
> *Shakes his ambrofial Curls, and gives the nod,*
> *The Stamp of Fate, and Sanction of the God:*
> *High Heav'n with trembling the dread Signal took,*
> *And all* Olympus *to the Centre fhook.*

His Thefeus, and other Pieces.

THE Hair of *Euphranor*'s *Juno* is much commended (75). His Picture of *Thefeus* founding the Democracy in the midft of the People, has been already mentioned. It was of this, or another *Thefeus*, painted by *Euphranor*, that he faid, on comparing it with one by *Parrhafius*, that the latter looked like one fed with Dew, but his was ftrong and mafculine, like one nourifh'd by more folid Food (76). His Excellence confifted in giving Heroes their proper Afpects and fuitable Qualities of Body and Mind. He painted a Battle called the Cavalry-Battle, becaufe there were no Foot-Soldiers in the Piece: It was the famous Battle at *Mantinea* againft *Epaminondas*. And this Picture, *Plutarch* fays, was wrought with a noble Enthufiafm (77); it was full of Life, Spirit, and Expreffion. The fame Picture is commended by *Paufanias* in his firft Book of Atticks, as well as the other of *Thefeus*. He did two Philofophers deeply mufing; a General putting up his Sword; and *Ulyffes* in his counterfeit Madnefs, yoking a Cow to the Plough with a Horfe (78). In all *Euphranor*'s Pictures there was great Propriety, and Strength of Expreffion; and they are no lefs extolled for their ex-

His Character, and wonderful Abilities.

cellence in the mechanical part. *Philoftratus* in his Life of *Apollonius* fays (79), his Pictures were alive; fo rounded that they appeared folid, fubftantial Bodies; and that fuch was his Art and Skill in painting, that fome parts feemed to come out, and offer themfelves to be grafped, while others preferved their due *Lontannezza* as it is called by Painters; that is, were duely diminifh'd, obfcured, and therefore appeared as if feen from far.

Of Cydias's *Works. The Argonautick Expedition.*

AT the fame time flourifh'd another very great Painter, *Cydias*, who painted the *Argonautick* Expedition; for which the famous Orator *Hortenfius* gave a great Sum (80): It came afterwards into the poffeffion of *Marcus Agrippa* (81), who confecrated it in the Portico of *Neptune*, as a proper Ornament for a Monument erected in Memory of naval Victories; and too noble a Work to be hidden in a private Villa. We cannot doubt of the Excellence of this Picture when we confider in what high efteem it was held by fuch intelligent Judges; but have good reafon to conclude that fo noble and worthy an Argument, was reprefented in a Stile fuitable to its Dignity.

The excellent Qualifications of Nicias.

NICIAS is mentioned with high Encomiums by feveral excellent Writers. *Plutarch* fpeaks of him with great Applaufe, he claffes him with the beft Painters of the *Athenian* School; and we may form fome Notion of the diftinguifhing Character and Excellence of that School, by what he fays of the *Athenian* Painters he commends. *Athens*, fays he, was a

fruitful

---

(73) *Dialoghi di D'Ant. Agoftini, Dial.* 5. *p.* 159. See *Ovid. Met. l.* 14. *v.* 60. & *Silius Ital. l.* 5.
Scylla fuper fracti contorquens pondera remi
Inflabat, fævofque canum pandebat hiatus.

(74) *Val. Max. lib.* 8. *c.* 11. *Exe. ext.* 5. *Macrobius* in like manner fays, that *Phidias* having made his *Olympian Jupiter*, which pafs'd for one of the greateft Miracles of Art, was afk'd from what Pattern he had fram'd fo divine a Figure; and anfwer'd, from thofe Verfes of *Homer* juft quoted. *Saturnal. l.* 5. *c.* 14. So foon as *Æmilius* faw this Statue, he faid, there is indeed the *Jupiter* of *Homer. Plut. in Æmilio.*

(75) *Lucian. in Imaginibus.*

(76) *Thefeus* in quo dixit, eundem apud *Parrhafium* rore paftum effe fuum Vero carne. *Plin.* 35. And *Plutarch. Bellone an Pace,* &c.

(77) *Plin. ibid.* Pinxit etiam equeftre adverfus Epami-

nondam prælium ad Mantineam, non fine quodam divino inftinctu Euphranor. *Plut. Bellone an Pace.*

(78) Nobiles ejus tabulæ Epheſi, Ulyxes fimulata veſania bovem cum equo jungens; & Palliatæ cogitantes; dux gladium condens. *Plin. ibid.* A Picture of *Ulyffes* in his counterfeited Madnefs is fully defcribed by *Lucian de Domo.*

(79) Οἶον εἰ ζεύξειας ἵππω τε, ἡ Πολυγνότε, ἡ Εὐφράνορος εἰ τὸ ἐνεῦχον βολιόωντι, ἡ τὰ ἱντεια, καὶ τὰ ὑπίχοντα καὶ ἐξέχον. lib. 2. c. 20.

(80) Eodem tempore fuit & Cydias, cujus tabulam, Argonautas, H. S. 144. Hortenfius orator mercatus eft, eique ædem fecit in Tufculano fuo. *Plin.* 35.

(81) M. Agrippa porticum Neptuni dictam propter victorias navales extruxit, & Argonautarum pictura decoravit. *Dion. Caffius, lib.* 53.

fruitful and kindly Mother, and Nurfe to all the fine Arts (82); fome it firft conceived and brought to Light; and to others it added great increafe of Excellence and Honour.   The Art of Painting was not a little promoted and improved by her.   For *Apollodorus* who firft invented the delicate Mixture of Colours, and found out the agreeable Diftribution of the Maffes of Lights and Shades, was an *Athenian:* Upon his Works it was infcribed, it is eafier to *carp at them, than to cope with them.*   So were *Euphranor, Nicias, Afclepiodorus* and *Plifti-nætus* Brother to *Phidias,* who painted Battles, and Generals leading Armies to War, and other great Subjects: He makes mention of the fame *Nicias* in another place, where he extols his indefatigable Diligence in improving himfelf and his Art, and the noble Enthufiafm with which he wrought (83).   *Paufanias* fpeaks highly in praife of his Paintings, in a fepulchral Monument at *Tritia,* a city of *Achaia;* which tho' finely adorned by feveral ancient Sculptures, was yet more diftinguifhed by *Nicias*'s beautiful Pictures.   There was painted, faith he (84), a beautiful, gracefulYouth fitting in a Chair, with aWoman on one fide holding a Parafol over his Head; and on the other a beardlefs Youth with a purple Robe hanging about him; near to whom is a Servant with a Spear in one hand, leading with the other fome Dogs to the Chace.   He did a Picture of *Hyacinthus,* with which *Auguftus* was fo delighted and charmed, that he brought it with him to *Rome,* from *Alexandria* (85).

His Danae.

BY him was painted a charming *Danae* fporting with little *Cupids,* while the Shower of Gold begins to fall which was to enfnare her: And *Ulyffes*'s Defcent into Hell as it is defcribed in the *Odyffey.*   But thefe Pieces were in Miniature.   His more capital Works were, the Story in the *Odyffey* of *Calypfo*'s detaining *Ulyffes* in her inchanted Ifland, and endeavouring to confole him by her Careffes: The Metamorphofis of *Io* into a Cow: *Juno* enraged againft *Jupiter* for his unfaithful Gallantries: *Perfeus* having killed the Monfter, handing down *Andromeda* from the Rock: An *Alexander* of exquifite Beauty; and another Picture of *Calypfo* in a different Attitude from the former, fitting on the Sea-fhore, and in the Action of looking after *Ulyffes,* with great Grief mixed with Anger at his Departure (86).   Thefe Pictures are praifed by feveral Authors, and fhew how converfant *Nicias* was with the Poets, and his poetical Genius; that he delighted in employing his Art upon Subjects which required a very fine Imagination and great Judgment; and could render Painting a Rival to her Sifter-Art.   He was fo greatly efteemed at *Athens,* that after his Death he was honoured with a fepulchral Monument amongft thofe who had been reckoned worthy of having fuch a publick Teftimony to their Merit (87).   He is particularly commended for fhunning in his Pictures what is called the *Triteria* by *Italians;* or filling Pictures with many fmall Objects which fplit or diffipate the Sight, and deftroy the Unity of Compofition (88).

Calypfo.

TIMOMACHUS (89) feems to have been a tragick Painter; he delighted and excelled moft in melancholy and horrible Subjects: And fhewed that the tragick Stile may be attained to in Painting as well as in Poetry; or that the former is no lefs capable of moving, and purging, (as *Ariftotle* calls it) our Pity and Horrour than the latter.   And therefore his Pictures are highly celebrated by the *Greek* and *Latin* Poets.   He painted *Ajax* become frantick upon his Difappointment in not having the Arms of *Achilles* adjudged to him by the *Greeks:*
                                                                                    Likewife

Timomachus a tragick Painter.

His Ajax.

(82) *Plutarch. Bellone an Pace, ab initio.*   Cujus operibus infcribebatur μωμησεται τις μαλλον, η μιμησεται, &c.

(83) *Plutarch. an Seni gerenda fit Refpublica.*   And in his other Treatife, *Non poffe fuaviter vivi,* &c.   So *Ælian, Var. Hift. lib.* 3. *c.* 31.   *Stobæus, Serm.* 29. *de Affiduitate.*   There we are told how fevere, temperate, and affiduous he was.

(84) It is not defcribed by *Paufanias,* as *Junius* and the Commentators on *Pliny* fay : For what he defcribes in his third Book is not Painting but a Piece of Sculpture, upon an Altar devoted to *Hyacinthus.*   " Upon it were " reprefented, faith that Author, in fine Relief, on one " fide *Neptune* with *Amphitrite,* on the other *Beris* one of " the *Nereids;* on another *Jupiter* and *Mercury* in con-" ference, and near to them *Bacchus, Semele* and *Ino;* " on the fourth *Ceres, Proferpine* and *Pluto,* and in their " Train the *Fates* and the *Hours:* After whom follow " *Venus, Minerva,* and *Diana,* carrying up *Hyacinthus* " to Heaven, with his Sifter *Polybaa,* who died a Virgin." The miftake feems to have been occafion'd by what *Paufanias* adds to this Defcription.   " As for the Statue " of *Hyacinth,* it reprefented him with a Beard, whether " he had one or not.   (*Nicias* in a Paffage, where he " hints at *Apollo*'s being in love with *Hyacinthus,* fpeaks of " his furpaffing Beauty.")   There is an Epigram in *Martial* upon the beautiful *Hyacinth* of this Painter : *Hyacinthus in tabula pictus,* l. 14. Ep. 165.
        Flectit ab invifo morientia lumina difco
        . *Oebalius, Phœbi culpa, dolorque puer.*
His *Perfeus* and *Andromeda* is thus defcribed in the *Greek* Epigrams. *Anthol. l.* 4. *c.* 9.

Æthiopum regio eft; qui fert talaria, Perfeus;
    Hæc adjuncta feris cautibus, Andromede :
Gorgonis hoc fectum caput eft; certamen amoris
    Bellua : Caffiopis garrula fertilitas.
Liberat illa pedes longa torpedine fegnes
    A fcopulo : potitur virgine victor amans.
Again, *Cepheus Andromeden, an pictor rupe ligavit ?*
    Namque oculus non quit cernere, credat utrum
    Picta fuper fcopulos oftenditur horrida Piftrix,
    An de vicino tollitur illa mari ?
    Agnofco vix figna manus : O! magnus in arte,
    Lumina qui potuit fallere, quique animos.

(85) *Paufanias Laconica,* p. 101.   Hyacinthus quem C. Auguftus, delectatus eo fecum deportavit Alexandriâ captâ; & ob id Tiberius Cæfar in templo ejus dedicavit hanc tabulam & Danae.   *Plin.* 35.

(86) Fecit & grandes picturas; in quibus funt, Calypfo, & Io, & Andromeda; Alexander quoque, in Pompei porticibus, præcellens ; & Calypfo fedens.   *Plin. ibid.*

(87) *Paufanias, lib.* 1. *p.* 57.   Paffage quoted above.

(88) *Demetrius Phalereus de Elocutione.*   The Paffage was quoted above.   The Words are remarkable, και μα καταχρυσωπη'ειν την τεχνην εις μικρα.   See a Picture of *Hyacinth* in *Philoftratus*'s *Icones.*

(89) Timomachus Byzantius, Cæfaris dictatoris Ajacem & Medeam pinxit, ab eo in Veneris genetricis æde pofitas octoginta talentis venumdatas.——Timomachi laudantur & Oreftes, Iphigenia, &c. *Plin.* 35.

His Medea. Likewise *Medea,* who in killing her Infants is not able to restrain her Tears, tho' transported to that barbarous Cruelty by the most violent of all Passions. *Ovid* alludes to both these:

> *Utque sedet Vultu falsus Telamonius, iram*
> *Inque oculis facinus barbara mater habet* (89). Triftium l. 2.

His Orestes, Iphigenia, *and* Medusa.   HE painted *Orestes; Iphigenia* acknowledging her Brother, and saving him out of the Hands of the *Barbarians;* a *Medusa's* Head, and several other Pieces. *Philostratus* speaking of his *Ajax,* very justly observes how well one must be acquainted with the human Mind and Passions in order to paint such Subjects (90). "As one, (says he) must know a Horse exactly, in order to represent it to the Life; so must one be intimately skilled in the Heart of Man, in order to paint its Motions, Affections, Sentiments and Passions, and to be able to touch and work them." I cannot however chuse but observe on this occasion, how reasonably *Plutarch* censures those who delight in painting base, barbarous, or cruel and horrible Actions (91). It requires a great deal of Delicacy and Judgment to treat them rightly, or without being offensive; and to deserve the Character which *Timomachus* gives of a Picture of *Pylades* and *Orestes* killing *Clytemnestra* and *Ægisthus,* due in a great measure to *Timomachus's Medea.* He calls it a most decent, virtuous Picture, because what was barbarous and inhumane in the Action was not represented in it (92). The Slaughter of the Innocents even by a *Raphael* will ever be a Subject too horrible to be beheld without suffering. *Horace's* Rule is as necessary in Painting as in Poetry:

Certain Subjects of Painting censured.

> *Nec pueros coram populo Medea trucidet.*

There are Examples among the Ancients of all sorts of Painting.   WE find Examples of all the Variety of Painting amongst the Antients: *Antiphilus* did a Boy blowing the Fire in a House, which is all enlightened by the Reflection from it. *Comus* in *Philostratus* is an Image of Debauchery; it is likewise a Night-piece, where all is seen by the Light of a Torch. *Pausias,* painted a muddled Woman drinking out of a Glass, in which her Image was seen distinctly reflected. *Socrates* is famous for having painted *Æsculapius* with his four Daughters; probably representing symbolically the different Branches of Medicine. He delighted in allegorical Pieces, and painted one to represent a too easy Husband ruin'd by an extravagant Wife. A Man is painted plaiting a Rope, and a She-Ass eating it up as fast as he made it. The Piece was called *(Ocnos).* Such a Picture with that Name is described by *Pausanias* (93), but he ascribes it to *Polygnotus.*

Aristophon's Ancæus.   *ARISTOPHON* is greatly renowned for two excellent Pictures. The Subject of one was *Ancæus* wounded by a wild Boar, and his Wife *Astypale* condoling him, and kindly sharing his Pain. The other is a much larger Piece, consisting of several Groupes: On the one side is *Priam, Helen,* and the rest of his Family, with *Credulity* flattering them: On the other *Ulysses, Deiphobus* and some other Generals, with *Cunning* teaching them Expedients
to

(89) See *Heinsius's* Notes upon the place. There are two *Greek* Epigrams upon the *Medea,* both translated by *Ausonius* :

> *Medeam vellet cum pingere Timomachi mens*
> *Volventem in natos crudum animo facinus;*
> *Immanem exhausit rerum in diversa laborem,*
> *Fingeret affectum matris ut ambiguum:*
> *Ira subest lachrymis; miseratio non caret irâ,*
> *Alterutrum videas ut sit in alterutro*
> *Cunctantem satis est. Nam digna est sanguine mater*
> *Natorum, tua non dextra, Timomache.*

Anthol. Ep. lib. 4. c. 9.   Vertit Auson. Ep. 122.

> *Quis te pictorum simulavit, pessima Colchis,*
> *In natos crudum volvere mente nefas?*
> *Usque adeone sitis puerorum haurire cruorem*
> *Ut ne picta quidem parcere cæde velis?*
> *Numnam te Pellex stimulat? numne alter Iason,*
> *Altera vel Glauce, sunt tibi causa necis?*
> *Quin ne picta quidem sis barbara; namque tui vim*
> *Cera tenax zeli concipit immodicam.*
> *Laudo Timomachum, matrem quod pinxit in ensem*
> *Cunctantem prolis sanguine ne maculet.*

Ausonius, Ep. 202.

There are several other *Greek* Epigrams in the *Anthol.* upon this *Medea.* This Subject, finely done in Marble, is described by *Calistratus. Calistrati ἐκφραϭις in signum Medeæ* 13.

(90) Quapropter dixerim ego, & eos, qui pictoriæ artis opera aspiciant, imitatrice opus habere facultate. Nemo enim laudaverit pictum equum, aut taurum, qui animal illud mente non intueatur, cujus similitudinem refert: Neque Vero Timomachi Ajacem quisquam miretur, qui furens ab illo pictus extat, nisi aliquam mente, Ajacis, speciem complexus fuerit, utque eum verosimile fit, interemptis ad Trojam armentis concidisse sessum, id-

que animo agitantem ut seipsum quoque interimat. *Philost. de vit. Apol. lib.* 2. *c.* 23.

(91) Quidam pingunt actiones turpes: ut Timomachus Medeam liberos necantem, Theon Orestem manus inferentem matri, Parrhasius Ulyssis simulatam insaniam, & Chærephanes libidinosos mulierum cum viris congressus. Plutarch. de poet. audien.

(92) *Lucian. de Domo.* Here he describes a very gay pleasant Picture. Post hæc autem Deus est formosus & adolescentulus venustus, amatorum quoddam ludicrum: Branchus puta in rupe sedens tenet leporem, & alludit cani. Hic autem afflicenti ad ipsum in sublimi, similis est: Et Apollo adstans arridet. Delectatur videlicet utroque & puero ludente, & cane saltum meditante. He here describes likewise a Picture of *Medea,* Æmulatione atque invidia flagrans, pueros aspiciens, & grave quiddam meditans, tenet quippe jam gladium: miseri autem illi adstant ridentes, nihil eorum quæ futura erant, scientes, & hunc aspicientes in manibus gladium. A little before the Picture of *Pylades,* &c. Is described. (γεγϑαμμεϑα·) Honestum quiddam pictor excogitavit, qui quod impium in hac re fuit id ostendit solum, & quasi jam peractum prætercurrit; sed adolescentes, in cæde adulteri, immorantes exprimit.

(93) Antiphilus, puero ignem conflante laudatus, ac pulchra domo flamma splendescente, ipsiusque pueri ore: ——Socrates jure omnibus placet; talesque sunt ejus cum Æsculapio filiæ, &c.——Et piger qui appellatur Ocnos. *Plin.* 35. *Pauf. Phoc.* 345. 20. Picta quoque ibi est Ebrietas, & ipse Pausiæ opus & Vitrea phiala bibens: videas autem in pictura Phialam vitream, ac per eam ipsius mulieris vultum. *Pausanias, lib.* 2. 134.

'to furprize the Befieged (94). This *Ariftophon* is a very ancient Painter, Son to *Aglaophon* already mentioned (95).

THERE was a *Danae* painted by *Artemon* that was extremely beautiful, with feveral Per-fons looking at her with Admiration.   *Jupiter* highly enamoured of her Beauty ; *Venus* fmiling at the vain Precautions taken to guard her ; and *Cupids* playing wantonly about her and them.   To fome fuch Picture *Horace* perhaps alludes:

> *Si non Acrifium, virginis abditæ*
> *Cuftodem pavidum, Jupiter & Venus*
> *Rififfent.*———   Hor. l. 3. Od. 16.

HE painted the Phyfician difcovering to *Seleucus* the Source of his Son's Sicknefs, even that he was defperately in love with his own Wife *Stratonice* ; a Subject that hath been often tried by modern Painters.   But his moft famous Picture was the Apotheofis of *Her-cules*, or *Hercules* having put off his Mortality, and left it in the Flames on Mount *Oeta*, afcending up triumphantly to Heaven, with the Confent of the Gods (96).   An-other reprefented the Ingratitude and Perfidy of *Laomedon* to *Neptune*, revenged by the Miniftry of *Hercules*.

IT is not furprizing to find Painters making as free with the Gods as the Poets.   *Cte-filochus* a Difciple of *Apelles*, and a very able Painter, but one who gave way to his pe-tulant libertine Imagination, had reprefented *Jupiter* drefs'd like a Woman and in travail, bringing forth *Bacchus*.   He feems to roar aloud (fays *Pliny*) and to call to all the Divi-nities for help (97).

THE *Venus* of *Nealces* was particularly efteemed, notwithftanding all the fine ones that had been done before him by fuch eminent Hands.   To one of Genius, a Subject is always new ; and there is a *Venus* in this Collection of ancient Paintings, which is indeed very beautiful, though perhaps not equal to that of *Nealces*.   This Painter had a ftrict regard to Truth, Nature, and the Coftume in his Pieces, which made them very intelligible, and added to their Beauty and Force exceedingly.   We have an inftance of this in one of his Pictures reprefenting a naval Fight between the *Perfians* and *Egyptians* : For having oc-cafion to paint the *Nile*, which is very large towards the End of its Courfe, and whofe Water there is hardly difcernible from the Sea ; he characterizes the *Nile* diftinctly by an Afs drinking, and a Crocodile, at a little diftance, half hid amongft the Bufhes, watching its opportunity to fpring upon the Afs (98).   Whence we fee how well the ancient Ma-fters underftood, by their Art, to give every thing its proper Character, and to determine by evident Marks the Scene of their Reprefentations.   *Plutarch* tells us in his Life of *Aratus* (99), how earneftly this Painter intreated *Aratus* to deftroy Tyrants, but not their Images, if they were well painted : For *Aratus*, though a great Lover of the Art, was fuch an Enemy to Tyranny, that he could hardly prevail upon himfelf to fuffer any me-morial of them to remain undeftroyed.

SIMUS painted the Goddefs *Nemefis* with all her Attributes; a Rule in her Hands to regulate our Words and Actions; a Bridle to reftrain our Paffions and Appetites; Wings to fly after the Guilty, that none may efcape, and a Crown to reward the Juft ; a Figure that muft have infpired Fear and Reverence (100).

> *Hæc Nemefis frænum geftans normamque monebit*
> *Nil effræne loqui, nil facere abfque modo.*   Anthol. lib. 4. c. 12.

THEODORUS had painted *Oreftes* killing Ægyfthus and *Clytemneftra* ; the Sub-ject of this Picture was taken from *Sophocles* (101).   He likewife had reprefented the whole War

---

(94) Ariftophon, Ancæo vulnerato ab apro cum focia doloris Aftypale : numerofaque tabula in qua funt Pria-mus, Helena, Credulitas ; Ulyxes, Delphobus, Dolus. *Plin. ibid.*

(95) *Plate in Gorgia.*

(96) Artemon, Danaen, mirantibus eam prædonibus ; reginam Stratonicen : Herculem & Dejaniram : Nobi-liffumas autem quæ funt in Octaviæ operibus, Herculem ab Oeta, monte Doridos, exuta mortalitate, confenfu deorum in cœlum euntem : Laomedontis circa Herculem & Neptunum.hiftoriam.   *Plin. ibid.*   Vid. *Ter. Eun. Act.* 3. *S.* 5.

(97) Ctefilochus, Apellis difcipulus, petulanti pictum innotuit, Jove liberum parturiente, depicto mitrato & mu-liebriter ingemifcente, inter obftetricia dearum. *Plin.ibid.*

(98) Nealces, Venerem ; ingeniofus & folers in arte,

&c.   *Plin. ibid.*   *Coppell* in his Pictures reprefenting *Mofes* faved by *Pharaoh's* Daughter, has imitated in feveral Cir-cumftances this Picture of *Nealces*.

(99) Arato poft liberatam Sicyonem volente una cum reliquorum tyrannorum imaginibus etiam tollere nobilem Ariftrati tabulam, pictam ab omnibus Melanthi affeclis, in qua tyrannus ille infiftebat currui triumphali cum victoria ; perhibent Nealcem pictorem, Arato carum, lacrymabundum dixiffe, Bellum gerendum cum ipfis tyrannis, minime vero cum eorum imaginibus. Sinamus igitur currum & Victoriam : Ariftratus ipfe faxo ut tolla-tur.   Quod cum ei indulfiffet Aratus, mox Ariftratum delevit pictor, palmamque in locum ejus fubftituit. *Plut. in Arato.*

(100) Simus, Nemefim egregiam. See the *French* Tranf-lation of *Pliny*, and the Notes.

(101) See the fame *French* Tranflation, and the Notes.

War of *Troy* in feveral Pieces; in which were painted all the moft remarkable Events as they are fung by *Homer.* Thefe Pictures were carried to *Rome* before *Virgil's* time; and 'tis highly probable that *Virgil* had his Eye upon them in defcribing the Pictures with which he adorns the Temple of *Juno* at *Carthage.* For there *Æneas* faw the whole *Trojan* War painted in order; and this Painter had painted the whole of it in a Suite of Pictures. *Theodorus* had alfo painted the unfortunate *Caffandra* (102); which Picture was like-wife brought to *Rome,* and placed in the Temple of *Concord*; and from it, no doubt, *Virgil* had taken affiftance in defcribing her tragick Story in fo pictorefque a manner as he does:

His Caffandra is defcribed by Virgil.

> Ecce trahebatur paffis *Priameia virgo*
> Crinibus, a templo, Caffandra adytifque Minervæ,
> Ad cælum tendens ardentia lumina, fruftra
> Lumina: nam teneras arcebant vincula palmas.
> Non tulit hanc fpeciem furiata mente Choræbus,
> Et fefe medium injecit moriturus in agmen. ·   Æn. 2. ver. 405.

The Alliance between Poetry and Painting.

NOW we may fee from thefe Examples how nearly allied Painting and Poetry are, and how they mutually affifted one another.

> Verfe and Sculpture bore an equal part,
> And Art reflected Images on Art.   Pope.

'Tis not in the leaft derogatory from *Virgil's* Genius, to fuppofe him gathering beautiful Images from all the fine ancient Sculptures, Statues, and Pictures that were brought from *Greece* to *Rome* in his time, fince he has made an excellent ufe of them. We cannot chufe but confider his Pictures in *Dido's* Temple as Defcriptions of real Pictures. For many ancient Painters, as well as *Theodorus,* had exerted their greateft Skill upon that noble Subject for Painting as well as Poetry. And no doubt the *Romans,* who were ac-quainted with thefe fine Pictures, muft have had a double pleafure in comparing the De-fcriptions with the original Pictures. I fhall juft add to thefe other Examples of the ufe *Virgil* made of the defigning Arts, that the Cloak upon which was interwoven the Story of *Ganymede* (which is recommended by Dr. *Trap* as a beautiful Subject for Painting) had been finely reprefented in Sculpture by *Leocharis* (103). He had reprefented the Eagle, carrying away *Ganymede,* as fenfible of his Charge, and for whom it was defign'd; and taking the tendereft Care not to hurt him.

Other Pictures de-fcribed or alluded to by Virgil.

TIS not improbably that or fome other fuch Work, that *Virgil* had in his Eye in this moft pictorefqne Defcription:

> ———— Quem præpes ab Ida
> Sublimem, pedibus rapuit *Jovis* armiger uncis:
> Longævi, palmas nequicquam ad fidera tendunt
> Cuftodes, fævitque canum latratus in auras.   Virg. Æn. 5. 254.

MARTIAL has defcribed the carrying up of *Ganymede* precifely, as *Leocharis* is faid to have reprefented it.

> Ætherias Aquila puerum portante per auras
> Illæfum timidis unguibus hæfit onus.   Lib. 1. Ep. 6.

AS for the other part of *Virgil's* Defcription:

> Intentufque puer frondofa regius Idâ,
> Veloces jaculo cervos curfuque fatigat
> Acer, anhelanti fimilis.————

WE have many Defcriptions of Statues and Pictures reprefenting young Hunters in that Attitude, as it were, quite out of breath; and *Pliny* in particular fpeaks of a Picture by *Parrhafius,* of one who having laid down his Arms, feemed to pant for Breath (104.)

The Oreftes of Theon.

THEON had painted *Oreftes,* who having killed his Mother through the violent Tranf-ports of his Vengeance, became mad; and the vain *Thamyras,* who had the prefumption

to

---

(102) Theodorus Vero & inungentem: idem, ab O-relte matrem & Ægyfthum interfici (c'eft une phrafe Grecque, familiere a notre auteur. Je n'en alleguerai qu'un example tiré du livre 34. §. 19. n. 4. ou il s'agit d'une antique de bronze de la façon de Pythagore le Sici-lien: Item, Apollinem, ferpentemque fagittis ejus con-fici:) The French Notes.——Bellumque Iliacum pluribus tabulis, quod eft Romæ, in Philippi porticibus; & Caf-fandram quæ eft in Concordiæ delubro. *Plin.* 35. Di-ogenes Laertius, Book 2d, in his Life of the Philofopher *Theodorus,* mentions twenty of that Name; Duodeci-mus eft ille Theodorus pictor, cujus meminit Polemon:

decimus tertius eft Theodorus Athenienfis pictor, de quo fcribit Menodotus: decimus quartus eft Theodorus pictor Ephefius cujus mentionem facit Theophanes in libro de pictura.

(103) *Plin. l.* 34. Leocharis fecit Aquilam fentien-tem quid rapiat in Ganymede & cui ferat, parcentem unguibus etiam per veftem.

(104) *Plin. lib.* 35. Arma deponens ut anhelare, fen-tiatur.

to enter into a Competition with the Muses; so confident was he in his Skill and Voice (105.) *Ælian* describes another Picture by the same *Theon* (106), which deserves to be taken notice of, on account of an ingenious Stratagem the Painter employed, in order to shew his Piece to the best advantage at the *Olympick* Prizes, according to the Custom of those Times. He had painted a Person in Armour, who seems to sally out upon the Enemy with Fury: He flies to the Combat with Eyes flaming with Rage: He brandishes his Sword, and lifts his Arm to reach a heavy Blow. Mean while there is no other Figure in the Picture; he is single and quite alone. Now the Method he took to display the Beauties of this Picture to the People assembled to judge of it, was this: He had hired Trumpets on purpose, and ordered them to be sounded on a private Signal; so that when the People were surprized with that unexpected Noise, and their Imaginations alarmed with the Fears of some sudden Irruption, he drew the Curtain and shewed this Piece to the great Astonishment of all the Spectators, who by this means were exceedingly struck with its Beauties.

Another famous Picture by him, and his Stratagem to shew it to advantage.

STRABO commends *Aregon* for having adorned the Temple of *Diana* in the *Aphionian* Grove sacred to her, near to the River *Alpheus*, with several beautiful Paintings; amongst which were the Burning of *Troy*, the Nativity of *Minerva*, and *Diana* carried up to Heaven upon a Gryphin (107): All noble and poetical Subjects.

Aregon's Works commended.

PAUSANIAS (108) mentions *Calyphon*, who, in a Picture of the Combat of the *Greeks* at their Ships, had painted a Figure of *Discord* in a most hideous Shape; but he had copied it from a Piece of Sculpture representing her, standing by *Ajax* and *Hector*, in their single Combat, by the same Hand that was celebrated for *Boreas* carrying off *Orythia*. He likewise painted *Theseus* playing on a Lyre, and *Ariadne* by him holding a Crown; the Combat between *Achilles* and *Memnon*, with their Mothers for Witnesses of their Valour; and several other excellent Pieces.

Discord by Calyphon, but copied from the Work of another Artist.

PLINY speaks of a *Dionysius* who was called the Man-Painter, because he only did Portraits. But there was another Painter of that Name, whom *Aristotle* reckons amongst those who understood Manners, and expressed them in their Pictures (109). He says, he painted Men just as they commonly are, in ordinary Life, neither better nor worse. *Plutarch* says, there was a great deal of Force, something very strong and nervous in *Dionysius's* Pictures; but that they had not the Charm, which an Air of Facility and Easiness gives (110). They had not, it seems, that great Beauty in Composition, which *Cicero* says is so charming, and so difficult to attain in Oratory and every Art, in consequence of which a Composition appears easily imitable to every one but to him who tries it (111). *Ælian* ranks him with those who excelled in representing the Affections and Manners, and in painting easy pictoresque-Draperies (112). Almost all the great Actions recorded by Historians, or sung by Poets, as we shall have occasion to observe more particularly in another place, have likewise been celebrated by the Pencil. *Pausanias* names one *Onatas* (113), who had painted the Battle of the *Argians* and the *Thebans*, which, he says, is the most considerable War amongst the *Greeks*, in those that are called the heroick Times. It cost so much Blood, that a *Theban* Victory was become a Proverb, signifying a very cruel and bloody one. This War, says he, was sung by some ancient Poet. The Poem is by some ascribed to *Homer*; but for my part (continues he) I must say that I have not seen any Poesy comparable to the *Iliad* and *Odyssey*. In that Picture this memorable Action was very well represented; the Heroes of both sides were properly distinguished, and a great variety of Bravery was admirably expressed.

Dionysius called the Man-Painter.

Another Dionysius. His Character.

The Battle of the Argians by Onatas.

THUS we see that ancient Artists delighted much in performing moral Pictures; that is, all sorts of judicious Representations of human Passions: In martial Pieces especially, in which were expressed, in lively Action, the several degrees of Valour, Magnanimity, Cowardice, Terrour, Anger, according to the several Characters of Nations, and particular Men. 'Tis here that we may see Heroes and Chiefs appear, even in the hottest of Actions, with a Tranquillity of Mind and Sedateness peculiar to themselves, which is indeed (as a noble Author (114) observes) in a direct and proper Sense, profoundly moral.

The Ancients delighted in martial Pieces, and these are truly moral Pictures.

THERE

(105) Theon Oreftis infaniam; Thamyram Citharædum. *Plin. ibid. Plutarch. de aud. Poet. ut fupra.*

(106) *Æl. var. Hift. lib. 2. cap. ult.*

(107) *Strabo, lib. 8. 343.*

(108) *Eliaca 1. 166.*

(109) *Arift. cap. 2. de re poet.*

(110) *Plut. in Timol. ut fupra.*

(111) *Cic. ad M. Brutum Orator.* He speaks of this Negligence in this manner——Non ingratam negligen-

tiam, de re, hominis, magis, quam de verbis, laborantis.——Sed quædam etiam negligentia eft diligens; nam ut mulieres dicuntur nonnullæ inornatæ quas idipfum deceat; fic hæc fubtilis oratio etiam incompta delectat. Fit enim quiddam in utroque quo fit venuftius, fed non ut appareat.——Again. Itaque eum qui audiunt, quamvis ipfi infantes fint, tamen illo modo confidunt fe poffe dicere: Nam orationis fubtilitas, imitabilis illa videtur effe exiftimanti, fed nihil eft experienti minus.

(112) *Æl. var. Hift. lib. 4. c. 3.*

(113) *Paufanias, lib. 9. p. 48.*

(114) *Tablat. of Hercules, Charact. 3d vol.*

There are a great many other Pictures described by ancient Writers.

THERE are a great many other ancient Pictures described by several Authors : The two *Philostratus's* have given us a particular Account of a great many. And several more Passages from the antient Poets might be brought, which are probably Descriptions of Pictures (115).

But those that have been mentioned suffice to prove the Excellency of the Art, its relation to Poetry and Philosophy.

What the Philostratus's say on that Subject.

BUT those that have been mentioned are sufficient to prove, that the ancient Painters could not only design correctly, which is all that Mr. *Perrault* allows them; but that they had Genius and Invention, understood all the Beauties of Disposition and Ordonnance, and could compose truly generous and pleasing, or truly great, majestick, and moving Pictures. And the Examples that have been brought do likewise fully confirm the Truth of the Observations, with which the two *Philostratus's* begin their Discourses on Pictures, upon the Usefulness of Painting, and its strict Connexion with Poetry and Philosophy. " He (say the (116) *Philostratus's*) who despises the Art of Painting is injurious to the Truth, and wrongs the " Wisdom of the Ancients; he injures also the poetical Art, for the principal End of both " these kindred Arts is to exhibit the great Virtues and great Actions of illustrious Heroes. " He must likewise contemn the Symmetry and Truth of Composition in Oratory. If " one had a mind to talk in the Stile of the Sophists and Declaimers, one might truly say " not only that it is a divine Invention; but that the Gods taught Men the Art by so beau- " tifully painting the Heavens with various Appearances, and the Earth with such innu- " merable beautiful Forms varying with the Seasons; and if we look narrowly into the " Origin of the delightful Art, we shall find that Imitation is very natural to Men, and " that all kinds of Imitation, or all the imitative and designing Arts must for that reason " be very ancient : Now all these, however classed and divided, have the same Founda- " tion, and proceed upon the same Principles. There is one kind, which whether mould- " ing with Clay, casting in Brass, or carving in Marble and Ivory, is properly called Plastick : " But Painting employs Colours, and with these is able to do more than any of those other " Arts can do. Tho' working always in the same way, or with the same Materials; yet " it is capable of a great variety : It marks the various Degradations of Lights and Shadows, " and emulates every Part and Appearance of Nature. It can imitate not only Woods, " Groves, Rivers, Mountains, Cities, Houses, and all sorts of Clothes, Arms, or what- " ever Ornaments; but it can likewise represent human Features, all the infinite Diversity " that is to be found in these, every Complexion, all kinds of Eyes and Countenances; " and which is still more, all the Sentiments, Passions, Motions, and Tempers, which " discover themselves in the Face or Gesture. *Aristodemus* of *Cana* hath wrote a full " History of the Art, and of its Progress and Improvements; an account of the States and Cities " in which it was cultivated and encouraged, and of the great Genius's who by their diffe- " rent Abilities and Talents added to it, and advanced it to perfection. I was four Years " in his House, in order to be instructed by him in the Principles and Beauties of the Art. " He himself was formed by *Eumelus*, an excellent Master, and painted according to his " Rules, and in his Manner; but gave more Grace to his Works than his Teacher was " able to do. It is indeed a great and comprehensive Art, and he who betakes himself to " any part of it must fully understand the Nature and the Beauties of that which he pre- " tends to imitate. But the noblest kind of it consists in imitating the highest Order of " Beauty, rational Life, of Men, Manners, and Characters. And must not such be throughly " skilled

(115) Such as, for instance, *Ovid's* Contest between *Minerva* and *Arachne.*

Augusta gravitate sedent. Sua quemque Deorum
Inscribit facies. Jovis est regalis imago,
Stare Deum pelagi, longoque ferire tridente
Aspera saxa facit, medioque e vulnere saxi
Exsiluisse ferum ;— Ovid. Met. lib. 6. ver. 73.

Such is his beautiful Description of the Seasons, *Metam.* l. 2. ver. 24.

————— *purpura velatus veste sedebat*
In solio, Phœbus claris lucente smaragdis.
A dextra lævoque dies, & mensis & annus,
Sæculaque & positæ spatiis æqualibus horæ.
Verque novum stabat cinctum florente corona :
Stabat nuda Æstas, & spicea serta gerebat :
Stabat & Autumnus calcatis sordidus uvis ;
Et glacialis Hyems canos hirsuta capillos,
Inde loco Medius, rerum novitate paventem
Sol oculis juvenem, quibus aspicit omnia, videt.

Compare this with the Description of the Seasons. *Ovid. Met. l.* 15. *ver.* 200, &c. No less picturesque is that Description of a Procession of the Seasons by *Lucretius :*

It Ver, & Venus, & Veneris præmuntius ante
Pimatus graditur Zephyrus vestigia propter :
Flora quibus mater præspergens ante viai
Cuncta coloribus egregiis, & odoribus opplet.
Inde loci sequitur calor aridus, & comes unâ.
Pulverulenta Ceres, & Etesia flabra aquilonum.
Inde Auctumnus adit : graditur simul Evius-Evan :
Inde aliæ tempestates, ventique sequuntur,
Altitonani Volturnus, & Auster fulmine pollens.
Tandem Bruma nives offert, pigrumque rigorem

Reddit. Hyems sequitur, crepitans, ac dentibus algor.
T. Lucr. Cari de rerum natura, l. 5.

And how delightful a Picture would this Description by *Ovid* make? Fast. l. 5. ver. 215.

Roscida cum primum foliis excussa pruina est,
Et variæ radiis intepuere comæ ;
Conveniunt pictis incinctæ vestibus horæ,
Inque cives Calothei munera nostra legunt.
Protinus arripiunt charites ; nectuntque coronas,
Sertaque cœlestes implicitura comas.

He mentions some Pictures in *Augustus's* House, some of which have been already taken notice of in speaking of the same or like Pictures.

Scilicet in domibus vestris ut prisca virorum
Artifici fulgent corpora picta manu ;
Sic quæ concubitus vanos Venerisque figuras
Exprimit, est aliquo parva tabella loco.
Utque sedet vultu fassus Telamonius iram,
Inque oculis facinus barbara mater habet :
Sic madidos siccat digitis Venus uda capillos :
Et modo maternis tecta videtur aquis.
Bella sonant alii telis instructa cruentis :
Parque tui generis, pars tua facta canunt.
Tristium, l. 2. ver. 521.

(116) *Philos. Icones Exord. & Philos. jun. Icones Exord.* In which there is this remarkable Passage : ἀδκϊν δὲ μοι παλαιοῖ τε ἣ σοφοί ἀνδρες πολλὰ ὑπὲρ ξυμμετρίας τῆς ἐν γεαφικῇ γεγφαι, οἷον ἰσονοῦν τὶζωνε τῆς ἐζαντῶι μελωι ἀναλογίαζ, ὡς ἂν οὖν τὸι τῆς ἐντιλοι ψυχωσει δεζε, μὴ οἶσω τὶ ἂν φύσιωι μέτρα τῆς ἁφμονίας πικυσε, τὸ γὰρ ἱκανωσι, ἣ ἔξω μέτρω, ἰκαπαϊ ἐχισταϊ φύσιι, ὀρθῶς ἰχιωσι κἰνισι.

" skilled in the Texture of the human Mind ? 'Tis not fufficient to know the outward Features
" only ; but he muft underftand fully the inward Operations, Features and Proportions of the
" Mind, that he may be able to reprefent any Paffion of whatever kind, and to give to every
" Affection and Movement of the Heart its peculiar and diftinguifhing Character.   To any one
" who gives himfelf leave to think of this Art, its near relation to Poetry muft be very evident.
" He will plainly fee that they have one common End, and a certain common Imagination.   For
" as the Poets introduce the Gods and Heroes, and paint all thofe things which have Gravity, Ma-
" jefty and Magnificence, or which are capable of moving, delighting or inftructing : In like
" manner the Painters, by virtue of their Out-lines, Colours, Lights and Shadows, repre-
" fent the fame Objects, and attain to the fame Ends of charming or teaching.   They are
" able to reprefent any Object as if it were really prefent, afpiring at no lefs than an ab-
" folute Command over our Senfes, by deceiving in not only an innocent, but a highly
" entertaining and ufeful manner.   And in order to this, Painters muft be great Students
" and Obfervers of Nature, underftand the natural Meafure and Proportion of every thing,
" and its higheft Perfection.   For which reafon feveral learned and wife Ancients have
" wrote much upon Symmetry in Painting, as being its principal Foundation ; they have
" laid down the Rules and Meafure, and as it were the Lines to be obferved in the Art,
" all of which are taken from Nature ; for every thing has its determinate Conftitution,
" its fixed Proportions, Limits and Degrees : And nothing can fubfift in Nature, or by
" confequence appear natural in Imitation, which is not conformable to its kind, and
" rightly difpofed according to the relative Laws of its Nature and Conftitution : It is fo
" in Minds as well as Bodies : And therefore the great Science of a Painter is the Science
" of Symmetry and Proportion, or of Truth, Nature, and Beauty."

TO thefe Reflections it may be added, That Painting plainly admits the fame variety as *It is plain that* Poetry ; and accordingly we find all the different parts, into which Poetry is divided, like- *Painting and Poetry* wife diftinguifhed in Painting.   One Painter is faid to have excelled in reprefenting the Vir- *admit of the fame* tues of Heroes, and fetting forth their noble Characters and Actions; another is faid to have *variety.* excelled in the tragick Kind; fome fucceeded beft in Comedy and Satire ; and others even *They were divided* delighted in Farce or Burlefque.   There is painly the Epick, the Lyrick, the Tragick, the *by the Ancients in* Comick, the Paftoral, the Elegiack in the one Art as well as in the other.   Thofe Pictures, *the fame manner,* for inftance, which defcribed the Siege of *Troy*, were as properly Heroick or Epick Pictures, *into the Epick, Tra-* as a Poem having that for its Subject is an Epick Poem.   As every kind of Poetry hath *gick, Comick, &c.* its particular Province and diftinguifhing Character ; fo, certainly, muft every particular kind of Painting.   And as it will afterwards appear that the general Rules of all po- etick Compofition, of that kind more efpecially which imitates Men and Manners, extend equally to Painting and Poetry : So were we to compare the particular Laws and Rules of any one kind of Poetry, with thofe of its correfponding part in Painting ; (as for ex- ample, the Tragedy of *Iphigenia*, or *Oreftes*, with the fuitable Difpofition of a tra- gick Picture to reprefent the fame Subjects, and to have the fame moving Influence on the Mind,) thefe Rules would be found to be fubftantially the fame, or to have a very near Affinity and Refemblance.   In order to give a full Account of the Art of Painting, one could not purfue a better Method, than by dividing it as Poetry is done, and by illuftrating the Rules of its feveral Parts, by proper Pictures compared with Poems of the fame Kinds; the Tragick with the Tragick, the Comick with the Comick, and fo on.   It is fufficient to my prefent purpofe to have obferved, that fuch a Divifion of Painting is fufficiently authorized by the an- cient ways of fpeaking about the Art, that have been taken notice of (117).   And indeed fince the Divifion of Poetry into its feveral Species or Branches, is purely taken from the dif- ferent Ends aimed at, and purfued by its feveral Parts; which are, either to convey Inftruction *Their End is the* to the Mind of one kind or other; or to touch and move this or the other particular Paffion ; *fame, to inftruct,* Painting, intending and purfuing the fame Defign of inftructing, delighting or moving, muft *move, and delight.* in like manner naturally diftinguifh itfelf according to the various Ends it purfues, or the dif- ferent Paffions it attempts to move.   If therefore it fooths the Mind with a delightful View of Nature, it is truly Paftoral; if it weeps over a departed Friend or Lover it is Elegiack; when the Subject moves my Pity or Horrour, it is Tragedy; when it fhews the Deformity of Ca- lumny or any Vice, it is Comedy or Satire.   And when it exhibits the Glory of great Deeds, it is Heroick.   And of all thefe kinds we have found Examples in ancient Pictures, as they are defcribed

(117) They have been all mentioned in their proper places, in treating on the Painters. To thefe may be added that pathetick Exclamation of *Hymerius*, apud Photium ex declamatione patris percufforis filii, *p.* 1090. *Quære plctorem tragicum quidem arte, & manu, animo vero magis tragicum : Jube vero feriem fortunarum me- arum in tabula depingat. Nihil ante narrationem pin- gat, neque dicentem, neque concionantem, neque coro- natum, nec quidquid eorum quæ fortunatis folent acci- dere. Plena fit tota meis calamitatibus tabula. Primo pingatur infelix pater fuis manibus infantem in folitudi- nem ferens, deplorans, lugens infortunium, exiens, re- diens, deponens, attollens, cedens naturæ & rurfum ne- ceffitate victus : Imitetur pictor, quoad ejus fieri poteft, fermonem gemibundo vultu, ut omnes per picturam Verba intelligant. Dein pinge infignes illos amores : potiffimum vero nihil in depingendo filio temere fingas, fac illum tar-* *dum, mox rem aggredientem, refpuentem, animo per- turbatum, metu autem coactum, refugientem adulterium, nondum intelligentem, quia a matre cogitur. Stet & alibi infelix anus, & eam fi lubet amore correptam de- fcribe, jam rugofam, & crinibus canam, ut rei novitate magis obftupefcas. Venias demum ad picturæ caput ; arma infelicem pauperem in cariffimos, & talia excogita, quæ licet ficta, crudelitatem tuam valeant explere. Im- pone denique dramati finem, teipfum fcilicet fignis qui- bufdam eminentem, ridentem, & quafi te bene gefta exultantem. Serva & mihi per Deos aliquam partem ta- bulæ nequis quæfierit ubi infelix pauper; quomodo vixit, qua ratione poft tot cafus vitam egerit ? Verum non hæc tibi perpetua fuerit felicitas, O Dives, & te oportet dra- matis partem effe. Nemo unquam infignem aliquam fpectavit tragœdiam, in qua tyranni non e priftina for- tuna exciderint.*

described to us by Writers, who well underſtood when the Cothurnus of Tragedy, the Comick Mask, or the Epick Enthuſiaſm and Sublimity, belonged to any Compoſition whether inWords or in Colours. An Art, according to them, which does not delight and move, does by no means reach the End of Art. *Ars enim cum a natura profecta ſit, niſi natura moveat ac delectet, nihil ſane egiſſe videatur.* Cic. de Orat. l. 3. ſ. 1.

CHAP. IV.

Farther Remarks on ſome of the more eſſential Parts of Painting, as they are explained to us by ancient Authors ; the poetical Parts chiefly, Truth, Beauty, Unity, Greatneſs, *and* Grace *in Compoſition.*

IT appears from the Titles of ſeveral ancient Treatiſes on Painting, that all the Parts of it had been handled by ancient Writers. *Apelles* wrote three Volumes on Painting for the Uſe of his Scholar *Perſeus.* *Euphranor* wrote of Colouring, and Symmetry or Deſign. *Democritus* the Philoſopher had likewiſe compoſed a Treatiſe on Painting, in which he conſidered three Qualities as eſſential to compleat the Art ; Diſpoſition or Ordonnance ; Symmetry or Truth of Deſign ; and bold Pronouncing, or Energy of Expreſſion : And accordingly in his Work he had treated of Unity of Compoſition ; true Proportions, or juſt Drawing ; and Poſition of Figures, which in order to ſignify ſomething diſtinct from the other Parts muſt mean Grouping, Contraſt, and Diſtancing. But, theſe Pieces being loſt, let us inquire what other Authors, ſuch as *Socrates, Ariſtotle,* and *Cicero,* have ſaid occaſionally of Painting, in diſcourſing of other Arts ; what Notions they had of this Art, and wherein they placed its chief Excellency.

Stobæus Eclog. Phyſ. c. 19.

WE have a ſhort but beautiful Deſcription of Painting, and the End it ought chiefly to aim at, in a Conference of *Socrates* with *Parrhaſius* that hath been already commended. I ſhall give it here in *Engliſh,* as well as I can, becauſe I am to keep it in View throughout the following Remarks.

" WHEN *Socrates* (ſays *Xenophon*) had occaſion to diſcourſe with Artiſts, his Converſa-
" tion was of great advantage to them (1.) For example, happening to go to *Parrhaſius* the
" Painter, he diſcourſed with him of his Art, to this purpoſe. What is Painting, *Parrha-*
" *ſius?* Is it not an Imitation of viſible Objects ; for do you not expreſs or repreſent by Colours,
" the Concave, and the Eminent ; the Obſcure, and the Enlightened, the Hard and Soft, the
" Rough and Smooth, the New and Old, and, in fine, all ſorts of Objects, and all the various
" Appearances of Nature? That is indeed our Aim, anſwered *Parrhaſius.*

" BUT when you propoſe to imitate beautiful Forms, ſince, for inſtance, 'tis not eaſy to
" find any one Perſon all whoſe Members are abſolutely faultleſs, do you not ſelect from
" many human Bodies thoſe parts which are beſt proportioned and moſt beautiful in each ;
" and by combining them, make whole Figures that are beautiful? We do, ſaid *Parrhaſius.*

" BUT what more? replied *Socrates:* Do not you attempt to repreſent the Temper, Diſ-
" poſition, and Affections of the Mind ; that Genius, and Habitude chiefly, which is the moſt
" engaging, ſweet, friendly, lovely, and deſirable? Or are theſe quite inimitable? How can
" we, ſays *Parrhaſius?* for how can that be imitated which hath neither Meaſure nor Co-
" lour, nor any of thoſe viſible Qualities you have juſt now enumerated, and which can not
" indeed be ſeen? Doth not a Man ſometimes look upon others with a friendly pleaſant Aſ-
" pect, and ſometimes with the contrary one? I can't deny that, ſays *Parrhaſius.* And can't
" you imitate that in their Eyes? Certainly, replies the Painter. Have our Friends, ſays *So-*
" *crates,* the ſame Countenance when their Affairs ſucceed well, or ill? Are the Looks of
" the Anxious the ſame with thoſe of the Man that is not oppreſſed by ſollicitous Cares? No
" at all, anſwers *Parrhaſius,* they are cheerful in Proſperity, but ſad and dejected in ad-

" verſe

(1) Ἀλλὰ μὴν κỳ ἐι ποτε των τὰς τέχνας ἐχόντων, κỳ ἐργασίας ἕνεκα χρωμένων αὐταῖς, διαλέγοιτό τιςι, κỳ τῆτοις ὠφέλιμO᾽ ἦν.——Εἰσελθὼν μὲν γὰρ ποτε πρὸς Παρράσιον τὸν ζωγράφον, κỳ διαλεγόμενO᾽ αὐτῷ, Ἆρα, ἔφη, ὦ Παρράσιε, Γραφική ἐςιν ἡ εἰκασία των ὁρωμένων ; τὰ γὰν κοῖλα κỳ τὰ ὑψηλὰ, κỳ τὰ σκοτεινὰ κỳ τὰ Φωτεινὰ, κỳ τὰ σκληρὰ κỳ τὰ μαλακὰ, κỳ τὰ τραχιὰ κỳ τὰ λεῖα, κỳ τὰ νία κỳ τὰ παλαιὰ σώματα, διὰ των χρωμάτων ἀπεικάζοντες ἐκμιμεῖσθε. Ἀληθῆ λέγεις, ἔφη.

Καὶ μὴν τὰ γε καλὰ εἴδη ἀφομοιοῦντες, ἐπειδὴ ὠ ῥάδιον ἐνι ἀνθρώπῳ περιτυχεῖν ἄμεμπτα πάντα ἔχοντι, ἐκ πολλῶν συνάγοντες τὰ ἐξ ἑκάςτων κάλλιςα, ὅτως ὅλα τὰ σώματα καλὰ ποιεῖτε Φαίνεσθαι. Ποιῆμεν γὰρ (ἔφη) ὅτως.

Τί γὰρ ; (ἔφη) τὸ πιθανώτατόν τι, κỳ ἥδιςον, κỳ φιλικώτατον κỳ ποθεινότατον, κỳ ἐραςμιώτατον ἀπομιμεῖσθε τῆς ψυχῆς ἦθO᾽ ; Ἠ ὐδὲ μιμητόν ἐςι τῦτο ; Πῶς γὰρ ἂν (ἔφη) μιμητὸν εἴη, ὦ Σώκρατες, ὃ μήτε συμμετρίαν, μήτε χρῶμα, μήτε ὦν σὺ εἶπας ἄρτι μηδὲν ἔχει, μηδὲ ὅλως ὁρατόν ἐςιν ;

Ἆρ᾽ ὖν (ἔφη) γίγνεται ἐν ἀνθρώπῳ πώποτε Φιλοφρόνως κỳ τὸ ἰχθρῶς βλέπειν πρός τινας ; Ἔμοιγε δοκεῖ, ἔφη. Οὐκῦν τό γε μιμητὸν ἐν τοῖς ὄμμασιν ; Καὶ μάλα, ἔφη. Ἐπὶ δὲ τοῖς των Φίλων ἀγαθοῖς κỳ τοῖς κακοῖς ὁμοίως σοι δοκοῦσιν ἔχειν τὰ πρόσωπα, κỳ τι Φροντίζοντες κỳ οἱ μὴ ; Μὰ Δί᾽ ὐ δῆτα, ἔφη. Ἐπὶ μὲν γὰρ τοῖς ἀγαθοῖς Φαιδροὶ, ἐπι

3

" verfe Circumftances. But thefe Differences can be expreffed or reprefented? faid *Socrates.*
" They can, replies *Parrhafius.*

" WHICH is more, continues the Philofopher, doth not a noble and liberal Spirit, or a
" mean and ignoble one; a prudent and well-governed Mind, or a petulant and diffolute
" one, difcover itfelf in the Countenance, Air, and Gefture of Men whether they ftand or
" move ? That is very true, anfwers the Painter. But all thefe Differences furely, faid *So-*
" *crates,* can be expreffed by Imitation ? They can indeed, replies *Parrhafius.* Which
" then do you think, fays *Socrates,* Men behold. with greateft Pleafure and Satisfaction,
" the Reprefentations by which good, beautiful, and lovely Manners are expreffed, or thofe
" which exhibit the bafe, deformed, corrupt and hateful ? As to that, in truth, fays
" *Parrhafius,* the difference is fo great, that it is diftinguifhable to every body."

IN this fhort Dialogue, it is firft obferved, that Painting in general propofes to give *The End of Paint-*
a true Image or Likenefs of every vifible Object : In the next place, that even with regard *ing is to imitate all*
to merely fenfible Forms, 'tis neceffary that the Painter fhould have a juft Notion and Tafte *vifible Appearanc.*
of Beauty. And laft of all, the chief Defign of it is to teach that Painting may be rendred
ferviceable in Morality, in fhewing the Deformity of Vice, and the Beauties of Virtue.

I fhall therefore, keeping this Defcription of Painting in my Eye, make fome Obfervations
on Drawing and Colouring, the Imitation of moral Life, or the Expreffion of Manners, and
Truth, Beauty, Grace, and Greatnefs of Compofition in Painting : that is, I fhall endeavour
to fhew how thefe Qualities are explained by ancient Authors.

WITH regard to Defign and Colouring, it appears from *Socrates's* Defcription of Paint- *The Drawing and*
ing, that the Artifts in his time were able to reprefent any Appearance of Nature what- *Colouring of the An-*
foever. He is very particular and full in his Enumeration of vifible Objects, in order to *cients is generally*
give a View of the Extent of the Art, or of the manifold Skill required in Drawing and *allowed to have*
Colouring all forts of Objects. And his Expreffions to fignify the Truth and Life in Imi- *been perfect.*
tation of Objects of every kind, Painters ought to aim at, and then attained to, are exceeding ftrong, ἀπεικάζοντες ἐκμιμεῖσθε. Thefe Words fignify what *Ovid,* fpeaking of
Dreams, calls Reprefentations,——*Quæ veras æquent imitamine formas.* Such Copies
as are hardly diftinguifhable from the Originals. But indeed many ancient Authors, *Pliny*
in particular (2), fpeak fo explicitly and clearly about the Drawing, the Colouring, and the
Intelligence of Light and Shade, in their Accounts of ancient Painters and their Works,
that they are generally acknowledged to have greatly excelled in thefe parts of Painting.
It is their Knowledge of Perfpective alone that is difputed.

I would therefore juft obferve on this head, that it feems highly probable that the *Arguments to prove*
Science of Perfpective was not unknown to them, from the following Authorities. *Pliny* *that the Science of*
                                                                                    Perfpective was not
                                                                                    unknown to the An-
ἐπὶ δὲ τοῖς κακοῖς σκυθρωποὶ γίγνονται. Οὐκῶν (ἔφη) κ)   that relates to the Clair-obfcure, the Middle Lights, and *cients.*
ταῦτα δυνατὸν ἀπεικάζειν ; κ) μάλα, ἔφη.   the Harmony or Union of Colours. What *Pliny* calls
                                                            the *Tranfitus* or *Commiffuræ,* cannot be better explained
Ἀλλὰ μὴν κ) τὸ μεγαλοπρεπές τι κ) ἐλευθέριον, κ) τὸ   than by *Ovid's* Defcription of the Rainbow. *Met. lib.*6.
ταπεινόν τε κ) ἀνελεύθερον, κ) τὸ σωφρονικόν τε κ) φρόνι-   *ver.* 61.
μον, κ) τὸ ὑβριστικόν τε κ) ἀπειρόκαλον, κ) διὰ τῦ   *Illic & Tyrium quæ purpura fenfit aërnum*
προσώπε, κ) διὰ των σχημάτων, κ) ἐστώτων κ) κινωμένων   *Texitur, & tenues parvi difcriminis umbræ :*
ἀνθρώπων διαφαίνει. Ἀληθῆ λέγεις, ἔφη. Οὐκῶν κ)   *Qualis ab imbre folet percuffis folibus arcus*
ταῦτα μιμηπά ; Καὶ μάλα, ἔφη. Πότερον ἂν (ἔφη) νο-   *Inficere ingenti longum curvamine cœlum :*
μίζεις ἥδιον ὁρᾷν τυς ἀνθρώπυς, δι᾿ ὧν τὰ κάλα τε κἀγαθὰ   *In quo diverfi niteant cum mille colores,*
κ) ἀγαπηπὰ ἤθη φαίνεται, ἢ δι᾿ ὧν τὰ αἰσχρά τι κ) πο-   *Tranfitus ipfe tamen fpectantia lumina fallit.*
νηρὰ κ) μισηπά ; Πολύ νὴ Δί᾿ (ἔφη) διαφέρει, ὦ Σώκρατες.   *Ufque adeo quod tangit idem eft : tamen ultima diftant.*
Ἀπομνημ. lib. 3. c. 10. ab initio.   'Tis to this Paffage *Seneca* refers, *Nat. Quæft. lib.* 1. *c.* 3.
                                                            Videmus in Iride aliquid flammei, aliquid lutei, aliquid
[This Note refers to *Democritus,* line 4. of Chap. IV.]   cærulei, & alia in picturæ modum fubtilibus lineis ducta,
The Writings of *Apelles* and *Euphranor,* have been al-   ut ait poeta ; ut an diffimiles colores fint, fcire non poffis,
ready mentioned ; as for *Democritus,* we are told by *Sto-* nifi cum primis extrema contuleris. Nam commiffura
bæus, Eclog. Phyfic. c. 19. Democritus contendebat co-   decipit : ufque adeo mira arte naturæ, quod a fimillimis
lores naturâ fua nihil effe : quæ vero ex iis coagmentan-   cœpit, in diffimilia definit. See what *Felibien* fays of
tur, colorari διαταγῇ, κ) ῥυθμῷ κ) προτροπῇ. Accord-   Colouring, *tom.* 3. *p.* 13. But fo many Paffages have
ingly he diftinguifhes three parts, τάξις, σχῆμα, θέσις.   been already quoted, that we may juftly conclude :
'Tis remarkable, that *Quintilian* ufes the fame Terms in   Quant au clair-obfcur & à la diftribution enchantereffe
fpeaking of Oratory, *Inft. lib.* 8. *c.* 3. Quod male dif- des lumieres & des ombres, ce que *Pline* & les autres
pofitum eft, id ἀνοικονόμητον : Quod male figuratum, id   ecrivains de l'antiquité en difent eft fi pofitif, leurs recits
ἀσχήματον : Quod male collocatum, id κακοσύνθετον vo-   font fi bien circonftanciés & fi vraifemblables, qu'on ne
cant. *Vitruvius, lib.* 1. *c.* 2. ufes the fame Divifion. fauroit difconvenir que les anciens n'egalaffent du moins
                                                            dans cette partie de l'art, les plus grands Peintres mo-
(2) Tandem fe ars ipfa diftinxit, & invenit lumen   dernes. Les paffages de ces auteurs que nous ne com-
atque umbras, differentia colorum alterna vice fefe ex-   prenions pas bien quand les Peintres modernes ignoroient
citante ; poftea deinde adjecta eft fplendor, alius hic   encore quels preftiges on peut faire avec le fecours de cette
quam lumen ; quem, quia inter hoc & umbram effet, ad-   magie, ne font pas fi embroüillés & fi difficiles depuis que
pellaverunt τόνον : Commiffuras vero colorum & tranfitus,   *Rubens,* fes Eleves, *Michel Ange de Caravage,* & d'au-
ἁρμογὴν. *Plin.* 35. 12. Here are plainly mentioned all   tres Peintres les ont expliqués bien mieux les pinceaux à
                                                            la main que les commentateurs les plus érudits ne le pou-
                                                            voient faire dans les livres. *Refl. crit. fur la poefie & fur*
                                                            la peinture, f. 38.

fays exprefsly, that *Pamphilus,* Mafter to *Apelles,* added Geometry to Painting (3) ; as à Science without which it was impoffible to compleat the Art, or bring it to full Perfection. And what other part of Geometry can this be fuppofed to be but Perfpective ? Befides, in fpeaking of the Parts of Painting in which *Apelles* was inferiour to others, he plainly diftinguifhes between the Meafures and the Pofition (4). So that the firft muft neceffarily mean the Proportions of Parts to one another in a fingle Figure, and the other muft mean giving Objects their proper places in the Plan of a Picture, in order to their reprefenting different Diftances : For without taking *Pliny* in that obvious Senfe, it feems hardly poffible to conceive any difference between two Talents or Excellencies which he exprefsly diftinguifhes : And to explain what he calls (*pofitio*) he adds (*quanto quid a quoque diftare deberet*), which plainly denotes the Art of placing Figures in a Picture, in fuch a manner as that any Diftance may be reprefented with regard to the other Objects in it.

'ADD to this, that *Vitruvius* mentions fome Authors (5), who had wrote upon the Art of determining by Geometry, and Lines, the Places of Objects in the Plan of a Picture, in order to reprefent any propofed degrees of Diftance, of Sinking, or Projecting, Vicinity or Remotenefs. *Philoftratus,* in the place above quoted (6), fays, many learned Men had wrote on Symmetry, and he gives a Definition of it that feems to comprehend both lineal and aërial Perfpective ; all that relates to the Reprefentation of Diftance.

MANY other Authorities might be produced to fhew that Perfpective was not abfolutely unknown to antient Painters : But the Abbé *Sallier* (7) having publifhed a long Differtation to prove it, and to refute Mr. *Perault's* Objections, I fhall only add, that whatever reafon there may be to doubt whether Perfpective was well underftood by the Ancients ; or whether the ancient Painters had Rules of Perfpective to work by in their Imitations of Nature ; there is none at all to doubt, but they were able, at leaft, by the Judgment of the Eye, to reprefent and counterfeit any vifible Appearances ; to bring Objects near to the Eye, or make them retire and fly off ; to project or fink, to caft at a diftance and degrade in any Degree, or contrariwife to give Relief, Strength and Nearnefs. For all thefe excellent Effects are afcribed to their Works (8). *Socrates* is often introduced in the Dialogues of *Plato* taking his Illuftrations on various Occafions (9), from the Plaftick Arts, and difcourfing in fuch a manner of them,

At leaft they were able, by the Judgment of the Eye, to paint agreeably to Perfpective.

(3) Sed primus, in Pictura, omnibus literis eruditus, præcipue Arithmetice & Geometrice, fine quibus negavit artem perfici poffe. *Plin.* 35. 17.

(4) *Plin.* 35. *in Apelles.* Demontiofius obferves upon that place, Difpofitio eft partium fingularum fitus, & recta collocatio. Symmetria commenfus partium fibi invicem. Optice earundem pro varietate fitus, & pofituræ, diffimilis & inæqualis delineatio.——Sed non adduci poffum ut credam autorem ita fcripfiffe—Quocirca ut membrum luxatum in fuos artus redeat locum ita legemus. " Nam cedebat Amphioni de pofitione, hoc eft quantum " quid a quo diftaret. Afclepiodoro de Menfuris." Vid. loc. *Demon. de pict. vet. ab initio.*——This Paffage is underftood to mean Perfpective, by a very good Author, *Scannelli da Forli, Microcofmo della pittura,* p. 57. l. 1. Ed ad Eclipiodoro nella Profpettiva, &c.

(5) Agatharchus primum Athenis, Æfchylo docente, tragœdiam fcenam fecit, & de ea commentarium reliquit. Ex eo moniti Democritus & Anaxagoras, de eadem re fcripferunt, quemadmodum oporteat ad aciem oculorum, radiorumque extenfionem, certo loco centro conftituto, ad lineas naturali ratione refpondere : Uti de incerta re certæ imagines ædificiorum in fcenarum picturis redderent fpeciem, & quæ in directis planifque frontibus fint figuratæ, alia abfcedentia, alia prominentia effe videantur. *Vitr. in præf. lib.* 7^{mi} compare *lib.*7. *c.*5. Etenim etiam trallibus cum Apatureus Alabandeus eleganti manu finxiffet fcenam, &c. See likewife *Plin. lib.* 35. *c.* 10. Habuit & fcena, Ludis Claudii pulchri, magnam admirationem picturæ, &c.

(6) In the End of the former Chapter.

(7) *Mem. de Liter.* tom. 8. p. 97.

(8) To the many Paffages already quoted in the Account of the Painters and their Works, others might be added, but the following feems fufficient. Τὰ μὲν ἄυ ἄλλα τῆς γραφῆς. κ. τ. λ. At reliquæ picturæ partes, propter quas non ubique accurata ai..s præftantia nobis Idiotis comperere folebat, nihilo fecus tamen fumma induftria erant elaboratæ, videlicet linearum ductibus atque extenfionibus rectiffimis, colorum commixtionibus fcientiffimis, neque non tempeftivarum adjectionum circumductionibus. Infuper decentibus inumbrationibus, neque neglecta magnitudinis ratione, & menfurarum totius ope-

ris æqualitate atque harmonia. *Lucian. Zeuxis. Philof. Icon. lib.*1. 6. *in Menœtio.* Jucunda pictoris ars. Armatos enim Viros poft mænia repræfentans, alios quidem totos oculis fiftit, alios Vero crurum tenus tectos, nonnullos dimidiatos, quorundam pectora & capita tantum & galeas folas, inde haftarum tantum extrema. Hoc eft proportionem obfervare, O puer. Oportet enim oculis fubduci difparentes pro ratione ambientium eos murorum. See *Junius de Pict. Vet. lib.* 1. *c.* 3. See *Pomponius, Gauricus de Perfpectiva, c.* 5.

(9) The Paffage that the Abbé *Sallier* founds upon, is in *Plato's Sophifta,* tom. 1. p. 235. *Edit. Steph.* Τἰ δ'; ϰ πάντες ὁι μιμάμενοι τι. κ. τ. λ. Quid nonne omnes qui aliquid imitantur, id facere inftituunt ? *Hofp.* Nequaquam fané ii quidem qui magna aliqua opera fingunt aut pingunt. Nam fi veram pulchrorum proportionem repræfentarent, ita certò habe futurum, ut fuperiores quidem partes præter modum minores, inferiores Vero majores apparerent : quum aliæ quidem eminus, aliæ cominus a nobis confpiciantur, &c. Compare what is faid upon Imitation, in his Book *de Rcpub.* p. 606. The Abbé *Sallier* takes notice, that Diminution and Degradation are Very well obferved in feveral ancient engraved Stones, that in particular which is well known by the Name of *Michael Angelo's* Seal : And he likewife takes notice of what *Frefnoy* fays in his Poem *de Arte Graphica,* and *Du Pile* in his Notes on that Paffage.

Regula certa licet nequeat perfpectiva dici
Aut complementum Graphidos ; fed in arte juvamen,
Et modus accelerans operandi : at corpora falfo
Sub vifu in multis referens, mendofa labafcit :
Nam Geometralem nunquam ficut corpora juxta
Menfuram depicta oculis, fed qualia vifa.

Du Pile in his Remarks confiders what is objected againft ancient Artifts, on account of the *Trajan* and *Antonine* Pillars. See what *Shaftefbury* has obferved on the fame Subject. *Trattato della Pittura,* p. 29, and *p.* 247. I fhall only add, that Lord *Shaftefbury* has obferved to the fame purpofe in his Notion of the Tablature of the Judgment of *Hercules* : For the ordinary Works of Sculpture, fuch as the Low-relieves, and Ornaments of Columns and Edifices, great allowance is made. The Very Rules of Perfpective are here wholly reverfed, as neceffity requires ; and are accommodated to the Circumftances and Genius of the Place or Building, according to a certain Oeconomy or Order of a particular and diftinct kind ; as will eafily be obferved by thofe who have thoroughly
studied

them, and of the Painters, Statuaries, and Sculptors in his time, as plainly fhews that the Art was then compleatly illufive; and that they could moft accurately reprefent to the fight all the different Appearances of Objects by which we judge of Magnitudes and Diftances in Nature. And feveral Pictures have been mentioned, in which thefe Qualities and Effects are commended by ancient Writers.

IT would be but tedious to give an Account of the Colours the ancient Painters made ufe of (10). It is agreed on by all, that they knew nothing of the way of preparing Colours with Oil: But as feveral excellent Authors obferve (11), thofe who have feen the many excellent Paintings of *Raphael, Guido,* and other great modern Mafters in Frefco, will not entertain any prejudice againft the ancient Painters on that fcote. That their Colouring was very durable is beyond all controverfy; fince *Petronius, Pliny, Plutarch, Paufanias* and others had feen Pictures of *Zeuxis, Apelles* and *Protogenes* that were as frefh as if they had been lately painted. *Pliny* mentions fome Pictures older than *Rome,* that were, in his days, not in the leaft or very little injured by age. And fuch Accounts will not appear incredible to thofe who have feen the better Remains of the Paintings of the Ancients at *Rome,* fome of which are ftill of a very furprizing Frefhnefs; notwithftanding the carelefs, not to fay bad, ufage they have met with. There will be occafion to fpeak of thefe afterwards; Prints of feveral of them being annexed to this Effay.

Their Colouring lafted long.

BUT what is well worth our Attention with regard to the Colouring of the ancient *Greek* Mafters is, what we are told of their Care not to difplay it too much. They avoided the gaudy, lufcious, and florid; and ftudied Chaftity and Severity in their Colours. It was not till Painting was in its decline, that Luxury and Libertinifm in Colouring, fo to fpeak, came into vogue; or that gorgeous, fplendid, expenfive Colours were efteemed, and the Pleafure arifing from thefe preferred to Truth of Defign, Unity and Simplicity of Compofition, with due Strength of Expreffion (12). This imitative Art, in the Senfe of all the better Ancients, tho' it requires help from Colours to execute its illufive Defigns; and ufes them as means to render its Copies of Nature fpecious and deceiving: Though it is indeed only by Colours, that Painting can attain to that Command over the Senfe, which is its high and diftinguifhing Aim; yet it hath nothing wider of its real Scope, than to make a fhew of Colours, or by their Mixture to raife a feparate and flattering Gratification to the Senfe. " This Pleafure, fays an " Author well acquainted with the Ancients, is plainly foreign and of another kind, as " having no fhare or concern in the proper Delight and Entertainment which naturally arifes " from the Subject. For the Subject, in refpect of rational Pleafure, is abfolutely com- " pleated when the Defign is executed. And thus it was always beft, in their Opinion, " when the Colours were moft fubmitted, and made wholly fubfervient."

The care they took to fubdue the florid.

MANY Authorities might be brought to prove this (13). *Apelles* is faid, by *Pliny,* to have invented a kind of Varnifh which ferved to preferve his Pictures neat and clean : It
could

The Varnifh of Apelles.

---

ftudied the *Trajan* and *Antonine* Pillars. In the fame manner, as to Pieces of engrav'd Work, Medals or whatever fhews itfelf in one Subftance, (as Brafs or Stone) or only by Shade and Light, (as in ordinary Drawings, or Stamps) much alfo is allow'd, and many things admitted of the fantaftick, marvellous, or hyberbolical kind, &c.

(10). See the Subject fully handled by *Bulengerus, lib.*1. *c.* 4, & 5.

(11) On ne fauroit former un préjugé contre le Coloris des anciens de ce qu'ils ignoroient l'invention de detremper les Couleurs avec de l'huile, laquelle fut trouvée en Flandres fi n'y a gueres plus de trois Cens ans. On peut très bien Colorier en peignant à Frefque. La meffe du Pape Jules, un ouvrage de Raphaël dont nous avons déja vanté le Coloris, eft peinte à Frefque dans l'appartement de la fignature au Vatican. *Reflex. &c. ibid.* See What is faid by *Lomazzo* in his *Idea del tempio della Pittura,* of Oil and Frefco-Painting, *p.* 72, and 74.

(12) See *Plin. lib.* 35. *c.* 2. Primumque dicemus quæ reftant de pictura : Arte quondam nobili——Nunc vero in totum marmoribus pulfa, jam quidem & auro, &c. *c.*15. Qua contemplatione tot Colorum, tanta varietate, fubit antiquitatem mirari ! Quatuor coloribus folis immortalia illa opera fecere ; ex albis Melino ; ex filaceis, Attico ; ex rubris, Sinopide Pontica ; ex nigris attramento ; Apelles, Echion, Melanthius, Nicomachus, clariffumi Pictores : Quum tabulæ eorum fingulæ oppidorum venirent opibus. Nunc & purpuris in parietes migrantibus, & India Conferente fluminum fuorum limum, & Draconum ac Elephantorum faniem ; nulla nobilis pictura eft. Omnia ergo meliora tunc fuere, quum minor Copia. Ita eft, quoniam, ut fupra diximus, rerum non animi pretia excubabar. Quare vincat veritatem ratio falfa non erit alienum exponere. Quod enim antiqui infumentes laborem & induftriam probare contendebant artibus, id nunc

coloribus & eorum eleganti fpecie confequuntur ; & quam fubtilitas artificis adjiciebat operibus auctoritatem, nunc Dominicus fumptus efficit ne defideretur. Quis enim antiquorum, non uti medicamenta, minio parce videtur ufus effe ? At nunc paffim plerumque toti parietes inducuntur. Accedit huc Chryfocolla, Oftrum, Armenium. Hæc vero cum inducuntur, etfi non ab arte funt pofita, fulgentes tamen oculorum reddunt vifus ; & ideo, quod pretiofa funt, legibus excipiuntur, ut a domino, non a redemptore, repræfententur. *Vitr. lib.* 7. *c.* 1.

(13) To thefe juft mentioned may be added the famous Saying of *Apelles.* Cum vidiffet quendam ex fuis difcipulis pinxiffe Helenam multo auro ornatam : O adolefcens, inquit, cum non poffes pingere pulchram, fecifti divitem. *Cl. Alex.*——Sic hæc fubtilis pictura etiam incompta delectat. Fit enim quiddam in utroque quo fit venuftius, fed non ut appareat. Tum removebitur omnis infignis ornatus quafi margaritarum. Ne calamiftri quidem adhibebuntur. Fucati vero medicamenta candoris, & ruboris, omnia repellentur : Elegantia modo, & munditia remanebit. *Cic. Orat.* 23. Virgo minime quidem fpeciofa, formofa tamen, vera pariter atque antiqua pulchritudine referta, qualia funt antiquæ artis fimulacra, quæ ad fui admirationem temporis moram atque accuratiores oculos requirunt. *Themiftii Orat.* 3. *de Amicit.* Recentiores deorum imagines in admiratione funt propter operis dignitatem, veteres vero propter operis fimplicitatem, magis vero Deorum majeftati congruentem. *Porphyr. de Abft. lib.* 2. So *Silius Ital. lib.* 14. *circa fin.* fpeaking of the ancient Images of the Gods :

———fimulacra Deorum
Numen ab arte datum fervantia.

Non ideo tamen fegnius precot, ut quandoque veniat dies ; utinamque jam venerit ; quo aufteris illis feverifque dulcia hæc blandaque, ut jufta poffeffione decedant. *Plin. jun. lib.* 3. *Ep.* 8. See *Cicero de Orat. lib.*3. 25. *Quint. lib.*8. *c.* 3. *lib.* 12. 10.

'could not be difcerned unlefs one came very near, and looked narrowly to his Pictures: But it gave them a charming Tranfparency at a due diftance: It likewife render'd the Colouring wonderfully mellow: But it was chiefly intended by him to darken the too florid Colours, and to give them a certain Aufterity (14).. *Nicias* had likewife difcovered a Varnifh which was of great ufe to Statuaries, as well as Painters (15), and had much the fame effect in Painting, as hath been defcribed.

THE Truth of this Obfervation is likewife evident from the high efteem in which the imperfect or unfinifh'd Pictures of the great Mafters were held by the Intelligent; when the Subject was fo compleated by the Drawing, that the noble Ideas, the Invention, Genius, and Judgment of the Painters were as much feen in them, as in their finifhed Pictures (16). It was for the fame reafon that their mere Drawings were fo highly valued. Of this kind were the *Monochromata* of *Apelles*, the *Rudimenta* of *Protogenes*, and the *Veftigia* of *Parrhafius*, that are faid to have contended with Nature in Truth and Beauty; and that were fo earneftly fought after by the Students and Lovers of the Art (17). Thefe *Monochromata* were very different, as *Quintilian* obferves, from the rude Drawings of the firft Defigners, called *Monochromatifts*, in which Objects were very imperfectly delineated, there being in them no Light and Shade, or Intelligence of the Clair-obfcure (18). " On " the contrary, they were of that kind of Drawings which another Author defcribes, that " might be very juftly called Pictures, (though, properly fpeaking, faith he, it is only Works " executed with Colours that are fo denominated,) becaufe they expreffed not only outward " Likenefs, but inward Affections, Characters, Actions, and Manners: They conveyed fine " Ideas and Sentiments, and were able to touch the Heart; which are the principal Ends of " Imitation (19)." If *Menander* had reafon to fay, that he looked on his Work as finifhed, when he had concerted the Difpofition and Plan of his Drama (20); a Painter's Work may with much better reafon be faid to be fo, when his Subject is compleatly expreffed by his Defign. For though Painting and Poetry, being Sifter-Arts, are often very fitly compared together, and in this Comparifon the Language in the one is likened to the Colours in the other; yet in this refpect the Comparifon manifeftly fails, that whereas the Sentiments of a Poet cannot be conveyed to others without Words, thofe of the Painter may be ftrongly expreffed without Colours.

IN truth, Drawings, properly fpeaking, are the Originals, Pictures are but Copies after them. And for that reafon it is juftly obferved by good Judges, that the Genius of a Mafter is beft learned from his Drawings. " There is a *Grace*, (fay very good ones) a Delicacy, " a Spirit in them, which, when the Mafter attempts to give in Colours, is commonly " much diminifhed. They are, in one word, generally fpeaking, preferable to Paintings; " as having thofe Qualities which are moft excellent, in a higher degree than Paintings " commonly have, or poffibly can have, and the others, Colouring excepted, equally with " them (21). Thofe who have no relifh for Drawings, in which the Subject is fully ac- " complifhed, in refpect of Invention, Difpofition, and Expreffion, certainly feek after " fome Entertainment that muft be far inferiour to that which arifes to the Underftanding " from truly poetick Compofition."

THOUGH the Analogy between Poetry and Painting does not hold in that refpect which has been juft now mentioned; yet by comparing them together we fhall be led to form very juft Notions of Colouring in Pictures. For whatever is laid to make the Beauty of Language, will be found to conftitute, for the fame reafons, the Beauty of Colouring. If Simplicity be the Perfection of Writing, it muft, for the fame reafon, be the Perfection of

---

(14) Inventa ejus & ceteris profuere in arte: Unum imitari nemo potuit, quod abfoluta opera atramento inlinebat ita tenui, ut idipfum repercuffu claritates colorum excitaret cuftodiretque a pulvere & fordibus; admotum intuenti demum adpareret: fed & tum ratione magna, ne claritas colorum oculorum aciem offenderet; veluti per lapidem fpecularem intuentibus e longinquo; & eadem res nimis floridis coloribus aufteritatem occulte daret. *Plin.* 35.

(15) Hic eft Nicias, de quo dicebat Praxiteles, interrogatus quæ maxime opera fua probaret in marmoribus? Quibus Nicias manum admovifiet: tantum circumlitioni ejus tribuebat. *Plin.* 35. See French Notes ad loc.

(16) Illud vero perquam rarum ac memoria dignum, etiam fuprema opera artificum imperfectafque tabulas, ficut Irin Ariftidis, Tyndaridas Nicomachi, Medeam Timomachi & quam diximus, Venerem Apellis, in majore admiratione effe quam perfecta: Quippe in iis lineamenta reliqua, ipfæque cogitationes artificum fpectantur, atque in lenocinio commendationis dolor eft: Manus, cum id agerent extinctæ defiderantur. *Plin.* 35. 32.

(17) Zeuxis pinxit & Monochromata ex albo.——— Graphidis veftigia extant in tabulis ac membranis ejus (Parrhafii) ex quibus proficere dicuntur artifices. *Plin.* 35.

In Pinacothecam perveni vario genere tabularum mirabilem. Nam & Zeuxidos manus vidi, nondum vetuftatis injuria victas; & Apellis, &c. *Petro. Arb. Satyr. ut fupra.*

(18) Qui finguli pinxerunt coloribus, alia tamen eminentiora, alia reductiora fecerunt, fine quo ne membris quidem fuas lineas dediffent. *Quint. lib.* 11. *c.* 3.

(19) *Philoft. de vit. Apol. lib.* 2. *c.* 22. Picturam enim non eam folum mihi videris putare, quæ coloribus abfolvitur, nempe unus etiam color veteribus illis pictoribus fatis erat, incrementa vero capiens ars, quatuor adhibuit, inde plures etiam; imo & linearum picturam, & quod coloribus deftituitur opus, quod ex umbra & luce compofitum eft plectuam fas eft adpellare. In talibus enim etiam fimilitudo cernitur, figura item, & mens, & pudor, & audacia, &c.

(20) Menander cum fabulam dipofuiffet, etiamfi non verfibus adornaffet, dicebat tamen fe jam compleffe. *Commen. vet. ad illud Horat. de Art. Poet. Verbaque provifam rem non invita fequuntur.*

(21) Mr. *Richardfon* in his Difcourfe on Painting. See likewife *De Pile l'Idée d'un Peintre parfait.*

of Colouring. Whatever is said against the gaudy, the pompous, the florid, and luxuriant on the one hand; or in praise of the chaste, the pure, the subdued, and unaffected on the other, doth equally agree to Colouring and Discourse. And accordingly ancient Authors speak of the one and the other almost in the same Phrases (22):

PAINTING is frequently considered, as a poetical Art, by ancient Writers: *Plutarch* tells us it was an ancient Apophthegm, that a Poem is a speaking Picture, and that good Painting is silent Poesy: And he adds, to confirm and illustrate this Saying of *Simonides*, That the Actions which are described by Speech or Writing as past, are represented by Painters as if they were done in our sight. Painters express by Lines and Colours what Writers paint by Words: They therefore only differ in the manner of Imitation. They both propose to themselves the same End which is to tell a Story well; that is, to exhibit the Action or Event to our sight, as if it were really done before us. And therefore he is reckoned the best Historian, for instance, who describes Persons and Actions in so lively a manner; and touches on such proper Circumstances in every Story, that his whole Description is an admirable Picture. His Reader thus becomes a kind of Spectator, and feels in himself all the Variety of Passions which are correspondent to the several parts of the relation (23).

IF we pursue this Comparison a little, between good Writing and good Painting, it will lead us to form juster Ideas of the Design and Merit of Painting than are commonly conceived; or of the Ends it ought to propose; and of the different Degrees of Merit, that different Talents in the Art, and different Pictures ought to hold, corresponding to the respective Excellencies of various sorts of Writing or Description.

The Comparison between poetical Description and Painting, naturally lead s to a just Notion of Painting and the different Qualities requisite to it.

THE End of Description is certainly to convey a true and lively Idea into the Mind, by Words: And this is likewise the Design of Painting. Both therefore must be clear and intelligible; and are excellent in proportion to the Clearness, the Truth and Liveliness of the Images they excite in the Mind. But every Description, however true, and clear, or strong it may be, is not equally pleasing and acceptable to the Mind, because all Objects are not equally so.

LET us therefore inquire, what are the Circumstances and Causes that recommend some Descriptions more than others.

FIRST (24) of all then, it is obvious that a Description of what is little, common, or even deformed and monstrous, is in some degree entertaining to the Imagination, when it is presented to it by suitable Expressions. The Mind, in this case, says *Aristotle*, is delighted not so much with the Image contained in the Description, as with the Aptness of the Description to excite the Image (25). This Pleasure arises solely from Imitation and Likeness;

---

(22) *Cic. Orator*, Nº. 23. & *de Oratore*, lib. 3. Nº. 26.——In qua vel ex poetis, vel oratoribus, possumus judicare, concinnam, distinctam, ornatam, festivam, sine intermissione, sine reprehensione, sine varietate, quamvis claris sit coloribus picta vel poesis, vel oratio non posse in delectatione esse diuturna.——In scriptis & in dictis non aurium solum, sed animi judicio etiam magis, infuscata vitia noscuntur.——Sed habeat tamen illa in dicendo admiratio, ac summa laus umbram aliquam ac recessum, quo magis id, quod erit illuminatum, extare atque eminere videatur.——Ita sit igitur nobis ornatus, & suavis orator ut suavitatem habeat austeram & solidam, non dulcem, atque decoctam, &c. So *Quint.* lib. 8. c. 3. Sed hic ornatus virilis fortis & sanctus sit, nec effeminatam levitatem, nec fuco eminentem colorem amet, sanguine & viribus niteat.——Quare nemo ex corruptis dicat me inimicum esse culte dicentibus. Non nego hanc esse virtutem, sed illis eam non tribuo. An ego fundum cultiorem putem, in quo mihi quis ostenderit lilia, & violas, & amœnos fontes scaturientes, quam ubi plena messis, aut graves fructu vites erunt?—— Ad aspergendam illam quæ etiam in picturis est gravissima, Vetustatis inimitabilem arti auctoritatem, &c. See the Whole Chapter, and likewise the Prooemium to that Book, Namque & colorata, & astricta, & lacertis expressa sunt, sed eadem siquis vulsa atque fucata muliebriter comat fœdissima sunt ipso formæ labore. Et cultus concessus atque magnificus addit hominibus ut græco versu testatum est, auctoritatem. At muliebris & luxuriosus, non corpus exornat, sed detegit mentem. Similiter illa translucida & versicolor quorundam elocutio res ipsas effœminat, quæ illo verborum habitu vestiuntur. Curam ergo verborum, rerum volo esse sollicitudinem: Nam plerumque optima rebus cohærent, & cernuntur suo lumine, &c. Unumquidque genus cum pudice casteque ornatur, fit illustrius; cum fucatur atque prælenitur, fit præstigiosum. *Aul Gel. Noc. Att.* 14. Grandis, & ut ita dicam, pudica oratio non est maculosa, nec turgida, sed naturali pulchritudine exurgit. Nuper ventosa isthæc & enormis loquacitas Athenas

ex Asia commigravit, animosque juvenum ad magna surgentes veluti pestilenti quodam sidere afflavit, semelque corrupta eloquentia regula stetit & obmutuit. Ac ne carmen quidem sani coloris enituit: Sed omnia quasi eodem cibo pasta non potuerunt usque ad senectutem canescere. Pictura quoque non alium exitum fecit, postquam Ægyptiorum audacia tam magnæ artis Compendiariam invenit. *Petr. Arb. Satyr.*

(23) Quamobrem etiam non ineleganter Simonides dixit, Picturam esse Poesin tacentem; Poesin vero Picturam loquentem. Quas enim res ac si coram agerentur, pictores repræsentant, eæ oratione ut præteritæ enarrantur; atque conscribuntur. Cumque pictores idem coloribus & figuris exprimant, quod scriptores verbis & vocibus, differunt tantum inter se materia & modo imitationis. Utrisque autem idem propositus est finis: Et is habetur historicorum optimus, qui narrationem personis & figuris animum moventibus, haud aliter ac picturam conformat. *Plut. Bello an Pace.* So *Longinus* speaks of Oratory, *De Sublim.* f. 15. Rhetorica vero imaginatio illa pulcherrima est ac præstantissima, quæ sibi res, voces, actus denique omnes evidentissime & ad ipsam veritatem fingit, atque auditoribus ante oculos ponit. Turpis autem ac pravus, & plane, quod aiunt, extra lineas procurrens error est, quum in oratione civili ac pedestri ad poeticas & fabulosas, atque impossibiles fictiones progreditur.

(24) See the Essays on the Pleasures of Imagination in the Spectator, vol. 6. whence these Reflexions are taken.

(25) *De Poet.* r. 4. Et gaudere omnibus rebus imitatione expressis, naturale est; veluti picturis, sculpturis & similibus. Cui quidem rei, signo est id, quod contingit in operibus artificum: Quæ enim ipsa per se, non sine molestia quadam cernimus, horum Imagines exactissime expressas dum intuemur, gaudemus; veluti belluarum formas immanissimarum, & cadaverum; in quibus nisi imitatio gigneret voluptatem, nihil illic erat, quod oblectaro

U

nefs; the Action of the Mind in comparing and perceiving Similitude being made agree-able to us by Nature, becaufe it is ufeful, or rather neceffary to our acquiring Knowledge. But muft not a Picture of the fame nature pleafe, as he obferves it does, in the fame way, in the fame degree, and for the fame reafon; that is, on account of the Agreement of the Copy with the Original? It is owing intirely to the Pleafure which Imitation and Similarity afford to the Mind, that Pictures or Defcriptions of fuch Objects, as it is painful to be-hold in real Life, are capable of delighting us. But if fuch Defcriptions give a lower En-tertainment to the Fancy, and are juftly reckoned of a meaner kind, than Defcriptions of more agreeable Originals; Pictures of that fort muft likewife be accounted of the fame rank in Painting, as the other in Writing. It is when the Objects themfelves defcribed, are great, furprizing, or beautiful, that Defcriptions are moft delightful: Becaufe in this cafe we are not only pleafed with comparing the Reprefentation with the Original; but we are highly delighted with the Original itfelf. The Ideas excited are in themfelves noble and elevating: They agreeably fill and employ the Mind. Now if this be true, Pictures which reprefent great, noble, and beautiful Objects; or convey fublime and pleafing Ideas, muft alfo neceffarily be more agreeable to the Fancy, and of a higher Order, than Pictures of mean and low Objects, not to fay deformed ones. It will likewife be granted, that new and uncommon Objects give greater pleafure than ordinary, common, and familiar ones. Nor is the final Caufe, or moral Fitnefs of this Effect of Newnefs difficult to be found out. It is highly proper that a Being made for Progrefs and Improvement in Knowledge, fhould be fond of Novelty in fome degree, and be agreeably affected by every frefh Acquifition, that he may thereby be excited to take due pains to make new Improvements in Know-ledge, and to add to his treafure of Ideas.

BUT there is yet another Circumftance which will be owned to recommend a Defcrip-tion more than all the reft; and that is, if it reprefents fuch Objects as are apt to raife a fecret Ferment in the Mind, and to work ftrongly on the Paffions. In this cafe the Heart is moved, at the fame time that the Imagination is delighted: We are at once enlightened and warmed. Now muft it not be fo likewife with regard to Paintings, that touch and move the Heart by the lively Images they prefent to the Fancy? Accordingly let any one make the Experiment, and he muft unavoidably obferve upon the firft trial, that, in Paint-ing, it is pleafant to look on the Picture of any Face, when the Refemblance is hit; but the pleafure increafes, if it be the Picture of a Face that is beautiful; and is ftill greater if the Beauty be foften'd by an Air of Melancholy and Sorrow.

LET any one carry on in his own Mind this comparifon between Difcourfe and Paint-ing, and he will foon be able to fatisfy himfelf with refpect to the Ranks, the different Qualities of a Painter and various forts of Pictures deferve; becaufe he muft clafs them in the fame way as he does Defcriptions. This is the Gradation *Socrates* makes in his Defcription of Painting; from Truth and Likenefs to external Beauty; and from thence to the Beauties of the Mind, and what moves the Heart and Affections. And we find him con-verfing with *Clito*, a Statuary, to the fame purpofe.

Socrates reafons in this manner.

"I know and fee, *Clito*, (fays (26) *Socrates*) that you make Runners, Wreftlers, thofe
" that play at the Gantlet, and all forts of Combatants. But that which is moft delightful
" to our Eyes, in your Works, is the Life and Spirit you exprefs in your Figures: Pray
" therefore how do you thus animate them? *Clito* not anfwering him readily, *Socrates*
" asks him again: Do you not infpire your Images with much more Vivacity by affimila-
" ting them to living Forms, and ftudying real Life? Juft fo, faid the Statuary. Don't
" you therefore render your Imitations liker, and more conformable to Nature and Truth,
" when you artfully exprefs all the Changes in the Mufcles and Nerves, that are occa-
" fioned by various Poftures and Attitudes; all their Contractions, Diftortions, Shorten-
" ings, Bracings, and Relaxations? That is the very thing, replies *Clito*. But when you
" exprefs

His Conference with Clito.

---

lectare poffet. Caufa vero etiam hujus rei eft, quod dif-
cere, non folum philofophis (quod quidam cenfent) jucun-
diffimum eft, fed etiam aliis, qui fimiliter quidem, tametfi minus exacte, jucunditatis fejus participes fiunt.
Ob hanc enim caufam gaudio afficiuntur, dum cernunt
imagines rerum; quia contingit fpectando perdifcere, &
quid unumquodque fit, ratiocinari; veluti hanc imaginem, illum effe: fiquidem nifi tibi illum prius Contige-
rit vidiffe, tabula hæc, non propter effigiem imitatione
expreffam voluptatem feret, fed propter artificis feduli-
tatem, aut Colorem, aut ejufmodi aliquam aliam caufam.
So *Plutarch de aud. Poetis.* Pictam Lacertam, aut Simiam,
aut Therfitæ faciem videntes delectamur & moramur;
non pulchritudinis, fed fimilitudinis caufa. Suapte enim
natura id quod turpe eft, pulchrum fieri non poteft: imitatio autem, five pulchræ five turpis rei fimilitudinem
exprimat, laudatur. See his *Sympofiacon, l. 5. qu. 8.*

(26) Πρὸς δὲ Κλείτωνα τὸν ἀνδριαντοποιὸν ἰσελθὼν πο-
τι, καὶ διαλεγόμεν⸮ αὐτῷ, Ὅτι μὲν, ἔφη, ὦ Κλείτων,
ἀλλοίες ποιεῖς δρομεῖς τε καὶ παλαισ͂ας, καὶ πύκλας, καὶ

παλκραλιασ͂ὰς, ὁρῶ τί κỳ οἶδα· ὃ δὲ μάλιςα ψυχαγωγεῖ
διὰ τῆς ὄψεως τὲς ἀνθρώπες, τὸ ζῳλικὸν Φαίνεθαι, πῶς
τᾶτο ἐνεργάζη τοῖς ἀνδριάσιν.
Ἐπεὶ δὲ ἀπορῶν ὁ Κλείτων ἐ ταχὺ ἀπεκρίνατο· Ἀρ'
[ἔφη] τοῖς τῶν ζώντων ἰδέσιν ἀπεικάζων τὸ Ἔργον, ζωτικω-
τέρες ποιεῖς Φαίνεθαι τὲς ἀνδριάντας; Καὶ μάλα, ἔφη.
Οὐκᾶν τά τε ὑπὸ τῶν σχημάτων καταπωμενα κỳ τὰ ἀνα-
σπώμενα ἐν τοῖς ζώμασι, κỳ τὰ ζυμπιεζόμενα κỳ τὰ διελ-
κόμενα, κỳ τὰ ἐντεινόμενα κỳ τὰ ἀνιέμενα ἀπεικάζων, ὁμοι-
ότερά τε τοῖς ἀληθινοῖς κỳ πιθανώτερα ποιεῖς Φαίνεθαι;
Πάνυ μὲν ᾦν, ἔφη.
Τὸ δὲ κỳ τὰ πάθη τῶν ποιούντων τι ζωμάτων ἀπομι-
μεῖσθαι, ἆ ποιεῖ τινα τέρψιν τοῖς θεωμένοις; Εἰκὸς γ᾽ ᾦν,
ἔφη. Οὐκᾶν κỳ τῶν μὲν μαχομένων ἀπειλητικὰ τὰ ὄμματα
ἀπεικαςέον, τῶν δὲ νενικηκότων ἐυφραινομένων ὄψις μιμη-
τέα. Σφόδρα γε, ἔφη. Δεῖ ἄρα (ἔφη) τὸν ἀνδριαντοποιὸν
τὰ τῆς ψυχῆς ἔργα τῷ ἴδιῳ προσεικάζειν. κ. τ. λ. Mem.
Soc. lib. 3. c. 10. fect. 6.

" exprefs the Paffions in your Figures, that are difcernible in the Looks and Geftures of
" Actors, proper to their different Characters and Circumftances, is it not that which
" chiefly delights an intelligent Eye? It is fo, faid *Clito.* For that reafon, replies *So-*
" *crates,* the Eyes of Combatants' ought to threaten; and Conquerors fhould have cheer-
" ful Countenances. Very true. It is then, faid *Socrates,* the Statuary's chief Bufinefs
" and higheft Effort, to reprefent the Actions of the Mind by their outward Indications
" in the Face and Gefture."

I am not a little furprized to find the ingenious Author of the *Reflexions on Poetry*
and Painting, afferting, that it is to no purpofe to inquire, which is the moft eftimable
Quality or Part in Painting, Defign and Expreffion, or Colouring (27). For if it be not
in vain to inquire what are the beft and nobleft Ends of Poetry, and what Parts of it are
moft agreeable and ufeful; it cannot be fo to inquire into the beft Ends of Painting;
or what are its nobleft and moft valuable Performances. And which-ever way the one
Queftion is decided, the fame Judgment muft of neceffity determine the other; becaufe
the Pleafures, which both are qualified to afford our Minds, proceed from the fame Sources,
and are nearly of the fame kind. If thofe are the beft Pieces in Poetry, which entertain
the Reafon as well as pleafe the Fancy; which exprefs and convey great Sentiments and
Ideas, and at the fame time move our Affections; it muft be fo likewife with regard to
Pictures. What are the nobleft, the moft pleafing, and at the fame time the moft ferious, and
inftructive Parts of Poetry? Are not thofe pronounced fuch by *Ariftotle,* and all Criticks,
which ftir up our Pity and Horrour, in order to refine and direct them (28): Or, in other
words, which exercife our greater Paffions, in a way that hath a wholefome Influence upon
the Mind? And if this be true, whatever the reafon of it may be, thofe Pictures which
are fitted to work upon the fame Affections in a ftrong and proper manner, muft be the
nobleft Pieces of Painting; becaufe they are at the fame time the moft entertaining and the
moft ufeful. Accordingly we have found that Mafter-Critick of all the fine Arts, giving the
preference to fuch Pictures above all others, and cenfuring the fineft Colourift of Antiquity
for not expreffing Manners in his Pictures (29.)

Obfervations on the Difpute about Colouring and Expreffion, which is preferable.

THE Author of the *Reflexions, &c.* very juftly obferves in another place (30), "That
" a Painter may pafs for a confiderable Artift in quality of an excellent Defigner, or a beau-
" tiful Colourift, tho' he be not able to reprefent affecting Objects, or to animate his Pic-
" tures with that Soul, and Truth of Expreffion, which makes itfelf felt in the Works of
" *Raphael* and *Pouffin.* The Painters of the *Lombard* School are admired, though they
" aimed at nothing beyond pleafing the Senfe, by the Richnefs and Variety of their Co-
" louring. Yet their moft zealous Partizans acknowledge, that in the Pictures of that
" School a great Beauty is wanting; and that even thofe of *Titian,* for inftance, would
" be vaftly more precious if he had oftener joined, to the Talents of his own School, thofe
" of the *Roman.* A Picture of this great Mafter, reprefenting the Martyrdom of a *Do-*
" *minican* Friar, is not perhaps the moft valuable of his Works in refpect of Colour-
" ing: In the Opinion however of Cavalier *Ridolfi,* who has wrote the Hiftory of the *Ve-*
" *netian* Painters, it is that which is moft univerfally known and moft highly efteemed.
" The reafon is, the Action is interefting, and *Titian* has handled that Subject with a more
" touching Expreffion than appears in his other Works."

BUT how very differently doth this Author talk, in his Chapter, about Expreffion
and Colouring (31)? He decides the Queftion with, *Trahit fua quemque voluptas;* All is
Tafte, and it is in vain to difpute about Tafte.

(27) *Tom. 1. f.* 50. Qu'il eft inutile de difputer fi la
partie du deffein & de l'expreffion eft preferable a cette
du coloris—Vouloir perfuader à un homme qui prefere
le coloris a l'expreffion en fuivant fon propre fentiment,
qu'il a tort c'eft lui vouloir perfuader de prendre plus de
plaifir a voit les tableaux du Pouffin que ceux de Titien.
La chofe ne depend pas plus de lui qu'il depend d'un
homme dont le palais eft conforme de maniere, que le
vin de Champagne lui faffe plus de plaifir, que le vin
d'Efpagne, de changer de gout, & d'aimer mieux le vin
d'Efpagne que l'autre, &c.

(28) Eft igitur Tragoediæ imitatio actionis ftudiofæ,
& perfectæ, magnitudinem idoneam habentis,——Et non
per enarrationem rei, fed per mifericordiam, metumque
factis expreffum, ejufmodi vehementis animorum pertur-
bationes undequaque purgans expianfque. *De Poet. c.* 6.
Quoniam vero imitatio tragica non folum eft perfectæ
actionis imitatio, fed etiam terribilium & miferabilium,
c. 9. Reliquis igitur, qui maxime idoneus habendus eft
inter hos interjectus. Eft autem talis, qui neque virtute
infigni eminet, & juftitia; fiquidem facinus admifit ul-
tione dignum, &c. *ib.* 13. Utra vero fit melior imitatio,
epica an tragica dubitare poffit quifpiam, *c.* 26.

(29) *Ib. c.* 6. Veluti etiam ex pictoribus, &c.

(30) *Tom. 1. f.* 6. L'Imitation ne fcauroit donc nous
emouvoir quand la chofe imitée n'eft point capable de le
faire. Les fujets que Teniers, Vovermans, & les autres
Peintres de ce genre ont reprefentées, n'auroient obtenu
de nous qu'une attention tres ligere——nous tenons l'Art
du Peintre a bien imiter, mais nous le blamons d'avoir
choifi pour l'objet de fon travail des fujets que nous in-
tereffent fi peu.——Les Peintres intelligents ont fi bien
connu, ils ont fi bien fenti cette verité, que rarement ils
ont fait des payfages deferts & fans figures, &c. And *Sect.*
10. Un Peintre peut donc paffer pour un grand artifan en
qualite de colorifte rival de la nature, &c.

(31) *Sect.* 50. La prédilection qui nous fait donner la
preference a une partie de la Peinture fur une autre partie,
ne depend donc point de notre talfon, non plus que la
prédilection qui nous fait donner un genre de poefie prefera-
blement aux autres. Cette prédilection depend de notre
organifation, de nos inclinations prefentes & de la fitua-
tion de notre efprit, &c.

*Tastes may be dis-
puted.*
I am far from charging that ingenious Author with the abfurd Confequences which ne-ceffarily follow from his Maxim. But certainly if it be falfe, it is not in vain to difpute whether the preference ought to be given to the mere Colourift, or to one who excels in Expreffion and Defign. And if the Maxim be true in one cafe, it muft be univerfally true; upon which fuppofition it would be ridiculous to lay down Rules about the Perfections and Faults of any Art; or indeed about a right Tafte of Life and Happinefs: Right Education, which is nothing elfe but the Art of forming and perfecting good Tafte in Life, and in Arts, would be vain labour. In truth, when it is faid that Taftes may not be called in queftion, and examined, in order to their being amended, the propereft Refutation is that propofed by an excellent Author, which is to prefent thofe who maintain that Abfurdity, with a Picture of a Fly, or a certain groffer Animal at its beloved Repaft, with this Motto, *Trahit sua quemque voluptas.*

'TIS true, ancient Authors have faid, that in Poetry, Oratory, Painting, or any Art, good Tafte can no more be communicated by Art and Teaching, than Tafte or Smell (32). And fo have the beft ancient Moralifts faid, that Virtue cannot be taught. But 'tis plain their Meaning is not, that the Beauties of Life and Arts cannot be explained; that the Nature of Virtue cannot be defined; or that Arts and Life do not admit of Rules, pointing out what is beautiful and excellent in the one or the other, and their contraries. For don't the fame Philofophers, who tell us that a moral Senfe muft be from Nature, and that it cannot be acquired, fhew us the Rules of Conduct, the Obfervance of which produces Harmony and Confiftency of Life and Manners; *Numeros modofque vitæ?* Is it not the chief End of their excellent Writings, to correct and improve our Tafte of Happinefs and moral Beauty? And in like manner do not thofe Authors, who tell us, that good Tafte in any of the fine Arts cannot be acquired by mere Inftruction, but muft be fundamentally from Nature, fhew us, how good Tafte in the Arts may be cultivated, and brought to due Perfection; and point out the Perfections and Imperfections, or, to fpeak in their own Stile, the Virtues and Vices belonging to thefe Arts? All that is meant by them is Indeed felf-evident; namely, that Morality or tight and wrong Conduct in Life, prefuppofes a natural Tafte of moral Beauty and Fitnefs in Actions: And in like manner all the Arts prefuppofe a natural Senfe of Harmony, Beauty, Proportion, Greatnefs and Truth; and that as neceffarily, in both cafes, as Taftes and Smells prefuppofe Faculties or Senfes fitted to receive thefe Senfations. As no Art can fupply the outward Senfes where they are abfolutely wanting; fo neither can Art produce the other internal ones where they are totally deficient. But in both cafes Art can cure and improve, reform and perfect. It is in Morality and all the Arts, as *Horace* fays it is in Writing:

Scribendi recte sapere est principium & fons.   Hor. Art. Poet.

Good Senfe is the Source and Fountain of all; but good Directions are ufeful to guide it into its proper Channels (33), and lead it to a proper place, where it may dilate and fpread it felf with Pleafure and Ufe.

*What is meant by
Expreffion, what
by Paffion, and
what by Colouring.*
BUT not to infift longer upon what is fo evident, I would only fuggeft, that in the Difpute about Colouring and Expreffion, which of the two ought to be preferred, Expreffion is of-ten confounded with Paffion; and hence arifes great Confufion and Jangling. Yet thefe, in truth, are very diftinct things; every Paffion is Expreffion, but all Expreffion is not Paffion, or of the pathetick kind. As it is in Writing, fo is it in Painting; there may be Loftinefs in Sentiments where there is no Paffion. The Pathetick, as *Longinus* hath obferved (34), may animate and inflame the Sublime; but is not effential to it. And therefore, in comparing Painting with Defcription, I mentioned four forts of Expreffion; which, tho' the diftin-guifhing Character of the Object defcribed may be clearly and ftrongly delineated in each, are however very different in refpect of their Excellence, or of the Pleafure they are qualify'd to afford the Mind: The Expreffion of low, mean, and vulgar Objects; the Expreffion of lofty, noble, beautiful and delightful Ideas; the Pleafure which arifes from the Newnefs or Uncommonnefs of the Ideas that are convey'd by Defcription and Pictures; and the Expref-fion of Objects that touch the Affections. The laft Clafs is properly the pathetick fort. Ex-preffion is a general Term, that fignifies reprefenting any Object agreeably to its Nature; or giving it its true and proper Character. Paffion denotes thofe Motions in the Face and Gefture,

(32) Non magis arte traditur quam guftus aut odor. *Quint. Inft.* Whether Virtue could be taught or not, is a Queftion often handled by *Plato,* and other ancient Philofophers. This *Horace* tells us, *Epift. l.* 1. *Ep.* 18.
    *Inter cuncta leges & percuntabere doctos
Vertutem doctrina paret, naturæne donet.*

(33) So *Longinus* fpeaks, *De Sublim. f.* 2.——Atta-men quo modo, loco, tempore, & ad quos & quatenus eam conveniat adhiberi, unumque adeo rectum illius at-que emendatam ufum & excercitationem ab arte ac me-thodo definiri & proficifci.——Atque ut quod de Communi vita Demofthenem pronuntiaffe ferunt, primum omnium bonorum effe felicitatem: proximum vero huic ac tin-tum non par, felicitate illa fapienter uti; quo deficiente & illius hominibus fructus intereat atque evanefcat; id ipfum quoque in dicendi ratione commode ufurpari poffe;

naturam quidem felicitatis vias fuftinere, artem vero pru-dentiæ.

(34) Prima eaque luculentiffima præftantiffimaque fub-limitatis fcaturigo, eft nobilis & felix in concipiendis grandibus ac excelfis fenfibus animi magnitudo.———-Altera eft vehemens & ad concitandos perturbandofque animos efficax affectus: atque hæ quidem duæ fublimi-tatis fcaturigines maxima fui parte homini ingenitæ funt & naturales.——Qui fi fublimitatem & hanc animo-rum perturbationem rem unam effe cenfuit, & cum na-tura tum conftitutione ea rdem, vehementer errat. Nam & affectus aliquot inveniuntur a fublimitate remotiffimi, immo humiles plane & abjecti; quod genus miferatio, triftitia, metus: & vice verfa fublimia multa omni om-nino affectu deftituta. *Long. f.* 8.

Gefture, by which Affections of the Mind are expreffed. Colouring therefore, as it is diftinguifh'd from both, muft mean no more than the artful Imitation of the real Appearance of Objects in refpect of Colour; as for inftance, in the human Body.   Now without all doubt to be able, by a thorough Intelligence of local Colouring, and of Light and Shade, as by a kind of Magick, to imitate real Flefh and Blood, fo as to impofe almoft upon the Senfe, and deceive the Eye, is a wonderful Art.   But let any one ask himfelf, whether it is not a yet higher and more entertaining Art, to give a Face a fagacious, graceful, or majeftick Air; to mark the diftinguifhing Character of a *Jupiter*, a *Pallas*, or an *Apollo :* Whether, in one word, the moft perfect Refemblance to Flefh and Blood, without any other Ideas fuggefted to the Mind, is the higheft pleafure (35) he can conceive a Picture capable of giving: Or whether he is not more delighted, when, tho' the Colouring is not fo perfect, a particular Character is fo marked, that he diftinctly perceives what it is, and is natually led into pleafing Reflections in his own Mind upon it, and the Propriety with which it is expreffed.

IT may therefore be laid down as a general Rule, which refpect to Pictures, that they are proportional in Merit, to the Dignity of the Ideas they are qualified to convey to the Mind. If the Truth, Strength, and Propriety of the Reprefentation are equal, they are as the Ideas or Objects that are reprefented: And if the Ideas or Objects reprefented are the fame, or equal, they are as the Truth, Strength, and Propriety of the Reprefentation.

SOCRATES and *Ariftotle* have not hefitated to pronounce the Talent of Imita-
ting moral Life, and expreffing the Affections of the Mind, the chief Excellence in all *The Opinion of So-crates and Ari-ftotle.*
the imitative Arts (36).   And the latter divides moral Imitation in Painting and Poetry
into three forts.   " Men, faith he, are either good or bad; they are chiefly diftinguifh'd *The latter's Account of moral Imitation.*
" by their Manners, that is, by their Virtues and Vices.   Thofe therefore who propofe
" to imitate human Life, muft either paint Men better or worfe than they are in the
" ordinary Courfe of human Affairs; or fuch as they commonly are.   There are but thefe
" three Kinds of Reprefentation.   Now *Polygnotus* excelled in the firft, exhibiting Men of
" great, illuftrious, and uncommon Virtues; *Pouffin* in the fecond, painting extraordinary
" *Scelerates*, or the vileft and moft abominable Characters; and *Dionyfius* drew the more
" common Manners, Difpofitions, and Qualities of Mankind (37)."

THIS Paffage is mifunderftood by thofe who imagine the *Stagyrite* to be fpeaking of mere Face or Portrait-Painters.   He is difcourfing of moral Imitation in Poetry; and is illuftrating it by fuch Painting as aimed alfo at the Reprefentation of Manners, Actions, and Characters.   He adds, that the Tragedies of fome young Men were like the Pictures of *Zeuxis*, in which Manners were not painted; not properly diftinguifhed or characterized.

PROPRIETY and Truth of Characters do therefore belong no lefs to Painting than to Poetry; and according to *Ariftotle* and *Socrates*, it is the principal End of both to exprefs Manners and to touch the Mind.   But whatever thefe Arts propofe to imitate, 'tis *Painting ought to aim at Truth.*
Truth and Nature muft be their guide.   Then is Art, fays *Longinus*, perfect when it is Nature (38).   *Socrates* begins both his Difcourfes with obferving, that Nature is the Stan-
dard

(35) What *Felibien* fays in the Life of *Tintoret* deferves our attention.   Quoiqu'il eut toujours en Vuë le coloris du Titien & le deffein de Michel Ange, il craignoit bien plus de manquer dans le deffein que dans la couleur, di-fant même quelquefois, que ceux qui vouloient aVoir de belles couleurs pouvoient en trouVer dans les boutiques des marchands: mais que pour le deffein, il ne fe trouvoit que dans l'Efprit des excellens Peintres.———Le blanc & le noir font les couleurs les plus precieufes dont un peintre pouvoit fe fervir; parce qu'avec celles-la feules, on peut donner relief aux figures & marquer les jours & les ombres—il prefervit le feu de l'imagination & l'abon-dance des expreffions à l'achevement d'un ouVrage; c'eft pourquoi certains peintres Flamands, qui venoient a Rome, lui aYant montré quelques têtes qu'ils avoient peintes & finies aVec beaucoup de foin & de tems, il leur demanda combien ils avoient eté de tems a les faire?——Il prit du noir aVec un pinceau & en trois coups deffina, fur une toile, une figure qu'il rehauffa aVec du blanc: puis fe tournant Vers les Etrangers, Voila, leur dit il, comme nous autres pauVres peintres Venitiens, aVons accoutumé de faire des tableaux—Un jeune peintre de Boulogne l'etoit allé Voir, & lui demandant fes aVis pour devener bon peintre, il ne lui dit autre chofe, finon qu'il falloit deffiner——fon fentiment etoit qu'il n'y aVoit que ceux qui etoient deja bien aVancez dans le deffein, que devoient traVailler d'apres la nature: parce que la plufpart des corps naturels marquoient beaucoup de grace & de beauté—que cet art eft tel, que plus on y aVance, plus on y trouVe de difficultes: qu'il reffemble à une mer qui n'a point de bornes, & qui paroit toujours plus grande à mefure que l'onVogue deffus.   *Entret. fur les Vies, tom.* 3. *p.* 154.

(36) *Arift. de Poet. c.* 6.   Prima igitur pars, & velut anima tragœdiæ eft ipfa fabula.   Proxima autem loco funt mores: His enim affimile quiddam eft etiam in re pictoria.   Siquis namque tabulam pigmentis licet pulcher-rimis temere fufimque illeverit; non perinde fpectantem oblectet, ac fi, albo licet colore imaginem delinearit cer-tam: pari modo in tragœdiis abfque conftitutione rerum, magis Valent mores quam morum expers fabula.   Eft etiam omnis imitatio, proprie quidem, ipfius actionis & per hanc, eorum eft maxime qui agunt; quibus primitus hærent mores.   So likewife *Horace de Arte Poet.*
     Non fatis eft pulchra effe poemata dulcia funto:
     Et quocunque volent animum auditoris agunto.
Again.   *Si plauforis æges Aulæa manentis & ufque*
     Seffuri, donec cantor, vos plaudite dicat;
     Ætatis cujufque notandi funt tibi mores, &c.
And again. *Interdum fpeciofa locis, morataque recte*
     Fabula nullius Veneris, fine pondere & arte
     Valdius oblectat populum, meliufque moratur,
     Quam verfus inopes rerum, nugæque canoræ.

(37) See *Arift. de re Poet.* the whole 2d Chapter, and compare it with the laft Paragraph of the 15th Chapter.   Quoniam autem Tragœdia, meliorum imitatio eft: (ut Comœdia fequiorum) fictores imaginum bonos imitari debemus; qui cum fingulis fuam propriamque dent for-mam, faciendo fimiles; quantum res patitur, pulchriores fingunt.   Ita & Poeta, &c.

(38) This appears from the Paffages of *Xenophon* and *Ariftotle* already quoted.   So likewife *Longinus.*——Tum demum ars confummata eft atque abfoluta, quum naturæ
                                                                                    fpeciem

X

dard of the imitative Arts : And this is indeed manifeftly included in the very idea of Imitation.   But both *Ariftotle* and *Socrates* tell us, that the imitators of Nature muft aim not only at Truth but at Beauty : becaufe Probability is the Truth of Art (39), or with refpect to Art, Nature and Probability mean the fame thing.   This term Nature, not only comprehends what actually does exift, but whatever may exift or is confiftent : It includes, in its Meaning, not only what is called by fome Moderns Real Truth ; but alfo what is called by the fame Criticks, Ideal Truth.

Probability is the Truth of Art.

And Painting ought to aim chiefly at Beauty.

IN order therefore to paint agreeably to Truth, it is not neceffary to adhere too ftrictly to Nature ; but the Imitator may chufe and collect from various Parts of Nature, or from all her immenfe Riches, in order to make his Reprefentations more grand, beautiful, inftructive or moving, than common Nature ; and whilft he does fo, what he paints will be Nature.

Of the Liberty of Poets and Painters to mend Nature.

THE Art, Genius, Tafte, and Judgment of Poets and Painters, difcovers itfelf in chufing well, in order to fet off their Subjects to the beft advantage.   This, in *Ariftotle's* Phrafe, is to know how to lye as one ought (40).   When Poets or Painters are faid to have the Power or Liberty of heightening and mending Nature, the Meaning is, that they are at liberty to felect from the various Parts of Nature, and to combine Circumftances according to their Fancy, as may beft fuit their end (41).   But their Compofitions muft be confiftent and probable : they muft be congruous Wholes.   And whatever is fuch, becaufe it may exift, is Nature, tho' it be not copied after any particular Object of Nature.   All this is charmingly explained by *Horace* in his Art of Poetry.

> —————— *Pictoribus atque poetis*
> *Quidlibet audendi femper fuit æqua poteftas.*
> *Denique fit quodvis fimplex duntaxat & unum*
> *Infelix operis fumma, quia ponere totum*
> *Nefcit :*—————
> *Atque ita mentitur, fic veris falfa remifcet*
> *Primo ne medium, medio, ne difcrepit imum.*

It is on account of this extenfive Liberty of Poets and Painters, reaching as far as Probability extends, that the imitative Arts are faid by *Ariftotle* to be more Philofophical than Hiftory (42) : Becaufe the Hiftorian is tied down to a faithful Reprefentation of Facts as they really happened ; but the imitative Arts are more univerfal, having a greater Latitude in chufing and combining proper Circumftances, and therefore are better adapted for teaching and exhibiting human Nature : They are fitter to exhibit Men and Manners ; and confequently to inftruct in the Knowledge of Mankind (43) and Morals.

IT is almoft needlefs to obferve, that Truth or Probability of moral Reprefentation muft comprehend, not only regard to what may be called univerfal Truth, that is, to the Fabrick of the human Mind, or the Nature of human Affections ; but likewife regard to accidental or variable Truth, the Differences of Times, Countries, Climates, Cuftoms, Habits, and all that is properly denominated by the modern Painters, *Coftume*.   He who draws Battles, or other Actions of any diftinct and peculiar People, ought to draw the feveral Figures of his Piece in their proper and real Proportions, Geftures, Habits, Arms ; or at leaft with as fair Refemblance as poffible : Accordingly *Nealces* and feveral other ancient Painters are highly commended on this account, as hath been obferved.   Every Imitation ought to be performed with fuch Intelligence of human Nature, which is ever-fubftantially the fame, that it may be univerfally inftructive and moving.   But every Imitation being
particular,

fpeciem induit ; & viciffim natura tum denique felix & emendata dicenda eft, quum ab arte latenter adjuvatur. *De Subl. fec.* 22. So *Vitruvius,* particularly with regard to Painting, and the ancient Artifts, Quod non poteft in Veritate fieri, id non putaverunt, in imaginibus factum, poffe certam rationem habere.   Omnia enim certa proprietate, & a Veris naturæ deducta moribus, traduxerunt in operum perfectiones ; & ea probaverunt, quorum explicationes in difputationibus rationem poffunt habere veritatis. *Lib.* 4. *c.* 2. & *lib.* 7. *c.* 5.   Pictura fit imago ejus quod eft, feu poteft effe ; ut hominis, ædificii, naVis, reliquarumque rerum, e quarum formis certifque corporum finibus figurata fimilitudine fumuntur exempla.   Itaque in conclavibus Vernis & autumnalibus, æftivis etiam Atriis & Periftyliis, conftitutæ funt ab antiquis ex certis rebus certæ rationes picturarum.   Sed hæc quæ a veteribus ex Veris rebus exempla fumebantur, nunc iniquis moribus improbantur ; nam pinguntur Tectoriis monftra potius, quam ex rebus finitis imagines certæ.   At hæc falfa Videntes homines, non reprehendunt, fed delectantur : Neque animadvertunt fiquid eorum fieri poteft, necne.   Judiciis autem infirmis obfcuratæ mentes, non Valent probare quod poteft effe cum auctoritate·& ratione decotis : Neque enim picturæ probari debent, quæ non funt fimiles veritati.

(39) Compare with the Paffages of *Ariftotle* already quoted, *c.* 9. *ob initio.*   Manifeftum eft, non effe poetæ munus, ea quæ fingulatim fiunt, dicere ; fed ea memorare, qualia factum iri contigerint, & quæ poffibilia fuerint, fecundum verifimile, vel neceffarium, &c.

(40) Διδάχει δὲ μάλιϛα ὍμηϱΘ· ϰỳ τὰς ἄλλυς ψυδῆ λέγειν ὡς δεῖ.   Ἔϛι δὲ τῦτο παϱαλογισμὸς.

(41) Compare with *Ariftotle* the Paffages from *Vitruvius* and *Longinus* above, and what the latter fays, *Sect.* 36. ——Præftiterit, inquam, artem naturæ auxiliatricem adjungere.   Ubi namque hæ duæ amice confpiraverint fieri nequit, quin idipfum, quod communi opera effecerint omnibus fuis numeris fit abfolutiffimum.

(42) Διὸ ϰỳ Φιλοσοφώτεϱον ϰỳ σπυδαιότεϱον ποίησις ἱϛοϱίας ἐϛί.   Ἡ μὲν γὰϱ ποίησις μᾶλλον τὰ ϰαθόλυ, ἡ δ' ἱϛοϱία τὰ ϰαθ' ἕϰαϛον λέγει.   De Art. Poet. *c.* 9.

(43) Compare the Paffages in *Ariftotle's* Art of Poetry already quoted, with what he fays of Manners. *Polit. Ed. Wechel. p.* 225.

particular, or reprefentative of one certain Action; the Action painted ought to be told with fuch a ftrict regard to the accidental *Coftume*, that the Subject and Scene may be eafily diftinguifhed by thofe who are verfed in Hiftory.

IT is then evident from what hath been faid, that there is no kind of Compofition re- lating to Men and Manners, in which it is not equally neceffary for the Author to under- ftand moral Truth. 'Tis not enough that the moral Painter hath ftudied the Features, Pro- portions, and Graces of the human Body; he muft be profoundly knowing in thofe of the Mind (44). How elfe can he juftly reprefent Sentiments and Characters; diftinguifh the Beau- tiful from the Deformed; mark the Sublime of Tempers and Actions; and give a moral Whole its juft Body and Proportions? How elfe can he note the Boundaries of the Paffions, and difcern their exact Tones and Meafures? This therefore is the Study which *Socrates* recommended to *Parrhafius* and *Clito*: This is the Study *Horace* recommends to all the Imitators of rational Life.

Painters as well as Poets ought to ftudy Mankind, and true moral Philofophy.

> *Refpicere exemplar vitæ, morumque jubebo*
> *Doctum imitatorem, & veras hinc ducere voces.*

AND for this end he advifes them to ftudy the *Chartæ Socraticæ*, the Dialogues of *Plato*, in which *Socrates* is the Hero or principal Character (45); becaufe thefe Writings are Imi- tations which have the effential Quality of fuch Compofitions, MANNERS. "The philofo- " phical Writings, (fays a noble (46) Author) to which *Horace* in his Art of Poetry refers, " were in themfelves a kind of Poetry like the Mimes, or perfonated Pieces of early Times, " before Philofophy was in vogue, and when as yet dramatical Imitation was fcarce form'd; " or at leaft, in many parts, not brought to due Perfection. They were Pieces, which, be- " fides their Force of Stile, and hidden Numbers, carry'd a fort of Action and Imitation, the " fame as the epick and dramatick Kinds. They were either real Dialogues, or Recitals of " fuch perfonated Difcourfes; where the Perfons themfelves had their Characters preferved " throughout; their Manners, Humours, and diftinct Turns of Temper and Underftanding " maintained, according to the moft exact poetical Truth. It was not enough that thofe " Pieces treated fundamentally of Morals, and in confequence pointed out real Characters " and Manners; They exhibited them alive, and fet the Countenances and Complexions of " Men plainly in view. And by this means they not only taught us to know others; but, " what was principal and of higheft Virtue in them, they taught us to know ourfelves. The " philofophical Hero of thefe Poems, whofe Name they carry'd both in their Body and Front, " and whofe Genius and Manner they were made to reprefent, was himfelf a perfect Cha- " racter; yet, in fome refpects, fo veil'd, and in a Cloud, that to the unattentive Surveyor, " he feemed often to be very different from what he really was: and this chiefly by reafon " of a certain exquifite and refined Raillery, which belong'd to his Manner, and by virtue of " which he could treat the higheft Subjects, and thofe of the commoneft Capacity both to- " gether, and render them explanatory of each other. So that in this Genius of Writing, " there appeared both the Heroick and the Simple, the Tragick and the Comick Vein. How- " ever, it was fo ordered, that notwithftanding the Oddnefs or Myfterioufnefs of the prin- " cipal Character, the under-parts or fecond Characters fhew'd human Nature more diftinctly, " and to the Life. We might here, therefore, as in a Looking-Glafs, difcover ourfelves, " and fee our minuteft Features nicely delineated, and fuited to our own Apprehenfion and " Cognizance."

Why Horace recom- mends the Chartæ Socraticæ to their ftudy.

I could not chufe but take notice here of this excellent Reflection on *Horace's* Precept to the Imitators of moral Life, becaufe it is not obferved by the Commentators on *Horace*, and it is an excellent Remark upon our main Subject, the ftrict relation of all the imitative Arts; the relation of moral Painting to moral Poetry, and of both to moral Philofophy; not merely in refpect of the Subject, but likewife in the manner of teaching it, according to the beft ancient Models of philofophical Writing.

BUT to proceed; what is called by the Ancients the τὸ καλὸν in Compofition (47), comprehends that exquifite Tafte in the Choice of a Subject and its Parts, and in the Dif- pofition and Subordination of every part to one excellent principal End, by which a noble and beautiful Whole is formed, that may be diftinctly comprehended, and yet wonderfully fill and occupy the Mind. It arifes, according to *Ariftotle's* Account, in all the imitative Arts, from the Expreffion of Greatnefs with order; or is accomplifhed by exhibiting the Principal in the largeft Proportions in which it is capable of being viewed. It muft not be gigantick, for thus it is in a manner out of fight, and cannot be comprehended in a fingle united View: On the contrary, when a Piece is of the miniature kind; when it runs into the Detail, and a nice Delineation of every particular, it is, as it were, invifible, for the

Of Beauty in Paint- ing according to Ariftotle.

---

(44) See the Prefaces to the *Icones* by the two *Philo- ftrates*, above cited.

(45) ——*Scribendi recte, fapere eft principium & fons. Rem tibi Socraticæ poterunt oftendere chartæ.*
     De Art. Poet.

(46) *Charact.* vol. 1. p. 193. Advice to an Author.

(47) Ἔτι δ' ἐπεὶ τὸ καλὸν, ἢ ζῶον ἢ ἅπαν πρᾶγμα ὃ συνέστηκεν ἐκ τινῶν, οὐ μόνον ταῦτα τεταγμένα δεῖ ἔχειν, ἀλλὰ ἢ μέγεθΘ ὑπάρχειν μὴ τὸ τυχόν· τὸ γὰρ κα- λὸν, ἐν μεγέθει ἢ τάξει ἐςί. Arift. de Art. Poet. c. 7.

the ſame reaſon; becauſe the ſummary Beauty, the Whole itſelf, cannot be comprehended in that one united View; which is broken and loſt, by the neceſſary Attraction of the Eye to every ſmall ſubordinate Part. In a poetical Whole, the ſame regard ought to be had to the Memory, as in Painting to the Eye. The dramatick Kind is confined within the convenient and proper time of a Spectacle. The Epick is left more at large. Each Work, however, muſt aim at Vaſtneſs, and be as great, and of as long Duration as poſſible; but ſo as to be comprehended (as to the main of it) by one eaſy Glance or Retroſpect of Memory. And this the Philoſopher calls εὐμνημόνευτον, Eaſineſs or Unity of Comprehenſion. The noble Author, who thus comments on *Ariſtotle*, adds, " I cannot better tranſlate the " Paſſage than I have done in theſe explanatory Lines. For beſides what relates to mere " Art, the philoſophical Senſe of the Original is ſo majeſtick, and the whole Treatiſe ſo " maſterly, that when I find even the *Latin* Interpreters come ſo ſhort, I ſhould be vain " to attempt any thing in our own Language. I would only add a ſmall Remark of my " own, which may perhaps be noticed by the Studiers of Statuary and Painting: That the " greateſt of the ancient as well as modern Artiſts, were ever inclin'd to follow this Rule " of the Philoſopher; and when they err'd in their Deſigns, or Draughts, it was on the ſide " of Greatneſs, by running into the unſizable and gigantick, rather than into the minute and " delicate. Of this *Michael Angelo*, the great Beginner and Founder among the Moderns, " and *Zeuxis* the ſame among the Ancients, may ſerve as inſtances (48)." The ſame hath been already obſerved with reſpect to *Euphranor*, and *Nicias*, and in general, all the beſt ancient Maſters.

Of Ordonnance and Eaſineſs of Sight.

THIS Beauty of Compoſition, was likewiſe very emphatically called by the Ancients, in one word, εὐσύνοπτον (49), Eaſineſs or Unity of Sight. And it cannot be better defined, as it relates to Painting, than in the Words of the ſame noble Author juſt cited. " When the Ordonnance is ſuch, that the Eye not only runs over with eaſe the ſeveral Parts " of the Deſign, (reducing ſtill its View each moment to the principal Subject on which all " turns) but when the ſame Eye without the leaſt Detainment in any of the particular Parts, " and reſting, as it were, immovable, in the Middle, or Centre of the Tablature, may " ſee, at once, in an agreeable and perfect Correſpondency, all which is there exhibited to " the Sight (50.) Thus alone can the Subordination be perfect. And if the Subordination " be not perfect, the Order (which makes the Beauty) remains imperfect."

THIS Unity and Eaſineſs of Sight and Comprehenſion, neceſſarily requires Unity of Action, Time, and Place; and that what is principal or chief ſhould immediately ſhew itſelf, without leaving the Mind in any uncertainty.

BUT all that relates to Unity and Simplicity of Deſign, and to the one Point of Time in hiſtorical or moral Painting, are fully explained by my Lord *Shafteſbury* in his Notion of the hiſtorical Draught or Tablature of the Judgment of *Hercules* (51); where he indeed ſhews moral Painting to be a truly profound and philoſophical Art.

WHAT

(48) *Charact. vol. 1. Eſſay on Wit and Humour, p.* 143. I uſe that noble Author's Words. It is an excellent Commentary on that Paſſage of *Ariſtotle.*

(49) Ὥστε δεῖ καθάπερ ἐπὶ τῶν σωμάτων, καὶ ἐπὶ τῶν ζώων ἔχειν μὲν μέγεθος, τοῦτο δὲ εὐσύνοπτον εἶναι· οὕτω καὶ ἐπὶ τῶν μύθων ἔχειν μὲν μῆκος τοῦτο δ' εὐμνημόνευτον εἶναι. Ariſt. de Art. Poet. c. 7.

(50) *Charact. vol. 3. Tablature, &c. p.* 38.

(51) See particularly what is there explained concerning the Conſiſtency of Anticipation and Repeal with Truth and Credibility: Or that Law of Unity and Simplicity of Deſign, which conſtitutes the very Being of a hiſtorical Picture. " To preſerve therefore a juſt Con- " formity with hiſtorical Truth, and with the Unity of " Time and Action, there remains no other way by " which we can poſſibly give a hint of any thing future, " or call to mind any thing paſt, than by ſetting in " view ſuch Paſſages or Events as have actually ſubſiſted, " or, according to Nature, might well ſubſiſt or happen " together in one and the ſame inſtant. And this is " what we may call the Rule of Conſiſtency. Now " is it therefore poſſible, ſays one, to expreſs a Change " of Paſſion in any Subject, ſince this Change is made " by ſucceſſion; and that in this caſe the Paſſion which " is underſtood as preſent, will require a Diſpoſi- " tion of Body and Features wholly different from the " Paſſion which is over and paſt? To this we anſwer, " that notwithſtanding the Aſcendency or Reign of the " principal and immediate Paſſion, the Artiſt has power " to leave ſtill in his Subjects the Tracks and Footſteps of " its Predeceſſor: So as to let us behold not only a riſing " Paſſion, together with a declining one; but what is " more, a ſtrong and determinate Paſſion, with its con- " trary already diſcharg'd and baniſh'd. As for inſtance, " when the plain Tracks of Tears new fall'n, with " other freſh Tokens of Mourning and Dejection, re- " main ſtill in a Perſon newly tranſported with joy at " the ſight of a Relation or Friend, who the moment " before had been lamented as one deceas'd or loſt. " Again, by the ſame means which are imploy'd to " call to mind the paſt, we may anticipate the future: " as would be ſeen in the caſe of an able Painter, who " ſhould undertake to paint this Hiſtory of *Hercules*, ac- " cording to the third Date or Period of Time propos'd " for our hiſtorical Tablature, (when the Diſpute be- " tween the two Goddeſſes *Virtue* and *Pleaſure* is already " far advanced, and *Virtue* ſeems to gain her Cauſe.) " For in this momentary Turn of Action, *Hercules* " remaining ſtill in a Situation expreſſive of Suſpenſe " and Doubt, would diſcover nevertheleſs that the " Strength of this inward Conflict was over, and that " Victory began now to declare herſelf in favour of " *Virtue.* This Tranſition, which ſeems at firſt ſo my- " ſterious a Performance, will be eaſily comprehended, " if one conſiders, that the Body which moves much " ſlower than the Mind, is eaſily out-ſtripp'd by this " latter; and that the Mind on a ſudden turning itſelf " ſome new way, the nearer ſituated, and more ſprightly " Parts of the Body, (ſuch as the Eyes and Muſcles " about the Mouth and Forehead) taking the Alarm, " and moving in an inſtant, may leave the heavier and " more diſtant parts to adjuſt themſelves, and change " their Attitude ſome Moments after." The ſame Author adds, that if this Queſtion concerning the inſtantaneous Action or preſent Moment of Time were applied to many famous hiſtorical Pictures much admired in the World, they would be found very defective; as we may learn by that ſingle inſtance of *Acteon*, one of the commoneſt in Painting. Hardly is there any where ſeen

a

WHAT I chiefly propoſed was, to mention ſome of the more important Obſervations of ancient Philoſophers on the Art of Painting. And, from what hath been ſaid, it mani-feſtly appears; in what they placed the chief Excellence of Painting. A Picture muſt be a true Imitation, a true Likeneſs; not only the Carnation muſt appear real, but even the Stuffs, Silks, and other Ornaments in the Draperies. Without Truth no Imitation can pleaſe. But the great Merit of Painting conſiſts, in making a fine and judicious Choice of Nature; in exhibiting great, rare, ſurprizing, and beautiful Objects in a lively manner; and thus conveying great and pleaſing Ideas into the Mind. But becauſe rational is the higheſt Order of Life, the Source whence the greateſt, the loftieſt, as well as the moſt inſtructive and touching Sentiments are derived; the higheſt Merit and Excellence of Painting muſt con-ſiſt in a fine Taſte of moral Truth; in exciting in our Minds great and noble Ideas of the moral Kind, and in moving our Paſſions in a ſound and wholeſome way: For ſuch is our Frame and Conſtitution, that what hath a virtuous Effect is at the ſame time moſt pleaſant and agreeable.

Socrates *repreſents moral Imitation as the chief End of Painting.*

PARRHASIUS ask'd *Socrates* how this could be done; and the Philoſopher an-ſwers, that if all that is viſible may be painted, all the Paſſions and Affections of the Mind may be painted, for all theſe have their viſible Characteriſticks. Whatever is great, generous, beautiful, or graceful in the Mind, ſhews itſelf by plain Marks in the Countenance, and Geſture: And ſo likewiſe do mean, low, baſe, unworthy Sentiments and Affections. And therefore all theſe may be exhibited to the Sight by a Painter who hath ſtudied Mankind, and is profoundly skilled in the human Heart, and the natural Language of the Paſſions. So *Horace* .

> *Format enim Natura prius nos intus ad omnem*
> *Fortunarum habitum: juvat, aut impellit ad iram;*
> *Aut ad humum mœrore gravi deducit, & angit :*
> *Poſt effert animi motus interprete lingua.*   De Art. Poet.

And *Pliny* gives us a long and elegant Account of the Force of Expreſſion in the Eye, that well deſerves the Conſideration of Painters (52).

BUT *Socrates*, ſpeaking of moral Painting, or of the Expreſſion of Manners, goes farther, and leads *Parrhaſius* to give the Preference to thoſe Pictures which expreſs the Beauties of Virtue; amiable and worthy Characters; truly good and great Actions; pure and virtuous Manners. Theſe the Mind contemplates with the higheſt Delight and Satisfaction: Theſe raiſe our Admiration, and inſpire us with the moſt pleaſing Sentiments and generous Diſpoſitions. Merely corporeal Beauty hath a wonderfully charming Influence upon the Mind : But 'tis moral Beauty, the Graces of the Soul, the Fair, Lovely and Decent in Characters and Actions that moſt highly raviſhes and tranſports us. We find this Philoſopher often diſcourſing to his Diſciples in *Plato* and *Xenophon*'s Works, upon the Excellence of Virtue; often telling them, ſuch is the Force of its Charms that it appears in its higheſt Glory when we ſee its Behaviour in diſtreſs. 'Tis then moſt lovely and engaging when it is put to the ſevereſt Trials. Then do we ſee all its Majeſty and Firmneſs, all its Strength, Reſolution, and Sublimity: Then is it we are moſt deeply intereſted in its behalf; our Hearts are then filled with the higheſt Ad-miration and Aſtoniſhment, and at the ſame time melted into the moſt tender, generous Pity. So virtuous is our Frame, (according to the Doctrine of that moſt excellent Moraliſt) that no Act of the Mind yields it ſuch a complicated Contentment, or ſo high a Reliſh of Pleaſure, as the ſelf-approving Complacency and Affection with which it embraces ſuffering Virtue and Magnanimity. Now the ſame Philoſopher, conſiſtently with his conſtant Doctrine, tells *Par-rhaſius* and *Clito*, that in order to give us the higheſt Satisfaction, and the moſt delightful as well as wholeſome Entertainment by Art or Imitation, they ought to paint the Beauties of Vir-tue; and for that end, that they ſhould make a wiſe Choice of proper Circumſtances, to ex-hibit its greateſt Force and Excellence; or, in one word, that they ſhould ſtudy Human Nature and the Beauty and Sublime of Characters and Actions, in order to paint theſe truly amiable Virtues, the Contemplation of which exalts, enlarges and tranſports the Mind.

What may be infer-red from his Con-verſation with Par-rhaſius with regard to painting Virtue.

SUCH, no doubt, were thoſe Pictures amongſt the *Greeks*, done in Memory of their Heroes, and their glorious Atchievements for their Country and the publick Good. And 'tis of ſuch pictures *Ariſtotle* ſpeaks, when he juſtly aſſerts that Painters and Sculptors may teach Virtue and recommend it, in a more ſtriking, powerful, and efficacious Manner, than Phi-loſophers

So Ariſtotle.

a Deſign of this poetical Hiſtory without a ridiculous Anticipation of the Metamorphoſis. The Horns of *Actæon*, which are the Effects of a Charm, ſhould naturally wait the execution of that Art in which the Charm conſiſts. Till the Goddeſs therefore has thrown her Caſt, the Hero's Perſon ſuffers not any change. Even while the Water flies, his Forehead is ſtill ſound. But in the uſual Deſigns we ſee it otherwiſe. The Horns are already ſprouted, if not full grown, and the God-deſs is ſeen wattering the Sprouts.

(52) Neque ulla ex parte, majora animi indicia cunc-

tis animalibus, ſed homini maxime, id eſt, moderationis, clementiæ, miſericordiæ, odii, amoris, triſtitiæ, læti-tiæ. Contuitu quoque multiformes, truces, torvi, fla-grantes, graVes, tranſverſi, limi, ſummiſſi, blandi. Pro-ſecto in oculis animus inhabitat. Ardent, intenduntur, humeſcunt, conniVent. Hinc illæ miſericordiæ, lacrymæ, &c. *Plin. Hiſt. Nat. lib.* 11. *c.* 37. So *Seneca, Epiſt.* 106. Annon Vides quantum oculis det Vigorem fortitudo? Quantam intentionem prudentia ? Quantam modeſtiam & quietem reverentia ? Quantam ſerenitatem lætitia ? Quantum rigorem ſeveritas ? Quantum remiſſionem hi-laritas ? See *Quint. lib.* 2. *c.* 3.

Y

loſophers can do by their Differtations and Reaſonings; and that Pictures are more capable of exciting Remorfe in the Vitious, and of making them enter into a ferious Converfation with their own Hearts, and return to a right Judgment of Life and Conduct, than the beſt moral Precepts can do without fuch affiſtance (53).

PARRHASIUS is led by *Socrates* to acknowledge that the Virtues are the moſt agreeable Objects Pictures can reprefent; and that the Vices cannot be beheld without Abhorrence and Deteſtation. Whence *Parrhaſius* might have learned, that the Deformity and Vilenefs of vitious Characters, is then moſt pleafantly reprefented in Pictures, when the hateful Characters are introduced into a Piece, fo as to ferve by way of Contraſt or Foil, to fet off and heighten the Beauty of the virtuous Action which is the principal Subject. At leaſt this Conclufion naturally follows from what *Socrates* leads *Parrhaſius* to perceive and confefs with great Emphafis (54). Nothing can be more inſtructive, with regard to Painting, than this fhort Converfation when it is duly attended to. " Painting can give an Appearance of Reality to " any Object; but is this all it propofes? Can it not paint more beautiful Objects than " are to be feen in Nature? And how is it able to do that? Is it not by chufing out of " the vaſt Riches of Nature, and by combining difperfed Beauties with Taſte and Judg- " ment? But does it aim at nothing higher than reprefenting merely fenfible and corpo- " real Beauties and Proportions? Can it not imitate the Motions, Actions and Affections " of the Mind? Are not thefe likewife vifible, and if they can be difcerned by the Eye in " real Life, may they not be painted? But do all Sentiments, and Motions or Affections " of the Mind equally pleafe? Is there not a Beauty and a Deformity belonging to them? " What do you fay of a noble and heroick Mind; and of a mean and groveling fordid one? " What do you fay of great, generous and lovely Actions; and of bafe, abominable and " flagitious ones? Here indeed (faid the Painter) there is a moſt fenfible difference between " Beauty and Deformity."

· HIS Conference with *Clito* the Statuary (as we have feen) is to the fame effect. And the Philofopher concludes : " Thus then you fee what ought to be your chief Study, and what " is the nobleſt Attainment your Art can afpire at." It ought to be your principal Employment to exhibit the Beauties and Proportions of the Mind; to recommend Virtue, and to abaſh and difcountenance Vice : Thus it is that your Art may be at once ufeful and pleafing; for virtuous Manners well painted cannot fail to charm and delight. The Philofopher's Defign is plainly to lead the Painter at once to juſt Notions of Virtue, and of his own Art, by an Argument taken from his Art, and to fhew how ferviceable it might be rendered to true Philofophy, by difplaying the Beauties of Virtue, and the Turpitude of Vice.

SO fenfible have all Sects of ancient Philofophers been of the Power of the Painting-Art, that it feems thofe who taught the contrary Doctrine to that of *Socrates,* concerning the Beauty of Virtue; and maintain'd that Pleafure ought to be confulted, and not Virtue, in our Determinations and Purfuits; were wont likewife to try to bring Painting over to *Other Philofophers* their fide. For *Cicero* tells us, that *Cleanthes* ufed frequently to defire his Hearers to ima- *endeavoured to make* gine to themfelves *Pleafure,* painted in regal Pomp, beautifully arrayed, fitting upon a mag- *ufe of Painting to* nificent Throne, with the *Virtues* attending her like Waiting-Maids, who had no other *the Advantage of a* Employment but to receive and execute her Orders; and whifpering her in the Ear only to *contrary Philofophy.* take care to do nothing rafhly, or that might offend and bring pain after it. How charmingly does *Cicero* reafon on this Subject? *Cleanthes* painted this Tablature elegantly enough in Words; but can you, *Torquatus* (fays he) look into your Mind, confult your own honeſt Heart, and the Purfuits to which it generoufly impels you, without being afhamed of this Picture? Can you bear that fervile Language he gives to the *Virtues,* that they are born to be Slaves to *Pleafure,* and not to rule? If *Pleafure* is indeed the lawful Miſtrefs, it is impoffible to maintain *Virtue,* or to be fteady to her Dictates. For can he be reckoned a good or a juſt Man who abſtains from doing Injuries, merely through fear? Sure you well know the Force of that honeſt ancient Saying; *Nemo pius eſt qui pietatem metu capit* (55).

TWAS

---

(53) *Ariſt. Polit. lib.* 5. So *Quintilian, lib.* 11. *c.* 3. Nec mirum, fi iſta quæ tamen in aliquo pofita funt motu, tantum in animis Valent, cum pictura, tacens opus, & habitus femper ejufdem, fic in vitioſos penetret affectus ut ipfam vim dicendi nonnunquam fuperare videatur. So *Seneca, lib.* 2 *.de ira.* Movet mentes & atrox pictura, & juſtiſfimorum fuppliciorum triſtis eventus. So *Val. Maximus, lib.* 5. *c.* 4. *Exemplo ext.* 1. where he mentions an ancient Picture : Idem de pietate filiæ exiſtimetur quæ patrem fuum, Cithona confimili fortuna affectum; parique cuſtodiæ traditum tam ultimæ fenectutis, Velut infantem pectori fuo admotum aluit. Hærent ac ſtupent hominum oculi cum hujus facti pictam imaginem Vident, cafufque antiqui conditionem, præfenti fpectaculi admiratione renovant; in illis mutis membrorum lineamentis Viva ac fpirantia corpora intueri credentes.

(54) See the 15th Chapter of *Ariſt. de re Poet.* Boni imaginum fictores quantum res patitur, pulcriores fingunt, &c.

(55) Omnis eſt enim de virtutis dignitate contentio, at cum tuis differas, multa funt audienda etiam de obfcœnis voluptatibus de quibus ab Epicuro fæpiffime dicitur. Non potes ergo iſta tueri, Torquate, mihi crede, fi te ipfe, & tuas cogitationes, & ſtudia perfpexeris. Pudebit te, inquam, Illius tabulæ, quam Cleanthes, fane commode Verbis depingere folebat. Jubebat eos, qui audiebant, fecum ipfos cogitare pictam in tabula Voluptatem, pulcherrimo veſtitu, & ornatu regali, in folio fedentem : Præſto effe virtutes, ut ancillulas, quæ nihil aliud agerent, nullum fuum officium ducerent nifi ut voluptati miniſtrarent, & eam tantum ad aurem admonerent, (fi modo

'TWAS quite the reverſe of that corruptive Doctrine of *Cleanthes*, which we find *Socrates* teaching, in *Xenophon* and *Plato's* Works; and making uſe of the moſt ancient Poets to prove and enforce; of that ancient Fable in particular, of the Choice of *Hercules* (56); when, *Virtue* and *Pleaſure* appearing to him, he bravely diſdains all the ſoft, enchanting Allurements of Vice; and prefers the arduous but glorious Purſuits to which *Virtue* prompts, for their intrinſick Beauty and Excellence: A Subject of Painting full of noble Inſtruction, and that hath been often tried; but by none more ſucceſsfully with reſpect to the Deſign, than by a Painter at *Naples*, under the Direction of the Earl of *Shafteſbury*. And it is indeed to *Virtue* only that the Muſes willingly lend their Charms: they delight not in Varniſh and Diſguiſe, but in diſplaying real Beauties; and when they are forced into the Service of *Vice*, and conſtrained to give falſe Colours to Deformity, the Diſagreeableneſs of the Task, the Compulſion is diſcernible in every Feature.

HITHERTO I have chiefly had two Dialogues of *Socrates* in view, one with a Painter, the other with a Statuary; but left any one ſhould imagine, I have inferred too much from theſe with regard to the Connexion of the fine Arts with Virtue and true Philoſophy; I ſhall now endeavour to enforce the ſame Concluſion, by conſidering the more eſſential Qualities of good Painting, that are mentioned by ancient Authors, in another light. Let it only be premiſed, that the Beauties and Graces of the polite Arts, like the Virtues and Graces of the Mind and Behaviour are ſo inſeparably connected together, ſo intimately involved one in another, that none of them can be intirely divided from the reſt, or conſidered quite independently from the others. In both caſes Explication is nothing elſe but giving different Proſpects, as it were, of the ſame beautiful Figure: The Terms which ſeem at firſt ſight to ſignify Qualities eſſentially different, do, in reality, only denote the different Effects of the ſame Quality ſurveyed in various Circumſtances, or, as it were, from divers Points of Sight. And therefore in ſpeaking whether of the one or of the other kind of Beauties and Excellencies, Repetitions muſt be almoſt unavoidable. We cannot have a full and adequate Idea of an Object but by going round it, and viewing it in many different Situations and Lights: But a Deſcription of the ſame Object in one particular Situation, will neceſſarily coincide in many reſpects with the Deſcription of it in any other View.

Of other Qualities of good Painting.

How they are all connected together, in like manner as the moral Virtues.

IN the Hiſtory that hath been given of the more famous ancient Painters, many are praiſed for the Sublimity of their Ideas, and the admirable Efficacy of their Works in exalting and enlarging the Mind of every intelligent Spectator. Now to what Pictures is this noble Influence aſcribed? Is it not to thoſe which repreſented great Subjects with a ſuitable Greatneſs of Manner; to thoſe which by exhibiting ſublime Objects in a proper Light, that is, with all their natural Strength and Loftineſs, inſpired great Sentiments into the Minds of Beholders, and mightily moved and elevated them (57)?

Of the Great and Sublime.

THE Sublime in Writing, as we have had occaſion already to obſerve in the Character of *Timanthes* (58), who is ſaid to have been a very ſublime Painter, conſiſts, according to *Longinus*, in exciting noble Conceptions, which by leaving more behind them to be contemplated than is expreſſed, lead the Mind into an almoſt inexhauſtible Fund of great thinking: And if Painting can really produce the like Effect, it ought to be called in that Art likewiſe by the ſame Appellation, as it accordingly is by ancient Criticks. None of the ancient Treatiſes that are ſaid to have been written by Artiſts upon Painting being now extant; it is no wonder that nothing is handed down to us concerning the mechanical Part of it, or the Management of the Pencil and Handling: Other Authors would naturally take notice of thoſe Qualities only that belong to Painting, in common with Poetry and Oratory, and other Subjects of which they were expreſſly Writing; or of what more immediately relates to Invention, Diſtribution, Compoſition, Truth, Beauty, Greatneſs and Grace, and their delightful Effects on the Mind. And indeed all that can be ſaid, except by Artiſts to Artiſts, about the technical Part, can amount to little more than what is ſaid in general of Words and Phraſes by thoſe rational Criticks on Writing, who meddle more with Sentiments than Words; That the Strokes of the Pencil, like Words, ought to be the propereſt that can be choſen for conveying the Ideas and Sentiments, that are Intended to be expreſſed by them with due Warmth and Vigour, or, in other terms, that they ought to be ſuitable to the Subject. Learning to manage the Pencil, is to Painting, what acquiring a Language is to Writing: In order to paint or write ſublimely, the chief thing is to be able to think ſublimely. And therefore as all the Obſervations, which ancient Criticks have laid down concerning ſublime Thinking, muſt equally relate to all Compoſition; to Painting as well as to Poetry and Oratory; ſo they not only tell us, that good Writing is good Painting by

modo id pictura intelligi poſſet) ut caveret, nequid perficeret imprudens, quod offenderet animos hominum, aut quidquam, equo oriretur aliquis dolor. Nos quidem virtutes, ſic natæ ſumus, ut tibi ſerviremus: aliud negotii nihil habemus, &c. *Cic. de fin. lib.* 2. N° 21.

(56) *Xenophon. Memorab. Socratis.* c. 22.

(57) It is needleſs to repeat here the Paſſages that were quoted in ſpeaking of the Greatneſs of *Apelles, Euphranor, Niceas, Nealces,* and others. Grandeur, Majeſty, Sublimity, are expreſſly aſcribed to their Works, &c.

(58) See *Longinus,* Sect. 7. & *Plin. l.* 35.

by Wörds (59), but they have treated all thefe Arts conjunctly, and have chofen to illuftrate each of them by comparifon with the others (60).

THESE Authors have remarked, that different Subjects touch and affect the Mind differently, or excite different Thoughts; and hence it is, that Subjects are divided into different Claffes; as for inftance, the Sublime, the Pathetick, and the Tender; Anger, Fury, and the rough Paffions awaken ftrong Thoughts; Glory, Grandeur, Power, move great Thoughts; Love, Melancholy, Solitude, and whatever gently touches the Soul, infpire tender ones. They have obferved, that it's fublime Thinking that alone can produce Sublimity in Compofition; and that the true Sublime can only proceed from a great Mind: *it is its Image or Sound reflected.* But tho' Greatnefs of Mind muft be original or from Nature, yet it may be exceedingly improved by the Study of fublime Writings and Paintings, joined with the Contemplation of Nature; or, in general, by being converfant about great Objects and fuitable Reprefentations of them: Natural Greatnefs of Mind (fay they) ftands in need of reftraints, and may be guided and affifted by Art, or judicious Rules. And, in fine, he who underftands thoroughly the Management of a Pencil, like one who is abfolutely Mafter of a Language, if he is able to conceive great Thoughts and Images in his Mind, by which he is himfelf greatly moved, will not fail to move others, by expreffing himfelf naturally, and as he is moved within. Upon thefe, and many other Topicks relating to the Sublime, have ancient Criticks largely infifted (61).

BUT hardly will any one expect that I fhould, in an Effay of this kind, repeat what hath been faid by ancient Criticks upon the Sublime, and its Sources and Effects. It will be readily acknowledged, that the Ancients thoroughly underftood the Sublime: And it cannot be imagined, that thofe Authors who have fo well defined the Sublime in Writing, would have afcribed the fame Excellency to Paintings, had they not felt them, to deferve fo noble a Character, by producing the fame Effect on their Minds. They could not furely miftake with regard to a Power and Efficacy they have fo compleatly defcribed, and concerning which they have laid down fuch excellent Rules. We may therefore juftly conclude, that thofe Painters who are commended by *Ariftotle, Varro, Cicero,* and other Ancients, for reprefenting the nobleft, the fublimeft, the moft heroick Subjects, with due Force and Energy, were really fublime Painters.

WHAT I would chiefly obferve on this Head is, that thofe ancient Painters who are faid to have excelled in the Sublime, chiefly painted moral Subjects: And that all the ancient Criticks have owned that the Perfection of the Sublime is to be found in truly virtuous and generous Sentiments and Actions. It is indeed of thofe principally that the Mind naturally fays, " It is Sublime, Divine, God-like." Whence it follows that a Poet or Painter who doth not underftand the Sublime of Sentiments and Actions cannot poffibly produce Works of the nobleft and fublimeft Kind. *Longinus* cenfures (62) *Homer* for attributing feveral things to the Gods, which if they are not taken in an allegorical Senfe, are impious, being far beneath the Majefty of the immortal Powers: And how much more excellent and fublime (faith he) are thofe Paffages in which the Poet defcribes them, as they really are, majeftick, great, and pure? The fame Critick (63) obferves in another place, that there is nothing in this Life fo great as the juft Contempt of Riches, Honours, Dignities, Empires, and all thofe pompous Appearances of Grandeur, which are fo apt to dazzle vulgar Eyes, and to attract their Admiration, when thefe come into competition with Virtue and Duty. Nothing raifes or exalts the Mind fo highly as virtuous Sentiments, becaufe nothing is in itfelf fo great and noble as a truly good and virtuous Mind. He therefore who would merit the Character of a fublime Painter, muft have a ftrong and lively Senfe of Virtue; true Greatnefs of Mind; and employ his Pencil to difplay the Beauties and Excellencies of Virtue, and the Turpitude of Vice.

Of Greatnefs in the Manner.

BUT befides the Greatnefs, ftrictly fo called, which belongs properly to the Subject, and arifes from its Greatnefs, there is another Greatnefs in Painting which lies in the Manner; by which a Picture may be rendered great, whatever the Subject may be, that is, however familiar and common. Now this may be refolved into thefe three fineft Secrets of almoft every Art; for they extend not only to Poetry and Painting, but in a confiderable degree

(59) See *Longinus de Sublimitate, Sect.* 15. περὶ φαν. ἰασίας. Definitur vulgo vifio, quivis conceptus mentis orationem generans, undecunque ille excitetur: peculiariter autem in illis nomen obtinuit, quum quis earum, quas dicit, rerum imagines adeo efficaciter cogitatione fua depingit, ut affectuum vehementia, velut inftinctu quodam numinis extra fe raptus, cernere eas oculis, ipfifque oftendere auditoribus Videatur——oratorius vero, ut, quidquid dicitur non tam dici Videatur, quam fub afpectum ipfum fubjici.——

(60) So *Ariftotle, Cicero, Horace, Quintilian,* &c. as has been already remarked. So likewife *Longinus* very frequently. See particularly *Sect.* 17. Nec multum differt quod in pictura evincere folet, &c.

(61) All thefe Obfervations are fully difcourfed upon by *Longinus.* See what he fays of Nature and Art, *f.* 2. Naturam in elato dicendi genere plerumque fui juris effe & arbitrii; veruntamen non ita temere ferri, omnifque omnino rationis expertem effe, ut non quibufdam quafi fraenis artis, &c. And *Sect.* 8. De quinque fublimitatis veluti fontibus. And *Sect.* 9. De fenfuum altitudine; where he fays, Sublimitatis hocce genus veræ animi magnitudinis tanquam *imaginem quandam effe, feu repercuffum fonum,* &c.

(62) *Longinus de Sublimitate, Sect.* 9.

(63) *Sect.* 7.

3

degree even to Gardening, or the laying out of Fields with good Tafte. For what elfe is that but producing a fine Landfcape, or rather a variety of them?

A Picture ought to have variety enough to fill the Mind agreeably; and to entertain *Of Variety and Sur-* the Eye while it travels over it with many delightful Surprizes. So ftrict ought the Unity *prizes.* of a Picture to be, as it hath been already obferved, that the Eye may be neceffarily reduced by every part it contemplates, to what is principal in the Compofition: But, at the fame time, fo curious, fo nice and exquifite ought the Choice of the Parts to be, that the Uncommonnefs of each Figure in its kind may wonderfully ftrike the Beholder, and raife his Admiration of the Genius that could fet his main Subject in fo fine a light, by fuch a happy variety of fubaltern Parts, fo excellently adapted to his purpofe; whilst each of them fingly confidered is exceedingly rare and entertaining, natural, but uncommon, or fuch Nature as one feldom fees. *Annibal Carrache* (64) faid, that a Picture ought not to confift of more than twelve Figures. But with refpect to number of Figures, perhaps no general Rule can be laid down befides this, that the Piece ought to fill and occupy the Mind without fatiguing or over-ftraining it, in order to comprehend the whole. The Mind, in order to be pleafed, muft be put to fome trial of its Force: It muft not however be over-powered; for thus it is vexed and fretted, becaufe it is in a manner upbraided. But the Force of the Mind to comprehend a Whole, in the juft Senfe of this Rule, ought not to be meafured from the Strength or rather Weaknefs of thofe who are not yet able to take in, at one view, a very complex Piece; but from the greater Capacity and higher Reach of thofe, who by due Culture and Practice, have attained to a very vigorous comprehenfive Imagination. Otherwife great Genius's would be fadly cramp'd in their Works. It is the. fame here as in Poetry, or in Architecture and Mufick.. On the contrary, tho' thofe Pictures are far from being defpicable, which every ordinary Mind yet unpractifed in judging of fuch Compofitions, may eafily compafs at firft fight; yet it is not the Painter's, nor the Poet's Bufinefs to lower himfelf in his Performances to the reach of weaker and unimproved Minds; but it is ours to raife and improve our Imaginations to fuch a pitch of Perfection, that we may be able to comprehend with tolerable cafe, whatever the greateft Painter was himfelf able to conceive in his own Mind as one Whole.

THIS is certain, that as the Mind, in order to be pleafed, muft perceive Unity of Defign; fo its delight will be exceedingly heightened, if every Figure in the Picture, at the fame time that its Aptitude to the principal Scope of the Piece is clearly perceived, agreeably ftrikes and furprizes us by its Newnefs or Uncommonnefs; and thus is by itfelf capable of affording very confiderable Entertainment to the Eye.

ANOTHER Quality in Pictures which fhews Strength of Genius, and gives Greatnefs *Of Contrafl.* to a Work, whatever the Subject of it may be, is an apt and elegant Choice of Contrafts. Figures muft be fo placed in a Picture as to produce Harmony to the Eye, as a Concert of Mufick does to the Ear; but this Harmony is then moft delightful and entertaining, when it is perceived to refult from a very nice Diverfity of Characters, Ages, Paffions, Complexions, Airs, Forms, Geftures, and Attitudes. Then is the Piece moft charming, when all the Figures in it mutually fet off one another to great advantage, and thus make a beautiful melodious Whole; when every Pofture, Complexion, Action, and, in one word, every piece of Drapery, and every Ornament, gives force to all the reft of the Parts, and Beauty and Harmony, as well as Spirit and Relief, to the Whole. The pleafing Effect of this Art, and its neceffity in order to make an agreeable Picture, may be eafily comprehended, if one will but reflect upon the manner in which different Characters in a Poem heighten and illuftrate one another by Contraft; and on the neceffity of this, in order to make a dramatick Piece, or even a Dialogue truly entertaining. But it will be beft underftood in Painting, by giving attention to the Contrafts that charm us in any Piece of Nature; for that is indeed one of the principal Sources of our Delight and Admiration, when we behold any beautiful Landfcape in Nature; or any real Affemblage of living Figures, when they are gather'd together in different Groupes, to hear a Difcourfe, or to behold any amufing or interefting Sight.

NOW many ancient *Greek* Painters are highly commended for their excellent Tafte *The ancient Painters* in the Choice of rare uncommon furprizing Figures; and for the variety of their Airs of *ftudied and excelled* Heads, Actions, Pofitions, and Characters, while, at the fame time, every part was duly *in thefe.* adapted and fubordinated to what was principal in their Pictures. And *Quintilian* (65) juftly obferves,

(64) See *Du Pile's* Notes on *Frefnoy's* Poem *De Arte Graphica,* upon thefe Lines:
    Pluribus implicitum perfonis d'tama fupremo
    In genere ut rarum eft; multis ita denfa figuris
    Rarior eft tabula excellens. ———
The Reafons which he gave were, firft, that he believ'd there ought not to be above three Groupes of Figures in any Picture: And fecondly, that Silence and Majefty were of neceffity to be there, to render it beautiful; and neither the one nor the other could poffibly be in a Multitude and Croud of Figures.

(65) *Quintilian, Inftit. l.* 2. *c.* 13. Expedit autem fæpe mutare ex illo conftituto, traditoque ordine, aliqua, & interim decet, ut in ftatuis, atque picturis videmus, variati habitus, vultus, ftatus, &c. *Horace* fpeaking of painting a variety of Characters in Poetry, calls thefe *opetum colotes.*
    Defcriptas fervare vias operumque colores,
    Cur ego, fi nequeo ignoreque, poeta falutor. Art.Poetica.
Colores, f. e. fay the Scholiafts, varietates, naturæ difcrimina, caracteres.

obferves, that without thefe Qualities, without variety of Contraft in particular, no Picture can long detain the Eye, or agreeably employ the Imagination. Many however of the great Mafters among the Moderns have fallen into what is called the Manierato, and have not ftudied enough to give Diverfity of Complexions and Characters; or at leaft of Attitudes and Draperies in their Pictures: And not a few of the ancient *Roman* Pieces now publifhed, tho' there is a great deal of Beauty in them all, have the fame fault.

Of concealing Bounds.

A N O T H E R moft important Secret in Painting may be called concealing Bounds. It confifts in giving a very large, and, as it were, unbounded Profpect to the Eye. It is needlefs to infift long on this head. Every one feels that the Eye hates to be ftinted and confined; and that the Imagination is wonderfully charmed by wide expanding Views. Hence it is, that placing feveral living Figures, and other Objects in a Picture at a great diftance, reprefenting a fine open variegated Sky, an extenfive Landfcape, noble Pieces of Architecture; or on other occafions, huge Mountains, Rocks, and other fuch towring, awful Objects, have fuch a wonderful Effect upon the Mind. Whatever is pleafing and delightful in Nature, will be fo when it is well reprefented; and who is not fenfible of the difference between one Scene in Nature and another; and whence that proceeds? Commonnefs, Want of Diverfity, Defect in Colouring and Contraft, but above all Narrownefs and Confinement, are the Caufes to which our Diffatisfaction with any real Landfcape is chiefly owing. This Rule extends not only to Landfcape-Painting, properly fo called, but to moral or hiftorical Pieces; for tho' in all Imitations of Nature by the Pencil, as well as by Defcription, every thing ought to be fubmitted to what is chief in the Piece; yet even in reprefenting an hiftorical Subject, in which moral Life is neceffarily principal, the Scene of the Action ought not to be neglected, but ought to be as pleafant and entertaining as may be, confiftently with hiftorical Truth, and the Subject itfelf: it ought to be fitted to fet off the Story to the beft advantage.

A L L thefe Qualities are requifite to truly beautiful Compofition in Painting; and wherever they are found, there, is Greatnefs felt in the Invention, in the Tafte and Manner, that exceedingly tranfports the Mind, affording it variety of furprizing and agreeable Entertainment. Thofe who have great Minds will naturally feek after Greatnefs in the Subjects; yet there is a very confiderable Satisfaction arifing even from the lowest, that is, the moft ordinary Subjects, when by thofe happy Circumftances that have been mentioned, they are exceedingly raifed and greatned above common ordinary Nature. A Subject which cannot be naturally wrought into a beautiful pleafing Whole, by means of fuch Art and Contrivance, is by no means proper for the Pencil: However naturally it may be reprefented, the Choice of it will be juftly looked upon as an Argument of a very low and unafpiring Genius; or of a mean and groveling Tafte.

Of Eafy Painting.

T H E R E is another Quality often recommended as abfolutely neceffary to the Perfection of Painting by ancient Authors, which may feem at firft fight not compatible with Strength, Force, and Greatnefs; and that is an appearance of Freedom and Eafe. It confifts in hiding Art by Art; or in giving an agreeable Semblance of unlaboured and natural to a Work, which for that very reafon coft the fevereft Study; as every one who fets himfelf to try muft find. It is well obferved by feveral Ancients, that Flatnefs and Puetility are not more oppofite to the Sublime than that Fury, Violence, or Extravagance which is ofen miftaken for Strength and Energy of Expreffion. This laft is called by *Longinus*, (who treats (66) of both thefe Oppofites to the Sublime) the Παρευθηρσοι; and he gives an excellent Defcription of that fault in Writing, which is eafily applicable to the other Arts, to Painting and Sculpture. Every thing, as he obferves, hath its proper Meafures and Bounds. A Bully is not more different from a Hero, or a drunken Man from a fober, than true and becoming Expreffion is from the wild, the affected, or over-done.

O N the other hand, as in Poetry there are fome things which muft be written with ftrength, that neverthelefs are eafy; fo is it with regard to the other polite Arts. The Statue of the Gladiator, though reprefented in fuch a Pofture as ftrains every Mufcle, is as eafy as that of *Venus*; becaufe the one expreffes Strength and Fury as naturally as the other doth Beauty and Softnefs. The Satyr in the Collection of ancient Paintings annexed, though it is a Character very boldly and ftrongly marked, is as eafy as the young Faun offering a Gift to *Pomona*, which is exceeding faft; or as that Goddefs, which is indeed a very fimple, eafy, and graceful Figure; or as any of the Figures in the Marriage, which are fo light and charming.

T H E Paffions are fometimes to be roufed, as well as the Fancy to be entertained; and the Soul to be exalted and enlarged as well as foothed. And as in Writing (67) this often requires a raifed and figurative Stile, that Readers of low cold Imaginations, or foft and languid Tempers, are apt to reject as forced and affected Language; fo in Painting, to
Spectators

(66) *Longinus de Sublimitate*, Sect. 3, & 4.——Quippe qui furere apud fanos, & quafi inter fobrios bacchari violentus videtur.

(67) See *Guardian*, Tome 1. Number 12, and 15.

Spectators of the same Make and Temperament, due Strength of Expreſſion, a proper heightning of the Features, and ſuch a bold Pronunciation of the Muſcles as the Subject requires, often appear wild and extravagant. Nature hath given every thing its peculiar and diſtinguiſhing Properties and Characteriſticks, and hath, as it were, appointed even different Garbs for different Things. And as in Writing, every thing that is agreeable to Nature, and expreſs'd in Language ſuitable to it, is juſtly ſaid to be written with eaſe; ſo in the other Arts, for the ſame reaſon, whatever Object is exhibited agreeably to its Character, whatever is ſet to view in its propereſt Light, and with the Colouring and Dreis that is moſt ſuitable to it, is repreſented naturally, without Affectation, or with Freedom and Eaſe. There is an eaſy Mien, an eaſy Dreis, peculiarly ſo called; and ſo likewiſe there is an eaſy ſort of Writing, properly ſo denominated. And thoſe who underſtand what that is, will be at no loſs to find out its analogous kind in Painting. Different Subjects affect the Mind differently. The Thoughts which love Melancholy, Solitude, the paſtoral Life, and whatever gently touches the Heart and ſoftens it, are thoſe, which ſtrictly ſpeaking, are called eaſy ones. Such were the Subjects *Protogenes* and others amongſt the Ancients painted, and among the Moderns *Parmegiano, Guido,* and *Albano.*

BUT the Notion of Eaſe, as it is oppoſed to what is ſtiff, laboured, and affected, cannot be better ſtated than by the above-mentioned Explication of it. It conſiſts in concealing Labour and Art (68). And with regard to it, no other Rules can be laid down but thoſe which are given about eaſy Writing. In order to attain to that Charm in any Compoſition of whatever ſort, one muſt think eaſily : And when the Subject is clearly and diſtinctly conceived; when the Thoughts are natural, juſt, and rightly digeſted, then will the Author or Painter acquit himſelf with eaſe in his Performances. This Talent, like every other Quality of the Mind, muſt be in ſome degree natural; it can never be acquired by ſome, no more than an eaſy Behaviour by all the aſſiſtance of Rules. But it may be improved into Perfection by reading the beſt Authors, and above all by Converſation with the politer Part of Mankind. The mere Scholar can never have it in any conſiderable degree. All who have been moſt diſtinguiſh'd for it in their Works of whatever kind, have been Men verſed in the World, and of a truly genteel, eaſy, elegant Turn of Mind. The two beſt Advices that can be given concerning it are to conſult our Genius, and to attempt nothing above it, or repugnant to it.

Sumite materiam veſtris qui ſcribitis æquam
Viribus, & verſate diu quid ferre recuſent
Quid valeant humeri : cui lecta potenter erit res;
Nec facundia deſeret hunc, nec lucidus ordo.   Hor. de Arte Poetica.

And not to endeavour to communicate to others what we do not clearly perceive, and ſtrongly feel within ourſelves.   .

——*ſi vis me flere, dolendum eſt*
Primum ipſi tibi; tunc tua me infortunia lædent.   Hor. ibidem (69).

WHATEVER really comes from the Heart will go to it, and appear eaſy and natural; becauſe in that caſe the Author is guided by Nature, and moves as it dictates, without any Reſtraint, Diſguiſe, or Affectation. Theſe Precepts of *Horace* do not merely relate to Poetry; but extend equally to Painting. And indeed as he ſets out by comparing the one with the other, ſo he ſeems to have both in view throughout that whole Maſter-piece of Criticiſm. ·

BUT to proceed : The Perfection of Oratory, Poetry, Painting, and of every Art, is ſaid by *Cicero* to conſiſt in the τό πρῖπον, that is, Decorum (70). " It is this (ſaith he) " that is moſt difficult to obtain in Life, or in Art : It is the ſupreme Beauty in both : " And it is to our Ignorance of this, that many Faults not in Life and Conduct only, but " in Poems and Orations are owing. The good Painters have exceedingly ſtudied it. *Ti-* " *manthes* ſhewed his juſt Taſte of it in his Picture of *Iphigenia,* by veiling the Father: " This was not only a moſt happy way of expreſſing his extreme Grief, by a tacit Confeſ- " ſion of the impoſſibility of painting it; but a more judicious, decent way, as it could " not have been repreſented more bitter and vehement than that of all the other Perſons " in the Picture, who were each ſo violently afflicted, without being diſagreeable, or giv- " ing too much pain to the Spectators; which ought carefully to be avoided in Painting " as well as in Poetry (71).

Of Decorum.

" THIS

(68) *Interea niveum mira feliciter arte*
Sculpſit ebur; formamque dedit qua fæmina naſci
Nulla poteſt : operiſque ſui concepit amorem.
Virginis eſt vera facies quam vivere credas:
Et ſi non obſtet reverentia, velle moveti.
Ars adeo latet arte ſua.
                                    Ovid. Metam. l. 18. ver. 247.

(69) So *Quintilian* in ſeveral places. Nec agamus rem alienam, ſed aſſumamus parumper illum dolorem. *Inſt.* *l.* 6. *c.* 1.—Imagines rerum quiſquis bene conceperit, is

erit in affectibus potentiſſimus. *Ibidem.* Primum eſt bene affici, & concipere imagines rerum; & tanquam veris moveri. *l.* 2. *c.* 3.

(70) *Cicero ad M. Brutum Orat.* N° 21.

(71) *Longinus de Sublim. ſ.* 9. cenſures this Fault. At vide quam diſſimile ſit Illud ex Aſpide Heſiodum de Juſtitia, ſi tamen hoc Heſiodi poemation eſt. Non enim tam horribilem nobis ejus imaginem objecit quam ingratam odioſamque.

"THIS Decorum is of vaft extent ; it comprehends, according to *Cicero,* good Tafte in
" the Choice of the Subject, and in the Difpofition of every part with relation to the prin-
" cipal End of the Whole. It confifts chiefly in Juftnefs, Truth, and Beauty of Sentiments;
" in Propriety of Expreffion, and in giving every Object its proper Character and Place
" in a Compofition : But it extends, as in Oratory, fo likewife in Painting, not to the
" Sentiments only, but to the Diction in the one, and to the Colouring in the other.
". The Subject muft be decent ; and the Expreffion muft be agreeable to the Subject ; every
" Ornament muft be correfpondent to the Genius of the whole Piece; all the Colouring
" muft be on the fame Key ; or partake of the Character of the principal Figure. It is
" not enough that a part be beautiful in itfelf, it muft belong to the Defign, and be ftrictly
" fubfervient to it." This, I think, is a juft Commentary upon what *Cicero* fays of the
Decorum. And *Vitruvius* (72) fpeaking of Painting, tells us, that Truth is not fufficient
to recommend it, but that Decorum is alfo abfolutely requifite ; and that, not only in the
Compofition itfelf, but in the Adjuftment of Paintings to the Nature, End, and Genius of
the Places .they are intended to adorn.

Of Simplicity, or
Frugality. BUT the full Meaning of what the Ancients underftood by this Decorum will be more
evident, if we confider that it is often called by them by another Name, that fignifies (73)
Frugality and good Oeconomy, and is often illuftrated in their Writings by Similitudes
taken from Simplicity, Elegance, and good Tafte in Drefs ; in giving Entertainments, and
in the whole of true Management and Behaviour in Life. Nothing is more repugnant to it
than Profufion of Ornaments. It is in Art, what *Horace* calls in Attire, *Simplex mun-
ditiis* ; a Character that is literally due to all the Draperies of the Figures in the ancient Pieces now publifhed. " Every thing, fays *Cicero,* has its Meafure, and the greateft
" Secret in Compofition of every kind is to know how far to go. But yet the too much is
" more offenfive than the too little (74)." True Elegance is rather frugal and referved, than
lavifh and exceffive, like Nature itfelf, the true Rule and Standard of all Art and Tafte. The
Perfection of true painting of Nature, whether by Words, or by the Pencil, lies in felecting proper Circumftances, and placing them in agreeable Lights; that is, in fuch as will
affect the Fancy in the moft delightful manner. And therefore not only Livelinefs of
Fancy is requifite to be able to call up a great variety of Images, but alfo Accuracy of
Judgment, and Elegance of Tafte, to chufe thofe that are fufficient, and moft proper to
fet forth an Object in its beft, its moft pleafing and inftructive View. The Painter, as well
as the Poet, of a rich Imagination, muft therefore learn to deny himfelf, and to be able to
reject fine Embellifhments and Decorations, when the Subject does not require them ; or
when they would not be in their place : more efpecially in reprefenting thofe Subjects,
which, the more fimply they are conceived, and the more plainly they are expreffed, give the
Soul proportionably the more pleafing Emotions : Other Embellifhments added to them, as it
is well faid by fome Author, ferve only to hide a Beauty ; however gracefully they are put
on, and are thrown away like Paint on a fine Complexion. Many Painters, as well as
Poets, have difplayed in their Works a great Fertility and Livelinefs of Imagination ;
but few have been able to controul their Fancy, conceal their Art, and reprefent Objects
in their fimpleft and propereft Light, without any foreign, borrowed, unneceffary Ornaments ; by felecting fuch Circumftances, as fhine by their own intrinfick Beauty. All
this is admirably explained by *Horace,* with refpect to both the Sifter-Arts.

> *Inceptis gravibus, plerumque & magna profeffis*
> *Purpureus, late qui fplendeat, unus & alter*
> *Affuitur pannus : cum lucus & ara Dianæ,*
> *Et properantis aquæ per amænos ambitus agros,*
> *Aut flumen Rhenum, aut pluvius defcribitur arcus :*
> *Sed nunc non erat his locus : & fortaffe (75) cupreffum*
> *Scis fimulare : quid hoc fi fractis enatat exfpes*
> *Navibus, ære dato qui pingitur.*

The

---

(72) *Vitruvius, l.* 7. *c.* 5. Neque picturæ probari debent quæ non funt fimiles veritati ; nec fi factæ funt
elegantes ab arte, ideo de his ftatim debet repente judicari, nifi argumentationis habuerint rationes fine offen-
fionibus explicatas. Etenim etiam Trallibus cum Apaturius Alabandeus eleganti manu finxiffet fcenam, in eaque feciffet pro columnis figna, centaurofque fuftinentes
Epiftylia, coronafque capitibus leoninis ornatas : præterea fupra eam nihilominus epifcenium, in quo Tholi,
Pronai, femifaftigia, omnifque tecti varius pictoris fuerat
ornatus. Itaque cum afpectus ejus fcenæ propter afperi-
tatem eblandiretur omnium vifus, & jam id opus probare
fuiffent parati, tum Licinius mathematicus prodiit, &
ait Alabandeos fatis acutos ad omnes res civiles haberi, fed
propter vitium indecentiæ infipientes eos effe judicatos ;
quod in Gymnafio eorum quæ funt ftatuæ, omnes funt
caufas agentes ; in foro autem difcos tenentes, aut cur-
rentes, feu pila ludentes. Ita indecens inter locorum pro-
prietates ftatus fignorum, publice civitati vitium exifti-

mationis adjecit. Itaque Apaturius contra refpondere
non eft aufus, fed fuftulit fcenam, & ad rationem veritatis commutatam, poftea correctam approbavit.

(73) Compare what *Cicero* fays, *Orator. n.* 25. Nam
ficut in Epularum apparatu, &c. with *Quintilian, Inft.
l.* 8. *c.* 3. Nam ipfa illa, ἀφέλεια fimplex & inaffectata, &c.

(74) *Cicero ibidem.* In omnibufque rebus videndum eft
quatenus. Etfi enim fuus cuique modus eft, tamen magis
offendit nimium quam parum, &c.

(75) The old Scholiaft obferves on this Paffage, Ineptus pictor vix aliud noverit, quam denique depingere cu-
preffum ; a quo cum naufragus quidam peteret, ut vultum fuam & naufragium exprimeret, interrogavit, num
ex cupreffo aliquid vellet appingi.

The Rule is, *Denique fit quodvis, fimplex duntaxat & unum.*

And in this does Beauty, Simplicity, and Order confift, even in difpofing all things juftly, and in being able to rejeét whatever is not ftrictly relative to the Subject.

> *Ordinis hæc virtus, erit & Venus, aut ego fallor*
> *Ut jam nunc dicat, jam nunc debentia dici*
> *Pleraque differat, & præfens in tempus omittat :*
> *Hoc amet; hoc fpernat promiffi carminis autor.*   Hor. Art. Poetica.

IN fine, the Quality which is pronounced by the Ancients moft effential to good Paint- *Of Grace.* ing, is called by them Grace (76). This we are told comprehends Truth, Beauty, Eafe, Freedom, Spirit, Greatnefs, all thefe are neceffary to it ; yet it fuperadds fomething to them, which it is exceeding difficult to defcribe by Words. We find by their Accounts of it, that its greateft oppofite is the καxoζηλοr, or over-diligence in finifhing. The Pictures of *Protogenes* wanted Grace, becaufe he did not know when it was time to give over. It is extremely rare and difficult to give Grace to a Piece ; and yet there is a certain Air of Negligence, fays *Cicero*, that is a main Ingredient in every kind of Grace, as well as in that of Drefs. Simplicity is infeparable from it. It is far removed from Superfluity and Af-fectation. Whatever is graceful is likewife truly beautiful and great; yet Grace is fome-thing diftinct from both : For it is Grace that diftinguifhes Greatnefs from the Rough and Savage ; and it is Greatnefs, on the other hand, that fupports Beauty from degenerating into the Languid and Infipid. It is withal a miftake to imagine, that Grace is peculiar to one Character ; on the contrary, each Character hath its peculiar and diftinguifhing Grace. Meeknefs hath its Grace as well as Majefty. Humility hath its Grace as well as Magna-nimity. Cheerfulnefs may be graceful ; and Tears are often exceedingly fo. Even Anger and a Frown may be graceful ; and Fear itfelf frequently adds a very great Beauty and Grace (77). It refults from the whole, and yet belongs to every part, the very Folds of the Draperies not excepted.

BUT it is vain to attempt to define that Charm which the Ancients themfelves have pronounced fo inexplicable by Words. It may be clearly difcerned, or rather felt in the Works of *Raphael*, and in the Antiques upon which that moft perfect Mafter of Great-nefs and Grace formed, or rather perfected his Tafte. And feveral Writers on Painting have made many very ufeful Remarks upon the Proportions obferved in the Antiques, and by thofe who ftudied and imitated them ; upon their beauteous Airs of Heads, the Eafinefs of their Attitudes, the juft Ponderation, as it is called by Artifts, of Figures ; the Largenefs, the Squarenefs, the bold Pronunciation of the Contours, or their delicate Wav-ings and Contrafts ; their exquifite Tafte of Draperies ; and many other Excellencies in the Defign and Workmanfhip of the beft Mafters, from which Greatnefs and Grace refult. There are many excellent Obfervations in *Lomazzo's* Treatifes on Painting (78), to this effect. But none perhaps hath better treated this Subject than Mr. *Richardfon* (79). It is well worth while to infert here fome of his judicious Obfervations.

" WHAT it is that gives the Grace and Greatnefs I am treating of, faith he, is hard to fay. " The following Rules may however be of fome ufe on this occafion.

" THE Airs of the Heads muft be efpecially regarded. This is commonly the firft thing " taken notice of when one comes into Company, or into any publick Affembly, or at " the

---

(76) See what is faid in the Notes on the fecond Chap-ter of *Apelles*. And to the Paffages of *Cicero* and *Quin-tilian* referred to concerning the Decorum, may be added what *Cicero* fays (*De Orator. l.* 1.) Rofcium fæpe audio dicere, caput effe artis docere ; quod-tamen unum effe quod tradi arte non poffit. See *Quint. Inft.* l. 8. *c.* 3. Virtus & gratia in omnibus operibus efflorefcens, res eft prorfus admiranda, & quamvis difertæ orationis vim ex-fuperans. Maxime quidem idonea eft confpici, omnibuf-que pariter idiotis, atque artium harum intelligentibus per-fpiciendam fe præbet ; oratione tamen eam explicari etiam iis eft arduum, qui plurimum dicendo valent. Quifquis itaque qualemcunque hanc vim explicari fibi verbis requi-rit, plurimarum quoque aliarum infignium atque ineffa-bilium rerum rationem pari jure poftulabit. Quidnam videlicet in corporum pulchritudine vocamus ἄραν. Quid in mobili illa modulatione ac flexu vocum ἕυαρμοϛοr, quid in omni convenientia temporum fit ϊάξις atque ῥυθμων. In omni denique opere atque in omni re ge-renda, quifnam fit ille qui dicitur χαιρόν, quemadmodum etiam τὸ μἰγριον in quo confiftat. Senfu enim horum fingula, non oratione comprehenduntur. *Dion. Halic. in Lyfia.*

(77) *Dulce ridentem Lalagen amabo*
Dulce loquentem.   Hor. Car. l. 1. Od. 22.
Dulce ridere.   Hor. Ep. 7. l. 1.

Tutatur favor Euryalum, lacrymæque decoræ
Gratior & pulchro veniens in corpore virtus.
        Virg. Æn. 5. ver. 313.

In gremio vultum depofuit que fuum
Hoc ipfum decuit : lacrymæ cecidere pudicæ
Et facies animo dignaque parque fuit.
        Ovid. Faft. l. 2. ver. 755.

Ingentes animo & dignas Jove concepit iras.
        Ov. Met. l. 1. 166.

Et timor ipfe novi caufa decoris erat.
        Ov. Faf. l. 5. ver. 608.

——— *pavit illa ; metuque*
Et colus, & fufus digitis cecidere remiffis.
Ipfe timor decuit.——   Ov. Met. l. 5. 229.

Mifcetur decori virtus, pulcerque fevero
Armatur terrore pudor.   Claud. de Prob. &c.

Nefcia quid fit amor ; fed erubuiffe decebat.
        Ov. Met. l. 4. 330.

(78) *Lomazzo* in his *Trattato della Pitura* of the Bel-lezza of the Antique, *p.* 291, 296. and of Draperies, *p.* 445.

(79) Mr. *Richardfon's* Difcourfe on Painting.

A a

" the firſt ſight of any particular Perſon, and this firſt takes the Eye, and affects the Mind
" when we ſee a Picture, a Drawing, *&c.*

" THE ſame regard muſt be had to every Action and Motion. The Figures muſt not
" only do what is proper, and in the moſt commodious manner, but as People of the beſt
" Senſe and Breeding (their Character being conſidered) would or ſhould perform ſuch Ac-
" tions. The Painters People muſt be good Actors, they muſt have learned to uſe a hu-
" man Body well; they muſt fit, walk, lie, ſalute, do every thing with Grace. . There muſt
" be no aukward or affected Behaviour, no ſtrutting, or ſilly pretence to Greatneſs; no
" Bombaſt in Action : nor muſt there be any ridiculous Contorſion of the Body : nor
" even ſuch Appearances, or Fore-ſhortnings as are diſagreeable to the Eye, *&c.*

" THE Contours muſt be large, ſquare, and boldly pronounced, to produce Greatneſs;
" and delicate, and finely waved and contraſted to be Gracious. There is a Beauty in a
" Line, in the Shape of a Finger or Toe, even in that of a Reed or Leaf, or the moſt
" inconſiderable things in Nature. I have Drawings of *Giulio Romano* of ſomething of
" this kind; his Inſects and Vegetables are natural, but as much above thoſe of other Painters
" as his Men are, *&c.*

" BUT this is not all; Nature with all its Beauties has its Poverties, Superfluities, and
" Defects, which are to be avoided and ſupplied, but with great Care and Judgment, that
" inſtead of exceeding Nature, it be not injured. There is (for example) great Beauty
" in a certain Squareneſs in pronouncing a Feature, or any part of a Figure : This ſome
" have carried to exceſs, and have thereby diſcovered they knew ſomething, but not enough,
" which is the caſe in many other inſtances. What is here ſaid of Drawing is applicable alſo
" to Colouring.

" THE Draperies muſt have broad Maſſes of Light and Shadow, and noble large Folds
" to give a Greatneſs; and theſe artfully ſubdivided add Grace. The Linen muſt be clean
" and fine; the Silks and Stuffs new, and the beſt of the kind. But Lace, Embroidery,
" Gold and Jewels muſt be ſparingly employed. It is of Importance to a Painter to con-
" ſider well the manner of cloathing his People. Howſoever a Figure be clad, this gene-
" ral Rule is to be obſerved, that neither the Naked muſt be loſt in the Drapery, nor too
" conſpicuous. The Naked in a cloathed Figure, is as the Anatomy in a naked Figure, it
" ſhould be ſhewn, but not with Affectation, *&c.*"

NOW are not all theſe Excellencies very remarkable in the ancient Pieces of Art that
are juſtly admired ? Are they not likewiſe very obſervable in the Works of *Raphael,* and of
the other beſt modern Painters? And are they not what chiefly conſtitute the Beauty of ſeveral
of theſe ancient Paintings which are added to this Treatiſe ? I am far from imagining thoſe
Pieces equal to the Works of *Apelles, Protogenes, Euphranor,* or *Nicias,* ſo highly renowned for the Beauty, Grace and Greatneſs of their Works. The greater part of them;
are not improbably but Copies by the Pencil from *Greek* Bas-reliefs. But how ſweet,
pleaſant, comely and gracious are almoſt all the Heads and Attitudes, that of the Bride in
particular, and of the Figure touching a muſical Inſtrument in the Marriage ? And to mention no more of them at preſent ; all the Airs of the Heads in the Rape of *Europa,* have
they not indeed that very ſame Character of Sweetneſs and Beauty for which *Guido* is ſo
juſtly celebrated ? How eaſy and natural are the Attitudes in all theſe Pieces ? And as for
the Draperies throughout them all ; are they not in a moſt exquiſite Taſte ? How ſimple,
genteel, eaſy, natural, and flowing are they ? The Naked is neither too conſpicuous nor
loſt, it is ſhewn, but without Affectation. But whatever may be thought of theſe ancient
Paintings, to which all who have ſeen the Originals will own, that both the Drawer and
the Engraver have done juſtice ; theſe Excellencies which Mr. *Richardſon* points out as
neceſſary to produce Grace and Greatneſs, are the very Attainments for which we have
already found ancient Painters ſo highly praiſed by Authors, whoſe good Taſte will no more
be called into queſtion, than their Acquaintance with the Works they deſcribe. We have
no reaſon to think, that they have exaggerated in commending ancient Works ; for they
do not always ſpeak of Beauties and Perfections, but often cenſure and blame ; and many
of the ancient Remains in Sculpture and Statuary do no wiſe fall ſhort of the higheſt Beauties and Excellencies aſcribed by ancient Authors to any ſuch Performances.

Lucian's *perfect Beauty.*   BUT that no room may be left to doubt of the vaſt Perfection to which all the Arts
of Deſign were advanced amongſt the ancient *Greek* Maſters, in reſpect of Truth, Beauty, Grace,
and Greatneſs ; it is not amiſs to add at full length the delightful Account *Lucian* (81) gives
of the diſtinguiſhing Talents and Excellencies of the moſt renowned ancient Artiſts, when
he calls upon them to aſſiſt him in painting the Portrait and Character of his perfect
Woman.

" LET her Head (ſays he) be as that of the *Cnidian Venus,* that Maſter-piece of Art : She
" muſt have the flowing Locks, and graceful Eye-brows, which *Praxiteles* gave to that lovely
                                                                          " Figure,

(80) *Lucian. de Imaginibus.*

" Figure, and the like sparkling rolling Eyes instilling Love and soft Desire. But let her
" have the Breasts of *Alcamene's Venus* in the Gardens at *Athens*, and such slender, delicate, rosy
" Fingers: let the Tenderness and Softness of the Cheeks, the straight Nose, and all the Fea-
" tures resemble those of the *Lemnian Venus* by *Phidias.* The Mouth too must be by him,
" and the milky Neck like that of his *Amazon.* The *Sosandra* of *Calamis* will furnish us
" with the modest Vermilion, the pleasing amiable Smile, and the neat simple Dress; only
" our Lady's Head must be without any artificial Ornaments. We will paint her of the same
" Age the *Cnidian Venus* appears to be; for that we may see the Artist designed to express in
" her Look. But this is not sufficient; it remains to give all the Members of the Body their
" proper Colouring: For that contributes not a little to the Perfection of Beauty, and great
" regard ought to be had to the Propriety and Decency of Colours, in painting a compleat
" Beauty: That the Shades may fall as they ought, that what is darken'd may be agreeably so,
" and that the White may be of the fairest sort; while at the same time all is enlivened with a
" fit and becoming Red, celestial, rosy Red, Love's proper Hue. Whence then shall we fetch
" Assistance for this part of our Work, but from the Painters who have excelled most emi-
" nently in the fine Mixture of their Colours, and in a pleasant, charming Carnation? Let
" *Polygnotus* therefore, *Apelles, Euphranor,* and *Echion,* divide this Task among them.
" *Polygnotus* shall open, and spread her Eye-brows, and give her that warm, glowing, de-
" cent Blush, that so inimitably beautifies his *Caſſandra.* He likewise shall give her a flowing,
" easy, genteel Dress, with all its tender delicate Weavings, part clinging to her Body, and
" part fluttering in the Wind. *Apelles* shall finish the other Parts after the Model of his ad-
" mired *Pancaſté;* only she must not be altogether so pale; a little more Colour must be in-
" termingled. We cannot give her more charming Lips than those of *Roxana* by *Echion;*
" unless *Homer,* the best of Painters, would lend us his Help, that her whole Body might be,
" as the Limbs of *Menelaus,* like Ivory dipp'd in Purple. Shall not he likewise give some
" Touches of Life and Cheerfulness to the Eyes, and add some Grace to the Smile?
" This is work for the Painters, Statuaries, and Poets. But that the whole may be Grace-
" ful as well as Beauteous, the *Graces* themselves must compleat the Piece: The whole
" Choir of *Graces* and *Cupids* must dwell in her Looks. We must paint her in some
" Action, and it shall be just as when I saw her walking with a Scroll in her Hand;
" one Page she had read, and she was running over the other with her Eye; but talk-
" ing at the same time to one of her Attendants, not so loud as to be heard at any di-
" stance, but with a gracious enchanting Smile that shewed her ivory Teeth so fitly join-
" ed, and set together. But to make a perfect Picture, corporeal Beauty is not sufficient; it
" must be set off by its truest Ornaments, not purple and gold Stuffs, but Elegance and Sim-
" plicity of Manners; a virtuous, modest, humane, winning Air. And therefore the Phi-
" losophers must be called to aid us, in order to produce a compleat Beauty, according to
" the Manner and Taste of the ancient plastick Arts."

THIS masterly Passage of *Lucian* hath been often referred to in the Notes; but I re-
served it to be inserted in this place, because it is hardly possible to imagine a finer Illustration of the many different Accomplishments it requires to make a truly beautiful and
graceful Picture; or to give a better Account of the chief Excellencies of the Antique.

TO conclude, it hath been justly remarked by many, that a Painter in order to infuse
Greatness and Grace into his Works, must have noble and fine Ideas; a very elegant and
refined Taste; he must have a beautiful and graceful Turn of Mind. Such were *Nicoma-*
chus, Nicias, and other ancient Painters who arrived to the greatest Perfection in their Art;
such most eminently was *Apelles.* They could not otherwise have painted in such a masterly, sublime, great and graceful manner. For here certainly the received Maxim takes
place, that one cannot communicate what he does not possess. He alone can give Grace
and Greatness to his Productions, who possesses these Qualities not in Idea only, but in his
Form and Make: and such will do it naturally, without labouring to attain to them, in
consequence of their own great and graceful Manner of thinking. Grace will insinuate it
self into all their Works who really have it in Possession and Habit, as it did into the
Pictures of *Apelles, Raphael,* and *Corregio,* without the assistance of Rules; and operate in
the same manner upon every one who sees them, as the Poet most charmingly and gracefully describes the Influence of Grace in outward Behaviour upon all who behold it.

> *Illam quicquid agit, quoquo vestigia flectit*
> *Componit furtim, subsequiturque decor.*
> *Seu solvit crines, fusis decet esse capillis;*
> *Seu compsit, comptis est veneranda comis.*
> *Urit, seu Tyria voluit procedere palla;*
> *Urit, seu nivea candida veste venit.*
> *Talis in æterno felix Vertumnus olympo,*
> *Mille habet ornatus, mille decenter habet* (81). Tibul. l. 4. El. 2.

BUT

(81) *Quintilian* plainly alludes to this Passage in his   aliquid ex hac exercitatione puerili unde nos non id
Description of graceful Behaviour. Neque enim gestum   agentes furtim ille discentibus traditus prosequatur:
componi ad similitudinem saltationis volo; sed subesse

3

To what that Per-
fection was owing.

BUT to aſcribe all the Perfection the Arts of Deſign had attained to in Grace, merely to the extraordinary Genius of the *Greek* Artiſts, would be doing injuſtice to a Country which is known to have produced at that time the moſt perfect Models of every Beauty, Virtue, and Grace. And therefore the ſame excellent Author we have already quoted on this Subject obſerves, that the principal reaſon why the *Greek* Artiſts, at the time that the Arts were in their Glory among them, arrived at ſuch truly wonderful Perfection, is, that, " They painted and carved the *Greeks.* When you ſee and admire (ſays he) what they " have done in Braſs and Marble, what Majeſty, what Beauty, what Grace their Figures " expreſs, remember *Salamis,* and *Marathon,* where they fought, and *Thermopylæ,* where " they devoted themſelves for the Liberty of their Country."

RUBENS (82) is ſaid to have given this reaſon why the *Grecian* Statues are ſo exceedingly beautiful, ſo far beyond common Nature, that the *Greeks* were really ſo themſelves in their Perſons, far ſuperiour in Beauty, Proportion, and Grace to what we now commonly ſee. And that happened, as he obſerves, naturally and neceſſarily in conſequence of their Temperance, and the Exerciſes that made a part of their liberal Education. There were Maſters or Profeſſors, as is well known, amongſt them for forming the Youth early to Beauty, Activity, Vigour, and Grace. The Statuaries therefore and Painters amongſt them had moſt perfect Originals, in reſpect of outward Grace to imitate. If they were but able to come up to thoſe they had continually before their Eyes, they muſt have performed Works exceedingly perfect in Beauty and Proportion. But we are told, that not contented with what they ſaw, they endeavoured to improve upon Nature, and to out-do it. 'Tis not then to be wondered at, that their Performances are ſo noble ; ſo inimitable, ſince they had ſuch uncommon Originals to equal, which they ſtrove to excel.

BUT this Reaſon extends farther than *Rubens* carries it, and accounts likewiſe for their being able to paint and exhibit not only the outward Graces of the Body in their higheſt Perfection ; but the Sublime of Actions and Characters ; the Majeſty and Grace of Gods and Heroes in ſuch a maſterly and truly wonderful manner. It was becauſe no Nation ever produced ſuch great Men, ſuch eminent Virtue, ſuch compleat Models of moral Perfection. What ſets this Obſervation beyond all doubt is, that as the Arts never arrived at ſuch a heighth of Excellence, or continued to flouriſh ſo long in any Country as in *Greece* ; ſo it is remarkable that they degenerated among them in proportion as Virtue and publick Spirit declined. The Arts were at their higheſt pitch of Glory amongſt them, whilſt they had the moſt noble Examples before them, to inſpire them with great Ideas, warm their Fancy with the nobleſt Enthuſiaſm ; and to copy and emulate in their Repreſentations of Men and Manners. It is commonly ſaid of *Rubens,* that though he had a very extraordinary Genius, he could never, even after he had ſeen the Antiques, and the excellent Works of the beſt *Italian* Maſters, get the better of that original Taſte of Beauty he had early contracted. He ſtill continued to paint *Flemiſh* Features and Proportions, and could riſe to no higher Ideas of Beauty. And it is for the ſame reaſon morally impoſſible that the *Greek* Painters, Sculptors, and Statuaries could ever have attained to ſuch ſublime, noble Ideas ; to ſuch a truly admirable degree of Excellence and Perfection in their Imitations of Nature, (that the greateſt Genius's have ever ſince beheld their Productions with Aſtoniſhment, and have owned their Inability to equal them) if the Nature they had before them to imitate had not been of the ſublimeſt and moſt perfect kind ; far exalted above common Nature. What *Cicero* ſays of their Oratory, may very juſtly be applied to the other Arts amongſt them, to their Painting and Sculpture in particular, which were at leaſt in equal Perfection with their Oratory. " It was owing (ſays he) to the extraordinary Politeneſs and Juſtneſs of " Taſte, that prevailed almoſt univerſally at *Athens.* Their Orators could not have ob " tained a Hearing, far leſs have gained Honour and Reputation amongſt them, but by the " pureſt and moſt perfect Eloquence. And all who ſeek Applauſe, naturally conform them " ſelves to the Temper and Taſte of their Judges ; they exert themſelves to the utmoſt to " pleaſe them (83)."

THE great modern Maſters ſeem to have fallen ſhort of the ancient Artiſts, not in Genius, but chiefly on this account, that they had not ſuch noble living Forms before their Eyes to raiſe and exalt their Conceptions. It is to the Study of the Antiques, that the Perfection the Art was brought to in *Italy,* is principally aſcribed by the Maſters themſelves, as well as other Writers. The beſt Ideas of the moſt eſteemed modern Maſters, if they are not entirely taken from the ancient Remains ; it was theſe excellent Works certainly that elevated and inflamed their Imaginations, while they ſtrove to keep up to their Truth,

(82) So *Felibien* and *De Pile* tell us, who mention a Treatiſe of his *De uſu Statuarum in Pictura.* So the Author of the *Reflections ſur la Poeſie & ſur la Peinture, tom.* 1. *ſect.* 38. Rubens dans un petite traité Latin que nous avons de lui ſur l'uſage des ſtatues antiques qu'on doit faire en Peinture, ne doute point que les exerciſes en uſage chez les anciennes donaſſent aux corps une perfection a laquelle ils ne parviennent plus aujourd'hui.

(83) Semper oratorum eloquentiæ moderatrix fuit au-

ditorum prudentia. Omnis enim qui probari volunt, voluntatem eorum qui audiunt, intuentur, ad eamque, & ad eorum arbitrium & nutum totos ſe fingunt & accommodant itaque Caria, &c.——Athenienſes vero funditus epudiaverunt quorum ſemper fuit prudens ſincerumque judicium, hihil ut poſſent niſi incorruptum audire & elegans. Eorum religioni cum ſerviret orator, nullum verbum inſolens, nullum odioſum ponere audebat. *Cicero, Orator.* N° 8.

Truth, Grandeur, Beauty and Grace. This they themfelves acknowledged. If therefore they were not able to come up intirely to the Perfection of the ancient Artifts, to what Caufe is it more natural to afcribe it than to this, that the later had far fuperiour living Models before their Eyes to copy after and emulate, in the Perfons and Conduct of the great Men of thofe Times. *Pliny* (85) gives this remarkable Reafon for the Decay of Painting in his Time, even the Decay of Virtue, or the Want of good Models to infpire the Artifts with noble Ideas, and to raife their Minds to great Thoughts. And *Lomazzo* makes the fame Obfervation about Painting in his time.

NONE who are converfant in the *Greek* Hiftory will think this Obfervation is carried too far. For what Hiftory, what Times, afford fuch amazing Examples of every great, joined with every amiable Quality and Virtue? But not to infift too long on what is fo well known; what a high Opinion does it neceffarily raife in our Minds of *Greece* in its beft Eftate, when we confider that *Rome*, proud haughty *Rome*, long after the better Days of *Greece*, fent thither her moft illuftrious Youths to be formed, or at leaft perfected? There they ftudied Philofophy and all the Sciences, moral Philofophy, juft Reafoning, and true Eloquence. *Cicero*, even after he had gained great Reputation, was confcious to himfelf that fomething was wanting to make him a more compleat Orator; and was not afhamed to become a Scholar in *Greece*. It was from *Greece*, even after it was fadly degenerated, that *Rome* derived its Philofophy and Oratory, all Sciences, all Arts, and all Politenefs. What then muft *Greece* have been in its better State (86)? And it cannot, furely, be thought to have been of fmall confequence to the imitative Arts, to have had the moft perfect Originals to copy.

HAVING thus briefly confidered the more effential Qualities of good Painting, mentioned by ancient Authors, have we not reafon to infer, that *Socrates, Ariftotle, Cicero, Quintilian*, and others, had a very full and compleat Notion of that Art, and that it was indeed in very high Perfection amongft the *Greeks*? From what hath been faid, it plainly follows, that, according to their Ideas of it, a moral or hiftorical Picture ought to be confidered as a Poem, and ought to be examined in the fame way, or by the fame Rules and Queftions, to prove which is one of the Points chiefly aimed at in this Effay.

IS the Subject worthy of being reprefented; and doth the Reprefentation excite a lively and juft Idea of it? To what End is the Compofition adapted, and what Effect doth it produce on the Mind? Doth it duly fill and employ it? Have all the Parts a juft relation to the principal Defign? Doth it clearly ftrike, or is the Sight fplitted, divided, and confounded, by Parts; either not effential, or not duly fubordinated to the Whole? Is the Colouring proper to the Subject and Defign; and is it of a proportional Character throughout the whole, to that of the principal Figure? Doth the fame Genius and Spirit reign throughout all the Work? Is there a fufficient and well-chofen variety of Contrafts? Is there too little or too much? Of whatever kind it is, whether Landfcape or Hiftorical, doth it make a beautiful and great Whole? Is it a true and compatible Choice of Nature? Is there nothing repugnant to Nature's Laws and Proportions, her fixed and unalterable Connections? And above all, what Influence hath it upon the Mind? Doth it inftill great, rare, beautiful, or delightful Ideas? Doth it fpread the Imagination, light up the Underftanding, and fet the Mind a thinking? Doth it fhew a fine Tafte of Nature; an exalted Idea of Beauty and Grace; and raife the Mind to the Conception and Love of what is truly great, beautiful, and decent in Nature, and in Arts?

BY thefe and fuch like Queftions ought Pictures, as well as Poems, to be tried and canvaffed. And therefore the Examination of both is a truly philofophical (87) Employment,
as

(85) Ita eft profecto, artes Defidia perdidit, & quoniam animorum imagines non funt, corporum negliguntur. *Plin. l.* 35.

(86) Nothing can give us a higher Opinion of the *Greeks* in their beft Eftate, than the following Letter of *Pliny* the younger to *Maximus*, when *Trajan* gave him the Government of *Achaia*. " Remember *Maximus*, that you are " going to *Achaia*, the true *Greece*, the Source of all " Learning and polite Tafte; where even Agriculture it " felf was firft found out. Suffer not yourfelf ever to for- " get that you are fent to govern Freemen, if ever any " deferved that Name. Men who by their Virtues, their " great Actions, their Treaties, their Alliances, have " preferved to themfelves the Liberty they received from " Nature. Revere the Gods their Founders. Refpect " their Heroes; the ancient Glory of their Nation, and " the Venerable, facred Antiquity of their Cities; the " Dignity, the glorious Atchievements, the very Fables " of that People. Remember that from them we de- " rived our Laws; and that after we had conquered " them, we did not impofe our Laws upon them; but that " they gave us ours when we entreated it of them, and

" before they felt the Weight of our Arms. In one " word, it is to *Athens* you go, it is at *Lacedemon* you " are to command. It would be Barbarity and Inhu- " manity of the blackeft kind, to rob them of that " Shadow of ancient Liberty which remains to them, " &c."——He adds, " Power is ill fhewn by infulting. " Veneration is not gained by terror; and Love has " a far greater Efficacy towards the Attainment of your " end than Fear. Fear vanifhes in your abfence, Love " remains, but fo that one is turned into Hatred, the " other into Refpect." *Pliny, Ep. l.* 8. *Ep.* 24.

(87) The Art is called by *Philoftratus* in his Life of *Apollonius, lib.* 6. *c.* 9. μίμῶν σοφίας πράγμα. The younger *Philoftratus* calls the good Artift ἀγαθὸς δημιουργὸς ἣ διτός τῆς ἀληθείας, Calliftratus calls him δημιργὸς ἀληθίας. *Plutarch,* the *Philoftrates,* and others frequently fpeak of the ἰσχὺς, the κρατὸς, the σοφίσματα τῆς ἐπιστήμης. And the Artift is faid to work δαιμονίως, αμηχανῶς, ἀρρήτῳ λογῳ. αληθεια, καιρῷ, δικαιοσύνη, and the το καλον are often afcrib'd to the Art. The Subject of a Picture is called ἔννοια, and

as having a direct Tendency to advance and improve our Taste of Truth, Beauty, Simplicity, and Unity; or, in one word, of Nature, and of all the imitative Arts.

CHAP. V.

Observations on the Rise and Decline of PAINTING *among the* Romans; *the State of the other Arts, while it flourish'd among the* Greeks *and* Romans; *and the Causes, natural and moral, to which its Declension is ascrib'd.*

'Twas long before Painting was esteemed by the Romans.

THAT Philosophy and all the Liberal Arts came from *Greece* to *Rome*; and that it was very late before they were encourag'd by the *Romans*, is confessed by *Virgil* (1), *Cicero* (2), *Horace* (3), and all their best Authors.

PLINY indeed, as has been already observed, mentions some Paintings at *Ardea, Lanuvium,* and *Cære,* older than *Rome*; but these were done by *Greek* Masters; and for 450 Years we do not find so much as the Name of any Painter among the *Romans.*

Fabius is the first Roman Painter mention'd in History.

FABIUS PICTOR is the first who is mentioned (4). His Works were burnt in the time of *Claudius:* And so *Pliny* could not have seen them after he was capable of passing a Judgment on Pictures, that may be depended upon.

BUT it appears from *Cicero* (5), and other Writers, that he neither was an extraordinary Painter, nor much honour'd by his Countrymen for professing that Art. *Livy,* who frequently mentions the *Fabian* Family, says not a Word of this Painter, even when he speaks of the Dedication of the Temple he painted: And Names and Surnames were not, as is known, always Marks of Honour.

Pacuvius, the second.

THE second who is celebrated is *Pacuvius* (6), Nephew to the famous *Ennius*; who flourish'd in the sixth Age of the Republick. He was a very good Poet; excelled in writing Tragedy: and is likewise said to have been a very skilful intelligent Painter. He was highly esteem'd and honour'd by the younger *Scipio Africanus,* one of the first among the *Romans* who had an elegant Taste of the fine Arts. And *Pacuvius's* poetical Talents contributed not a little to usher the Art of Painting into Reputation. Yet after him, it doth not appear that the Art was professed by any Person of Distinction, unless *Turpilius* (7), a *Roman* Knight may be reckon'd such; whose Pictures at *Verona,* as *Pliny* assures us, were very beautiful; and who was remarkable for Painting with his left Hand. He lived in *Vespasian's* Reign.

No Person of Distinction after him follow'd that Profession till Turpilius.

AS

---

sometimes γνωμη, ὁ λογ℈, το ϑραμα, ἱςορια, &℈. And the Artist is often called πϑοποιητ℈. See *Junius de Pictura veterum.*

(1) *Excudent alii spirantia mollius æra,*
   Credo equidem: vivos ducent de marmore vultus;
   Orabunt causas melius: Cælique meatus
   Describent radio, & surgentia sidera dicent;
   Tu regere imperio populos, Romane, memento:
   Hæ tibi erunt artes————*Æn.* 6. ver. 846.
So *Livy,* Multas artes ad animorum corporumque cultum nobis eruditissima omnium gens Græca invenit. L. 39. N°. 8.

(2) —— Sed meum semper judicium fuit, omnia nostros aut invenisse per se sapientius, quam Græcos: aut accepta ab illis, fecisse meliora, quæ quidem digna statuissent, in quibus elaborarent.——Doctrinâ Græciâ nos, & omni literarum genere superabat; in quo erat facile Vincere non repugnantes.——An censemus, si Fabio, nobilissimo viro, laudi datum esset, quod pingeret, non multos etiam apud nos futuros Polycletos, & Parrhasios fuisse, &c. *Cic. Tuf. Quæst. lib.* 1. N°. 1. & 2.

(3) Hor. Epist. lib. 2. Ep. 1. ver. 161.
   Serus enim Græcis admovit acumina chartis,
   Et post Punica bella quietus, quærere cæpit:
   Quid Sophocles, & Thespis, & Æschylus utile ferrent.

(4) Compare what *Pliny* says, *lib.* 35. 8. with *c.* 18. The Passages have been already quoted.

(5) Apud Romanos quoque honos mature huic arti contigit: Siquidem cognomina ex ea Pictorum traxerunt Fabii, clarissimæ gentis; princepsque ejus cognominis ipse, ædem salutis pinxit A. U. C. 450. Quæ pictura duravit ad nostram memoriam, media æde, Claudii principatu exusta. What *Pliny* says here of the Honour paid

to *Fabius* does not agree with the Passage in *Cicero* just now quoted, nor with what *Valerius Maximus* says of him. Illa vero gloria interdum etiam a claris viris, ex humilibus rebus petita est. Nam quid sibi voluit C. Fabius, nobilissimus civis, qui cum in æde salutis quam C. Junius Bubalcus dedicaverat, parietes pinxisset, nomen his suum inscripsit? Id enim demum ornamentum familiæ, consulatibus, & sacerdotiis, & triumphis celeberrimæ, derat! ceterum sordido studio deditum ingenium, qualemcunque illum laborem suum silentio obliterare noluit. Nor is it consistent with what *Pliny* himself says afterwards of *Pacuvius, Antistius Labeo,* &c. See the French Notes on *Pliny,* 35. 9. where 'tis justly observ'd: Ajoutez qu'à l'egard des ouvrages de pictor, il ne pouvoit les avoir vûs que dans sa jeunesse, puisque le temple en question fut brûle sous l'empire da Claude: au lieu que Ciceron avoit eû tout le loisir d'en bien juger, &c.

(6) Proxime celebrata est in foro Boario, æde Herculis, Pacuvii poetæ pictura, Ennii sorore genitus hic fuit, clarioremque eam artem Romæ fecit gloria scenæ. *Plin. ibid.* See what *Cicero* says of this *Pacuvius, lib. de Amic. c.* 7. Qui clamores tot cavea nuper in hospitis, & amici mei M. Pacuvii, novâ fabula, &c. See *Quintilian, lib.* 10. *c.* 1. Virium tamen actio plus tribuitur. Pacuvium videri doctiorem, qui esse docti affectant, volunt, &c. Hor. Ep lib. 2. Ep. 1. ver. 55.
   —— *Aufert*
  Pacuvius docti famam senis.——

(7) Postea non est spectata honestis manibus: Nisi forte quis Turpilium equitem Romanum nostræ ætatis, e Venetia, Vellet referre; pulchris ejus operibus, hodieque Veronæ extantibus. Læva is manu pinxit, quod de nullo antea memoratur. *Plin. lib.* 35. The famous *Holbein* and *Nicholas Mignard* both painted with the left Hand.

. AS for the learned *Antiſtius Labeo*, he ought rather to be number'd amóngſt thoſe who lov'd and encourag'd the Art, than among the Painters; he uſed the Pencil only for his Diverſion; and ſo much was Painting even then deſpiſed, that this Amuſement was laughed at by the *Romans*, and was reckon'd beneath his Rank and Dignity. He however, far from being aſhamed of it (8), gloried in it as one of the beſt and moſt becoming Recreations for a Man of Learning and polite Taſte.

ABOUT this time the general Contempt of Painting as a Profeſſion, was a little diminiſh'd among the *Romans*. For *Q. Pedius* (9), a young Gentleman of high Extraction being born dumb, *Meſſala* the Orator in a Conſultation of this young Gentleman's Relations about the propereſt way of diſpoſing of him, urged ſtrongly that he ſhould be bred a Painter; which Advice was generally approv'd of by them all; and in particular, by *Auguſtus*.

PAINTING began to come into ſome repute, after *Valerius Meſſala*, who was Conſul with *Ottacilius Craſſus*, U. C. 489, having defeated *Hiero* in *Sicily*, expoſed a Picture of that Battle to publick View at the *Curiæ Hoſtiliæ* (10). This Piece being admir'd, it conduced not a little to raiſe the Reputation of the Art. This warlike People began to have a higher Opinion of it when they ſaw how fit it was to celebrate the Glory, and perpetuate the Fame of heroick military Atchievements. After him *L. Scipio* made the ſame uſe of Painting (11), and expoſed in like manner a Picture of his *Aſiatick* Victory in the Capitol. *Hoſtilius Mantinus* did the ſame ſome time afterwards.

THE firſt time that Painting began to be uſed in ſcenical Decorations was at the publick Entertainments given by *Claudius Pulcher* (12), U. C. 633. In which all the rare Pieces of Nature or Art that he could collect, were diſplayed to publick View; and among other curious Pieces of Workmanſhip the famous *Cupid* of *Praxiteles*. Certain Buildings on this occaſion were painted with ſuch Dexterity that the Birds are ſaid to have been deceived, as much as they had been formerly by ſome Paintings of *Zeuxis*, and to have perched upon the illuſive Tiles.

BUT Painting came yet into greater eſteem at *Rome*, when foreign Pictures were brought thither. The firſt who did ſo was *L. Mummius Achaicus* (13), from *Corinth*, which was razed by him the ſame Year that *Carthage* was reduced by *Scipio*. From that time the Taſte and Love of Painting began to grow and ſpread; and in what high regard it was held at laſt by *Varro*, *Cicero*, *Hortenſius*, *Atticus*, *Aſinius Pollio*, *Agrippa*, and all the greateſt Men of that polite Age of *Rome*, is too well known to be long inſiſted upon.

HOWEVER, we do not find any conſiderable Painters amongſt the *Romans*, mentioned even during the Reign of *Auguſtus*.

PLINY mentions but very few *Roman* Painters, and gives no very great Character of moſt of them. Firſt of all he names *Ludius* (14), who chiefly painted little Pieces on the Walls and Cielings, repreſenting Sea-ports, Porticoes, Landſcapes, Gardens, Villages, Country Feſtivals, and other Subjects of that inferiour kind.

'TIS remarkable enough, that there was a Painter of the ſame Name about 700 Years before him, who painted in the ſame manner upon Stucco in little Compartiments. And that

this

(8) Parvis gloriabatur tabellis, extinctus nuper in longa ſenecta, Antiſtius Labeo prætorius, etiam proconſulatu provinciæ Narbonenſis functus : ſed ea res in riſu & jam contumelia erat. *Plin. ibid.*

(9) Fuit & principum virorum non omittendum de pictura celebre conſilium. Q. Pedius, nepos Q. Pedii conſularis, triumphaliſque, & a Cæſare dictatore cohæredis Auguſto dati; quum natura mutus eſſet, quum Meſſala orator, ex cujus Familia Pueri avia erat Picturam docendam cenſuit : idque etiam D. Auguſtus comprobavit. Puer magnos profectus in ea arte obiit. *Plin. 35.*

(10) Dignatio autem præcipua Romæ increvit, ut exiſtimo, a M. Valerio Maximo, qui Martius princeps, tabulam pictam prælii quo Carthaginienſes & Hierohem in Sicilia devicerat, propoſuit in latere curiæ hoſtiliæ, &c. *Plin. ibid.*

(11) Fecit hoc idem & L. Scipio, tabulamque victoriæ ſuæ Aſiaticæ in capitolio poſuit.—L. Hoſtilius Mancinus, qui primus Carthaginem inruperat, ſitum ejus oppugnationemque depictam proponendo in foro, & ipſe adſiſtens populo ſpectanti ſingula enarrando : qua comitate proximis Comitiis conſulatum adeptus eſt, &c. *Plin. ibid.*

(12) Habuit & ſcena, ludis Claudii pulchri magnam admirationem picturæ ; quum ad tegularum ſimilitudinem corvi decepti advolarent. *Plin. ibid.*

(13) Tabulis autem externis auctoritatem, Romæ publice fecit primus omnium L. Mummius, cui cognomen Achaici Victoria dedit. *Plin. ibid.* See what *Cicero* ſays of him *de Off. lib. 1. c. 11.* where he regrets the Deſtruction of *Corinth*, Nollem Corinthum, &c. and the fine Character he gives of him *de Off. lib. 2. c. 22.* Italiam ornare quam domum ſuam maluit, &c. He is ſaid however by *Val. Maximus* and *Pliny* not to have been a very great Connoiſſeur.

(14) Decet non ſileri & ardeatis templi pictorem præſertim civitate donatum ibi, (Ludius Eloras)—— non fraudando & Ludio, Divi Auguſti ætate, qui primus inſtituit amœniſſimam parietum picturam :. Villas & Porticus, ac topiaria opera, Lucos, Colles, Piſcinas, Euripos, Amnis, Llttora ; qualia quis optaret : Varias ibi obambulantium ſpecies ; aut navigantium ; terráque Villas adeuntium Aſellis aut Vehiculis ; item Piſcantis, aucupantiſque aut venantis, aut etiam vindemiantis. Sunt in ejus exemplaribus nobiles, paluſtri acceſſu villa, ſuccolatis ſponſione mulieribus labantes trepidique. That theſe Paintings were upon the Walls in Freſco, appears from what *Pliny* adds : Idemque ſubdialibus maritimas urbis pingere inſtituit, blandiſſimo aſpectu minimoque impendio. The *French* Tranſlator gives the Meaning of the Paſſage thus ; Il le peignoit dans les maiſons, ou dans les veſtibules pourvû que ce fut à couvert du ſoleil & de la pluye. *Plin. 35. 18.*

this Taste always prevail'd at *Rome* while Painting subfisted there, is plain from the Remains of that fort yet extant, of which some Specimens are added to this Treatise which are almost all in that Taste and Manner.

A Remark of Pliny.

BUT *Pliny* makes a very just Remark on this occasion, and speaks like a warm and intelligent Lover of Painting (15). " It must be acknowledg'd (says he) that the true Glory of the " Art belongs not to those who painted in this lower Manner; but to those who painted on " Boards great Subjects, and capital Pictures. In this the Prudence and Oeconomy of " the Ancients is truly praise-worthy. For they chose rather to imploy their Talents upon " Works worthy of being preserv'd, and that might easily be saved from Fire, and very con- " veniently carried by the Curious into any part of the World, to spread the Fame and Love " of the delightful Art."

SOME short time before this *Ludius,* was one *Arellius* (16), who (according to *Pliny*) would have deserved very great praise as a Painter, had he not prostituted his Qualifications, and exercised his Pencil in a very lewd libertine way.

Fabulus.

AFTERWARDS arose a Painter of a quite opposite Character, *Fabulus* (17), a very grave Man, and who had no fault but a little too much Precisenefs and Affectation in his Dreis. He was an excellent Artist; but *Nero* having bought up all his Pictures to adorn his golden House, they were burnt with it. *Pliny* calls this magnificent Palace the Prison of *Fabulus's* Works (18); as indeed any Palace may be justly termed, when the Curious have not free access to see the Pictures in it.

Pinus *and* Priscus.

SOME time after *Fabulus, Cornelius Pinus* (19), and *Accius Priscus* had considerable Reputation. They painted the Temple of Honour when it was repaired by *Vespasian.* These two good Painters, says *Pliny,* studied and follow'd the ancient *Greek* Pictures as their Models: But *Priscus* painted more in their Taste, or came nearer to their grand and noble Manner than the other.

Dorotheus.

PLINY likewise mentions *Dorotheus* a Painter, in *Nero's* time. A Picture of his was placed by *Nero's* Order in the room of the famous *Apelles's Anadyomené* when it was quite destroyed or worn out (20).

How little we know of Roman *Painters.*

NOW this is almost all that we know of the *Roman* Painters, except in general, that the Art flourish'd very remarkably under *Vespasian, Titus,* and yet more under *Nerva, Trajan, Adrian, Antoninus Pius,* and *Antoninus Philosophus,* who were great Encouragers of all polite Literature (21), and the fine Arts, and indeed of Virtue and Merit. We are told that Painting, with all the other Arts and Sciences, was promoted by these good Princes, and made considerable Progress under their auspicious Influence: Yet we hardly know the Names of any of the Painters who flourish'd in these Reigns; and none of their Works are particularly describ'd to us by any Writer; so imperfect are our Accounts of those Times. It is not however

(15) *Pliny* allows that there was some Wit and Humour in those little Pieces; Feruntur plurimæ præterea tales argutiæ facetiffumi falis. But he adds, Sed nulla gloria artificum eft, nifi qui tabulas pinxere: eoque Venerabilior antiquitatis prudentia adparet. Non enim parietes excolebant Dominis tantum nec domos uno in loco manfuras, quæ ex incendiis rapi non poffent. Cafula Protogenes contentus erat in hortulo fuo. Nulla Apellis in Tectoriis pictura erat. Nondum libebat parietes totos pingere. What follows is exceeding emphatick. Omnium eorum ars urbibus excubabat, pictorque res communis terrarum erat. *Plin. ibid.*

(16) Fuit & Arellius Romæ celeber, paulo ante Divum Auguftum, ni flagitio infigni corrupiffet & artem, femper alicujus amore feminæ flagrans; & ob id Deas pingens, fed dilectarum imagine. Itaque in pictura ejus fcorta numerabantur. *Plin. ibid.*

(17) Fuit & nuper gravis ac feverus, idemque floridus humilis rei pictor, Fabulus, fpectantem fpectans quacunque adfpiceretur. Paucis Diei horis pingebat, id quoque cum gravitate; quod femper togatus, quanquam in Manicis. See the *French* Notes upon this Paffage, where he fhews that Mr. *Perrault* has no reafon to laugh as he does on this occafion: Since the moft ancient Manufcript of *Pliny* has not thofe Words, which are the Foundation of his Triumph: (Hujus erat Minerva fpectantem fpectans.) 'Tis however pretty extraordinary to find fome very good Authors bringing this Paffage to prove that *Fabulus* underftood Perfpective.

(18) Carcer ejus artis domus aurea fuit, & ideo non extant exempharia magnopere, &c. *Plin. ibid.* See likewise

Book 36. 24. See *Suetonius's* Account of this golden Houfe, in *Nerone, c.* 31.

(19) Cornelius Pinus & Accius Prifcus, qui honoris & virtutis ædis imperatori Vefpafiano Augufto, reftituenti pinxerunt: fed antiquis fimilior, &c. *Plin. ibid.* This Edifice was very ancient: *Cicero* mentions it *De Nat. Deor. lib.* 2. N°23. Vides Virtutis templum, Vides honoris a M. Marcello renovatum, quod multis ante annis erat bello Liguftico a Q. Maximo dedicatum, &c. There is a Plan of it in *Montfaucon's* Antiquities, it confifted of two Twin-Temples, the one (*viz.* that of Virtue) ferving as an Antichamber to the other of Honour; to teach the *Romans* the Road to true Glory.

(20) Confenuit hæc tabula carie, aliamque pro ea fubftituit Nero principatu fuo, Dorothei manu. *Plin.* 35. 17. *Saturn. lib.* 2. *c.* 2. *Macrobius* commends one *Lucius Mullius,* and tells a very witty Repartee by him to *Servilius Geminius,* who fupping with him, when he faw his Sons, who it feems were extremely ugly, faid, Non fimiliter, Mulli, fingis, & pingis. To which the Painter replied, In tenebris fingo, luce pingo. *Horace* mentions a few trivial Painters:

  —— Fulvi, Rutulæque;
  Aut Placidiani contento poplite miror
  Prælia, &c.   Sat. l. 2. Sat. 7. ver. 96.

(21) We know that thofe good and generous Emperors were great Lovers and Promoters of the fine Arts; but the Accounts of their Times are very defective. This Fact is however fufficiently Vouched, with refpect to *Nerva* and *Trojan,* by *Tacitus:* The Paffages to this purpofe are afterwards quoted.

1

however improbable, as fhall be obferved afterwards, that the greateft part of the Remains of Painting that have been difcover'd at *Rome* are of that laft Age.

WE learn from *Seneca, Pliny,* and other Authors, that all the Arts were fadly degenerated in the time of *Claudius* and *Nero.* The latter loved Shew and Magnificence, and fent *Carinas* and *Acratus* into *Afia* and *Achaia* to collect, or rather to rob, for him : But the fine Arts were in a wretched Condition in his time ; and in a very falfe and corrupt Tafte. *Juvenal* alludes to his barbarous inhuman way of plundering Pictures and Statues, in order to fatiate, not his Love of the Arts, but his Pride, Vanity and Arrogance. *The Art in a bad way in the time of Claudius and Nero.*

> *Et pater Armenti caput eripiatur agello :*
> *Ipfi deinde Lares, fiquid fpe{t}abile fignum,*
> *Siquis in ædicula Deus Unicus.*   Sat. 8. ver. 110.

And *Tacitus* gives the worft of Characters to thofe who were fent by him into *Greece* to rifle Pictures and Statues. He fays, they were very wicked, profligate Fellows, pretending to Tafte, but whofe Minds were far from being humanized by the fine Arts (22). *Pliny* (23) fpeaking of his own time, calls Painting a languifhing expiring Art. And indeed all the good Writers, after *Auguftus's* time, are full of Complaints (24) of the fad Decay of Virtue, and of all the ingenious Arts and Sciences, of Painting in particular.

" 'TIS no wonder, fays *Junius,* (25), that *Pliny* calls Painting a dying Art in his Days; *Nay even in the time of Auguftus,*
" for 'tis plain from *Vitruvius,* and feveral other Authors, that it was beginning to take a wrong
" Turn and to be difcoloured in *Auguftus's* time : that is, almoft fo foon as it came into
" vogue or credit amongft the *Romans.* It began immediately to depart from its ancient
" Simplicity and true Grandeur, and to be tainted with the falfe Magnificence of the Times."
The Fact is beyond all controverfy. No doubt there were then at *Rome* many *Greek* Artifts. But at that time the Intelligent admired the Paintings of the ancient *Greeks,* and made but little account of modern Pictures. The more they ftudied the former, the more they were charm'd and fatisfy'd with them; whereas the Works of later Mafters foon cloy'd and fated them. And the reafon they give is, that in the older Pictures there was a Simplicity of Tafte, a Truth of Workmanfhip, a Spirit and Juftnefs of Defign and Expreffion, which fupported the Admiration of underftanding Examiners, and perpetuated, or rather augmented their Entertainment : But in the Performances of modern Mafters, there was nothing but variety of gaudy, gloffy Colours.

" CICERO fays (26) expreffly, that the Pictures of modern Artifts were florid and fhi- *What Cicero fays of ancient and modern Painters.*
" ning; that they had a Richnefs and Splendour of Colouring, which the Works of the more
" ancient ones had not, their Colours being rather auftere and fubdued. But thefe modern
" Pieces, fays he, which fo ftrongly ftrike and enchant the Eye at firft fight, are not able very
" long to detain our Admiration; they foon furfeit the Spectator, and are quickly naufeated.
" Whereas notwithftanding the Simplicity and Aufterity of the ancient Colouring, we are
" never weary of admiring their Pictures : They never become tirefome or infipid, but our
" efteem grows and increafes, the more we examine them." He then carries on a Parallel between Eloquence and Painting in that refpect, and philofophizes upon the matter with great Judgment and Tafte. " 'Tis the fame, fays he, with regard to all our natural Senfes, that
" which is moft lufcious fooneft difgufts the Palate, and it is fo likewife with refpect to our
" Smell and Touch, and all fenfible Gratifications."

ANOTHER

<hr>

(22) Enimvero pet Afiam atque Achaiam non dona tantum, fed fimulacra numinum abripiebantur, miffis in eas proVincias Acrato, ac Secundo Carinate. Ille libertus cuicunque flagitio promptus : Hic Græca doctrinæ ore tenus exercitus, animum bonis artibus non induerat. *Annal. lib.* 15. *Tacitus* calls *Nero* elfewhere incredibilium cupitor : A Lover not of the Beautiful but of the Vaft.

(23) Arte quondam nobili——nunc Vero in totum marmoribus pulfa jam quidem & auro——non jam placent abaci,——cœpimus & lapide pingere. Hoc Claudii principatu inventum ; Neronis Vero maculas qua non effent, cruftis inferendo, unitatem variare,——qualiter illas nafci optaffent deliciæ——nec ceffat luxuria id agere ut quamplurimum incendiis perdat——adeo materiam maluit quam fe nofci; &c.

(24) See befides the Authors already quoted, the Dialogue afcribed to *Quintilian de corrupta Eloquentia.*

(25) ——Bene morientis, quandoquidem fupra ex Vitruvio & Plinio didicimus artem hanc olim fæculorum plurimorum ftudio, & confummatiffimorum artificum cura perfectam, circa tempora Augufti animam cœpiffe agere : Tunc enim ars, vitiis evincentibus, paulatim victa ceffit ; & artifices ultra modum curam cultui impendentes, relicta priorum ingenua fimplicitate, tabulis fuis commen-

dationem potius quærebant ex fumptuofis coloribus quam ex ipfius artis finceritate atque elegantia, donec omnem gratiam rei nimia captatione confumpliffent. *Jun. de Pict. vet. lib.* 3. *c.* 6. See the Paffages of *Pliny* and *Vitruvius* quoted above, in fpeaking of the ancient Colouring.

(26) Difficile enim dictu eft, quænam caufa fit, cur ea quæ maxime fenfus noftros impellunt voluptate, & fpecie prima acerrime commovent, ab iis celerrime faftidio quodam & fatietate abalienemur. Quanto colorum pulchritudine, & varietate floridiora funt in picturis noVis pleraque quam in veteribus? Quæ tamen etiamfi primo afpectu nos ceperunt, diutius non delectant : Cum iidem nos in antiquis tabulis illo ipfo horrido, obfoletoque teneamur. —— Licet hoc videre in reliquis fenfibus ; unguentis minus diu nos delectari, fumma & acerrima fuavitate conditis, quam his moderatis ; & magis laudari quod ceram, quam quod crocum olere Videatur. In ipfo tactu effe modum & mollitudinis & lævitatis.——Sic omnibus in rebus, voluptatibus maximis faftidium finitimum eft, quo hoc minus in oratione miremur : In qua vel ex poetis, vel oratoribus poffumus judicare, concinnam, diftinctam, ornatam, feftivam, fine intermiffione, fine reprehenfione, fine varietate, quamvis claris fit coloribus picta vel poefis, vel oratio, non poffe in delectatione effe diuturnâ. *Cic. de Orator. lib.* 3. *c.* 25.

C c

What Dionyfius Halicarnaflus fays.

ANOTHER learned Critick (27), a *Greek* originally, but bred at *Rome*, and of the *Auguftan* Age, makes the fame Remark. " The Ancients, fays he, were perfect Mafters " of Defign and Expreffion, and delineated in a noble ftrong manner, or with great Spirit " and Truth. Their Colouring was not florid, but rather fevere, and fubmitted to the Sub- " ject and Defign; they underftood Expreffion and Characterizing : But the Moderns do " not draw fo correctly, nor have they that mafterly Skill of expreffing great and noble " Ideas, and of touching the Paffions, in which the Ancients excelled. All their ftudy is " to gratify and flatter the Senfe by a various injudicious Mixture of fine Colours.

It therefore only re- mains, to inquire what is faid by an- cient Authors, of the Progrefs and De- cline of Painting, and all the Arts.

BUT if the Account of Painting amongft the *Romans* (28) be fo lame and deficient, and confifts rather in Complaints of its Decay than any thing elfe ; what remains but that we fhould enquire into the more important Remarks of ancient Authors with re- fpect to the Arts, while they flourifh'd in *Greece*, or among the *Romans* ; and to what Caufes they have afcribed their Declenfion, Fall, and Ruin.

FIRST of all, 'tis obferved by feveral Authors, that all the great Men for Science or Art, in *Greece* or *Rome*, were nearly contemporary ; and that all the politer Arts flourifh'd and perifh'd together. We learn from *Diodorus Siculus* that it was fo in *Greece* (29) ; and *Velleius Paterculus* (30) obferves, that it was the fame among the *Romans*.

AT the fame time that *Greece* produced an *Apelles*, it not only produced a *Praxiteles* and *Lyfippus* ; but it was then that its greateft Philofophers, Poets, and Orators flourifh'd. *Socrates, Plato, Ariftotle, Demofthenes, Ifocrates, Xenophon, Thucydides, Æfchylus, Euripides, Sophocles, Ariftophanes, Menander,* and feveral others were of the fame Age. And what great Men were the Generals of that time ! What vaft Exploits did they per- form with fmall Armies ! If you gather together (fays an ingenious Author) all the illu- ftrious Men *Greece* produced, from *Perfeus* King of *Macedonia*, to the taking of *Conftan- tinople* by the *Turks*, you fhall not find in all that long Period of feventeen hundred Years, fuch a number of great Men of whatever fort of Profeffion, as is to be found in the Life- time of *Plato* only. All Profeffions and all Virtues degenerated at the fame time with polite Letters, and the fine Arts.

AMONGST the *Romans* in like manner, all their greateft Poets, Orators, Philofo- phers and Artifts ; *Lucretius, Virgil, Horace, Propertius, Tibullus, Catullus, Ovid, Cornelius Gallus, Fundanus, Pollio* and *Varius, Hortenfius* and *Cicero, Titus Livius, Sal- luft,* and *Vitruvius,* the moft celebrated of the *Roman* Architects, all thofe were almoft contemporary (31) ; *Auguftus* might have feen them all, and they might all have feen and con- vers'd with one another. In fine, as *Seneca* obferves (32), whatever *Rome* had to oppofe or compare to the *Grecians,* who boafted fo highly of their Oratory, and their fine Ge- nius for all the Arts, appeared about the time of *Cicero.* All the great Genius's who ad- vanced or improved Literature and Science amongft the *Romans,* flourifh'd about that Pe-

Whence this pro- ceeds.

riod. *Velleius Paterculus* feems to marvel at this Phænomenon, and to be at a lofs how to account for it : But one moral Reafon or Caufe of it is very evident. Does it not

Firft from the natu- ral Union and De- pendance of all the Arts.

prove that ftrict and intimate relation of all the Arts and Sciences, of which *Cicero,* and other ancient Authors fo often fpeak (33) ? It appears to have happen'd naturally, and in consequence

---

(27) Veteres tabulæ coloribus fimpliciter illitæ, & nullam in mixturis habentes varietatem, accuratæ Vero delineationis & multum venuftatis in iis habent. Recen- tes autem accurate minus delineatæ, in varietate & mul- titudine mixturæ vim repofitam habent. *Dion. Halicar. in Ifæo.* So likewife *Themiftius* in *Oratione de Amicit.* The Place was quoted before.

(28) The *Roman* Painting is always faid by *Roman* Writers to have been inferiour to the *Greek :* And amongft the Vaft number of *Roman* Statues and Bas-Reliefs that remain, how few are in a very fine Tafte ? And thofe few when compared with the *Greek* ones that are pre- ferved, how far fhort do they fall of them ?

(29) Xerxis in Græciam expeditio, propter ftupendam exercitus multitudinem, fummum Græcis terrorem in- cuffit, cum extremæ fervitutis periculum hoc bello adire fibi viderentur. Ceterum bello præter omnium expecta- tionem fecundum eventum fortito, non modo a tanto difcrimine Græcorum gens liberata eft, fed ingentem præ- terea gloriam obtinuit. Et tantis tunc opibus fingulæ Græcorum civitates repletæ funt, ut cuncti relapfas in contrarium fortunæ Vices demirarentur : Ex eo namque tempore per annos quinquaginta infignes ad fummam fe- licitatem progreffus fecit. Temporibus enim hifce omnes bonæ artes magnopere excultæ, & artifices maximi fæcu- lum illud gloria auxiffe memorantur, ut quorum numero eft Phidias ftatuarius, &c. *Diod. Sic. lib.* 12. *ab initio.*

(30) See *Vell. Pat. lib,* 1. *c.* 16, & 17. The Paffage is quoted almoft at full length before.

(31) *Horace* mentions feveral of thefe as his Contempo- raries, *Sat.* 10. *lib.* 1. *ver.* 40.
　Argutâ Meretrice potes, Davoque Chremeta
　Eludente fenem, comis garrire libellos
　Unus vivorum, Fundani. Pollio regum
　Facta canit pede ter percuffo. Forte epos acer,
　Ut nemo varius ducit : molle atque facetum
　Virgilio annuerant gaudentes rure Camenæ.
This Obfervation hath been often made. *Felix Faber* in his *Hiftoria Suevorum, lib.* 1. *c.* 8. Revixit in Germania fcientia & eloquentia, & ex confequenti quæque ingeniofæ artes, ut Picturæ & Sculpturæ : Amant enim hæ artes fe ad invicem, Ingenium pictura expetit ; ingenium elo- quentia cupit, non vulgare fed altum & fummum. Mi- rabile dictu eft, dum viguit eloquentia, viguit pictura ; ficut Demofthenis & Ciceronis tempora docent : Poft- quam cecidit facundia jacuit & pictura, &c. See like- wife the *Reflexions Critiques fur la Poefie,* tom. 2. *fect.* 13. *Tacitus* makes a very fage and comprehenfive Reflection in his Life of *Agricola.* Virtutes iifdem temporibus op- time æftimantur quibus facillime gignuntur.

(32) Quicquid Romana facundia habet quod infolenti Græciæ aut opponat aut præferat circa Ciceronem efflo- ruit. Omnia ingenia quæ lucem ftudiis noftris attule- runt, tunc nata funt. In deterius deinde quotidie data ces eft. *Sen. de Confol. lib.* 1.

(33) Eft etiam illa Flatonis vera, &c. *Cic. de Orat. lib.* 3. N° 6. And in his *Oratio pro Archia Poeta ab initio.* The Paffages have been often quoted.
I

confequence of the infeparable Union and Connection amongft all the Liberal Arts. For, if we confider and attend to the Nature of things, is it not the fame Soil managed by the fame Culture, and cherifh'd by the fame benign Influences, that produces all the Arts? And thefe generous Plants, as they beautify, fo do they not ftrengthen one another by their conjunctive Growth? On the other hand, whatever in Climate or Soil, fo to fpeak, tends to weaken, or deftroy any one of them, is equally dangerous to them all. They have indeed but one Object, and one Meafure or Standard, *Nature* : They have one common genuine Scope and End, which is to promote Virtue and polifh Mankind : And they have therefore but one common Enemy, Luxury or falfe Pleafure, the Mother of all thofe noxious Weeds; amidft which, how is it poffible for Virtue, or wholefome Science, to thrive and profper? All Works of Genius and Tafte borrow Charms and Graces reciprocally from one another. " Art reflects Images on Art." They muft therefore thrive and flourifh beft; or be moft ftrong, lively, and beautiful, when they are all duly promoted and encouraged. This is the conftant Language of ancient Authors concerning the neceffary *How this was fig-* Union and Connection of the Liberal Arts and Sciences : And poffibly they might intend *nify'd by the An-* fomething like this in their Figures of the Graces, which were reprefented as link'd toge-*tients.* ther, in a perpetual Union, either ftanding hand in hand, or dancing to regular Meafures, where the Motions of each muft give a mutual help to the others, and make all of them more charming (33). In like manner the Mufes, that is the Sciences and Arts, according to the ancient Mythology are Sifters : And it hath been obferv'd by the Learned, that their Symbols reprefent their different Provinces and Employments : And their Names with the other mythological Fables concerning them, are appofite and proper Allegories, fignifying their noble End and Aim, and the means by which they are improv'd and per-fected; or contrariwife are corrupted, abufed and deftroyed; together with the many happy Advantages, as well as the glorious Luftre, Society receives from their Cultivation and Im-provement.

BUT another moral Caufe to which the mutual Growth, or Declenfion of all the Arts *Civil and moral* and Sciences is afcrib'd by ancient Authors, is the Prevalence or Fall of Liberty and pub-*Liberty the Parent* lick Spirit. Liberty and publick Virtue are the common Parent under whofe Favour and *and Patron of the* Patronage alone they can profper and flourifh; and with it they fink, decline and perifh. *Arts.*

LIBERTY or a free Conftitution is abfolutely neceffary to produce and uphold that Freedom, Greatnefs and Boldnefs of Mind, without which it cannot rife to noble and fub-lime Conceptions. Slavery foon unmans and difpirits a People; bereaves them of their Virtue and Genius, and finks them into a mean, fpiritlefs, enfeebled Race that hardly de-ferves to be called Men.

> Jove *fix'd it certain, that whatever* Day
> · *Makes Man a Slave, takes half his Worth away.*
>   Odyff. l. 17. ver. 392. Pope's Tranfl.

LONGINUS (34) introduces a Philofopher very juftly afcribing the miferable Decay *What Longinus* of Eloquence, of all the ingenious Arts, and of all that is truly great, or really ornamental *fays on that Subject.* in human Society, to the Lofs of Liberty, and with it, of that publick Spirit, which alone
                                                                                                      can

(33) *Segnefque nodum folvere gratiæ.*Hor.Car.l.3.Od.21.
Gratia cum nymphis geminifque fororibus audet
Ducere nuda choros. Hor. l. 4. Od. 7.
Jam Cytherea choros ducit Venus, imminente Luna :
Junctæque nymphis gratiæ decentes
Alterno terram quatiunt pede. Hor. lib. 1. Od. 4.
Vid. *Fulgentii Mythol. lib.* 1. *de novem Mufis.* They are painted in that manner, like Virgins and Sifters attending *Apollo,* in the juftly celebrated *Parnaffus* of *Raphael* in the *Vatican.* See alfo *Sen. de Benefic. lib.* 1. *c.* Nam dicam quare tres gratiæ, & quare forores fint, & quare manibus implexis, quare ridentes juvenes, & virgines, fo-lutaque & pellucida vefte? Alii quidem videri volunt unam effe quæ det beneficium; alteram quæ accipiat; tertiam quæ reddat : Alii tria beneficiorum genera.——Quid ille confertis manibus in fe redeuntium chorus? A hoc, quia ordo beneficii per manus tranfeuntis, ni-hilominus ad dantem revertitur, & totius fpeciem perdit fi ufquam interruptus eft : pulcherrimus fi cohæfit, & Vices fervavit. Ideo ridentes, quia vultus promerentium hilares funt, quales folent effe qui dant vel accipiunt be-neficia. Juvenes, quia incorrupta funt & fincera, & omnibus fancta, in quibus nihil effe alligati debet, nec ad-fcripti; folutis itaque tunicis utuntur, &c.
. They are often reprefented in Statues and Bas-Relief; and there is a Drawing of the elder *Bartoli* from an an-cient Painting, in the *Maffimi* Collection, now Dr. *Mead's,* that reprefents them in that manner linked together Arm in Arm.
' See *Paufanias, l.* 9. *Bæotica.* Of the Statues of the Graces naked and cloathed, *p.* 262. *Ed. Wechel.*
' See fome Difcourfes on the Graces in the Memoirs of the *French* Academy *des Belles Lettres,* and *Lomazzo della*

forma delle Mufe Cavata da gli antichi Autori Greci &
Latini; and likewife his *Trattato della Pittura, libro fet-*
timo, of the Mufes.
See *Paufanias Bæotica, l.* 9. *p.* 256.

(34) Quemadmodum igitur audio——Arculas illas lig-neas, in quibus Nani quos vulgus Pygmæos appellant, enutriri folent, non incluforum modo corporis obftare incremento, verum etiam illos ipfos ob circumdatum corpori vinculum contrahere : Ita & omnis fervitus, etiamfi ju-ftiffima fuerit, animæ velut arcula quædam ac publicus Carcer dici merito poffit.——Adde etiam, fi vis, affectus noftros, qui feculi hujus mores tanquam præfidiis infident, eofque per caput & pedis præcipitant. pecuniæ namque, cujus æftuabili nunc omnes æftuamus fiti, & huic fuc-centuriatus voluptatis amor in fervitutem rapit; aut fi ita mavis, ipfam una cum hominibus vitam deprimit ac demergit humanam : Nam avaritia quidem animi mor-bus eft pufilli & fordidi; amore autem voluptatis non abjectius quidquam, & ab omni animi magnitudine magis afienum, &c. *Longin. de Sublim. Sect.* 44. The Verfes of *Homer* above quoted are to be found in *Plato de Legi-bus,* with fome little Alteration from the Common Read-ing. *Tacitus* makes an excellent Reflection to the fame purpofe, *Hift. lib.* 4. Etiam fera animalia fi claufa teneas virtutis oblivifcuntur. There is a famous Saying of the Poet *Alcæus* to the fame purpofe, recorded by *Photius* in his *Bibliotheca, p.* 1290. Solus porro vel inter paucos ad-modum videtur hoc dictum Themiftocles comprobaffe, quod cum Alcæus poeta protuliffet olim, multi poftea ufurparunt. " Non lapides, non ligna, nec Fabrorum " artem Civitates efficere; fed ubi Viri funt, qui feipfos " liberos fervare noruit, ibidem & urbes effe & Mænia."

can engender noble Sentiments, generous Defigns, and ufeful Arts. When the Sciences flourifh'd in *Greece*, what a noble Spirit of Liberty and Independency reign'd there?

'Tis evident from the Hiftory of Greece.

'TIS known to all who are converfant in the *Greek* Hiftory (35), that the Arts declin'd amongft them after the lofs of their Liberty: Yet it is remarkable, that even after *Greece* was abforbed in the *Roman* Empire, and became a Province to it under the Name of *Achaia*, it did not lofe with its Power and Sovereignty, that lively Senfe and Love of Liberty which was the peculiar Chara&er of that People, amongft whom the Arts were produced and brought to Perfe&ion. The *Romans* when they had fubdu'd *Greece*, left that generous, brave and polite People in poffeffion of many of their Rights and Privileges. And they maintain'd fuch an ardent Zeal for Liberty (36), that, to name no other Inftances of it at prefent, when the civil Wats happen'd in *Italy*, the *Athenians* very warmly efpoufed the Party of *Pompey* who fought for the Republick: And, after *Cæfar* was killed, they ere&ed Statues in honour of *Brutus* and *Caffius* near to thofe of *Harmodius* and *Ariftogiton* their ancient Deliverers. · It was hence *Greece*, *Athens* in particular, after it was very much fallen and degenerated, continued ftill to be the Metropolis of Sciences, the School of all the fine Arts, the Standard and Center of good Tafte in all Works of Genius, to *Cicero*'s time, and long afterwards; infomuch that *Rome* fent its moft illuftrious Youth to be perfe&ed there in polite Literature, Eloquence, Philofophy, and all the ingenious Arts and Sciences; and the Emperors who loved Learning, if they could not go to *Greece*, and become Scholars there, as fome of them did (37), brought *Greece* to them, by inviting and receiving into their Palaces, its moft celebrated Profeffors and Artifts, and even intrufting the Education of their Children with *Greek* Mafters. Now their continuing to excel in the Arts and Sciences, to what elfe can it be attributed, but to this, that with fome fmall Remains of Liberty, they had retained the Spirit of Liberty, the Love of it and Zeal for it? It was indeed in confequence of this alone, that they maintain'd, in fome degree, even till *Italy* was quite over-run with Barbarifm; a Sovereignty the *Romans* could not take from them; a Sovereignty in Science, Arts, and good Tafte. 'Tis impoffible to account for it any other way: They preferved the Arts in a very great degree, becaufe they retained the Spirit of Liberty in a very extraordinary one.

From the Hiftory of Rome.

A noble Author has given us this true Account of the Fall of the Arts at *Rome*.

" Twas (38) the Fate (fays he) of *Rome* to have fcarce an intermediate Age, or fingle Period
" of Time between the Rife of Arts and Fall of Liberty. No fooner had that Nation begun
" to lofe the Roughnefs and Barbarity of their Manners, and learn of *Greece* to form their
" Heroes, their Orators and Poets on a right Model, than by their unjuft Attempt upon the
" Liberty of the World, they juftly loft their own. With their Liberty they loft not only
" their Force of Eloquence, but even their Stile and Language itfelf. The Poets who rofe
" afterwards among them, were mere unnatural and forc'd Plants. Their two moft accom-
" plifh'd, who came laft, and clos'd the Scene, were plainly fuch as had feen the Days of Li-
" berty, and felt the fad Effe&s of its Departure. Nor had thefe been ever brought into play,
" otherwife than thro' the Friendfhip of the fam'd *Mæcenas*, who turned a Prince, naturally
" cruel and barbarous, to the Love and Courtfhip of the Mufes. Thefe Tutoreffes form'd in
" their royal Pupil a new Nature, they taught him how to charm Mankind. They were
" more to him than his Arms or military Virtue; and, more than Fortune herfelf, affifted
" him in his Greatnefs, and made his ufurp'd Dominion fo enchanting to the World, that
" it could fee without regret its Chains of Bondage firmly rivetted.

" THE corrupting Sweets of fuch a poifonous Government were not indeed long-liv'd.
" The Bitter foon fucceeded; and in the iffue the World was forc'd to bear with patience
" thofe natural and genuine Tyrants, who fucceeded to this fpecious Machine of arbitrary and
" univerfal Power. And now that I am fallen unawares into fuch profound Refle&ions on
" the Periods of Government, and the Flourifhing and Decay of Liberty and Letters; I can't
" be contented, merely to confider of the Enchantment which wrought fo powerfully upon
" Mankind, when firft this univerfal Monarchy was eftablifh'd. I muft wonder ftill more,
" when I confider, how after the Extin&ion of the *Cæfarean*, and *Claudian* Family, and a
" fhort Interval of Princes rais'd and deftroy'd with much Diforder and publick Ruin, the
" *Romans* fhould regain their perifhing Dominion, and retrieve their finking State, by an
" After-race of wife and able Princes fucceffively adopted, and taken from a private State to
" rule the Empire of the World. They were Men who not only poffefs'd the military Virtues,
" and fupported that fort of Difcipline in the higheft degree; but as they fought the Intereft of
" the World, they did what was in their power to reftore Liberty, and raife again the perifhing
" Arts, and decay'd Virtue of Mankind. But the Seafon was now paft! The fatal Form of Go-
" vernment was become too natural; and the World, which had been under it, and was become
" flavifh and dependent, had neither Power nor Wili to help itfelf. The only Deliverance it
" could expe&, was from the mercilefs Hands of the Barbarians, and a toral Diffolution of that

---

(35) *Plutarch. in Vita Philopæmen. ab initio.*

(36) So *Dion. Caffius* tells us.

(37) 'Tis well known that *Marcus Aurelius*, even

" enormous
whilft he was Emperor, went to hear the Philofophers
Apollonius and *Sextus*; he difdained not to take Leffons
from them, and to become their Scholar.

(38) *Shaft. Chara&*. Advice to an Author, p. 219.

" enormous Empire and defpotick Power, which the beft Hands could not preferve from being
" deftructive to human Nature.   For even Barbarity and Gothicifm were already entred into
" Arts, e'er the Savages had made any Impreffion on the Empire.   All the Advantage which,
" a fortuitous and almoft miraculous Succeffion of good Princes could procure their highly
" favour'd Arts and Sciences, was no more than to preferve, during their own time, thofe
" perifhing Remains, which had for a while with difficulty fubfifted, after the Decline of
" Liberty.   Not a Statue, not a Medal, not a tolerable Piece of Architecture could fhew
" itfelf afterwards. Philofophy, Wit, and Learning, in which fome of thofe good Princes
" had themfelves been fo renown'd, fell with them; and Ignorance and Darknefs over-fpread
" the World, and fitted it for the Chaos and Ruin which enfu'd."

THIS is the very Language of ancient Authors themfelves concerning the Decline of Li-   *This afferted by an-*
berty, and Arts at *Rome*.   *cient Authors.*

SENECA in feveral Epiftles informs us, that Eloquence and all the Arts were fadly de- *By Seneca.*
generated in *Nero's* time; and that this could not but naturally, and of itfelf, happen after
fuch a Corruption and Diffolution of Manners, confequent to the Change of Government,
and the horrid Luxury and Effeminacy of the *Roman* Court, even before the time of a *Claudius* or a *Nero* (39).   There was no more poffibility of making a ftand for Purity of Tafte than
for Liberty.   The fine Arts in fuch a Relaxation of Manners .became Minifters to Vice,
Senfuality, and fervile Flattery.   Being corrupted, they became in their turn Corrupters.

WITH regard to Painting in particular, *Pliny* fhews it (40) to have been, while it *By Pliny.*
flourifh'd amongft the ancient Artifts, not only fevere in refpect of the Difcipline, Stile,
and Defign, but of the Characters and Lives of the noble Mafters; and not only in the
Effect, but in the very Materials of the Art, the Colours and Ornaments.   The Art, he
tells us, was fadly declin'd in his time, and juft upon the point of being extinguifh'd and
loft.   And the deadly Symptom upon which he pronounces the fure Death of this noble
Art not long Survivor to himfelf, was what belong'd in common to all the other perifhing
Arts, after the Fall of Liberty, the Luxury of the *Roman* Court, and the Change of Tafte
and Manners enfuing upon fuch a Change of Conftitution and Government.   This excellent Critick traces the falfe Tafte, that corrupted all the Arts, to its Source, and reprefents
it fpringing from the Court itfelf; and from that Affectation of Splendour, Opulence, and
Expence proper to the Place and Times.   Thus in the Statuary, and Architecture then in
vogue, nothing could be admir'd befide what was fumptuous and coftly in the mere Materials of the Work : Precious Metals, glittering Stones, every thing that was merely fhewy and
glaring, and poifonous to Art, came every day more into requeft; and were impofed as
neceffary Materials on the beft Mafters.

'TWAS in favour of thefe Court-Beauties, and gaudy Appearances, that all good Drawing, juft Defign, and Truth of Work began to be defpifed.   Care was taken to procure
from diftant Parts the moft gorgeous fplendid Colours of the moft coftly Growth or Compofition; not fuch as had been ufed by *Apelles*, and the great Mafters who were juftly fevere,

(39) Quare quibufdam temporibus provenerit corrupti
generis oratio quæris; & quomodo in quædam vitia in-
clinatio ingeniorum facta fit.———Quemadmodum
uniufcujufque actio dicenti fimilis eft, fic genus dicendi
imitatur publicos mores.——Si difciplina civitatis labora-
vit, & fe in delicias dedit, argumentum eft luxuriæ publicæ, orationis lafcivia——hon poteft alius effe ingenio,
alius animo color.——Hæc vitia unus alfquis inducit, ceteri imitantur, & alteri tradunt.——Quomodo Convivio-
rum luxuria, quomodo veftium, ægræ Civitatis indicia
funt, fic orationis licentia oftendit animos quoque a quibus
verba exeunt procidiffe.——Oratio nulli molefta eft, nifi
animus labat.   Ideo ille curetur, ab illo fenfus, ab illo
verba exeunt.   Illo fano ac valente, oratio quoque ro-
bufta, fortis, virilis eft : Si ille procubuit, & cetera fequuntur ruinam.   Rex nofter eft animus.   Hoc incolumi
Cetera manent in officio, parent & obtemperant.   Cum
vero ceffit voluptati, artes quoque marcent, & omnis ex
languido fluidoque conatus eft.——Nimis anxium effe te
circa verba, mi Lucili, nolo : Habeo majora quæ cures.
Quære quid fcribas, non quemadmodum.   Cujufcunque
orationem videris follicitam & politam, fcito animum
quoque non minus effe pufillis occupatum.   Magnu ille
remiffius loquitur & fecurius : Quæcunque dicit, plus habent fiduciæ quam Curæ.   Nolli complures, juvenes,
barba & Coma nitidos, de capfula totos : Nihil ab illis
fperaveris forte, nihil folidum.   Oratio vultus animi eft :
fi circumtonfa eft, & fucata, & manufacta, oftendit illum quoque non effe fincerum, & habere aliquid fracti.
Senec. Epift. 114, & 115.

(40) Ita eft profecto, artis Defidia perdidit.   *Plin.* 35.
2, *&c.*   Hactenus dictum fit de dignitate artis morientis.

Ib. c. 12.   Qua contemplatione tot colorum tanta varietate fubit antiquitatem mirari.   Quatuor coloribus folis
immortalia opera illa ferceë, ex albis, Melino; ex Sila-
ceis, Attico; ex Rubris, Sinopide Pontica; ex Nigris,
Atramento; *Apelles*, Echion, Melanthius, Nicomachus,
clariffimi pictores : cum tabulæ eorum fingulæ oppidorum
venirent opibus.   Nunc & purpuris, in parietes migrantibus, & India conferente fluminum fuorum limum, &
Draconum & Elephantorum faniem; nulla nobilis pictura eft.   Omnia ergo meliora tunc fuere, cum minor
Copia.   Ita eft, quoniam ut fupra diximus, rerum non
animi pretiis excubatur.   Et noftræ ætatis infaniam non
omittam.   Nero princeps jufferat fe Coloffeum pingi,
120 pedum, in linteo : Incognitum ad hoc tempus, &c.
Plin. 35. 15.   Hic multis jam fæculis fummus animus in
pictura.   Pingi autem gladiatoria muneta atque in publico exponi cœpta a C.Terentio, Lucano, &c. c. 16.   See
the Dialogue *de Oratoribus* afcribed to *Quintilian*.   See
Lord *Shaftesbury's* Comment on thefe Words of *Pliny*
juft quoted : in his Advice to an Author, *p.* 340.   To
the fame purpofe is what *Pliny* fays, *lib.* 34. 2.   Quondam æs confufum auro argentoque mifcebatur, & tamen
ars pretiofior erat, nunc incertum eft, pejor hæc fit an
materia : Mirumque, cum ad infinitum operum pretia
creverint, auctoritas artis extincta eft.   Quæftus caufa
enim, ut omnia, exerceri cœpta eft, quæ gloria folebat.
So *Horace de Art. Poet.* ver. 323.
 Graiïs ingenium, Graiïs dedit ore rotundo
 Mufa loqui, præter laudem nullius Avaris.
 Romani pueri longis rationibus affem
 Difcunt in partis centum diducere——
 ——*At hæc animos ærugo & cuta peculi*
 Cum femel imbuerit; fperamus carmina fingi, &c.

D d

vere, loyal, and faithful to their Art. This newer Colouring *Pliny* calls the florid kind. The Materials were too rich to be furnish'd by the Painter; but were befpoke or provided at the Coft of the Perfon who employed him. The other he calls the auftere kind. And thus, fays he, the Coft, not the Life and Art is ftudied. He fhews, on the contrary, what care *Apelles* ufed, as hath been already obferv'd, to fubdue the florid Colours by a darkening Varnifh: And he fays juft before of fome of the fineft Pieces of *Apelles,* that they were wrought in four Colours only: So great, fo venerable was Simplicity among the Ancients; and fo certain was the Ruin of all true Elegance in Life or Art, where this Miftrefs was once quitted or contemned.

By Tacitus.

TACITUS often fpeaks in the fame manner of the conjunct Ruin of Liberty, publick Virtue, and of all the Arts. He obferves, that foon after the fatal Change of Government, an avaritious mercenary Spirit began to prevail; and that vile Senfuality had quite extinguifh'd every Spark of Generofity and Virtue, and by confequence of good Tafte. And how virtuous and good were thofe Emperors, according to his Accounts, under whom the Arts began to revive, lift up their Heads, and even made very confiderable Progrefs! Was not publick Good their Aim? Did they not rouze the dead Arts by awakening publick Spirit, and a Senfe of the Dignity of human Nature? Did they not, as it were, mix Liberty with Defpotifm, as far as it is poffible to mingle things of fo contrary and oppofite a Temper (41)?

By Petronius.

IN fine, to what is it that the Decay and Ruin of all the fine Arts, of Painting in particular, is affign'd even by the diffolute *Petronius* himfelf (42), but to the Lofs of Liberty and the Corruption that naturally followed upon it; to the univerfal Prevalence of a mean, corrupt, mercenary, fenfual Spirit: When all was Avarice, and Ambition was no more: When Men were quite immerfed in grofs Voluptuoufnefs.

How civil and moral Liberty may be painted.

LIBERTY therefore is very juftly reprefented, by an ingenious Author often quoted, who well underftood the Genius and Tafte of the Ancients, as fhe (very probably) was painted by them: In her *Amazon* Drefs, with a free manly Air becoming her; her Guards, the Laws, with their written Tables like Bucklers furrounding her: Riches, Traffick, and Plenty, with the Cornucopia, ferving as her Attendants; and in her Train, the Arts and Sciences playing. The reft of the Piece (fays he) is eafy to imagine,—her Triumph over Tyranny and lawlefs Rule of Luft and Paffion.———But what a Triumph (faith he) would that of her Sifter and Guardian Liberty be? What Monfters of favage Paffions would there appear fubdued? There fierce Ambition, Luft, Uproar, Mifrule, with all the Fiends which rage in human Breafts, would be fecurely chain'd. And when Fortune herfelf, the Queen of Flatterers, with that Prince of Terrors, Death, were at the Chariot-wheels as Captives, how natural would it be to fee Fortitude, Magnanimity, Juftice, Honour, and all that generous Band, attending as the Companions of our inmate Lady, Liberty! She, like fome new-born Goddefs would grace her Mother's Chariot; and own her Birth to humble Temperance, that nurfing Mother of the Virtues; who like the Parent of Gods, (old reverend *Cybele*) would properly appear drawn by reined Lions patient of the Bit, and on her Head a Turret-like Attire; the Image of defenfive Power and Strength of Mind.

THIS Topick hath often been infifted upon, and cannot indeed be too frequently, or too ftrongly reprefented. For what is it that more nearly concerns Mankind? But I fhall only obferve farther on this head:

Of the Philofophy that produces the Arts.

THAT the Philofophy which prevailed in *Greece,* while the Arts were in their higheft Glory, the Philofophy of *Socrates,* is the only Philofophy than can infpire publick Spirit, or fupport Virtue and Liberty, produce Heroes, Patriots, brave and worthy Men, and Authors and Artifts of a fublime daring Genius. On the other hand, the Philofophy which

came

---

(41) This is a Reflection of *Tacitus :* Quod fi vita fuppeditet, principatum Divi Nervæ, & imperium Trajani, uberiorem fecurioremque materiem fenectuti fepofui : rara temporum fælicitate, ubi fentire quæ velis, & quæ fentias dicere licet. *Hift. lib.* 1. *ab initio.* And in his Life of *Julius Agricola* at the beginning : Scilicet illo igne vocem populi Romani & libertatem fenatus, & confcientiam generis humani aboleri arbitrabantur, expulfis infuper fapientiæ profefforibus, atque omni bona arte in exilium acta, nequid ufquam honeftum occurreret. Dedimus profecto grande patientiæ documentum, & ficut vetus ætas vidit, quid ultimum in libertate effet, ita nos quid in fervitute, adempto per inquifitiones & loquendi audiendique commercio. Memoriam quoque ipfam cum voce perdidiffemus, fi tam in noftra poteftate effet oblivifci quam tacere. Nunc demum redit animus, & quanquam primo ftatim beatiffimi fæculi ortu, Nerva Cæfar res olim diffociabiles mifcuerit, principatum ac libertatem, augeatque quotidie facilitatem imperii Nerva Trajanus; nec fpem modo ac votum fecuritas publica, fed ipfius voti fiduciam, ac robur affumferit : Natura tamen infirmitatis humanæ, tardiora funt remedia quam mala. Et ut corpora lente augefcunt, cito extinguuntur ; fic in-

genia ftudiaque facilius opprefferis, quam revocaveris. Subit quippe etiam ipfius inertiæ dulcedo : & invifa primo Defidia, poftremo amatur.

(42) Cœpi prudentiorem confulere ætatis tabularum, & quædam argumenta mihi obfcura, fimulque caufam Defidiæ præfentis excutere, cum pulcherrimæ artis periffent, inter quas pictura ne minimum quidem fui veftigium reliquiffet. Tum ille, pecuniæ, inquit, cupiditas hæc tropica inftituit. Prifcis enim temporibus, cum adhuc nuda virtus placeret, vigebant artes ingenuæ, fummumque certamen inter homines erat nequid profuturum feculis diu lateret. Verum ut ad Plaftas convertar, Lyfippum, ftatuæ unius lineamentis inhærentem inopia extinxit ; & Myron, qui pœne hominum animas ferarumque ære comprehenderat, non invenit hæredem. At nos vino fcortifque demerfi ne patatas quidem artes audemus cognofcere ; fed accufatores antiquitatis, vitia tantum docemus & difcimus. Noli ergo mirari fi pictura defecit, cum omnibus Diis hominibufque formofior videatur maffa auri, quam quicquid Apelles, Phidiafve græculi delirantes fecerunt. *Petr. Arb. Satyr.* See *Vell. Pat.* *l.* 2. *initio, & Saluft. Catil.* 2.

came afterwards to gain a great Afcendant in *Greece*, and that was almoft univerfally received at *Rome*, fo foon as the *Grecian* Arts and Sciences were admitted amongft them, was of a quite contrary Nature and Tendency : A Philofophy, which reprefented an interefted felfifh Temper as Wifdom ; and taught Men to liften to the foft effeminating Language of Pleafure ; inftead of that which calls upon us to confider the Dignity of Human Nature, to keep it always before our Eyes, and to accuftom ourfelves to ask our own Hearts; What is great and good, whatever it may coft ; or what is bafe and unworthy, whatever Pleafures it may bring.

WE are told by *Cicero* (43), That in his time the Image of *Epicurus* was not only in every Houfe, but on every Hand. So great was their Veneration for that Philofopher, whofe pretended, falfe Philofophy feem'd to give a fort of Sanction and Authority, to their Luxury, Avarice and Senfuality, from Reafon. *Pliny* (44) gives the fame Account of After-times. How earneftly and beautifully do we find *Cicero* (45) combating this poifonous corrupt Doctrine in his philofophical Works? Were ever the Names (fays he) of *Lycurgus, Solon, Leonidas, Epaminondas*, and other ancient Heroes heard in the School of *Epicurus?* Which however are the conftant Subject of the better Philofopher's Praifes : Did his School ever produce Men of a generous, noble, difinterefted Spirit? Or can indeed that Philofophy ever animate and incite Men to truly laudable and glorious Actions? *Torquatus*, you muft either quit the Defence of Pleafure, mere fenfual Gratification, or give up all our own Patriots and Deliverers. Fortitude and publick Spirit, or Contempt of Riches and Pleafures, and a generous Love of Mankind and publick Good, are of the very Effence of Virtue. The very Arts themfelves which feem to be the moft nearly allied to Pleafure, of any thing that hath any Communion or Partnerfhip with Reafon, have a higher View than Pleafure. Can then that Philofophy be confiftent with Virtue, which teaches us folely to calculate the Advantages and Pains that an Action or Purfuit may occafion ; and not to think of the *Honeftum*, the fit, the becoming, the good, and the worthy part? The Philofophy that alone can produce a great Mind, muft teach us to chufe the Beautiful, the Reafonable, the Virtuous and Laudable, whatever Confequences may enfue upon it ; whatever Pleafures muft be facrificed to the Choice, or in whatever Hardfhips it may involve us. Thefe cannot alter the Nature of moral Good and Evil. And therefore, the firft Leffon of Virtue is, to learn to abftain from inviting tempting Pleafures ; (46) and to contemn Dangers and Difafters, and to think only of the Goodnefs and Merit, or Bafenefs and Deformity of Actions ; that is, of their Tendency to publick Good or Hurt. Virtue confifts in being able to bear and forbear ; it looks beyond ourfelves, (*foras fpectat*) and fteadily eyes the Good of Society. Its Ways are truly, throughly pleafant, becaufe it brings no Remorfe, but fpreads Peace, Contentment, Satisfaction, Self-approbation, and pure unfading Joy over the whole Soul. But it may often be oppofed by mercenary felfifh Appetites; it may often demand a Sacrifice at our Hands, to which not merely the animal Paffions, but Paffions of a higher and nobler Nature, cannot eafily be brought to furrender. It may therefore occafion violent Struggles in the Breaft ; fo that without a ftrong Senfe of the Excellence of Virtue ; without exercifing ourfelves to Self-denial, and a Contempt of all inferiour Pleafures, which it is indeed greater to defpife than to poffefs (47), it is impoffible to make any confiderable Progrefs in Virtue.

THIS

(43) Nec tamen Epicuri licet oblivifci, fi cupiam : Cujus imaginem non modo in tabulis noftri familiares, fed etiam in poculis, & in annulis habent. *Cic. de fin. lib.* 15. N° 1.

(44) Iidem Palæftras Athletarum imaginibus & ceromata fua exornant, & Epicuri vultus per Cubicula geftant ac circumferunt fecum : Natali ejus, decima Luna facrificant, feriafque omni menfe cuftodiunt, quas Icadas vocant. *Plin.* 35. 3.

(45) We learn from *Cicero* that this was the Philofophy which prevail'd in *Greece* in its better days ; and he reafons againft the Contrary Philofophy in feveral parts of his Works, as I have here reprefented him. See particularly *De fin. lib.* 2. 21. Nunquam audivi in Epicuri fchola Lycurgum, Solonem, Miltiadem, Themiftoclem, Epaminondam, nominari : Qui in ore fun, ceterorum omnium philofophorum——At negat Epicurus (hoc enim veftrum lumen eft) quenquam qui honefte non vivat jucunde poffe vivere. Quafi ego id curam quid ille aiat aut neget ; illud quæro, quid ei qui in voluptate fummum bonum putat confentaneum fit dicere.——Jam fi pudor, fi modeftia, fi pudicitia, fi uno verbo temperantia, pœnæ, aut infamiæ metu coercebuntur non fanctitate fua fe tuebuntur : Quod adulterium, quod ftuprum, quæ libido non fe proripiet, ac projiciet, aut occultatione propofita, aut impunitate, aut licentia?——Paceres tu quidem Torquate hæc omnia. Nihil enim arbitror magnâ laude dignum, quod te prætermiffurum credam aut mortis aut doloris metu. Non quæritur autem, quid naturæ tuæ confentaneum fit, fed quid difciplinæ. Ratio ifta, quam defendis ; præcepta, quæ didicifti, quæ probas,

funditus evertunt amicitiam, &c. Compare with this *De Legibus, lib.* 1. 14, 15. What *Tacitus* fays in his Character of *Helvidius Prifcus* is very remarkable. Helvidius Prifcus——ingenium illuftre altioribus ftudiis juvenis admodum dedit : Non ut plerique, ut nomine magnifico fegne otium velaret, fed quo firmior adverfus fortuita, rempublicam capefferet. Doctores fapientiæ fecutus eft, qui fola bona quæ honefta, mala tamen quæ turpia ; potentiam, nobilitatem, ceteraque extra animum neque bonis neque malis annumerant, &c. *Tacitus Hift. lib.* 4. *circa initium.* So *Lucian* in his Character of *Cato.*

— *hi mores, hæc duri immota Catonis
Secta fuit, fervare modum, finemque tenere,
Naturamque fequi, patriæque impendere vitam,
Nec fibi, fed toti genitum fe credere mundo.
Juftitiæ cultor, rigidi fervator honefti :
In commune bonus, nullofque Catonis in actus
Subrepfit, partemque tulit fibi nata voluptas.*
                                        Lucan. l. 2. ver. 300.

(46) See how *Socrates* defcribes the good Man. *Xenoph. Apom. c. ult. p. ult.* Ἐγκρατὴς δὲ, ὥστε μηδὲ πότε προαιρεῖσθαι τὸ ἥδιον ἀντὶ τε βελτίονος. See *Epictetus*, and *Arrian* upon him, his Divifion of Virtue into ἀνέχειν and ἀπέχειν.

(47) Quemadmodum nihil in hac vita magnum eft, cujus defpectus in rebus magnis numeretur.——Adeoque illos, qui cum ea adfcifcere fibi poffunt animi adducti magnitudine refpuunt ac fpernunt, majorem fui Concitare admirationem, quam qui illa ipfa poffident. *Long. de Sublim. Sect.* 7.

The true Philofophy
prevail'd in Greece,
while the Arts were
in their greatest
Perfection.

THIS was the prevailing Philofophy in *Greece* in its beft and moft glorious Days: And we may be very fure, from the nature of things, that where the contrary Scheme of Philofophy begins to prevail, Men will foon run 'headlong into Corruption ; and even the Arts themfelves will not only partake of the Infection, but become Panders to Vice. Nothing can be more true than that Saying of the beft Philofopher of Antiquity, that is brought by *Cicero* as an Inftance of his manner of Reafoning. " Such as the Man is, fuch will his " Difcourfe and Productions be : His Actions will be like to his Speeches, and his whole " Life will be of a piece with his Temper and Difpofition." A Man's Deeds and Sayings are the Image of his Mind. If therefore Men are not of a fublime and great Difpofition, the Arts, amongft fuch, will very foon become low and groveling.

THE Conclufion (48) with which this Reafoning ends, contains the very Subftance of his Philofophy concerning Virtue and true Happinefs. The Affections of a good Man are truly noble, generous, and praife-worthy ; they do not hide themfelves or fhun the Light, they are not afraid to ftand the Examination of Reafon and Confcience : And therefore all his Actions will likewife be good and laudable. Whence it follows that the good Man alone can be happy, fince fupreme, independent Happinefs confifts chiefly in that Satisfaction which the Confcioufnefs of a well-govern'd Mind, pure Affections, and correfponding Actions only can afford.

AN excellent Author well obferves (49), that what Philofophy did for the Prefervation and Happinefs of *Greece* is almoft incredible. But why fpeak we of their Philofophers ? (faith he) the Poets themfelves, who were in every one's hands, inftructed them yet more than they diverted them.

HOMER hath delightfully reprefented the Reluctance with which Poetry is dragged into the Service of Vice ; and the fame muft hold equally true with refpect to her Sifter-Arts. They cheerfully impart their Ornaments and Graces to Truth, Virtue, and found Philofophy ; but fervile Flattery and immoral corruptive Doctrines are not more contrary to true Worth and Greatnefs of Mind, than they are repugnant to the real Beauty and genuine Spirit of the elegant Arts.

> *For dear to Gods and Men is facred Song,*
> *Self-taught I fing ; by Heav'n, and Heav'n alone,*
> *The genuine Seeds of Poefy are fown ;*
> *And (what the Gods beftow) the lofty Lay*
> *To Gods alone, and god-like Worth we pay.*
>
> *That here I fung was Force, and not Defire,*
> *This Hand reluctant touch'd the warbling Wire ;*
> *And let thy Son atteft, nor fordid Pay,*
> *Nor fervile Flatt'ry ftain'd the moral Lay.*   Odyff. l. 22. ver. 382.

THE Ancients have given an enchanting Voice and Air to the *Syrens*, that emphatical, fignificative Emblem of falfe Pleafure.

> *Sirenum voces & Circis pocula nofti,*
> *Quæ fi cum fociis ftultus cupidufque bibiffet*
> *Sub domina meretrice fuiffet : turpis & excors*
> *Vixiffet canis immundus, vel amica luto fus.*   Hor. l. 1. Ep. 2.

BUT it was, according to them, the proper Bufinefs of the Mufes to difcomfit the *Syrens* or falfe Pleafure, and accordingly they are faid to have fought the *Syrens*, and to have plucked their Wings (50). And therefore, as *Paufanias* tells us, the Statues of the Mufes are often adorn'd with Crowns of Feathers, or carried Feathers in their Hands in memory of that glorious Defeat ; and there are Statues of them ftill at *Rome*. And in this Collection of ancient Paintings the *Syren* is moft beautifully reprefented, juft as the Poets defcribe her.

THE Ancients have alfo charmingly pointed out to us, in their allegorical way, by feveral Emblems, the true Character of that Philofophy which ought to give Laws to all the fine Arts; and employ them as its beft Minifters in reforming, polifhing, and humanizing Mankind: And which alone can be beneficial to a State by infpiring the Love of Juftice, Benevolence, Mankind and Liberty. The Mufes and Graces are ever reprefented by them in the Train of the God or Goddefs of Wifdom. *Amphion* and *Orpheus* by their mufical Philofophy tamed favage Monfters, and enchanted rude Rocks into the Forms of faireft Cities: And *Orpheus* was the Son of *Apollo* and *Calliopé*, according to the ancient Mythology. How inftructive is *Horace's* Defcription of the true Philofophy, and of the Origin of truly divine Poetry, agreeable to this allegorical Theology ?

                                                    Sylveftres

(48) *Cic. Tufc. Quæft. lib. 5. N° 16.*

(49) *Boffuet Difcours fur l'Hiftore Univerfelle.*

(50) *Paufanias Bœotica, l. 9. p. 261. Ed. Wechel.*

Acheloi enim filias narrant Junonis fuafu in cantus certamen Mufas provocafle aufus: victis Mufas pinnas in alis convelliffe ; deque illis coronas fibi feciffe, &c.——See *Baconi Opera de Sapientia veterum*, 31 *Sirenes five voluptas.*

Sylvestres homines sacer interpresque Deorum
Cædibus & victu fœdo deterruit Orpheus ;
Dictus ob hoc lenire Tigres rapidosque Leones.
Dictus & Amphion, Thebanæ,conditor arcis,
Saxa movere sono testudines & prece blanda
Ducere quo vellet.　Fuit hæc sapientia quondam,
Publica privatis secernere, sacra profanis ;
Concubitu prohibere vago, dare jura maritis ;
Oppida moliri, leges incidere ligno,
Sic honor & nomen divinis vatibus, atque
Carminibus fuit.——Hor. de Art. Poet. ver. 391.

THESE Fables of *Orpheus* and *Amphion, Philostratus* (51) deſcribes beautifully painted; and *Callistratus* (52) gives us an Account of the Story of *Orpheus* repreſented with wonderful Elegance and Force in Sculpture.　We learn from *Martial,* that there were ſuch Pictures at *Rome* in his time (53).

AND to ſuch *Horace* plainly alludes, *Car. l. 1. Od. 12.*

Unde vocalem temere insecutæ
Orphea Sylvæ,
Arte materna rapidos morantem
Fluminum lapsus celeresque ventos :
Blandum & auritas fidibus canoris
Ducere quercus.

And lib. 3. Od. 11.

Mercuri (nam te docilis magistro
Movit Amphion lapides canendo)
Tuque testudo resonare septem
Callida nervis (54).

THUS, according to the beſt Authors of Antiquity, 'tis only when the Muſes or ingenious Arts are directed by true Wiſdom, Virtue, and a ſound publick-ſpirited Philoſophy, that they can attain to their natural worthy End, or diſplay their real Beauty and genuine Charms. With regard to theſe Fables, and other ſuch like Allegories, I cannot chuſe but take notice of what Lord *Verulam* remarks (55) : Theſe Inventions, ſaith he, are either great or happy : Great, if they were contrived and imagined purpoſely : Happy, if without any Intention they have afforded ſuch noble Matter of worthy Inſtruction.

'TIS the generous Mind enlarging and greatening Philoſophy which raiſes to the Love of Society and Mankind, and infuſes juſt Notions of rational Happineſs and Grandeur, aided, ſtrengthned, and ſweetned, or embelliſh'd, by the fine Arts, that alone can early fire the Youth with a truly laudable Ambition ; inſpire with noble Sentiments and Diſpoſitions, and fit them for publick Service.

BUT one thing more I would call to mind on this Subject is, That while this Philoſophy prevail'd in *Greece,* and produc'd its moſt glorious Effects, every kind of Philoſophy had fair play ; Truth and Virtue maintain'd the Aſcendant over all falſe, narrow Notions of human Nature, Virtue and Happineſs by the mere Force of Reaſon and Truth : Every Encroachment upon Liberty of Examination, Wit and Argument, is diametrically oppoſite to the Spirit and Genius of true Philoſophy.　Truth and Virtue can only make Proſelytes by perſuaſion : They deſire no other Conqueſt : 'Tis Reaſon alone that makes rational : 'Tis true Philoſophy alone that can detect the Abſurdity of the falſe : 'Tis by Teaching and Inſtruction alone that Men can be enlighten'd and informed.

The true Philoſophy was not promoted by force.

ANOTHER

(51) *Philostratus Iconum, lib.* 1. 10. *Amphion.* Amphion autem quid præ ſe fert ? Quid aliud quam cantum ? Et altera quidem manus mentem ad plectrum intendit, ipſeque tantundem exerit dentium, quantum canenti ſit ſatis. Canit autem, ut puto, terram, quod omnium ſit genetrix atque mater.　Iila vero muros dat ſpontaneo motu conſurgentes.　Coma autem jucunda etiam ſine ornatu eſt, fronti quidem oberrans, una vero cum lanugine ſecundum autem deſcendens eamque fulgore colluſtrans. Gratiam autem majorem mitta quoque addit, quam gratias ei texuiſſe ferunt.——In tumulo autem ſedet, pede pulſum edens cantui reſpondentem, dextráque fides tractans fallit : Et altera manus recta promiſſos habet digitos quod ſolam fingendi artem exprimere auſuram crederem.　Eſto. Quæ vero ad lapides pertinent quomodo ſe habent ? Omnes ad cantum concurrunt, & audiunt, ac mutus fiunt, & pars quidem jam ſurrexit, pars in eo eſt ut conſurgat,

pars modo aſſecuta eſt ceteros.　Æmuli lapides ac jucundi, Muſicæque obſequentes.　Mutus autem portis patet ſeptem, quot nempe lytæ fuere toni.　See a like Picture of *Orpheus* by the younger *Philostratus,* N° 6.

(52) *Callistrati Statuæ,* N° 7. *in Orphei Statua.*

(53) *Illic Orphea protinus videbis*
Udi vertice lubricum th eatri,
Mirantesque feras, avemque regis
Raptum quæ Phryga pertulit ſonanti.
　　　　　　　　Mart. l. 10. Ep. 19.

(54) So *Propertius,*
Saxa Cithæronis Thebas agitata per artem
Sponte ſua in muri membra coïſſe ferunt. Lib. 3. El. 2.

(55) *De Sapientia veterum in Præfatione.*

*An Observation
of Strabo, and
other Ancients, con-
cerning good Authors
and Artists.*

ANOTHER Obfervation with refpect to the Progrefs and Declenfion of the Arts is, that good Authors always have been and muft neceflarily be good Men. The learned and wife *Strabo* (56) makes this Remark, and reafons upon it at great length.

" THE Ancients (faith he) confider'd Poetry as the moft proper Art to teach Morals, or to
" form the Youth early to the Love of Virtue, and to point out the Rules of Life and Con-
" duct to them; on account of its being capable of rendring its Leflons at once fo agreeable
" and fo inftructive, or of giving Beauties and Charms to what is really ufeful and profitable.
" For this reafon anciently throughout *Greece*, the Youth were early inftructed in all the Vir-
" tues and Duties of Life by truly philofophical Poetry ; not merely for Pleafure and Amufe-
" ment, but to form them early to a perfect Notion of Harmony of every kind, by one and
" the fame Labour; of moral Harmony above all others. And who can think a true Poet,
" when he introduces Orators, Generals, and other great Perfonages acting noble, con-
" fiftent, and becoming Parts; a mere Trickfter or Babbler, who only propofes to aftonifh
" his Readers with pompous Tales, or fpecious flattering Fables that have no farther, or
" more ferious and ufeful Intent? Can we poflibly imagine, that the Genius, Power and Ex-
" cellence of a real Poet confifts in aught elfe, but the juft Imitation of Life, in form'd Dif-
" courfe and Numbers? But how fhould he be that juft Imitator of Life, whilft he himfelf
" knows not its Meafures? For we have not furely the fame Notion of the Poet's Excellence
" as of the ordinary Craftfman's, the Subject of whofe Art is fenfelefs Timber or Stone,
" without Life, Dignity or Beauty; whilft the Poet's Art turning principally on Men and
" Manners, he has his Virtue and Excellence as Poet, naturally annexed to human Excellence,
" and to the Worth and Dignity of Man : Infomuch that it is impoflible he fhould be a great
" and worthy Poet, who is not firft a worthy good Man."

CICERO and *Quintilian* obferve the fame with refpect to Orators: And according to all the Ancients it is impoflible that true Judgment and Ingenuity fhould refide, where Harmony and Honefty have no Being; or where there is not a full and ftrong Senfe of the Excellence of Virtue, and of the Diffonance of Vice; of the noble End to which human Nature is framed to afpire, and of the Meannefs of all inferiour Purfuits.

NOW what *Strabo*, and thefe other Authors fay of Poets and Orators, extends equally to all the Imitators of moral Life : For tho' the Artifts, who defign merely after Bodies and the Beauties of the corporeal kind, can never with all their Accuracy or Correctnefs of Defign, be able to mend their own Figure, or become more fhapely and proportion'd in their Perfons; yet as for all thofe who copy from another Life, who ftudy the Graces and Perfections of Minds, and are real Mafters of thofe Rules which conftitute this moral Science, 'tis impoflible they fhould fail of being themfelves improv'd and reform'd in their better part. But this is no lefs the Study of the Painter, Statuary, and Sculptor, than of the Poet. For the Perfection of thefe Arts, as well as that of their Sifter Poetry, lies in reprefenting or imitating the Fair and Beautiful of Sentiments and Affections, Actions and Characters.

THE noble Author (57) fo often already quoted, takes notice of this Remark with great applaufe. And he adds, that the Maxim will hardly be difproved by Hiftory or Fact, either in refpect of Philofophers themfelves, or others who were the greateft Genius's or Mafters in the Liberal Arts. The Characters of the two beft *Roman* Poets are well known : Thofe of the ancient Tragedians are no lefs : And the great *Epick* Mafter, though of a far obfcurer and remoter Age, was ever prefum'd to be far enough from a vile or knavifh Character. The *Roman* as well as *Grecian* Orator was true to his Country ; and died in like manner a Martyr for its Liberty. And thofe Hiftorians, who are of higheft Value, were either in a private Life approv'd good Men, or noted for fuch by their Actions in the publick.

. AS for the beft ancient Painters, it hath already been remark'd, that they were not only faithfully attach'd to their Art, and to that moral Truth and Beauty in which its Excellence principally confifts ; but that they were far removed from Senfuality, and a mercenary, unfocial, ungenerous Spirit ; or at leaft not addicted to any folitary, inhuman,
cruel

(56) Quamobrem Græcorum civitates, ab ipfo primordio, eorum liberos in poetica erudierunt, non nudæ utique voluptatis, fed caftæ moderationis gratia.——Quæ ab ineunte nos ætate ad vivendi rationes adducat quæ res gerendas cum jucunditate præcipiat. A qua quidem ipfi mufici cantus, & lyræ, & tibiarum modos edocentes, hanc fibi virtutem vendicant, feque morum magiftros, & emendatores effe profitentur. Hæc ipfa non modo a Pythagoricis audire licet, Verum etiam Ariftoxenus hujus eft fententiæ. Et Homerus cantores, calligatores appellavit, ficuti Clytemneftræ cuftodem illum, &c. *Strab. lib.* 1. *p.* 14. And again, *p.* 16. Quis igitur poeta, qui alios oratores, alios imperatores, alios reliqua virtutis opera demonftrantur decenter inducat, nugatorem quem-

piam & hiftrionem effe putet, qui auditorem magnificis tantum miraculis afficere, & affentationibus demulcere valeat, cum nihil afferre queat adjumenti? Num poetæ virtutem aliam dixerimus quam quæ verbis ad imitandum vivendi rationem excitaret ? Quonam vero modo is imitaretur, qui vivendi rationis imperitus & infipiens foret ? Non enim ficuti vel fabrorum vel ædificatorum, ita & poetarum effe memoramus. Sed hanc quidem nihil boni, nihil honefti conchnere. Ipfa vero poetæ virtus & hominis boni conjuncta eft : Sed vero poetam bonum effe poffe, nifi prius vir bonus exiftat.

(57) *Char. Vol.* 1. *p.* 208.

I

cruel Vice. The beſt of them, on the contrary, were ſevere in the Diſcipline and Cónduct · of their Lives, as well as in that of their Works (58).

THESE, together with a few others that were mentioned in former Chapters, are the principal moral Cauſes to which the Progreſs and Decline of the Liberal Arts are aſcribed by ancient Writers. The ingenious Author of the *Refleétions on Poetry and Painting*, gives a full and true Detail of the Facts relating to this Queſtion, in that Seétion wherein he inquires into the Cauſes of the Improvement and Deciiſie of the Arts in *Greece* and *Rome*. But he thinks moral Cauſes, tho' they muſt certainly have a very great Influence, are not ſufficient fully to explain this Phenomenon. " He remarks (59), with good reaſon, *Remarks on what*
" that 'twas not in the Times of profoundeſt Peace and Quiet, that the Arts were at the greateſt *is ſaid by an inge-*
" Heighth amongſt the *Greeks* and *Romans*, or amongſt the *Italians*, in the latter Age *nious Author in na-*
" of Painting and Sculpture. The Wars (faith he) between the *Athenians*, the *Thebans*, *tural Caufes.*
" and the *Lacedemonians*, and thoſe of *Philip* againſt the other *Greeks*, were much more
" direful in their Conſequences and Duration, than thoſe of *Alexander*, his Succeſſors, or
" of the *Romans* in *Greece :* Yet thoſe firſt Wars hinder'd not that wonderful Progreſs of
" the Arts and Sciences there, which is ſuch a Glory to human Genius. The *Greeks* after
" they became a *Roman* Province, enjoy'd for the moſt part a profound Tranquillity ; their
" Subjeétion to the *Romans* was rather a kind of Homage that ſecured their Peace and Eaſe,
" than a heavy oppreſſive Servitude. In like manner the great Men who compoſed what
" is called the *Auguſtan* Age, were already form'd before the more peaceful Days of that
" Reign commenc'd. Who knows not how cruel and bloody the firſt Years of that Age
" were? *Virgil* himſelf thus deſcribes them :

" *Quippe ubi fas verſum atque nefas, tot bella per orbem*
" *Tam multæ ſcelerum facies : Non ullus aratro*
" *Dignus honos, ſqualent abduétis arva colonis,*
" *Et curvæ rigidum falces conflantur in enſem.*
" *Hinc movet Euphrates, illinc Germania Bellum :*
" *Vicinæ ruptis inter ſe legibus urbes*
" *Arma ferunt : ſævit toto Mars impius orbe.*   Geor. 1. ver. 505.

" THE Men of the greateſt Diſtinétion and Merit were terribly haraſſed by the Pro-
" ſcriptions. Did not *Cicero* fall a Martyr to his Talents and Merit in that miſerable time?

" *Largus & exundans Letho dedit ingenii fons*
" *Ingenio manus eſt & cervix cæſa.*———Juv. Sat. 10. ver. 118. ·

" HORACE was Thirty at the Battle of *Aétium*; and in fine, tho' the Magnificence of
" *Auguſtus*, encouraged the great Poets and Genius's of every kind, yet the beſt Authors were
" already become great Men before that Encouragement.

" IN the ſame manner, the Declenſion of the Arts happened in *Italy*, preciſely in the
" moſt peaceable Times that Country had ſeen ſince the Deſtruétion of the *Roman* Empire.
" During thirty-four Years, *Italy* (as her own Hiſtorians expreſs it) was trod under foot by
" barbarous Nations; the Kingdom of *Naples* was conquer'd four or five times by different
" Princes; and the State of *Milan* changed Maſters much oftener; *Rome* was ſacked by
" *Charles* the Vth; and *Florence* was almoſt in continual War, either againſt the *Medici* who
" endeavoured to ſubdue and enſlave it, or againſt *Piſa* which they would gladly have brought
" under their Yoke : yet it was preciſely in theſe Years, that Letters and the fine Arts made
" ſuch Progreſs in *Italy*, as ſeems yet ſo prodigious and aſtoniſhing."

HENCE this Author infers, that Peace, Tranquillity, Plenty and other moral Cauſes are not ſufficient to produce the fine Arts and bring them to Perfeétion, or to account for their Riſe, Progreſs and Declenſion.

NOW here I would beg leave to obſerve that ancient Authors, *Cicero* (60) in particular, have very juſtly remark'd, on the one hand, that Eloquence and all the fine Arts are the Fruit and Produét, the Companion of Peace, Proſperity, and outward Eaſe.· In an expoſed, indigent State, a People cannot have either that full Leiſure, or eaſy Diſpoſition, which are requiſite to raiſe them to any Curioſity of Speculation. They who are neither ſafe from Violence,

(58) Inſtances of their Auſterity, Attachment to their Art, and Regularity in their Conduét, have been mentioned in the Account given of them. They were found to have obſerv'd the Rule recommended by *Petronius* to all who aim at Perfeétion in any Art or Science, the ſublimer ones more eſpecially.

   Artis ſeveræ ſiquis amat effeétus,
   Mentemque magnis applicat ; prius more
 · *Frugalitatis lege polleat exaéta,* &c.

(59) *Reflexions Critiques, &c. Seét.* 13. *part* 2. Qu'il eſt probable que les cauſes phyſiques ont auſſi leur part aux progrez ſurprenants des Lettres & des Arts.

(60) Sed tum ſere Pericles, Xantippi filius de quo ante dixi, primus adhibuit doétrinam : Quæ quanquam tunc nulla erat dicendi, tamen ab Anaxagora phyſico eruditus, exercitationem mentis a reconditis, abſtruſiſque rebus ad cauſas forenſes popularſque facile traduxit.——Hæc igitur ætas prima Athenis oratorem prope perfeétum tulit. Nec enim in conſtituentibus rempublicam, nec in bella gerentibus, nec in impeditis, ac regum dominatione devinétis naſci cupiditas dicendi ſolet. Pacis eſt comes, Otiique ſocia, & jam bene conſtitutæ civitatis quaſi alumna quædam eloquentia. Itaque ait Ariſtoteles, &c. *Cicer. de Clar. Orat.* N° 11, & 12.

lence, nor fecure of Plenty, are not in a Situation to engage in unneceffary Studies. When a Republick is unfettled, or in time of ravaging Wars, the Defire of Knowledge and the Love of Arts is not likely to rife and fpread. This Temper, Difpofition, and Genius, is the Product of Peace and Security; but of what Peace? Of Peace which refults from a well-eftablifh'd Government, from Profperity and Liberty fixed upon a fure and folid Foundation, and guarded by the Love of Liberty's watchful jealous Eye. 'Tis not under Slavery and lawlefs Domination; 'tis not among a fubdued, conquered People (whatever Peace they may enjoy) that the Arts can begin, or make proficiency.

The Danger of Peace and Plenty.

BUT, on the other hand, 'tis equally true that Opulence and profound Quiet, if due care be not taken to prevent it, are apt to lull the Mind into a profound Lethargy, apt to effeminate and enervate It. And therefore the Evils flowing from Peace are often pronounced by the Ancients, more dangerous to Virtue, Liberty, and all that is Good and Great in Society, than thofe Wars and Contefts which keep the Mind awake, lively and vigilant, roufe the Spirits, inflame the Love of Liberty, by keeping up a warm Senfe of publick Good, and of our Obligations to contend for it vigoroufly. Nothing hath ever prov'd fo fatal to Virtue, Science, and good Tafte, as the poifonous Sweets of Riches and profound Tranquillity : Thefe unbend, foften and unman the Soul, and are therefore juftly called Corrupters; againft which every particular Perfon for his own fake; and every Society for its Prefervation (60) cannot keep too ftrict and fevere a guard. In fuch a State, Vice rufhes up as in its proper Soil; Indolence, Senfuality and Avarice are naturally engendred, and quickly fpread their Contagion far and wide. "And "what place is there amidft thefe Vices (faith an excellent (61) Author) for the good Arts? No "more certainly than for wholefome Fruits and Grains in a Field over-run with rank and "hurtful Weeds." In fact, the greateft Genius's for any of the Arts have always appeared in times that tended to ftir up and awake the generous manly Temper, and to keep the Mind from finking into Sloth and Effeminacy. Hence it was an ancient Proverb, " *Plus nocuere* " *toga, quam lorica* (62)."

'TIS well worth the Politician's Thoughts to confider ferioufly this Tendency amongft Mankind to Corruption and Degeneracy, in confequence of, what on other accounts is fo highly defirable, Peace and Plenty ; and to inquire if any effectual Remedy may be provided againft it. No Topick hath indeed afforded a greater Source of Railing againft human Nature, to thofe who delight to paint Mankind in the worft Colours; and to gather together all that tends to blacken and reproach our excellent Frame. But was this the proper place for engaging in fo profound an Enquiry, I think it might be made appear, that even this Phenomenon, however ftrange and unaccountable it feems to be at firft fight, takes its rife from Principles and Caufes that are in themfelves exceeding good and ufeful, and that afford a moft convincing proof of our being made to be active and virtuous, and to be happy only in being fo. The Ancients have made feveral very deep and profitable Reflections on this Subject : We are here in a probationary State; this Life is but the firft School of Virtue : And therefore not merely Adverfity, but chiefly Profperity is intended to be a Trier, an Explorer; and, by that means, the Occafion and Means of exerting, proving, and perfecting many great and noble Virtues (63).

BUT not to leave our prefent Subject, the ingenious Author whofe Remarks I am now tracing and criticizing, hath laid together feveral very curious Obfervations to prove the Power of phyfical Caufes in producing Effects that may be properly called moral. He feems to think that the Differences of Character, whereby Nations are fo remarkably diftinguifh'd ; the Changes in refpect of Character, Temper, and Genius, which happen in the fame Nation ; and by confequence the Rife, Progrefs and Declenfion of Arts, muft in a great meafure be owing to Air, Diet, Climate, Soil, bodily Conftitution, and fuchlike continually varying Caufes.

Phyfical Caufes have, and ought to have fome Influence on our Minds.

AND here again I would obferve, that without doubt, phyfical Caufes have a very great Influence upon our Minds, in confequence of our Frame and Conftitution, and all our

(60) *Cum tu inter Scabiem tantam & Contagia lucri*
Nil parvum fapias ;——
Hor. Epift. lib. 1. Ep. 12. ver. 14.
So Cicero : Ex hac copia, atque omnium rerum affluentia, primum illa nata funt arrogantia, quæ a majoribns noftris alterum Capua confulem poftulavit : Deinde ea luxuries, quæ ipfum Hannibalem armis ipfis etiam tum invictum, voluptate vicit. Cic. Orat. de Leg. Agraria, N° 35. So Pliny, lib. 36. 6. Poftquam altæ fecuræque pacis mala in republica invaluere, picturæ quoque dignatio imminuta eft, & marmoris ac ligni maculis pretium acceffit.
Nihil eft tam mortiferum ingeniis quam luxuria, fays Seneca, lib. 1. Controv. in Proæm. So Salluft frequently both in his Bell. Catil. & Jugurt.
Nunc patimur longæ pacis mala : Sævior armis Luxuria incubuit, victumque ulcifcitur orbem.
Juv. Sat. 6. ver. 291.
(61) *Quint. lib.* 12. *c.* 1. Et quis inter hæc bonis artibus locus? Non Hercle magis quam frugibus in terra

fentibus ac rubis occupata.——Where he goes on to the fame purpofe. Age, non ad perferendos ftudiorum labores neceffaria frugalitas ? Quid ergo ex libidine aut avaritia fpei ? Non præcipue acuit ad cupiditatem literarum amor laudis ? Num igitur malis effe laudem curæ putamus.

(62) *Tertul. de Pallio.*

(63) *Tacitus* makes a very fagacious and ufeful Reflection on this Subject, in the Speech he makes Galba pronounce to Pifo. Fortunam adhuc tantum adverfam tulifti, fecundæ res acrioribus ftimulis animum explorant : Quia miferiæ tolerantur, felicitate corrumpimur. Fidem, libertatem, amicitiam, præcipua humani animi bona, tu quidem Conftantia retinebis : Sed alii per obfequium imminuent, irrumpet adulatio, Blanditiæ peffimum veri affectus venenum, fua cuique utilitas, &c. *Hift. lib.* 1. *p.* 189. *Lip. Fol.*

our intellectual or moral Powers and Faculties: The Obfervation is very ancient (64); many Authorities might be added to thofe our Author hath brought to prove it. And though perhaps we are hardly able to fay more of this Phænomenon in the phyfical way, than in general, that it is the natural and unavoidable Refult of the reciprocal Union and Connection of our Mind and Body ; fince it is hardly conceivable that an organical Frame or Syftem of Senfes can fubfift, without a dependence upon the Laws of Matter and Motion : Yet as for the moral or final Gaufe of this mutual Dependence of Body and Mind, it is very manifeft ; for without an organical Frame, or without Bodies, we could not have communication with the fenfible World, from which however, fuch Ideas, Perceptions and Images; fuch Materials of Knowledge and Arts; and fuch Subjects, Means and Occafions of Virtues are derived, as plainly conftitute a very noble firft State of progreffive Being (65), without which Nature would not be full or coherent. But leaving this Reflection to the Purfuit of Philofophers, I fhall obferve in the next place.*

THAT as dependent as the human Mind is upon the Body in its prefent State of Exiftence ; and by confequence upon every thing that influences or affects the Body, that is upon all the Laws of Matter and Motion ; yet this Dependence extends not fo far as that Virtue and Genius can be faid to depend chiefly upon mechanical Caufes not within our power ; fince we are confcious to ourfelves of being capable of improving in Virtue and in Knowledge, in proportion to our Zeal and Affiduity to improve and advance in every rational Quality and Perfection, without arriving at any unfurmountable Obftacle.

But this Influence does not extend fo far as to render Progrefs in Virtue and Knowledge quite beyond our power.

THE chief or moft remarkable Dependence of Mankind in refpect of Caufes not entirely fubject to the fingle Will of every one, is our dependence on Education, and the right Frame of civil Government, which is in its Nature a focial Dependence: The Progrefs of the Arts and Sciences, as well as innumerable other Bleffings of Life, depend greatly on the Care of Society to encourage, affift, and promote them ; and particularly on its Care about Education. Nor can it be otherwife with regard to Beings made for Society, and fitted to acquire Knowledge, and to refine and polifh Life gradually, by united Study and Induftry. This is the Law of Nature, with refpect to our Improvement in Sciences, and all ufeful or ornamental Arts : " That Knowledge fhall " be advanced and improved in proportion to our Application to cultivate and promote " it in a focial confederate way, by joining and combining our natural Stocks and Forces " for that end." And this Law of our Natures is admirably well fuited to us as focial Beings ; it is excellently adjufted to every Affection of our Mind, and to every Circumftance in our prefent State and Condition. Yet the natural and neceffary Confequence of fuch a Conftitution is, that Men muft be formed into regular and well-conftituted Societies and Governments, in order to bring human Life to its Perfection, and to attain all thofe valuable and glorious Advantages which the Virtues and Arts, if duly cultivated, would naturally produce. If Society is agreeably framed and modelled for producing and perfecting the Arts and Sciences, no Climate, no Soil will be found fo repugnant and averfe to Genius, Learning, and polite Tafte, but that thefe will quickly grow up in it to a very great heighth of Beauty and Vigour. But on the other hand, however favourable all other outward Circumftances may be, 'tis no lefs impoffible, that the Arts and Sciences fhould profper in a State, where it is no part of its Aim and Scope to encourage and promote them ; than that the Fruits peculiar to any Soil or Climate fhould come to perfection in it, without the proper Culture they neceffarily require. Education muft be taken care of with that View, and all the neceffary means of their Improvement muft be fkilfully and honeftly imployed. The Arts and Sciences did not fpring up at *Athens* fpontaneoufly, and as it were of themfelves ; their Conftitution was excellently adapted to breed, nourifh and perfect them ; and no proper appofite Means were neglected for their Cultivation and Improvement.

The chief Dependence of Virtue and the Arts on Caufes beyond our power, it a focial Dependence.

OUR Author in purfuance of his Conjectures about the Influences of natural Caufes upon the Progrefs and Decline of Arts, pays no fmall Compliment to the *Englifh* Genius ; and takes particular notice of the Efteem and Love of Painting and Sculpture that hath eminently appear'd in *England* on many occafions. For which reafon he feems

to

(64) *Cicero Oratio de Lege Agrar.* Nº 35. Non ingenerantur hominibus mores tam a ftirpe generis, ac feminis, quam ex iis rebus, quæ ab ipfa natura loci, & a vitæ confuetudine fuppeditantur ; quibus alimur & vivimus. Carthaginienfes, fraudulenti, & mendaces, non genere, fed natura loci, quod propter portus fuos, multis & variis mercatorum, & advenarum fermonibus, ad ftudium fallendi, ftudio quæftus vocabantur. Ligures, Montani, Duri atque Agreftes. Docuit ager ipfe, nihil ferendo, nifi multa cultura & magno labore quæfitum. Campani, femper fuperbi, bonitate agrorum & fructuum magnitudine, urbis falubritate, pulchritudine. Singularis homo privatus, nifi magna fapientia præditus, vix facile fefe regionibus officii magnis in fortunis & copiis continet : Nedum ifti, ab Rullo, & Rulli fimilibus conquifiti, atque electi Coloni; Capuæ, in Domicilio fuperbiæ, atque in fedibus luxuriæ collocati non ftatim conquifituri funt aliquid fceleris & flagitii.

(65) *Pope's* Effay on Man.

F f

to imagine, that this Country's not having produc'd, wholly of its own Growth, any confiderable Hiftory-Painter, can hardly be attributed to any thing elfe, but to our Climate, Air, Diet, or fome fuch other phyfical Caufe.

BUT, in truth, other reafons are not far to feek, by which this Effect may be fufficiently explained and accounted for. The fine Arts have never had any place in Liberal Education amongft us: We have not yet had the neceffary Means for improving, or even for calling forth Genius of this kind, duly eftablifh'd and fupported amongft us. Academies or Schools for thefe Arts, well furnifh'd with the requifite Models for Study and Imitation, are even yet wanting. No Country, in modern Times, hath produced better Painters with Words: And therefore without entring farther into the Enquiry, why Painting hath never been promoted and encouraged amongft us as it deferves; we may teft fatisfied that there can be no phyfical Obftacle in the way: For furely the Climate cannot be too cold, nor the Air too grofs, to bring forth even an *Apelles* or a *Raphael*, that produced a *Milton*.

FROM what hath been faid we may fee how neceffary a free, generous, publick-fpirited Government or Conftitution is to produce, but more efpecially to uphold and promote, the Liberal Arts and Sciences; and how amicably they all confpire to illuftrate and perfect one another; and to fupport and improve the virtuous Temper, from which alone they can receive proper Nourifhment, Beauty, and Vigour. This was the conftant Doctrine of the better Ancients, and is very evident from Hiftory.

CHAP. VI.

Obfervations on the Ufes to which Painting and Sculpture were employed among the Ancients; the noble Purpofes to which they ought to be apply'd in order to adorn human Society, promote and reward Virtue and publick Spirit; and on the Objections that are brought againft the Encouragement of them.

Of the Ufes to which Pictures were applied.

EVERY one knows that Painting and Sculpture were the principal Ornaments of Temples, Schools, Academies, Theatres, Portico's, and in general of all publick Buildings in *Greece*, at *Athens* in particular. But in order to have a Notion of the excellent Purpofes to which the defigning Arts ought to be employed; it is not amifs to obferve, that while Virtue, publick Spirit, and the Arts prevailed in *Greece*, due Honour was paid by them to the Merit of every worthy and deferving Citizen : Pictures and

To preferve the Memory of great Men and ufeful Deeds.

Statues were erected in publick Places to preferve the Memory of their Virtues, and to excite others to follow their excellent Example. This Honour was done to all who had deferv'd well of their Country, and had diftinguifh'd themfelves either in the Arts of War or of Peace; to every virtuous good Man; to Philofophers, Poets, Painters, and to every ingenious Artift; but chiefly to thofe who had ferved the Publick with Integrity, Bravery, and Wifdom as Magiftrates or Generals. *Paufanias* abounds with Defcriptions of Images of this kind, Portraits, Statues, or Bufts. At *Athens*, in the place called the Court of the Five Hundred, there were many fuch Monuments. With the Statues of *Jupiter* and *Apollo* by *Pifias*, and one reprefenting the People of *Athens* by *Lyfon*, were placed feveral Pictures of Legiflators and Patriots, among whom was *Olbyades*, who had remarkably exerted himfelf at *Thermopyle* : All which were painted by the famous *Protogenes* (1). The fame Author mentions a Picture of *Themiftocles*, confecrated to his Memory by his Son in the *Parthenion*, or the Temple of *Minerva* the Virgin, at *Athens*: A little after, is mentioned one of *Leofthenes*, and his Children. And in the fame Book he fpeaks of Statues not only of illuftrious Men, but likewife of illuftrious Women. There were confecrated in Temples, and in other publick Places, Statues or Portraits of all their Heroes, as of *Lycurgus, Callias, Demofthenes, Pericles, Ariftides,*

Some Inftances.

Miltiades, Iphicrates, Olympiodorus, and many others. *Ifocrates* (fays *Paufanias*) was placed among the greateft Heroes, becaufe he had left three excellent Examples to Pofterity for their Imitation : One of his Conftancy and Perfeverance in teaching the Youth, which they confidered as a very noble and ufeful Employment (2) to the State, having continued to reach till he was ninety-eight : Another, of fingular Modefty, which made

him

---

(1) *Paufanias, lib.* 1. The Examples here named are in the firft Book of *Paufanias*. But in every Page almoft of that Author, there are Inftances of this Ufe of the defigning Arts.

(2) This was the Sentiment of all the greateft Men of Antiquity about the Importance of Education to pri-

vate or publick Happinefs. Quod enim Munus reip. afferre majus, meliufve poffumus, quam fi docemus, atque erudimus juventutem ? His præfertim moribus, atque temporibus: quibus ita prolapfa eft, ut omnium opibus refrænanda ac coercenda fit. *Cicero de Dam. l.* 2. *init.*

him fhun all other publick Offices, and devote himfelf intirely to the Bufinefs of Education : And a third, of Love and Zeal for Liberty (3).

ALL the Poets had likewife this honour paid to them ; *Homer, Hefiod, Sophocles, Euripides, Menander, Æfchylus ;* to the Memory of the laft, *Paufanias* tells us, a Picture was confecrated on account of his brave Behaviour at the Battle of *Marathon.* The Philofophers were not neglected ; nor indeed were any Perfons of Merit overlooked. This appears from the Statue of *Æfop* erected at *Athens,* to fhew, fays *Phædrus,* that the Road to true Honour lies open to all in a well-govern'd State.

Perfons of Merit of all Ranks.

A Statue of Æfop.

> *Æfopi ingenio ftatuam pofuere Attici,*
> *Servumque collocarunt æterna in bafi ;*
> *Patere honoris fcirent ut cuncti viam,*
> *Nec geneti tribui, fed virtuti gloriam.*   Phædrus.

SOON after *Socrates* was cruelly condemned, the *Athenians* repented bitterly of it, and banifhed fome of his Accufers, and punifhed others of them with Death, and erected a brafs Statue of *Socrates* in the moft remarkable place of *Athens* (4).

AS their Gods (5) were diftinguifh'd in Painting and Sculpture by certain Attributes or Symbols ; fo were the Images of their Great Men. They were not merely Portraits of their outward Forms, but they were principally intended to commemorate their noble Virtues and ufeful Deeds ; and to ftir up a worthy Emulation in the Breaft of every Beholder.

Proper Symbols were given to Heroes and others.

HEROES were often reprefented without Sandals, with Beards, and the Lion's Skin, fuch as *Hercules* wears in Statues, and as he was anciently painted (6). They were frequently reprefented as carried up to Heaven by an Eagle, and with a kind of bright Cloud about their Heads, and the *Medufa* upon their Breaft-plates ; as *Pallas* is painted by *Virgil.*

Some Examples, Heroes.

> *Jam fummas arces Tritonia, refpice, Pallas*
> *Infedit, nimbo effulgens, & Gorgone fæva :*   Æn. 2. ver. 613.

To this Cuftom he alfo alludes. *Æn.* 6. 779.

> ————*Viden' ut geminæ ftent vertice criftæ,*
> *Et pater ipfe fuo fuperûm jam fignet honore* (7) ?

THE

---

(3) *Pauf. lib.* 1. *p.* 16. *Edit. Wechel.*

(4) Poft damnatum Socratem, tanta mox pœnitentia ejus rei Athenienfes cœpit, ut gymnafia clauderent ; ut accufatores Socratis partem exilio, partem morte mulctarent : at Socrati ipfi ftatuam æneam ftatuerent in loco Celeberrimo Athenis. Sentit Plutarchus in eo libello cui titulus eft *De odio & invidia,* quod Athenienfes adeo oderunt, averfatique funt Socratis calumniatores, ut neque eis ignem accendere, neque interrogantibus refpondere, neque aqua illa in qua hi fe abluiffent uti voluerint, fed eam petinde ac fceleratam eff undi jufferint : proinde illi cum odium tam atrox perpeti diutius non poffent fufpendio fefe necaverunt. Verum non folum puniendi fuerant accufatores Socratis, verum etiam Judicis mulctandi, qui damnantes Socratem injuftiffimo judicio, ipfam virtutem damnare atque exfcindere vifi funt. Quod crimen eo atrocius judicandum quod Athenienfes & erant & habebantur prudentes, eruditi, humani & legiflatores optimi : unde humanitas, religio, doctrina, Jura, leges ortæ, atque in omnes diftributæ putantur. See *Apuleii Afin. Aur. l.* 10. *cum Commentar. Philippi Beroaldi.*

(5) What *Plutarch* tells us of the ancient Images of the Gods, is very remarkable. Prifci theologi, philofophorum vetuftiffimi, inftrumenta mufica in manus deorum imaginibus pofuerunt : non fane quod eos lyra aut tibia ludere putarent ; fed quod nullum Deo opus convenientius effe judicarent, quam confonantiam & harmoniam. *Pluarch. περι της εν Τιμαιω ψυχογονιας.* And *Ælian* makes the following Remark on the ancient Images of the Mufes: Statuas & imagines, quas nobis ars fictorum exhibet, non ofcitanter aut obiter fpectare foleo : nam in his etiam ars manuaria judicium aliquod fapientiamque adhibet. Atque id fic fe habere, cum ex multis aliis confici poteft, tum ex eo potiffimum, quod nemo pictorum feu plaftarum aufus eft unquam mufis, filiabus Jovis, adulterinas atque alienas fpecies effingere ; neque quifquam opificum tam eft a ratione

alienus, qui eas armatas exhibuerit. Certiffimo argumento, vitam qnæ mufis tribuitur placidam, facilem, tranquillamque iis effe oportere. *Ælian. var. Hift.* 14. 37.

(6) Heroas quoque in pellibus olim pingebant fingebantque, fays the old Scholiaft upon *Apollonius Rhodius, Argonaut. lib.* 1. *veri* 324. Pellem habere Hercules fingitur, ut homines cultus antiqui admoneantur, fays *Feftus.* Suidas in his Ἡρακλῆς tells us how *Hercules* was reprefented in Statues ; and *Cedrenus,* how he was painted. Lautia, fandalia, crepidæ, calcei, ægrotantium funt geftamina, vel fenum. Pictores itaque muniunt Philoctetum Calceis, tanquam claudum & ægrum : Sinopenfem vero philofophum, & Thebanum Cratetem, & Ajacem, & Achillem difcalceatos pingunt : at Jafonem ex parte dimidia. Fertur enim fluvium Anaurum tranfiturus. *Philof. Epif. in Epif. ad excalceatum Adilefcentem.* See likewife *Hyginus, fab.* 12 ; and *Macrob. in fomn. Scip. lib.* 5. *c.* 18. Hence *Val. Maximus* takes notice of it as fomething unufual. *L.* Scipionis Afiatici ftatuam chlamydatam & excalceatam in capitolio fuiffe, *lib.* 3. *c.* 6. So *Cicer. Orat. pro Rabirio pofthumo. L.* Scipionis qui bellum in Afia geffit, Antiochumque devicit, non folum cum Chlamyde, fed etiam cum Crepidis in capitolio ftatuam vidimus. Heroes non fuerunt folliti tondere barbam. See *Servius in Æn.* 3. *ver.* 393. They ufed likewife to have a Dog by them. See *Pollucis Onomafticon, lib.* 1. *c.* 4.

(7) See *Servius* upon thefe places. As for their being carry'd up to Heav'n, there is a beautiful Agate in the King of *France's* Cabinet, reprefenting *Germanicus* carried up to Heaven upon an Eagle, with the augural Batton in one hand, and a Cornucopia in the other, while the Ægis on his Breaft, and a Victory crowning him. This was made by the Monks of *St. Evre* at *Toul* for St. *John* upon an Eagle crown'd by an Angel. When they found it to be Pagan, they made no difficulty of parting with it. There is another Agate of an exquifite

THE Serpent was not the Symbol of *Æscupalius* only, but was confecrated to *Jupiter, Apollo,* and other Gods; and likewife to Heroes (8).

THUS on the Shield of *Epaminondas,* which was fixed on a Pillar, erected to his Memory, was engraved a Serpent.

MARTIAL Heroes were frequently done with Thunder in their Hands, as *Alexander* was painted by *Apelles.*

THEY are called by the Poets, as *Virgil* does the *Scipio's,*

——— *Fulmina belli* (9). Æn. 6. 841. (10)

THOSE who excelled in the Arts of Peace were crowned with Olive, and held fre. quently fome religious Utenfil in their Hand; as *Virgil* defcribes *Numa Pompilius* appearing to *Æneas.*

> *Quis procul ille autem ramis infignis Olivæ,*
> *Sacra ferens? Nofco crines incanaque menta*
> *Regis Romani; primus qui legibus urbem*
> *Fundabit, curibus parvis & paupere terra*
> *Miffus in imperium magnum.* Æn. 6. 808.

THOSE who had polifhed Life with ufeful Arts had their Heads wreathed with Fillets; to which Cuftom *Virgil* likewife alludes:

> *Quique facerdotes cafti, dum vita manebat:*
> *Quique pii Vates, & Phœbo digna locuti:*
> *Inventas aut qui vitam excóluere per artes:*
> *Quique fui memores alios fecére merendo:*
> *Omnibus his niveâ cinguntur tempora vittâ.* Æn. 6. 661.

WE fee *Apollo* giving a Crown to a Poet in one of the Pictures now graved; and there is the Portrait of another in the fame Piece encircled with Laurel.

ÆLIAN tells us, that *Homer* was painted with Streams of pure Water iffuing out of his Mouth, and a Croud of Poets drinking largely of it (11). To fuch a Picture *Ovid* plainly alludes:

> *Adjice Mæoniden, a quo, ceu fonte perenni,*
> *Vatum Pieriis ora rigantur aquis.* Ovid. Amor. El. 9. ver. 25.

So *Manilius,*

> ——— *Cujufque in ore profecto*
> *Omnis pofteritas latices in carmina duxit.* Man. l. 2.

THEY erected Temples to *Homer* in *Smyrna,* as appears from *Cicero* (12); one of thofe is fuppofed to be yet extant, and the fame which they fhew for the Temple of *Janus.* Mr. *Spon* denies this to be the true *Homereum;* but it agrees with *Strabo's* Defcription, a fquare Building of Stone near a River, thought to be the *Meles,* with two

Doors

---

fite Tafte in the fame Collection, in which *Agrippina* and *Germanicus* are reprefented under the Images of *Triptolemus* and *Ceres.* See both thefe defcrib'd in the *Memoirs of the* French *Academy of Literature, tom.* 1. *p.* 276.

(8) *Plutarch* gives the reafon of it in his Life of *Cleomenes:* Where he tells us, that a Serpent being found wreath'd about *Cleomenes's* Head, fo covering all his Face, that no ravenous Creature durft come near him. The King who had put him to death, and all the Ladies of his Court, began to fear that they had highly provok'd the Gods, and made many expiatory Sacrifices for the Purification of this Crime. *Plutarch* adds, that this coming to the knowledge of wife Men, they confecrated the Serpent to Kings and Princes, as friendly unto Men. *Plut. in Cleom. ad fin.* Heroum pictis fictifque imaginibus appofitos olim Dracones. *Macrob. lib.* 1. Saturnal 20, where he likewife gives the reafon, Cur ædium, adytorum, oraculorum, Thefaurorum cuftodia Draconibus affignatur. Junguntur figuræ Draconum quia præftant ut humana corpora, velut infirmitatis pelle depofita ad priftinum revirefcant Vigorem: Ut virefcunt Dracones per annos fingulos pelle fenectutis exuta. *Pompeius Feftus* gives another reafon: Clariffi-

mam dicuntur habere oculorum aciem, qua ex caufa incubantes eos Thefauris cuftodia caufa finxerunt antiqui. Serpenti creduntur multa ineffe remedia, & ideo Æfculapio dicatur. *Plin.* 29. *c.* 4.

(9) So *Lucretius* before him. Scipiades belli fulmen, Carthaginis horror, *l.* 3.

(10) There is an Agate of a very fine Tafte in the King of *France's* Collection, reprefenting *Jupiter* with his Mantle and the Thunder in his Hand, on one fide of an Olive; and *Minerva* on the other with her Cafque on her Head: A Serpent wreaths itfelf about the Tree; and feveral Animals are on the Exerg. It was for a long time underftood to mean *Adam* and *Eve* in Paradife. See it explain'd in the *Memoirs of Literature, tom.* 1. *p.* 373.

(11) Æl. *var. Hift.* 13. 22. Hence probably it is that *Pliny* calls him *Fontem Ingeniorum. Plin. Hift. Nat. l.* 17. *c.* 5.

(12) *Cic. Orat. pro Archia Poeta,* N° 8. Smyrnæi vero fuum effe confirmant. Itaque etiam delubrum ejus in oppido dedicaverunt.

Doors oppofite to each other, North and South, and a large Niche within the Eaſt Wall where the Image ſtood (13). There is a *Greek* Epigram defcribing a Statue of him, in which he is reprefented in a different manner from the ancient Buſts of him that fub- fift at prefent (14). For in thefe he hath a ſhort curl'd Beard, and his Hair comes over his Forehead; but in that Statue he was reprefented according to the Defcription, with a large and long Beard, his Forehead without Hair, and his Head turned afide in a liften- ing Pofture. *His Statue.*

I have an Intaglia of him that agrees exactly with that Defcription; it is finely en- graved, very deep, and *in faccia.*

THE famous Marble in the Palace of *Colonna* at *Rome*, called his Apotheofis, the *His Apotheofis.* Work of *Archelaus* of *Priene*, is well known to the Curious. We fee there a Tem- ple hung with its Veil, where *Homer* is placed on a Seat with a Footſtool to it, juſt as he has defcrib'd the Seats of his Gods; fupported by Figures on each fide, reprefent- ing the Iliad and the Odyffey; the one by a Sword, the other with the Ornament of a Ship, which denotes the Voyages of *Ulyffes*: On each fide of his Footſtool are Mice, in allufion to the Batrachomuomachia: Behind is Time waiting upon him, and a Figure with Turrets on its Head, which fignifies the World, crowning him with Laurel: Before him is an Altar, at which all the Arts are facrificing to him as to their Deity: On one fide of the Altar ſtands a Perfon reprefenting Mythology; on the other, a Woman repre- fenting Hiſtory: After her is Poetry bringing the facred Fire; and in a long Train, Tragedy, Comedy, Nature, Virtue, Memory, Eloquence, and Wifdom, in all their proper Attitudes.

AT the *Panathenæan* Solemnities (15) in honour of *Minerva*, certain Perfons called 'Ραψῳδοὶ, were appointed to fing fome Verfes of *Homer*; and in the fame Feſtival a Herald pronounced with a loud Voice, that the People of *Athens* had given a Crown of Gold to the famous Phyfician *Hippocrates*, for the fignal Services he had done them in the time of the Plague.

ACHILLES is faid to have found out fome Remedy for Wounds, and in me- mory of that he was painted ſhaking fomething from the Point of his Spear into the Wounds of *Telephus* (16).

HEROES were reprefented with their Armour when they had conquer'd and put an Enemy to flight; or with the Spoils and Trophies they had gain'd in Battle, and crown'd with Victory: Emperors, with famous Nations or Cities fupplicating them, offering them a Crown or other Gifts (17). And in one word, every Perfon was exhibited with fuch Symbols as were moſt fignificant of that in which he excelled; whether Fortitude, or Science. Particular care was taken that the Images ſhould be expreffive of their Cha- racters and Difpofitions: And thofe who are acquainted with the Remains of Antiquity *The Excellency of ancient Statues and Pictures.* know, that the Accounts we have of the wonderful Skill of the Ancients in this prin- cipal Quality of the defigning Arts are not exaggerated. They will not think that *Phi- loſtratus* magnifies Matters, when defcribing the Picture of *Antilochus*, he fays, "*Ulyf- "* fes is manifeſtly diſtinguiſh'd by his fevere vigilant Look; *Menelaus* by his gentle Mild- " nefs; *Agamemnon* by a certain fuperiour divine Majeſty above all the reſt; *Diomede* " is the very Picture of a free bold Spirit; *Ajax* is known by his terrible grim Look; " *Locrus* by his alert Forwardnefs; *Hector* is a Demi-god, his Statue expreffes many " Paffions, if one attends accurately to it; for he is great and awful; he hath a won- " derful Alacrity, and a mafculine Softnefs; he is without Hair, but comely: And the
" Statue

---

(13) *Strabo, lib.* 14. Habet etiam Bibliothecàm & Homereum & porticum quadratum, cum Homeri tem- plo & ſtatua. Nam & hi maxime hunc poetam fibi vendicant. Unde & nummus quidam æneus apud eos Homerus vocatur.

(14) *Æs vita vigetum, nobis oſtendit Homerum: Non animus, non fenfus abeſt: fed folius illæ Vocis æget: mirum quo vis procefferit artis.*

——— *fenium præferre videtur Dulce fed hoc fenium eſt, & ab illo ditior æri Gratia: conveniunt gravitas & amabile quiddam: Blanda verecundæ majeſtas lucet in ore: Innata in curva canus cervice Corymbus Vertice defcendens, & circumfunditur auret. Mento barba cadens fpatio difpefcitur amplo,. Mollibus illa pilis multoque volumine, nec fe Cogit in anguſtum, fed late excurrit, & infra Et veſtis fimul eſt ea pectoris, & decus oris: Nuda canis frons eſt: & adeſt fapientia.fronti..*

Afpiciens cæcum non poſſis credere: tanta Ofcuris oculis admixta eſt gratia: felix Hoc vitium eſt, labefque oculorum profuit arti.

Nonnihil introrfum fefe cavat utraque mola Utraque fulcatur rugis, fed utrique venuſtus Eſt pudor, in focia recipit qui fede pudorem. ——————— *fed & arrigit aures Dextra fe, Phœbum cupiens audire loquentem, &c,* Anthol. Græc. lib. 5. tranflated by Grotius.

(15) See *Hiſtoire ancienne, par M. Rollin, tom. cinquieme p.* 10. *& tom.* 3. *p.* 421.

(16) *Plin.* 25. *c.* 5. *& 34. c.* 15.

(17) Imperatoriis imaginibus alii imperatores aliud. quiddam appingi gaudent; quidam clariſſimas quafque urbes dona offerentes: alii victorias caput eorum corona cingentes: Nonnulli magiſtratus adorantes, &c. See *Junius de Pict. vet. lib.* 3. *c.* 1.

G g

" Statue is so lively that it seems to breathe, to accost you and invite you to touch it.
" *Amphiaraus* the Prophet has a reverend Aspect, and seems to pour out some divine
" Oracle (18)."

*Great Deeds
painted.*
ALL their great Actions or meritorious Inventions were beautifully represented by Pictures or Sculptures, in which one might see their whole History. Thus was painted the famous Cavalry-battle between *Gryllus*, Son to *Xenophon*, at the Head of the *Athenians*, and *Epaminondas* who commanded the *Thebans*; the *Trojan* War; the Battle of *Marathon*; the famous Stand at *Thermopylæ*; the brave Behaviour of *Olympiodorus*; all the great Actions, or remarkable Events in their History, were transmitted to Posterity by the Chissel and Pencil, as well as by the Pen. They consecrated Statues and Pictures, to the honour even of such foreign Princes and great Men as had render'd Services to them: As for instance, to the *Ptolemys* of *Ægypt*, *Ptolemy Philometer* in particular, and his Daughter *Berenice*. Near to these Memorials of the *Ptolemys* at *Athens*, were the Kings of *Macedon* placed. But what *Pausanias* says on this occasion is very remarkable. " The " *Ptolemys* owed their Statues to the Love and Gratitude of the *Athenians*; whereas " *Philip* and *Alexander* were only obliged, for the honour done them, to the Fickleness " of the Populace and Flattery. The *Athenians* did the same honour to *Lysimachus*, but " rather out of Politicks than Affection; and to accommodate themselves to the " times (19)."

*Shields how adorn'd
by the Ancients.*
ANCIENTLY Shields were adorn'd with the Images and Actions of their Possessors; such were those used in the time of the *Trojan* War, says *Pliny*: And this Custom, according to the same Author, prevailed likewise among the *Carthaginians* (20). It was indeed very universal: such a one *Marcius* brought with him, with his other rich Booty, from *Carthage*, with *Asdrubal* engraved on it. The Poets often describe this Usage, or allude to it.

Et Sacranæ acies, & picti scuta Labici.   Æn. 7. ver. 796.

*At Nileus, qui se genitum septemplice Nilo
Ementitus erat, clypeo quoque flumina septem
Argento partim, partim cælaverat auro.*   Ovid. Met. lib. 5. ver. 187.

*Flumineaque urna cætalus Bragada parmam,
Et vastæ Nasamon syrtis populator Hyempsal, &c.*   Sil. Ital. l. 1. ver. 407.

*Ipse tumens atavi Brenni se stirpe ferebat
Chryxus, & in titulos Capitolia capta trahebat :
Tarpeioque jugo demens, & vertice sacro
Pensanteis aurum Celtas umbone ferebat.*   Sil. Ital. lib. 4. ver. 150.

*At contra ardenti radiabat Scipio cocco,
Terribilem ostentans Clypeum, quo patris, & una
Cælarat Patrui spirantes prælia dira
Effigies : flammam ingentem frons alta vomebat.*   Ibid. lib. 17. ver. 400.

PLINY calls it a noble Use of the designing Arts; a great Incentive to true Bravery, and a Custom full of Glory. Hence the practice in the first Ages of Christianity, described by *Prudentius*.

————*Clypeorum insignia Christus
Scripserat, ardebat summis crux addita cristis.*

THIS Subject is fully handled in a Dissertation upon dedicated Shields, in the *Memoirs of the Academy of the Belles Lettres*: In which the famous Shield of *Scipio* is describ'd. It was found in the *Rhone*, A. 1566, and is now in the King of *France*'s Cabinet (21). It represents that heroick Action that hath been often painted by modern Masters, and is indeed a most noble Subject, commonly called the *Continence of Scipio*. 'Tis beautifully related

(18) *Philostratus in Iconum lib. 2. in Antilochi pictura.* Agnoscitur autem Ithacensis quidem ex severa & excitata facie. Menelaus vero lenitate, Agamemnon divina quadam majestate, Tydidem sua libertas designat : Telamonium vero dignoscas ex terribili, & Locrum ex prompto aspectu.—Amphiarus ipso aspectu sacer atque fatidicus. *In Amphiar. Pictura, tom. l. 1.* Quæ est Illi Hectoris statua, semideum refert hominem, multosque præ se fert affectus, si quis diligenter accurateque aspexit. Etenim elata est ac terribilis, alacrisque & cum mollitie vigens, ineståque ei absque ulli coma pulchritudo. Est autem usque adeo spirans, ut ad se tangendum spectatores attrahat. *In Heroicis.*

(19) See *Pausanias, lib. 1.* particulatly *pag. 7.* Phi-

lippo vero & Alexandro adulationi potius multitudinis, nam & Lysimacho, &c.

(20) Scutis enim quałibus apud Trojam pugnatum est continebantur imagines ; unde & nomen habuere Clypeorum, non ut perversa grammaticorum subtilitas voluit, a cluendo. Origo ; plenam virtutis faciem reddi in scuto cujusque, qui fuerit usus illo. Pœni & ex auro factitavere & Clypeos & imagines ; secumque in castris vexere. Certe captis iis, talem Asdrubalis invenit Marcius, Scipionum in Hispania ultor, &c. *Plin.* 35. 6. For this Shield see *Livy, lib. 25. c. 39.*

(21) *Dissertation sur les Boucliers votifs, par M. l'Abbé Massieu. Hist. de l'Academie Royale, tom. 1. p. 177.*

related by *Livy* (22). And Mr. *Thomson*, in his *Sophonisba*, hath told it with the noble Fire virtuous Subjects always inspire into him. These votive or confecrated Bucklers were not only called in general *Clypei*, *Disci*, *Cycli*, but by the particular Name of (*Pinaces*) or Pictures, because they painted great Men and their glorious Actions.

How Philopæmon *recover'd the A-chaian Youth from Effeminacy.*

PHILOPÆMON, who is called by *Livy* the laft of the *Greeks*, made a fine ufe of this Cuftom of adorning Shields and other Parts of Armour (23). The young Men in his time being exceffively effeminate, and fond to extravagance of rich Apparel, fumptuous Furniture, curious Services at Table, and delicate Difhes; this brave and publick-fpirited *Achaian*, in order to give this their Love of Finery in all fuperfluous unneceffary things a good turn, and bring them to like things that were manly and profitable, endeavour'd to make them think of fhining in the Field, and coming out for the Defence of their Country with magnificent Armour: And it had the defigned effect. For the fight of finely adorned Arms breathed a new Spirit into them, and fired them with an Emulation of trying who fhould moft diftinguifh himfelf in the Service of his Country. " Indeed, faith " *Plutarch*, Sumptuoufnefs and Finery in Drefs, Equipage and Table, do fecretly lead " away Mens Minds from manly Purfuits, and allure them to feek after Vanities that ren- " der them foft and inactive : Luxury melts and diffolves the Strength and Courage of the " Mind ; but the fumptuous Coft beftowed upon warlike Furniture, animates a noble " Heart ; as *Homer* fays it did *Achilles*, when his Mother brought him the new Armour " fhe had caufed *Vulcan* to make for him, and laid them at his Feet : For the moment " he fees them, he is fired with the fight, and impatient for fome Action to try them, and " fhine in them.   So when *Philopæmon* had brought the Youth of *Achaia* to this good " pafs, to come thus bravely arm'd and furnifh'd into the Field; he begun then continually " to exercife them in Arms, wherein they did not only fhew themfelves obedient to him, " but did moreover ftrive to excel one another."

THERE is indeed a Tafte of Beauty and Elegance in our Natures, that may eafily be improved to very good ufes : This Defire will neceffarily be difcovering itfelf, if not in the Purfuit of the true, the real Beauty in Characters, Affections, and Actions, and in the Study of pure, chafte Arts ; in a faife Affectation and Defire of Symmetry and Elegance, in merely external Ornaments, in Equipage, Table, Drefs, and fo forth. 'Tis therefore of the higheft confequence to give a good Turn, by proper Education, to this natural Paffion (24).

The Monument of Archimedes.

TO name but a few more Inftances of the Honours paid to Virtue, we have an Account from *Cicero* of the Monument erected to *Archimedes*. How earneftly did *Cicero* fearch after it in *Syracufe* ! And how does he lament that it was over-grown with Weeds and fadly neglected ! He found it out with great difficulty after much hunting and fearching. It was adorned with the Sphere and Cylinder; and he was probably reprefented drawing Diagrams upon the Sand (25).

The Monument of Duilius's *naval Victory.*

HOW naval Victories and Triumphs were commemorated, we may fee by that Monument in the Capitol at *Rome*, in honour of *Duilius* (26), juft as it is defcribed by *Silius Italicus* ; where he likewife mentions feveral other Pictures and Monuments of great Deeds and illuftrious Men : which, whether they are real or imaginary Pictures, equally ferve to fhew us to what noble purpofes Painting may and ought to be employed in the Opinion of the Ancients.

———*varia fplendentia cernit*
Pictura, belli patribus monumenta prioris
Exhaufti.   Nam porticibus fignata manebant.
Quis inerat longus rerum, & fpectabilis ordo,
Primus bella truci fuadebat Regulus ore :

Bella

(22) *T. Liv. l.* 26. *c.* 50. *& Polybius* L 10. *p.* 593. Ed. *Cafaub.*

(23) See his Life in *Plutarch.* I have given this Paffage in the Words of the old *Englifh* Tranflation.

(24) See this Reflexion delightfully purfued at great length in the Characterifticks, *tom.* 1. *p.* 138. Every one is a Virtuofo of a higher or lower degree : Every one purfues and courts a *Venus* of one kind or another. And *tom.* 3. *p.* 184, &c.

(25) Cujus (Archimedis) ego quæftor ignoratum ab Syracufanis, cum effe omnino negarent, feptum undique & veftitum vepribus, & dumetis indagavi fepulchrum. Tenebam enim quofdam fenariolos quos in ejus monumento effe infcriptos acceperam : Qui declarabant, in fummo fepulchro fphæram effe pofitam cum Cylindro. Ego autem cum omnia colluftrem oculis

(eft enim ad portas Agragianas magna frequentia fepulchrorum) animadverti Columellam non multum e dumis eminentem : in qua inerat fphæræ figura & Cylindri. ——— Quo cum patefactus effet aditus, ad adverfam bafin acceffimus. Apparebat epigramma exefis pofterioribus partibus verficulorum dimidiatis fere. Ita nobiliffima Græciæ civitas quondam vero etiam doctiffima, fui civis unius acutiffimi monumentum ignoraffet, nifi ab homine Arpinate didiciffet. Quis eft omnium, qui modo cum mufis, id eft, cum humanitate, & cum doctrina habeat aliquid commercium qui fe non hunc mathematicum malit, quam illum tyrannum, &c. *Tufc. Quæft. lib.* 5. 23.

(26) *Pliny* tells us that this Monument was in the Forum in his time. *P. Ciacconius* has explain'd this Monument *fingulari opere.* See likewife *Gruter in Lapide Capitoline, p.* 297.

Bella neganda viro, ſi noſcere fata daretur.
At princeps Pœnis indictæ more parentum
Appius aſtabat pugnæ, lauroque revinctus
Juſtum Sarranâ ducebat cæde triumphum.
Æquoreum juxta decus, & navale trophæum
Roſtra gerens, nivea ſurgebat mole columna,
Exuvias Marti donum, quæ Duilius alto
Ante omnes merſa Pœnorum claſſe dicabat:
Cui nocturnus honos, funalia clara, ſacerque
Poſt Epulas Tibicen adeſt, caſtoſque Penates
Inſignis læti repetebat murmure cantus. Sil. Ital. lib. 6. 651.

IN fine, due Honour was done by Statues, Pictures, and other Monuments, to every great Action, in ancient Times, by the *Greeks* eſpecially; to every one who had been ſerviceable to his Country in whatever Station of Life, and not to thoſe only in the higher Spheres of Action.

Of the Battle of Marathon. AFTER the famous Battle of *Marathon,* there were erected, on the Spot where the Battle was given, noble Monuments, on which were inſcribed the Names of all thoſe who had bravely died for their Country; one for the *Athenians,* another for the *Platæans;* and a third for the Slaves that had been put in arms on that occaſion (27). Afterwards one was erected for *Miltiades. Cornelius Nepos* makes a fine Reflexion upon what was done by the *Athenians* to honour the Memory of this General (28). "Formerly, ſays he, "(ſpeaking of the *Romans*) our Anceſtors recompenſed Virtue by Marks of Diſtinction, "not indeed very pompous, but which they rarely beſtowed, and that were for that very "reaſon highly eſteemed; whereas now that they are laviſh'd ſo promiſcuouſly they are not "regarded. It had been ſo likewiſe among the *Athenians;* all the Honour paid to *Mil-* "*tiades* the Deliverer of *Athens,* and of all *Greece* was, that in a Picture of the Battle of "*Marathon* he was repreſented at the Head of the ten Chiefs, exhorting the Soldiers to Cou- "rage, and ſhewing them a noble Example of it: But this ſame People in after-times, becom- "ing more powerful, but at the ſame time more corrupt, appointed three hundred Statues "of *Demetrius Phalereus* to be erected." *Plutarch* makes the ſame Obſervation (29), and remarks wiſely, that the Honours rendred to great Men ought not to be conſider'd as a recompence for their glorious Actions; but purely as a Mark of the high Eſteem in which they were held, and of a deſire to perpetuate their Memory and the Imitation of them. 'Tis not, ſays he, the Riches nor the Magnificence of publick Monuments that makes their Value or renders them durable; but 'tis the ſincere Love and Gratitude of thoſe who erect them: The three hundred Statues of *Demetrius Phalereus* were thrown down in his own time; but the Picture of *Miltiades* ſubſiſted many Ages after him.

PLATO often ſpeaks of this glorious Day of *Marathon* as the Source of the *Athenian* Bravery and Succeſs. For on all occaſions of Importance the Example of *Miltiades* and his invincible Troop, was recalled to their Remembrance, and ſet before their Eyes as an Example of what a little Army of Heroes was able to do. It was this glorious Inſtance that inſpired them for a long time afterwards, with a noble Emulation to imitate thoſe brave Anceſtors, and not to degenerate from their Virtue, Love of Liberty and their Country: And no doubt the excellent Pictures of that glorious Action contributed not a little to produce that noble Effect.

Of the Monuments at Thermopylæ. BY publick Order there was likewiſe erected, near to *Thermopylæ,* a glorious Mo- nument, to the Memory of theſe brave Defenders of their Country, with two Inſcrip- tions; one that regarded all thoſe in general who had died there, and bore that the *Greeks,* to the number of four thouſand, had bravely made head againſt an Army of three Millions of *Perſians.* The other Inſcription was peculiar to the *Spartans:* It was written by *Simonides* (30), in theſe plain ſtrong Words:

Ξεῖν᾽, ἀγγειλον Λακεδαιμονίοις, ὅτι τῇδε
Κείμεθα, τοις κείνων πειθόμενοι νομίμοις.

Of funeral Pane-gyricks among the Greeks and Ro-mans. DIODORUS SICULUS tells us likewiſe, that the *Athenians* inſtituted cer- tain funeral Games in honour of thoſe who had died in the War againſt the *Perſians* (31), and

(27) So *Pauſanias* tells us in his Atticks.

(28) *Nepos in Miltiade.*

(29) *Plut. in præceptis de Repub. gerenda.*

(30) See *Cicero Tuſc. Quæſt.* lib. 1. 42. Pari animo now cited.

Lacedæmonii in Thermopylis occiderunt, in quo. Si-monides:
Dic, Hoſpes Spartæ, nos te hic vidiſſe jacenteis,
Dum ſanctis Patriæ legibus obſequimur..
See alſo *Pauſanias, p.* 95. *Laconica.*

(31) Lib. 2. See likewiſe *Pauſanias* in the place juſt now cited.

and a folemn yearly Panegyrick was pronounced in their praife. In the firft general Affembly of *Greece* after the Victory of *Platæa*, *Ariftides* propofed a Decree, which was pafs'd; that all the Cities of *Greece* fhould fend Deputies yearly to *Platæa* to facrifice to *Jupiter* the Deliverer, and to the Gods of that City, and that every five Years a Feaft of Liberty fhould be celebrated there. The *Platæans* refolved to keep an annual Feftival in memory of thofe who had died in Battle. The Ceremonies of it are fully defcribed by *Plutarch* (32). *Polybius* gives us an Account of an ancient Cuftom among the *Romans*, before the Arts were much cultivated amongft them; " which, " fays he, contributed exceedingly to infpire them early with noble Ambition, and to " form great Minds; and fhews the extraordinary Care and Diligence of the Repub- " lick to promote the Defire of Glory and Reputation. When any Perfon of Meri't " and Renown died, his Body was carried in great State, and expofed to publick View " at the Roftra; where one of his Children, if any of them was of Age, and qualify'd " to undertake it, or if not, fome other of his Family or Race harangu'd the People, " fetting forth his excellent Virtues, and exhorting all to imitate his noble Example: " Whence it came about that many by fuch lively Commemorations of great Virtues and " Actions, were filled with laudable Emulation, and excited to merit equal Praife and " Honour. After having perform'd the funeral Rites and Obfequies, the Image of the " Defunct was placed in the moft confpicuous part of the Houfe, an Image taken after the " Life, and exactly reprefenting his Likenefs (33)."

IN funeral Ceremonies the Badges or Enfigns of the publick Employments any one had filled were difplay'd. And can we imagine a nobler Spectacle than a young Man proclaiming the due Praifes of Virtue, Merit, and publick Services? Muft not the fight of thofe Images of Perfons thus glorify'd by their Virtues, have awaken'd and inflam'd every one with ardent, generous, heroick Sentiments and Refolutions. By this practice the Senfe of Honour was kept lively and vigorous; and the Youth were fired with an Ambition able to incite to great Atchievements, able to undergo any Hardfhip, or forgo any Pleafure for the publick Good. 'Tis plain from feveral Paffages of ancient Authors, that fuch Images were amongft the old *Romans*, their Titles or Patents of Nobility (34). Amongft the *Greeks* fepulchral Monuments were either adorned with Bas-reliefs or painted. *Paufanias* and other Authors mention many that were painted; and this was alfo a practice among the *Romans*; for feveral fuch Monuments are yet to be feen at *Rome*, and about *Baiæ* and *Cumæ*.

THE Antiquarians have been often puzzled to find out the reafon why the Maufolea, Sarcophagi, fepulchral and other funeral Monuments are often adorn'd with Reprefentations of Vintages, Huntings, Feftivals, and fuch gay Subjects. But 'tis worth obferving, that the ancient *Greeks* and *Romans* inftead of adding artificially to the natural Horrors of Death, took all pains on the contrary to allay that Dread. This at leaft is certain, that they took care to make Death in the Service of the Publick defirable and glorious.

AMONGST the *Greeks*, the Pictures and Statues of great Men, and in memory of their great Deeds, were placed in the Temples amidft the Images of their Gods, and Pictures and Sculptures reprefenting religious Rites and Cuftoms. In the Temples were likewife Pictures recommending the Virtues, and pointing out the Errors and Miferies into which Ignorance and falfe Pleafure miflead. This is evident from one Example out of many that might be brought: The famous allegorical Picture in the Temple of *Saturn*, defcribed at large by *Cebes* (35), commonly called his Table. This is a charming allegorical Picture of human Life, and fufficiently fhews us what fine Notions the ancient Philofophers in the Age of *Socrates*, had of the ufe that might be made of Painting to inftruct in the profoundeft Doctrines of Morality. But I fhall fay nothing of this Picture at prefent, being fully determin'd to publifh a correct Edition of it in *Greek*, and an *Englifh* Tranflation, with feveral Remarks upon allegorical Painting, illuftrated with a good Print done after an old one, far furpaffing any other of this piece I have feen in Drawing and Tafte. One thing however which I have not hitherto had occafion to remark, is worth our attention: The Symbols in ancient Allegory, by which the Affections of the Mind, the Virtues, and the Vices are reprefented, are well known to the Learned; they make

a

Pictures of great Men, and great Actions placed in Temples.

So likewife moral Pictures.

(32) *Plutarch in Ariftide.*

(33) *Polybius, lib.* 6. *p.* 495. *Ed. Cafaub.* Oris fimillitudinem artificiofe effictam (fays the *Latin* Interpreter) coloribus, pigmentifque adumbratam referens.

(34) Nunc fum defignatus Ædilis, habeo rationem quid a populo Romano acceperim.——Ob earum rerum laborem & follicitudinem fructus illos datos, antiqui-

orem in fenatu fententiæ dicendæ locum, togam prætextam, fellam curulem, jus imaginis ad memoriam pofteritatemque prodendam. *Oratio* 5. *contra Verrem*, N° 15.

(35) See the Table of *Cebes*. See *Suidas & Sam. Petit. Mifcell. l.* 4. *c.* 4. *& Junius de Pictura veterum,* l. 2. *cap.* 6. and the Paffages in *Meurfii Athenæ Atticæ* already quoted.

H h

a fix'd determinate Language, from which when Painters depart, they fpeak an unknown Tongue, to which there can be no Key, unlefs they give us a Dictionary for explaining their capricious Inventions. *Rubens* (35) is juftly blamed for mixing Allegory with Hiftory; two Subjects that ought to be kept diftinct from one another; and not only for mixing profane Theology with Chriftianity, but for inventing in Allegory, and not conforming himfelf to the ancient known Language or Symbols. Such moral Pictures had place in the Porticoes and Schools where the Philofophers taught. For all the Schools, Academies, and Places of Exercife amongft the ancient *Greeks* were adorned with Pictures proper to them; and that often furnifh'd the Philofophers with very fuitable Arguments for moral Leffons. To this Cuftom *Perfius* alludes, as hath been already obferv'd:

Such Pictures plac'd in Schools, Academies, &c.

> *Haud tibi inexpertum curvos deprendere mores,*
> *Quæque docet fapiens Braccatis illita Medis*
> *Porticus.*───

THAT in the Schools of the Liberal Arts were plac'd the Statues of the nine Mufes and *Apollo*, might be prov'd by many Authorities: And that the famous Philofophers were reprefented in thefe is plain, fince it was become a Proverb; *Qui nunquam Philofophum pictum viderunt* (36). *Sidonius Apollinaris* gives us an Account of the Pictures of Philofophers in the *Gymnafia* fubfifting in his time (37): And *Pliny* mentions feveral Artifts that were famous for doing Philofophers only (38).

In places throughout all Greece for Converfation caled Lefchæ.

PAUSANIAS tells us, that there were in all the Cities of *Greece*, certain Places defign'd for Affemblies of the Learned and Ingenious for Converfation; and that thefe were adorned with Pictures, Statues, and Sculptures. He defcribes two Pictures in one of thefe Schools or Academies called *Lefchæ*. And he quotes *Homer* to fhew that fuch places of Meeting were very ancient. 'Tis where *Melanthus* upbraids *Ulyffes* for pratling as if he was at the *Lefchæ* (39). He mentions two Places of that Name at *Sparta* (40). Of this kind at *Rome* were the Schools in the Porticoes of *Octavia*, where *Pliny* tells us feveral *Greek* Pictures were put up (41).

PLINY

(35) *Reflections fur la Poefie & fur la Peinture*, tom. 1. fect. 24.

(36) *De fin. lib.* 5. 27. The Meaning of which will eafily be underftood by the ufe *Cicero* makes of it. Dicis eadem omnia & bona & mala; quæ quidem dicerent qui nunquam philofophum pictum viderunt. Gymnafiis præfidebant Mercurius, Hercules, Thefeus, atque ideo ftatuas eorum in Gymnafiis paffim confecrabant. See *Paufan.* l. 5. p. 276. *Mercury* is called in the *Greek* Epigrams, *Antholog.* l. 7. c. 25. τῶν γυμναςίων ἐπίσκοπον. See *l.* 4. *cap.* 12. Cur Vero amorem quandoque in Gymnafiis una cum Hercule & Mercurio confecraverunt, See *Athenæus Deipnofoph.* L 13. c. 1. See *Junius de Pictura veterum*, l. 2. c. 8. See *Cicero Ep.* ad *Atticum*, l. 1. *Ep.* 1. Hermathena tua valde me oblectat, & pofita ita belle eft, ut totum gymnafium, πλιν ανάθημα effe videatur. *Ep.* 4. Quod ad me de Hermathena fcribis, per mihi gratum eft, & ornamentum Academiæ proprium meæ, quod & Hermis commune omnium, & Minerva fingulare infigne ejus gymnafii. Quare Velim, ut fcribis, ceteris quoque rebus quamplurimis eum locum ornes. *Ep.* 6. Tu, Velim, fi quæ ornamenta γυμναςιωδη reperire poteris, quæ loci fint ejus, quæ tu non ignoras, ne prætermittas. *Ep.* 8. Hermæ tui pentelici cum capitibus æneis, jam nunc me admodum delectant, quare velim, & eos, & figna, & cetera, quæ tibi ejus loci & noftri ftudii, & tuæ elegantiæ effe videbuntur, quamplurima & maxime tibi quæ gymnafii, xyftique, &c. See *Meurfii Lect. Attic.* l. 5. c. 6. Alla fcuola over ginnafio delle fcienze, conVengono filofofi, con fentenze illuftri & libri tenuti in mano con belliffime attitudini. Adornerà fommamente, ad immitatione degli antichi, quella ftatoua da loro chiamata Hermathena, ove erano Pallade & Mercurio abbracciati la quali i filofofi antichi dedicaVano & pone Vano ne i fuoi Ginnafi, come ne fa in più Luochi mentione Marco Tullio. Et intendeVano per Pallade la fapienza & per Mercurio l'eloquenza. *Lomazzo della Pittura*, l. 6. c. 26.

(37) Per Gymnafia pinguntur Areopagitica vel Prytanæum, Speufippus cervice curVa, Aratus panda, Zeno fronte contracta, Epicurus cute diftenta, Diogenes barba comante, Ariftoteles brachio exferto, Xenocrates crure collecto, Heraclitus fletu oculis claufis, Democritus rifu labris apertis, Chryfippus, digitis propter numero-

rum indicia conftrictis; Euclides, propter menfurarum fpatia laxatis; Cleanthes, propter utrumque corrofis, &c. *Sidon. Apollin. lib.* 9. *Epift.* 9.

(38) *Plin.* 34. 8. Apollodorus, Androbulus, Afclepiodorus, Alevas, fecerunt philofophos.

(39) Supra Caffiotidem ædificium quoddam eft: In quo picturæ aliquot Polygnoti, quas Gnidiæ dedicarunt: Locum Delphi Lefchen vocant (quafi confabulationem aut ftationem dicas) quod eo convenientes prifcis olim temporibus feria & joca inter fe conferebant. Talia fuiffe multa in omni Græcia conciliabula Homerus docuit, quo loco Melanthus in Ulyffem convitium exponit:

> Οὐδ᾿ ἰθύλιις εὔδιιν χαλκήϊον ἐς δόμον ἐλθών,
> Ἠέ πη ἐς λέσχην, ἀλλ᾿ ἐνθάδε πολλ᾿ ἀγορεύεις.

Ubi in hoc ædificium introiris pictam videas in dextro tempii pariete Ilii everfionem, & Græcorum claffem domum folventem. After this follows a particular Account of the Pictures. There is a Difcourfe on two of them in the *Memoirs of Infcriptions* and *Belles Lettres*.

(40) *Paufan. Laconic.* l. 3. See the *French* Tranflator of *Paufanias* on this place, Le Lefché eft tout contre, &c. where he remarks, Il y avoit à Sparte deux endroits qui portoient ce nom, l'un dit le Lefché des Crotanes; l'autre le Lefché Pœcile du mot ποικίλος varius, a caufe de la varieté de ces peintures comme le Pæcile d'Athénes. C'etoit apparemment deux portiques où l'on venoit fe promener & converfer, &c.──Par la Lecture d'Homere on voit que dans toutes les bonnes Villes de la Grece il y avoit de ces Lefchez, c'eft-à-dire des lieux où les gens d'oifif venoient jafer, comme au jourd'hui nos caffez, &c.

(41) *Hiftoire de la Peinture ancienne, p.* 89. *ad fin.* On trouve ces deux piéces à l'Académie, dans le portique d'Octavie, &c. His Remark is, où les philofophes & autres gens de lettres s'affembloient ordinairement. Pour ce qui eft du portique d'Octavie, bâti par Augufte, il renfermoit deux temples, celui de Junon, pour potioent ce nom, l'un dit le Lefché des Crotanes; pour potioent ce nom, l'un dit le Lefché des Crotanes; celui d'Apollon; la cour, l'ecole & la Bibliotheque, c'eft cette ecole que j'ai nommée Académie, deftinée uniquement aux conférences des philofophes & des fçavans. *Voy.* Suet. *dans la Vie d'Augufte*, c. 29.

PLINY juſtly celebrates *Aſinius Pollio* for founding publick Libraries at *Rome*, and adorning them with the Pictures of thoſe great Men, whoſe immortal Souls ſpoke by their Writings (42). This *Aſinius Pollio* was the firſt who dedicated publick Libraries, that is, founded them and conſecrated them to publick Uſe, thus making, ſays *Pliny*, (*ingenia hominum Rempublicam*) Learning a common Good: This was a generous Action, worthy of that illuſtrious *Roman*, the Friend of *Cicero*, *Virgil* and *Horace*; who was Conſul, General, Orator, Poet, and Hiſtorian; and a great Patron of Ingenuity, polite Literature, and of all the fine Arts. *Virgil* has immortalized his Name.

Of publick Libraries at Rome, how adorned with the Pictures of great Men: Of Authors eſpecially. One founded by Aſinius Pollio.

> *Pollio amat noſtram, quamvis ſit ruſtica, muſam :*
> *Pollio & ipſe facit nova carmina———* Virg. Ecl. 4.

ISIDORUS gives ſome Account likewiſe of this Library (43). The Dedication of ſuch Libraries was ſolemnly made by a Diſcourſe which was commonly publiſh'd afterwards. *Pliny* the Younger, who had founded a publick Library at his own Expence, for the Uſe of his Compatriots, mentions a Diſcourſe that he pronounc'd on that occaſion (44). And that ſuch Libraries were adorn'd with Pictures of Philoſophers, Learned Men and the Encouragers of Letters, appears from another of his Epiſtles, in which he expreſſes his deſire to get a good Painter to copy the Portraits of *Cornelius Nepos*, and *T. Caſſius*, that they might be plac'd in the Library of one of his Friends (45).

How thoſe Libraries were dedicated.

PLINY likewiſe informs us, that *Atticus* had been at great pains to preſerve the Memory of illuſtrious Men, and that he had publiſh'd a Volume of their Images and Lives (46). *Cornelius Nepos* gives us a fuller Account of this noble and generous Work. He was a great Lover of Antiquity, ſays *Nepos*, and of the ancient Manners; and he was ſo well acquainted with Hiſtory, and the Lives of great Men, that, in his Book of illuſtrious ones, there is no War, no Peace, no Law, no remarkable Event in the *Roman* Hiſtory which he has not accurately related : And he had likewiſe given ſuch a diſtinct Account (which was extremely difficult) of the *Roman* Families, that the Genealogies of all that great Men may be found there : He likewiſe gave their Images, or Portraits; under each of which there were four Verſes comprehending the Subſtance of their Hiſtory and Character (47).

Of the Zeal of Atticus to preſerve the Fame of great Men.

MARCUS VARRO wrote ſeveral Volumes on various Subjects, and theſe were adorn'd likewiſe with the Images of great Men, to the number of ſeven hundred (48). And this Honour he did to Foreigners as well as to *Romans*. *Pliny* calls this a moſt noble and glorious Undertaking, thus to preſerve the Memory of Men of Merit, that they might be every where preſent and known: " *Inventor muneris etiam Diis invidioſi,* " *quando immortalitatem non ſolum dedit, verum etiam in omnes terras miſit, ut præ-* "*.ſentes eſſe ubique & videri poſſent.*" Thoſe then who are careful in collecting the Images of illuſtrious Men follow the beſt and nobleſt Examples of Antiquity. *Pliny* tells us, that tho' it was not uſual to place the Portraits of the Living in publick Libraries; yet *Aſinius Pollio* thought it an Honour due to *Varro*, and accordingly put up his Picture in the Library he had devoted to the Uſe of the Publick (49). The Images of

Of the Zeal of Marcus Varro, &c.

---

(42) Aſinii Pollionis hoc Romæ inventum, quoniam primus, Bibliothecam dicando, ingenia hominum rem publicam fecit. *Plin.* 35. 5. A little above he ſays, In Bibliothecis dicantur illi, quorum immortales animæ in locis iiſdem loquuntur. Concerning the *Greek* Libraries, ſee *Meurſii Ath. Att.* and *Monſfaucon's Palaeographia Graeca.*

(43) See the *French* Notes upon this Paſſage in *Pliny*. Romæ primus librorum copiam advexit Æmilius Paulus, Perſeo Macedonum rege devicto : Deinde Lucullus e Parthica praeda. Poſt hos, Caeſar dedit M. Varroni negotium cauſa maxime Bibliothecae conſtruendæ : Primum autem Romæ Bibliothecas publicavit Pollio, Graecas ſimul atque Latinas, additis imaginibus in Atrio quod de Dalmatarum manubiis magnificentiſſimum inſtruxerat.

(44) *Epiſt.* 8. *lib.* 1.

(45) *Lib.* 4. *Epiſt.* 28.

(46) Imaginum amore quondam flagraſſe teſtes ſunt & Atticus ille Ciceronis edito de his volumine. *Plin.* 35. 5.

(47) Moris etiam majorum ſummus imitator fuit, antiquitatiſque amator : Quam adeo diligenter habuit cognitam, ut eam totam in eo volumine expoſuerit quo

magiſtratus ornavit. Nulla enim lex, neque pax, neque bellum, neque res illuſtris eſt populo Romano quæ non in eo, ſuo tempore ſit notata : Et, quod difficillimum fuit, ſic familiarum originem ſubtexuit, ut ex eo Virorum clarorum propagines poſſimus cognoſcere.——— Quibus libris nihil poteſt eſſe dulcius, iis, qui aliquam cupiditatem habent notitiæ clarorum virorum. Attigit quoque Poëticen, credimus, ne ejus expers eſſet ſuavitatis. Namque verſibus, qui honore, rerumque geſtarum amplitudine ceteros Rom. populi præſtiterunt expoſuit ; ita ut ſub ſingulorum imaginibus facta, magiſtratuſque eorum non amplius quaternis, quiniſve verſibus deſcripſerit : Quod vix credendum ſit tantas res tam breviter potuiſſe declarari. *Cor. Nep. in Attico.*

(48) ——— Et M. Varro, benigniſſimo inventu, inſertis voluminibus ſuarum fœcunditatum, non nominibus tantum ſeptingentorum illuſtrium, ſed & aliquo modo imaginibus ; non paſſus intercidere figuras, aut vetuſtatem ævi contra homines Valere : Inventor muneris etiam Diis Invidioſi quando immortalitatem non ſolum dedit, &c. *Plin.* 35. 5.

(49) *Plin. lib.* 7. *c.* 30. We find *Horace* complaining of the Honour done to *Fannius*, by placing his Books and Image in a publick Library.
——— *Beatus Fannius, ultro*
Delatis capſis & imagini : H. l. 1. Sat. 4.

of the Living were placed among thoſe of the Deceaſed in private Libraries, as appears from *Martial* :

> *Hoc tibi ſub noſtra breve carmen imagine vivat,*
> *Quam non obſcuris, jungis, Avite, viris.*   L. 9. Ep. 1.

A N D the ſame Poet tells us, that the Author's Picture was ſometimes prefixed to his Book.

> *Quam brevis immenſum cepit membranâ Maronem !*
> *Ipſius Vultus prima tabella gerit.*   L. 14. 174.

Of private Libraries.

T H A T private Libraries were adorned with the Portraits and Buſts of great Men, we learn from *Cicero,* who ſpeaks of Reading under the Image of *Ariſtotle,* or ſome other great Philoſopher, as ſomething that inſpired and elevated him exceedingly (50). So likewiſe do *Seneca* (51), and all the good and great *Romans* ſpeak.

The Concluſions that follow from all this concerning the true uſe of the deſigning Arts, to celebrate the praiſe of good and great Men, and their uſeful Deeds and Inventions.

F R O M what hath been ſaid two things are evident, that well deſerve our Attention. Firſt of all, the great care that was taken, among the *Greeks* in particular, to preſerve the Memory of great Men and their Virtues, and thereby to promote, and maintain the Love of true Glory. 'Twas to this excellent Uſe that the deſigning Arts were chiefly employed by them.

And for that reaſon theſe ought to be erected in publick places.

A N D for that Effect 'tis obſervable in the ſecond place, that ſuch Memorials of Merit of whatever ſort were ſet up in publick Places, and expoſed to general View : They were the Ornaments of publick Buildings. The *Romans* for ſome time imitated the *Greeks* in this practice. The Pictures and Statues that were brought to *Rome* by *Mummius,* were not employed to adorn his own Houſe, but for the Ornament of *Rome.* Even *Julius Cæſar* and *Auguſtus* plac'd Pictures and Statues brought from *Greece,* in Temples, the Capitol, and other publick Edifices of *Rome* (52). But it ſeems it ſoon became too common a practice to deprive the Publick of them, and to make them the Ornaments of private Houſes. *Pliny* tells us to the honour of *M. Agrippa,* that he publiſh'd an Oration againſt this Cuſtom, which was extant in his time. He ſpeaks like a true Lover of the Art; with great warmth, about the generous and noble Spirit of this Speech; the Intent of which was to ſhew how unfriendly to the Arts, and ungenerous to the Publick it was to baniſh or impriſon fine Pieces of Art : And that they ought to be expoſed to the Publick in order to call forth Genius, and to be ſtudied by Artiſts deſirous of improving themſelves and the fine Arts (53).

Of the Zeal of M. Agrippa againſt baniſhing Pictures and Statues into private Villas.

T H E Speeches made at the Conſecration of publick Libraries adorn'd with Pictures and Sculptures, as well as Books, were probably of this nature (54). And this, it ſeems, was an Evil that had already begun to prevail in *Agrippa*'s time, and was likely to ſpread ; exiling Pictures or Statues ; locking them up where they could not be ſeen ; or denying free acceſs to the Curious to ſee and ſtudy them. 'Tis ſaid that a great Man who had all the Inclination in the World to have a fine Collection of Drawings and Pictures, juſt come from *Athens,* would not however conſent to their being made publick ; or that they ſhould be plac'd where there might be ready admittance to all who deſir'd to ſee them : And that upon this account he was generouſly told, that it would be an Injury to Mankind, and the polite Arts, to give them into his poſſeſſion on ſuch cruel Terms. It was certainly on ſome ſuch occaſion that *M. Agrippa* publiſh'd his Diſcourſe upon the Advantages of making them publick Ornaments inſtead of private Furniture. The Deſign of his Speech was to ſhew the bad Conſequences to the Arts of ſuch a narrow Mind. I cannot forbear taking notice to the Honour of our Country, that

The Topham Collection given to Eton College on excellent Terms.

the fine Drawings after Antique Paintings, Statues and Sculptures at *Rome,* collected by the ingenious Mr. *Topham,* were, after his Death, depoſited in *Eton* College, for the Uſe not only of the Maſters and Students there, but upon Terms in the true Spirit of

a

---

(50) *Epiſt. ad Att. lib.* 4. *Epiſt.* 10. Literis ſuſtentor & recreor maloque in illa tua ſedecula quam habes ſub imagine Ariſtotelis ſedere quam in iſtorum ſella curuli.

(51) Quidni ego magnorum virorum & imagines habeam, incitamenta animi & natales celebrem ? Quidni illos honoris cauſa ſemper appellem ? Quam Venerationem præceptoribus meis debeo, eandem illis præceptoribus generis humani a quibus tanti boni initia fluxerunt. *Sen. Epiſt. Ep.* 64.

(52) So *Pliny* tells us, lib. 35. And we have often

had occaſion to obſerve from *Pauſanias,* that among the *Greeks,* Pictures and Statues were the Ornaments of publick Buildings.

(53) Poſt eum M. Agrippa vir ruſticitati propior quam deliciis. Extat certe ejus oratio magnifica & maximo civium digna de tabulis omnibus ſigniſque publicandis : Quod fieri ſatius fuiſſet, quam in villarum exilia pelli. *Plin.* 35. 11.

(54) See *Pliny*'s Account of ſuch a Speech of his above quoted.

a *Varro*; an *Agrippa*; or *Asinius Pollio:* It being wrote upon the Door of the Room where they are kept, that they are there for the Use of all the Lovers of the Arts.

IF the Arts are indeed worthy of Encouragement in a State; the fine Models, which alone can invite Genius to disclose itself, or form and improve it, ought not to be hid. And if the Arts are applied to their principal End, which is to give due Fame to Merit, and thereby to quicken and animate us to Virtue; nothing can be more absurd than to keep such Incentives to laudable Emulation out of sight. It is disappointing the very End and Scope of them. *Pictures and Statues ought to be publick, in order to excite worthy Emulation.*

IN modern Policy, employing proper means of kindling, maintaining and invigorating publick Spirit and the Love of Praise, is much neglected. Yet sure, as the desire of Fame was implanted in us to be an Incentive to glorious Actions, so it is the Motive that hath produced the greatest Virtues, the most heroick Spirits, and likewise the brightest Genius's, and all the high Improvements of the useful or ornamental Arts. *The Love of Praise ought to be encouraged in a State.* " They whose Hearts are sincerely good and virtuous, says *Cicero*, do not pursue the Re
" wards of Virtue so much as Virtue itself: For nothing is in their Persuasion so ex
" cellent as to deliver their Country from Dangers, and to be useful to it by their
" Studies or Labours; they think they have done nothing in Life, if they have done
" nothing that is praise-worthy: They reckon those happy who are honour'd by their
" Fellow-Citizens for their Merit and Services; yet they do not account those mise-
" rable who have repaid Good to their Country for Evil: But of all Rewards the no-
" blest is Glory; it is this which by perpetuating our Memory to future Ages, com-
" pensates the Brevity of human Life, preserving us present, in our absence, and alive
" after Death: 'Tis, in fine, by the Steps of Glory that Men on Earth seem to ascend
" to Heaven (55). He defines Glory to be the illustrious Fame of meritorious and bene-
" ficent Deeds to our Country, or to Mankind (56), willingly spread abroad by all, by the
" Great and Good especially. 'Tis something solid and real, not a Shadow; 'tis the con-
" senting cheerful Approbation of the Good; the uncorrupted Voice of those who know
" the Excellence of Virtue: It reflects the Image of Virtue(57). Honour and Fame are the
" Reward of Virtue conferred upon one by the sincere Approbation and Esteem of his
" Countrymen: He who is thus distinguish'd is at once honourable and honoured. But he
" who on any occasion obtains Places of Power and Dignity, which were the sole Object
" of his Ambition, in opposition to the Will and Desire of his Country; such a one, I
" think, hath not obtained Honour, but merely the Name of it (58). Honour rightly be-
" stow'd nourishes the Virtues, and all the Arts; it quickens to noble Pursuits, and to an
" active Exertion of our best Powers and Faculties. Whatever is not duly encouraged by
" Praise and Honour, will lie dead and dejected. If *Fabius*, for instance, had been ho-
" nour'd for the Improvements he made in the Art of Painting, should we not, do you
" think, have seen in *Rome* many *Polycletus's* and *Parrhasius's*? 'Tis the same with re-
" spect to all the Virtues; all truly noble and honourable Qualities and Arts are exceed-
" ingly strengthen'd and quicken'd by Honours wisely and impartially bestowed (59). 'Tis
" Virtue's best recompence, nay the Love and Desire of it is itself a Virtue; far from be-
" ing a low and mercenary Passion, it burns strongest in the most virtuous Bosom. It
" cannot reside but where the Love of Mankind is ardent and vigorous. 'Tis impossible
" to delight in reputable Actions and Employments without desiring Reputation. And as
" he who loves Virtue will feel pleasure in praising and honouring it; so he who is con-
" scious of a sincere Affection to Mankind and publick Good, must wish that Mankind
" may be sensible of his generous Disposition, and gratefully make him suitable Returns
"   " of

(55) Addit hæc quæ certa vera sunt, forteis & sa-
pienteis viros non tam præmia sequi solere recte factorum quam ipsa recte facta : se nihil in vita, se nihil
præclare fecisse; siquidem nihil sit præstabilius Viro
quam periculis patriam liberare : Beatos esse, quibus ea
res honori fuerit a suis civibus : Nec tamen eos miseros,
qui beneficio civeis suos vicerint : Sed tamen ex omnibus præmiis Virtutis, si esset habenda ratio præmiorum
amplissimum esse præmium gloriam : Esse hanc unam,
quæ brevitatem vitæ posteritatis memoria consolaretur ;
quæ efficeret ut absentes adessemus, mortui viveremus :
Hanc denique esse cujus gradibus etiam homines in
cœlum videantur ascendere, &c. *Oratio pro Rabirio*,
N° 35.

(56) Gloria est illustris & pervulgata multorum &
magnorum, vel in suos, vel in patriam, vel in omne
genus hominum fama meritorum. *Oratio pro Ligario* 9.

(57) Est enim gloria solida quædam res & expressa
non adumbrata. Ea est consentiens Laus bonorum,

incorrupta vox bene judicantium de excellente virtute.
Ea Virtuti res sonat tanquam imago. *Tusc. Quæst. lib.*
3. *ab initio.*

(58) Cum honor sit præmium virtutis judicio, stu-
dioque civium delato ad aliquem, qui eum sententiis,
qui suffragiis adeptus est, is mihi & honestus & hono-
ratus videtur. Qui autem occasione aliqua etiam invi-
tis suis civibus, nactus est imperium, ut ille cupiebat ;
Hunc nomen honoris adeptum non honorem puto. *Cic.*
de Clar. Orator. 81.

(59) Honos alit artes, &c. *Tusc. Quæst. lib.* 1. N° 3.
Neque enim est hoc dissimulandum quod obscurari non
potest : sed præ nobis ferendum, trahimur omnes laudis
studio : Et optimus quisque maxime gloria ducitur. *Pro*
Arch. Poet. N° 2. Adhibenda est quædam reverentia
& optimi cujusque & reliquorum. Nam negligere quid
de se quisque sentiat, non solum arrogantis est, sed omnino dissoluti. *De Off. lib.* 1.

" of Efteem and Approbation. Indeed to have no concern about Reputation, one muft
" not only be arrogant but diffolute. The Senfe of Shame, and the Love of Glory, are
" the beft Handles that Civil Policy can employ in the Government of Mankind. Hardly
" will any Laws be able to reprefs Vice ; far lefs to promote Virtue, if Men are become
" infenfible to Ignominy and Honour." Now 'tis not merely by Hiftory, but chiefly by
Poetry, and by the Arts of Defign, that Virtue and Vice are fet in their due lights. It is
by thofe Arts that Infamy and Praife are moft forcibly imprefled upon Actions and Perfons : And therefore it is by means of thofe Arts, when rightly cultivated and employed,
that the Senfe of Shame and Honour is preferved delicate and lively. Several excellent
Authors, modern as well as ancient, have made this Remark, and highly commended
ancient Policy in making ufe not only of Painting and Statuary, but of the current
Coins of their Country, to preferve the Memory of great Actions and ufeful Inventions, thereby rendering them inftructive in Hiftory, and Incentives to Virtue and
Merit (60). The excellent Influence of fuch Methods of preferving the Memory of
great Men and their good Actions, is charmingly exprefled by *Salluft,* who tells us, that
Fabius, Scipio, and other illuftrious *Romans,* have often declared, that at the fight of
the Statues or Portraits of their glorious Anceftors, they felt their Minds animated with
a very ftrong Senfe of the Beauty of Virtue, and with a truly noble Ambition to imitate
their meritorious Example : Not that the Wax of which thefe Images were made, or
the Figures themfelves, had any magical Force ; but it is the lively Memory of great Deeds
revived by thefe Monuments, that kindles the virtuous Flame, and infpires with a Zeal
that cannot be fatisfied but by having deferved the fame Glory (61).

Ingenious, ufeful,
and ornamental
Arts aggrandize a
State.

THUS we have feen what a high Opinion fome of the beft Men of all Ages have
had of the fine Arts ; and their Sentiments about the Ufes to which they ought to be
applied. And indeed what is it that gives either Grace, or Dignity, or relifh to human
Life, but the ingenious Arts ? What elfe is it that raifes Society to true Grandeur ?
Take away the Virtues and Arts, and what remains but merely fenfual or animal Gratifications ? What remains that is peculiar to Man, that exalts him above the groveling Brutes,

It is Virtue and the
purfuit of ufeful
Studies that alone
can make even a
rich Man happy.

or intitles a Society of Men to the Character of Rational Society ? Can there be a
more ignominious Name than that of a rich Man whofe Plenty fpreads Vice, Effeminacy, Idlenefs, and Corruption over the Land ; his Riches being flung away on Pleafures
far beneath the Dignity of a rational Being, and which he dares not review, or reviewing
dares not approve ? What a vaft Drawback is it upon Enjoyments and Purfuits, when
one cannot reflect on them without Shame and Remorfe ? When one cannot fay to
himfelf thefe are Exercifes, thefe are Deeds, thefe are Joys which truly become a Man
and ennoble him ; in thefe appear the Talents and Endowments which really dignify
Man, and make him fuperiout to all Beings void of Reafon and Underftanding. And
of what elfe can one pronounce that fatisfactory Sentence in his own Breaft, but the
Exercifes of Virtue, Reafon, and a well-improv'd Imagination ? Let any one but afk
his own Heart the queftion, and it will immediately tell him what it is alone that kind
Nature hath made to be pure, uncloying, ever-growing Pleafure ; even the Exercifes of
Reafon, Underftanding and Virtue ; and the Confcioufnefs of Worth and Merit, generous and noble Deeds, and ufeful Studies. It hath been often obferv'd, that none are
more apt to Fretfulnefs and Difcontent ; to reproach Nature for not having made fufficient Provifion for our Happinefs, and to complain of the tedious Round of Life's dull
Pleafures ; than thofe who are plac'd in the happieft Circumftances of outward Enjoyment. But the very Source and Caufe of thefe Murmurings againft Nature is the ftrongeft
Proof of her Wifdom and Benignity. Whence proceeds this, but becaufe mere Affluence
cannot in the nature of things make a reafonable Being happy ? It is becaufe generous virtuous Nature hath made us for a higher and nobler kind of Happinefs, than the moft
exquifite Titillations of Senfe can yield ; the Pleafures of the Mind. When we arraign
Nature for her Niggardlinefs towards us, we in effect defire to have been made with
more capacious Senfes, but without Reflection, Reafon, a moral Senfe, and Confcience :
As if fenfual Enjoyments were preferable to thofe which Reafon, Virtue, and elegant
Studies afford to him ; who can bring his Conduct, his Purfuits, and Employments to
their Tribunal, and receive their Approbation for acting and beftowing his time as it
becometh the Excellence and Dignity of his Nature. Let any one, whofe Time hangs
heavy upon his hands, and whom neither Drefs, Pageantry, Table nor Play, can make
eafy and cheerful ; but amidft Plenty is ever complaining of the narrow tirefome Circle of human Pleafures ; let him but try the virtuous Employments, lay out his Time
                                                                                     and

(60) So *Spanheim, Scipio Maffei,* and our own *Spec-*
tator and *Guardian.* See *Bulengerus de Pictura vete-*
rum, L 1. c. 3. Ea eft vitæ memoria, lux vitæ, teftis
temporum, nuncia virtutis, mortuorum a morte refti-
tutio, famæ gloriæque immortalitas, vivorum propaga-
tio ; quæ facit ut abfentes præfto fint, & Variis diffitif-
que locis uno tempore repræfententur.

(61) Sæpe audivi Q. Maxumum, P. Scipionem, præ-

terea civitatis noftræ præclaros viros folitos ita dicere ;
quum majorum imagines intuerentur, vehementiffime
fibi animum ad virtutem accendi, fcilicet non ceram
illam, neque figuram tantam vim in fefe habere ; fed
memoria rerum geftarum, eam flammam egregiis Viris
in pectore crefcere ; neque prius fedari quam virtus eorum famam atque gloriam adæquarent. *Salluft. in*
Bello Jugur. See likewife *Valerius Maximus,* l. 5. c. 8.
Ex. 3.

and Fortune in manly Studies, and in doing good ; and then let him say, whether Man hath not a large fhare of true Happinefs in his power, that brings no Remorfe along with it, and that never furfeits.   The younger *Pliny* had but a fmall Eftate , but what true Luxury did he enjoy who knew fo well how to employ it in great and generous Deeds, and how to divide his time between polite ufeful Studies and good Actions? To name no other Examples from ancient Hiftory, which affords fo many, let us take a fhort review of what he did with a Fortune that now-a-days would hardly be reckon'd a tolerable Competency ; for falfe Pleafure is as avaritious as it is prodigal and diffolute. *Pliny*, the greateft Lawyer and moft elegant Writer of the Age he lived in, in feveral of his Epiftles fhews a generous Sollicitoufnefs in recommending to the Public fome young Men of his own Profeffion ; and very often undertakes to become an Advocate, upon condition that fome one of thafe his young Favourites might be join'd with him, in order to produce Merit which Modefty otherwife would have fuppreffed. This great Man is ever relieving his Friends.   He makes a prefent to one of a confiderable Sum he had at firft but lent him.   He pays the Debts of another that were juftly and honour-ably contracted.   He augments the Portion of a young Lady, that fhe might be in a con-dition to fupport the Dignity of him to whom fhe was about to be married.   He fur-nifhes one Friend with what was neceffary to be a *Roman* Knight ; to have the means of ferving another, he fells a fmall Eftate for ready Money below its Value.   He provides another with Money to return to his own Country, and end his Days in Tranquillity. It was the Poet *Martial*.   He generoufly refigns fome Rights in order to put an end to Family-Divifions and Quarrels.   He fettles a Competency upon his Nurfe for her comfortable Subfiftence.   He founds a publick Library for the ufe of his Country : And provides Salaries for Profeffors to inftruct the Youth in all ufeful and polite Sciences. He made an Eftablifhment for maintaining and educating Orphans and poor Children. And all this he did out of a very fmall Revenue.   But his Frugality was to him a Fund of Riches, which fupplied the Scantinefs of his Fortune, and enabled him to do all thefe generous Offices.   " *Quod ceffat ex reditu, frugalitate fuppletur ; ex qua, ve-* " *lut ex fonte liberalitas noftra decurrit* (62)."   At what a diftance does this glorious Example caft thofe, who, though born to great Fortunes, live as if they were made for themfelves only, and for the loweft Purfuits and Gratifications ; who look upon Wealth only as the Inftrument of Senfuality, Luxury, and vain Oftentation ; and give them-felves up to Enjoyments, which inftead of being ufeful are equally pernicious to them-felves and to the Publick ; who abandoning the real Joys of Friendfhip, Generofity, Science, good Tafte and Virtue, act as if they owed nothing to their Blood, their Fa-mily, their Friends, their Fellow-Creatures, their Country ; as if they owed nothing to Merit, to Humanity, to Virtue, to Ingenuity, to Society and publick Good ? Riches are no more than Means of being great and happy, and not the abfolutely neceffary Means neither.   For 'tis poffible to be extremely happy without great Affluence.   And how mife-rable may one be in the moft luxurious Condition of outward Gratifications ? In what Na-ture, affectionate, kind, wife Nature, (to whom Man is dearer than to himfelf) hath plac'd our Happinefs, even the ancient Poets have often told us (63) ; but none hath better de-fcribed the trueft Happinefs of Man, which Virtue alone can yield, than one of our own from Experience and the Heart.

> *Know then this Truth, (enough for Man to know)*
> *Virtue alone is Happinefs below :*
> *The only Point where human Blifs ftands ftill,*
> *And taftes the Good without the Fall to Ill :*
> *Where only Merit conftant Pay receives,*
> *Is blefs'd in what it takes and what it gives :*
> *The Joy unequall'd, if its End it gain ;*
> *And if it lofe, attended with no pain.*
> *Without Satiety, though e'er fo blefs'd,*
> *And but more relifh'd as the more diftrefs'd ;*
> *The broadeft Mirth unfeeling Folly wears,*
> *Lefs pleafing far than Virtue's very Tears.*

Good

The younger Pliny's Generofity and Vir-tue, a noble Ex-ample.

(62) See his Life by Mr. *Henley*, prefix'd to the *Eng-lifh* Tranflation of his Epiftles, *lib.* 2. *Epift.* 4. *lib.* 3. *Ep.* 2. *ver.* 2. *lib.* 6. *Ep.* 32. *lib.* 1. *Ep.* 19. *lib.* 7. *Ep.* 2. 18, & 19. *lib.* 3. 21, *lib.* 4. *Ep.* 10. *lib.* 8. *Ep.* 2. *lib.* 5. *Ep.* 19. *lib.* 1. *Ep.* 8. *lib.* 4. *Ep.* 13. *lib.* 8. *Ep.* 30. which he concludes in this manner : A Pattern of Li-berality, though imperfect, is at prefent extremely rare ; the defiring of getting prevails fo far upon Mankind, that they feem not fo properly to poffefs their Wealth as to be poffefs'd by it. Many Paffages might be brought from his Letters to prove his Tafte of the fine Arts ; fee particularly *lib.* 3. *Ep.* 6. to *Severus* upon a *Corin-thian* Statue. Where, after an elegant Defcription of its Beauties, he concludes : I bought it indeed not with

any view of placing it at home, but of fixing it in fome famous place of our Country, and to chufe in the Temple of *Jupiter* ; for it feems a Prefent worthy of the Temple, worthy of the God.

(63) How excellent is *Horace's* Advice and Caution ?
——————— *Si non*
Intendes animum ftudiis, & rebus honeftis,
Invidia vel amore vigil torquebere :
Incipe : qui recte vivendi prorogat horam.
Rufticus expectat, dum defluat amnis.
———————————— *fapere aude.*
                                     Hor. l. 1. Ep. 2.

Good from each Object, from each Place acquir'd,
For ever exercis'd, yet never tir'd.
Never elated while one Man's opprefs'd,
Never dejected while another's blefs'd.
And where no Wants, no Wifhes can remain,
Since but to with more Virtue, is to gain.
See the fole Blifs Heav'n could on all beftow ;
Which who but feels, can tafte ; but thinks, can know.

Effay on Man, Ep. 4.

The Opulence of a State ought to be employed in encouraging Virtue, Induftry, and the ingenious Arts and Sciences.

NOW as it is with regard to particular Perfons, fo is it likewife with refpect to Societies or Bodies of Men. Wealth in a State is a Nufance, a poifonous Source of Vilenefs and Wickednefs, if it is not employed by publick Spirit and good Tafte in promoting Virtue, Ingenuity, Induftry, and all the Sciences and Arts, which employ Mens nobleft Powers and Faculties, and raife human Society to its moft amiable glorious Eftate. 'Tis not Opulence pilfered by unfair means, or difhoneft Commerce ; but Riches procured by Virtue, Ingenuity and Induftry, maintain'd by Temperance and Frugality, and laid out in the Encouragement of Virtue, Induftry, and all ingenious Arts, that aggrandizes a Nation. Let us but imagine to ourfelves a Country over-flowing with Wealth, that produces nothing but fuperfluous Tables, gaudy, fplendid Equipages, Horfe-Races, gladiatorial Combats and Bull-baitings ; and in which the moft ingenious Entertainment is Rope-dancing or a Puppet-fhew, and the only cultivated Science, Cookery : Let us imagine fuch a Country fupplied with Riches by the Labour of the common People, in Tillage, Manufactures and Commerce, who content themfelves with a poor Maintenance ; while a fmall number confume the Produce of their Sweat and Drudgery, in every way of Enjoyment to which Senfe alone is requifite, and to which Reafon is rather a Diminution and Hindrance than advantageous : Let us figure to ourfelves fuch a State, without Sciences and Arts of any kind, except fuch a fmall Portion as is abfolutely neceffary to Agriculture, Manufactures and Navigation : And then let us oppofe to this Picture that of another Country, in which not only all the Virtues and Arts that are requifite to bring in Riches are duly cultivated and rewarded ; but, where Riches being employed in the Encouragement of every kind of Ingenuity and Invention, Philofophy moral and natural, Mathematicks, Poetry, Architecture, Painting, Statuary, Sculpture, and all the Arts, are daily making new Improvements and Advances; no Man of Merit is unprovided for or unrelieved ; due Provifion being made for the Succour of the Unfortunate, and for rewarding the Good and Ufeful ; Senfuality is ignominious ; all the publick Entertainments and Diverfions are ingenious and virtuous ; and the Great and Rich do not wafte their Eftates in maintaining idle, wanton, infolent Domefticks, and deftroying their Health by unnatural, not Food but Poifon ; or in Furniture, the coftly Materials of which only fhew how much good they have in their power to do ; contenting themfelves with what is neat, and eftimable rather upon account of Art and Work than Subftance (64) : And thus every degree and kind of Virtue, Genius, Science, Art, Induftry is encourag'd, flourifhes and exerts itfelf with Spirit and Alacrity. Let us oppofe, I fay, thefe two Pictures to one another ; and then pronounce which is the greateft, the moft defirable State ; which beft deferves to be called a Society of Men, of rational Creatures, ingenious virtuous Beings ; for thofe alone certainly are reafonable Beings, who delight and exert themfelves in fuch Productions, Works and Actions as are truly worthy of and becoming the noble Faculties and Powers with which Nature hath adorned them. Can any one hefitate about giving the preference in this cafe ? What is it that hath perpetuated the Glory of *Athens*, a fmall State ; and that hath made it the Subject of Wonder and Admiration in every enlighten'd Age ? Is it not chiefly the publick Spirit, the Virtue, the Ingenuity of that People, and the immenfe Height to which all the Arts and Sciences arofe amongft them.

Ariftotle and Plato cenfured the Laws of Lycurgus, becaufe they were not calculated to promote Politenefs and Science.

ARISTOTLE in his Politicks, and others, have juftly found fault with the Laws of *Lycurgus*, becaufe they were merely calculated to produce a military People, a Nation of Soldiers. This Legiflator, fay they, had only in view fortifying the Body, and not at all the Culture of the Mind. Why muft he banifh from his Republick all the Arts, one of the chief Fruits of which is the Polifh they give to Life and Manners ? They fweeten the Heart, infpire a focial benign Temper, and render Society lively and agreeable. Hence it came that the *Lacedæmonians* had fomething in their Temper and Character too rough, auftere, and ferocious ; this Fault refulted chiefly from their Education, the fine Arts having no place amongft them. The liberal Arts mightily humanize :

Adde, quod ingenuas didiciffe fideliter Artes
Emollit mores, nec finit effe feros.   Ovid. Ep. ex Ponto I. 2. Ep. 9.

They

(64) What a glorious Character does *Nepos* give of *Atticus* in this refpect ? Elegans non magnificus ; fplendidus, non fumptuofus, omni diligentia munditiam non affluentem affectabat. Supellex non modica, non mufta ; ut in neutram partem confpici poffet, &c. *In Vit. Attici.*

They soften, but far from effeminating, they add Strength to the Mind :

> *Doctrina sed vim promovet insitam*
> *Rectique cultus pectora roborant* (65).   Hor. l. 4. Od. 4.

LET us enquire, on the other hand, what Objections are brought against the En. *Objections against* couragement of the ingenious Arts ; those principally of which I am now treating. *encouraging the* And what is commonly laid against them may be summ'd up in these four Articles. *Plato* *Arts, consider'd and* banish'd them from his Commonwealth. *Pericles* is blam'd for encouraging them at *answer'd.* *Athens*, by very grave and wise Men. They were no inconsiderable Cause of the Ruin and Fall of the *Roman* State. And they naturally tend to effeminate the Mind and promote Luxury.

FIRST of all it is said, that *Plato* banish'd all the fine Arts from his Republick. *Plato banish'd them* Now 'tis not pretended that *Plato* treated the Arts of Design worse than he did Poetry. *from his Republick.* And who, even in deference to so great a Man, would banish from a State that divine Art, of which that excellent Philosopher was himself so great a Lover and Imitator ? But if Poetry is left, her Sisters must likewise have place ; for without them, that is, without continually borrowing from them, and calling them to her assistance, she could not long subsist, or at least, arrive to any very considerable degree of Perfection. 'Tis the same common Genius that maintains and animates them all. But, the truth of the matter is, *Plato* was not for banishing the fine Arts ; he was too sensible of their ad. mirable power to convey moral Instructions into the Heart, and to recommend Virtue in the powerfullest manner, to have thought of depriving Philosophy of its best Ministers and Servants. He was only for bringing all the Arts and Sciences under the Cognizance of his philosophical Magistrates ; that the Laws and the Arts might speak the same Lan- guage, and these might not be employed to pull down what those were intended to build (66). And what honest Man and true Lover of the Arts, doth not heartily regret that ever they should be alienated from Virtue, and prostituted to give false Charms to Vice ? 'Tis needless to lose time in shewing, that *Plato*'s Scheme of regulating the Sciences is impracticable. 'Tis not by establishing an Orthodoxy in Poetry and her Sister Arts, that they can be kept steady to Virtue : But the Example of Magistrates and great Men would do in such Cases what Laws cannot possibly effectuate. Here, good Example which is always more powerful than Laws, is the only proper Remedy (67). No Statutes can be contriv'd which would not bring very great Inconveniences along with them, not merely to Wit ; and it seems to be *Plato*'s chief Scope to prove, in his Ideal Republick, the Weakness and Insufficiency of the best Laws, unless Magistrates or Rulers set a good Example, and take proper care of Education.

IN the next place it is said, that *Pericles* is blam'd by good Men for giving too *Pericles censured* large Encouragement to the fine Arts. Let us then inquire what is said on this head. *for encouraging* 'Tis indeed observ'd by *Plato* (68), after *Socrates* his Master, in more than one place, *them too much.* that *Pericles*, with all the fine Works he did to adorn *Athens*, had contributed very little to make his Fellow-Citizens better Men ; but rather a great deal to corrupt the Purity and Simplicity of their ancient Manners. He is not blam'd by them for adorn- ing *Athens* or encouraging the fine Arts ; but for not taking more pains to promote, at the same time, virtuous and pure Manners ; by others he was censured, not for pro- moring the fine Arts, and beautifying *Athens*, but for bestowing the Money in that way, which was allotted for other Exigencies. *Cicero* indeed tells us in his Offices, that *Demetrius Phalereus* blam'd *Pericles* exceedingly, for squandring away such a vast Sum of Money upon one magnificent Building at the Entrance of the *Acropolis* (69). But *Cicero* calls him one of the greatest Men amongst all the *Grecians*. And *Plutarch* (70) gives an account of the Methods he took to employ all the ingenious Artists in adorn- ing *Athens*, that is well worthy the Imitation of great Men. In fine, without going further into the Examination of *Pericles*'s Character, if we will allow *Cicero* to decide in this question about the true Magnificence of great Men, Magistrates, or Ministers of State, his Opinion amounts to these two excellent Observations.

FIRST, " that even great Men ought to take care, not to be too extravagant in their " Magnificence and Expences ; which is a very ill thing, though it had no other harm in
" it

(65) See how *Polybius* speaks of the happy Effects of Musick, and all the ingenious Arts in humanizing the Minds of a People in the strongest Terms, *l.* 4. *p.*289, & 291.

(66) See his Books *De Legibus & de Repub.* and a Dissertation on this Subject, in the *Memoirs of the Aca- demy of Belles Lettres*, by the Abbé Fraguier.

(67) Præcipuus adstricti moris auctor Vespasianus

fuit antiquo ipse cultu victuque, obsequium deinde in principem, & æmulandi amor validior quam poena ex legibus, & metus. *Tac. Annal. lib.* 3. *c.* 55.

(68) *Gorgias, p.* 515. and *Alcibiades* 1, *p.* 119. *Edit. Steph.*

(69) *De Off. lib.* 2. *c.* 17.

(70) *Plutarch. in Pericle.*

" it but only that one of giving a bad Example (71) : For moſt Men are apt to imitate
" the great ones in this particular, more than in any thing elſe : Where, for example, (ſays
" he) ſhall we find the Man that rivals the famous *Lucullus* in his Virtues ? Whereas, how
" many have done it in the Statelineſs and Magnificence of his Country-Houſes? But
" there certainly ought to be ſome Bounds fix'd and preſcrib'd to theſe things, and thoſe to
" be according to the Rules of Moderation ; but the Meaſure whereby we are to judge of
" their being moderate, is their Subſerviency to the Ornaments and Conveniencies of Life.
" Now the main End of Building is Lodging, and other neceſſary Uſes of a Houſe ; and
" therefore the Draught and Contrivance of it ſhould be ſuited accordingly. But we
" ſhould not ſo much regard bare Neceſſities as not to have an Eye likewiſe to Conve-
" nience and Magnificence. A Houſe ought to be ſuited to a Perſon's Rank and Dignity;
" as in all other caſes a Man ſhould not have reſpect to himſelf alone, but to other People
" alſo ; ſo it is in this of a Nobleman's Houſe, which ought to be very large and capaci-
" ous, becauſe he ought to keep up the Laws of Hoſpitality, and entertain in it multitudes
" of Perſons of all ſorts. For a fine and large Houſe, that gives Entertainment to ho
" body, ſerves but to upbraid its Owner ; and eſpecially if it was uſed to be frequently
" viſited under its former Maſter. For 'tis an odious thing to have Paſſengers cry as they
" go along, *O domus antiqua, heu ! quam diſpari dominare domino !* 'Tis well if a Man
" can enhance that Credit and Reputation, he has got by the Splendour of his Houſe,
" but he muſt not depend upon his Houſe alone for it ; for the Maſter ought to bring Ho-
" nour to his fine Seat, and not the fine Seat bring Honour to his Maſter."

IN the ſecond place he obſerves, " that the beſt way of laying out Money is not in
" giving Entertainments and Shews to the People ; but in publick and uſeful Works, in
" repairing City-walls, High-ways, making Docks, Havens, Aqueducts, and the like things,
" that may ſerve to the general Uſe and Advantage of the Publick (72)." There is a manifeſt difference between thoſe ſumptuous uſeleſs Works of Tyrants, which *Pliny* calls their
vain Oſtentation of Riches, *Regum pecuniæ otioſa ac ſtulta oſtentatio* (73) ; and on
account of which *Tacitus* condemns the falſe Magnificence of *Nero*, and calls him *Incredibilium Cupitor* (74) ; and ſuch Works as are really uſeful, tending either to the
Advantage or proper Ornament of a Country. The Encouragement of the fine Arts is
ſo far from requiring Sumptuouſneſs and Coſtlineſs in the Materials, that it hath been
obſerv'd on the contrary that this falſe Taſte hath ever prov'd their ruin. It is the Art
and Work that ought to be valued, not the Subſtance. And as the Arts ought chiefly
to be employed in rendring juſtice to Merit, and in teaching and recommending Virtue
by praiſing it ; ſo ought they, for that effect, to be chiefly employed in adorning publick Buildings ; the Houſes where the States of a free People aſſemble to deliberate about
the common Intereſts of their Country ; Schools and Academies of Arts and Sciences,
and other ſuch places of common and publick Utility. 'Tis not againſt the Arts that
Seneca rails, but againſt the horrid Corruption and Abuſe of them when they are made
Miniſters to Luxury and Vice (75).

*'Tis ſaid they tend
to effeminate the
Mind, and that
they contributed to
the Ruin of the
Roman State.*

IF it is ſaid, that the fine Arts were no inconſiderable Cauſe of the Fall and Ruin of
the *Roman* (76) State ; and that they tend to promote Luxury, and effeminate the
Mind : It may be anſwer'd, that *Polybius* had foretold the ſad Change in the *Roman*
Government, juſt as it happen'd, in conſequence of other Cauſes (77). He obſerves,
that the Corruption of Manners, which muſt inevitably bring after it a fatal Change of
Government, from Liberty to Slavery, is in human Affairs the ordinary effect of happy
Succeſſes and long Proſperity.

" WHEN a Republick, ſays he, after having gone through many Dangers, comes
" forth victorious, and arriving to the very Summit of Power and Glory, hath no longer
" any Rivals to diſpute Power and ſupreme Empire with it ; ſuch Proſperity, if it is
" high and permanent, never fails to introduce the Luxury and corrupt Ambition, which
                                                                                    " muſt

(71) ―――― Dicendum etiam eſt qualem hominis ho-
norati & principis domum placeat eſſe, cujus finis eſt
uſus : ad quem accomodanda eſt ædificandi deſcriptio:
Et tamen adhibenda dignitatis, &c.——ornanda eſt enim
dignitas domo, non ex domo tota quærenda. *Off. lib.*
1. 39.

(72) *De Off. lib.* 2. *c.*17.   Atque illæ etiam impen-
ſæ meliores, muri, navalia, portus, aquarum ductus,
omniaque quæ ad uſum reipublicæ pertinent, &c.

(73) *Plin.* 36. 12.

(74) *Annal.* 15. 42.

(75) Non enim adducor ut in numerum liberalium
artium pictores recipiam, non magis quam ſtatuarios
aut marmoreos aut ceteros luxuriæ miniſtros. *Sen. Ep.*

88.   He had good ground to ſay ſo of them in his time.
He ſpeaks of Libraries in the ſame Strain, *de Tranquilli-
tate animi*, N°6.——Bibliotheca quoque ut neceſſarium
domus ornamentum expolitur.   Ignoſcerem plane, ſi e
ſtudiorum nimia cupidine oriretur : nunc iſta exquiſita,
& cum imaginibus ſuis deſcripta ſacrorum opera ingeniorum, in ſpeciem & cultum parietum comparantur.

(76) So *Velleius Paterculus, l. 1. c.* 13.   Non puto,
dabitis, Venici, quin magis pro rep. fuerit, manere
adhuc rudem Corinthiorum intellectum, quam in tantum ea intelligi ; & quin hac prudentia, illa impruden-
tia decori publico fuerit convenientior.

(77) *Polyb. Hiſt. lib.* 6.   See *Velleius Paterculus, l.* 2.
ab initio. Salluſt and *Livy* in many places of their Writings.

" muſt infallibly be the Ruin of the moſt flouriſhing potent State. The Love of Mag-
" nificence, falſe Pleaſures and Luxury, demanding vaſt Supplies of Money continually,
" ſoon engender Avarice, and that produces Injuſtice and Rapine ; it leaves no Stone un-
" turn'd to accompliſh its Ends ; now it plunders, now it flatters and bribes ; and thus
" the People provoked on one hand by unjuſt cruel Exactions, and corrupted on the
" other by the poiſonous Flatteries and Largeſſes of the Ambitious, no longer conſult
" their Intereſts, but liſtening to their Paſſions and Caprices, become licentious and un-
" governable. Accuſtomed to live upon Spoil and Bribes, and to fatten in Sloth and
" Wickedneſs, if a hardy enterprizing Leader, who, tho' he be not able to ſupply their
" Wants himſelf, appears however bold and daring enough to find out means of ſatiſ-
" fying them ; if ſuch a one offers himſelf, they will attach themſelves to him, ſupport
" and ſtand by him in all his Attempts. Hence muſt come Seditions, Murders, Exiles,
" Proſcriptions, Abolition of juſt Debts, and an unjuſt Diviſion of Eſtates ; till at laſt
" ſome one ariſes, who, being more powerful than all the reſt, ſeizes the ſupreme
" Command, and renders himſelf abſolute Maſter, or rather Tyrant."

SUCH in effect were the diſmal Revolutions which ſo miſerably chang'd the Face of the *Roman* Republick, according to that great Politician's moſt ſagacious Prediction. The Arts did not in this caſe corrupt the *Roman* People ; but coming amongſt them when they were very deprav'd, were corrupted by them : And then indeed, as it muſt happen in the nature of things, being vilely abuſed, they in their turn ſerved to promote Vice and Diſſoluteneſs of Manners.

WHAT a glorious Character does *Cicero* give of thoſe great Men, who firſt brought Statues and Pictures, and the fine Arts from *Greece*, not to adorn their own Houſes, but *Rome* (78) ? *Paulus Æmilius* had all the Wealth of *Macedonia* in his power, which amounted to almoſt an infinite Value : So that he brought ſuch a Sum into the Treaſury, as that the ſingle Booty of that one General ſuperſeded the Neceſſity of all Taxes for the future : And yet he brought nothing into his own Houſe but the eternal Memory of his Name and Atchievements. *Africanus* followed the Example of his Father, and returned nothing richer from the Overthrow of *Carthage*. So *Mummius*, who was afterwards his Partner in the Cenſorſhip, did he make himſelf ever a farthing the wealthier, by razing one of the wealthieſt Cities in the World ? No ; he rather choſe to make *Italy* fine with the Spoils of his Enemics, than his own Houſe : " Tho' " in my Opinion (ſaith *Cicero*) the Fineneſs of *Italy* reflects a bright Luſtre upon his " Houſe too." *Cicero* remarkably ſhews his Love to the fine Arts in another place (79), when he regrets the razing of *Corinth*, becauſe it had been long a School for the fine Arts.

THE good Emperors, under whom they flouriſh'd moſt, were celebrated Ehemies to falſe Luxury and Magnificence ; they were ſober and frugal in their private Expence. Such was *Veſpaſian*, who did his utmoſt to put a ſtop to all Luxury, eſpecially that of the Table. *Nerva, Trajan*, the two *Antonines*, all of them were Examples of Modera-tion, Temperance and Frugality in their own Perſons : And yet it was chiefly under them that the Arts revived and proſpered at *Rome* (80). Did the Arts effeminate thoſe excellent Princes ? Did they effeminate a *Socrates*, who was brave in the Camp, in De-fence of his Country, as any of the moſt veteran Captains (81) ? Did they effeminate a *Xenophon*, an *Aratus*, the Deliverer of his Country, or a *Scipio*, the Glory of his ? Did they render a *Polybius* too ſoft and indolent ? And yet his Love of the Arts ſuffi-ciently appears, from the pain with which he ſaw the fine Pieces of curious Art de-ſtroy'd by the common Soldiers at *Corinth* (82). Did they, in fine, render a *Cicero* leſs fit for ſerving his Country on every occaſion ? Leſs ſevere and rigid in his Oppoſition to Corruption, Luxury and Tyranny ? " As for the Judgment of *Cato* (ſays my Lord " *Verulam*) he was well puniſh'd for his blaſpheming againſt Learning, in the ſame " kind wherein he offended ; for when he was paſt threeſcore Years old, he was taken " with an extreme deſire of going to School again to learn the *Greek* Tongue, to the " end

They flouriſh'd un-
der the good and
frugal Emperors.

They did not effe-
minate a Socrates,
a Xenophon, a
Scipio, a Cicero, a
Polybius, &c.

(78) *De Off. lib.* 2. *c.* 22. Upon which occaſion he makes this excellent Remark : Nullum igitur Vitium tetrius, quam aVaritia, in principibus præſertim & rem-publicam gubernantibus. Habere enim quæſtui rem-publicam non modo turpe eſt, ſed ſceleratum etiam & nefarium.. Itaque quod Apollo Pythius oraculo edidit Spartam nulla re alia niſi aVaritia perituram, id vide-tur non ſolum Lacedæmoniis, ſed & omnibus opulentis populis prædixiſſe, &c.

(79) *Cicero de Offic. l.* 1. *c.* 11.

(80) See *Sueton. in Vita Veſpaſ.* The Paſſages of *Ta-citus* already cited. *Plin. Paneg. Capitol. in Vita Anto-*nin. *Aurel Victor. Epitom. Eutrop. & Jul. Cæſares.*

(81) See *Plutarch's* Life of *Alcibiades*, and his *Sym-poſiacum.*

(82) Polybius ſane, quæ in urbis captivitate obvene-runt in commiſerationis partem colligens, injuriam mi-litum addit atque ludibria, quæ in artes & præclara ex-ercuerunt opera, Vetiis oblata dona. Ait enim præ-ſente ſeſe, abjectas in paVimenta vidiſſe tabulas, ſu-perque illas talis luſitaſſe milites, eaſque nominatim ex-plicat. Ariſtides de libero Patro pinxerat, &c. *Strabo, l.* 8. *p.* 367. And ſee likewiſe what *Polybius* ſays of the Fine Arts, *l.* 4. *p.* 289, & 291.

" end that he might perufe the *Greek* Authors : Which doth well demonftrate, that his
" former Contempt of the *Greek* Learning was rather an affected Gravity, than according
" to the inward Senfe of his own Opinion (83)." Did they effeminate a *Julius Cæfar* or
an *Alexander ?* How happy had it been for the Times in which they liv'd, if thefe
humane Arts had more humanized their Minds; and turn'd into Ambition into a more
benign and kindly Courfe with regard to Mankind, and their Country! In fine, if we
look about in our own Country, who are the moft fteady to its Interefts, the moft im-
pregnable to Corruption, and the moft capable to ferve it either in Peace or War ;
Are they not known to be Lovers of true Philofophy and the fine Arts, and thoroughly
acquainted with them? The Arts, indeed, are not only capable of being abufed, but
have been fo moft wickedly. But what hath not been corrupted and abufed? Or what

will not vitious Men corrupt and abufe? The Arts when employed to their natural,
genuine, beft Purpofes, will not foften the Mind ; but muft on the contrary infpire it
with true Virtue and laudable Ambition. But the Arts alone are not indeed fufficient
to compleat Education :·The manly Exercifes ought alfo to have their place, according
to the ancient Method of Education ; when nothing was neglected in it that could
either fortify the Body or the Mind, promote Virtue or good Tafte ; fit for doing ufeful Services to the Publick, or for worthy and becoming Recreations at Hours of leifure : When nothing was neglected that could qualify for oppofing Corruption with
Stedfaftnefs in times of Peace, Plenty and Profperity ; or for defending their Country's
Rights in juft War, with prudent Bravery: And when, at the fame time, nothing was
neglected in Education (84) that could capacitate for agreeable and ufeful Converfation,
or truly profitable as well as pleafant Studies, in the Retirements from publick Bufinefs,
which are fo requifite to unbend the Mind, or rather to recruit it with new Vigour.
Ingenious Study and polite Converfation are equally refrefhing and improving : And even
the Amufements, the Exercifes and Diverfions of the virtuous Man will be far removed
from Vice.

THUS we have feen to what generous and noble Ufes the fine Arts are fitted to ferve ;
and in purfuance of what Defign it is that they ought to be employed agreeably to
their Nature and Genius; as well as for the Intereft and Honour of Society. But let us
inquire more particularly whence it is that they are capable of yielding fuch delight ; of
what kind the Pleafure is which they afford ; or to whom it is that they give the higheft
Satisfaction and Entertainment, and how that Tafte muft be cultivated and improved,
upon which a juft and thorough Relifh of them depends.

(83) See *Bacon's* Effay on the Advancement of
Learning.

(84) See what *Cicero* fays of the Liberal Arts.——
Iis artibus quibus ætas puerilis ad humanitatem infor-
mari folet.——Quam multas nobis imagines, non totum
ad intuendum, Verum etiam ad imitandum, fortiffi-
morum virorum, expreffas, fcriptores & Græci &
Latini reliquerunt ? Quas ego femper in adminiftranda
rep. animum & mentem meam ipfa cogitatione ho-

minum excellentium conformabam.——Quod fi non hic
tantus fructus oftenderetur, fi in his ftudiis delectatio
fola peteretur : tamen ut opinor, hanc animi adver-
fionem, humaniffimam, ac liberaliffimam judicaretis.
Nam ceteræ neque temporum funt, neque ætatum
omnium, neque locorum. Hæc ftudia adolefcentiam
alunt, fenectutem oblectant, fecundas res ornant, ad-
verfis perfugium ac folatium præbent, delectant domi,
non impediunt foris, pernoctant nobifcum, peregri-
nantur, rufticantur. *Cicero Orat. pro Archia Poeta.*

CHAP. VII.

Observations on the Samenefs of good Tafte in all the Arts, and in Life and Manners ; on the Sources and Foundations of rational Pleafures in our Natures, and the Ufefulnefs of the fine Arts in a liberal Education.

WHAT hath been hitherto obferv'd concerning the Arts of Defign, Painting in particular, is chiefly intended to prepare the way for fhewing their Ufefulnefs in Education, by pointing out their Foundation in our Nature, and their Conneƈion with true Philofophy ; that true Philofophy which explains the τὸ καλὸν, or Beautiful in Nature, in Conduƈt, and in Arts, and fhews it to be the fame in them all.   Now as in giving an Account of the Rife, Progrefs, and Decline of Painting amongft the Ancients, and the Caufes to which thefe Effeƈts are principally afcribed, I have only commented and enlarged a little on fome Teftimonies of ancient Authors ; fo even in this more philofophical Part of my Plan, my Defign is merely to fet the Sentiments of the better Ancients concerning good Tafte and liberal Education in the cleareft Light I can, by reafoning from their Principles and Maxims. *The chief Defign of this Effay.*

THE Doƈtrine of the beft ancient Philofophers concerning our Powers and Faculties, true Happinefs, good Tafte, and right Education, amounts briefly to this. *A Summary of the Doƈtrine of the better Ancients, concerning the Sources of our nobleft Pleafures.*

THE Pleafures of the Mind are far fuperiour to thofe of the Body : We have, (fay they) by our Frame and Conftitution but a very fcanty Provifion for Enjoyment in the way of Senfe and common Appetite ; but we have a very noble and ample one for rational Happinefs ; fince even our Senfes in that refpeƈt make a very proper and ufeful part of our Stock or Furniture ; whereas confidered abftraƈtly from our intelleƈtual Powers and Capacities, or otherwife than as Minifters to them, they are a moft mean and narrow Pittance.   A very flight Review of our Make and Contexture is fufficient to convince us, that the chief Enjoyments our Senfes are capable of affording us, are thofe which they adminifter to us, as Inlets of Materials for Imagination, Reafon, and our inward Senfe of Beauty, natural and moral, to work upon and employ themfelves about : And that if we were not indued with thefe fuperiour Faculties, all the barely fenfual Gratifications our outward Organs can receive or convey, would conftitute but a very low degree of Happinefs.   Our higheft Pleafures are thofe which accompany, or refult from the Exercifes of our moral Powers ; the Pleafures of Imagination, Underftanding, Virtue, and a moral Senfe : Otherwife indeed thofe Powers which diftinguifh a Man from the lower Herds of Animals could not be called his moft noble and honourable Faculties ; or be faid to raife him to a higher Rank and Dignity in Being (1).   But what are the Objeƈts adapted to thefe Faculties, or how do they employ themfelves about them ? What is it the Underftanding delights to know ; Fancy to defcribe, or Art to imitate ? Is it not Nature ? And what is it that Virtue emulates ? Is it not likewife the Benevolence, the Beauty and Harmony of Nature ?   Nature being therefore the fole Objeƈt of Knowledge, and of Imitation whether in Arts or Life ; all our greateft Pleafures and Enjoyments, all our nobleft and worthieft Exercifes muft be very nearly allied.   It is the fame Stock of Powers and Faculties that capacitates us for them all : They have the fame Objeƈt, Rule, Meafure and End : And confequently good Tafte in Science, in Arts, and in Life, muft be the fame ; that is, it muft be founded on the fame Principles ; lead to the fame Conclufions ; and be improveable in the fame manner.   Accordingly, the Perfeƈtion of our Underftanding, does it not confift in as full and compleat a Knowledge of Nature as we can obtain by Study and Contemplation ;

or

---

(1) Compare what *Cicero* fays *De finibus Bonorum, lib.* 2. N° 33, & 34.   Quod Vero a te difputatum eft majores effe voluptates, & dolores animi quam corporis——Ad altiora quædam & magnificentiora nati fumus : Nec id ex animi folum partibus, in quibus ineft memoria rerum innumerabilium, ineft conjeƈtura confequentium, non multum a divinatione differens, ineft moderator cupiditatis pudor, ineft ad humanam focietatem juftitiæ fida cuftodia : Ineft in perpetiendis laboribus, adeundifque periculis, firma & ftabilis doloris mortifque contemtio.   Ergo hæc in animis : Tu autem membra ipfa fenfufque confidera : Qui tibi ut reliquæ corporis partes, non comites folum virtutum, fed miniftri etiam videbuntur, &c.   *De Nat. Deor. lib.* 2. N° 58, & 59.   Omnifque fenfus hominum multo antecellit fenfibus beftiarum.   Primum enim oculi in iis artibus quarum judicium eft oculorum, in piƈtis,

fiƈtis, cælatifque formis, in corporum etiam motione atque geftu multa cernunt fubtilius.   Colorum etiam & figurarum venuftatem atque ordinem, & ut ita dicam decentiam oculi judicant : atque etiam alia majora, nam & Virtutis & Vitia cognofcunt : Iratum, propitium, &c.——Auriumque item eft mirabile quoddam artificiofumque judicium, &c.

The whole Defign of *Marcus Antoninus*'s Meditations is to fhew, that we are made not merely for the Pleafures of Senfe, but for thofe of Reafon, Virtue, and Religion.   There are feveral Difcourfes of *Socrates* in the memorable things by *Xenophon* to the fame purpofe.   See in particular l. 4. *cap.* 5.   See to the fame effeƈt a beautiful Paffage of *Plato* quoted by *Longinus, de Sublimitate, feƈt.* 13. as an inftance of *Plato*'s fublime way of Writing.

or in a just Comprehension of its Order, Wisdom, Beauty, and Greatness in all its Operations? The Perfection of Life and Manners, does it not consist in conforming our Affections and Actions to that beautiful Model of Simplicity, Consistency, Greatness, and Goodness, which a right understanding of Nature sets before us for our Imitation? And the Perfection of all the Arts of Imagination, in what else does it consist but in emulating the Beauty, the Harmony, the Grandeur, and Order of Nature, in Systems or Works of our own Invention and Formation (2)?

Another View of the same Doctrine concerning Man, and the Improvement of his best Powers and Faculties.

MAN, say the Ancients, is made to contemplate and imitate Nature, and to be happy by so doing (3). His Dignity, his Duty, his Happiness, principally consist in these two. The Dignity, Duty, and Felicity of a Being, must be but different Names signifying the same thing; they cannot be really different: And how can they be ascertain'd or determin'd, but from the Consideration of the highest and noblest End, to which the Frame and Constitution of a Being is adapted? That is, from the Consideration of that End, towards which its Powers, Faculties, Instincts, and Affections consider'd, as making by all their mutual Respects one Whole, or one certain determinate Frame and Constitution, are fitted to operate (4). Now if the Frame of Man be thus consider'd, we shall find that he is made, chiefly, to contemplate and imitate Nature: Because his Senses, Powers, Faculties, Instincts, and Affections qualify him for that end; and the highest and noblest Pleasures he is capable of, arise from these Sources. Every other inferiour Exercise or Gratification, in the way of ordinary Appetite, rather terminates in Dissatisfaction and Nauseating, than in solid and pure Pleasure.

IF therefore it be the great Business of Education, to improve the Capacity and Taste of those Employments and Satisfactions, which are the remotest from all Grossness and Disgust, and yield the highest and most lasting delight; Education ought, by consequence, to aim chiefly at improving those natural Powers, Capacities, Affections, and Senses, by which we are capable of contemplating and imitating Nature; that is, at bringing to perfection that Sense of Beauty, Order, Harmony, Goodness and Greatness, by which alone we can enjoy Nature in Contemplation; and which alone fits for imitating it in Arts and Manners; or for receiving Satisfaction from Conformity with it in Speculations and Imitations of whatever kind.

NOW this 'tis evident must be but one Work; for from what hath been said it necessarily follows, that good Taste of Beauty, Order and Greatness in Nature, transferred to Life and Conduct, or to the Arts, must produce an equally good Taste in them, and reciprocally good Taste of Order, Beauty, and Greatness, transferred from the Arts, or from Manners to Nature, must produce a good Taste of Nature. A sound and thorough Sense of Beauty, Greatness, and Order in Nature, in Life, or in the fine Arts, will therefore be best form'd, by such a Course of Instruction and Education, as exercises the Mind in passing from Nature to Imitations, and reciprocally from Imitations to Nature; and in observing that the Beauty and Perfection of Arts, of Life, and of Nature, is the same (5).

THE End of Philosophy, is it not to form a good Taste of what is beautiful and admirable in Nature, orderly in Life, Conduct and Society, and true and perfect in Arts? But that Philosophy must be one, into whatever different Parts it is branched

---

(2) *Cicero* tells us, that, according to the Doctrine of *Plato*, all the liberal Arts and Sciences are strictly united, and gives this as the Reason for it, that Nature their Object is one throughout all her Works. *De Orat. lib.* 3. N° 6. Ac mihi quidem veteres illi majus quiddam animo complexi, multo plus etiam vidisse videntur quam quantum nostrorum ingeniorum acies intueri potest: Qui omnia hæc quæ supra & subter unum esse & una vi atque una consensione naturæ constricta esse dixerunt. —— Est etiam illa Platonis Vera, omnem doctrinam harum ingenuarum, &c. See *de finibus, lib.* 4. N° 21. Physicæ quoque non sine causa tributus idem est honos; propterea quod qui convenienter naturæ victurus sit, ei & proficiscendum est ab omni mundo & ab ejus procuratione. Neque Vero potest quisquam de bonis aut malis vere judicare nisi omni cognita ratione naturæ, & utrum conveniat necne natura hominis cum universa, &c. Compare with this *De Leg. lib.* 2. N° 22, & 23. and the Passages that are afterwards quoted.

(3) *Cicero de Senect.* N° 21. Sed credo Deos immortaleis sparsisse animos in corpora humana ut essent qui terras tuerentur, quique cælestium ordinem contemplantes imitarentur eum Vitæ modo, atque constantia. Nec me solum ratio impulit ut ita crederem, sed nobilitas etiam summorum philosophorum & auctoritas, &c. *De Nat. lib.* 2. N° 56.——Qui primum eos humo excitatos celsos & erectos constituit ut Deo-

rum cognitionem cælum intuentes capere possent. Sunt enim e terra homines non ut incolæ atque habitatores sed quasi spectatores superarum rerum atque cælestium quarum spectaculum ad nullum aliud genus animantium pertinet, &c. And again in the same Book, Ipse homo ortus est ad mundum contemplandum & imitandum.

(4) *Cicero de Nat. Deor. lib.* 2. N° 13. Neque enim dici potest in ulla rerum Institutione non esse aliquid extremum atque perfectum. Ut enim in Vite, ut in pecude, &c. *De Leg. lib.* 1. N° 7. Animal hoc providum, sagax, multiplex, memor, plenum rationis & consilii, quem vocamus hominem præclara quadam conditione generatum esse a supremo Deo, &c. *Acad. lib.* 2. N° 41. Est enim animorum ingeniorumque naturale quoddam quasi pabulum consideratio, contemplatioque naturæ: Erigimur, elatiores fieri videmur, humana despicimus: Cogitantesque supera atque cælestia hæc nostra ut exigua & minima contemnimus, &c. See his elegant Description of Philosophy, *Tusc. Quæst. lib.* 5. N° 2. O Vitæ philosophia dux, &c. Compare, with these Passages, the Reasoning in the 5ᵗʰ Book *de Finibus*, N° 9. to shew how the ultimate End of any Being may be determin'd, *Ergo Instituto veterum, &c.*

(5) Such Philosophy or Education may (as *Junius* observes *de Pictura veterum, l.*1. *c.*4.) be rightly called Φιλοσοφια εκ παραδειγματων, philosophiam salubrium exemplorum intuitu spectantium oculos conformantem.

and divided; or, all the Sciences which conduce towards this End, muſt be very ſtrictly and intimately related; and have a very cloſe Union and Connection; becauſe the Tranſition from Beauty and Truth, in any one kind, to Beauty and Truth in any other kind, is not only very eaſy and natural; but Beauties of different kinds being compar'd and brought to the ſame common Standard, muſt mutually illuſtrate and ſet off one another to great advantage. And.it is indeed impoſſible to give a juſt and adequate Notion of Truth and Beauty, whether in Nature, in Manners, or in Arts, otherwiſe than by ſhewing from proper Examples, that wherever it is found, it is the Reſult of the ſame ſettled Laws and Connections in Nature, together with the Conſtitution of our Mind, as it is adjuſted by Nature to theſe Laws and Connections. Our Reaſonings upon Truth and Beauty of whatever ſort, if they do not proceed in this manner, muſt be not merely very narrow and confined, but very lame and defective; we cannot have a clear and full Idea of Truth and Beauty in any Subject, without comparing it with Truth and Beauty in many, or rather in all Subjects; for it is by means of Oppoſition and Compariſon that Truth and Beauty are diſplay'd to the beſt advantage.

· THIS is the Sum of what the better Ancients have ſaid of the natural Union and Connection of all the Sciences which form good Taſte, and of the Deſign of Liberal Education. *The chief Points of this Doctrine more fully illuſtrated.*

BUT it is well worth while to ſet this important Doctrine in a fuller and clearer Light, by inquiring more particularly, what is meant by contemplating and imitating Nature; and by conſidering thoſe Faculties, Inſtincts and Affections, by which we are qualify'd for contemplating and imitating Nature.

THE Study of Nature, is nothing elſe but that accurate impartial Enquiry into Nature itſelf, by which the general Laws it obſerves in all its Productions, may be inveſtigated and determin'd. Phyſiology conſiſts in reducing all particular ſimilar Effects to general Laws. ·'Tis too obvious to be inſiſted upon, that the Laws of Nature cannot be found out otherwiſe than by attending to Nature itſelf; by diligently tracing its Operations, and comparing Appearances with Appearances. Nor is it leſs evident, that if Nature did not obſerve general Laws in its Productions, but work'd in a deſultory, inconſtant manner, it could not be the Object of Science : It would be an unintelligible inexplicable Chaos. Did not Nature always ſpeak the ſame Language, it would be abſolutely incomprehenſible; that is, were not its Connections fix'd, ſteady, and uniform, we could not know by any Marks or Signs what Qualities are co-exiſtent, or what Effect would be produc'd in any given Circumſtances; we could not know, for inſtance, when Fire would give a pleaſant degree of Heat, and when it would burn and deſtroy : We could not know when to plow and ſow, nor indeed what it was ſafe to eat or even to touch. On the other hand, Nature, by obſerving general Laws, and operating always uniformly, or according to the ſame ſettled Rules and Connections, becomes orderly and the Object of Science; it is regular, and therefore it may be ſtudied, traced and underſtood. A Phenomenon is then ſaid to be fully explained in a phyſical way, when it is reduced with ſeveral other like Effects to a uniform general Law of Nature. For thoſe are juſtly concluded to be general Qualities, Laws or Connections, which are found to work ſteadily and uniformly; and to which many Effects being analogous are . reducible. And indeed what elſe doth or can the Analogy or Likeneſs of Effects mean, beſides their ſimilar Method of Production, or Nature's analogous manner of Operation in producing them? Thus, for inſtance, it is reaſonably concluded, that Gravity is a general Law of Bodies prevailing throughout our mundane Syſtem, becauſe every Body gravitates; no Body is found devoid of that Quality, and many very diſtant Operations are reducible to it as their phyſical Cauſe, becauſe of their Likeneſs to Effects of the ſame nature, that fall more immediately under our Cognizance. *Of the Contemplation of Nature, and how we are qualiſy'd for it.*

NATURAL Philoſophy is, then, nothing elſe but the Knowledge of the general Analogies and Harmonies which take place in Nature, to which particular Appearances are reducible.

BUT how are we fitted and qualify'd by Nature for this Science; or for finding out the general Laws and Connections, the Harmonies and Analogies, which conſtitute the Order of the ſenſible World? Is it not by our natural Senſe of Beauty ariſing from Regularity and Order, or, in other words, from Uniformity amidſt variety? 'Tis this natural Senſe improv'd and cultivated by Exerciſe, that chiefly diſtinguiſhes the natural Philoſopher from the common Herd of Spectators; all his Satisfactions ariſing from the Contemplation of Nature's Unity, Beauty, and Harmony, are owing to this Senſe; that is, they belong as properly to it as thoſe of hearing to the Ear, or of taſting to the Palate. For as without the Organ of Hearing we could not perceive Sounds, or *By our natural Love of Order, Analogy, Unity amidſt variety, or of general Laws.*

without

without the Palate, taftes; fo no more could we perceive Unity, Beauty, Simplicity, and be pleafed with thefe Perceptions, without a Senfe and Difpofition adapted to them.

This Tafte ferves to put us into the right way of difcovering Truth, and fatiffying our natural defire of Knowledge.

THERE is indeed implanted in our Natures a ftrong defire after Knowledge; Light is not more fweet and agreeable to the Eye, than Truth to the Underftanding: The Mind of Man is naturally curious and inquifitive about the Reafons and Caufes of Things; it is impatient to underftand and comprehend every thing; what is dark to it or hid from it, gives it Uneafinefs and Difquiet; whereas what we know, we look upon ourfelves as in fome degree Poffeffors and Mafters of, and fo far we are eafy and contented. But befides the Satisfaction Knowledge gives to our Curiofity, and the Pleafure that attends the Exercife of our reafoning Faculty, there is another Enjoyment arifing from the Perception of Beauty and Unity; which, as it is exceedingly agreeable to the Mind, fo we are directed and guided by our natural Love of it, delight in it, and defire after it, to that right Method of enquiring into the Nature and Order of Things, that alone can fatisfy our Thirft after Knowledge. For by it we are led to fearch after Harmonies and Analogies; to compare Effects with Effects, and to reduce like ones to like Caufes; which is the only way of coming at the Knowledge of Nature. We are delighted with Analogy; we are exceedingly charm'd with Unity amidft variety; and hence we are determined to feek after Unity and Regularity, or, in one word, fettled Analogies and general Laws. And this we foon find to be an equally pleafing and profitable Employment, leading us very fuccefsfully into the Knowledge of Nature, and giving us higher and higher delight the further we advance. Thus it is that Nature points out to us the Method of coming at the Knowledge of its Operations and Orders. How Men ever came to purfue the Knowledge of Nature, in any other way than this to which we are fo ftrongly directed and invited by Nature, or by our internal Senfe of Beauty, is a Queftion that would lead us into too long a Digreffion. 'Tis fufficient to our prefent purpofe, to have obferved how we are qualify'd by Nature for phyfical Knowledge, and the Pleafures attending it.

We are by our moral Senfe difpos'd to inquire after moral or final Caufes, and to delight in the Contemplation of Good.

BUT this is not all: We have likewife by Nature a moral Senfe, or we receive Pleafure and Satisfaction from Effects that produce Good and Happinefs in Nature: Not only are we pleafed with the Contemplation of Effects, Laws, and Caufes, that tend to our own Good; but we are delighted with the Perception of Good and Happinefs wherever we obferve or behold it; though no other Portion of that Good and Happinefs fhould fall to our fhare, befides the Pleafure which the View of it affords us. Now by this moral Senfe, we are naturally led to inquire into the good Effects of the general Laws of Nature. In confequence of it we are not contented with the barely phyfical Explication of Appearances; but are chiefly prompted to fearch after the moral Ends or final Caufes of Effects, or rather of the general Laws from which Effects refult. We perceive high delight in contemplating natural Beauty and Uniformity; but it is moral Beauty that is moft fatisfactory and delighting to our Mind: For thus, together with Unity of Defign, Goodnefs and Benevolence are perceived; and therefore, at the fame time that our natural Senfe of Beauty is entertain'd, our natural Love of generous Intention is gratify'd; and all our benign, focial Affections are moft agreeably exercifed.

WE fhall not now inquire how it ever came about, that inveftigating, moral, or final Caufes hath been at any time excluded from Philofophy; but certainly thofe who content themfelves with reducing Effects to their phyfical Caufes, without any Reflections upon the Wifdom, Goodnefs, and Benevolence, that appear in the Laws of Nature, deprive themfelves of the higheft Satisfaction the Study of Nature affords. For can there be a more refin'd Joy than to range at large through Nature, perceiving every where not only Unity of Defign, Harmony, and Analogy; but Beneficence, Kindnefs, Bounty, and Goodnefs? Now for this Satisfaction we are qualify'd by our moral Senfe. Thefe Pleafures do as neceffarily pre-fuppofe it, as Light and Colours do the Senfe of feeing; or Mufick, the Capacity of diftinguifhing Harmony and Difcord in the Combination of Sounds.

THUS then we are fitted to receive Pleafure from the Study of Nature, by our Curiofity, or Thirft after Knowledge; by our Senfe of Beauty arifing from Unity of Defign, or Uniformity amidft Diverfity; and by our moral Senfe, or our Senfe of Beauty and Fitnefs refulting from the Purfuit of Good; or, in other words, from our Difpofition to delight in the Happinefs of Beings, and in the Contemplation of the Good of a Whole, fteadily purfued by excellent general Laws, or by wifely and generoufly contrived Analogies and Harmonies.

1   BUT

BUT there is yet another Source of Pleasure to our Minds, in the Contemplation of Nature, that deserves to be consider'd, depending on our natural Sense of Great-ness, or our Disposition to be struck with pleasing Admiration by the Greatness of Ob-jects, or by the Greatness of the manner in which they exist and operate (6). The Mind of Man is naturally great and aspiring : It hates every thing that looks like a Re-straint upon it : It loves to expatiate and dilate itself, prove its Force and range uncon-fin'd. And therefore it is wonderfully pleas'd with every thing that is noble and ele-vated, that fills it with lofty and sublime Ideas, and puts its Grasp to the trial. Hence an inexhaustible Source of Entertainment to the Mind in the Contemplation of Na-ture : For there is an Immensity every where in Nature, that flings the Mind into a most agreeable Astonishment, not only in the greater Prospects it affords in contempla-ting the Orbs that compose the vast and mighty Frame of the Universe, amidst which our Earth is so small a point ; but even in considering those Objects, which in respect of our Senses are called minute : In every Insect, for instance, there is an endless Source of Wonder and Amazement, or Marks of Wisdom and Contrivance of an astonishing unmeasurable Greatness.

Another Source of Pleasure to our Minds in the Con-templation of Na-ture, is our natural Sense of Greatness, or our Disposition to admire great Ob-jects, or Greatness in the manner of Objects.

THIS must be allowed to be a just Account of the Contemplation of Nature, or of natural Philosophy, and the Pleasures which it yields. *Socrates* long ago found fault with those pretended Enquirers into Nature, who amused themselves with unmeaning Words, and thought they were more knowing in Nature, because they could give high-founding Names to its various Effects ; and did not inquire after the wise and good gene-ral Laws of Nature, and the excellent Purposes to which these steadily and unerringly work (7). My Lord *Verulam* tells us, that true Philosophy consists in gathering the Knowledge of Nature's Laws from Experience and Observation. And Sir *Isaac New-ton* hath indeed carried that true Science of Nature to a great height of Perfection ; of which he himself thus speaks in his Opticks,

This is a true Ac-count of natural Philosophy, and the Pleasures arising from the Study of Nature, according to Socrates, Lord Bacon, and Sir Isaac Newton.

" LATER Philosophers (8) banish the Consideration of such a Cause out of natural Phi-
" losophy, feigning Hypotheses for explaining all things mechanically, and referring other
" Causes to Metaphysicks : Whereas the main Business of natural Philosophy is to argue
" from Phenomena without feigning Hypotheses, and to deduce Causes from Effects, till
" we come to the very first Cause, which certainly is not mechanical ; and not only to
" unfold the Mechanism of the World, but chiefly to resolve these and such like Que-
" stions. What is there in Places almost empty of Matter, and whence is it that the Sun
" and Planets gravitate towards one another, without dense Matter between them ?
" Whence is it that Nature doth *nothing in vain* ; and whence arises all that *Order*
" and *Beauty* which we see in the World ? To what end are Comets, and whence is
" it that Planets move all one and the same way in Orbs concentrick, while Comets
                                                                              " move

(6) The Passages of antient Authors relating to our Sense of Beauty in natural Objects, and our Sense of moral Beauty, shall be quoted afterwards when I come to speak of Virtue. Let it only be observ'd here, that the Nature of this Discourse does not allow me to en-large more fully upon the reality of these Principles in our Natures, far less to answer the Objections that have been made against the Writings in which they are ex-plain'd : Let those who desire to be satisfy'd upon this head, have recourse to the *Characteristicks, Traité de Beau*, par M. *Crousaz*, Mr. *Hutchinson's* Enquiry, and his Illustrations on a moral Sense. As for this Principle of Greatness, see *Longinus de Sublim. sect.* 35. Ut mul-ta alia omittam, hoc eos præcipue intuitos existimo : Naturam non humile nos quoddam, aut contemptum animal reputasse : Verum cum in hanc Vitam, & in hunc universum terrarum orbem, ceu in amplissimum quoddam nos mitteret amphitheatrum, invictum una simul & insuperabile mentibus nostris omnis magnæ rei, & humanam conditionem excedentis, adeoque divinio-ris, ingeneravisse desiderium. Atque hinc fieri, ut hu-manæ mentis contemplationi & conjectuique ne totus quidem orbis sufficiat ; sed ipsos sæpenumero ambientis omnia cœli terminos immensa animi agitatione trans-cendat : Quare si quis undequaque Vitam hanc omnem confideraverit, & quantum quod grande & excel-lens in cunctis rebus pulchro nitidoque prævaleat, intel-liget e vestigio, cui nos rei nati simus. Itaque instinctu illo ducti naturæ non exiles miramur rivulos,——Verum ad conspectum vel Danubii vel Rheni resistimus atto-niti ; maxime omnium autem ad ipsius intuitum Oceani. Ad eundem modum non igniculum aut flammulam, &c. So *Cicero*. Est id omnino Verum, nam omnium magnarum artium sunt arborum altitudo nos delectat. *Ad M. Brutum Orator.* N° 43.

(7) See *Platonis Phædo, Edit. Steph. tom.* 1. *p.* 97.

At cum ego aliquando audirem legentemque ex quodam libro, ut ipse dicebat, Anaxagoræ, mentem esse quæ omnia ordine disponat regatque omniumque sit causa : Hac nimirum causa delectabar, mihique illa quodammodo recte comparata esse videbatur, mentem nimirum omnium rerum esse causam : Et ita apud me statuebam, si ita res habeat, confici mentem illam gu-bernatricem atque dispositricem omnia ita disponere, itaque res singulas eo in loco collocare ubi fuerint rec-tissime constitutæ.——Cum hæc in animo meo reputa-rem, cum magna voluptate arbitrabar me præceptorem comperisse, qui me ex animi mei sententia rerum causas edoceret, illumque mihi explicaturum, primum an terra lata sit an rotunda : Illisque rebus expositis adjuncturum etiam copiosiorem explicationem causæ & necessitatis : Id est, ecquid melius, & cur ita omnino melius fuerit. ——A mirifica tamen illa spe, crede mihi, excidi : Quan-doquidem cum ulterius in illorum lectione progrederer, hominem video nec mente quidem nec judicio ullo uten-tem, neque ullas causas ad rerum compositionem ordi-nemque commodi assignantem sive digerentem : At aëras quofdam & ætheras, aliaque multa & absurda quæ-dam pro rerum causis collocantem. Et mihi quidem Videtur idem omnino illi contingere ac ei qui diceret, quicquid agit Socrates, mente & ratione agit : Deinde instituens explicare causas singularum rerum quas agam, diceret me primum quidem hic federe, quia corpus meum ex ossibus & nervis conflet : Ossa Vero sint so-lida & firma & juncturarum discrimina seorsim a se in-vicem habeant :——Cum ergo ossa in suis commissuris elevantur nervi qui modo laxantur, modo intenduntur, efficiunt ut membrorum incurvandorum inflectendorum-que habeam facultatem, atque hac de causa hic sedeam incurvus, &c.

(8) Opticks by Sir *Isaac Newton*, Book 3. *p.* 345.

" move all manner of ways in Orbs very excentrick ; and what hinders the fix'd Stars
" from falling upon one another ? How came the Bodies of Animals to be contrived
" with fo much Art, and for what Ends are their feveral Parts ? Was the Eye contrived
" without Skill in Opticks, and the Ear without Knowledge of Sounds ? *&c"*.

What we may infer
from this Account
of natural Philofo-
phy, concerning the
right Method of im-
proving moral
Knowledge, or the
Science of the moral
World.

I fhall only obferve farther on this Head, that if this be the right Method of improving and purfuing natural Philofophy, it muft neceffarily follow, that the Knowledge of
the moral World ought likewife to be cultivated in the fame manner, and can only be attain'd to by the like Method of enquiry : By inveftigating the general Laws, to which, if
there is any Order in the moral World, or if it can be the Object of Knowledge, its
Effects and Appearances muft in like manner be reducible, as thofe in the corporeal
World to theirs ; and the moral Fitnefs of thefe general Laws, or their Tendency to
the greater Good of the whole Syftem to which they belong.   A little Reflection upon
the Conftitution of our Minds, or our intellectual and moral Powers, will fhew us, that
general Laws obtain with regard to thefe, as well as in the fenfible World.

FOR, to name but two Inftances ; there is, with refpect to us, a Law of Knowledge
as fix'd and uniform as the Law of Gravity ; in confequence of which, Knowledge is
acquir'd by Experience and Application, in proportion to our Situation for taking in
Views, and to our Affiftances by focial Communication.

AND there is alfo a Law of Habits, in confequence of which, repeated Acts produce a Propenfity to do, and a Facility of doing ; and, in confequence of which, we
can acquire the Mafterfhip of ourfelves, or the Habit of acting deliberately, and with
mature Examination.   ·

NOW the many Effects that will foon be found on Reflection, to be reducible to
thefe two excellent general Principles or Laws of our Nature, muft convince every thinking
Perfon, that were moral Philofophy ftudied and purfued in the fame way as natural Philofophy hath been for fome time, we fhould quickly fee another kind of it produc'd, than
what hath hitherto appear'd.   This is perhaps what Sir *Ifaac Newton* means, when he
fays, " And (9) if natural Philofophy in all its Parts, by purfuing this Method fhall at
" length be perfected, the Bounds of moral Philofophy will be alfo enlarged.   For fo
" far as we can know by natural Philofophy what is the firft Caufe, what Power he
" has over us, and what Benefits we receive from him, fo far our Duty towards him,
" as well as that towards one another, will appear to us by the Light of Nature".

Of the Imitation of
Nature, and the
Pleafures accruing
from that Source.

BUT having thus briefly fhewn by what Faculties, Powers, and Senfes Man is fitted
for the Contemplation of Nature, and directed to the right Method of acquiring natural Knowledge ; let us next confider what is meant by the Imitation of Nature, and
the Pleafures arifing from it, and how we are qualify'd for them.

NATURE may be imitated two ways, by ingenious Arts ; and in Life and Manners.
And Man will be found fitted for both thefe kinds of Imitation by the fame Powers, Faculties, and Senfes that render him capable of contemplating and underftanding Nature.

How we are fitted
for the Imitation of
Nature in Life and
Conduct, by the
fame natural
Powers and Senfes,
or Taftes above
mention'd.

MAN is impelled to imitate Nature in the Regulation of his Affections and Actions,
and fitted for it by his Senfe of Beauty and Regularity ; his publick Senfe, or Delight
in publick Good, and in the Affections and Actions that purfue it ; and his Magnanimity, or Senfe of Greatnefs.   And accordingly, all the Virtues and Excellencies of human Life are reducible to thefe four ; Prudence, Benevolence, Fortitude or Magnanimity,
and Decency, or orderly and beautiful Oeconomy.

THESE virtuous Affections are pleafant and agreeable in the immediate Exercife,
becaufe we are fo made and conftituted as to receive Pleafure from them by our inward Senfes, in the fame manner as Light is pleafant to the Eye, or Harmony to the Ear.
And they afford a yet higher and nobler Pleafure upon Reflection, in confequence of
our Capacity of reviewing our Conduct, and approving it when it is perceiv'd to be
becoming the Dignity of our Nature, and conformable to the Temper and Difpofition
of Nature's all-governing Mind.

Cicero's Account of
the Virtues corre-
fponding to the di-
ftinguifhing Princi-
ples in human Na-
ture.

THE Cardinal Virtues are reduced by *Cicero* to thefe four above mentioned, becaufe
there are four Principles in our Natures, which exalt us to the Rank and Dignity of Being
we hold above merely fenfitive Creatures.   The Defire and Love of Knowledge ; our
focial Feeling, Love of Society or Delight in publick Good ; Greatnefs of Mind, or a
Defire of Power and Perfection ; and a Senfe of Beauty and Decorum in Characters and
Actions.   All the Virtues, Duties or Excellencies of human Life can be nothing elfe
(faith

(9) Opticks by Sir *Ifaac Newton, Book* 3. *p.* 381.   *The fourth Edition.*

(faith he) but thofe our principal Powers, Faculties or Senfes operating, conjunctly each with proper force, towards the Perfection and Happinefs of our Minds, and the Beauty and Regularity of our Conduct. All thefe mix'd with Art and confin'd to due Bounds, make and maintain the Ballance of the Mind; and by their well-accorded Contrafts produce a lovely Harmony and Confiftency of Life and Manners. *Cicero* fhews us in many different parts of his Writings, that all the Virtues are thefe Powers and Principles duly regulated, or mixing and combining with well-proportion'd Strength to give Nerves, Beauty, and Grace to Life. The Whole of Virtue confifts (according to that Philofophy) in living agreeably to Nature; agreeably to what we perceive by our moral Senfe and Confcience to be fuitable to the Dignity of our Nature; agreeably to what we perceive, by the fame Senfe and the Study of Nature, to be the End appointed to us by Nature; agreeably to the End purfued by Nature itfelf in all its Works (10).

HAD we no Senfe of moral Beauty and Perfection, no Senfe of Harmony and Decorum in Life and Manners; no moral Senfe, fhewing us the Subordination in which all the interiour merely fenfitive or animal Appetites and Affections ought to be maintain'd, we could not be capable of Virtue, we could not approve or difapprove Affections and Manners. Without a Senfe of Beauty and Harmony, Greatnefs and Becomingnefs of Affections and Actions, we could no more have any Senfe of the Dignity of our Natures, and of acting a right part, than a blind Man can have of Colours. 'Tis in confequence of moral Confcience, or of our moral Senfe of the Beauty, Dignity, Worth, and Merit of Characters, Affections and Actions, that though we may be brib'd or terrify'd into the doing a bafe Action; yet we can neither be brib'd nor terrify'd into the Approbation of it. It is in confequence of it that we are able to form any other Idea of an Action, befides that of the Quantity of fenfible Pleafures it may bring, and that we are capable of framing to ourfelves general Rules of Life, by the Study and Obfervance of which, Life is render'd uniform, confiftent, regular and beautiful; and of delighting in that moral Harmony and Beauty.

THUS it is evidently the fame Senfes, Difpofitions, and Powers, which fit and qualify us for contemplating Nature with fatisfaction; and for imitating in our Conduct the moral Perfections of its Creator and Governour, which are clearly manifefted by the Frame, Conftitution and Laws of Nature. And then it is that the Study of Nature muft afford the higheft Joy, when we feel the fame Temper and Difpofition prevailing in

Virtue neceffarily pre-fuppofes a Senfe of moral Beauty and Perfection, and Greatnefs of Mind.

(10) See *Marcus Antoninus*'s Meditations, *Collier's* Tranflation, *p.* 140. *c.* 26. Pleafure and Satisfaction confifts in following the Bent of Nature, and doing the things we are made for. And which way is this to be compafs'd? By the practice of general Kindnefs, by neglecting the Importunity and Clamour of our Senfes, by diftinguifhing Appearances from Truth, and by contemplating Nature and the Works of the Almighty. All this is acting according to kind, and keeping the Faculties in the right Channel, &c. And *p.* 77. *c.* 21. Among all things in the Univerfe direct your Worfhip to the Greateft; and which is that? 'Tis that Being which manages and governs all the reft. And as you worfhip the beft thing in Nature, fo you are to pay a proportionable regard to the beft thing in yourfelf: You'll know it by its relation to the Deity, &c. *Cic. de Off. lib.* 1. N° 4. From autem quod rationis eft particeps, per quam confequentia cernit, caufas rerum videt, earumque progreffus & quafi antecefliones non ignorat, fimilitudines comparat, & rebus praefentibus adjungit, atque annectit futura: Facile totius vitae curfum videt, ad eamque degendam praeparat res neceffarias: Eademque natura, vi rationis hominem conciliat homini & ad orationis & ad vitae focietatem:— In primifque hominis eft propria veri inquifitio atque inveftigatio. Itaque—cognitionemque rerum aut occultarum aut admirabilium, ad beate vivendum neceffariam ducimus. Ex quo intelligitur, quod verum, fimplex, fincerumque fit, id effe naturae hominis aptiffimum. Huic veri videndi cupiditati adjuncta eft appetitio quaedam principatus, ut nemini parere animus bene a natura informatus velit, nifi praecipienti, aut docenti, aut utilitatis caufa, jufte & legitime imperanti: Ex quo animi magnitudo exiftit, humanarumque rerum contemtio. Nec vero illa parva vis naturae eft, rationifque quod unum hoc animal fentit quid fit ordo, quid fit quod deceat, in factis dictifque qui modus. Itaque rorum ipforum, quae adfpectu fentiuntur, nullum aliud animal pulchritudinem, venuftatem, convenientiam partium fentit, quam fimilitudinem natura, ratioque ab oculis ad animum transferens, multo eff magis pulchritudinem, conftantiam, ordinem in confiliis factifque confervandum putat:—Omne quod honeftum eft, id quatuor partium oritur ex aliqua. Aut enim in perfpicientia

veri, folertiaque verfatur: aut in hominum focietate tuenda, tribuendoque fuum cuique & rerum contractarum fide, aut in animi excelfi, atque invicti magnitudine ac robore; aut in omnium quae fiunt, quaeque dicuntur, ordine & modo, in quo ineft modeftia & temperantia. Quae quatuor quanquam inter fe colligata atque implicita funt, ramen ex fingulis certa officiorum genera nafcuntur, &c. De *Ciceto de Oratore, lib.* 1. N° 3, 4, & 5. *De Partitione Oratoria,* N° 22, & 23. Eft igitur vis virtutis duplex, aut enim fcientia cernitur virtus aut actione. Nam quae prudentia quaeque graviffimo nomine fapientia appellatur, haec fcientia pollet una. Quae vero moderandis cupiditatibus, regendifque animi motibus laudatur, ejus eft munus in agendo, cui temperantiae nomen eft.—Quae autem haec uno genere complectitur magnitudo animi dicitur: Cujus eft liberalitas in ufu petuniae: fimulque altitudo animi in capiendis incommodis & maxime injuriis:—Cuftos vero virtutum omnium eft verecundia, &c. De *fin. Bon. & Mal. lib.* 2. N° 14. Honeftum igitur id intelligimus quod tale eft ut detracta omni utilitate fine ullis praemiis, fructibufque per fe-ipfum poffit jure laudari.— Homines enim etfi alliis multis tamen hoc uno a beftiis plurimum differunt, quod rationem habeant a natura datam mentemque, & aerem & vigentem quae caufas rerum, &c.—Eademque ratio fecit hominem hominum appetentem, cumque his natura & fermone, & ufu congruentem, ut profectus a caritate domefticorum ac fuorum, ferpat longius, & fe implicet primum civium deinde omnium mortalium focietate :—Et quoniam eadem natura cupiditatem ingenuit homini veri inveniendi, &c. His initiis iuducta omnia vera diligimus, id eft fidelia, fimplicia, conftantia, &c. Eadem ratio habet in fe quiddam amplum, atque magnificum ad imperandum magis, quam ad parendum accomodatum : Omnia humana non tolerabilia folum, fed etiam levia ducens : Altum quiddam & excelfum, nihil timens, nemini cedens, femper invictum. Atque his tribus generibus notatis, quartum fequitur, & in eadem pulchritudine, & aptum ex illis tribus; in quo ineft ordo & moderatio. Cujus fimilitudine perfpecta in rerum fpecie; a dignitate tranfitum eft ad honeftatem dictorum atque factorum, &c. Of Greatnefs of Mind, fee *Cicero de Off. lib.* 1. N° 20. Of Beauty or Decency, *ibid.* 28, & 29.

in our own Minds which Nature difplays; and we are confcious of our earneft Endeavours to tranfplant into our Minds and Lives, all the moral Beauties that appear in it; the Benevolence, the Harmony, the Simplicity, the Truth, and Greatnefs that reign throughout univerfal Nature; and to become like to our Creator the all-perfect Mind, who made, upholds, and governs all.

We can only know whether we have thefe Powers or Principles, and Difpofitions inherent in our Natures, by turning our Eyes inward, and by reflecting on our own Minds, and their Operations.

WHETHER we have thofe Senfes that have been mention'd, is matter of Experiduce; it can only be known by Confcioufnefs. And therefore in fpeaking of them, an Appeal muft be made to what we feel and perceive. It is the fame with regard to all our other Faculties and Perceptions: There can be no other way of convincing one that he hath certain Powers, Ideas and Feelings, but by endeavouring to make him turn his Eyes inward, look attentively into his own Mind, and obferve what paffes in it. Mean

Yet it is certain that our Capacity of contemplating Nature with delight, or of imitating it by the Study and Exercife of Virtue, pre-fuppofes thefe Principles. Every Pleafure pre-fuppofes a correfponding Appetite, Affection, or Difpofition.

time 'tis certain, that if we had not thefe Faculties and Difpofitions, Nature could not pleafe us by its Unity, Regularity and Beauty; or by its fteady purfuance of univerfal Good; nor could we be delighted with amiable, lovely, and praife-worthy Characters and Actions. Thefe would neceffarily be to us as Harmony to one who has no Ear. Unity, Beauty and Grace would be empty, infignificant Sounds to us. For it muft be true in general, that every Gratification or Pleafure neceffarily pre-fuppofes an Affection, Appetite, or Difpofition fuited to it: And that without natural Affections, Difpofitions and Appetites, no one thing could pleafe us more than another.

THIS alfo is certain, that if Beauty, Harmony, Unity of Defign, Regularity, and wife generous Adminiftration, are real things in Nature, they muft be fo in our Conduct; or reciprocally, if they are real Qualities, and not Words without any Meaning with regard to our Conduct and Manners, they muft likewife be real with refpect to the Oeconomy of Nature. 'Tis impoffible to have a Seufe of them in one of thefe, without transferring them to the other. To own their Reality in the one cafe, and deny it in the other, is a Contradiction in terms: For how can Order, Beauty, Goodnefs, and Greatnefs belong to certain Affections and Actions; to the Character of one rational Being, or to any moral Object; and not likewife as neceffarily belong to all analogous Affections, Actions, and Characters, or to every like moral Object? If the generous Purfuit of publick Good be laudable and excellent in Nature; it muft likewife be valuable and praife-worthy in us, and its contrary be hateful and bafe: And, on the other hand, if benevolent generous Affection be amiable and commendable in us, and its oppofites be mean, ignoble, and unworthy; the fame muft likewife be true with regard to the Adminiftration of Nature, and the Temper and Difpofition of its Author and Governour.

Of the Imitation of Nature by ingenious Arts, and the Pleafures arifing from that Source.

BUT there will be occafion to carry this Reafoning yet farther, in confidering the imitative Arts, to which I now proceed. Man is not only capable of imitating Nature in Life and Manners, but likewife by feveral Arts. All Arts are Imitations of Nature, or Applications of its known Laws to the Ufes and Purpofes of human Life; as of Gravity, Elafticity, &c. But the Arts that are more properly called imitative, are thofe of Fancy and Genius, fuch as Poetry, Painting and Sculpture. Now 'tis the fame Senfes, Difpofitions, Inftincts and Powers, that render us capable of contemplating Nature, and of imitating its Order, Beauty, and Greatnefs in Life and Manners; that likewife fit and qualify us for the Imitation of Nature by thofe ingenious Arts.

THERE is implanted in our Minds not only a ftrong defire of underftanding Nature's Methods of Operation, and all its various Appearances; but alfo a very ftrong Difpofition to imitate Nature, emulate it, and vie with it; and thus to become as it were Creators ourfelves. Hence the Origin of Poetry, Painting, and of all the noble and afpiring, imitative Arts: Hence all the bold Efforts of the human Mind to add as much as it poffibly can, to our Happinefs by our own Invention, Genius, and Induftry. Man is very wifely made by his Creator, an imitative Being; this Propenfity to copy after Nature, and to emulate it, is indeed a Principle of wonderful ufe in fuch a Conftitution as ours is. But to what purpofe could it ferve; or what could it produce that is great and excellent, were we not at the fame time indued with the other Faculties and Senfes that have been defcribed, to guide and affift in the Imitation of Nature; that is, with a Senfe of Beauty, Order, and Greatnefs, and with a moral Senfe, or a focial, affectionate, generous Difpofition? The chief Qualities of good Imitation by Poetry, Painting and Sculpture, that have been already enumerated and explained, do they not all of them evidently pre-fuppofe thefe Faculties and Difpofitions in order to relifh them, or indeed to have any Notion of them? What elfe is it that could prompt us to purfue and endeavour after Truth, Beauty, Confiftency, Decorum, Greatnefs and Grace in Compofitions of any kind; or that could be delighted and charmed by thefe Qualities when they are attained to in any human Production, but a natural Senfe of Beauty, Unity, Decorum, Grace and Greatnefs? In like manner, if we had nothing of Sympathy, Compaffion, Benevolence

Benevolence and Generofity in our Frame, could we think of calling forth fuch Affections into Action, and giving them agreeable Exercife by moving and interefting Reprefentations : Or could we be delightfully touched and affected by the imitative Arts in
a tender focial manner, without any Difpofition, or Principle in our Nature fit to be
worked upon? Nothing can be more ridiculous than to fpeak of perceiving any Qua- *We are qualify'd*
lity, without a Senfe qualified to perceive it : Beings can neither defire nor relifh any *for that by the fame*
Entertainment for which they are not fitted by Nature, or for which, fo to fpeak, *Powers and Difpo-*
they have no natural Appetite.   On the one hand therefore, if Truth, Beauty, Great- *tion'd.*
nefs and Grace, and all the other Qualities that are afcribed to the fine Arts, as confti-
tuting their Perfection, are not mere Sounds without a Meaning, we muft have naturally
implanted in us thofe Faculties and Difpofitions that are requifite to comprehend and
enjoy them.   And, on the other hand, if we really are poffefs'd of Faculties and Senfes
qualify'd to underftand and tafte thefe Qualities, the chief Excellence of the imitative
Arts muft neceffarily confift in their being able to give fuitable Entertainment to fuch
noble Faculties and Senfes : Or their Productions can only be excellent in proportion
to the Satisfaction they are able to afford to them.

THAT it is the very fame Faculties and Difpofitions which qualify us for underftanding and relifhing the Beauty and Perfection of Nature, the Beauty and Perfection of
moral Conduct, and the Beauty and Perfection of the imitative Arts is fo evident, that
it is indeed unaccountable how any who pretend to Tafte or Intelligence of thefe
Arts, can doubt of the Reality and Naturalnefs of Virtue, and of a moral Senfe in our
Make and Frame ; or entertain wrong Conceptions of Nature, and doubt of the moral
Senfe and good Difpofition of our Contriver and Author.

BUT fince it is no rare thing to meet with Virtuofi or profeffed Admirers of the
fine Arts, who call into queftion all other Beauty but that of their beloved Arts, I cannot chufe but call upon them to reflect, that they muft either give up the reality of the
Tafte-upon which they fo highly value themfelves, and which is indeed a very fine Accomplifhment ; or they muft of neceffity own the reality of Virtue and of a moral Senfe ;
and confequently acknowledge the Wifdom and Goodnefs of our Maker, the Creator and
Upholder of all things, who hath inlaid it into our Natures, and made us capable of
receiving fuch noble Entertainment from it in various ways.

SO ftrictly are all Truths bound and united together, that having firft eftablifhed a right
Idea of Virtue, and of thofe Faculties that capacitate us for perceiving and delighting in
it ; or of Nature's wife and regular Oeconomy in purfuing the general Good of the Whole ;
it is very eafy by obvious Confequences to deduce and eftablifh a juft Notion from thence,
of the fine Arts and their principal Excellencies : And, on the other fide, if we begin by
fettling a true Idea of the Excellencies of the fine Arts, and of thofe Faculties and Difpofitions in our Minds which qualify us for purfuing them, and receiving pleafure from
them, it is very eafy by natural confequences from thefe Principles to fix the true Notion
of Virtue and moral Excellence, whether in the Government of our own Affections and
Actions, or in the Adminiftration of Nature.   For if the Perfection of Nature confifts
in working unerringly towards the Beauty and Good of the Whole by fimple confiftent
Laws; and the Perfection of Life and Manners confifts in acting in concert with Nature,
and in purfuing fteadily the Good of Mankind by well-poifed, regular and generous
Affections ; then muft the Perfection of the imitative Arts confift in like manner in making regular and beautiful Syftems, in which every part being duly adapted and fubmitted to what is principal, the Whole hath a great, noble, and virtuous Effect upon the
Mind : And reciprocally, if the Beauty and Perfection of the imitative Arts is acknow- *If the Reality of thefe*
ledged to refult from a due Subordination of Parts to the main End, and from Harmony *Qualities is ac-*
and a noble virtuous Tendency in the Whole ; then muft our Conduct and the Admini- *knowledg'd in any*
ftration of Nature be beautiful and perfect, only in proportion to the juft Subordination, *one of thefe Inftances,*
Harmony and good Tendency that prevails in the Whole. *in the Contemplation*
or Imitation of Na-
ture, whether in
IF Unity, Decency, Truth and Greatnefs are acknowledged in the imitative Arts, *Life or Arts ; their*
they muft likewife take place with regard to Nature, for Nature itfelf muft be capable *reality muft likewife*
of affecting us in the fame manner.   And they muft likewife take place in Life and Man- *be own'd in all the*
ners, in Affections, Actions and Characters ; for thefe muft be capable of touching and *other Inftances.*
affecting us in the fame manner in real Life as in Imitation.   The Artift derives all his
Ideas from Nature, and does not make Laws and Connexions agreeably to which he
works in order to produce certain Effects, but conforms himfelf to fuch as he finds to be
neceffarily and unchangeably eftablifhed in Nature : All his Attempts pre-fuppofe certain
Difpofitions implanted in the Breafts of Mankind originally by Nature itfelf, which he
cannot produce if wanting, but may fuit himfelf to and work upon in the way that Nature
hath appointed, and thereby render his Works exceeding pleafing and agreeable.   If
therefore the imitative Arts are really capable of producing beautiful, great, and noble Effects
upon us, there muft be fomething beautiful, great and noble in our Minds, the Improvement of

which is neceffarily our Excellence and Perfection, for which we could not have been fuited, but by a Mind of fuperiour Beauty, Noblenefs and Greatnefs, whofe Perfection confifts in producing Beings capable of noble Ends and Purfuits, and in framing and adapting each kind of Beings in every refpect as may beft fuit to the higheft Perfection in the Whole.

TO acknowledge a real Excellence and Beauty in any imitative Art, without confeffing a real Excellence and Beauty in Nature, and the real Excellence and Worth of Virtue, is abfurdly to afcribe a Power and Influence to Copies which the Original hath not : It is the fame as to affert, that a real Object of which an exact Copy is taken, would not have the fame effect upon us by its real Qualities, which thofe Qualities have upon us in the Imitation : It is to affert not only that the Artift can form Ideas which have no Foundation in Nature itfelf, or are no wife fuggefted to him by it ; but that he can give Powers and Qualities to Objects which he copies from Nature, that are quite independent of all Nature's Laws and Eftablifhments, and in which Nature hath no part or fhare.

BUT this way of reafoning may appear to fome too abftrufe and metaphyfical ; and therefore I fhall endeavour to fet the Analogy between the moral Virtues and Graces, and the Beauties and Graces of the fine Arts in another light, by fuggefting briefly a few Obfervations of the Ancients upon this Subject : For, according to them, to illuftrate, prove and enforce this infeparable neceffary Connexion, (of which I am now treating) between the reality of Beauty, Unity, Order, Grace and Greatnefs in Nature, and their reality in *Farther Illuftrations* the Conduct of our Affections and Actions, and in all ingenious Imitations of Nature by *upon the Foundations* Arts, is the chief Scope of true Philofophy, the fitteft Method of forming betimes in *of the Arts, and of* young Minds an univerfal good Tafte ; and therefore it is the proper Bufinefs of Educa*good Tafte in our* tion. It is only fuch Philofophy that deferves to be called the Guide of Life (9), and the *Natures, and the* Difcerner of Excellence, and the Source of all truly manly, rational, and pure Happi*proper ways of cul* nefs : Or that can produce a right Tafte of Life, and of Man's beft Purfuits, Employ*tivating it.* ments and Diverfions. And therefore it is this Philofophy that the Formers of Youth ought to have ever in their View throughout the whole of Education.

A ftrict Connection THE Ancients have often obferv'd, that there is a ftrict Analogy between our Senfe *and Analogy between* of Beauty in fenfible Objects, and our moral Senfe, or our Senfe of Beauty in Affec*our Senfe of natural* tions, Actions and Characters. So nearly are thefe related, or fo intimately are they *and our Senfe of* blended together in our Natures; that he who hath any Tafte of Beauty in fenfible *moral Beauty.* Forms, any Notion of Harmony, Regularity and Unity in Bodies, muft neceffarily be led to transfer that Senfe to moral Objects : And therefore if fuch a one is diffolute or irregular in his Conduct, he muft live at continual variance with himfelf, and in downright contradiction to what he delights in and highly admires in other Subjects. So ftrictly, fo nearly are thofe two Senfes allied to one another, that it is hardly poffible to fpeak of moral Objects in any other Language, than that which expreffes the Beauties of the other kind. Hence it is that the beft Authors of Antiquity fpeak of the Meafures and Numbers of Life ; the Harmony, Unity and Simplicity of Manners ; the Beautiful, the Decent in Actions; the Regularity, the Order, the Symmetry of Life ; the Proportions, the Graces of the Mind ; Truth, Sublimity, Greatnefs, and Confiftency of Manners. Such is the Style of the beft ancient Moralifts (10). And in explaining thefe moral Qualities, they are conftantly referring to thofe which are analogous to them in fenfible Forms, and in the Productions of Fancy and Genius in Imitations of Nature. On account of this Affinity and Analogy, they have juftly concluded, that the Admiration, and Love of Order, Harmony and Proportion in whatever kind, muft be naturally improving to the Temper, advantageous to focial Affection, and highly affiftant to Virtue, which is itfelf no other than the Love of Order and Beauty in Society : That all the Arts which have Truth, Order and Beauty for their Object and Aim, muft have a Tendency to advance the Love of moral Beauty in Life and Conduct, and to check Diforder and Irregularity : But chiefly the Contemplation of the Order of Nature, from which all our Ideas of Order and Beauty are originally copied. One of the moft pleafant and entertaining Speculations in Philofophy is the univerfal Analogy that prevails throughout Nature : The Analogy between the natural and moral World in every refpect. Tis this Analogy that lays the Foundation (as it hath been frequently obferved by many Authors), for what is principal in the Works of Genius, the cloathing moral Objects with fenfible Images, or the giving them Bodies, Shapes, and Forms in Defcription, Sculpture, and Painting.

                                                                          BUT

(9) So *Cicero* addreffes true Philofophy, O philofophia vitæ dux, O virtutum indagatrix, expultrixque vitiorum? Quid modo non nos, fed omnino vita hominum fine te effe potuiffet ? &c. *Tuf. Quæft. l.* 5. N° 2.

(10) See the Paffages already quoted, at the Beginning of this Chapter, about the Contemplation of Nature, and thofe juft now quoted concerning the Decorum. So *Horace,*
    Sed veræ numerofque, modofque edifcere vitæ.
                                    Epiſt. l. 2. Ep. 2.
    Eſt modus in rebus ; funt certi denique fines,

Quot ultra, citraque nequit confiftere rectum.
                                    Sat. l. 1. Sat. 1.
*Quid verum atque decens, curo & rogo,& omnis in hoc
    fum.
Effluat, & vitæ difconvenit ordine toto.*
                                    Ep. l. 1. Ep. 2.
Qui quid fit pulcrum, quid turpe quid utile, quid non.
                                    Ep. l. 1. Ep. 2.
- So *Plato, Cicero,* and all the beft Philofophers are ever fpeaking of the το καλον, the το πρεπον, the *pulcrum,* the *decens,* the *honeftum, convenienter naturæ vivere,* &c.

BUT this Analogy between the natural and moral World reaches much farther; and indeed if it did not, Man would neceſſarily be incapable of one of his nobleſt Pleaſures; for unleſs there was ſuch a Similitude or Analogy between the natural and moral World, that all Objeĉts of the later ſort may be painted under Images taken from the former, we could not at all have any Intercourſe or Communication with one another about moral things. It hath been often remarked, that the greater part of the Words denoting Affeĉtions and Operations of the moral kind, do in their original Signification expreſs ſenſible Perceptions. But the truth of the matter is, that if inward Sentiments, Affeĉtions, and Aĉtions could not be piĉtured to us by means of ſome things analogous to them in the ſenſible World, Language and Diſcourſe could not extend any farther than to the Objeĉts perceivable by our outward Senſes, and thoſe of the moral kind could not be deſcribed or conveyed at all. · But not to dwell longer on that Reflexion, though it well deſerves the Attention of thoſe who are concerned in Education, and naturally leads to a juſter Notion of the moſt profitable as well as agreeable Method of teaching Language, or explaining Words, than is commonly entertained : It is ſufficient to the preſent purpoſe to obſerve, that Beauty in its firſt Meaning ſignifies a Satisfaĉtion which certain viſible Objeĉts are adapted to give to the Sight ; and it is fitly applied to denote a ſimilar Satisfaĉtion which certain moral Objeĉts are equally adapted to give to the Underſtanding or Eye of the Mind, becauſe of the Similarity of the Pleaſures perceived, and becauſe of their Analogy in all other reſpeĉts. For as by Induĉtion, in the former caſe it is found to be the Regularity of Objeĉts that gives that Satisfaĉtion ? or, in other words, that whatever Objeĉt of Senſe gives it is a regular Whole, that hath Variety amidſt Uniformity ; and yet it is alſo found, that Uſefulneſs is always conneĉted with Regularity and Beauty : So in the later caſe by Induĉtion it is likewiſe found, that the ſame Connexions take place with regard to every moral Objeĉt that is pleaſing and agreeable to our Contemplation : Theſe alſo are regular Objeĉts, or have Variety with Unity, and are in like manner profitable or uſeful. The Perception of Pleaſure called Beauty in both caſes is diſtinĉt from the Reflexion upon Utility, or upon Regularity and Unity ; it is perceived immediately, or at firſt ſight previouſly to all Conſideration of theſe Concomitants. Theſe Connexions between Beauty, Regularity and Utility, are found out afterwards by Enquiry ; and it is becauſe they are diſcovered to take place in many Examples, and no contradiĉtory Inſtance appears, that it is eſtabliſhed into an univerſal Canon by Induĉtion, agreeably to all the Rules of Philoſophy and good Reaſoning ; that whatever is beautiful in the moral, as well as in the natural, or ſenſible World, is regular, hath Unity of Deſign, or Variety with Uniformity, and is uſeful. It is upon this Connexion between Beauty and Utility, that the Ancients have greatly inſiſted.

The inſeparable Connexion of Beauty and Truth with Utility and Advantage.

THEY have often remarked, that as in Nature, ſo in all the Afts, Beauty, Truth, and Utility are inſeparably conneĉted, or more properly are one and the ſame. Beauty and Truth are plainly join'd with the Notion of Utility and Conveniency, in the Apprehenſion of every ingenious Artiſt ; the Statuary, the Painter, the Architeĉt : And for what reaſon, but becauſe it is ſo in Nature ? The ſame Shapes and Proportions, which make Beauty, afford advantage, by adapting to Aĉtivity and Uſe. The ſame Features which occaſion Deformity, create Sicklineſs and Diſeaſe. The proportionate and regular State is the truly proſperous, ſound, and natural one in every Subjeĉt. Health of the Body is the juſt Proportion, Ballance and regular Courſe of Things in a Conſtitution. And what elſe is Health or Soundneſs of Mind but the harmonious State, or true and juſt Ballance of the Affeĉtions (11) : Or what elſe is it that produces Deformity of the moral kind, but ſomething that tends to the Ruin and Diſſolution of our mental Fabrick ? *Cicero* and *Quintilian* have illuſtrated this Truth (*nunquam veri ſpecies ab utilitate dividitur*) by a variety of Examples, from the Struĉtures of animate and inanimate things ; the Fabrick of the human Body, and the Beauty of the human Mind ; and then by analogous Inſtances from Architeĉture and all the Arts (12). And hence the Ancients have laid it down as an univerſal Maxim in Life and Manners, in Nature and

in

(11) Et ut corporis eſt quædam apta figura membrorum cum coloris quadam ſuavitate : Eaque dicitur pulchritudo, ſic in animo, opinionum, judiciorumque æquabilitas, & conſtantia, cum firmitate quadam & ſtabilitate virtutem ſubſequens, aut Virtutis vim ipſam continens, pulchritudo vocatur. Itemque viribus corporis, & nervis, & efficacitati ſimiles, ſimilibus verbis, animi vires nominantur. Velocitas, ſanitas, morbi, &c. *Cic. Tuſcul. Quæſt. lib.* 4. N° 13. *De Off. lib.* 1. N° 28, & 36. Every thing is at eaſe when the Powers of it move regularly and without interruption. Now a rational Being is in this proſperous Condition, when her Judgment is gain'd by nothing but Evidence and Truth ; when her Deſigns are all meant for the adVantage. of Society. When her Deſires and Averſions are confined to Objeĉts within her power, when ſhe reſts ſatisfied with the Diſtributions of Providence : for which ſhe

has great reaſon, ſince ſhe is a part of it herſelf. And with as much propriety, as a Leaf belongs to the Nature of the Tree which bears it, &c. *Marcus Antoninus*'s Meditations, *Collier*'s Tranſlation, *p.* 134.

(12) *Cicero Orator. lib.* 3. 45, 46. Sed ut in pleriſque rebus incredibiliter hoc natura eſt ipſa fabricata : ſic in oratione, ut ea, quæ maximam utilitatem in ſe continerent, eadem haberent plurimum vel dignitatis, vel ſæpe etiam venuſtatis. Incolumitatis, ac ſalutis omnium cauſa, videmus hunc ſtatum eſſe hujus totius mundi atque naturæ.——Hæc tantam habent vim ut paulum immutata cohærere non poſſint : Tantam pulchritudinem, ut nulla ſpecies ne excogitari quidem poſſit ornatior. Referte nunc animum ad hominum, vel etiam eeterarum animantium formam, & figuram. Nullam partem corporis ſine aliqua neceſſitate affiĉtam, totamque

in all the imitative Arts; That what is beautiful is harmonious and proportion'd, what is harmonious and proportion'd is true; and what is at once both beautiful and true, is of confequence agreeable and good. And accordingly, Affections, Manners, and all the Arts are to be judged by this Rule (13). That which in Art is not ufeful to the Whole, cannot be beautiful; all Ornaments which do not naturally rife out of the Subject, and tend to fupport and maintain it, and promote the defign'd Effect of the Whole, are, for the fame reafon that they are an Incumbrance, not merely fuperfluous, but noxious and hurtful with regard to the propofed End and Effect of the Whole.

THIS *Cicero* illuftrates particularly by Architecture, which one is apt to confider at firft fight as a merely ornamental Art; and fo does *Vitruvius* more fully. *Cicero* and *Quintilian* fhew it to be fo in Oratory; and 'tis evidently fo in Painting and Sculpture : For is not the Truth and Beauty of every Figure meafured in thefe Arts, from the Per- fection of Nature, in her juft adapting of every Limb and Proportion, to the Activity, Strength, Dexterity, Life and Vigour of the particular Species or Animal defign'd ? And in a Whole confifting of many Figures relative to one main End, doth not that fpoil the Unity, Simplicity and Correfpondency of the Whole, which hath no neceffary or proper Connection with its principal Scope, but diftracts the Eye, and diverts the Atten- tion from what is chiefly intended.

ALL Pieces of Art, like all Pieces of Nature, muft make one Body, found and well- proportion'd in its Parts, without any cumberfome Excrefcencies, or without Parts of another kind, and not belonging to it as one particular Whole, however beautiful thefe may be confider'd apart. We cannot indeed advance the leaft in any Relifh or Tafte of Symmetry and Proportion, without acknowledging the neceffary Connection betwixt the Ufeful and the Beautiful. And as no Reflection on Nature, and on Arts is of larger Extent, fo none can have a better, or more benign and wholefome Influence upon the Mind. 'Tis by it chiefly, that the Mind is improv'd to perfect good Tafte in all the Arts; confirm'd in its Love and Admiration of the beautiful and ufeful Order that prevails throughout Nature; and kept fteady to Virtue, or the Purfuit of moral Beauty in Life and Manners. And therefore a great part of moral Philofophy, in the ancient way of treating it, is juftly taken up in fhewing the Connection of Virtue with Inte- reft; or, that Virtue is private as well as publick Good; and Vice, on the other hand, private as well as publick Mifery; and that Nature purfues Beauty and Utility by the fame excellent Laws and Methods of Operation.

In what Senfe inge- nious Imitations, or Works of Imagina- tion and Genius are Imitations of the Whole of Nature.

IN the third place, another Method of explaining the Beauty of Works of Genius, of Painting in particular, among the Ancients, is by confidering them as good Imita- tions, not of a part of Nature, but of Nature in general.

THE Meaning of this is, that as Nature is in itfelf a beautiful Whole, in which all is fubordinate to the general Good, Beauty and Perfection of the Whole, (and therefore Perfection is not to be look'd for in any particular Part feparately, but in the Whole; the Perfection of fingle Parts being only purfued by Nature fo far as the general Good per- mits;) fo ought it alfo to be in Pictures : Every Picture ought to be a perfect Whole by itfelf, and its Beauty ought to refult from the whole Compofition; not from the Per- fection of fingle Parts, but from the Subferviency of all the Parts to one main beau- tiful and great End. The Artift cannot bring all Nature into his Piece; he muft there- fore imitate the Whole of Nature in his Work, by chufing a noble, a great, or beauti- ful Plan, and by adapting and difpofing every particular part of his Piece in the manner that may beft fuit to the main End of the Whole. He therefore ought not to paint De- formity, for the fake of expreffing or reprefenting Deformity; but as Nature in the Whole is beautiful, fo ought his Works to be; and the Deformities in fingle Parts, ought, as in Nature, to ferve as Foils or Contrafts to fet off fome principal Beauty to the greater advantage. In one word, whatever particular parts are confider'd by themfelves, the Whole ought to be harmonious and beautiful : And as in Nature, fo in Imitations, it muft only be to the greater Beauty of the Whole that any particular part is fubmitted; and that fo far only as the greater Beauty of the Whole requires it.

THIS

totamque formam quafi perfectam reperietis arte non eafu. Quid in arboribus, in quibus non trancus, non rami, non folia funt denique, nifi ad fuam retinendam, confervandamque naturam ? Nufquam tamen eft ulla pars nifi venufta. Linquamus naturam, arteifque Vide- amus. Quid tam in naVigio neceffarium quam latera, quam carinæ, quam mali, quam Vela, quam prora, quam puppis, quam antennæ ? Quæ tamen hanc ha- bent in fpecie venuftatem; ut non folum falutis fed etiam voluptatis caufa inVenta effe videantur. Colum- næ, & templa, & porticus fuftinent. Tamen habent non plus utilitatis quam dignitatis. Capitolli faftigium illud, & ceterarum ædium, non venuftas fed neceffitas ipfa fabricata eft. Nam cum effet habita ratio, quem- admodum ex utraque tecti parte aqua delaberetur : Uti-

litatum templi, faftigii dignitas confecuta eft : Ut etiam fi in cœlo ftatueretur, ubi imber effe non poffet nullam fine faftigio dignitatem habiturum fuiffe videatur. Hoc in omnibus item partibus orationis evenit ut utilitatem, ac prope neceffitatem fuavitas quædam ac lepos confe. quatur, &c. See *Vitruvius, lib.* 4. *c.* 2. The Paffage was already quoted. *Quintilian, lib.* 8. *c.* 3. where he treats the fame Subject at great length, particularly towards the end of that Chapter. Nam ipfa illa ἀφίλια fimplex & inaffectata, &c. See likewife *Cicero, Orator.* N° 25. Nam fic ut in epularum apparatu, &c.

(13) Compare with the Paffages already quoted, what *Cicero* fays of the *Utile* in the 3d Book of his Offices.

THIS is the Meaning of what they fay, of gathering from the various Parts of Nature to make a beautiful Whole. This is particularly the Meaning of what *Cicero* fays in the Place already quoted ; where he tells us, that *Zeuxis,* from the Confideration of many Beauties, formed his Idea of a perfect Beauty : " Becaufe Nature purfues the Beauty, and " Good or Perfection of the Whole, and not of particular Parts" (13). The Sum of this Obfervation amounts briefly to this, That what is called properly Shade, is not more neceffary to fet off the enlighten'd Parts, in refpect of Colouring, than fomething which, being analogous to it, may likewife be called Shade, is requifite, with regard to the Choice and Difpofition of the Subject, or to poetical Compofition in Painting. And it muft be fo in copying from Nature, fince 'tis fo in Nature itfelf : Whatever is heightened, or hath Relief, whether in the natural or moral World, is raifed, diftinguifhed, or made ftrong and confpicuous by Shade or Contraft.

BUT in the fourth Place, 'tis obvioufly our moral Senfe, and our focial Affections, which afford the Mind the moft agreeable Touches of Joy and Satisfaction. Let one examine himfelf narrowly and impartially, and he fhall find that the largeft Share, even of all thofe Gratifications which are called fenfible Pleafures, is owing to a focial Principle deeply inlayed into his Nature. What are Riches, Titles, Honours, a Table, Drefs, and Equipage, abftractedly from all Regard to Society? What is even Love itfelf, without the *Spes animi credula mutui?* And if we attend to the Pleafures which Arts and Imitation yield, thefe are a fufficient Proof of the Tendernefs and Humanity, fo to fpeak, of our Make and Frame. For whence elfe is it, that where a Succeffion of the kindly Affections can be carried on, even thro' Fears and Horrors, Sorrows and Griefs, the Emotion of the Soul is fo agreeable; or, that when the Paffions of this kind are fkilfully excited in us, as in a Tragedy, we prefer the Entertainment to any one of Senfe ? 'Tis certainly, becaufe exerting whatever we have of focial Affection and generous Sympathy in our Natures, is of the higheft Delight, and produces a greater Enjoyment in the way of Sentiment, than any thing befides can do in the way of mere Senfe and vulgar Appetite.

The chief Pleafures produced or excited in us by ingenious Imitations of human Life, prefuppofe a moral and publick Senfe. And reciprocally, from the Reality of a moral and publick Senfe, it may be inferred, that our chief Pleafures, arifing from Imitations or Fictions, muft be of a moral and focial kind.

TIS the fame with refpect to the Defigning Arts : Whatever touches our publick Senfe, and calls into Action our generous, tender, and kind Affections, is that which moft agreeably detains our Mind, and employs it. Reprefentations of fuch Subjects, fo foon as they are fet to our View, immediately attract us, working upon us in the moft pleafing, becaufe in the moft humane and focial Manner. ·

SOME have faid, that Works of Genius and Fancy pleafe us, becaufe they employ the Mind, which naturally delights in Exercife; and this is undoubtedly true : But 'tis not merely becaufe they employ us, that they pleafe us; for tho' the human Mind be naturally active, and made for Exercife, yet all kinds of Exercife do not equally pleafe and delight. If we attend to our own Feelings, it will evidently be perceived, that of all Exercifes the focial and affectionate, or the Operations of the focial Affections, are the moft fatisfactory and lafting. Who was ever cloy'd by Acts of Friendfhip, Generofity, and a publick difinterefted Spirit? Or did ever the Workings of good and kind benign Affections, when excited by artful Illufion, leave Remorfe, Bitternefs (14) and Difquiet behind 'em? Some have afcribed all the Pleafure arifing from the imitative Arts, to the Power of Illufion, as if we were only pleafed, becaufe we are deceived into imagining a Reprefentation real. But hardly does any one abfolutely forget, that it is Imitation he beholds in Dramatick Pieces, or in Pictures, and fancy the Objects before him real. Or, if he fhould, yet the Pleafure he feels while he imagines fo, cannot be owing to this Deceit: Such Pleafure muft be pofterior, and can then only take Place, when the Mind reflects, that what it took to be real, was merely Imitation; and wonders at the Dexterity by which it was deluded. If, therefore, Fictions are capable of entertaining the Mind, previoufly to fuch Reflection, that Pleafure muft be owing to fome other Difpofition or Senfe within us, upon which the Objects reprefented are fitted to work. And a little Reflexion upon the Fictions or Reprefentations which affect us moft agreeably, or give us the greateft Pleafure, will fhew us, that it is thofe which excite our focial Affections, and call forth generous Sentiments, that yield us the higheft and moft fatisfactory and lafting Entertainment. In fine, we may reafon in this manner about the Conftitution of our Mind, and Imitations fitted to delight or pleafe our Mind; if thofe Imitations, which call forth our Pity and Compaffion into Exercife, and intereft us in behalf of Virtue and Merit, are indeed the Reprefentations that give us the higheft Satisfaction, it muft be confeffed that we are qualified by Nature to receive high Pleafure

(13) *De Invent. Rhetor. lib.* 2. *ab Initio.*

(14) See what is faid on this Subject by the Author of the *Reflexions fur la Poefie & fur la Peinture, T.* 1. *Sect.* 1. La reprefentation pathetique du facrifice de la fille de Jepthé enchaffée dans un bordau dorée, fait le plus bel ornament d'un cabinet qu'on a voulu rendre agreable par

les meubles, on neglige pour contempler ce tableau tragique, les grotefques, & les compofitions les plus riantes des pientres galands. —— En fin plus les actions que la poefie & la peinture depeignent, auroient fait foufrir en nous l'humanité, fi nous les avions vues veritablement, plus les imitations que ces arts en prefentent ont de pouvoir fur nous pour nous attacher. *& Sect.* 3.

Pleafure from focial Affections, and virtuous Exercifes; and that our Frame and Conftitution is focial and virtuous, or deeply interefted by Nature itfelf in behalf of Worth and Merit. Reciprocally, if our focial Affections, and a publick Senfe, are the Sources of our higheft Satisfactions in real Life, then muft thofe Fictions or Reprefentations which are fuited to them, afford us the higheft Pleafure, the beft and moft agreeable Exercife. On the one hand, if we confult our natural Difpofitions, as thefe difcover themfelves on other Occafions, we muft quickly be led to a right Judgment, concerning the Imitations which, in Confequence of our Frame, muft needs be moft acceptable and pleafant to us: On the other hand, if we attend to the Effects of Imitation on our Minds, we muft immediately perceive the Reality of Virtue; or that there is a natural Difpofition in us to be delighted by focial and publick Affections, in a Degree far fuperior to all the Enjoyments of mere Senfe. Thus the Excellence and Naturalnefs of Virtue may be inferred from the Excellencies that belong to the fine Arts; and if the former is owned, there can be no Difpute wherein the latter confift.

TO thefe Obfervations it may be juftly added, that there is a very great Pleafure in reflecting on Arts and Works of Genius and Fancy, as the fkilful Productions of human Invention. For fo great, fo noble, and afpiring hath our Creator made the human Mind, that whatever gives it a high Idea of human Power and Perfection, or of the Force of our intellectual Faculties, to rife to noble Productions, fills it with a moft tranfporting Satisfaction: It exalts the Mind, makes it look upon itfelf with laudable Contentment, and infpires it; with worthy Ambition. We are fo framed as to be highly delighted with what may be confidered as our own Acquifition, or the Product of our own Powers, that we may be thereby impelled to exert and improve ourfelves. And hence it is that we cannot confider the Works of human Genius, the great Actions of Men, or the ufeful Arts difcovered and perfected by them, without faying to ourfelves, with a fecret kind of Joy, Such Works are Men capable of performing, if they take fuitable Pains to improve the Faculties Nature hath kindly conferred on us!

HAVING thus briefly fuggefted the chief Sources of our higheft and nobleft Pleafures, of whatever kind; may we not juftly conclude, that Man is fitted by Nature for a very great and noble Share of rational Happinefs and Perfection, by being made capable of contemplating and imitating Nature? When we confider the Pleafures the Senfes are able to afford us, in the way of common Gratification, as our chief Provifion and Allowance; then it is no Wonder, that Men arraign Nature, and complain of her Niggardlinefs. But all that can be faid of the Impoffibility of attaining Happinefs by fenfual Enjoyments; what does it prove, but that our Happinefs lies not in thefe low Pleafures, and muft be derived from another Source? It was truly kind in Nature, to accompany thofe Exercifes of our Senfes, which are requifite to uphold our organical Frame, with certain Degrees of rewarding Pleafure, and thofe that tend to hurt or deftroy it, with certain Degrees of admonifhing Pain. But our Senfes are chiefly noble and dignifying, as they are fuited to furnifh Materials, and give Employment to Imagination, Invention, Art, Reafon, and Virtue. Our Eyes and Ears, fays *Cicero,* are fuperior to thofe of the Brutes; becaufe there is in our Minds a Senfe of Beauty and Harmony in fenfible Objects, by means of which thefe outward Senfes may be improved into Inftruments, or rather Minifters, of feveral beautiful, highly entertaining Arts (15). 'Tis our intellectual Powers, Taftes, and Senfes that truly ennoble us; becaufe, in Confequence of thefe, our outward Organs may be made, as it were, rational Sources of pure, reafonable, and uncloying Pleafures, far beyond the Reach of

merely fentitive Beings. It may be faid, That if our chief Happinefs does indeed confift in Enjoyments of the rational kind, then are Mankind upon a very unequal Footing with regard to Happinefs. I anfwer, That fome Inequalities amongft Mankind, even in refpect of rational Powers, are as abfolutely neceffary to the General Good, Perfection, and Beauty of the kind, as Shades in a Picture, or Difcords in a mufical Compofition. But notwithftanding thefe neceffary Inequalities, all Men may have the Pleafures of Virtue and Religion in a very high Degree.

> *Take Nature's Path, and mad Opinion's Leave,*
> *All States can reach it, and all Heads conceive;*
> *Obvious her Goods, in no Extreme they dwell;*
> *There needs but thinking right, and meaning well!*
> *And mourn our various Portions as we pleafe,*
> *Equal is common Senfe, and common Eafe.* Effay on Man, Epif. 4.

SECONDLY, their having the Pleafures of natural Knowledge, or thofe the fine Arts afford, chiefly depends, as the Happinefs of a Syftem of rational Beings muft do, upon Government rightly modelled; upon a Conftitution, Laws, and Policies that have the Publick Good for their End, and are duly adapted to obtain it. But in fuch Society, or under good

(15) *De Nat. Deorum, lib. 2. No. 56. 57 58. & 59. De fin. bon. lib. 2. No. 34.*

good Government, the People will not be artificially kept in Darknefs,· but will be generoufly provided with all the neceffary Means of Education, with publick Teachers to
inftruct them in that wife and good Adminiftration of Providence, which they ought to
approve, adore, and imitate, in order to be happy; and to recommend themfelves to the
Divine Favour here or hereafter. In fuch a State Ignorance will not be look'd upon, either
as the Source of Religion, or of civil Submiffion and Obedience; and confequently, its
Subjects will not be hood-wink'd, or deny'd the Advantages of Inftruction in Virtue, the
Rights of Mankind, and true Happinefs.

· I N·the third Place, where the Arts are duely encouraged and promoted, in the manner
that hath been already fuggefted, even the common People, like thofe of *Athens*, will be no
Strangers to the Pleafures which the fine Arts are qualify'd to give, by their Power to teach
and reward Virtue, and to reproach and ftigmatize Vice, while all publick Places are
adorn'd with proper Works of that Nature.

THE Ancients had likewife good Reafon to conclude, from this View of the human *Another Conclufion*
Nature, and of the Pleafures for which we are principally fitted by our Frame, that the *concerning the Be-*
Author of Nature could not have implanted a Senfe of Beauty, Order, Greatnefs, and *nignity of the Di-*
Publick Good in us, were he not poffeffed of it himfelf in the higheft and moft perfect *vine Mind, the Cre-*
Degree. Not only is it neceffarily true, faid they, that the firft independent Mind can *ator, Governor, and*
have no Malice, becaufe fuch a Mind can have no private Intereft, oppofite to or diftinct *Upholder of All.*
from that of the whole, his own Creation: But a malignant Mind, an Enemy to Order,
Beauty, Truth, and Goodnefs, could not poffibly be the Author of thofe noble and
generous Difpofitions which he hath fo deeply inlaid into our Conftitution, to be improved
into Perfection and Happinefs by due Culture (16). · Far from being capable of purfuing
throughout all his Works, Order, Wifdom, and the greateft Good of the whole Syftem, he
could not have difpofed and fitted us for delighting in the Contemplation and Purfuit of
Beauty, Order, and publick Good. Without fuch a Difpofition in his own Nature, he
could not have implanted it in his Creatures; becaufe he could not have had any Motive to
implant it in them, but what muft be fuppofed to proceed from the like Difpofition in
himfelf: Nay, he could not have produced it,· becaufe he could not have had any Conception of it. It was thus the better Ancients reafoned concerning the all-governing Mind;
and confequently, they confidered the Contemplation of Nature as his Workmanfhip; due
Affection towards him,· and the Imitation of his Perfections and Works, as the principal
Sources of human Happinefs; as the Exercifes and Employments that conftitute our fupreme
Dignity and Perfection (17).

BUT the Conclufions that belong more immediately to our Defign, are thofe that may *Other Conclufions*
be drawn from the preceding Account of human Nature, its Powers and Capacities, with *more nearly relating*
refpect to Education and the polite Arts. Had not then the Ancients good Ground to *to the prefent Defign*
infer, ·from the Principles that have been explained, that it ought to be the great End of *concerning Educati-*
Education, to improve our natural Senfe of Beauty, Order, and Greatnefs, and fo to lead *on, and the beft Me-*
to juft Notions of Nature, Conduct, and Arts: And that good Tafte in all thefe muft be *thod of Improving*
the fame, and can only be cultivated and perfected by uniting all the liberal Arts and *Virtue and good*
Sciences in Education, agreeably to their natural Union and Connexion? All the Arts, *Tafte.*
faid they, however divided and diftributed, are one; they have the fame Rule and Standard,
tend

(16) See *M. Antoninus's Meditations, Collier's Tranflation*,
p. 52, *c.* 27. Now can any Man difcover Symmetry in
his own Shape, and yet take the Univerfe for a Heap of
Rubbifh? *&c.* —— So *p.* 57. *c.* 40. and *p.* 85. *book 6.*
As Matter is all of it pliable and obfequious, fo that So-
vereign Reafon which gives Laws to it, has neither Motion nor inclination to bring an Evil on any thing. This
great Being is no way unfriendly or hoftile in his Nature.
He forms and governs all things, but hurts nothing.——
That intelligent Being that governs the Univerfe, has perfect Views of every thing : his Knowledge penetrates the
Quality of Matter, and fees through all the Confequences
of his own Operations. —— This univerfal Caufe has no
foreign Affiftant, no interloping Principle, either without
his Jurifdiction, or within it. And fee what he quotes
from *Plato, p.* 121. See how *Socrates* writes to the fame
Purpofe. *Xenop. Apomn. Soc. p.* 4. *c.* 4.

(17) Compare with the Paffage quoted from *Antoninus, Cicero de Nat. Deorum, lib.* 2. *No.* 6. Si enim eft
aliquid in rerum natura quod hominis mens, quod ratio,
quod vis, quod poteftas humana efficere non poffit; eft
certe id quod illud efficit, homine melius. Atque res
cœleftes, omnefque eæ, quarum eft ordo fempiternus, ab
homine confici non poffunt. Eft igitur id quo illa confi-
ciuntur, homine melius. —— Et tamen ex ipfa hominum
folertia effe aliquam mentem, et eam quidem acriorem,
et divinam exiftimare debemus. Unde enim hanc homo *&c.*

arripuit? ut ait apud Xenophontem Socrates —— Rationem, mentem, confilium, cogitationem, prudentiam, ubi
invenimus? unde fuftulimus? —— Quid vero? tanta
rerum confentiens, confpirans, continuata cognatio, quem
non coget ea comprobare? —— Hæc ita fieri omnibus
inter fe concinentibus mundi partibus profecto non poffent, nifi eo uno divino, & continuato fpiritu contineren-
tur. *No.* 10. Natura eft igitur, quæ contineat mundum
omnem, eumque tueatur, & ea quidem non fine fenfu
atque ratione. Omnem enim naturam neceffe eft, quæ
non folitaria fit, neque fimplex, fed cum alio juncta atque
connexa, habere aliquem in fe principiafum, ut in homine
mentem, in bellua quiddam fimile mentis. Itaque neceffe
eft illud etiam, in quo fit naturæ totius principatus, effe
omnium optimum, omniumque rerum poteftate domi-
natuque digniffimum, *&c.* *No.* 35. ·Hi autem dubitant
de mundo, cafune ipfe fit effectus, aut neceffitate aliqua, an
ratione ac mente divina : Et Archimedem arbitrantur plus
valuiffe in imitandis fphæræ converfionibus, quam naturam in efficiendis, præfertim cum multis partibus fint
illa perfecta, quam hæc fimulata folertius. Atque ille apud
Attium paftor, qui navem nunquam ante vidiffet, ut procul
divinum, & novum Vehiculum, e monte confpexit.——
Ex iis enim naturis quæ erant, quod effici potuit optimum
effectum eft; doceat aliquis potuiffe melius. Sed nemo
unquam docebit: Et fiquis corrigere aliquid volet, aut
deterius faciet, aut id quod fieri non potuit defiderabit,
&c.

tend to the same End, and must therefore be mutually assistant to one another, in promoting and improving that good Temper and good Taste, the Foundations of which Nature hath laid in our Minds, but hath left to Education and Culture to finish and bring to Perfection; that Men may be early wise, good, and virtuous, capable of the best Pursuits and Employments, disposed to seek after them, and averse to every Pleasure and Amusement that sinks and degrades the Man. If Education and Instruction are not in the least calculated to fit for Life and Society, or to give a just Notion of Pleasure, Worth, and Happiness, what is its Business; or what Name can be given to its Designs and Pretensions? But if this be really the Scope it ought to aim it, how can that End be more effectually accomplished, than by exercising our Reason and our Sense of Truth and Beauty about a Variety of proper Objects; and by observing the Sameness of Truth and Beauty in every Subject, throughout Nature, Life, and all the Arts (18)?

Illustrations of this, by considering how several liberal Arts and Sciences were taught by the Ancients, or ought to be taught.

THE Ancients considered Education in a very extensive View, as comprehending all the Arts and Sciences, and employing them all to this one End; to form, at the same time, the Head and the Heart, the Senses, the Imagination, Reason, and the Temper, that the whole Man might be made truly virtuous and rational. And how they managed it, or thought it ought to be managed, to gain this noble Scope, we may learn from their way of Handling any one of the Arts, or of Discoursing on Morals: Whatever be the more immediate Subject of their Enquiries, we find them, as it hath been observed, calling upon all the Arts and Sciences for its Embellishment and Illustration. Let us therefore consider a little the natural Union and close Dependence of the liberal Arts, and enquire how these were explain'd by the Ancients.

Oratory, how philosophical an Art, and its relation to Poetry and Painting.

IF we suppose teaching Oratory to make one principal Part of liberal Education, as it was justly considered at *Athens* and *Rome* to do, while these States were free; ought it not to be taught, as ancient Authors handle it, by tracing and unfolding the Foundations of that Art in our Natures, in the Texture and Dependence of our Affections, in our Sense of the Beautiful, the Sublime, and the Pathetick in Sentiments; and in our Sense of Harmony, even in Sounds, Phrases, and the Cadences of Periods? Ought not the Teachers of Oratory to distinguish true Ornaments, and the native, genuine Embellishments and Graces of Speech, from the false, affected, and unnatural; the Force which Sentiments give to Language, when it is elevated by them, from the pompous and swelling, that is empty Sound? Is it not his Business to criticise the various Sorts of Evidence and Argumentation; and to teach to discern Sophistry, artful Chicane, and false Wit, from true, clear, solid Reasoning, Strength of Argument, and Wit that is able to stand the Test of grave Examination? Now, must he not, for that End, compare Oratory with Poetry, and both with the simple didactick Manner of Teaching; and enter profoundly into the Structure of the human Mind, and into the Nature of Truth and Knowledge, as *Aristotle, Cicero,* and *Quintilian* have done? And are not the properest Subjects for the Exercises that are requisite to form the Orator, as they have likewise shewn, truly philosophical and moral; such as regard Nature, Society, Virtue, Laws, and the Interests of a State, that of one's own Country in particular? The whole Art is therefore truly philosophical, and it cannot be taught without having Recourse to the other Sciences, in order to explain its Rules, or set its Beauties in full Light. It must be ever borrowing from moral Philosophy, that is often called by *Cicero,* for that Reason, *The Fountain of Oratory.* And it hath been already remarked, that we owe our Knowledge of the Painting and Sculpture of the Ancients, in a great measure, to the excellent Use ancient Writers on Oratory and Poetry have made of the former in explaining the latter (19).

Poetry, how philosophical an Art, and its relation to Oratory and Painting.

IF the Art of Poetry ought to be taught, must not the Teacher proceed in the same manner, by tracing its Foundations in our Nature; shewing its best Subjects, and properest Ornaments, its various Kinds, and the respective Provinces and Laws peculiar to each Sort? And can this be done more agreeably or advantageously, than by comparing Poetry, which gave Rise to Oratory, with its own Offspring, and the other Sister-Arts Painting and Sculpture, as *Aristotle* hath done (20).   THE

(18) Compare the Passages of *Cicero* already quoted, concerning the natural Union of the Sciences, with what he says, *De fin.* l. 4. No. 13. where Education is compared to the Art of *Phidias.* Ut Phidias potest a principio instituere signum, idque perficere: Potest ab alio inchoatum accipere ac absolvere: Huic est sapientia similis. Non enim ipsa genuit hominem, sed accepit a natura inchoatum. Hanc intuens debet institutum illud quasi signum absolvere. Qualem igitur natura hominem inchoavit? Et quod est munus, quod opus sapientiæ? Quid est, quod ab ea absolvi ac perfici debeat, si nihil in eo quidem perficiendum est, præter rationem? Necesse est, huic ultimum esse, ex virtute vitam fingere. Rationis enim perfectio est virtus. Si nihil nisi corpus: summa erunt illa, valetudo, vacuitas doloris, pulchritudo, &c. Nunc de homini summo bono quæritur. Quid

ergo dubitamus in tota ejus natura quærere quid sit effectum? See likewise what he says of the Pleasures of the Body, *De fin. lib.* 2. No. 33. Fluit igitur voluptas corporis, et prima quæque avolat, sæpiusque relinquit causas poenitendi, quam recordandi. —— Ad altiora quædam et magnificentiora, mihi crede, Torquati, nati sumus, &c.

(19) This is *Aristotle's, Cicero's,* and *Quintilian's* Method. See likewise *Longinus, Sect.* 39. Harmoniam non modo natura ad persuadendum delectandumque esse accommodatam, sed ad implendos generoso quodam celsoque spiritu, &c.

(20) See his *Poeticks,* and *Andreas Mintærnus de Porta,* his best Commentator.

THE two laſt may therefore be taught, as it were by the by, in explaining the other Arts. But if one was to difcourfe on them, or teach them by themfelves, it hath already appeared, that they may make Reprifals upon Oratory and Poetry; or that the propereſt Similitudes and Illuſtrations in that Cafe muſt be brought from thefe Arts.

'T IS certainly one main End of Education, to form betimes a Taſte for reading Hiſtory with Intelligence and Reflection, and not merely for Diverfion : Now what elfe is this but teaching or inuring Youth to make ufeful Remarks, in reading Hiſtories, upon Men and Manners, Actions, Characters, and Events; the moral Springs and Caufes of moral Appearances; the Beauty of Virtue, and the Deformity of Vice; the good Confequences of the one, and the bad Effects of the other? And is not this true Philoſophy, found Politicks, and the Knowledge of Mankind? But what could have a greater Influence in attracting the Attention of young Minds, or impreffing remarkable Paffages of Hiſtory upon their Me-mories, than to fhew them how the Poets have defcribed the fame or like Actions, and how the Pencil alfo hath, or may do it; and to accuftom Students to entertain themfelves in reading Hiſtory, with Reflexions on the different Methods, the feveral Arts, Philoſo-phy, Hiſtory, Poetry, and Painting, confpiring to the fame End, take to inſtil the fame ufeful important Leffohs? To this we may add, that, in reading Hiſtory, the Progrefs or Decline of Arts ought not to be flightly paffed over; fince thefe afford fure Symptoms of rifing or falling Liberty, in any Country, that well deferve the matureſt Confideration.

IF Logick is taught, what elfe is its Province, but to examine the Powers and Faculties of our Minds, their Objects and Operations; to enquire into the Foundations of good Taſte, and the Caufes of Error, Deceit, and falfe Taſte; and for that Effect to compare the feveral liberal Arts and Sciences with one another, and to obferve how each of them may derive Light and Affiſtance from all the reſt? Its Bufinefs is to give a full View of the natural Union, Connexion, and Dependence of all the Sciences, and fo to complete what I have been now attempting to give an imperfect Sketch of, and as it were to draw the firſt Outlines (21).

BUT if we confider what Philoſophy is, we fhall yet more fully perceive what excel-lent Ufe may be made of the Arts of Defign in Education; if teaching either natural or moral Philoſophy in the propereſt Manner be any Part of its Aim and Scope. Philoſophy is rightly divided into natural and moral; and in like manner, Pictures are of two Sorts, natural and moral: The former belong to natural, and the other to moral Philoſophy. For if we reflect upon the End and Ufe of Samples or Experiments in Philoſophy, it will immediately appear that Pictures are fuch, or that they muſt have the fame Effect. What are Landfcapes and Views of Nature, but Samples of Nature's vifible Beauties, and for that Reafon Samples and Experiments in natural Philoſophy? And moral Pictures, or fuch as reprefent Parts of human Life, Men; Manners, Affections, and Characters; are they not Samples of moral Nature, or of the Laws and Connexions of the moral World, and there-fore Samples or Experiments in moral Philoſophy? In examining the one, we act the Part of the natural Philoſopher; and in examining the other, our Employment is truly moral; becaufe it is impoffible to judge of the one, or of the other, without comparing them with the Originals from which they are taken, that is, with Nature: Now what is Philoſophy but the Study of Nature? And as for the Advantage of ſtudying Nature by means of Copies, 'tis evident: For not only does the double Employment of the Mind, in comparing a Copy with the Original, yield a double Satisfaction to the Mind; but by this comparing Exercife, the Original is brought, as it were, nearer to our View, and kept more fteadily before us, till both Original and Copy are fully examined and comprehended: The Mind is pleafed to perceive an Object thus doubled, as it were, by Reflexion; its Curiofity is excited narrowly to canvafs the Refemblance; and thus it is led to give a clofer and more accurate Attention to the Original itfelf.

IF Pictures of natural Beauties are exact Copies of fome particular Parts of Nature, or done after them, as they really happened in Nature; they are in that cafe no more than fuch Appearances more accurately preferved by Copies of them, than they can be by Ima-gination and Memory, in order to their being contemplated and examined as frequently and as ferioufly as we pleafe. 'Tis the fame as preferving fine Thoughts and Sentiments by Writing, without trufting to Memory, that they may not be loſt. This is certainly too evident to be infiſted upon. On the other hand, if Landfcapes are not copied from any particular Appearances in Nature, but imaginary; yet, if they are confotmable to Nature's Appearances and Laws, being compofed by combining together fuch fcattered Beauties of Nature as make a beautiful Whole; even in this cafe, the Study of Pictures is ſtill the Study of Nature itfelf: For if the Compofition be agreeable to Nature's fettled Laws and Pro-portions,

(21) See the Paffages referred to in the Preliminary Remark. *Milton* particularly in his Effay on Education:

portions, it may exiſt : And all ſuch Repreſentations ſhew what Nature's Laws would produce in ſuppoſed Circumſtances. The former Sort may therefore be called a Regiſter of Nature, and the latter a Supplement to Nature, or rather to the Obſervers and Lovers of Nature. And in both Caſes Landſcapes are Samples or Experiments in natural Philoſophy : Becauſe they ſerve to fix before our Eyes beautiful Effects of Nature's Laws, till we have fully admired them, and accurately conſidered the Laws from which ſuch viſible Beauties and Harmonies reſult.

THO' one be as yet altogether unacquainted with Landſcapes (by which I would all along be underſtood to mean all Views and Proſpects of Nature) he may eaſily comprehend what ſuperior Pleaſures one muſt have, who hath an Eye formed by comparing Landſcapes with Nature, in the Contemplation of Nature itſelf, in his Morning or Evening Walks, to one who is not at all converſant in Painting. Such a one will be more attentive to Nature, he will let nothing eſcape his Obſervation; becauſe he will feel a vaſt Pleaſure in obſerving and chuſing pichtureſque Skies, Scenes, and other Appearances, that would be really beautiful in Pictures. He will delight in obſerving what is really worthy of being painted ; what Circumſtances a good Genius would take hold of; what Parts he would leave out, and what he would add, and for what Reaſon. The Laws of Light and Colours, which, properly ſpeaking, produce all the various Phænomena of the viſible World, would afford to ſuch an inexhauſtible Fund of the moſt agreeable Entertainment; while the ordinary Spectator of Nature can hardly receive any other Satisfaction from his Eye, but what may be juſtly compared with the ordinary Titillation a common Ear feels, in reſpect of the exquiſite Joy a refined Piece of Muſick gives to a ſkilful, well-formed one, to a Perſon inſtructed in the Principles of true Compoſition, and inured to good Performance.

NOR is another Pleaſure to be paſſed by unmentioned, that the Eye formed by right Inſtruction in good Pictures, to the accurate and careful Obſervance of Nature's Beauties, will have, in recalling to mind, upon ſeeing certain Appearances in Nature, the Landſcapes of great Maſters he has ſeen, and their particular Genius's and Taſtes. He will ever be diſcerning ſomething ſuited to the particular Turn of one or other of them ; ſomething that a *Titian,* a *Pouſin,* a *Salvator Roſa,* or a *Claud Lorrain,* hath already repreſented, or would not have let go without imitating, and making a good Uſe of in Landſcape. Nature would ſend ſuch a one to Pictures, and Pictures would ſend him to Nature : And thus the Satisfaction he would receive from the one or the other would be always double.

IN ſhort, Pictures which repreſent viſible Beauties, or the Effects of Nature in the viſible World, by the different Modifications of Light and Colours, in Conſequence of the Laws which relate to Light, are Samples of what theſe Laws do or may produce. And therefore they are as proper Samples and Experiments to help and aſſiſt us in the Study of thoſe Laws, as any Samples or Experiments are in the Study of the Laws of Gravity, Elaſticity, or of any other Quality in the natural World. They are then Samples or Experiments in natural Philoſophy. The ſame Obſervation may be thus ſet in another Light : Nature hath given us a Senſe of Beauty and Order in viſible Objects ; and it hath not certainly given us this or any other Senſe, for any other Reaſon, but that it might be improv'd by due Culture and Exerciſe. Now in what can the Improvement of this Senſe and Taſte conſiſt, but in being able to chuſe from Nature ſuch Parts, as being combined together according to Nature's Laws, would make beautiful Syſtems ? This is certainly its proper Buſineſs and Entertainment : And what elſe is this but Painting, or a Taſte of Nature ? For Painting (22) aims at viſible Harmony, as Muſick at Harmony of Sounds. But how elſe can either the Eye or the Ear, the Senſe of viſible or audible Harmony, be formed and improved to Perfection, but by Exerciſe and Inſtruction about theſe Harmonies, by means of proper Examples? Pictures, therefore, in whatever Senſe they are conſidered, have a near Relation to Philoſophy, and a very cloſe Connexion with Education, if it be any Part of its Deſign to form our Taſte of Nature, and improve our Senſe of viſible Harmonies and Beauties, or to make us intelligent Spectators and Admirers of the viſible World.

Hiſtorical or moral
Pictures areSamples
or Experiments in
moral Philoſophy ;
and the Uſeſulneſs
of ſuch Samples in
teaching Morals.

BUT I proceed to conſider hiſtorical or moral Pictures, which muſt immediately be acknowledged, in Conſequence of the very Definition of them, to be proper Samples and Experiments in teaching human Nature and moral Philoſophy. For what are hiſtorical Pictures,

(22) Theſe Reflexions I owe to *Plutarch*: Haud omnibus idem eſt judicium videndi : Etenim viſus viſu, ut audituͻ auditu, vel natura perfectior eſt, vel arte exercitatior ad pulchri explorationem. Ad harmonias nimirum & modulos muſici ; ad formas vero & ſpecies judicandas pictores ingenio ſenſuque plus Valent. Quemadmodum aliquando Nicomachum reſpondiſſe ferunt cuidam idiotæ, qui Helenam minime pulchram ſibi videri dixerat, Sume oculos meos, & dea tibi videbitur. Ex *Plutarcho de Amore Stobæi, ſermo 61, de Venere & Amore.*——— So *Plutarch, de genio Socratis, ab Initio,* ſpeaking of a

Painter : Aiebat rudes & artis ignaros ſpectatores ſimiles eſſe eorum, qui magnam ſimul turbam ſalutant ; ſcitos autem & artificii ſtudioſos, eorum, qui ſingulatim obvios compellant. Illos nempe non exacte in artificum opera inſpicere, ſed informem quandam operum concipere imaginem. Hos autem cum judicio partes operis perluſtrantes, nihil inſpectatum, nihil inobſervatum relinquere eorum qui vel bene vel male ficta ſunt. Prorſus quemadmodum communis quiſpiam auditus dici recte queat, qui tantum Voces valet diſcernere : qui vero ſonos, non jam amplius communis, ſed artificioſus.

Pictures, but Imitations of Parts of human Life, Reprefentations of Characters and Manners? And are not fuch Reprefentations Samples or Specimens in moral Philofophy, by which any Part of human Nature, or of the moral World, may be brought near to our View, and fixed before us, till it is fully compared with Nature itfelf, and is found to be a true Image, and confequently to point out fome moral Conclufion with complete Force of Evidence? Moral Characters and Actions defcribed by a good Poet, are readily owned to be very proper Subjects for the Philofopher to examine, and compare with the human Heart, and the real Springs and Confequences of Actions. Every one confents to the Truth of what *Horace* fays on this Subject:

Trojani belli fcriptorem, maxime Lolli,
Dum tu declamas Romæ, Prænefte relegi:
Qui, quid fit pulchrum, quid turpe, quid utile, quid non,
Plenius ac melius Chryfippo & Crantore dicit. Hor. Ep. L. i. Ep. 2.

But moral Pictures muft be for the fame Reafon proper Samples in the School of Morals: For what Paffions or Actions may not be reprefented by Pictures; what Degrees, Tones, or Blendings of Affections; what Frailties, what Penances, what Emotions in our Hearts; what Manners, or what Characters, cannot the Pencil exhibit to the Life? Moral Pictures, as well as moral Poems, are indeed Mirrours in which we may view our inward Features and Complexions, our Tempers and Difpofitions, and the various Workings of our Affections. 'Tis true, the Painter only reprefents outward Features, Geftures, Airs, and Attitudes; but do not thefe, by an univerfal Language, mark the different Affections and Difpofitions of the Mind? What Character, what Paffion, what Movement of the Soul, may not be thus moft powerfully expreffed by a fkilful Hand? The Defign of moral Pictures is, therefore, by that Means, to fhew us to ourfelves; to reflect our Image upon us, in order to attract our Attention the more clofely to it, and to engage us in Converfation with ourfelves, and an accurate Confideration of our Make and Frame (23).

AS it hath been obferved, with refpect to Landfcapes, fo in this Cafe likewife, Pictures may bring Parts of Nature to our View, which could never have been feen or obferved by us in real Life; and they muft engage our Attention more clofely to Nature itfelf, than mere Leffons upon Nature can do, without fuch Affiftance; nothing being fo proper to fix the Mind, as the double Employment of comparing Copies with Originals. And in general, all that hath been faid to fhew that Landfcapes are proper Samples or Experiments in natural Philofophy, as being either Regifters or Supplements to Nature, is obvioufly applicable to moral Pictures, with relation to moral Philofophy. We have already had Occafion to remark, that it is becaufe the Poet and Painter have this Advantage, that whereas the Hiftorian is confined to Fact, they can felect fuch Circumftances in their Reprefentations as are fitteft to inftruct or move; that it is for this Reafon *Ariftotle* recommends thefe Arts as better Teachers of Morals than the beft Hiftories, and calls them more catholick or univerfal. I fhall only add upon this Head, that as certain delicate Veffels in the human Body cannot be difcerned by the naked Eye, but muft be magnified, in order to be rendered vifible; fo, without the Help of Magnifiers, not only feveral nice Parts of our moral Fabrick would efcape our Obfervation, but no Features, no Characters of whatever kind, would be fufficiently attended to. Now the Imitative Arts become Magnifiers in the moral way, by means of chufing thofe Circumftances which are propereft to exhibit the Workings and Confequences of Affections, in the ftrongeft Light that may be, or to render them moft ftriking and confpicuous. All is Nature that is reprefented, if all be agreeable to Nature: What is not fo, whether in Painting or Poetry, will be rejected, even by every common Beholder, with *Quodcunque oftendis mihi fic, incredulus odi*. But a Fiction that is confonant to Nature, may convey a moral Leffon more ftrongly than can be done by any real Story, and is as fure a Foundation to build a Conclufion upon; fince from what is conformable to Nature, no erroneous or feducive Rule can be inferred.

THUS, therefore, 'tis evident that Pictures, as well as Poems, have a very near relation to Philofophy, a very clofe Connexion with moral Inftruction and Education.

THE chief Advantage which Painting hath above Poetry, confifts in this:

Segnius

The Advantages of Painting above Poetry.

---

(23) Confidering what has been fo often faid, upon the Union of the Sifter Arts with Philofophy, it may not be amifs to refer my Readers to the Confeffion of one of the greateft and moft learned of the Moderns, upon this Head. See therefore *Ifaaci Cafauboni liber commentarius in Theophrafti notationes morum, in prolegomenis :* Enimvero morum conformandorum, quod ethicus philofophus prærogativæ jure quodam quafi proprium fibi affumit, non una eft a veteribus fapientibus inventa & exculta ratio. Nam idem hic, fi propius attendimus, et ethici philofophi, et hiftorici, & poeræ finis eft. —— Quare tendunt quidem eodem omnes quodammodo, fed diverfis tamen itineribus. —— Omnis enim poeta μιμητὴς, ait Plato. —— Fit autem hoc a Theophrafto magna ex parte μιμηλικῶς. —— Mores hominum ita hic olim erant defcripti, ut liceret tanquam in fpeculo hinc Virtutis fplendorem et pulcherrimam intueri faciem, &c. Compare with this his Preface to his Commentary on *Perfius*.

Segnius irritant animos demissa per aurem,
Quam quæ sunt oculis subjecta fidelibus, et quæ
Ipse sibi tradit spectator.

And of Poetry above Painting.

POETRY, on the other Hand, hath a very great Superiority over Painting, because it can give proper Language to each Character and Personage, according to a very ancient Apophthegm (24) :

Pictura est poesis muta, poesis pictura loquens.

BUT without entering into the Dispute about Pre-eminence between the two Sister Arts, that are both so excellent, each in its Province, 'tis worth while to observe, with regard to both, that human Nature may be better and more securely learned from their Representations, than from mere Systems of Philosophy, for a Reason that hath not yet been mentioned; because both Poets and Painters exhibit Affections and Characters as they conceive, or rather as they feel them, without suffering themselves to be byassed by any Scheme or Hypothesis. They follow the Impulse of Nature, and paint as she dictates; Whereas the Philosopher has often a favourite Supposition in View, and is thereby tempted to strain and wiredraw every Appearance into a Congruity with, if not a Confirmation of his peculiar System.

How they are mutually assistant one to the other.

AND let even that be as it will, it is obvious, from what hath been said of the Affinity between Poetry and Painting, that the Imagination, by being conversant with good Pictures, must become abler to keep Pace with the Poet while he paints Actions and Characters; and on the other hand, Acquaintance with the Works of good Poets must add mightily to one's Pleasure in seeing good moral Paintings; since by that Means the proper Sentiments each Figure seems disposed, as it were, to speak, in a good Picture, will readily occur to the Spectator, in the properest and most affecting Language. The same will likewise hold with regard to Landscapes: For, on the one side, as a poetical Description of any natural Beauty will be better relished, in Proportion as the Reader, in Consequence of being accustomed to study Nature, and compare good Pictures with it, is abler to paint in his Imagination; so, on the other side, fine Prospects of Nature's Beauties will be more highly delightful, when they recall to the Mind a beautiful lively Description of it, or of any like Prospect in some good Poet.

Moral Imitations ought therefore to be made use of in teaching moral Philosophy.

BUT the Conclusion I have now chiefly in View is, that good moral Paintings, whether by Words, or by the Pencil, are proper Samples in moral Philosophy, and ought therefore to be employed in teaching it, for the same Reason that Experiments are made use of in teaching natural Philosophy. And this is as certain, as that Experiments or Samples of Manners, Affections, Actions, and Characters, must belong to moral Philosophy, and be proper Samples for evincing and enforcing its Doctrines; for such are moral Paintings.

WHEN one considers moral Philosophy in its true Light, as designed to recommend Fortitude, Temperance, Self-denial, Generosity, Publick Spirit, the Contempt of Death for the sake of Liberty and general Happiness, and all the Virtues which render Men happy and great; when moral Philosophy is considered in this View, how many Pictures must immediately occur to those who are acquainted with the best Works of the great Masters, that naturally, and as it were necessarily, call up in the Mind the most virtuous Sentiments, and noblest Resolutions, or that are qualified to operate upon our Minds in the most wholsome, as well as agreeable Manner? And how many more Subjects might easily be named, that if well executed by a good Pencil, would have the like excellent Effects!

Several Pictures mentioned, that are proper Samples in teaching Morals.

IT is indeed just Matter of Regret, that at all times moral Subjects have been too much neglected, and Superstition hath had too great a Share of the Pencil's marvellous Art. But hath not her Sister Poetry had the same Fate? And, while I cannot forbear making this Complaint, yet, to do Justice to Painters antient and modern, I must own, that at this very Moment, my Imagination being carried with Transport thro' the Pictures I have seen, or read Descriptions of, one calls upon me, in the strongest manner, to submit to the cruellest Torments, rather than forego my Honour, Integrity, Country, Religion and Conscience: Another, methinks, enables me to prefer Continence and Self-command to the highest Delights of Sense. One fills my Soul with the noblest Opinion of Publick Spirit and Fortitude, and the sincerest Contempt of a selfish mercenary Temper: Another raises my Abhorrence of base, ungenerous, cruel Lust. One warns me to guard against Anger and Revenge, shewing the Destruction that is quickly brought upon the Mind by every unbridled Passion : Another makes me feel, how divine it is to conquer ourselves, forgive Injuries, and load even the Unthankful with Benefits. In one, I see the Beauty of

Meekness

(24) *Plato de Rep. Arist. Poet. Plutarch. in Simonide.* So likewise *Horace : Mutum est pictura poema.*

Meekness and Goodness; in another, the Firmness and Steadiness that becomes a Patriot in the Caufe of Liberty and Virtue, and it infpires me with the moft heroick Sentiments. On one hand, I am loudly called upon to examine every Fancy and Appetite, maintain the Mafterfhip of my Mind, and not rafhly to truft to the moft fpecious Appearances of Plea-fure : On the other, I fee and tremble at the direful Confequences of the leaft immoral Indulgence.

WITH what a Variety of human Nature doth one admirable Piece prefent me (25) ; *Pictures defcribed.* where almoft all the different Tempers of Mankind are reprefented in a polite elegant Audience to a truly divine Teacher ! I fee one incredulous of all that is faid ; another wrapt up in deep Sufpenfe : One fays, there is fome Reafon in what he teaches ; ano-ther is unwilling to give up a favourite Opinion, and is angry with the Preacher for attacking it : One cares for none of thefe Things ; another fcoffs ; another is wholly con-vinced, and holding out his Hands in Rapture, welcomes Light and Truth ; while the Ge-nerality attend and wait for the Opinion of thofe who are of leading Characters in the Af-fembly. Who can behold, unmoved, the Horror and Reverence which appears in that whole Affembly, where the mercenary Man falls down dead ? With what Amazement doth that blind Man recover his Sight ! How do thofe Lame, juft beginning to feel Life in their Limbs, ftand doubtful of their new Strength ! How inexpreffible is the gracelefs Indignation of that Sorcerer who is ftruck blind ! But how fhall I fignify by Words, the deep Feeling which thefe excellent Men have of the Infirmities which they relieve, by Power and Skill which they do not attribute to themfelves ! Or the generous Diftrefs they are in, when divine Honours are offered to 'em ! Are not thefe a Reprefentation in the moft exquifite Degree of the Beauty of Holinefs ! As for that inimitable Piece, in which is drawn the Appearance of our Saviour, after his Refurrection, who will undertake to defcribe its Force and Excellency ? Prefent Authority, late Suffering, Humility, and Ma-jefty, defpotick Command, and divine Love, are at once fettled in his celeftial Afpect. The Figures of the Eleven Apoftles are all in the Paffion of Admiration, but difcovered dif-ferently, according to their Characters ; *Peter* receives his Mafter's Orders on his Knees, with an Admiration mixed with a more particular Attention ; the two next, with a more open Ecftafy, tho' ftill conftrained by their Awe of the divine Prefence : The beloved Dif-ciple, who is the Right of the two firft Figures, has in his Countenance Wonder drowned in Love ; and the laft Perfonage, whofe Back is toward the Spectator, and his Side toward the Prefence, one would fancy to be St. *Thomas*, as abafhed at the Confcience of his former Diffidence ; which perplexed Concern, 'tis poffible, the great Painter thought too hard a Task to draw, but by this Acknowledgment of the Difficulty to defcribe it. The whole Work is indeed an Exercife of the higheft Piety in the Painter ; and all the Touches of a religious Mind are expreffed in a manner much more forcible than can poffibly be per-formed by the moft moving Eloquence.

BUT when I reflect upon the Power of the Pencil to exprefs Subjects of all Sorts, my *Pictures defcribed.* Mind is immediately carried into another more diftant Gallery, and prefents me with a moft beautiful Picture of the fine Arts, and of *Apollo* the God of Wifdom, their Father and Lawgiver. See *Apollo* fitting on Mount *Parnaffus*, under a Laurel, with a delightful Fountain at his Feet ; he is playing upon a mufical Inftrument, attended by the Mufes, and the moft famous Poets, with their immortal Crowns on their Heads, all in Poftures of Ad-miration, which is differently expreffed according to their Characters. How lovely is the God, and how charming doth his Mufick appear to be, by its wonderful Effects on all about him ! Upon his right Hand fits *Clio* with her Trumpet, ready to found with higheft Tranf-port the Praifes of Gods and godlike Men : Upon the Left is *Urania*, who, turned towards *Apollo*, liftens with Rapture to his divine Harmony ; fhe holds a Lyre in her Hand, and her celeftial Robe fhews her divine Birth, and high Employment. The other Mufes ftand be-hind, in two Choirs, with Books and Mafks ; and tho' each hath a diftinguifhing Counte-nance and Mien, they are evidently Virgins and Sifters, the Daughters of *Jove*. Not far from *Clio*, on her right hand, ftands *Homer*, in a long Robe, full of Infpiration, and accompanying a Heroic Song with correfpondent Action. There he is, the old, venerable, blind Bard, the Father of Poets, juft as the Ancients have reprefented him, with the fame fweet, yet grave, majeftick, prophetical Air ! How agreeable is it to fee *Virgil* leading *Dante* to *Apollo* ; and how charming, how inexpreffibly delightful is the whole Reprefen-tation ! How pleafantly doth it point out the Confent and Harmony of all the Arts ; and how powerfully doth the Place given to the Ancients, recommend the Study of 'em to all who would arrive at any Perfection in good Tafte, and ufeful Science ! See again, in ano-ther Piece, the ancient Philofophers, and their Scholars ; with what profound Meditation do fome ftudy ! With what divine Joy do others teach and impart found Philofophy, and pro-fitable Science ; whilft feveral Students of different Ages and Characters, quite in Love with true Learning, drink in Inftruction, or take Notes with the keeneft Attention, the moft agreeable

(25) This Defcription of the Cartoons is taken from one of the *Spectators*, No. 226, T. 3.

An ESSAY *on the Rise, Progress,*

agreeable Docility, and higheft Satisfaction! How pleafantly is the true Philofophy of *Py-thagoras* reprefented, who taught that all Nature is Mufick, perfect Harmony ; and that Virtue is the Harmony of Life ; or its Conformity to the Harmony of the all-govern-ing Mind, and his immenfe melodious Creation (26)!

WHAT cannot Painting teach or exprefs in the moft forcible Manner! For fee there in another Piece the Conftancy, the Serenity, the Fortitude of Heroes in the Fury and Dan-ger of Action : How hot and terrible is the Battle! and with what intrepid Bravery does the Chief rufh into the thickeft of the Enemy! His Countenance befpeaks Victory, ere yet the Tyrant's Defeat is declared : One of the Captains, fraught with glad Tidings, is but beginning to declare his Overthrow, and to point at him, juft falling with his Horfe thro' the Bridge into the River. How eager do many appear to tell the whole Conqueft, and to fhew the Emperor the dread Trophies of their Victory ; while other Commanders, flufhed with Succefs, eagerly purfue the flying Enemy! But how vain is it to attempt to equal by Words the ineffable Force of fuch a Pencil!

Hence we fee that the liberal Arts ought not to be fe-vered from Philo-fophy, or from one another, in Educa-tion.

FROM what hath been faid 'tis manifeft, that all the liberal Arts and Sciences have the moft clofe and intimate Relation, Dependence and Connection, and that they cannot be fevered from one another in Education, without rendering it very incomplete, and indeed incapable of accomplifhing its noble End, which is to form betimes the Tafte and Love of Beauty, Truth and Harmony in Nature, in Life, and in all the Arts which imitate Nature and moral Life.

In whatever View Education is confi-dered, the Affift-ance of the Defign-ing Arts is of the greateft Ufe.

IN whatever View Education is confidered, whether as it is defigned to improve the Senfes and Imagination, or as it is defigned to improve our reafoning Powers, and our inward Senfe of Beauty natural and moral ; or, laftly, as it is defigned to form a benevo-lent, generous, and great Temper of Mind ; in which ever of thefe Lights it is confidered, all the Arts and Sciences amicably confpire towards it ; and it is by mixing and combining them together, that all or any of thefe Ends may be moft effectually and agreeably accom-plifhed : How can the Temper be better improved, than by Reflections on the Greatnefs and Benevolence of Nature, and upon the beautiful Effects of like Benevolence and Greatnefs of Mind in our own Conduct? And when is it that Poetry and Painting fhew their Charms, their divine Power to the greateft Perfection? Is it not when they are employed to difplay the Beauties of Nature, and the Beauties of thofe Virtues which emulate Nature, and when their Productions are truly beautiful natural Wholes? Is not the Imagination a powerful Faculty, that well deferves Culture and Improvement? Nay, is it not of the greateft Importance to have it early interefted in Behalf of true Beauty, and fecured againft the Delufions of Vice, Luxury, and falfe Pleafure? And how can this be done, but by early employing it in the Contemplation of Nature, and of the true Beauties of Life, and confequently by calling in all the Arts to exhibit thefe in their livelieft Colours? What doth the Improvement of Imagination mean, but, in one Word, teaching it to paint, with Spirit and Life, after Nature, according to Truth? Have we a Senfe of natural Beauty and Harmony capable of giving us fuch a vaft Variety of truly pure and noble Pleafures? and ought this Senfe to be neglected in Education? Is it worth while to form the Ear, as moft certainly it is? and ought not the Eye likewife to be formed to a luft, quick, and perfect Relifh, of the Har-monies it may be fitted to perceive, and delight in, by due Culture and Exercife? About what ought our reafoning Powers to be exercifed, but the Harmonies and Beauties of Nature, the Harmonies and Beauties of Life? The chief Employment of Man's Underftanding, is the Order and Regularity he ought to promote within his own Breaft, by the right Manage-ment of his Affections, and the Order, Harmony and Good, that wholefome Laws, impar-tially executed, produce in human Society. But what is it can more powerfully inforce the Senfe and Love of moral Order, than the Contemplation of the wife and good Order of Nature, and frequent Reflections upon that which conftitutes true Order, Beauty and

A Saying of Atticus.

Greatnefs, in the Arts which imitate Nature? *Atticus* is introduced by *Cicero* (27), after a long Conference about the Foundation of Virtue in our Natures, making a very beautiful Reflection, which muft naturally lead every intelligent Reader to the Conclufion I have been all along aiming at ; even that Beauty, Truth and Greatnefs, are the fame in Nature, in Life, and in all the Arts. If we attend, fays he, to what it is that chiefly pleafes us even

(26) See *Diogenes Laertius, lib.* 8. Pythagorei affirmare non dubitabant virtutem harmoniam effe, fanitatem, nec-non omne bonum, Ipfumque adeo Deum : Proptereaque univerfa hæc harmoniæ potiffimum beneficio confiftere.

(27) *De legibus, lib.* 2. ab initio. Equidem, qui nunc potiffimum huc venerim, fatiari non queo : Magnificafque villas, & pavimenta marmorea, &. laqueata tecta con-temno. Ductus vero aquarum, quos ifti tubos & Euripos vocant, quis non, cum hæc viderit, irriferit? Itaque, ut tu paulo ante de lege & Jure differens, ad naturam refere-bas omnia ; fic in his rebus, quæ ad requietem animi,

delectationemque quæruntur ; natura dominatur.——— Quin ipfe vere dicam, fum illi villæ amicior modo factus, atque huic omni folo, in quo tu ortus, & procreatus es. Movemur enim nefcio quo pacto locis ipfis, in quibus eorum quos diligimus, aut admiramur, adfunt veftigia. Me quidem illæ noftræ Athenæ non tam operibus mag-nificis, exquifitifque antiquorum artibus delectant, quam recordatione fummorum virorum, ubi quifque habitare, ubi federe, ubi difputare fit folitus : Studiofaque etiam eorum Sepulchra contemplor. Quare iftum; ubi tu es natus, plus amabo pofthac locum, &c.

in

in rural Profpects, we fhall find that it is the fame natural Tafte and Difpofition, from which you have derived Virtue : And now that I feel a particular Attachment to this Place where we are, to what is this Pleafure owing? is it not to my Delight in the Remembrance of great Men and their Virtues, or to fome other focial affectionate Tie, and kindly Principle deeply inlaid into our Natures? There is likewife a famous Saying of *Æmilius* recorded by *Plutarch*, very much to the prefent Purpofe (28). Having given a very elegant Entertainment after the Conqueft of *Macedonia*, he was asked how it came about that a Man always employed in great Affairs, the Difcipline of Armies, Battles, and military Arts, underftood fo well the Management even of a Feaft: To this he is faid to have replied, that 'tis the fame Tafte that qualifies for the one and the other, to range an Army in Battle-array, or to order a publick Entertainment. Thefe and feveral fuch-like antient Apophthegms are pregnant with Inftruction, and well deferve to be unfolded and explained to Youth, becaufe they afford Occafion of difcourfing fully upon what I have now been endeavouring to fhew to be the chief End of Education, and the propereft Method it can take. The Sum of all which amounts to this; " That the readieft, the moft effectual and moft agreeable Manner " of forming an univerfal good Tafte, is by fhewing from proper Examples, that good Tafte " is the fame every-where, always founded on the fame Principles, and eafily transferred " from any Subject whatever to any other ".

Another of P. Æmilius.

Thefe lead us to the Conclufion now aimed at.

BUT left, after all that hath been faid, this Scheme of Education fhould appear to any one too complex, and for that Reafon hardly practicable; let us but imagine to ourfelves a School confifting of different Apartments for Inftruction in the feveral Parts of ufeful Learning and Philofophy, fuitably adorned with Pictures and Sculptures, or good Prints of them; and all I propofe muft be immediately perceived to be very fimple, and eafily reducible to Practice. For in reading the antient Poets and Hiftorians, for Example, what could have a better Effect than having recourfe to fuch Pieces of Painting and Sculpture as exhibit the Cuftoms, Rites and Manners defcribed or alluded to by them? How agreeable would it be to fee the Images of antient celebrated Heroes, while we read their Lives and Characters, or to compare the Gods as they are defcribed by Authors, with the Reprefentations of them that are given us by the Pencil or Chezil? And how much more delightful ftill would it be to compare Fables or Actions as they are told by an Hiftorian or Poet, with the Reprefentations of 'em the other Arts have given? I need not tell thofe who are ac-quainted with the antient Remains in *Italy*, or with the Works of the great modern Mafters (29), that almoft the whole antient Mythology and Hiftory, all the Fables, and almoft all the great Actions that are the Subjects of antient Poets, or that make the greateft Figure in Hiftory, are to be found reprefented in a very beautiful expreffive Manner upon Antiques of one kind or other; and many of thofe Subjects have been likewife painted by excellent modern Mafters. And I think 'tis too obvious to be infifted upon, that fuch Works, that is, good Defigns or Prints of 'em, would have their proper Place, and be of great Ufe in the Schools, where antient Poets and Hiftorians are read and explained. To be convinced of this, one need only read Mr. *Addifon's* Dialogues on Medals, in which he fhews what Ufe may be made of thefe in explaining the antient Poets, or giving a more lively Idea of the Beauties of their Epithets and Defcriptions. Now, if the Schools of natural and moral Philofophy were in like manner furnifhed with proper Pictures of the natural and moral Kinds; would it not render Leffons on any Subject in Philofophy exceedingly agreeable, and confequently much more ftrong and infinuating, if to philofophical Reafonings and Arguments, was added an Explication of the ingenious Devices and Contrivances of the Imitative Arts to illuftrate the fame Subject, or to inforce the fame Leffon? Thus, for Inftance, in difcourfing upon any Virtue, any Vice, any Affection of the human Mind, and its Operations, Effects and Confequences, would it not neceffarily have a very pleafant, and therefore a very powerful Effect upon young Minds, if they were fhewn, not only the Fables, the Allegories, the dramatic Reprefentations, and the other different Methods Poetry hath invented to explain the fame moral Truth, but likewife fome Paintings and Sculptures of that fame Nature and Tendency?

A View of the eafy Practicablenefs of this Method of Education by uniting the Defigning Arts with the other Parts of liberal Education.

THIS Plan only requires that our Youth fhould be early inftructed in Defign or Drawing. For thus in teaching other Sciences, the Beauties of Painting and Sculpture might be fully explained in any Part of their following Studies occafionally, and in Subferviency to a greater Defign. And as for teaching the Art of Defigning early, the good Confequences of fuch a Practice in other refpects, or with regard even to mechanical Arts, are too evident to need any Proof : 'Tis indeed furprifing that an Art of fo extenfive Ufe fhould be fo much neglected. *Ariftotle* recommends it ftrongly as a very neceffary Part of Education with refpect even to the lower Ranks of Mankind (30); and we learn from him, that it was

This Manner of Education only re-quires that Defign be taught early, and the other Advan-tages of this Prac-tice are evident.

(28) Plutarch. in vita Æmilii.

(29) On'y fee what Account *Felibien* gives of the Works of *Giulio Romano*, and of *Polydore* and *Marburino*, and like-wife of *Ligrio*.

(30) Ariftot. Polit. Ed. Wechel. p. 218. 13. p. 219. 12. p. 220. 4. p. 225. 2. See *Plutarch's* Life of *Peri-cles*, where he gives an Account of his Education.

the

the Practice in *Greece* to instruct the better Sort early in it. The *Romans* too, so soon as they began to educate their Youth in the liberal Sciences, followed this Method. *Paulus Æmilius,* who is celebrated for having taken particular Care of the Education of his Children, employed not only Rhetoricians and Philosophers, but likewise Painters to instruct them (31). It hath been already observed, that *Pamphilus* not only established Academies in *Greece* for the Formation of Painters, but that by his Means it became an universal Custom over all *Greece* to teach the Principles of Design amongst the other elementary Sciences in liberal Education.

The Education of the antient Greeks well deserves our Attention in every respect, since Education is the very Basis of publick or private Happiness.

IN Truth, the Care that was antiently taken of Education in general, well deserves, on every account, the most serious Attention of those, who having the Interests of their Country at Heart, look upon it (to use the Words of a very great Man) as that by which the Foundation-Stones are laid of publick or private Happiness (32). No Part of it seems to have been overlooked by the *Athenians* in their better Times ; and hence chiefly their immortal Glory.

I SHALL only add, that what was called by the Antients Musick (33), seems to have been a very comprehensive Part of Education, and very different from what now passes under that Name. The Design of it was to form the Ear, the Voice, and the Behaviour, or to teach a graceful Way of reading, speaking, and carrying the Body, not only on publick Occasions, but at all Times, or even in ordinary Conversation. *Cicero* regrets that this Part of Education was so much neglected amongst the *Romans* : And as for the manly Exercises, which had so great a Share in antient Education among the *Greeks* and *Romans,* not merely to form the Body to Vigour and Agility, but chiefly to fortify the Mind, and to fit for Action, Suffering and Hardship in the publick Service ; though the same Exercises may perhaps not be the propereft in present Circumstances to gain these Ends, yet the Scope intended and pursued by them must be acknowledged to be of lasting Use, or rather Necessity.

But my present Design was only to give some Notion of the Usefulness of the Designing Arts in Education.

BUT I have accomplished my present Aim, if what hath been said of the Arts of Design, and of their Usefulness in Philosophy and Education, shall be found in any Degree conducive to give a juster Idea of those Arts than is commonly entertained, and a larger and better Notion of the Ends Education ought to have in View ; for we have seen that a good Taste of Life and of all the fine Arts being the same, it must be improved and perfected by the same Means, even by uniting and conjoining all the liberal Arts in Education agreeably to their natural and inseparable Connection and Dependency.

C H A P. VIII.

Some Observations on the particular Genius, Characters, Talents and Abilities of the more considerable modern Painters, and the commendable Use they made of the antient Remains in Painting as well as Sculpture ; and upon the Pieces of antient Painting now published.

Some Conclusions that follow obviously from the Analogy between Poetry and Painting.

ENOUGH hath been said in the preceding Chapters concerning the chief Qualities of a Painter, to lead every one to infer, " That whatever different Talents it may require " to be a good Poet, and to be a good Painter, a right Notion or Taste of poetical or true " Composition is equally necessary to both ". Nor is it less obvious from what hath been just now laid down concerning those natural Faculties and Dispositions of our Minds, which being duly cultivated by Education, form a good Taste of Imitation, whether in Poetry or Painting ; " That whoever is capable of receiving truly rational Entertainment

It is as easy to become a good Judge of the one Art as of the other.

" from the former, if he is not likewise an intelligent Judge of the latter, it must only be " because he hath not turned his Mind toward the Consideration of that other Kind of " Imitation by Drawing and Colours ; it can proceed from this alone, that he hath not had " Opportunity of seeing and examining Pictures, or hath not reflected, that Painting is a " Sort of poetical Composition, which ought to be examined in the same Manner as that " which is peculiarly so called ". Like that other, it only presupposes a just Idea of the Part of Nature represented, and requires Comparison with it, in order to be able to form a true Judgment concerning it ; Truth of Composition in order to affect every one suitably, who is not a Stranger to natural Sentiments, being all that is necessary with regard to the one or the other : For both these Arts aim at the same End, as we have found *Socrates, Aristotle, Cicero, Plutarch, Philostratus,* and other Antients observing, though by different Means and Instruments, which End is a true Representation of well chosen Nature.

THE

(31) Plutarch. in vita Æmilii. And in like manner we are told, several of the best Emperors, *Marcus Antoninus Philosophus* in particular, had Painters to Instruct them in Drawing, and a Taste of Painting.

(32) Lord *Molesworth* in his Preface to his Account of Denmark.

(33) This is plain from the Definition of it by *Aristides Quintilianus, lib.* 1. Ars decens in voctbus & motibus. Necessary to all the Ages of Life.——See what *Quintilian* says of it, *Inst. lib.* 1. c. 3, 6, & 12. But see of this, Reflexions Critiques sur la Poesie & sur la Peinture. Troisieme part.

THE Analogy between Poetry and Painting likewife leads very naturally to another Con- *There is the like Charatter with re- gard to Painting, as that of the verbal Critick in Wri.ing.*
clufion with refpect to both thefe Arts : " One may have a very good Tafte of *Homer*, *Virgil*,
" or *Horace*, without being deeply verfed in the Niceties of Philofophy, or verbal Criticifm ;
" Arts which, however ufeful, do not indeed belong to thofe whofe high Birth and Fortune
" loudly call upon them to devote themfelves to more important Studies, and to feek after
" more ufeful Knowledge from fuch excellent antient Authors, the Knowledge of Men and
" Things : In like manner, one may have a very juft Notion of Painting, and be capable of
" receiving very ufeful Inftruction, as well as very great Pleafure, from good Pictures, without
" being profoundly skilled in the Mixtures of Colours, and in the other merely mechanical
" Secrets of Painting, which cannot be learned without much Practice, or rather ferving a
" long Apprenticefhip to the Art ; and ought therefore to be left to thofe who choofe
" Painting for their Profeffion, as philological Difcuffions ought to be to Etymologifts, Gram-
" marians, and Editors ". One who in examining Pictures never thinks of the Truth, Beauty
and Spirit of a Compofition, but is wholly taken up in criticifing the Handicraft, or mecha-
nicai Part, may he not be juftly compared to him, who; without entering into the Sentiments, the Characters, the Spirit, Unity, Beauty, Truth and Morality of a good Poem,
is intirely employed about the Style and Words, the Alterations, Adulterations and Inter-
polations that may have crept into the Text by various Accidents, and other fuch Inquiries
of very inferior Concernment ? If he would juftly be accounted a Perfon of no Tafte, who
neither admires or blames, nor forms any Judgment at all of an Author, till he knows his
Name and Reputation in the World ; ought not the fame to be concluded of him, who,
though he had feen a Picture ever fo often; was not at all touched by it, till fome Perfon,
in whofe Judgment he confides, affured him it was done by *Raphael*, or fome other renowned Painter, and then was fuddenly filled with the higheft Admiration ?

TIS Truth and Beauty of Compofition that ought to be chiefly attended to in Paint- *All the Inquiries with regard to Au- thors and their Wri- tings, take place likewife with re- fpect to Painters and their Works.*
ing, as well as in Poetry : But fo like are thefe Sifter-arts to one another, that there is no
Inquiry with regard to Authors or Performances in the one Way, that does not likewife
as properly relate to Artifts and their Perfotmances in the other. I fhall juft mention two
which are allowed to be very agreeable and ufeful Inquiries with refpect to Poets or Authors
in general and their Works ; that muft alfo be equally ufeful and pleafant with regard to
Painters and their Works ; for 'tis not the Defign of this Effay to purfue any other Inquiries
about Painting, befides thofe philofophical ones to which the ftrict Analogy and Affinity
between Painting and Poetry lead us as it were by the Hand.

AS the Works of antient Poets are the beft Models upon which modern ones can form *Both Arts have their antient Mo- dels.*
themfelves, fo likewife have the Painters their antient Models for their Study and Imita-
tion ; thofe exquifite Remains of antient Artifts in Painting, Statuary and Sculpture, upon
which the moft celebrated Mafters in modern Times are known to have formed their
Tafte.

NOW it muft be no lefs pleafing or profitable to trace and obferve the Ufes that Painters *It is very agreea- ble to obferve what Ufe modern Pain- ters have made of antient Works, in like manner as in Writing,* &c.
have made of antient Pieces of Art, than to trace and obferve the Ufes modern Poets
have made of their beft Patterns; the antient Poets. 'Tis very juftly faid with refpect to
Writers (1), " That over and above a juft painting of Nature, a learned Reader will find
" a new Beauty fuperadded in a happy Imitation of fome famous Antient, as it revives in
" his Mind the Pleafure he took in his firft reading fuch an Author ". And the fame muft
hold true with regard to Paintings, in which, one well acquainted with the Antiques, finds
a wife and happy Imitation of antient Works. In the one Cafe as well as the other, " fuch
" Copyings give that kind of double Delight which we perceive when we look upon the
" Children of a beautiful Couple, where the Eye is not more charmed with the Symmetry
" of the Parts, than the Mind, by obferving the Refemblance tranfmitted from Parents to
" their Offspring, and the mingled Features of the Father and Mother. The Phrafes of
" holy Writ, and Allufions to feveral Paffages in the infpired Writings, (though not pro-
" duced as Proofs of Doctrine) add Majefty and Authority to the noblest Difcourfes of the
" Pulpit : In like manner, an Imitation of the Air of *Homer* and *Virgil* raifes the Dignity
" of modern Poetry, and makes it appear ftately and venerable ". And the judicious Imitation of ancient Remains in the Works of a *Raphael* or a *Pouffin* have the fame great and
agreeable Effect.

AGAIN, if it be in any Degree entertaining or ufeful to inquire after the particular and *'Tis very agreeable to obferve the pe- cular Genius of the Painter difcovering itfelf in his Works.*
diftinguifhing Genius of a Writer, as it appears in his Performance, it muft be equally fo to
make the like Obfervations upon the particular Genius, Talents, and Characters of good
Painters, as thefe are difcovered by their Pictures. Such Inquiries cannot be called merely
ftudying Words, or Hands and Styles ; but are rather ftudying Men, Tempers, Genius's
and

(1) Guardian, No. 15.

R r

and Difpofitions ; 'tis tracing moral Effects to their proper Springs and Caufes. In truth, any other Marks or Characterifticks for diftinguifhing the Works of Authors or Artifts, befides thofe which are taken from their peculiar Turn of Mind, and their correfpondent Manner of thinking and of communicating their Thoughts, of whatever Ufe they may be to Artifts in the one Cafe, or to Philologifts in the other ; yet they do not belong to rational Criticifm, and fo neither fall into the Province of the Philofopher, nor of the polite Scholar.

'Tis worth while to make a few Remarks upon thefe two Heads juft mentioned.

THOUGH in purfuance of my Defign, (which is to point out the real Ufefulnefs of Painting, and the more important as well as pleafurable Inquiries with relation to it, to which the Confideration of its Analogy with Poetry obvioufly leads us) it might be reckoned . fufficient to have fuggefted and recommended thefe Inquiries ; yet in order to lead our young Travellers and thofe concerned in their Education to a better, a more philofophical Way of confidering Pictures, than feems to be the Employment of the greater Part of thofe who are called Virtuofi ; I fhall adventure to prefent my Readers with fome few of the beft Reflections that have occurred to me in reading the Lives of the more celebrated modern Painters, or in feeing their Works, upon the peculiar Genius, Character and Talents of fome of the greateft amongft them, and upon the commendable Ufe they made of the antique Remains in Painting as well as Sculpture. And this will naturally lead me to make a few Animadverfions upon the Pieces of antient Painting that are now publifhed ; rather to excite others, who are better skilled in antient Literature, to make proper Ufe of fuch Remains of Antiquity as are happily preferved to us, for the Illuftration of antient Authors, than to take an Opportunity of entering, for the prefent at leaft, into Difcuffions of that Kind. For all indeed intended from the Beginning was but to pave the Way for fuch more learned Undertakings, by endeavouring to revive a better Notion of the fine Arts, in refpect of their Ufefulnefs in Education, than is commonly entertained even by their greateft Admirers.

Of fervile Imitators.

'TIS obferved by one of the beft Writers on Painting (2), " That it is no lefs impoffible " for a Painter than for a Poet to fucceed in Attempts not fuited to his Genius, *invita* " *Minerva* (3), or unlefs he follows his natural Turn and Bent of Mind. Accordingly, " faith he, thofe Painters, who without confulting their own Genius, have fet themfelves " fervilely to imitate Mafters of great Fame, never came near to them, and confequently " never acquired any other Name but that of bad Copyifts ; whereas 'tis not improbable, " that if they had known their own true Genius, and had duly cultivated it, they might " have produced very good Works, and have gained very confiderable Reputation ".

PAINTERS ought to ftudy the Performances of the beft Mafters, and above all the Remains of antient Sculpture and Painting ; and thefe they ought to imitate. But how ? Juft as the Poets ought to imitate *Homer* and *Virgil* ; that is, as *Virgil* himfelf did *Homer*. And as a Poet will profit moft by *Virgil* in his Imitations of him, who thoroughly underftanding *Homer*, hath well obferved how *Virgil* hath imitated him ; fo Painters will learn moft from the beft modern Mafters who ftudied and imitated the Antiques ; if being intimately acquainted with the Antiques, they are able to difcern, what happy excellent Ufe thefe noble Imitators have made of fuch unrivalled Works. The antient Rule fo well expreffed by *Horace* ;

> *Sumite materiam veftris, qui fcribitis, æquam*
> *Viribus ; & verfate diu quid ferre recufent,*
> *Quid valeant humeri.*

And fo earneftly recommended by him at the fame Time that he preffes fo ftrongly the conftant Study of the *Greek* Examples or Models :

> ———*Vos exemplaria Græca*
> *Nocturna verfate manu, verfate diurna* (4).

That Rule, I fay, extends equally to Painters and Poets ; and fervile Imitation in the one Cafe as well as the other will ever be rejected by intelligent Judges (5), with

> *O Imitatores, fervum pecus !* ———

TIS

(2) Lomazzo Trattato della Pittura, *lib. 6. p.* 43. And in his Tempio della Pittura, *p.* 7, 10. & 39.

(3) Admodum autem tenenda funt fua cuique, non vitiofa, fed tamen propria, quo facilius decorum illud quod quærimus retineatur. Sic enim eft faciendum, ut contra univerfam naturam nihil contendamus ; ea tamen confervata, propriam naturam fequamur ; ut etiamfi fint alia graviora atque meliora, tamen nos ftudia noftra, naturæ regula metiamur. Neque enim attinet repugnare naturæ, nec quicquam fequi, quod affequi nequeas. Ex

quo magis emergit, quale fit decorum illud. Ideo, quia nihil decet invita Minerva (ut aiunt) id eft, adverfante & repugnante natura. Cicero de Off. *lib.* 1. No. 31.

(4) Hor. de Art. Poet. *v.* 39. & 268.

(5) Unde plurimi, cum in hos inexplicabiles laqueos inciderunt, omnem etiam, quem, ex ingenio fuo, potuerunt habere conatum, velut aftricti certis legum Vinculis, perdiderunt ; & magiftrum refpicientes, naturam fequi defierunt. Quint. Inft. *lib.* 5. *c.* 10.

'TIS obfervable that when the Art of Painting was perfected in *Italy*, under *Raphael* *The remarkable Dif-*
and *Michael-Angelo*, it was likewife very much cultivated and brought to a confiderable *ference between the*
Degree of Perfection on this Side the *Alps*, in *Germany*, *Switzerland*, *Holland*, *Flan-* *Painters who ftudied*
ders, and *France*. But a Superiority in Tafte of fine and beautiful Nature is unanimoufly *Antiques, and thofe*
given to the *Italians*, who ftudied the Antiques, after they became able to make a proper *who did not.*
Ufe of Statues and Baf-reliefs in Painting. It is indeed generally allowed, whatever may
be the Caufe of it, that the ·Painters of *Lombardy*, who had not feen, or at leaft had not
much ftudied the Antiques, far furpaffed the *German*, *Flemifh* and *French* Painters, in Tafte
of Beauty, Sweetnefs, Grace, and Greatnefs; or in other Words, ·in a delicate and fine
Choice of Nature : But at the fame time, 'tis yielded, that thofe *Lombardy* Mafters never
arriv'd to the Merit and Excellence of the *Roman* School, where the Antique was fedu-
loufly ftudied. This Obfervation hath been often made, and therefore I fhali not dwell
longer upon it.

ONE Thing however I would beg leave to fuggeft upon this Subject, that hath not
been 'taken Notice of, though it feems to me very probable. Thofe who ftudied the
antient Statues, Carvings, and Baf-reliefs, *Raphael* in particular, were for fome Time *How Raphael firft*
·fuch ftrict fervile Imitators of them, that their Painting was very dry, cold, and ftiff, or, *imitated the antient*
in one Word, Statue-like ; that is, liker Drawings after Statues and Baf-reliefs than Pic- *tures.* *Statues and Sculp-*
tures : But afterwards they became able to make a proper Ufe of Sculptures and Statues
without painting in fo rigid, hard, and fervile a manner.. Now, though this known Fact
be commonly attributed to their joining at laft the Study of Nature itfelf, and living Forms,
to that of the Antiques, and it muft undoubtedly have been· in a great meafure owing to
that ; yet may we not imagine that they were led and directed to this better Manner of
imitating Works in Marble, Brafs, and other Metals, by the Pencil ; or to the right Notion
they at laft acquired of the Difference there ought to be between Painting and Sculpture, by
the antient Paintings that were difcovered fome Time after the more famous Statues and
Baf-reliefs had been digged up ? It feems very probable that the greater Part of the Remains *Whence his better*
of antient Grotefque Painting in *Italy* were done after antient Sculptures, all of them having *Manner of imita-*
fo much of that Air in the Difpofition of the Figures : But is not each Figure done in fuch *ting them proceeded.*
a manner as fhews how Painting ought to borrow from or copy after Statues and Baf-
reliefs ?

HOWEVER that be, it is certain, that *Raphael* in particular was very ·fond of the
antient Grotefque Paintings difcovered in his Time at *Rome*, at *Puzzoli*, *Cumæ*, and other
Places in *Italy*. He admired and ftudied them much ; he fent his Scholars, where-ever any
thing of that Kind was difcovered, to copy it ; and fo had made a great Collection of
·Drawings after antient Paintings. This we are affured of by all the Writers of his Life.
Some (6) have invidioufly faid, that having taken Copies of them, he had them deftroyed,
that the World might not know how much he was indebted to them in his beft Performances.
But that is neither confiftent with his extreme Love of the Art, his profeffed Efteem of all
antient Works, nor with his generous, benign, amiable, unenvious Temper.

SO much did he and the whole *Roman* School ftudy the antient Grotefque Paintings, that *How much he*
they are faid to have tranfplanted feveral Figures and Groupes of Figures from them into all *efteemed and ftudied*
their Works ; into their Paintings particularly in the *Vatican Loges*, and upon the Walls and *the antient Paint-*
Ceilings of other Palaces at *Rome*; which are therefore confidered at *Rome* rather as Copies *ings.*
by thofe great Mafters from the Antique, than as original Works of their own.

· *GIOV. DUDINA*, a favourite Scholar of his Mafter *Raphael*, made it his whole
Bufinefs to make Collections of Drawings after the antient Grotefque Paintings on Stucco,
and other antient Stucco Works, and to imitate them ; and accordingly to him it is that
we owe the Revival of what is called Grotefque. *Polydore* and *Mathurin*, as I have obferved in another Place, likewife employed their whole Time in drawing after Antiques,
and copying them. ·

AFTER what hath been faid of right Imitation in Painting and Poetry, no one will
think it derogatory from the Merit of *Raphael*, and other great Mafters, to affirm that they
ftudied and copied the Antiques ; and that the Perfection of their Works is chiefly owing to
their fo doing. One might with equal Reafon fay, that it is a Reflection on *Virgil* to affirm
that he imitated *Homer*. *Felibien* did not furely defign to detract from *Nicolas Pouffin's* *Pouffin likewife*
·Merit, but rather to exalt him, by taking fo much Pains to fhew in what Veneration he *ftudied and imitated*
·held the antient Remains of every Kind, and the noble Ufe he made of them in all his beft *the antient Pain-*
Pictures. Of this he gives many Inftances, and we may add one he does not mention. 'Tis *tings.*
well known at *Rome*, *Pouffin* highly efteemed the celebrated antient Painting commonly
called the *Nozze Aldobrandine*. There is a very fine Copy of it by him in the *Pamphili*
Palace at *Rome*; and I think no one who has feen that famous antient Picture, will be at
a Lofs

(6) *Lomazzo* refutes this Story· Trattato della Pittura, *lib.* 6: *c.* 48.

So Frederico Zuccaro.
Carlo Marati.

a Loſs to find out that he, as it were, formed his Taſte on that Model ; and that he hath without Plagiariſm borrowed very conſiderably from it in almoſt all his Works, particularly in his famous Sacraments. *Frederico Zuccaro*, who was an excellent Painter, ſpeaks of this antient Piece with the higheſt Eſteem and Admiration. *Carlo Marati*, commonly called the laſt of the great Painters in *Italy*, is likewiſe known to have much admired and ſtudied all the antient Paintings that ſubſiſted in his Time. He was particularly fond of the *Venus* in the *Barberini* Palace : He retouched ſome Parts of it that were decayed, and he added a *Cupid* to this Piece; that his Eſteem for it might be known ſo long as the Picture is preſerved. My Deſign being to publiſh antient Paintings, I have only given the *Venus* the Drapery and the Vaſe.

HannibalCarrache.

HANNIBAL CARRACHE is likewiſe ſaid to have held the antient Paintings in the higheſt Veneration, and to have improved greatly at *Rome* by the Study of the Antiques. Mr. *Richardſon* has an Original Drawing by that great Maſter, after one of the Compartiments in *Titus's* Palace at *Rome*, repreſenting *Coriolanus* and his Mother diſſuading or rather upbraiding him. And, as hath been already remarked, every one who is acquainted with *Guido's* Works, will find a very great Likeneſs between his Idea of Beauty, his Airs of Heads and Attitudes, and thoſe in the *Europa*, and other Pieces now publiſhed. In fine, ſince I have had the Drawings by me of thoſe and other Remains of antient Paintings from which the Engravings annexed to this Eſſay are taken, I have been often very agreeably entertained in looking over the Deſigns of ſeveral of the greateſt modern Maſters in the Collections of the Curious here, by finding very conſiderable Borrowings in the latter from theſe antient Paintings. And ſome who are much better acquainted with the Pictures and Drawings of the moſt eſteemed Painters than I am, upon ſeeing my Drawings after antient Paintings now engraved, have aſſured me, that there is almoſt none of them that did not immediately recall to their Minds ſeveral Ideas in the Works of modern Maſters, that undoubtedly muſt have been taken from thoſe antient Pieces, ſince it is known that all the beſt Maſters ſtudied them ſo much. To give this additional Pleaſure to thoſe who like Painting, in examining the Drawings of the better Maſters, is one of the Reaſons for which theſe Samples of antient Painting are now made publick. But not to prevent the Satisfaction that the Curious may have in tracing by themſelves the laudable Uſes that the beſt Maſters in the latter Age of Painting have made of thoſe Remains of antient Painting, as well as of Sculptures and Statues, (which is generally acknowledged) I ſhall add no more on this Subject, but content myſelf with inſerting in the Notes a Part of what *Lomazzo* (8) ſays in general of the antient Groteſque Paintings, and of Compoſitions of that Kind, in his own Words : And the many remarkable Inſtances that are recorded by Writers in their Lives of the Painters and Sculptors, of their high Regard for all the antient Remains, I ſhall but mention one Story that is told of *Michael Angelo*, becauſe it hath not been very often repeated, and is very well vouched. We are told in the Memoirs of Monſieur *de Thou* this very curious Fact. Monſieur *de Thou*, when he was very young, accompanied into *Italy* Monſieur *de Foix*, whom the Court of *France* had ſent thither. When they were at *Pavia*, amongſt the other Rarities that *Iſabelle d'Eſte*, grandmother to the Dukes of *Mantua*, had collected and ranged into excellent Order in a moſt magnificent Cabinet ; there was ſhewn to Monſieur *de Foix* one very extraordinary and admirable Piece, a ſleeping *Cupid*, by *Michael Angelo Buonarotti*, of that fine Marble of *Spezzia* upon the Coaſt of *Genoa*. Monſieur *de Foix*, having heard very much of this Maſterpiece of Art, deſired to ſee it ; and all his Attendants (Monſieur *de Thou* in particular, who had had a very fine Taſte of all the polite Arts) after having moſt carefully conſidered and examined it, acknowledged with one Voice, that it far ſurpaſſed the higheſt Praiſes that Words could expreſs. But after leaving them for ſome Time in the higheſt Admiration of this *Cupid*, at laſt another was produced, that famous Piece of *Praxiteles* which is ſo celebrated by antient Writers (for there are above twenty *Greek* Epigrams upon it) : It was yet ſullied with the Earth, out of which it had been but lately digged ; and when the Company ſaw this marvellous Figure, and had compared it with that other of *Michael-Angelo*, they were aſhamed to have expreſſed

What Lomazzo *ſays of the antient Groteſques.*

Guido.

(8) Ho udito dire da molti, che Rafaello, Polidoro, il Roſſo, & Perino hanno levato via parte delle grotteſche antiche per non laſciar vedere le inventioni ſue ritrovare per quelle con ſommo artificio. Ma non ſo io come ſi poſſano le grotteſche levare ne manco biaſimare, Vedendoſene molte da gli antichi fatte in Roma a Pozzuolo & a Baie, dall' imitatione delle quali eglino, ſi come hanno ſempre fatto in ognialtra loro inventione, hanno riportato quell' honore che da ogniuno gli è conceſſo ; & appreſo la maniera d'eſprimere anco in quelle ſorti di pittura coſi ingenioſamente i capricci & ritrovati ſuoi, & inſegnato à gli altri a non partir ſi mai dall' orme & veſtigia ſegnate da gli antichi in ciaſcuna coſa, che s'imprenda a fare. Sono ſtati eccellenti per queſta parte anco molti altri, come Polidoro, Maturino, Giovani da Udine, il Roſſo, Giulio Romano, Franciſco Fattore, & Perino del Vaga che furono i primi introdurre nelle grotteſche animali, ſacrifici fogliami, feſtoni, trofei, & altre ſimili bizarrie ; togliendo dalle grotte antiche dipinte da ſerapione & dagli

altri il piu bello & vago che ſene poteſſe levare ; d'onde ne hanno poi ornato tutta l'Italia, & le altre Provincie con gli altri ſuoi ſeguaci come ſono ſtati Aurelio Buſſo, il Peſſa, il Soncino, & Giacobo Roſignolo da Livorno, i quali hanno fatto coſi maraviglioſamente, che Veramente fanno reſtare confuſi coloro che dicono le grotteſche eſſere ſogni, & confeſſare ch' eſſendo fatte con lanventione & diligenza, ſono di grandiſſimo ornamento & richezza all' arte.——Ma laſciando queſta curioſa inveſtigatione che il tutto importa come dianci propoſi mi ſtendero ſolamente a diſcorrere intorno alla compoſitione loro, laquale e di molta importanza.——La compoſitione adunque loro primamente vuole ſempre haver una cotal veriſimilitudine naturale, come nel mezzo di colonne arbori che ſoſtengono candelieri, & nelle partiche hanno piu del fermo e del groſſo templi, con ſimolacri & ſimili, & nel fondo per baſa animali bizarri, moſtri & ſimili che ſoſtengono, con ornamento di maſcheroni, arpie, ſcale, e cariozzi, che tengano del fermo, &c.

preſſed themſelves in ſuch ſtrong Terms about the one they had firſt ſeen; and agreed that when the two were ſet together, the antient one appeared animated, and the modern one a mere Block of Marble, without any Expreſſion or Life. Some of the Family then aſſured them, that *Michael Angelo* himſelf was ſo ſincere and impartial, that he had earneſtly begged the Counteſs *Iſabella*, (when he made her a Preſent of his *Cupid*, and ſhe had ſhewn him the other) not to let the antique one be ſeen till his had been produced, that the Intelligent might thus clearly ſee how far the Antients excelled the Moderns in Works of that Sort. He whoſe Performances had more than once deceived very good Judges, and been deemed by them real Antiques, on account of their almoſt inſurpaſſable Excellence, was however modeſt and ingenuous enough to own that he was far inferior in his beſt Works to the great antient Maſters. Every one who has been at *Rome* knows how much he is ſaid to have ſtudied a moſt curious Fragment of a Statue (9), which is for that Reaſon commonly called *Michael Angelo*'s Scuola or Studio, as the Nozze is called *Pouſſin*'s.

BUT as much as the greater modern Maſters ſtudied the antique Paintings, Statues, and Carvings, they cannot however be charged with Plagiariſm more than *Virgil* for borrowing from *Homer*. All the Antiques became their own by the happy Uſe they at laſt made of them in their beſt Works. They ſtudied them in order to raiſe their Fancy, and inrich their Minds with fine Ideas; they ſtudied them in order to learn from them the right Method of imitating Nature; and by ſtudying them, they became able to conceive Ideas in the noble Taſte of the antient Artiſts, and to perform in their maſterly Manner. So far are they from being juſtly chargeable with ſtealing, that whatever Likeneſs to the Antiques ſhews itſelf in their Works, their Performances are however abſolutely their own, their own genuine Productions; for every one's peculiar Genius appears in his Works diſtinguiſhing him from all the reſt, and the Uſe every one made of the ſame common Models upon which they all formed themſelves, or which were greatly eſteemed and ſtudied by them all, was proper to himſelf. *Though the more Maſters ſtudied and imitated the Antques, yet their Works were their own, and ſhew the peculiar Genius of each.*

I SHALL endeavour to illuſtrate this, by a few Remarks upon the peculiar Characters of ſome few of the moſt celebrated modern Maſters. I have already had Occaſion, in comparing the Progreſs of Painting amongſt the *Greeks*, with its Progreſs in *Italy*, till it was brought to Perfection there by *Raphael*, to give ſome ſhort Account of ſeveral Maſters of that laſt Age of Painting: But 'tis worth while to return to that Subject; for many of them well deſerve to have their Characters more fully ſet to View; and though nothing can be more tedious than the idle, minute, inſipid Particulars that have no Relation to the Painters as ſuch, and that are not worth being recorded upon any Conſideration, with which the Lives of Painters are generally ſtuffed; yet 'tis proper that thoſe who travel into *Italy*, to ſee the famous Works of certain Painters, ſhould have previouſly ſome Idea of their diſtinguiſhing Characters, Manners, and Excellencies; or at leaſt they ought to be put into the Way of ſtudying to know and diſtinguiſh Painters, by getting as it were acquainted with their Turn and Caſt of Mind, or with their Way of thinking, rather than by merely technical Marks much more eaſily counterfeited. For as a very low Genius, who is not capable of conceiving one Thought that can paſs for a great Author's with thoſe who are thoroughly converſant with his Sentiments, may eaſily forge his Hand; ſo one who only conſiders the penciling of a great Maſter, may be eaſily deceived by Imitations of his Style and Hand in that reſpect, which however cannot poſſibly be accounted genuine by thoſe who underſtand his Genius, his Thoughts, his Taſte of Compoſition, and the Soul, ſo to ſpeak, of his Works. *It is worth while to purſue this Reflection a little.*

LET me only add here, before I proceed to draw the Characters of any of the Painters, an excellent Advice of *Du Piles* (10) to thoſe who deſire to be able to diſtinguiſh Maſters by the beſt Characteriſticks; and that is to begin with ſtudying their Drawings; for 'tis in theſe, as he juſtly obſerves, that the Spirit and Genius of the Maſter is beſt diſcerned. *The Genius of a Painter is beſt known from his Drawings.*
" By Deſigns, he tells us, he would be underſtood to mean not only the Ideas which Painters
" on Paper had expreſſed for their Aſſiſtance in the Execution of any great Work they were
" meditating; but likewiſe all the Studies of the great Maſters, that is to ſay, all the Parts
" or Members they had drawn after Nature, as Heads, Hands, Arms, Feet, and whole
" Figures, Draperies, Animals, Trees, Plants, Flowers, and in fine, whatever can enter
" into the Compoſition of a capital Picture. For whether one conſiders a good Drawing
" with reſpect to the Picture, of which 'tis an Idea or Sketch; or with regard to ſome par-
" ticular Part of Nature, of which 'tis a Study; it well deſerves the Attention of the Curious.
" Deſigns, continueth he, ſhew the Character of a Maſter better than his Pictures; they
" diſcover his Genius whether it is lively or low; in theſe his Ideas and Manner of think-
" ing appear, and one ſees whether he hath ſublime, great, and elevated Sentiments, or
" mean, common, and groveling ones; and whether he hath a good Taſte of drawing in
" every thing that can be expreſſed by the Pencil: For in theſe he gives fair Play to his
" Genius,

(9) *Torſo d'Hercule.*   (10) In his *Idée d'un Peintre parfait.*

" Genius, and fuffers it to work and difplay itfelf as it really is. There is one Thing, faith
" he a little after, which is as it were the Salt or Spirit of Defigns, and without which I
" fhould not make any great Account of them; and this I cannot better exprefs than by the
" Word *Character.* This Character confifts in the Painter's Manner of conceiving Things:
" It is the Seal which diftinguifhes his Works from all others, and which he ftamps upon
" them as the Image of his Soul. It is by this Character, peculiar to every one, that Pain-
" ters of Genius, after having ftudied under Mafters, feel themfelves impelled to give free
" Scope to their own Tafte, and to fly as it were upon their own Wings. He tells us
" there are three Things that ought chiefly to be confidered in Defigns; *Science,* as he
" calls it, which he defines to be a good Tafte of Compofition, and of Correctnefs in
" Drawing, together with a fufficient Knowledge of the *Clair-obfcure ; Spirit,* under
" which he comprehends natural and lively Expreffion of the Subject in general, and of
" every Object in particular; and *Liberty,* which is nothing elfe but the Habit the Hand
" hath contracted of expreffing with Eafe, Boldnefs, and Freedom, any Idea the Painter
" hath formed in his Mind. Defigns, fays he, are excellent in Proportion as they have
" thefe Qualities. He diftinguifhes between the Character of Genius, and what he calls
" the Character in the practical or technical Part; and very juftly concludes, that Know-
" ledge of the latter Character of a Painter rather depends upon a long Habitude than a
" great Capacity; and for that Reafon it is not the ableft Painters whofe Decifions may be
" always moft relied upon in that Point. Others very inferior to them may furpafs them
" in that kind of Knowledge : The Knowledge of the other Character requires a very clear,
" diftinct Head, and a very folid Judgment; but it is the pleafanteft as well as the fureft
" Guide in judging of Mafters, and in diftinguifhing their Defigns.".

The beft way of di-
ftinguifhing Copies
from Originals.

WITH regard to diftinguifhing Originals from Copies, the fame Author tells us,
" That many Pictures have been done by Scholars, fo much in the Tafte, Manner, and
" Character of their Mafters, that they have paffed for the Works of their Mafters them-
" felves ; and that many Painters having imitated, even at home, the Tafte of a quite
" different School and Country; and feveral Mafters having paffed from one Manner to
" another, it is no Wonder that many Pictures are fo equivocal; or that it is fo hard to
" determine by what Mafter they were done. Yet this Inconvenience doth not want its
" Remedy, with thofe who, not fatisfied with ftudying the Character of a Mafter's Hand,
" have Penetration enough to difcover that of his Spirit and Genius. An able Mafter may
" eafily communicate to his Difciples his Manner of Handling; but he cannot fo eafily
" impart to them his Ideas, and Manner of Conception and Thinking." He diftinguifhes
three Sorts of Copies : " The firft are exact, but fervile; thefe are eafily known. The
" fecond are light and eafy, but not exact or correct; and Copies of this Sort, by reafon
" of their Freedom and Eafe, may deceive fome of lefs Experience; but the Inaccuracy of
" the Contours foon difcovers them to more intelligent Eyes. The third are exact, correct,
" and yet free and eafy; and therefore being done by a mafterly Hand, and, which is more,
" about the Time of the Original, it is no Wonder that Connoiffeurs are embarraffed
" with regard to them, and often know not what to determine. *Giulio Romano* was
" deceived by a Copy of a Picture of *Raphael,* in which he himfelf had had fome Hand,
" by *Andrea del Sarto :* He took it for the Original, till *Vafari* fhewed him the Mark he
" had feen *del Sarto* put upon the Back of it to diftinguifh it." It is fufficient for us to
obferve on this Subject, that he who hath a good Notion of Compofition, will not be
deceived in judging of the Goodnefs of a Picture, which is the chief Thing : And 'tis but
of very little Importance what the Mafter's Name was who painted it, if it be really a good
Picture, and hath all, or at leaft a great many of the effential Qualities of good Painting.
Hardly can any other Rule be given for diftinguifhing very good Copies from Originals,
except that antient Maxim, *That Copies are commonly ftiffer and colder than the Originals,*
tho' done by ever fo good a Hand (11), *or even by the Author himfelf, after his own Works.*
They have not the fame Freedom, Eafe, and Spirit; but if a Picture hath Spirit and Freedom, let it be Copy or Original, no Matter, it is an excellent Performance. That Copies
generally fhould not be fo free and eafy, or have fo much Fire and Life as Originals, is not
furprizing; fince Original Pictures have not the Spirit, Life, and Fire of the Drawings
from which they are compofed. Drawings are, in refpect of fuch Pictures, Originals :
And for that Reafon it muft be by the Study of Drawings, that one may not only beft
learn the Characters of Mafters; but likewife, in general, form to himfelf the jufteft Notion of Beauty, Truth, Spirit, Greatnefs, Grace, or of any other of the more effential
Qualities in good Compofition. Thofe who are not acquainted with Drawings, or who
do not begin by ftudying them, are very apt to mind nothing in Pictures but the Colouring ;

(11) Omnibus quidem archetypis naturalis quædam
gratia & pulchritudo decus addit. Iis vero quæ ex archetypis expreffæ funt, erfamfi ad extrema Imitationis perve-
nerint, ineft quippiam affectatum, & non naturale. Et
hoc præcepto non rhetores modo rhetoras difcernunt,
fed etiam pictores ea quæ funt Apellis ab Iis quæ eum
imitantur: Et ftatuarii quæ funt Polycleti, & fculptores
quæ funt Phidiæ. *Dio. Hal. in Dinarcho.* Quicquid alteri
fimile eft, neceffe eft minus fit eo quod imitatur; namque
his quæ in exemplum affumimus, fubeft natura, & vera
vis; contra omnis Imitatio ficta eft, &, ad alienum propofitum accommodatur. *Quint. Inft.* L 10. *c.* 2.

ng; and to prefer Pictures which pleafe in that refpect, to others which have far fuperior Excellences: which is like preferring a fine Complexion to Senfe, Goodnefs, and every other moral Qualification; the Beauties of the Skin to thofe of the Mind. But enough having been already faid on that Head, in feveral Parts of this Effay; I proceed now to make a few Obfervations on the Characters of fome of the principal Painters.

(12) *LEONARDO DA VINCI* was formed by *Andrea Verrocchio*, who was a better Sculptor than Painter, but well skilled in feveral other Arts; in Geometry, Architecture, and Mufick; a very elofe Student of Nature, but too ftrict a Copier of it.

Andrea Verroc.

LEONARDO muft, no doubt, have owed very much to fuch a Mafter; but having naturally a far fuperior Genius, he quickly made much greater Advances in all thefe Sciences and Arts, and in feveral others, Anatomy and Poetry in particular; and being withal a very well-bred Man, and very much converfant in the polite World, he was able to conceive much finer and nobler Ideas than his Mafter, and to felect out of the vaft Variety of Nature with much better Tafte than his Mafter, and to felect out of the vaft Variety of Nature with much better Tafte: yet partly thro' the Influence of his firft Inftructions and Habits, and partly thro' his Earneftnefs to attain to the higheft Pitch of Perfection, in exprefling his great Ideas by the Pencil, there is a remarkable Stiffnefs in his Pictures; they appear too laboured; the Contours are too ftrongly mark'd; and, inftead of having a natural Carnation, his Pieces, being too much finifhed and polifhed, look rather like Marble than Flefh. One fees, in his Drawings efpecially, an extraordinary Greatnefs of Genius, vaft Spirit, and Strength of Imagination, and a very accurate Judgment; tho' at the fame time all his Works fhew that he was nice and curious to a Fault, and very difcontented with his Hand, believing it could never reach to the Idea of Perfection, which he had conceived in his own Mind. There is evidently a violent Stretching to attain to fomething which he felt his Pencil fall fhort of, and hardly able to come near to: This is the Character given of him by Criticks; and 'tis natural to think, that in the Beginning of the Art, one of fo vaft a Capacity; and fo great and comprehenfive a Mind, muft have erred juft as he did, through this exceflive Ardour to bring his Pictures to a Height of Perfection, to which the Pencil could not, in the Nature of Things, yet all at once rife, from the low State in which he found the Art. A profound Scholar, a deep Thinker, who is at the fame time very well acquainted with all the Rules of juft Compofition, is very apt to fall into the fame Error in Writing. Learning, Science, Judgment, Imagination, and Genius, may appear in his Works; but Art not being hid, nor yet the Diffatisfaction of the Author with all his Corrections and Amendments, his Compofitions are not eafy: They would nave been more agreeable, and more perfect, if he had not laboured to make them more than perfect. The Stiffnefs and Overftraining that appears in the Works of *Leonardo da Vinci*, is however quite different from that Over-diligence which arifes from Timoroufnefs and Self-diffidence, of which we fhali have Occafion afterwards to fpeak: The one kind of Labour fhews a great and afpiring Mind, pleafed with its Ideas, but diffatisfied with the Execution; the other fhews a Lownefs of Genius, and a Confcioufnefs of Inability to conceive great Ideas without fevere plodding, fearching, and mufing. *Leonardo* was not diffatisfied with his Conceptions, but with his Hand or Pencil.

Leonardo da Vinci.

IN *Pietro Perugino* his Fellow Scholar's Works, there was all the Littlenefs, Drynefs, and Infipidity of a low Genius, who painted for Bread, and not for Glory. His Thoughts being intirely fet on making Money; and being of a very mean and fervile Spirit, it was no Wonder that he fcarcely furpaffed his Mafter, from whom his Scholars could learn little more than the Habit of ftudying Nature; which, tho' it be the Standard of all the Imitative Arts, and the beft Guide, yet the Study of it can never make a great Painter, if one hath not a fine Genius, or a good Eye, to contemplate Nature with; fomething naturally great in his Caft of Mind, to prompt and direct him to the right Study and Imitation of it, or to chufing out of Nature with Elegance and Judgment. Without that Turn of Mind, Painters will fatisfy themfelves, as many have done, with copying ordinary common Objects, inftead of more beautiful and perfect Nature.

Pietro Perugino.

RAPHAEL, in Confequence of that Veneration for a Mafter, which is natural to a good, docile, modeft Difpofition, followed at firft *Perugino*'s Manner; but becoming very quickly as perfect as he, or rather fomewhat above him, thro' the fuperior Strength of his natural Genius, upon the firft Sight of the greater Works of *Leonardo da Vinci*, and *Michael Angelo*, he was able to perceive what was defective and wanting in his Mafter, and how much higher the Art might rife than it had yet done. No fooner did he obferve the ftronger Relief, and the greater Force and Truth of Expreffion and Character in *Leonardo*'s Works, and the fublimer, bolder, grander Tafte of *Michael Angelo*, than he felt greater Ideas fpring up in his Mind; and with Greatnefs of Invention, his own fweet, gracious Temper naturally mixed Sweetnefs and Grace; fo that he very foon became that perfect

Raphael d'Urbino.

(12) In drawing the following Characters I have chiefly been found more conformable to *Du Piles, Felibien*, and followed my own private Judgment; but what I fay will *Lomazzo*, than to *Vafari*.

perfect Mafter whofe Works are always faid to have been the Pictures of his own Mind and Character; full of Strength, and yet exceedingly pleafing and graceful. No other Painter ever was able to give fo much Grace to his Works, becaufe no other Painter ever poffeffed fuch a Share of it in his Make and Temper, fince *Apelles*; unlefs it was *Corregio*, or *Par-meggiano* : For that Softnefs and Sweetnefs of *Guido* is of a quite different Character from the true Greatnefs of *Raphael*, juftly tempered by his Grace. *Vafari* and others of the *Florentine* School will not allow, that he ever defigned any thing with fo much Force as *Buonarotti* : But I do not hefitate to affert with *Felibien*, " That there is another kind of " Art in *Raphael*'s Figures, than in thofe which they fo highly exalt above all his Per-" formances; an Art which is by fo much the more marvellous, that it is more concealed " than that of all other Painters." And to prove his equal Skill of Anatomy, or in painting the Nerves and Mufcles, with *Michael Angelo*, *Felibien* juftly mentions a Figure in one of his Pictures in the *Vatican*, called *Incendio del Borgo*, reprefenting a young Man with an aged Perfon on his Shoulders, juft as *Virgil* defcribes *Anchifes*, when *Æneas* faved him from the Flames of *Troy*, and the Fury of the *Greeks*. He muft have had a very great Genius, to have profited fo much as he did by fo flight a View of fome of *Michael An-gelo*'s Paintings in the *Vatican*, which is all that is pretended. And he feems to have owed more to *Leonardo da Vinci* than to *Michael Angelo*; for his Expreffion of Mufcles and Nerves was always more pure and delicate than that of *Michael Angelo*, or freer from Affectation of fhewing particular Skill in Anatomy. It was perhaps owing to his Imitation of *Leonardo da Vinci*, that his Contours, except in his laft Pieces, are too hard and dry. The Antique, as hath been already obferved, was his Mafter, and by that alone was he furpaffed, in his laft Manner, in Invention, Force of Expreffion, or in Grace. He defigned correctly, and was very judicious in Ordonance and Difpofition; and being thoroughly in Love with his Art, none ever painted with more Tafte, Spirit, Freedom, and Pleafure. In his Pictures Force is duly mingled with Sweetnefs; and he underftood perfectly how to treat his Subjects with due Decorum, in reprefenting the different Cuftoms, Habits, Arms, Dreffes, and Ornaments of Nations, and all that is called the *Cuftume*, which Poets and Painters ought to underftand equally well. What he chiefly failed in, is the Clair-obfcure, and the Contrafte of Lights and Shadows; and tho' his Colouring be not difagreeable in feveral Pieces, yet he was excelled in that Part by *Titian*. Sometimes, however, he has admirably fucceeded even in that; for, to name but one Piece, of many that might be mentioned, the famous *Madonna*, with the *Chrift* and St. *John*, in the Duke of *Tufcany*'s Palace at *Florence*; Can any Picture be more charming than it is, even

with refpect to Colouring? *Raphael* was of a very generous Temper, exceeding affable and courteous to his Scholars, and to all Mankind in general; and therefore he was greatly beloved by all Men, and by his Scholars he was quite adored. He was very ready in giving them Affiftance; and the beft Rule, with regard to diftinguifhing the Pieces quite done by himfelf, from thofe of his Scholars, that have paffed for his, tho' they were only touched by him, is that laid down by *Felibien*. Thofe that are well painted, but are not correct in drawing, are of *Timotheo d'Urbina*, or of *Pellegrino de Modena*, who imitated his Colouring very well, but were incorrect Defigners. Thole in which the Defign is precife and exact, but the Colouring not fo agreeable, may be of *Francefco Penni*, another of his Scholars. Thofe in which *Giulio Romano* had any Share, have more Fire in the Actions, and more Blacknefs in the Flefh. *Perino del Vaga* is one of them who imitated him the beft; but in his there is rather Softnefs and Tendernefs, than Force and Greatnefs, fomething inclining to the feeble and languid. And now that I am fpeaking of Imitation, it is not amifs to obferve, that there was one *Lorenzo Credi*, a Fellow Scholar with *Leo-nardo da Vinci*, under *Verrocchio*, who quitting his Mafter's Manner, to imitate *Leonardo*, copied him fo exactly, that very often his Copies are miftaken for Originals.

WITH regard to *Raphael*'s Scholars, I fhall only add to what hath been faid, that *Penni*, commonly called *il Fattore*, becaufe he was fo quick and expeditious in Contriving and Defigning, tho' he drew well, yet he painted but indifferently. His quick impatient Ge-nius, after he underftood Drawing, did not allow him to fpend much Time upon the Study of Colouring, a more unpleafant, laborious Task. *Raphael* had fo high a Notion of his Talent at Defigning, that he employed him much in making Draughts for Tapeftries and other Ornaments. There are feveral Cielings at *Rome* painted by him; and it was he and *Giulio Romano* that finifhed the Hiftory of *Conftantine* in the great *Salle* of the *Vatican*, after the Defigns of their Mafter *Raphael*.

PERINO DEL VAGA had naturally no Vivacity, no Fire; whatever of that appears in any of his Works was borrowed from *Giulio Romano*, whilft they worked together. He was fitter to be a Copier than an Inventor, and to that he chiefly applied himfelf.

OF all *Raphael*'s Scholars, *Giulio Romano* came the neareft to him in Invention and Defign; but I think not in Colouring, as is faid by *Felibien*. It is obferved, that *Raphael*'s
                                                                                    Works

Works had more Fire while *Giulio* worked with him.   Such was *Giulio's* Vivacity, that he had not Patience to bestow Time on perfecting himself in Colouring : Whence it is, that his Drawings are far preferable to his Pictures.   He was learned in the Antique, and shewed accordingly great Erudition in all his Pieces.   He got both his Correctness in Design and his Taste of the Antique, from the Study of the antient Remains, under the Direction, of his Master; but his Boldness was chiefly owing to his own natural Genius.   And by comparing the Works he did under *Raphael's* Eye, with those he did entirely by himself, we may plainly see that his Performances differed from those of his Master, just as their Tempers differed.   In those of the Master, Sweetness and Grace are predominant ; tho' there is nothing of the languid or effeminate in them : In those of the other, Fire and Boldness prevail.   And while they.worked together, as *Raphael's* Pieces had more of the *Furia*, as it is called by the *Italians*; so the other's had less of the Ferocious, and were duly moderated by *Raphael's* naturally sweet and gracious Manner.

IN *Michael Angelo Buonarotti's* Works, an extraordinary Force of Imagination, and *Michael Angelo.* Greatness of Genius, even to Caprice and Wildness, appear ; for he erred in Design on the Side of Greatness.   None ever better understood the Principles of Design ; " that Art of " marking exactly all the Members of the human Body ; all the Bones, Veins, and Muscles; " and of giving a just Ponderation to Figures ; of making appear in the Arms, the Legs, and " in all the Parts, more or less Efforts, according to the Nature of the Actions or Sufferings " represented ; and of expressing in the Countenances all the different Passions of the Mind; " of disposing the Draperies, and placing all things that enter into a great Composition, with " Symmetry, Consistency, and Truth".   This is that great Art which is so justly admired in the Performances of the best Masters, and which is by itself sufficient, without the Aid of Colours, to give a clear and lively Idea of any Object.   *Michael Angelo* was Master of this great Art to vast Perfection; he excelled particularly in Skill of Anatomy; and seems rather to have affected too much to shew that Skill : A vast uncommon Strength of Genius something leaning toward the Savage and Furious characterizes all his Works, and clearly distinguishes them from those of any other Master.   He is indeed extravagant in many things ; he has taken great Licences contrary to the Rules of Perspective, and is frequently too bold in the Actions and Expressions of his Figures; in his Draperies there is not all the Grace one could wish; and his Colouring is frequently neither true nor agreeable : He was not Master of the *Clair-obscure*; and with respect to Decorum, and the *Costume*, he often erred ; but he had a masculine, daring, comprehensive Genius. As he studied *Dante* very much, so it is justly observed, that there is a great Likeness *Like to Dante,* between the Painting of the one, and the Poetry of the other.   This is certain, that the *whom he studied* greatest Errors *Michael Angelo* committed against Decency in his Pictures, in his famous *much.* Last Judgment in particular, if he was not misled into them by that Poet, he was at least not more culpable in them than the Poet, who had taken the like Licences in his Poems. *Raphael* is said to have learned a greater Manner from seeing some of *Michael Angelo's* Paintings, than he had been able to conceive before he saw them : But *Michael Angelo* seems to have been yet more indebted to the Painting of *Luca Signorelli* of *Cortona*, than *Raphael* was to him.   This *Luca Signorelli* was excellent at designing naked Bodies.   And from a Piece which he had painted in a Chapel of the great Church at *Orvietto*, *Michael Angelo* transferred several Figures into his Last Judgment.

FRANCESCO SEBASTIANO DEL PIOMBO, having studied Colouring *Francesco Sebasti-* at *Venice* under *Bellini*, and afterwards under *Georgione*, and being naturally of a light *ano del Piombo.* and airy Genius, had a very agreeable Colouring : But, though some of his Pictures after the Designs of *Michael Angelo* are highly esteemed, yet, when he was not supported by him, he was hardly able to go through with any great Work.   He was for some time set up against *Raphael*, because his Colouring was rather more perfect; and while *Michael Angelo* assisted him in the Invention and Design, his Pieces were preferred by some to *Raphael's*: But the Lightness and Airiness of his Temper, and his Want of Invention, Judgment, and Solidity, quickly appeared, so soon as he was left to himself.   And indeed, when he got Preferment from the Pope, he gave himself up to his natural Disposition, quitted the Pencil, or at least did nothing considerable, but lived in an idle, loose, and dissipated Manner.

ANDREA DEL SARTO understood the Principles of the Art very well ; he *Andrea del Sarto.* had studied them accurately ; and he put them in Practice in as great a Degree of Perfection as one of his Complexion of Mind was capable of.   " Be not surprized, says *Felibien*, that " I ascribe what was perfect or wanting in his Pictures to his Constitution and Genius ; " for 'tis certain, that what was deficient in his Performances may be justly attributed to his " natural Slowness and Heaviness.   If his Designs are correct, and in the Style of *Michael* " *Angelo*; if he has invented agreeably, and disposed Things with much Judgment; that " we may assign to his Accuracy, to his Solidity, and Deliberation.   And if his Pieces have

T t   " not

" not that Vivacity, that Force and Spirit for which other Pictures are fo much admired,
" it was becaufe he himfelf had naturally not enough.of that Fire and Livelinefs which is
" neceffary to animate Pictures". He was not fertile, but rather cloudy and tardy; and
hence it is that there is not Diverfity enough in his Draperies, nor a fufficient Variety of
Expreffion in his Countenances and Geftures. However, if we confider his Works without any Prepoffeffion, we fhall perceive that in many of his Women and Children there
are fine Airs of Heads; tho' they are not fufficiently diverfify'd, yet the Expreffion is fwcet
and natural, and the Draperies are difpofed in a very judicious agreeable Manner. The
Naked is well underflood, and correctly defigned; and in fine, tho' there is not that Greatnefs
of Tafte in his Works, nor that Strength and Heat which is admired in others, yet all he
did was accurate, correct and ftudied. The natural Melancholy, Self-diffidence, and Timoroufnefs of.the Painter appear, in fome Degree, in all he did. Confcious of his own Slow-
nefs and Heavinefs, he endeavoured to make up what was wanting .in Quicknefs and
Strength of natural Parts by Study, Thinking and Labour. In almoft all his Pictures,
thofe efpecially reprefenting Saints, and devout Characters, there is a very great Cloudinefs
about the Eyes, and a Kind of Gloominefs mixed with Wildnefs. And I remember one faid, on
feeing fome of his moft famous Pictures at *Florence,* " That he thought he excelled in
" painting a Kind of Enthufiafm, which might be miftaken for the Effect of new Wine,
" becaufe of the mifty Swimming he gave to the Eyes". Had he ftaid longer at *Rome,* he
might have improved greatly, confidering his Diligence and Application; but being
naturally timorous, he was difcouraged by the great Perfection that School had attained
to; and defpairing of ever being able to come near to it, he returned to *Florence,* purfued the Way of Painting to which his natural Genius had at firft led him, and produced
feveral Pictures, which, if they do not fhew great Genius, but rather Labour and Poring,
do at icaft evidence Accuracy and Correctnefs.

C O R R E G E's Genius appears in all he has done, that wonderful Greatnefs of natural
Genius, and fine Tafte of Beauty, which was able, without any Affiftance, to rife to a moft
fublime pitch of Perfection. 'Tis no Wonder he was not altogether correct, not having
any Affiftance from the Antique, nor indeed from any Mafter. How far was he fuperior
in his Tafte to the *German* and *Flemifh* Painters by means of a better, a nobler, and more
elegant Turn of Mind! and he feems only to have fallen ihort of *Raphael* in Correctnefs of
Defign, for want of the fame Helps from the Antique, which *Raphael* had. There is in
moft of his Pieces fomething of Greatnefs, even above *Raphael* himfelf; and his Tafte of
Grace and Beauty is, tho' quite different from that of *Raphael,* yet not lefs agreeable and
charming. He was excellent at fore-fhortening Figures, and his Pictures abound with
Inftances of it. It feems, he looked on that as a very difficult Part in Painting, had ftudied
it much, and underftanding it well, liked rather too much to fhew his Skill of it. Hiftory
hardly affords a greater Inftance of Strength of Genius, than in this excellent Painter: For
all his Sweetnefs and Greatnefs, confidering his Circumftances and Education, can be afcribed
to nothing elfe but to a very rare natural Stock of thefe excellent Qualities. But having
already faid a great deal of him in another Place, I fhall only add here, that one fees, or
rather feels very remarkably in his Pieces, the delightful charming Effects of a fine Genius
exerting itfelf naturally, without Conftraint, Violence, or Affectation, as Nature itfelf directs
and moves. He had no other Mafter but Nature; he imitated nothing but Nature; but by
a happy natural Genius he well knew how it ought to be copied, or how to diftinguifh
between the Parts that ought to be emulated, and thofe which not being agreeable in
Nature itfelf, can never be render'd fo in Imitation.

T I T I A N was a great Obferver of the rare and more agreeable Effects of the falling of
Light upon Bodies, and of Colours whether local or reflected. And as *Michael Angelo*
affected to ihew his Knowledge of Anatomy, to the Study of which his natural Genius
prompted him, fo the other delighted in difplaying his Intelligence of Light and Colours,
and their moft pleafing Appearances. He loved Show and Magnificence in. Drefs and
Equipage, and in the Furniture of his Houfe: He had naturally a voluptuous Eye, and
rather fought after the Pleafures it is capable of receiving, than thofe which are more intellectual, pure, and remote from Senfe. He had a Brother who imitated his Colouring very
well; which is indeed very natural, warm, and agreeable; perfect Flefh and Blood: And
he had a Son who came yet nearer to him, and many of his Scholars copied his Works fo
perfectly, that their Copies have paffed for his own original Pictures. *Calver,* a *Flemifh*
Painter, imitated him well; but the beft of them all was *Paris Bordon.* In general, his
own Works are correcter in the Defign, than thofe of his Imitators and Copiers, tho' he
did not excel in that Part. His Tafte of Landfcape plainly fhews his admirable Judgment
in choofing from Nature the moft beautiful Parts, and he remarkably avoided in his Performances what is called by *Italians* the *Triteria.* · In fine, he was fo excellent a Painter in
refpect of all that belongs to Colouring, and giving a true and pleafing *Carnaggione,* as it is
termed by Artifts; that it may be faid of him, that when *Michael Angelo* wifhed there had
been

been as much Truth of Defign in his *Danae,* as it has Beauty of Colouring, it was to defire a Picture more perfect than any that ever was painted by any Mafter.

THE Love of Magnificence difcovers itfelf yet more evidently in *Paul Veronefe's* Paulo Veronefe. Pictures, and he did really fhew it in all his Conduct. He payed no great Regard to hiftorical Truth, or the *Coftume,* in his Performances, but chiefly ftudied to pleafe the Eye by a fine Carnation, and rich Draperies. *Apelles* would certainly have defired him not to make his Pictures fo rich, as he is faid to have advifed a Painter in his Time, whofe Fictures glared with magnificent Apparel, Jewels, and other fhining Ornaments, but were incorrect in the Drawing, and had very little Meaning.

TINTORET, of all the *Venetian* Painters, ftudied moft after the Antiques. He Tintoret. took great Pains by ftudying Nature, the antient Remains, and by making Models in Clay of the Figures he intended to paint, to become correct in Defign, which he preferred to excelling in the colouring Part; yet he imitated the Colouring of *Titian,* and often came very near to it. He defpifed the Over-finifhing of the *Flemifh*; and as he painted very faft; fo Fruitfulnefs of Invention, Richnefs of Fancy, Force of Expreffion, great Warmth and Vivacity appear in his Pictures. As *Hannibal Carrache* obferved, he was not always equal to himfelf, nor could that be well expected of one who painted fo quick, and had fo much Life and Sprightlinefs: However, he, like the other beft Painters of all Ages, converfed much with all the learned Men of his Time; it is certain he painted rather for Glory than for the Love of Money; and in many of his Pictures, at the fame time that there is a great deal of Fire, great Freedom and Readinefs, there is alfo a Correctnefs in Defign far beyond any other of the *Venetian* School.

I HAVE already faid a great deal about the *Carraches,* who reftored Painting when it HannibalCarrache. was beginning to decline. One, I think, may fee the melancholy cloudy Temper of *Hannibal* in all his Countenances: He was often difpleafed with his Works, even after he had bellowed very great Pains upon them; and therefore he frequently deftroyed what he had almoft finifhed, and begun afrefh. The *Carraches* united their Talents in order to perfect the Art, and it was indeed only by fuch a Conjunction of many different Abilities and Accomplifhments, that Painting could have been brought to fuch Perfection as it was by them. After laying afide all their Quarrels and Jealoufies, they joined together in the firmeft Friendfhip, and mutually affifted one another. And it is no fmall Honour to them to have founded fo great an Academy, that produced fo many excellent Mafters. Let me only add, that tho' every one of the *Carraches* had his diftinguifhing Genius and Manner; yet they worked together fo jointly, and in fo friendly a Manner aided and affifted one another, that very good Judges have not feldom been miftaken in taking the Works of *Lewis* in particular for thofe of *Hannibal.* *Hannibal* however was Mafter, as it were, to the other two; and whatever other Accomplifhments they were poffeffed of, their Perfection in Painting was chiefly owing to his Inftructions and Affiftances, as foon appeared after they were feparated; for *Auguftin* applied himfelf wholly to Engraving; and *Lewis,* when left to himfelf, quickly loft his firft excellent Manner. *Hannibal* began firft to form himfelf by imitating the Sweetnefs, Purity, and Gracioufnefs of *Corrège.* Afterwards, he ftudied the enchanting Force of *Titian's* Colouring; but when he came to *Rome,* and had well confidered the Greatnefs of the Antique, and of the Works of *Michael Angelo* and *Raphael,* he then began not only to defign more correctly, but to form higher Ideas; and ever afterwards taking *Raphael* principally for his Pattern to copy after, his chief Endeavour was to unite with Nature a fine Idea of Beauty and Perfection, neither copying the common Appearances of Nature too fervilely, nor foaring too high above fomething too far above Nature, or rather quite out of it. It is remark'd of him, that with all his Melancholy and Cloudinefs, he had a great deal of Vivacity and Wit, and faid very fine Things in Converfation; and this Temper led him frequently to amufe himfelf with painting *Caricature,* as they are called, or whimfical over-charged Countenances and Characters, a kind of Painting like what is called Burlefque in Poetry : *Felibien* mentions (13) a large Book of fuch Defigns by him.

GUIDO had three Manners; the Firft was ftronger whilft he imitated his Mafter Guido. *Lewis Carrache,* the Second more agreeable, and the Third very negligent. There is indeed a great deal of Sweetnefs in his beft Manner : But after all, what *Felibien* fays of him appears to me very juft. " He ftudied a foft gracious Way, but there is not Strength " and Boldnefs enough in his Pictures : And withal, his Style is what is called *Manierato*; " there is no great Variety in his Airs of Heads, Attitudes and Draperies". He has defigned fome Figures very well in the Labours of *Hercules*; but ftill he is too languid and foft even in thefe; and it was his own Temper. Three different Manners are rather more diftinguifhable in *Guido* than in any other Mafter; yet there is hardly any one in whom we may not difcern his Beginning, Progrefs, and End, or three Manners: A firft, which always

(13) Tom. III. p. 266.

always hath a great deal of his Mafter, as even that of *Raphael* himfelf had of *Pietro Perrugino* ; a fecond, in which his own Genius difcovers itfelf with confiderable Evidence and Force. And a laft, which degenerates commonly into what is called Manner, becaufe a Painter having ftudied Nature a long time, at laft fatisfies himfelf with the Habitude he hath formed of imitating it, without giving himfelf the Trouble of more Study, or of acquiring new Ideas.

Albano.

ALBANO chiefly excelled in painting agreeable Women, Boys, and *Cupids*; not in painting Men. He formed himfelf not after the Antique, but after Nature entirely, after his Wife and Children ; his Wife giving him all the Affiftance fhe could by fitting to him in various Attitudes naked, and by placing her Boys before him in different picturefque Poftures. One may fee by his Works he was of a very light, eafy, chearful Difpofition. It is faid, that tho' he painted Nudities, yet he was very modeft and chafte : And Mr. *Bayle* has been at great Pains to prove this was often the Cafe with refpect to the moft lafcivious Writers. Yet, generally fpeaking, this Rule will hold true; " As the Heart is, " fuch will one's Studies and Employments be: As the Tree is, fo are its Fruits."

Dominichino.

DOMINICHINO, preferred by *Pouffin* (14) to all for painting the Paffions, thofe efpecially of the rough, fiercer Kind, fpent a great deal of Time in ftudying and digeft-ing his Plan before he took his Pencil, and began to compofe. He had applied himfelf with great Diligence to all the Arts that have any relation to Painting, to Mathematicks, Archi-tecture, Philofophy and Poetry, and he converfed much with the Learned. He thought he had got over the chief Difficulty, when he had once formed a Plan of his Works that pleafed him : And becaufe he judged it impoffible to paint any Paffion well without feeling it, he ufed to take all proper Methods to work himfelf into the Paffion he had a Mind to reprefent; but when he did fo, he ufed to fhut himfelf up in fome very private Place; for having been more than once furprized in thofe Studies, he was imagined to be fubject to mad Fits. *Annibal Carrache* happening to come upon him unawares, when he was paint-ing the Martyrdom of Saint *Andrew,* and finding him in a violent Fit of Paffion, becaufe he was juft then going to reprefent a Soldier threatening the Apoftle, owned he had learned a great deal from him in that Moment. His Pictures are not much admired by thofe who do not feek for Entertainment to the Mind; but better Judges have the fame Opinion of him with *Pouffin,* who reckoned him one of the beft, that is, one of the moft inftructive and moving Painters. He painted in that Way ; that is, he delighted moft in expreffing and moving the Paffions, becaufe he had a juft Notion of the nobleft Ufes and Ends of the Art, and was himfelf a very affiduous Student of human Nature, and of all the Authors who excelled in painting moral Life.

Salvator Rofa.

WHO does not fee in *Salvator Rofa's* Pictures, the Savagenefs of his Imagination ? His Genius led him moft ftrongly to paint Battles. He painted likewife *Paifages* and Sea-ports; but always in a whimfical, wild, and favage Tafte.

Pietro da Cortona.

PIETRO DA CORTONA's Pictures are, as he is faid to have been, lively, ingenious, eafy, agreeable. He wrought with great Expedition, Warmth, and Enthufiafm, and fucceeded beft in great Compofitions, the *Tout-enfemble* of which is always very noble as well as pleafing: Tho' painting faft, and in a Fit of Enthufiafm, as it were, he was not correct in his Defign, nor always true in his Expreffion, yet his Pictures are very great and entertaining. He was in his natural Temper very prompt and *vif,* as the *French* call it, and yet very engaging : He was fuch in his Converfation, and fuch alfo are his Pictures; they are the true Image of his Mind.

Reubens.

REUBENS failed in what regards Tafte of Beauty, and very often in Defign; his lively, great Mind not permitting him almoft ever to mend or change what he had done : All the Errors he committed, he was tranfported into them by the Rapidity and Impetuouf-nefs of his Genius. He improved a little by feeing the Pictures of the *Lombardy* Painters; but ftill his firft Notion of Beauty maintained the Afcendant : He always continued to paint *Flemifh* Faces and Proportions: Tho' he efteemed the Antique and *Raphael* exceed-ingly, yet he never imitated them; on the contrary, had he copied the Statues of *Apollo, Venus, Hercules,* the dying Gladiator, or any other of the famous antient ones at *Rome,* one could not certainly have known them, fo much would he have difguifed and changed them in Confequence of his own very different Tafte. His great Freedom is extraordinary : " But hence proceeded his Incorrectnefs, not in Defign merely, but likewife in Colouring, " as

(14) C'eroit dans le tems que la plupart des jeunes peintres qui etoient à *Rome,* attirez par la grande reputa-tion ou eroit le Guido, allolent avec empreffement copier fon tableau de Martyre de Saint *André,* qui eft à Saint G*regoire.* Le *Pouffin* etoit prefque le feul qui s'attachoit à deffeiner celui du Dominiquin, lequel eft dans le même endroit ; et il en fit fi bien remarquer la beauté, que la plupart des autres peintres, perfuadez par fes paroles, et par fon exemple, quitterent le Guide pour etudier d'apres le Dominiquin.--Il regardoit le Dominiquin comme le meilleur de l'ecole des Caraches, pour la correction du deffein, et pour les fortes expreffions. Fellbien *fur les vies,* &c. T. IV. p. 17.

" as *Felibien* and others have obferved, the Tints of his Carnations being often fo ftrong,
" and fo feparated the one from the other, that they feem like Spots". He was a very
uncommon Genius, had a very warm and lively Imagination, and was withal very learned,
extremely well acquainted with the beft Authors, and with Mankind. I have often wifhed
to have feen two Treatifes, which he is faid to have left behind him in Manufcript: It is,
no doubt, a very great Lofs to the Science that they have not been publifh'd; one was
about the proper Ufe that may be made of Statues in Painting, and the other contained
Obfervations upon Perfpective, Symmetry, Anatomy, Architecture, and upon the Actions
of the human Body, and the Expreffions of the Paffions, all which he had himfelf
defigned agreeably to the beft Defcriptions of antient Poets. He had likewife collected
from *Homer*, *Virgil*, and other Poets, Defcriptions of Battles, Shipwrecks, Feftivals,
Entertainments, Games, and of all the different Employments and Diverfions of Mankind,
together with fome Allegories and Fables, all which he had compared with Pictures of
Raphael, and other great modern Mafters reprefenting the fame or like Subjects. In fine,
his Learning, and his natural Fire, and Freedom of Mind, appear in his Works, and are indeed
highly admirable; but a good Tafte of Beauty, and of the Antique, is wanting. His
Paintings in the *Banqueting Houfe* are juftly reckoned his Mafter-piece, and do indeed fhew
a vaft Imagination, and a very fublime grand Genius.

THO' he himfelf followed his own Tafte, yet he advifed his favourite Scholar *Vandyck*,
to go to *Italy* for his Improvement; where, having ftudied the Works of *Titian*, he
foon became a more agreeable Colourift than his Mafter *Reubens*. He attended principally
to *Titian's* mafterly Portraits, and quickly became one of the beft Portrait Painters that
ever was; but he did not poffefs Defign, and the other Qualities neceffary to hiftorical Compofition, to an equal Degree of Perfection. His Portraits are well known in *England*, and
will ever be admired by all who like what is genteel, natural, eafy and lively: 'Tis faid he
was very open, free, genteel, and natural in his Converfation, and had an admirable
Talent at entertaining thofe whom he painted, in order to produce them in their gen-
teeleft, eafieft, and moft agreeable Likenefs.

Vandyck.

I SHALL conclude with *Nicolas Pouffin*, with whom died all the greater Talents
neceffary to good hiftorical Painting : For *Carlo Marratti*, commonly called the laft of the
good Painters, tho' indeed his Idea of Beauty is fomething peculiar to himfelf, and never
fails to pleafe at firft Sight; yet, when well confidered, it appears languid; and there being
very little Diverfity in his Airs of Heads and Countenances, his Pictures foon fatiate and
cloy.

Carlo Marratti.

" *NICOLAS POUSSIN*, fays the ingenious Author of the Reflections on
" Poetry and Painting, was juftly called by his Contemporaries *Le Peintre des gens d'efprit*;
" or, a Painter for thofe who look for Entertainment to their Underftanding, by Truth,
" Science, Learning, Correctnefs, and good Difpofition in Pictures, or for Exercife to
" their Paffions by juft Force of Expreffion": In all thefe did this excellent Scholar, and
accurate judicious Painter, eminently excel. Had he been a better, that is, a more agreeable Colourift, he would have been inferior to none of the Painters of any Age in which
the Art hath flourifhed. · He was well verfed in all the beft Authors, and in Geometry,
Anatomy, Architecture, and all the Sciences, the Knowledge of which is neceffary to
make an able Compofer in Painting, or a polite Scholar. At firft, he ftudied the charming
Colouring of *Titian* very much; but in Proportion as he improved in Tafte and Knowledge,
he more and more attached himfelf to what regards the Truth and Juftnefs of Drawing,
which he muft have confidered to be the principal, the moft effential Part of Painting; and
for which the beft Painters, fays *Felibien*, " Have ever abandoned the other Parts, fo foon
" as they had attained to a true Idea of the chief Excellence of the Art". This great Painter,
after having made very confiderable Progrefs in all the Parts of Learning and Philofophy, in
the Study of human Nature in particular; in order to perfect himfelf in the Art of Painting,
applied himfelf principally to the Study of the Antiques, and of *Raphael's* Pictures and
Defigns. It was upon thefe excellent Models that he formed his Ideas of Compofition, and
his Style in Painting. In his Pictures we fee all the Evidences and Advantages of Judgment, and a well regulated Fancy: No Painter ever took greater Pains to improve his
natural Genius and Abilities than *Pouffin*, and to acquire the Science requifite to make
Painting truly perfect by being truly ufeful. He perfectly well underftood every thing that
is neceffary to make a great Compofition, or judicious Ordonnance in Pictures. He could
diftinguifh what would be fuperfluous, and only produce Confufion in a Piece, from what
was proper to the Subject; and would fet it in its beft Light, by making the principal
Figures appear to the greateft Advantage; infomuch that in his Pictures there are neither
too few nor too many Figures, and they are all agreeably difpofed, and properly employed,
with relation to the main Subject, and the Action that is principally reprefented. " Of this,
" fays *Felibien* (15), his Seven Sacraments, and the Picture reprefenting the ftriking of the

Nicolas Pouffin.

U u   " Rock,

(15) *Entretien fur les vies & fur les ouvrages de Peinstres*, Tom. IV. p. 17,

" Rock, are a fufficient Proof; for in all thefe, all the Parts admirably contribute to the
" Perfection of the Ordonnance, and to the agreeable Difpofition of the Figures, as well
" proportioned Members ferve to render a Body completely beauteous. What Beauty,
" what Grace is there in his Picture of *Rebecca?* One cannot fay of *Pouffin* what *Apelles*
" faid to a Painter of his Picture of *Helen*, that not being able to make her beautiful, he
" had painted her very richly arrayed; for in that Picture her Beauty is the more ftriking,
" that her Attire is very fimple and plain: He hath in it, and almoft all his Pieces, carefully
" obferved the Decorum: And as for his Skill of human Nature, and his natural Difpofi-
" tion to moral Science, that fufficiently appears in his Works; for no one more efteemed
" the Painters who excelled in that Part, than he did, and all his Expreffions are true with-
" out any Exaggeration. He hath painted all the different Paffions of Mankind in all their
" various Tones and Modifications (15). His Figures do indeed fpeak to and moft effec-
" tually touch the Heart. His Learning fhews itfelf in the ftrict Regard to the *Coftume,*
" with which he always painted in every Circumftance. He hath been accufed, faith
" *Felibien*, of having preferred the Antique to Nature; but if thofe who fay fo, acknow-
" ledge that one cannot copy after more elegant and beautiful Proportions than thofe of
" the Antique Statues; and that the antient Sculptors fet themfelves to attain to Majefty
" and Grace in their Attitudes, by their great Correctnefs, and the Delicacy and Simplicity
" of all the Members in their Figures, avoiding carefully every thing that leffens the
" Beauty of Parts, or of the Whole; are not thefe the propereft Models for Imitation?
" And can the Antiques be praifed without inducing one to copy after them? But 'tis faid,
" One ought to know how to paint them without giving painted Figures the Drynefs and
" Hardnefs of Statues: This is certainly true, and one ought, befides that, to give particular
" Attention to the different Effects of Light upon Marble and other hard Subftances, and
" upon natural Bodies, real Elefh and Blood, and real Stuffs or Silks; and hath *Pouffin*
" made Men and Women, in any of his Pieces, of Brafs or Marble, inftead of Flefh? He
" knew that in order to make the moft graceful, beauteous, and well proportioned
" Bodies, there were no better Models to be ftudied and imitated than the Statues and
" Bas-reliefs of antient Artifts, thofe Mafter-pieces of Workmanfhip, which have ever been
" fo highly admired by all the Intelligent; and which, ever fince the Art was at fuch a
" Degree of Perfection as to have been capable of producing them, all Artifts have
" thought it the beft thing they could do to copy after them, and endeavour to come as
" near to their Excellence as poffibly they could. *Pouffin* was not fo prefumptuous as to
" imagine, that by his own Genius he could form fuch perfect Figures as the *Venus* of
" *Medicis, the Gladiator*, the *Hercules*, the *Apollo*, the *Antinous, the Wreftlers*, the
" *Laacoon*, and the other celebrated Pieces of antient Art, that are yet preferved to us in
" *Italy*. He likewife knew, that it was impoffible to find any where fuch perfect Bodies
" of Men and Women as Art had formed by the Hands of thofe excellent Mafters, to whom
" the Manners and Cuftoms of their Country had furnifhed all the moft advantageous and
" favourable Means of making a fine Choice of Nature: And that therefore, without
" ftudying and following thefe Models, a Painter would unavoidably fall into many Faults;
" as indeed all thofe have done, who ftudying Nature alone, took indifferently for their
" Models all Sorts of Perfons, as they chanced to prefent themfelves to them, without once
" thinking of fhunning what was defective, ill proportioned, imperfect or unbeauteous.
" One fees in *Pouffin's* Pictures, that he made a proper Ufe of thofe admirable Remains of
" Antiquity, and followed them in his Choice of Proportions, in Simplicity, Correctnefs,
" Beauty and Majefty, and even in the Difpofition of his Draperies, without falling into
" any thing that inclines to the Hard and Dry. He underftood how to take Affiftance
" from them, whether in reprefenting Divinities or Mortals, having himfelf entered into
" the Spirit and Tafte of antient Artifts, who have fo carefully diftinguifhed their Gods,
" Heroes, and more ordinary Men. He knew like them how to characterize Perfons of
" all Ranks and Conditions of Life, of all Tempers and Difpofitions; and to all this he
" has added a very confiderable Intelligence of the Effects of Light and Colours, as they
" are diverfified in Nature by different Caufes". In fine, his manly Temper, his Accuracy,
his penetrating folid Judgment, and his high Idea of the moral Ufes to which Painting
might be rendered conducive, and for which it ought chiefly to be employed, appear clearly
in all his Performances, and will ever exceedingly recommend them to all who have juft
Notions of the fupreme Excellence, to which Painting ought to afpire. In his Works,
without going any farther, we fufficiently fee to what excellent Purpofes Painting may be
employed, and what divine Leffons the Pencil is able to convey in the moft entertaining
forcible manner.

WHETHER thefe Obfervations are juft or not, muft be left to the Judgment of thofe
who are acquainted with the Works of thofe Painters who have been mentioned: They
are merely intended by way of Specimen to fhew what it is that Students of Painting
ought chiefly to look for in Pictures; or to point out the Marks and Characterifticks, by
which they ought to endeavour to be able to diftinguifh the Works of different Mafters. I
need

(15) Tom. IV. p. 90.

need not tell my Readers, that there is hardly any Mafter, who hath not done fome bad, or at leaft indifferent Pictures; and therefore one ought not to form a Judgment of a Mafter from one Picture, but from many of thofe which he did when he was at his greateft Perfection, or from the general prevailing Excellencies of his beft Pieces, in which he hath not copied after any one, but followed his own Genius, Temper and Tafte.

LOMAZZO, in his Treatife on Painting, and his Temple of Painting, hath gone feveral different Ways to work in order to give an Idea of the diftinguifhing Characters and Turns of feveral Painters. He likens one to one Poet, and one to another. He allots a different Planet to each, agreeably to the then received Opinion of the different Influences of the Planets upon Mens Difpofitions and Temperatures of Mind, as well as of Body. He gives every one, in another Place, a different Animal for his Attendant, as a Symbol of his peculiar Character; and elfewhere, he imagines a Temple with feven Pillars varioufly conftituted and adorned, to reprefent the diftinguifhing Excellencies of feven great Mafters. I have copied in the Notes the Subftance of what he has faid of the principal Painters (16). But I fhall only obferve here, that he, and Scanelli da Forli after him, have remark'd, that as amongft the antient Greeks, fo amongft the Moderns, the effential Qualities of a good Painter were divided amongft feveral Mafters; and that in order to make two perfect Pictures, one, for Example, of Adam, and another of Eve, the two moft perfect human Bodies that ever were, Adam muft have been defigned by Michael Angelo (17), and coloured by Titian, all the Proportions being taken from Raphael; and Eve muft have been defigned by Raphael, and coloured by Correge. Such two Pieces thus drawn and coloured, would be the moft perfect Pictures, fay they, that ever were painted.

Lomazzo takes different Ways to defcribe the diftinguifhing Qualities of the more famous Painters.

IF I durft attempt to imitate that beautiful mafterly Paffage of Lucian, in his Book of Images, to which I found it fo difficult to do Juftice in Tranflation, wherein he defcribes the different Talents of antient Mafters, by calling upon them to lend each the Strokes for which he was moft renowned in any of his Works, in order to make the Picture of a perfect Woman; I think I could point out what I would require from Raphael, Leonardo, Michael Angelo, Correge, Hannibal, Guido, Dominichin, and all the moft famous modern Mafters, in order to make a perfect Piece. But I rather chufe to endeavour to give an Idea of their diftinguifhing Abilities, by naming Subjects, according to my Idea of them, fuitable to the Genius of each, and which they either have, or would have executed to very great Perfection, had they fet about it.

What different Qualities are required to make a perfect Picture.

The different Qualities of the modern Painters might be reprefented as Lucian does thofe of the antient ones.

I WOULD have chofen to have had from Leonardo da Vinci, feveral Drawings, one reprefenting the Holy Supper, the divine Author of our Religion with all his Apoftles about him, inftituting that holy Rite, by which Chriftians were in all Ages to commemorate his Goodnefs in dying for them; and together with that feveral others, in which various Characters of Men, of great Men more particularly, were reprefented: Thefeus, for Example, founding the Democracy at Athens; Cato refufing to confult the Oracle whether he fhould adhere to the Interefts of Liberty and his Country, whatever it might coft him, or abandoning them. live an inglorious Life; and faying, Nature hath implanted in every Man an Oracle, that clearly points out what is Duty, to all who confult it, or will hearken to its Voice, &c. And with thefe not a few Caricature.

An Attempt to do it in another way, by affixing to each of them a Subject fuitable to his peculiar Genius. To Leonardo da Vinci.

FROM Raphael what can one wifh for, that is more inftructive than his Cartoons, or more fublime than his Transfiguration? But his School of Athens, and his Parnaffus, well deferve a Place in a Library, and would make the fineft Ornament for the beft furnifhed one. To Raphael every great and graceful Subject was proper, and I fhould have chofen

To Raphael.

. to

---

(16) Perche fi vede che Leonardo ha' efpreffo i moti, & decoro di Homero, Pofidoro la grandezza, & furia di Virgilio, il Bunarotto l'ofcurezza profonda di Dante, Raffaello la pura Maefta del Petrarca, Andrea Mantegna l'acuta prudenza dell' Ariofto, & Gaudentio la devotione che fi trova efpreffa ne' libri de Santi. Lomazzo della Pittura, p 283. ——— Et frá moderni fi vede per la maeftà, & bellezza, in Raffaello, per la furia & grandezza nel Roffo, per la cura & induftria in Petino, per la gratia et leggiadria nel Mazzolino, & per la fierezza in Polidoro, &c. p. 287. Of Raphael and Michael Angelo, p. 291. Guardifi auco il pittore che per dimoftrarfi perito nell' arte dell' Anatomia non efprima in tutti i corpi tutti i mufcoli che l'Anatomifta trova, quando effercita l'arte fua ne' corpi naturali; Come fece Michael Angelo, ma' imitando in ciò il prudentiffimo Raffaello feguitò la natura, la quale lo Hercole, &c. See his Tempio della Pittura, p. 7, 9, 10. Where he Compares them with the antient Maiters, and fhews that the effential Qualities of good Painters were in like manner divided amongft the Antients and Moderns. L'ifteffo fi può offervar ne gli

antichi. p. 15. Polidoro, Michael Angelo, & Raffaello, per abellire la noftra maniera moderna ai pari della antica. Et cio con grandiffimo gluditio, &c. p. 40. Governatori di pittura fono fimili a quelli de i Cieli——— p. 42. Michael Angelo formato del metalo del primo Governatore.———Imitatore di' Dante.———Gaudentio formato del metallo del fecondo Governatore ———Polidoro del terzo. ——— Leonardo del quarto.———Raffaello del quinto ——— Andrea Mantegna del fefto.———Titiano del fettimo. Pittori contrari——p. 45. Animali dedicati a Governatori della pittura. La onde anco gli antichiffimi Matematici Babilonii i quali attribuirono á ciafcun de i pianeti un animale di natura a lui conforme, Come a Saturno il Drago per la terribiltá, a Giove l'aquila per l'altezza, a Marte il Cavallo per la fierezza, al Sole il Leone per la fortezza, a Mercurio il Serpe per la Prudenza, alla Luna il Bue per l'humanità, a Venere attribuirono l'huomo per la ragione, con la quale egli che nafce animale ragione. vole dee reggere e moderate tutti i fuoi affetti, &c.

(17) Lomazzo Tempio della pittura, p. 60. So Scanelli da Forli il microcofmo della pittura, p 68,

to have had all the Muses, all the Graces, all the Virtues, painted by him, but with their antient Symbols and Attributes; the Choice of *Hercules*; the Continence of *Scipio*; all the great and generous Actions of antient Heroes; and the whole History of our Divine Teacher and his Apostles; and; together with these; all the pleasant Legends about Sta. *Cecilia.*

To Giulio Romano.

GIULIO ROMANO should have painted for me the monstrous Audacity of the Giants, and *Jupiter,* by his almighty Thunder, discomfiting their impious Enterprize. He should rather have painted for me profane than sacred History; and in that, whatever required the profoundest Learning, and the greatest Strength, or rather Fury of Imagination. *Homer* he loved; and he should have painted for me the whole *Iliad*; his Battles more especially.

To Jean d'Udina, Perino del Vaga, *&c.*

FROM *Jean D'Udina,* *Perino del Vaga, Mathurino,* and *Ligorio* (18), I should have had Copies after all the Antiques, containing a whole System of the antient Myrbology, and all their more remarkable Rites and Customs, civil or religious; all their Ships and Gallies, Instruments of War, Standards, Trophies, *&c.*

To Michael Angelo.

MICHAEL ANGELO should have been employed by me to represent the Labours of *Hercules,* and to have adorned a School of Exercises with *Fotze Academice,* with Postures of Strength and Activity, that shew all the Muscling of the human Body. I would rather, however, have chose Statues from him than Pictures; and he should have done for me all the antient Heroes, Patriots, and Legislators, as they themselves, and the antient Statues of them, are described; *Moses* in particular. Before he began, and while he was meditating such Subjects, I would rather have had him study *Homer* and *Virgil* than *Dante.*

To Titian.

TITIAN should have done for me many Portraits, very many Landscapes, and the whole History of *Venus,* from the antient Poets.

To Paul Veronese.

PAUL VERONESE should have done me one Festival or Coronation-Procession, in which I would have allowed him to bring out all his vast Stock of rich Draperies.

To Correge.

From *Correge* I would have demanded the Graces attending *Apollo,* playing upon his Harp, and civilizing savage Beasts by his divine Musick. *Correge* should have done for me the Holy Family, and the Light should have come from the divine Infant; not common, but celestial Light. *Correge* should have painted for me a St. *John,* in the sublimest Enthusiasm, composing the *Apocalypse,* with an inspired Pen, that seemed to be moved, not by his Direction who held it, but by an invisible Agent; the holy Man himself being, as it were, quite out of the Body, and filled with the Holy Ghost.

To Hannibal Carrache.

HANNIBAL CARRACHE should have painted for me just what he has done in the *Farnese* Palace; and out of the Sacred Writings, the Taking down of our Saviour from the Cross, the Veneration of the holy Men, mingled with deep Sorrow, the tender Compassion and devout Meltings of the good Women, the pious inexpressible Grief of his blessed Mother, who is not, however, without Hope, but believes his Resurrection.

To Guido.

FROM *Guido* I would have desired a Morning; a gay, sprightly Morning; *Phoebus* in his Chariot, attended by the Graces, and the Hours going before perfuming the Air with Roses.

To Guerchin.

GUERCHIN should have done for me a black, cloudy one, heavily bringing on some direful Day, big, as it were, with the Fate of *Cato* and of *Rome.* *Guido* should have done for me divers Animals, and several faint languishing Damsels: *Guerchin* a gloomy Night, Spectres, and frightful Forms.

To Albano.

ALBANO should have painted for me *Venus,* with many *Cupids* sporting about her, in wanton, gay, amorous Attitudes; or *Diana,* with her attendant Nymphs, all in the Dress of Huntresses; the Rapes of *Europa* and *Proserpina,* and several other poetical Fables.

To Dominichino.

BUT from *Dominichino* I should have intreated a whole Set of Tragedies; Pictures representing all the great and strong Passions; several Martyrdoms of Saints; and *Iphigenia, Ajax, Clytemnestra, Orestes,* and all the Subjects of the great antient Tragedians.

To Andrea del Sarto.

ANDREA DEL SARTO should have done for me the Descent of the fiery Tongues, and miraculous Gifts, upon the holy Apostles.　　　　　　*PAR-*

(18) Il y a plusieurs volumes dessinez de sa main dans la bibliotheque du duc de Savoye, ou les curieux pourtolent apprendre beaucoup des choses que nous ne voyons plus aujourdhui. Entre celles qu'il a recherchees avec soin, on voit toutes sortes de vaisseux qui etoient anciennement en usage. *Felibien,* T. 3. p. 111.

PARMEGGIANO fhould have painted for me feveral tender, foft, pleafaht; *To* Parmeggiano: melting Stories; any thing that gently touches the Soul.

TO *Pouffin*, however, would I have left it to paint me an *Arcadia*, juft as he hath *To* Pouffin. done it. For in a charming romantick Country, there is placed in the middle of a Field, the funeral Monument of a beautiful *Arcadian* Girl, who died in the Flower of her Youth; as is known by her Statue laid on her Tomb after the manner of the Ancients, and this fhort Infcription, *Et in Arcadia ego;* which leads two young Men and two young Wo. men decked with Garlands of Flowers to very ferious Reflections. They feem not a little furprized to find this mournful Monument in a Place where they came not to feek for any fuch grave melancholy Object. One of them points out the Infcription to the others; and one fees in all their Countenances Joy and Chearfulnefs beginning, and deep Sorrow beginning to feize them. One can hardly help imagining he hears them fpeak out their Thoughts about cruel Deftiny, which neither fpares Youth nor Beauty, and againft which the hap. pieft Climate, the molt inchanting Country, affords no Security.

NOT contented with this, from his admirable Pencil, he muft have done for me all the religious Inftitutions of Chriftianity; and alfo Subjects of a very different Character; as *Mofes* delivering the famifhed *Ifraelites* by Manna from Heaven, or by Water from a Rock, in a barren, parched Defart.

GASPAR POUSSIN fhould have done for me a Variety of pleafant beautiful *To* Gafpar Pouffin: Landfcapes, from his own fine Imagination.

AND *Salvator Rofa* fhould have painted for me feveral Battles; and a great Variety of *To* Salvator Rofa: wild favage Profpects.

TEMPESTA fhould have drawn for me a Hurricane at Sea, frighted Mariners, and *To* Tempefta. the Ship ready to be fhatter'd into Pieces, or fink to the Bottom. I fhould have defired from *Caftiglione* and *Mola* a great Variety of Animals.

AND from *Reubens*, Satyrs, *Silenus* quite drunk, *Bacchante* and *Saturnalian* Feftivals. *To* Reubens.

PIETRO DA CORTONA fhould have done for me all the Battles of *Alexander.* *To* Pietro da Cortona.

AND *Tintoret* the whole Hiftory of *Venice*, its Foundation and remarkable Deliverances. *To* Tintoret:

FROM *Holbens* I fhould have demanded many Portraits; more from *Rembrandt*, and *To* Holbens, Rem-yet more, of the fair Sex efpecially, from *Vandyck.* brandt, *and* Van-dyck.

AND thus I fhould have had Pictures for all the noble Ufes of Painting; to preferve the Memory of Friends; to reprefent the Characters of antient great Men; to raife my Ima. gination, move my Paffions and Affections of every kind, in a truly wholfome and moral Manner; and to inftruct me in the profoundeft Secrets of the human Heart, in all its various and complicated Workings and Motions; to convey agreeable Images, and footh my Mind; or to rouze it, and awaken great and ftrong Thoughts : Pictures to compofe me into Meditation, or to refrefh and chear me after Study and Labour : Pictures to com. pare with the fineft Defcriptions of the beft Poets of every kind; and Pictures to inforce the fublimeft pureft Doctrines of moral Philofophy, and true Religion : Pictures wherein to ftudy the vifible Beauties of Nature, and all the charming Effects of varioufly modified Light and Colours : And Pictures in which I might view myfelf, and contemplate human Nature as in a moral Mirror : Pictures of as many Kinds as there are of Poetry; Lyricks by *Raphael* and *Correge*; Epick by *Giulio Romano*; Tragedy by *Dominichino* and *Pouffin*; Comedy and Satire by *Reubens*; rural Beauties by *Titian*, with *Venus*, her Cupids, Nymphs, and Lovers; Defcriptions of Characters by *Leonardo da Vinci*; Fables and Allegories by *Guido* and *Albano*; great Feats of Heroes by *Michael Angelo*; Love or tender Tales by *Parmeggiano*; and melancholy gloomy Ideas by *Andrea del Sarto*, or *Hannibal Carrache.* And by way of Contrafte to a fublime and fine Tafte of Na. *To* Michael Angelo ture and Beauty, I would have had a few Pictures of *Carravaggio* of common ordinary Carravaggio. Nature (19).

I HAVE

(19) To juftify what I have often faid of that Painter, I fhall take a Quotation from *Felfbien*, T. 3. p. 194. Mr. Pouffin ne pouvoit rien fouffrir du Caravage, & difoit qu'il eftoit venu au monde pour detruire la pefnture; mals il ne fuut pas s'etonner de l'averfion qu'il avoit pour lui: Car fi le Pouffin cherchoit la nobleffe dans fes fujets, le Caravage fe lailloit entporter à la verité du naturel tel

qu'il le voyoit : Ainfi ils etoient bien oppofez l'un à l'autre. Cependant fi l'on confidere en particulier ce qui depend de l'art de peindre, on verra que Michel Angelo de Cara. vage l'avoit tout entier; j'entends l'art d'imiter ce qu'il avoit devant fes yeux. Le Caravage a eu fes fectateurs Manfrede & le Valentin, *&c.*

X x

I HAVE been all this while venturing, perhaps, too far, or taking too much upon me; but wherein I am wrong or miftaken, I fhall be glad to be fet right. And if I, by my Boldnefs, fhall put others upon confidering Pictures in another more profitable Way than the greater Part of thofe who are called, or love to be called *Virtuofi*, do; without any Prepoffeffion, or blind Attachment to great Names and Authorities, I fhall gain one of the main Points I have in View in this Effay.

IT only remains that I fay fomething about thofe Pieces of antient Painting now engraved. And I think I need not make any Apology to the Lovers of Antiquiry, for publifhing thofe curious Remains, that heretofore have been quite neglected; tho' they are, furely, in refpect of their Antiquity, a very valuable Treafure; as much fo, at leaft, as any thing can be merely on that Account. To fuch this muft needs be a very acceptable Collection. Far lefs need I make any Apology to the Lovers of Painting, for giving to the Publick good Engravings of antient Pieces of Painting, that were highly efteemed by the greateft modern Mafters, and from which they received great Affiftances. The few of them that have been formerly engraved (the *Venus*, the *Rome*, and the *Marriage*) are fo fadly done, that it was neceffary, in Juftice to the Antients, to publifh them in a truer Light. 'Tis no Wonder that thofe who had nothing elfe of antient Painting to judge by, but the bad Prints of thefe Pieces, have hitherto entertained no very high Idea of the antient *Roman* Painting, or at leaft of the Remains of it.

I HAVE, indeed, chiefly publifhed them along with this Effay, that they might ferve by way of Evidences to prove that the Accounts given in it of antient Painting are not exaggerated. We have no Reafon to think that antient Writers magnified Matters, when they fo highly commend the antient *Greek* Painters for all the more effential Qualities of good Painting. There are indeed no Remains of *Greek* Painting; but how can we doubt of their Fidelity and Impartiality in their Accounts of them, fince there are Statues, Bas-Reliefs, Intaglias, Cameos, and Medals, to vouch fufficiently for the Truth of what they have faid, at the fame time, concerning thefe Sifter Arts? of which it is hardly poffible to be an intelligent Judge, without being equally capable to form a very juft and true Opinion of Painting. But thefe Remains now publifhed from excellent Drawings, with the greateft Exactnefs, put this Matter beyond all Doubt; for they fhew what *Roman* Painting was, if not at the Time of *Auguftus*, yet in After-times, when the Art is faid to have been in greater Perfection than it was at that Period.

AND from them we may judge what the *Greek* Painting was, fince the *Roman* at no Time was reckoned, by the beft *Roman* Judges, who had feen feveral of the moft celebrated *Greek* Pictures, equal to the *Grecian*: And thefe Pieces, however beautiful, can by no means be reckoned the beft Performances of *Roman* Mafters, or Mafters of whatever Country, who painted at *Rome* in the Time of the better Emperors, that is, of thofe who moft loved and encouraged the Arts; being done upon the Walls and Cielings in the fubterraneous Apartments of great Palaces, built by *Titus, Trajan,* or the *Antonines;* where it is not likely that the better Mafters would have been employed, or, if they were, that they would have exerted themfelves fo much, as in doing capital Pictures for the Ornament of Apartments of greater State and Magnificence, and that were oftner vifited.

I SHALL now give fome Account of them in the Order they are here annexed. As to the Colouring, I have added fome number'd Sketches, by which that will be better underftood, than by any Defcription. He who would have a fuller Account of it in Words, will be fatisfied by having recourfe to *Bellori's* Account of the Paintings found in the *Sepulchro Nafonis,* and other fubterranean Places at *Rome;* for all the Remains of Painting that now fubfift, are much the fame in that refpect, as he defcribes thofe he has publifhed from *Bartoli's* Drawings. I have an excellent Copy of the *Marriage,* juft as it is at prefent. The famous Collection that belonged to the *Maffimi* Family at *Rome,* and was juftly reckoned by all; Strangers as well as *Italians,* one of the greateft Curiofities at *Rome,* is now in Dr. *Richard Mead's* Library: And there one may fee the Colouring of the antient *Roman* Paintings exactly imitated by *Bartoli;* thefe Drawings having been faithfully done by him from the Originals, at the Time they were difcovered, or while they were very frefh. But, which will be yet more fatisfactory to the Curious, Dr. *Mead* has lately got fome of the beft and moft entire, well-preferved Pieces of that Kind that were at *Rome,* from the fame Palace of the *Maffimi.* There they had been long kept as an invaluable Treafure, that was never to be parted with by the Family: But now thefe admirable Rarities are in the Poffeffion of one of the beft Judges, and greateft Encouragers of polite Literature, and all the ingenious Arts, in *England:* To whofe elegant Library, and moft valuable Collection of Pictures, Drawings, Medals, and other Curiofities, all the Lovers of the Arts have very free and agreeable Accefs.

I. & II.

I. & II.

THE firſt in Order repreſents *Rome ;* the ſecond *Venus,* or *Deſidia,* or *Volupia* (20) : The Originals are in the ſame Apartment ; the one over-againſt the other in the *Barberini* Palace at *Rome.* I have placed theſe two firſt, becauſe we are told by *Dion Caſſius* (21), That the Emperor *Adrian* built a Temple at *Rome,* dedicated to *Rome* and *Venus ;* in which the Images of both were placed upon magnificent Thrones. And it is not improbable, that this Painting of *Rome* was taken from that Statue (22). There is a Statue of *Rome,* with almoſt all the ſame Symbols, in the Capitol at *Rome.*

THESE two ancient Pieces, according to the Tradition at *Rome,* were found in a ſubterraneous Apartment, thought to belong to the *Circus* of *Flora,* in digging to lay the Foundations of the preſent *Barberini* Palace. The *Venus,* or *Volupia,* with the *Cupid* added by *Carlo Maratti,* is in Breadth nine *Roman* Palms, and in Height eight and one half. The *Rome* is in Height eight, and in Breadth nine. It puts me in Mind of the many grand Epithets given to *Rome* by the Poets and other Authors, and of many fine warm Addreſſes to her (23). Theſe two, we are told by a very good Author, paſſed, for a conſiderable Time, the one for the Work of *Raphael,* and the other for that of *Correge.*

THIS ingenious Author's Account of the antient Paintings he had ſeen is worth our Attention ; and therefore I have copied it into the Notes, in his own Words, the Language being univerſally underſtood (24).

THE

(20) Vide *Montfaucon*'s *Antiquities.*

(21) *Dion, p.* 789, *&c.*

(22) See the Deſcription of this *Rome* in *Montfaucon, b. 2. c. 5. part* 2. where he likewiſe deſcribes another antient Picture of *Rome,* dug out of the Ground near the Amphitheatre.

(23) See in particular *Rutilii Galli Itinerarium.* How *Rome* was commonly painted or repreſented by Statues, and in Medals, we learn from *Claudian de Prob. & Olyb. Conf. Paneg.*

Ipſa triumphatis qua poſſidet æthera regnis,
Aſſiſt, Innuptæ ritus imitata Minervæ.
Nam neque cæſariem crinali ſtringere cultu
Colla, nec ornatu patitur mollire retorto ; .
Dextrum nuda latus, niveos exſerta lacertos
Audacem retegit mammam, laxumque coercens
Mordet gemma ſinum. Nodus qui ſublevat enſem,
Album puniceo pectus diſcriminat oſtro,
Miſcetur decori virtus, pulcherque ſevero
Armatur terrore pudor, galeæque minaci, &c.

This is a very fine Deſcription : But ſhe was repreſented in various Manners ; moſt commonly as the Learned have obſerved, *Victoriolam manu oſtentans, palmam ac coronam offerens,* ut *ſcilicet de toto orbe triumphos ſignificaret, & virtutem militarem,* Every one knows that ſhe is frequently called *Mater & ſanctiſſima parens.*

(24) Before I give this Author's Words, I beg leave to obſerve, that there are more antient Paintings yet ſubſiſting, than he mentions, as appears by the preſent Collection. And tho' many antient Paintings periſhed ſoon after they were diſcovered, for want of proper Care about them, yet, luckily, Drawings were taken of moſt of them that are loſt, the Moment they were diſcovered ; which do, as much as can be, ſupply the Loſs of the Originals. I need not tell my Reader what antient Paintings are publiſhed by *Bellori,* from the Drawings of the elder *Bartoll, &c.* And there are a great many Pieces in the Poſſeſſion of the King of *Naples* and *Sicily,* that were taken from *Auguſtus*'s Palace in *Monte Polatino* at *Rome,* that have never been engraved. As for what our Author ſays of the antient Moſaïcks, I ſhall juſt take Notice, that the only two given in this Collection are very beautiful, as ſhall be afterwards obſerved. His Words are,

Je ne ſache point qu'il ſoit venu juſques à nous aucun tableau des Peintres de l'ancienne Grèce. Ceux qui nous reſtent des Peintres de l'ancienne Rome, ſont en ſi petite quantité, & ils ſont encore d'une eſpece telle, qu'il eſt bien difficile de juger ſur l'inſpection de ces tableaux de l'habileté des meilleurs ouvriers de ce tems-là, ni des couleurs qu'ils employoient. Nous ne pouvons point ſavoir poſitivement s'ils en avoient que nous n'ayons plus ; mais il y a beaucoup d'apparence qu'ils n'avoient point les couleurs que nos ou-

vriers ne tirent que de l'Amérique, & de quelques autres pays, qui n'ont un commerce reglé avec l'Europe que depuis deux ſiecles.

Un grand nombre des morceaux de la Peinture antique qui nous reſte, eſt executé en Moſaïque ou en Peinture faite avec de petites pierres coloriées, & des aiguilles de Verre compaſſées & raportées enſemble, de maniere qu'elles imitent dans leur aſſemblage le trait & la couleur des objets qu'on a voulu répréſenter. On voit par exemple dans le Palais que les Barberins ont fait bâtir dans la Ville de Paleſtrine, à vingt-cinq mille de Rome, un grand morceau de Moſaïque qui peut avoir dix pieds de long ſur dix pieds de largeur, & qui ſert de pavé à une eſpece de grande niche, dont la Voute ſoutient les deux rampes ſeparées, par leſquelles on monte au premier palier du principal eſcalier de ce bâtiment. Ce ſuperbe morceau eſt une carte géographique où le cours du Nil eſt répréſenté. L'Ouvrier s'eſt ſervi pour l'embellir de pluſieurs eſpeces de Vignettes telles que les Géographes en mettent pour remplir les places vuides de leurs cartes. Ces Vignettes répréſentent des hommes, des animaux, des bâtimens, des chaſſes, des cérémonies & pluſieurs points de l'hiſtoire morale & naturelle de l'Egypte ancienne. Le nom des choſes leſquelles y ſont dépeintes eſt écrit au-deſſus en caractères Grecs, à peu près comme le nom des Provinces eſt écrit dans une carte générale du Royaume de France.

Le Pouſſin s'eſt ſervi de quelques-unes de ces compoſitions pour embellir pluſieurs de ſes tableaux, entr'autres celui qui répréſente l'arrivée de la ſainte famille en Egypte. Ce grand Peintre vivoit encore quand cette ſuperbe Moſaïque fut détertée des ruines d'un Temple de Serapis, qui pouvoit bien être, pour parler à notre maniere, une Chapelle du Temple celebre de la *Fortune Préneſtine,* Tout le monde ſait que l'ancien Préneſté eſt la même Ville que Paleſtrine. Par bonheur elle en fut tirée très entiere & très bien conſervée ; mais malheureuſement pour les curieux, elle ne ſortit de ſon tombeau que cinq ans après que Monſieur Suarez Evêque de Vaiſions eut fait imprimer ſon livre *Præneſtes Antiquæ libri duo.* La carte dont je parle étoit alors enſevelie dans les caves de l'Evêché de Paleſtrine, où elle étoit comme inviſible. On en appercevoit ſeulement quelque choſe à lavel les endroits qui étoient déja découverts, & l'on ne les voyoit encore qu'à la clarté des flambeaux. Ainſi Monſieur Suarez n'a pu nous donner dans ſon Ouvrage que la deſcription de quelques morceaux que le Cavalier del Pozzo avoit fait deſſiner ſur les lieux. Le Cardinal Barberin a fait graver ce monument dont j'ai parlé plus au long que mon ſujet ne ſembloit le demander, parce que toutes les relations de voiages que je connois n'en diſent mot.

On voit encore à Rome & dans pluſieurs endroits de l'Italie des fragmens de Moſaïque antique, dont la plûpart ont été gravés par Pietro Sancti Bartoli, qui les a inſerés dans ſes differents recueils. Mais pour pluſieurs raiſons on jugeroit mal du pinceau des anciens, ſi l'on vouloit en juger ſur ces Moſaïques. Les curieux ſavent bien qu'on ne rendroit pas au Titien la juſtice qui lui eſt due, ſi l'on vouloit juger de ſon mérite par celles des Moſaïques de l'Egliſe de Saint Marc de Veniſe, qui furent faites ſur les deſſeins de ce Maître de

la

III.

THE third was dug up in fearching the Ruins in *Monte Palatino,* now called *Orti Farnéfiani,* and is at prefent in Dr. *Mead's* Poffeffion. The Figures in the Copy are of the fame Size as in the Original. It reprefents *Auguftus* giving a Crown : But the Figure who

la couleur. Il eft impoffible d'imiter avec les pierres & les morceaux de Verre dont les anciens fe fort fervis pour peindre en Mofaïque, toutes les beautés & tous les agrémens que le pinceau d'un habile homme met dans un tableau, où il eft maitre de Voiler les couleurs, & de faire fur chaque point phyfique tout ce qu'il imagine, tant par rapport aux traits que par rapport aux teintes. En effet les Mofaïques fur lefquelles on le récrie du vantage, celles qu'on prend d'une certaine diftance pour des tableaux faits au pinceau, font des Mofaïques copiées d'après de fimples portraits. Tel eft le portrait du Pape Paul V. qu'on voit à Rome au Palais Borghefe.

Il ne refte dans Rome même qu'un petit nombre de peintures antiques faites au pinceau. Voici celles que je me fouviens d'y avoir vues. En premier lieu la Nopce de la Vigne Aldobrandine, & les *Figurines* de la Pyramide de Ceftius. Il n'y a point de curieux, qui du moins n'en ait vu des eftampes. En fecond lieu les peintures du Palais Barberin dans Rome, lefquelles furent trouvées dans des grottes fouterraines lorfqu'on jetta les fondemens de ce Palais. Ces peintures font le Payfage ou le Nymphée, dont Lucas Holftenius a publié l'eftampe avec une explication qu'il avoit faite de ce Tableau, la Venus retouchée par Carle Maratte, & une figure de Rome qui tient le *Palladium.* Les connoiffeurs qui ne favent pas l'hiftoire de ces Frefques, les prennent l'une pour être de Raphaël, & l'autre pour être du Corrège. On voit encore au Palais Farnefe un morceau de peinture antique trouvé dans la Vigne de l'Empereur Adrien à Tivoli, & un refte de plafonds dans le jardin d'un particulier auprès de Saint Grégoire. On voyoit auffi il y a quelque tems plufieurs morceaux de peintures antiques dans les bâtimens qui font compris vulgairement fous le nom des ruines des Thermes de Titus ; mais les uns font peris, comme le tableau qui répréfentoit Coriolan, que la mere perfuadoit de ne point venir attaquer Rome, & dont le deffein fait par Annibal Carrache, lequel a été gravé plufieurs fois, eft adjourd'hui entre les mains de Monfieur Crozat le cadet, les autres ont été enlevés. C'eft de là que le Cardinal Maffimi avoit tiré les quatre morceaux qui paffent pour répréfenter l'hiftoire d'Adonis & deux autres fragmens. Ces favantes reliques font paffées à fa mort entre les mains du Marquis Maffimi, & l'on en voit les eftampes dans le livre de Monfieur de la Chauffe, intitulé, *La Pitura Antichè delle Grotte di Roma.* Cet Auteur a donné dans ce livre plufieurs deffeins de peintures antiques qui n'avoient pas encore été rendus publics, & entr'autres le deffein du plafond d'une chambre qui fut déterrée auprès de S. Etienne *In Rotonda* en mil fept cens cinq, c'eft-à-dire une année avant l'édition de cet ouvrage. La figure de femme peinte fur un morceau de Stuc qui étoit chez le Chanoine Vittoria, eft préfentement à Paris chez Monfieur Crozat le jeune.

Il ne refte plus dans les ruines des Thermes de Titus que des peintures plus qu'à demi effacées. Le Pere de Montfaucon nous a donné l'eftampe du morceau le plus entier qui s'y voye, lequel répréfente un payfage.

On voyoit encore en mil fept cens deux dans les ruines de l'ancienne Capoue, éloignée de la Ville moderne de Capoue, une Gallerie enterrée, en latin *Cripto Porticus,* dont la Voute étoit peinte & répréfenteoit des figures qui fe Jouoient dans differents ornemens. Il y a fept ou huit ans que le Prince Emanuel d'Elbeuf en faifant travailler à fa maifon de campagne, fituée entre Naples & le Mont Vefuve, fur la bord de la Mer, trouva un bâtiment orné de peintures antiques ; mais je ne fache point que perfonne ait publié le deffein de ces peintures, non plus que celles de la Veille Capoue.

Je ne connois point d'autres Peintures antiques faites au pinceau, qui fubfiftent encore aujourd'hui, outre les morceaux dont je viens de parler. Il eft vrai que depuis deux fiecles on en a déterré ; foit dans plus grand nombre, foit dans Rome, foit dans d'autres endroits de l'Italie : mais je ne fais par quelle fatalité, la plûpart de ces peintures font perdues, & il ne nous en eft demeuré que les deffeins. Le Cardinal Maffimi avoit fait un très beau recueil de ces deffeins ; & par une avanture bizarre, c'étoit d'Efpagne qu'il avoit rapportés à Rome les plus grandes richeffes de fon recueil. Durant fa Nonciature il y avoit fait copier un portefueïlle qui étoit dans le cabinet du Roi d'Efpagne, & qui contenoit le deffein de plufieurs peintures antiques, lefquelles furent trouvées à Rome lorfqu'on commença dans le feizième fiecle d'y fouiller avec ardeur dans les ruines & y chercher des débris de l'antiquité. Le Cavalier Del Pozzo, dont le nom eft fi celebre parmi les amateurs de la peinture, le même pour qui le Pouffin peignit fes premiers tableaux des fept Sacremens, avoit fait auffi un très beau receuïl de deffeins

d'après les peintures antiques que le Pape régnant à acheté depuis quelques années pour le mettre dans la Bibliotheque particuliere qu'il s'eft formée.

Mais prefque toutes les peintures d'après lefquelles ces deffeins furent faits font perdes, celles du tombeau des Nafons qu'on déterra près de Pontemole il y a quarante-quatre ans, ne fubfiftent déja plus. Il ne nous eft refté des peintures de ce Maufolée que les copies coloriées, que furent faites pour le Cardinal Maffimi, & les eftampes gravées par Pietro Sancti Bartoli, lefquelles font avec les explications du Bellori un Volume *in folio* imprimé à Rome. A peine demeuroit-il il y a déja quinze ans quelques veftiges des peintures originales, quoiqu'on eut attention de paffer deffus une teinture d'ail, laquelle eft fi propre à conferver les Frefques. Malgré cette précaution elles fe font détruites d'elles mêmes.

Les Antiquaires prétendent que c'eft la deftinée de toutes les peintures anciennes, qui durant un grand nombre d'années ont été enterrées en des lieux fi bien étouffé, que l'air exterieur ait été long-tems fans pouvoir agir fur elles. Cet air exterieur les détruit auffi-tôt qu'elles redeviennent expofées à fon action, au lieu qu'il n'endommage les peintures enterrées en des lieux où il avoit confervé un libre accès, que comme il endommage tous les tableaux peints à Frefque. Ainfi les peinture qu'on déterra il y a vingt ans à la Vigne Corfini, bâtie fur le Janicule, devoient durer encore long-tems. L'air exterieur s'étoit confervé un libre accès dans les tombeaux dont elles ornoient les murailles ; mais par la faute du propriétaire elles ne fubfifterent pas long-tems. Heureufement nous en avons les eftampes gravées par Bartoli. Cette avanture n'arrivera plus déformais. Le Pape régnant qui a beaucoup de goût pour les Arts, & qui aime les antiquités, n'ayant pû empecher la deftruction des peintures de la Vigne Corfini fous le Pontificat d'un autre, n'a point voulu que les curieux puffent reprocher au fien de pa reils accidens, qui font pour eux des malheurs fignalés. Il fit donc rendre un Edit dès le commencement de fon regne par le Cardinal Jean Baptifte Spinola, Camerlingue du Saint Siége, qui défend à tous les propriétaires des lieux où l'on aura trouvé quelques veftiges de peinture antique de démolir la maçonnerie où elles feroient attachées fans une permiffion expreffe.

On conçoit bien qu'on ne peut fans temerité entreprendre de décider de la peinture antique avec la peinture moderne fur la foi des fragmens de la peinture antique qui ne fubfiftent plus aujourd'hui : & du moins par le tems. Ce qui nous refte, & qui étoit peint fur les murailles, n'a été fait que long-tems & qui fe perdit à la mort des Peintres celebres de la Grèce. La peinture antique ne la peut être la mort des Peintres celebres de la Grèce. La peinture antique ne la peut être par les écrits des anciens que les Peintres qui travaillerent à Rome fous Augufte, & fous les premiers fucceffeurs, furent très inferieurs à Zeuxis, & à fes illuftres contemporains. Pline, qui compofoit fon hiftoire fous Vefpafien, quand les Arts avoient atteint déja le plus haut point de perfection où ils parvinrent fous les Céfars, ne cite aucun ta bleau de fon tems-là, parmi les tableaux qu'il compte comme un des plus beaux ornemens de la Capitale de l'Univers. On ne fauroit donc affeoir aucun Jugement certain en vertu des fragmens de la peinture antique qui nous reftent, fur le degré de perfection où les anciens poutroient avoir porté ce bel Art. On ne fauroit même decider par ces fragmens du degré de perfection où la peinture pouvoit être lorfqu'ils furent faits.

Avant que de pouvoir juger d'un certain ouvrage de l'Art étoit où l'Art étoit lorfque cet ouvrage fut fait, il faudroit favoir pofitivement en quelle eftime l'ouvrage a été dans ce genre, & s'y l y a plûle pour un ouvrage excellent en fon genre. Quelle Injuftice, par exemple, ne feroit-on pas à notre fiecle, fi l'on jugeoit un jour de l'état où la Poëfie Dramatique auroit été de nôtre tems fur les tragedies de Pradon, ou fur les Comedies de Hauteroche ? Dans les tems les plus feconds en artifans excellens, il fe rencontre encore un plus grand nombre d'artifans médiocres. Il s'y fait encore plus de mauvais ouvrages que de bons. Or nous courrions le rifque de prononcer fur la foi d'un de ces ouvrages médiocres, fi par exemple, nous voulions juger de l'état où la peinture étoit à Rome fous Augufte, par les figures qui font dans la Pyramide de Ceftius, quoiqu'il foit très probable que ces figures peintes à frefque ayent été faites dans le tems même où la Pyramide fut élevé, & par conféquent fous le regne de cet Empereur. Nous ignorons quel rang pouvoit tenir entre les Peintres de fon tems l'Artifan qui les fit ; & ce qui fe paffe aujourd'hui dans tous les pays nous apprend fuffifament que la cabale fait diftribuer fouvent les ouvrages les

who receives it is wanting.   It is not improbable that it reprefents *Auguftus* reftoring the Crown to *Phraates*, of which *Horace* fpeaks (25):

—— Jus imperiumque Phraates
Cæfaris accepit genibus minor.   Ep. L. I.   Ep. XII. V. 27.

THOSE who are acquainted with Medals will eafily find out his chief Attendants. *Mecenäs* and *Agrippa* are there, and the remoteft Perfon is, not improbably, *Horace*; at leaft it is as like to his Defcription of himfelf as any of thofe Figures in *Intaglia's*, that are called *Horace* by the Learned, and is not unlike to them (26).

IV.

THE fourth.reprefents the Ceremonies of an antient Marriage; the Original is well known by the Name of *Nozze Aldobrandine*: it is in the *Villa Aldobrandina* at *Rome*; and where it was found we learn fully from *Frederico Zuccaro*, that excellent Painter, who was prefent when it was dug out of the Ruins of *Mecenas's* Palace: He cleaned it himfelf, and placed it where it now is.   I have given his Account of it in his own Words (27), becaufe 'tis very different from that which is given of it at the Bottom of the common very bad Print of it.

THE Figures in this beautiful Piece are about three *Roman* Palms in Height.   I have a very fine and a very exact Copy of it in Colours, by *Camillo Paderni*, that was done from the Original when I was laft at *Rome* in the Year 1737.   The Marriage Pomp, and feveral other Ceremonies reprefented in this Piece (28), the Bafhfulnefs of the Bride in particular, are often defcribed by the Poets.

Jam nuptæ trepidat follicitus pudor,
Jam produnt lachrymas flammea fimplices.
                    Claud. in Nupt. Hon. Aug. & Mar. Fefcin.

THE fame Poet thus defcribes other Ceremonies of Marriage

Flammea virgineis accommodat ipfa capillis:
Ante fores jam pompa fonat, pilentaque facram
Præradiant ductura nurum.   Calet obvius ire
Jam princeps——   De Nup. Hon. & Mar.

THE remarkable Bafhfulnefs of the Bride in this Piece is charmingly expreffed by *Statius* (29):

Lumina demiffam, & dulci probitate rubentem.
                    Sylv. L. I. Epit. Stellæ & Violant. V. 12.

V.

les plus confiderables à des Artifans très inferieurs à ceux qu'elle fait négliger.

Nous pouvons bien comparer la fculpture antique avec la nôtre, parce que nous fommes certains d'avoir encore aujourd'hui les chef-d'œuvres de la fculpture Grecque, c'eft-a-dire, ce qui s'eft fait de plus beau dans l'antiquité. Les Romains dans le fiecle de leur fplendeur, qui fut celui d'Augufte, ne difputerent aux Illuftres de la Grece que la fcience du Gouvernement.   Ils les reconnurent pour leurs maitres dans les Arts, & nommément dans l'Art de la fculpture, &c.   *Reflections fur la Poefie & la Peintre.* T. I. S. 38.

(25) He feems to allude to fome fuch Munificence of *Auguftus*, Carm. L. II. Od. II.

(26) See Ep. L. I.   Ep. XX. and fee *Urfin's* Gems.

(27) Ma la pittura per vero non può havere fi lunga Vita, ne la fragilità de i fuoi colori fotto-pofta a femplici accidenti refiftere nelle tele, e tavole, come ancho pietre, e muraglie in che fi opera. Nientedimeno ella ancora ha' Vita di più fecoli, e più ancora ne haverebbe fe fi poteffe diffendere per fe fteffa dalli accidenti ftrani, tutta via anco effa tra le dette ruine e grotte di *Roma* fi va fcuoprende, e moftrando in qualche parte la fua durata, come pochi mefi fono, fu' fcoperto fu'l monte di fanta *Maria Maggiore* ne gli horti Mecenati da quei cavatori, che continuamente Vanno cercando qua e la fotto terra, per trovar ftatue, marmi, e figure fotterrate, in quelle ruine,

trovarano una ftanza, ove era rimafto un pezzo di muro In piedi nel quale era dipinta una gratiofa, e bella hiftoria a frefcho, con figure dentro, di tre palmi in circa alto, colorite da eccellente mano, che merito effer ftimato quel pezzo di muraglia, e portato alla luce, e pofto nel giardino del cardinale *Aldobrandino* a monte Magnapoli, e cofi ben confervata tra quelle ruine, che fu maraviglia, ed fo che ful per forte uno di quelli primi a vederla, e laVarla, e nettarla dl mia mano diligentemente, la viddi cofi ben confervata e frefcha come fe fuffe fatta pur all' hora, che n'hebbi un gufto fingulare e fui caufa di farla portare alla luce.   L. II. del difegno efterno, P. 37. del CaValier *Frederico Zuccaro* nel'idea d'pittore fcultori, &c.

(28) This Piece appears to me to be a copy from a Baf-relief; and there are feveral antient Baf-reliefs reprefenting the Ceremonies of Marriage at *Rome*.   See *Kennet's Roman* Antiquities, where a Very remarkable one Is mentioned.   And, indeed, as I have already faid, moft of the antient Paintings that haVe been, or are now publifhed, at leaft moft of them I have feen, appear to me to be only Copies in Painting from Statues or Baf-reliefs; but moft excellent ones.

(29) The Commentators obferve on that Paffage, *Hoc fox eft τῶν παρθένων,* &c. apud *Xenoph.* de rep. *Lced—* Videtur etiam *Papinius Violantillam* effingere ad Illud *φιδὲς ἀγαλμα* apud *Pauſan. in Atticis,* p. 103.   Scrfbit ab *Icario* erectam fuiffe *Lacedæmone,* eo loci ubi *Penelope* rogata

2 Y

V.

THE fifth is a fine Image of old Age, *Curva Senectus*; it puts me in Mind of the old Woman done by *Lala*, fo much commended by *Varro*, for a very natural Picture of that Age.

IT may perhaps reprefent *Pallas* difguifed in the Likenefs of an old Woman, when fhe came to chaftife the Vanity of *Arachne*, agreeably to *Ovid's* Defcription :

> Pallas *anum fimulat*; *falfofque in tempora canos*
> *Addit.* ———   Ovid. Met. L. VI. v. 26.

> *Talibus obfcuram refecuta eft* Pallada *dictis*
> *Mentis inops, longaque genas confecta fenecta.*   Ibid. v. 36.

OR it may reprefent one of the Fates; for as thefe and all other imaginary Beings are differently reprefented by the Poets, fo, no doubt, they were reprefented in very various Manners by Sculptors and Painters (30). The Original is in the *Barberini* Palace at *Rome*; 'tis very well preferved, and is about two Palms in Height.

VI.

THE fixth is a Piece very much admired for the Boldnefs and Strength with which the Character is mark'd. There is not, indeed, in any Remain of antient Workmanfhip, a better expreffed Character of a Satyr (31). The Original is in the *Barberini* Palace carefully preferved, and very frefh in the Colouring. It is about two Palms in Height.

VII.

THE feventh is a *Siren* (32), agreeable to *Ovid's* Defcription :

> ——— *Vobis*, Acheloides, *unde*
> *Pluma pedefque avium, cum virginis ora geratis?*
> *An quia, cum legeret vernos* Proferpina *flores,*
> *In comitum numero miftæ*, Sirenes *eratis ?*
> *Quam poftquam toto fruftra quæfiftis in orbe;*
> *Protinus ut veftram fentirent æquora curam,*
>
>   *Poffe*

rogata ab ipfo patre ut maneret fecum in patria, velata facie, &c.

It is often alluded to by the Poets; fo *Catullus in Nup. Jul. & Man.*

> *Tardat ingenuus pudor.*
> *Afpice, intus ut accubans*
> *Vir tuus, Tyrio in toro*
> *Totus immineat tibi.*

So *Tibullus*, L. 3. Eleg. 4.

> *Ut Juveni primum Virgo deducta marito,*
> *Inficitur teneras ore rubente genas.*
> *Ut cum contexunt amaranthis alba puellæ*
> *Lilia, & Autumno candida mala rubent.*
> *Ima videbatur talis illudere palla, &c.*

See likewife *Lucan. de Nupt. Caton. & Marc.* The Commentators have obferved on thefe Paffages of the Poets: *Diogenes*, verecundum illum ruborum, colorem virtutis effe dicebat: & *Pithias Ariftotelis* filia, interrogata qui fibi color videretur pulcherrimus, eum, refpondit, qui in ingenuis ex pudore enafceretur.

(30) See a fine Defcription of them in *Catullus de Nuptiis Pelei & Thetidos.*

> *Cum interea infirmo quatientis corpora motu,*
> *Veridicas Parcæ cæperunt edere cantus.*
> *His corpus tremulum complectens undique veftis,* &c.

See *Ov. Met.* L. IV. v. 34.

> *Aut ducunt lanas, aut ftamina pollice verfant, &c.*

(31) See *Paufanias*, L. I. in *Atticis*: Where there is a long Account of Satyrs. See *Plutarch in vita Sylla*, and the Commentators on *Horace*, L. I. Od. I.

> · *Nympharumque leves cum* Satyris *chori*, &c.

And L. II. Od. XIX.

> ——— *& aures*
> *Capripedum Satyrorum acutas.*

(32) See the Difference between the *Syrens* and *Harpyes*, &c. defcribed by *Montfaucon* In his Antiquities. See likewife his *Diarium Italicum.* See likewife *Ant. Augoftini* Dialog. Dial. V. It is well worth while to read my Lord *Verulam* on this allegorical Story. See alfo *Ælian. de Animal.* Cap. XXIII. l. 17. Mr. *Pope's* Notes on the *Odyffey*, L. XII. v. 51.

> *Next where th'* Sirens *dwell you plow the Seas ;*
> *Their Song is Death, and makes Deftruction pleafe,* &c.

The Criticks have greatly laboured to explain what was the Foundation of this Fiction of the *Sirens:* We are told by fome, that the *Sirens* were Queens of fome fmall Iflands named *Sirenufæ*, that fie near *Caprea* In *Italy*, and chiefly inhabited the Promontory of *Minerva*, upon the Top of which that Goddefs had a Temple, as fome affirm, built by *Ulyffes*, according to this Verfe of *Seneca*. Ep. LXXVII.

> *Alta procellofo fpeculatur vertice* Pallas.

Here there was a renowned Academy, in the Reign of the *Sirens*, famous for Eloquence and the liberal Sciences, which gave Occafion for the Invention of this Fable of the Sweetnefs of the Voice, and attractive Songs of the *Sirens*. But why then are they fabled to be Deftroyers, and painted in fuch dreadful Colours? We are told, that at laft the Students abufed their Knowledge to the Colouring of Wrong, the Corruption of Manners, and Subverfion of Government; that is, In the Language of Poetry, they were feigned to be transformed into Monfters, and with their Mufick to have enticed Paffengers to their Ruin, who there confumed their Patrimony, and poifoned their Virtues with Riot and Effeminacy. The Place is now called *Maffa*, &c.

Poſſe ſuper fluctus alarum inſiſtere remis
Optaſtis : facileſque Deos habuiſtis ; & artus
Vidiſtis veſtros ſubitis flaveſcere pennis.
Ne tamen ille canor mulcendas natus ad aures,
Tantaque dos oris linguæ deperderet uſum,
Virginei vultus, & vox humana remanſit.
                                  Ov. Met. Lib. V. v. 552.

S O *Claudian* in *Sirenas:*

Dulce malum pelago Siren, *volucreſque puellæ*
Scyllæos *inter fremitus, avidamq;* Charybdin, &c.

It is a *Moſaick*, and was dug up in the *Farneſe* Gardens at *Rome* in the Year 1737, and is about four Palms in Height, and almoſt the ſame in Breadth.

VIII.

T H E eighth is likewiſe a *Moſaick*, (and theſe are the only two Specimens I have given, in this Collection, of *Moſaick* Painting) it repreſents the Rape of *Europa*, and it reſembles, in ſeveral Circumſtances, a fine Picture of this Story, beautifully deſcribed by *Achilles Tatius*, and both do *Ovid's* Deſcription :

Fert prædam: pavet hæc: littuſque ablata relictum
Reſpicit ; & dextra cornu tenet ; altera dorſo
Impoſita eſt : tremulæ ſinuantur flamine veſtes.
                                  Ov. Met. L. II. v. 873 (33).

The Original is in the *Barberini* Palace, but I could not certainly learn where it was found. It is commonly ſaid to have been dug up near to the Ruins of the Temple of *Fortune* at *Preneſte*, now called *Paleſtrina*. It is in Height 4 P. and 4 on. and in Breadth 4 P. and 3 on.

IX.

T H E ninth is very curious, and well deſerves the Attention of the Learned. It is in ſeveral reſpects very like to a Gem deſcribed by *Lion. Auguſtini* (34). There is the *Mithra*, as *Statius* deſcribes it :

———— *Seu te roſeum* Titana *vocari*
Gentis Achæmeniæ *ritu, ſeu præſtat* Oſirin
Frugiferum, ſeu Ferſel *ſub rupibus antri*
Indignata ſequi torquentem cornua Mithram.
                                  Theb. L. I. v. 1717 (35).

                                                                    It

---

(33) See *Ovid. Faſt.* L. V. v. 607.

Illa jubam dextra, &c.

Bullengerus, de pictura veterum, gives us the Subſtance of what may be collected from the Antients concerning this Kind of Work, L. I. Cap. VIII. *De Muſivariis:* Where he ſpeaks firſt *de pavimentis,* and then of *Moſaick* Pictures——Sequitur itaque Muſivarios fuiſſe, qui ſolum, ſeu ſtratum, parietes & apſides, teſſeris ac ſcutulis marmoreis ad effigies rerum & animantium vermicularunt. Quare *Vitruvius* L. I. C. VII. dixit, Pulſa deinde ex humo pavimenta in cameras tranſiere ex Vitro. Sed diſerte *Procopius,* L. I. de *Ædif. Juſtiniani,* Omne faſtigium excultum eſt picturis, non cera iniuſa, & diffuſa eo loci fixum, ſed teſſulis minutis in omne genus coloris tinctis aptatum, quæ & res alias, & homines imitantur. Id genus muſivi deſcribitur a *Manilio,* L. V.

Artifices auri faciet, qui mille figuris
Vertere opas poſſint, caræque acquirere dotem
Materiæ, & varios lapidum miſcere colores.
Sculpentem faciet ſauctiſ laquearia Templis,
Candentemque novum cælum per tecta ſonantis.

Several Paſſages from *Pliny,* and other Authors, are quoted to the ſame Purpoſe. Copying Pictures in *Moſaick* is now brought to very great Perfection at *Rome.*

(34) Parte ſeconda, p. 42. Gemme Antiche di *Lion. Auguſtini.*

(35) The Commentators obſerve ; Quod autem dicitur *torquentem Cornua,* ad illud pertinet, quod ſimulacrum ejus fingitur reluctantis tauri cornua retentare: quo ſignificatur lunam ab eo lumen accipere, cum cæperit ab ejus radiis ſegregari. There is another Figure in this Piece, with ſome of the Symbols of the *Dea Magna,* but drawn by Horſes ; whereas ſhe is painted in a triumphal Car drawn by Lions. So *Ovid:*

———— *Cur huic genus acre leones*
Præbent inſolitas ad juga curva jubas ?
Deſieram. Feritas mollita per illam
Creditur, id curru teſtificata ſuo eſt.
At cur turrita caput eſt ornata corona ?
An Phrygiis *turres urbibus illa dedit ?*
Annuit, &c.   Faſt. L. IV. v. 215.

Many Divinities, however, are repreſented by the Poets drawn by Horſes. See *Ovid.* Faſt. L. V. V. 50. *Fortune* is beautifully deſcribed by *Ovid* thus :

Fortuna arbitriis tempus diſpenſat iniquis :
Illa rapit juvenes ; ſuſtinet illa ſenes.
Quæque ruit, furibunda ruit : totumque per orbem
Fulminat, & cæcis cæca triumphat equis.
                                  Ad. Liv. Aug. v. 371.

It is taken from *Bartoli's* coloured Drawing, done from the Original, upon Vellum, in the *Maffimi* Collection already mentioned, now belonging to Dr. *Mead.*

X. &c.

THE tenth, eleventh, twelfth, thirteenth, fourteenth, fifteenth, fixteenth, are like-wife taken from Drawings of *Bartoli* in the fame Collection, done after the Originals: They made the Ornament of one Ceiling in what is called *Titus's* Palace, now called *Orti Gualtieri.* We may guefs at the Sizes of thefe Compartiments from thofe that remain uneffaced, which are in Height a little more than two *Roman* Palms, and in Breadth two. The tenth reprefents *Jupiter* on his Eagle careffing *Juno,* probably, becaufe *Minerva* is there; yet he was wont to receive his Daughter *Venus* very kindly, according to *Virgil.*

> *Olli fubridens hominum fator atque Deorum*
> *Vultu, quo cælum tempeflatefque ferenat,*
> *Ofcula libavit natæ.* Æn. L. I. v. 259.

THE eleventh, twelfth, thirteenth and fourteenth, reprefent Nymphs mounted on different Animals, juft as *Claudian* defcribes the *Nereids:*

> —*Choris quatitur mare ferta per omnem*
> Neptuni *difperfa domum,* Cadmeia *ludit*
> Leucothoe, *frænatque rofis* Delphina Palæmon.
> *Canitiem* Glaucus *ligat immortalibus herbis* (36).
> *Nec non & variis vectæ* Nereides *ibant*
> *Audito rumore feris. Hanc pifce volutam*
> *Sublevat Oceani monftrum* Tarteffia *tigris.*
> *Hanc timor* Ægæi *rupturus fronte carinas*
> *Trux aries. Hæc cærulea fufpenfa leæna*
> *Innatat. Hæc viridem trahitur complexa juvencum,*
> *Certatimque novis ornant connubia donis,* &c.
> Claud. de Nup. Hon. & Mar.

THE fifteenth reprefents *Pan* piping, as *Ovid,*defcribes him:

> Pan *ibi dum teneris jactat fua carmina Nymphis,*
> *Et leve cerata modulatur arundine carmen.* Met. L. II. v. 153.

AND in the fixteenth, he is reprefented embracing the fame Nymph.

IT is fufficient for me to have given, in a few Inftances, a Specimen of the Pleafure that arifes from comparing antient Pieces of Painting or Sculpture, with the Defcriptions of antient Poets, fince it never was my Defign to enter much into claffical or mythological Difcuffions about thefe antient Pieces now publifhed, but only to adorn and illuftrate the Hiftory of the Art, with fome philofophical Remarks on the Ufes that were or might be made of it. And indeed, had I ever formed any fuch Scheme, I fhould have dropp'd it the Moment I came to know, that one fo much fitter for that Task had far advanced in a Work of that Kind, from which I promife myfelf more Inftruction and Satisfaction than is yet to be had from any Books of Antiquity or Mythology. That Author's Defign is to fhew what Lights the antient Poets, and the Remains of antient Arts, caft reciprocally upon one ano-ther; and this he does in feveral Dialogues; for which agreeable, but difficult Way of Writing, he hath already fhewn himfelf to be excellently qualified. The Publick will foon be favoured with that moft excellent Performance; and therefore I fhall fay no more about

---

(36) *Glaucus* is reprefented N° 26. As for the firft Part of this Defcription,

> —*Hoc navigat oftro*
> *Fulta Venus. Niveæ delibant æquora plantæ.*
> *Profequitur volucrum late comitatus amorum,* &c.

I have feen a Drawing after an antient Picture found in the fame Place, very agreeable to it; a Print of which, if I could have obtained Leave to have had it copied, fhould have been given in this Collection. See *Ovid. Met.* L. II. V. 10.

> *Doridaque & natas: quarum pars nare videntur,*
> *Pars in mole fedens virides ficcare capillos;*
> *Pifce vehi quædam. Facies non omnibus una,* •
> *Nec diverfa tamen: qualem decet effe fororum.*

Hence we may account for the remarkable Refem-blance, or Likenefs of Faces among thefe Nymphs. One of them is mounted on a very fprightly Sea-horfe. See *Statius.Theb.* L. II. V. 45.

> *Ille* Ægæo Neptunus *gurgite feffor*
> *In portum deducit equos: Prior haurit arenas*
> *Ungula; poftremi folvuntur in æquora pifces.*

And *Achill.* L. I. v. 56.

> —*Placidis ipfe arduus undis*
> *Eminet, & triplici telo jubet ire jugales.*
> *Illi fpumiferos glomerant a pectore fluctus:*
> *Pone natant, delentque pedum veftigia cauda.*

See Gemme Antiche di *Liona. Auguf.* Part II. P. 25.

about the reſt of theantient Paintings now publiſhed; but juſt tell where the Originals
were found, and where ſuch as are ſtill extant may be ſeen.

XVII.

THE ſeventeenth, which probably repreſents *Coriolanus* and his Mother.

XVIII.

. THE eighteenth repreſenting *Apollo* giving a Crown to a Poet.

XIX.

THE nineteenth repreſenting a Faun offering á Gift.

XX.

THE twentieth repreſenting *Minerva*, and ſome antient Hero.

XXI.

THE twenty-firſt repreſenting á Spectre.

XXII.'

THE twenty-ſecond repteſenting *Orpheus*.

XXIII, and XXIV.

AND the twenty-third and twenty-fourth repreſenting two Aerial Nymphs.' All theſe
are from Drawings of *Bartoli* the Elder, done from the Originals found in *Titus's* Baths
while they were freſh, and theſe Compartiments were of the ſame Size with the others juſt
mentioned.

XXV.

THE twenty-fifth is exceeding curious, becauſe it ſhews us a *Triremis.* The Original
is now quite gone, tho' it was found not very long ago in the *Orti Farneſiani*. *Palazzo*,
the Pope's Antiquary, aſſured me it was in very good Condition when it was diſcovered,
and a Drawing of it was then taken, which Cardinal *Alexander Albani* now hath. It was
in Height P. 4. and in Breadth P. 1½.

XXVI.

THE twenty-ſixth is *Glaucus* (37), from the Original in the *Maſſini* Palace at *Rome*,
'as it is repreſented in the Print of, 1 P. in Circumference.

XXVII.

THE twenty-ſeventh repreſenting ſome Sacrifice or Offering, is from a Drawing after
the Original one in Cardinal *Alexander Albani's* Collection. This Piece was dug up out
of the Ruins in *Monte Palatino*, in the Month of *September* 1724. The Pope's Antiquary aſſured me, that it was very freſh when it was dug up, and that the Drawing was
very faithfully taken. It was in Height 6 P. and ⅓, and in Breadth 7¾ P.

XXVIII.

THE twenty-eighth, repreſenting an Offering (38) of a Chaplet upon an Altar, is done
from the Original in *Auguſtus's* Palace in the *Orti Farneſiani*, and is in Breadth P. 4. and
in Height P. 1.

2 Z   XXIX.

---

(37) See *Statius Theb.* L. VII. v. 335. & *Ovid. Met.*
L. 13. v. 904, &c. and compare with theſe a curious
Paſſage in *Velleius Paterculus*, relating to *Plancus*. L. II.
Cap. 83. And It is worth while with reſpect to *Glaucus*
and the Nymphs above mentioned, to conſult *Servius*
on *Virgil. Georg.* I. v. 437. & *Georg.* IV. v. 338. &
Æn. V. y. 823.

(38) This Piece deſerves the Attention of the Curious.
We know that Flowers were offered to many Divinities,
as to *Juno Lucina*, as well as to *Venus*, *Flora* and *Ceres*.
See *Ovid. Faſt.* L. III. v. 253.

Ferte Dea flores: gaudet florentibus herbis
  Hæc Dea: de tener⁰ cingite flore caput.

We know it was cuſtomary to burn the Laurel on an
Altar. See *Tibullus* L. II. Eleg. V.

Et ſuccenſa ſacris crepitet bene laurea flammis
  Omine quo felix & ſacer annus eat.

Laurus ubi bona ſigna dedit, gaudete Coloni.
So *Ovid*:

Et crepet in mediis laurus aduſta focis. Faſt. L. IV.

XXIX.

THE twenty-ninth, a Woman with the *Modius* on her Head, as Fortune is fometimes reprefented, is given as a Specimen of Portrait Painting, from the Original in the *Maffimi* Palace at *Rome.* In Height P. 1⅘, and in Breadth P. 1. And 2 on.

XXX.

THE thirtieth, with the Arm lifted up, is remarkable for the bold Pronunciation of the Mufcles. The Original is now in Dr. *Mead's* Poffeffion.

XXXI. &c.

THE thirty-firft, thirty-fecond, thirty-third, thirty-fifth, and fo on to the forty-eighth; are from Originals in the *Rofpigliofi* Palace at *Rome*, where they are well preferved.

XXXIV.

THE thirty-fourth is from the Original in the *Farnefe* Palace, which is in Height almoft 6 P. and in Breadth a little more than two. The Length of the Figure is 3½ P. Thofe from the *Rofpigliofi* Palace were found in the Year 1718, in what is called *Terme di Con-ftantino.* And indeed the forty-fixth and forty-feventh (39), are bad enough to be of that *Thefe, and thefe on-* Age, and are given as a Specimen of the fad Decline of the Art about or rather before that *ly, are a good deal* Time. But the others feem to be of a better Age. There are fome Pieces of Landfcape *mended in the* amongft them, but what may be inferred from thefe, with Regard to Skill of Perfpective, *Drawings.* I leave to others to determine:

THE thirty-fifth a Piece of Landfcape and Architecture, is of the fame Size with the Original. The thirty-firft is in Height 1 P. and 4 on. and in Breadth 1 P. The thirty-third, in Height 1 P. and 3 on. and in Breadth fomething lefs than one P. And the Meafures of all the reft are much about the fame.

XLVIII, XLIX, and L.

THE remaining three, forty-eight, forty-nine, and fifty, are from *Titus's* Palace, and the Originals are of the fame Dimenfions with the others already mentioned that were found in the fame Ruins. So that upon the whole, there are in this Specimen of antient *Roman* Painting twenty-nine, done from Originals, yet fubfifting. And the other twenty-one are from excellent Drawings taken by very good Hands from the Originals, while they were frefh. The greater Part of thofe twenty-one are from Drawings of the elder *Bartoli.* There are befides thofe publifhed by *Bellori, Holftenius,* and others, and thofe in this Collection, a great many other Pieces in *Italy,* particularly in the Poffeffion of the King of *Naples* and *Sicily,* which are well worth engraving. But I found it diffi-cult and expenfive enough for me to get at thofe Originals, or original Drawings, from which this prefent Collection is taken. I employed one of the beft Hands in *Rome,* for copying the Antique, to Draw for me; and as his Drawings have given very great Satis-faction to all who have feen them, fo I hope the Engravings will gain Reputation and Bufi-nefs to one who now is certainly equal to any Work of the moft difficult Kind in that Way, and hath done his utmoft to pleafe in this, by keeping ftrictly to the Drawings. Before I engaged him to do the whole Work, he had given me a few Specimens, which were fully fatisfactory to fome of the beft Judges here, who did me the Favour to compare them carefully with the Drawings; and certainly pronounced very impartially, fince they did not know his Name, till they had declared themfelves entirely fatisfied with his Performance, and were very defirous to have the Engraving well performed, as well for my fake, as out of Regard to Truth and Art.

(39) Thefe two are the only Pieces in this Collection that are mended by the Drawer.

CONCLUSION.

THUS have I fet before my Readers, in the beft Order I could, the moft material Obfervations upon the Rife, Progrefs, Declint, and Ufefulnefs of Painting, that had ever occurred to me in my Reading, or Reflections, whilft I was in *Italy*, more efpecially, where every one who hath previoufly conceived any Notion of the Arts of Defign, is unavoidably engaged to purfue the Study of them to great Length.

BUT fince, whether in difcourfing of the Antiquity of Painting, and of the high Efteem in which it was held by antient Poets and Philofophers, or of the Authorities from which the Account I give of antient Painters, and their Works, is brought; whether in giving the Hiftory of the more celebrated antient Painters, and of the diftinguifhing Qualities and Excellencies for which their Works are commended by the beft antient Judges: In pointing out the State of the other Arts amongft the Antients whilft Painting flourifhed or declined, and the Ufes to which all the fine Arts either actually were employed in their beft Times, or thofe that were ever thought by the beft Judges of every Age to be their propereft and moft becoming Ends: In tracing the Pleafures which good Painting is qualified to afford us, to their Foundations and Sources in our Nature, which are found to be the fame with thofe that render us capable of good Tafte in Life, or of virtuous, happy, and becoming Conduct : Since in handling all thefe, and feveral other Subjects relative to Painting, the main Point aimed at and always kept in View, is the Connexion of Painting with Poetry, and of both with Philofophy, and the happy Ufe that might be made of them in Education : Since, in one Word, I have only chofen to treat of Painting for this very Reafon, that, by fhewing the ftrict Relation of an Art to Philofophy, which is commonly imagined to be very remote from it, and from all the ferious Purpofes of liberal Education, I might at the fame time do Juftice to that Art, and fet Philofophy and Education in a jufter Light. Upon all thefe Accounts, I fay, it will not be improper to conclude this Effay with a fhort Recapitulation of fome of the chief Principles it is defigned to confirm, and upon the Truth of which all the Reafoning in it wholly depends. Thofe on the one Hand, who have fully comprehended my Defign, will not be difpleafed to find fome Maxims of very great Importance, with Refpect to Education, fet in various Views. On the other Hand, thofe who have not perhaps hitherto fully entered into my Scope, may now at laft difcover it in the Conclufion, and fo be able to recal the Whole into their Minds with a more clear Comprehenfion of the chief Purpofe and Intent of every Part: And to thofe, who know that Mens Underftandings are rather more different from one another than their Eyes, 'tis needlefs to make an Apology for exhibiting Truths of any Moment in various Points of Sight, or in diverfe Lights.

NOW the natural Connexion and Dependence of all the liberal Sciences and Arts, and the Fitnefs of uniting them in Education, evidently appears, whether we confider the Objects and Ends of the Sciences and Arts; or the natural Connexion and Dependence of all thofe rational Faculties and Difpofitions in our Natures, which it is the End of Education, that is, of Science and Art to cultivate and improve. And it will be no lefs manifeft if we confider either our natural Propenfion to imitate, trace Analogy and Likenefs, compare and copy, and the agreeable Effects which Imitations or Copies naturally have upon our Minds; or in the laft Place, if we attend to the Advantages allowed to Poetry, which muft likewife belong to Painting, fince thefe Advantages do indeed only belong to Poetry, as it is a Painting Art. In one Word, in order to be convinced of the Fitnefs of combining all the liberal Arts and Sciences in Education, one need but reflect that there can be but two Objects of human Speculation and inquiry, Truths themfelves, and Languages, that is, the various Ways of expreffing, embellifhing, or enforcing Truths in our Minds.

ALL the Sciences muft be one, or very ftrictly connected and allied, becaufe Nature, their Object, is one. What doth any Science natural or moral, or howfoever it may be denominated, inquire into? Is it not into fome Part of Nature, fome Eftablifhment or Connexion in Nature; or, in other Words, is it not into the Frame and Conftitution, the Connexions and Dependencies of fome particular Object in Nature? But if univerfal Nature be one Whole, and all its Parts being Members, fo to fpeak of one Body, are intimately related to, or rather united with the Whole, and with each Part of the Whole, then the Confideration of any one Part muft lead to the Examination of many Parts, or rather of all the Parts to which our Refearches can reach; and our Knowledge of any one Member muft be more full and adequate, or more defective and imperfect, in Proportion to what Share of its Connexions in the Whole we are able to trace and difcover. To make this fufficiently clear, we need only to obferve, that Man himfelf is the propereft Object of

human

human Inquiries. But Man being evidently related to Nature as a Part, Inquiries about Man muft mean Inquiries about all Man's Connexions and Dependencies; for how elfe can his Rank and Situation be known, or how elfe can we form a true Judgment of his Relation to the Whole, and to the Authôr of the Whole, and of his natural End, Duty, and Dignity? To know, Man cannot mean to know only his corporeal Frame, his fenfitive Faculties, and his Connexions with fenfible Objects, fince he hath likewife moral Powers and Difpofitions: Nor can it mean merely to know his moral Powers and Difpofitions, fince he hath alfo fenfitive Faculties, and corporeal Dependencies: And in Truth, his fenfitive Faculties, and his Connexions with the fenfible World, are fo mingled and blended with his moral Powers; Difpofitions and Connexions, as making one Frame or Conftitution, that it is impoffible to underftand one or other of them by feparate Confideration.

BUT what plainly follows from this? Is it not, that the great Secret of Education, or of Inftruction in the Science of Man, muft confift in being able to lead Students in the moft natural Way and Order thro' the various Connexions and Laws of Nature, upon which Mán · hath any Dependence, or the Knowledge of which is neceffary to give him a juft View of himfelf, and of the Relation he bears to Nature, and Nature to him? I may, perhaps, foon attempt to give a Specimen of fuch Inftruction in human Nature, by which the Con- hexion of all the Sciences, by whatever different Names they are diftinguifhed, and of the Manner of conjoining them in Education, will evidently appear. Mean time 'tis obvious from the very Nature of Science, or the Science of Man in particular, that the chief thing to be ftudied by thofe concerned in Education, is the moft natural, or fimpleft and eafieft Order in which Students of Nature may be led gradually from one Connection in Nature to another, to as full a View of Nature as can be attained to. Since thus alone can Man have a juft Idea of himfelf, or of his Site, Dignity, Scope and End.

BUT, if Nature being one, all the Sciences which inquire into Nature as one Whole muft be One, or ftrictly and intimately related; all the liberal Arts are for the fame Reafon One, and clofely connected: For what are all thefe, as they are diftinguifhed from the merely didactick Art of fetting forth or difplaying Truths, that is, Facts, or the Connexions of Nature, with Simplicity and Perfpicuity; What are they but fo many different Ways of entertaining the Imagination with pleafing Views of certain natural Connexions, and their beauteous Effects; Or of impreffing on the Mind fome ufeful Rules and Maxims for our Conduct, founded upon Nature's Laws and Connexions, by fuch Reprefentations of them as are moft likely, in Confequence of our Frame and Conftitution, to find eafieft Accefs, fink deepeft into, and take firmeft Hold of our Hearts? Or Laftly, Of actually exciting fuch Workings of the natural Affections as are not only pleafant in the Exercife, but have a happy Influence on the Temper? If we examine all the liberal Arts, Poetry, Oratory, or the Arts of Defign, we fhall find that all their Aims and Efforts, in Confe- quence of their general Definitions, are reducible to one or other of thefe three Ends juft mentioned: Whence it muft follow, that the great Art in Education lies in knowing how to employ all thefe Arts or Languages in their Turn, by choofing proper Examples from each of them, in order to give pleafing, inftructive, or wholfome Views of any Con- nexion in Nature, fo foon as it is difcovered by Experience, or by Reafoning from Expe- rience: Of the Beauties of the fenfible World, by means of poetical Defcriptions and Landfcapes: For fuch Defcriptions and Landfcapes only are poetical which are true, or reprefent pleafing Effects agreeably to Nature's Laws and Connexions: And of the Beau- ties of the moral World, by fuch poetical Compofitions expreffed either by Words, or by Lines and Colours, as do likewife truly reprefent Nature's moral Laws, and their Effects and Operations; or ferve to fend home into the Mind with great Force fuch rules of Con- duct, and fuch moral Conclufions, as do naturally refult from the Knowledge of certain Connexions relative to Nature, and to us as Parts of Nature. If every Connexion in Nature be not only worth our knowing, but really relative to us in fome Refpect, then every Science, by whatever Name it is called, belongs to us in fome Degree; and if fo, then muft every Art likewife belong to us, and to right Education, which is capable of recommending, infinuating, or inforcing and impreffing any Piece of ufeful Knowledge. But there is no Connection in Nature, which Oratory, Poetry, and Painting, may not be employed to recommend, infinuate or inforce. They ought all therefore to be employed and made Ufe of in Education. I need not add that it muft neceffarily be true in the Nature of Things, that fome Objects of Nature will bear a nearer Relation to us, and confequently more intimately concern us than others, that have a remoter Connexion with us: And therefore the Bufinefs of Education is, ftill keeping the Unity of Nature in View, to lead in the firft Place, and with the greateft Attention, to thofe Relations which moft nearly regard us, and for that Reafon to employ the infinuating, recommending, or inforcing Arts chiefly, to imprefs ftrongly upon our Minds thofe Conclufions that refult from them.

- THE

THE natural Union and Connexion of all the liberal Arts and Sciences, and the Neceſſity or Fitneſs of uniting them in Education will likewiſe appear, if we attend to the natural Union and Dependence of thoſe Faculties, Capacities, and Diſpoſitions of our Minds, which it is the chief End of Education to improve and perfect. Our Underſtanding or Reaſon, our Imagination, and our moral Temper, are allowed to be the Faculties and Diſpoſitions which Education ought to be calculated to improve and perfect. Now the natural Union and Dependence of theſe Faculties is too evident to be inſiſted upon. Hardly can the moral Temper be moulded into a right Form, or long preſerve it, if Reaſon and Judgment are not found, or well repleniſhed with true and wholſome Science; or if the Imagination be quite neglected and left to ramble without any Inſtruction or Guidance: Nor can Science indeed have its due Influence upon the Heart and Temper, if Fancy is not employed to repreſent its Diſcoveries and Leſſons in its warming as well as enlightening Methods of Painting them; that is, in other Words, of giving them Strength, *Relief*, and Heat. It is Imagination, and not mere Teaching, that touches the Heart and moves the Affections. All the liberal Arts ought therefore to be employed in Education; Reaſon to lay open Truths and prove their Reality; and Oratory, Poetry, and Painting, to impreſs them upon the Mind, and to work the Affections into the Temper which Truths ought to produce correſpondent to them. What Virtue would a Teacher not only exhibit in the ſtrongeſt Light, but fully recommend to Students, and eſtabliſh in their Minds? Is it, for Example, publick Spirit, *the Mother of all the Virtues?* Then let Reaſon ſhew throughout all Nature as far as our Enquiries can extend, the Benevolence, the publick Love of Nature's Author ever purſuing the general Good of the Whole, by ſimple, uniform, general Laws. Let Reaſon prove its Fitneſs and Becomingneſs; but let Oratory, Poetry, and Painting, make us feel its ſweet Influence on the Mind while it prevails and operates, and all the direful Effects on the other Hand, as well as vile Deformities of every immoral Indulgence; that is, of every Purſuit that is repugnant to publick Spirit and true Benevolence. Let well painted Characters and Actions, Allegories, Fables, dramatick Compoſitions and Pictures, concur to this End, to kindle the noble Paſſion which Reaſon demonſtrates to be an Imitation of Nature, and as ſuch to be our greateſt Glory, our pleaſanteſt Exerciſe, the worthieſt Part we can act; to be at once our Dignity and Happineſs. In order to ſet forth the Fitneſs of employing all the Arts and Sciences in Education, I have inſiſted, in the ſeventh Chapter, at great Length, upon thoſe moral Diſpoſitions in our Natures, which it is the principal End of Education to improve by Inſtruction and Exerciſe, for both muſt be joined in order to form the Heart, or to eſtabliſh good Principles and good Habits. And let any one reflect upon the cloſe Union and Dependence of thoſe Diſpoſitions; namely, our Senſe of Beauty natural and moral, our generous, benevolent, ſocial Propenſity, and our Love of Greatneſs; and he will immediately perceive how imperfect Education muſt be with regard to their Improvement, if all the Arts are not called in to give proper Exerciſe and Inſtruction to theſe Diſpoſitions; for how can theſe be cultivated and improved but by taking a right View of their Nature and Operations; and, which is principal, by bringing them forth into Action by means of proper Examples. By ſhewing us how generous, beautiful, and great, Nature is in all her Productions; and by making us feel, as well as perceive, when it is that Imitations of Nature by any liberal Art give the higheſt, the nobleſt, the moſt tranſporting Touches of Joy to our Minds by their generous, beautiful, and great Effects upon them, in like manner as all the Parts of Nature itſelf move and affect us when we have a juſt View of them. Are theſe then our beſt and moſt dignifying Faculties and Diſpoſitions; are they the Sources of our beſt and moſt becoming Pleaſures; and ought we not chiefly to ſeek after Pleaſure in their ſuitable Exerciſes and Employments? It muſt be owned at leaſt, that Education does not take proper Method for gaining its main End, if it does not employ ſuitable Means to ſecure us againſt being miſled by our Imagination, and by falſe corrupted Arts into wrong Principles and Habits, by ſhewing us early their genuine Scope, and trueſt Excellence. This is leaving us open to one of the moſt dangerous Sources of Depravity, not only in Taſte but in Temper, for theſe will always go Hand in Hand: If the one be impure or corrupt, the other muſt be ſo too. And, indeed, whatever Philoſophers or others have ſaid concerning the wonderful Power of Imagination, are ſo many ſtrong Arguments for taking right Care about it in Education, to give it early a good, pure, and benevolent Turn.

THE Neceſſity, or at leaſt Fitneſs of uniting all the liberal Arts and Sciences in Education, does alſo appear from the Conſideration of one very remarkable Inſtinct or Diſpoſition, of very great Uſefulneſs, and of proportionable Strength in our Natures, and that is our Propenſity to imitate, our natural Delight in Copies, or in tracing Analogy and Likeneſs, and the wonderful Effect theſe have to excite our Curioſity and Attention, and to engage us in a cloſe and accurate Examination of Originals. Every one muſt needs have recognized this Principle in his Nature on many Occaſions. But if it ſhould be doubted of, let one but make the Experiment on himſelf, and obſerve whether a Portrait that

3 A immediately

immediately recals to his mind the Air and Countenance of a Friend, does not soon make him better acquainted with all the distinguishing Particularities in that Air and Face than ever he was before: It necessarily makes him recollect the Original with great Attention, and go over and over again every Turn, Cast, and Feature in it, with an Exactness he never thought of before, on Account of the double Satisfaction arising from the double Employment of the Mind in comparing the Copy with the Original. And does not the same happen in seeing well-painted Landscapes? It makes one advert to several beautiful Incidences of Light and Shade, which, tho' they may have been often seen in Nature, it is but now when they are recalled to Mind by Imitation, that one gives due Attention to them, and feels all their Beauty. It is just so with Regard to well-painted moral Characters and Actions, whether by the Pencil or by Poetry. True Representation makes us say this is Nature, and recals to our Mind many like Instances of it in real Life, that made however but a slight Impression upon us, till now that they are revived by a good Copy; and the Mind is delightfully engaged in passing from Imitation to Nature, and in making an exact Comparison. Now if this be true, all Imitations of any Connexions or Appearances in Nature worth our Attention, must be of excellent Use in Education, not only in recommending and enforcing known Truths, but likewise in gaining our Attention to Nature itself, in order to discover Connexions, and draw due Inferences from them. The Fitness of teaching Physicks by a Course of Experiments, is readily acknowledged; but so far as any Arts copy Nature, so far do they furnish us with Experiments; and for the same Reason that Experiments are useful, or have a good Effect in teaching any Part of Nature, or inforcing any Piece of Knowledge upon the Mind, all Imitations of Nature being Experiments, must have the same Effect with Regard to that Part of Knowledge of which they are Specimens or Experiments: And consequently, in general, the best Way of teaching Nature, physical or moral Nature, must be by calling all good Imitations of Nature, or all Experiments to our Assistance. This Reasoning is certainly good, unless it be said that Imitations of Nature, by Painting or Poetry, are not Imitations; or that Imitations and Copies are not Experiments. For if it should be said that Painting or Poetry can go but a little Way in Imitation: I answer, that so far as they can go they furnish Experiments; and as they go Hand in Hand, so there is no Part of the sensible World; none of its Laws or Appearances; and there is no Part of our moral Pabrick, or none of its Laws, Connexions and Operations: No beautiful Effect of Light, Colours and Shade, (that is all the visible World); no Affection or Passion of the Heart, no Air of Face, no Effort of Body, no Character, no Sentiment, no Struggling, no Emotion of the Mind, (that is all the moral World), that may not be painted by the Pencil as well as by Words.

THE Union and Connexion of all the Arts and Sciences, and the Fitness of uniting them in Education, appears when we attend to the necessary Consequences of what is generally acknowledged concerning the Excellence and Usefulness of Poetry either for instructing or moving: For if that be owned, the Arts of Design must likewise be allowed to be of great Usefulness for the same Ends and Purposes, since Poetry is only able to accomplish these Ends as it is a Painting Art; or since what renders it so excellent in moving or instructing us, is its being able to rear up, by Words, in the Imagination, true consistent lively Pictures. One of its most essential distinguishing Excellencies, consists in conveying pleasant, forcible, animating Images, into the Mind; and accordingly the surest Rule of trying Poetry is by examining the Pictures it raises in the Fancy, their Truth, Life and Vigour. As well therefore may we doubt, whether the Study of Nature itself is requisite to a Taste of Poetry, as whether Acquaintance with Pictures be so. Could no more be said either of Poetry or Painting, than that they are capable of affording us ingenious Amusement (which is however far from being the Case), yet, considering how becoming human Dignity, and of what Importance to the Mind and Temper it is, that all our Recreations and Pleasures should be ingenious, or partake in some Degree of our higher Faculties; for that very Reason is it fit that all the Arts that tend to improve and refine the Imagination, should have Place in Education. And a Taste of Poetry and Painting may be better, that is, more easily formed conjunctly, than a Taste of either of them can be separately; since, depending on the same Principles of Truth and Beauty, and upon the same Rules, Maxims and Foundations, they mutually illustrate and set off each other. Poetical Truth, whether in Painting or Poetry, being the same with Nature, the Study of Truth in both these Arts is the Study of Nature: And Nature will always be studied with most Satisfaction and Accuracy, when it is reflected back upon us by various Sorts of Copies or Imitations, and when these are compared with Nature, and with one another.

IT is allowed that Poetry can not only instruct in an agreeable, insinuating Manner, but that it is able to work upon our Minds directly by exciting good Dispositions, Resolutions and Affections in them. Its dramatick Pieces, more especially, are moral Imitations; which being consonant to the Principles of human Nature, and their Operations and Effects, do really demonstrate the fatal Consequences of bad Tempers, and wrong disproportioned

portioned Affections, and the moft eligible, amiable Confequences of Virtue. And therefore criticizing fuch Pieces, or examining their Conduct and Subferviency to fuch virtuous Ends, is really fearching into human Nature by means of Copies, fince all muft be founded upon our moral Frame and Conftitution. But fuch Pieces are more than a moral School; they not only teach, perfuade and convince, but they actually infufe good Paffions into the Mind, and work upon it in a wholfome, virtuous Manner, that leaves it an excellent Temper not eafily effaced or corrupted. They are powerful Leffons, but that is not all; their chief Excellence confifts in their being more than Leffons. They are good Exercife to the Mind; Exercife that really produces worthy Affections, with which the Mind is highly pleafed, and the Operations of which it cannot chufe but approve, whilft it actually feels their happy agreeable Influences. Now moral Pictures have the fame Properties, the fame Tendency, the fame excellent Influence. Criticizing fuch Compofitions therefore in like Manner, is ftudying human Nature; and the immediate Effect of good moral or hiftorical Pictures upon the Mind, is either directly virtuous, or at leaft exceedingly ftrengthening and affiftant to Virtue. *Scipio*'s Self-command, or *Hercules*'s brave Choice, will have not a lefs powerful Effect when they are well Painted, than when they are well told; and both Ways of reprefenting thefe Subjects being united, they muft have a doubly ftrong Influence upon the Heart : For thus feveral Charms combine to give Virtue its full Force; to fet its intrinfick Beauty in a due Light, and to inflame the Mind with a ftrong and lively Senfe of its divine Excellence and happy Effects (40). What Pity is it then that the fine Arts are not folely employed to their beft and nobleft, their only genuine Purpofes; and in purfuing which, they alone can difplay all their Beauty and Sublimity! What Pity is it that they are at any time vilely abufed and proftituted to give falfe deceitful Charms to Vice! It is by recommending Virtue that they will moft effectually recommend themfelves. *Virtue is the fupreme Charm in Nature, in Affections, in Manners, and in Arts.*

(39) See a juft Commendation of the Mufes, or Arts, *ad Auguftum.* And in Mr. *Thompfon*'s Liberty, Part 2. in thefe refpects, in *Theocriti Idyllion* 16. and in *Horace*, L. 285, &c.--and Part 5. L. 374, &c. *Carm.* L. 4. Od. 8. compared with Ep. L. 2. Ep. 2.

F I N I S.

BOOKS lately publifhed, printed for, and Sold by A. MILLAR, over-againft
St. CLEMENT's CHURCH, in the *Strand.*

I. A Complete Collection of the *Hiftorical, Political,* and *Mifcellaneous* Works of JOHN MILTON : Correctly printed from the *Original Editions.* With an *Hiftorical* and Critical Account of the *Life* and *Writings* of the AUTHOR ; containing feveral *Original Papers* of his, *never before publifhed*; and a large *Alphabetical Index.* By THOMAS BIRCH, A. M. and F. R. S. in two Vols. Folio, beautifully printed on a fine Paper, and adorn'd with a curious Head of the *Author*, engraven by Mr. *Vertue*, from a Drawing by Mr. *Richardfon.*

II. The *Oceana*, and other Works of JAMES HARRINGTON, Efq; collected, methodized, and reviewed ; with an exact Account of his *Life* prefix'd, by TOLAND. To which is added, an *Appendix* containing all the *Political Tracts* wrote by this *Author*, omitted in Mr. TOLAND's Edition.

III. An HISTORICAL and POLITICAL DISCOURSE of the *Laws* and *Government* of ENGLAND, from the *Firft Time* to the End of the Reign of QUEEN ELIZABETH. With a Vindication of the ancient Way of Parliaments in *England.* Collected from fome Manufcript Notes of JOHN SELDEN, Efq; By NATHANIEL BACON, of Gray's-Inn, Efq;
The Fourth Edition : Corrected and Improved by a GENTLEMAN of the *Middle Temple.*
N. B. *There are a few of the above Three, printed for the* CURIOUS, *on large Paper.*

IV. The *Political Works* of ANDREW FLETCHER, Efq; containing, 1. A Difcourfe of Government with relation to *Militia's.* 2, and 3. Difcourfes concerning the Affairs of *Scotland* ; written in the Year 1698. 4. Difcorfe delle Cofe di Spagni fcritto nel mefe di Luglio 1698. 5. A Speech upon the State of the Nation, in *April* 1701. 6. Speeches by a Member of the Parliament, which began at *Edinburgh* the 6th of *May* 1703. 7. An Account of a Converfation concerning a right Regulation of Governments for the common Good of Mankind : In a Letter to the Marquis of *Montrofe*, the Earls of *Rothes, Roxburgh* and *Haddington*, from *London* the 1ft of *December* 1703.

V. The Works of Mr. *Thomfon*, in 2 Vols. 8°.—Vol. I. containing *Spring, Summer, Autumn, Winter* ; a Hymn on the *Seafons* ; a Poem facred to the Memory of Sir *I. Newton*; *Britannia*, a Poem ; and *Sophonifba*, a Tragedy.—Vol. II. containing Ancient and Modern *Italy* compar'd; *Greece, Rome, Britain*, and the *Profpect*, being the five Parts of *Liberty*, a Poem ; a Poem to the Memory of the late Lord Chancellor *Talbot* ; and *Agamemnon*, a Tragedy. Either of the Volumes are to be had feparate.
N. B. *There are a few Copies remaining of thofe printed on a fuperfine Royal Paper, in 2 Vols.* 4°.

VI. TRAVELS into MUSCOVY, PERSIA, and Part of the EAST INDIES. Containing an accurate Defcription of whatever is moft remarkable in thofe Countries. And embellifhed with above 320 Copper Plates, reprefenting the fineft Profpects, and moft confiderable Cities in thefe Parts ; the different Habits of the People ; the fingular and extraordinary Birds, Fifhes, and Plants, which are there to be found : As likewife the Antiquities of thofe Countries, and particularly the noble Ruins of the famous Palace of PERSEPOLIS, called *Chelminar* by the *Perfians.* The Whole being delineated on the Spot, from the refpective Objects. To which is added, an Account of the Journey of Mr. ISBRANTS, Ambaffador from *Mufcovy*, through *Ruffia* and *Tartary*, to *China*; together with Remarks on the Travels of Sir *John Chardin*, and Mr. *Kempfer*, and a Letter written to the AUTHOR on that Subject. By M. CORNELIUS LE BRUYN. Tranflated from the Original FRENCH.

VII. SELECTUS DIPLOMATUM & NUMISMATUM SCOTIÆ THESAURUS; in duas partes diftributus: Prior Syllogen complectitur veterum *Diplomatum* five *Chartarum* Regum & Procerum SCOTIÆ, una cum eorum Sigillis, a *Duncano* II. ad *Jacobum* I. id eft, ab Anno 1094. ad 1412. Adjuncta funt reliquorum SCOTIÆ & MAGNÆ BRITANNIÆ Regum SIGILLA a prædicto *Jacobo* I. ad nuperam duorum regnorum in unum, Anno 1707, coalitionem : Item *Charactteres* & *Abbreviaturæ* in antiquis codicibus MSS. inftrumentifque ufitatæ. Pofterior continet *Numifmata* tam Aurea quam Argentea fingulorum SCOTIÆ Regum, ab ALEXANDRO I. ad fupradictam regnorum coalitionem perpetua ferie deducta ; fubnexis quæ reperiri poterant eorundem Regum *Symbolis Heroicis.* Omnia fummo artificio ad Prototyporum fimilitudinem tabulis æneis expreffa; adjectis fingulorum Diplomatum, recentiore fcripturæ formâ, æri iifdem incifis exemplis. Ex mandato Parlamenti *Scotici*

collegit, digeffit & tantum non perficienda curavit egregius ac patriarum Antiquitatum callentiffimus vir JACOBUS ANDERSONUS, Scriba Regius. Quæ operi confummando deerant, fupplevit, & Prefationem, Tabularum Explicatione, aliifque Appendicibus, rem Scotiæ diplomaticam, nummariam & genealogicam haud parum illuftrantibus, auxit & locupletavit THOMAS RUDDIMANNUS, A. M.

VIII. COLLECTIONS relating to the HISTORY of MARY QUEEN of SCOTLAND. Containing a great Number of *Original Papers* never *before* printed. Alfo a few fcarce Pieces reprinted, taken from the beft Copies. Revifed and publifhed by JAMES ANDERSON, Efq; with an explanatory *Index* of the obfolete Words, and *Prefaces* fhewing the Importance of thefe Collections. In 4 Vols.

IX. The Hiftory of the UNION of *Great Britain*, done from the *Publick Records* ; containing, 1. A general Hiftory of Unions in *Britain.* 2. Of Affairs of both Kingdoms introductory to the *Treaty.* 3. Of the laft Treaty properly called the *Union.* 4. Of the carrying on the Treaty in *England*, next in *Scotland.* 5. The Proceedings and Minutes of the Parliament of *Scotland*, with Obfervations thereon, as finifhed there, and exemplified in *England*; in which is contained the Right and Method of collecting the Peers and Commons ; and all the Articles relating to both Kingdoms, as confirm'd by the Parliament of *Great Britain* : To which is added an Appendix of *Original Vouchers.*

X. GEORGII BUCHANANI *Scoti*, Poetarum fui fæculi facile Principis, *Opera Omnia*, ad optimorum Codicum fidem fummo ftudio recognita, & caftigata: nunc primum in unum collecta, ab innumeris fere mendis, quibus plerique omnes Editiones antea fcatebant, repurgata ; ac variis infuper notis alliifque utiliffimis acceffionibus illuftrata & aucta, Folio, curante THO. RUDDIMANNO, A. M. 2 Tom.

XI. A Syftem of HERALDRY, *Speculative* and *Practical.* With the true Art of Blazon, according to the moft approved Heralds in *Europe* ; illuftrated with fuitable Examples of Armorial Figures and Atchievements of the moft confiderable Sur-names and Families in *Scotland*, &c. Together with *Hiftorical* and Genealogical Memorials relative thereto. By *Alexander Nifbet*, Efq; Folio.

XII. ELEMENTS of CHEMISTRY : Being the annual Lectures of *Herman Boerhaave*, M. D. formerly Profeffor of *Chemiftry* and *Botany*, and late Profeffor of Phyfick in the Univerfity of *Leyden.* Tranflated from the Original Latin, by *Timothy Dallowe*, M. D. with feveral Alterations and Additions communicated by the Author to the Tranflator, for the Improvement of this Edition. In 2 Vols.

XIII. An Enquiry into the Nature of the human Soul ; wherein the Immateriality of the Soul is evinced from the Principles of Reafon and Philofophy. In 2 Vols.
" He who would fee the jufteft and precifeft Notion of
" God and the Soul, may read this Book; one of the
" moft finifhed of the Kind, in my humble Opinion,
" that the prefent Times, greatly advanced in true Phi-
" lofophy, have produced."
WARBURTON's *Divine Legation of Mofes demonftrated*, Page 395. of the firft Edition.

XIV. The MYTHOLOGY and FABLES of the Antients, explain'd from Hiftory. By the Abbé BANIER, Member of the Royal Academy of Infcriptions and Belles Lettres. *Tranflated from the Original* FRENCH.

In the Prefs, and will be publifhed at *Lady-Day* 1740.

A NEW EDITION of the WORKS of the Lord CHANCELLOR BACON, in 4 Vols. Folio. To which will be prefixed, A *New Life* of the Author, with feveral Pieces of his Lordfhip's, not inferted in the laft Edition : And no Pains fhall be wanting to give all the Perfection that can be defired, both for Beauty and Correctnefs.
The Encouragers of this Undertaking are defired to fend in their Names to *A. Millar*, over-againft St. *Clement's* Church in the *Strand*; for, as there are but 500 Copies to be printed, If any remain unfubfcrib'd for, they will be fold at an advanced Price, as he did in his late beautiful Editions of HARRINGTON and MILTON : And the Time fixed for the Publication fhall be punctually kept, or the Money returned.
The Price of the fmall Paper, in Sheets, to the Subfcribers, is Three Pounds Ten Shillings, and the large Paper Five Guineas ; one Moiety of each to be paid down at fubfcribing, and the other on the Delivery of the Book.

WS - #0017 - 170622 - C0 - 229/152/13 - PB - 9780259395317 - Gloss Lamination